ALSO BY WILLA CATHER

Novels

Alexander's Bridge
O Pioneers!
The Song of the Lark
My Ántonia
One of Ours
A Lost Lady
The Professor's House
My Mortal Enemy
Death Comes for the Archbishop
Shadows on the Rock
Lucy Gayheart
Sapphira and the Slave Girl

Short Stories

The Troll Garden
Youth and the Bright Medusa
Obscure Destinies
The Old Beauty and Others

Poetry

April Twilights

Nonfiction

Not Under Forty

THE SELECTED LETTERS
OF WILLA CATHER

THE SELECTED LETTERS OF
WILLA CATHER

EDITED BY Andrew Jewell
AND Janis Stout

ALFRED A. KNOPF   NEW YORK

2013

THIS IS A BORZOI BOOK
PUBLISHED BY ALFRED A. KNOPF

The letters of Willa Cather copyright © 2013
by The Willa Cather Literary Trust

Introduction, annotation, commentary, and compilation copyright © 2013
by Andrew Jewell and Janis Stout

Library of Congress Cataloging-in-Publication Data

Cather, Willa, 1875–1947.
The selected letters of Willa Cather /
edited by Andrew Jewell and Janis Stout.—1st ed.
p. cm.
"This is a Borzoi book."
ISBN 978-0-307-95930-0 (hardcover)—ISBN 978-0-307-95931-7 (ebook)
1. Cather, Willa, 1873–1947—Correspondence.
2. Novelists, American—20th century—Correspondence.
I. Jewell, Andrew (Andrew W.)
II. Stout, Janis P.   III. Title.
PS3505.A87Z48 2013   813'.52—dc23
[B]   2012036882

Jacket photograph: Willa Cather in Jaffrey, New Hampshire, 1920s,
probably taken by Edith Lewis. Archives and Special Collections,
University of Nebraska–Lincoln Libraries.
Jacket design by Megan Wilson

Manufactured in the United States of America
First Edition

Contents

✦

Introduction

➤ ⬥ ⬥

BEFORE WILLA CATHER DIED, she did what she could to prevent this book from ever existing. She made a will that clearly forbade all publication of her letters, in full or in part. And now we flagrantly defy Cather's will in the belief that her decision, made in the last, dark years of her life and honored for more than half a century, is outweighed by the value of making these letters available to readers all over the world.

Why did she put such restrictions in her will? Various answers have been proposed. Some believe that Cather was guarding her privacy, perhaps worried that the letters she dashed off over the years, not thinking of herself as a public figure, would compromise her literary reputation. Some have wondered if she sought to conceal a secret buried in her years of correspondence, some sign of an indiscretion or uncontrolled passion. Many people, following James Woodress's characterization of her in *Willa Cather: A Literary Life*, are convinced that Cather was obsessed with her privacy and that the will—together with her supposed systematic collecting and burning of letters—was simply an expression of a personality seeking to control all access to itself. Many have believed she actually did burn all her letters, or almost all, and the will was a kind of backstop.

Our research on Willa Cather's letters calls into question all of these assumptions about Cather, her character, and her motivations. Except for an isolated incident or two, there is no evidence that she systematically collected and destroyed her correspondence. This claim is overwhelmingly demonstrated by the large volume of surviving documents: about three thousand Cather letters are now known to exist, and new caches continue to appear. If Cather or Edith Lewis, her partner and first literary executor, really and systematically sought to destroy all correspondence, would so many letters have survived? Moreover, at the end of Cather's life, people who were quite close to her and would have undoubtedly known about any preference for wholesale destruction did *not* destroy the letters in their possession; on the contrary, they were concerned, as her niece Virginia Cather Brockway wrote, to be "very careful of everything of Aunt Willies" and protect it from "fire or something unexpected."* Indeed, some of the largest and richest collections of existing Cather letters are those that have been protected for decades by members of her family. The episodes of destruction that have given rise to the supposition that Cather destroyed her letters—for example, Elizabeth Sergeant's report in her memoir that all of the letters Cather wrote to her dear friend Isabelle McClung Hambourg were shoved into her apartment's incinerator after Hambourg's death†—appear to be isolated incidents rather than part of a larger pattern of obliteration.

Nevertheless, Cather's testamentary restriction on the publication of her letters was clearly driven by a desire to restrict the readership of them. We do not believe that desire emerged from a need to shield herself or protect a secret, but instead was an act consistent with her long-held desire to shape her own public identity. In her maturity, Cather was a skillful self-marketer, and a major element of her marketing strategy was to limit her publicly available texts to those she had meticulously prepared. She did not fill shelves with hastily written novels or fleeting topical essays, but toiled over each book until it succeeded to the best of her ability. Sometimes she delayed the publication of a novel by months or even years in order to achieve her artistic goals. She even contributed to the design of the physical books, considering each element that might communicate something of her work to the reader. She specified her margin preferences for *My Ántonia*, had ideas about the font type for *Death Comes for the Archbishop*, and thwarted most efforts to create paperback editions during her lifetime. Her strategy was extremely successful. By positioning herself not as a "popular" writer but as a literary artist, she was able to give herself the space to *be* such an artist while also financially succeeding in the marketplace. Her lovely, quiet, episodic novel about seventeenth-century Quebec, *Shadows on the Rock*, was one of the top-selling books of 1931. It was not a success because readers were rushing to read a novel about colonial Canada, but because the novel was written by the celebrated author Willa Cather.

We can guess that Cather may have believed that an edition of her letters

---

* See the full letter from Virginia Cather Brockway to Meta Schaper Cather on page 676.
† Elizabeth Sergeant, *Willa Cather: A Memoir* (Athens: Ohio University Press, 1992), 275.

would shift focus away from her novels and onto her private self. She was impatient with writers who managed to sell their books by constructing dramatic images of themselves. Although she did at times contribute to publicity efforts by providing stories of her early life, her goal was to create a persona that practically disappeared behind the work; she sought to meld the art and the artist into one indivisible package. She wrote to her brother Roscoe in 1940 that she was satisfied to do what James M. Barrie and Thomas Hardy did: they "left no 'representatives' but their own books,—and that is best."* In this way, the resistance to the publication of her letters was consistent with her resistance, in her later years, to lecturing, interviews, and other forms of exposing her self to the public.

Cather's suppression of the publication of her letters may indeed have helped cement her reputation as a true artist, and today that reputation is virtually unchallenged. In the nearly seven decades since her death, her works have continued to be read, studied, and celebrated, and both general readers and contemporary writers as diverse as A. S. Byatt and David Mamet celebrate her fine artistry and her absolute dedication to her craft. And rightly so: many of Cather's novels and stories are among the finest writings of the twentieth century, rich and complex in their meaning-making, yet elegant and pristine on their surfaces. She manages both to enchant readers with her prose and to move them with her insights into human experience.

We fully realize that in producing this book of selected letters we are defying Willa Cather's stated preference that her letters remain hidden from the public eye. But even her will itself envisions a moment when her preferences would not rule the day; acknowledging her inability to govern publication decisions indefinitely from beyond the grave, it leaves the decision for publication "to the sole and uncontrolled discretion of my Executors and Trustee."† Observing this part of Cather's will, Norman Holmes Pearson noted more than half a century ago that the document recognizes "certain difficulties in regard to the future." "The future must make its own decisions," he wrote. "All Miss Cather could do was to make the future as remote as possible."‡

The concerns that we believe motivated her to assert her preference are no longer valid. Cather's reputation is now as secure as artistic reputations can ever be, and her works will continue to speak for themselves. These lively, illuminating letters will do nothing to damage her reputation. Instead, we can see

---

* See page 588.

† Willa Cather, will dated April 29, 1943, Paragraph Seventh.

‡ Norman Holmes Pearson, "The Problem of Literary Executorship," *Studies in Bibliography* 5 (1952–53), 8.

from our twenty-first-century perspective that her letters heighten our sense of her complex personality, provide insights into her methods and artistic choices as she worked, and reveal Cather herself to be a complicated, funny, brilliant, flinty, sensitive, sometimes confounding human being. Such an identity is far more satisfying—and more honest—than that of a "pure" artist, unmoved by commercial motivations, who devoted herself strictly to her creations and nothing else.

In the past—unless they were lucky enough to have sufficient resources of time and money to travel to the almost seventy-five archives that house the letters themselves—readers and scholars interested in Cather's life and works were able to read only summaries and paraphrasings of her letters, not her actual words. Having ourselves summarized thousands of letters for the original or the expanded *Calendar of the Letters of Willa Cather*, we can attest to the inadequacy of such paraphrases. Substituting our words (or anyone else's) for Cather's own expressions of her meaning is never satisfactory. Second-hand approximations can never precisely convey what she said herself. Could a summary ever communicate the cheeky, alliterative fun of a postscript like "Fremstad flees on Friday to the inclement wood of Maine," at the end of a 1914 letter to Elizabeth Sergeant?* Cather's restrictions in her will, then, by making paraphrases the only option available to scholars and biographers, created a situation that even Cather herself would surely consider far worse than the publication of her letters. Readers have been forced to encounter what she "said" in her letters through words supplied by scholars seeking to convey what they understood her to mean. Now we will all be able to read and interpret her letters for ourselves. We will also be able to draw more accurate connections between the letters and the fiction. By forcing a delay of many years in publishing a volume of her letters, Cather's restrictions did, however, ensure that there is no longer any possibility of harming or embarrassing the people who appear in her correspondence.

Cather is now a part of our cultural history. Her works belong to something greater than herself. It is time to let the letters speak for themselves.

BECAUSE OF THE PREVALENCE of Nebraska settings in her fiction, most readers know Willa Cather as a Nebraskan. In fact, she was born in Virginia and spent her childhood on a sheep farm near the town of Winchester. She told University of Virginia professor Stringfellow Barr in 1928, "I always feel

* See page 190.

very deeply that I am a Virginian."* She was nine years old in April of 1883 when her family moved to Webster County, Nebraska, where they joined other family members who had gone before. It was an enormous change to go from the green hills of northern Virginia, where the family had been established for generations, to the nearly treeless prairie of central Nebraska. In a 1913 interview in the *Philadelphia Record*, Cather recalled the jolt of her arrival:

I shall never forget my introduction to it. We drove out from Red Cloud to my grandfather's homestead one day in April. I was sitting on the hay in the bottom of a Studebaker wagon, holding on to the side of the wagon box to steady myself—the roads were mostly faint trails over the bunch grass in those days. The land was open range and there was almost no fencing. As we drove further and further out into the country, I felt a good deal as if we had come to the end of everything—it was a kind of erasure of personality.

I would not know how much a child's life is bound up in the woods and hills and meadows around it, if I had not been jerked away from all these and thrown out into a country as bare as a piece of sheet iron. I had heard my father say you had to show grit in a new country, and I would have got on pretty well during that ride if it had not been for the larks. Every now and then one flew up and sang a few splendid notes and dropped down into the grass again. That reminded me of something—I don't know what, but my one purpose in life just then was not to cry, and every time they did it, I thought I should go under.

For the first week or two on the homestead I had that kind of contraction of the stomach which comes from homesickness. I didn't like canned things anyhow, and I made an agreement with myself that I would not eat much until I got back to Virginia and could get some fresh mutton. I think the first thing that interested me after I got to the homestead was a heavy hickory cane with a steel tip which my grandmother always carried with her when she went to the garden to kill rattlesnakes. She had killed a good many snakes with it, and that seemed to argue that life might not be so flat as it looked there.†

Some of the first people she became acquainted with had immigrated to the Great Plains from Sweden, Norway, and Bohemia. These people were

---

* See page 413.

† "Willa Cather Talks of Work," in *Willa Cather in Person*, ed. L. Brent Bohlke (Lincoln, NE: University of Nebraska Press, 1986), 10.

extremely interesting to her. She said in the same interview, "I have never found any intellectual excitement any more intense than I used to feel when I spent a morning with one of those old women at her baking or butter making. I used to ride home in the most unreasonable state of excitement; I always felt as if they told me so much more than they said—as if I had actually got inside another person's skin."

These immigrant women—and others she knew in Webster County and the town of Red Cloud, Nebraska—would remain in Cather's memory and imagination until the end of her life. They populate much of her fiction. Indeed, the town of Red Cloud, where Cather lived from about age eleven until not quite seventeen, when she went away to school in Lincoln, served as a model for many small towns in her fiction: Black Hawk, Moonstone, Sweet Water, Hanover, Skyline, Haverford. Her life there as a child, reinforced by many long visits home over the years, made Red Cloud central to Willa Cather's life and self-conception.

When she went to Lincoln, to the University of Nebraska, in 1890, she planned to study science (she had befriended some of the doctors in Red Cloud and on one occasion reportedly helped administer chloroform during an amputation); however, she soon turned to writing and literature, editing the campus literary magazine and writing for the *Nebraska State Journal*. Her columns and reviews for that newspaper, which she began with gusto at age nineteen, started her on her first career as a journalist. After graduating from college, she got a job as the managing editor of a national magazine, the *Home Monthly*, and in 1896 moved to Pittsburgh, Pennsylvania. After the magazine collapsed, she worked for Pittsburgh newspapers and then as a high school teacher, spending nearly a decade in Pittsburgh in all. In 1906 she moved to New York City to join the editorial staff of *McClure's Magazine*. She soon became managing editor of this highly popular and important periodical and, until she left the position in 1912, was arguably one of the most powerful women in journalism.

She left *McClure's* because what she really wanted to do was to be a professional writer. During her years in Lincoln, Pittsburgh, and New York (which remained her permanent address until her death in 1947), she wrote and published many short stories in magazines, published a book of poems (*April Twilights*), and released a book of short fiction (*The Troll Garden*). Her first novel, *Alexander's Bridge*, appeared in 1912, the same year as her long short story "The Bohemian Girl." These two successes in the same year, along with a life-changing trip to the American Southwest, led to *O Pioneers!*, the 1913 novel that she said "was like taking a ride through a familiar country on a horse that knew the way, on a fine morning when you felt like riding."* After *O Pioneers!* Cather dedicated her working life to writing. Between 1913 and 1940 she published fourteen books, many of which—*My Ántonia, A Lost Lady, Death Comes for the Archbishop, The Professor's House*—are considered among the finest works of American literature. All of her novels and collections are engaging, ambitious works of art. She was honored with a Pulitzer Prize, a Howells Medal from the American Academy of Arts and Letters, the Prix Femina Americain, numerous honorary doctorates, and many other awards. She became, and remains, one of the most eminent of American writers.

Throughout her working years, Cather led an active, cosmopolitan life. She loved theater and, especially, music, devoting much time (and much of her fiction) to music, singers, actors, and actresses. She traveled to Europe many times, and, a lifelong Francophile, stayed for extended periods in France. She traveled often to Arizona and New Mexico, to New England, and to Canada. She loved to go horseback riding and hiking in the open country. In the 1920s, she and Edith Lewis purchased the only property she ever owned: a cottage on Grand Manan Island in the Bay of Fundy. This little cottage near a cliff that overlooked the Atlantic became an important refuge for Cather, a private space away from the congestion and heat of New York City.

As the letters in this collection reflect, Cather was sustained throughout this extraordinary life by many deep and long-lasting relationships. She was close with certain members of her family, especially her parents, her brothers Douglass and Roscoe, and several nieces and nephews. She maintained friendships from her early years in Red Cloud, Lincoln, and Pittsburgh for many years and also enjoyed new friendships. Though some of the people she befriended were fellow luminaries, like Robert Frost, Sarah Orne Jewett, Yehudi Menuhin, S. S. McClure, and Alfred Knopf, she seemed to get the deepest satisfaction out of old friends with whom she shared a long history. Unfortunately, the two relationships that were likely the most profound in her adult life—Isabelle McClung Hambourg and Edith Lewis—are not well represented in her correspondence. Only a small handful of letters from Cather to these two women are known to survive.

THOUGH THE MISSING LETTERS to Lewis and McClung Hambourg are a disappointing gap in the record, we are incredibly lucky in the range and rich-

---

*Willa Cather, "My First Novels (There Were Two)," in *Willa Cather on Writing* (Lincoln, NE: University of Nebraska Press, 1988), 93.

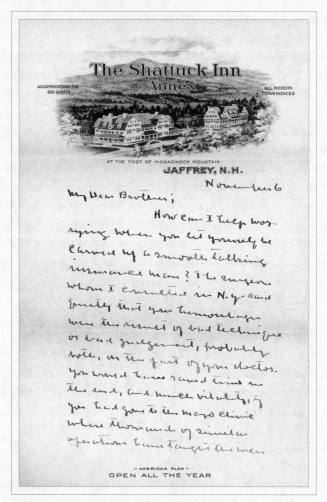

First page of November 6, 1938, letter from Willa Cather to her
brother Roscoe

ness of Cather letters that did survive. Thanks to the stewardship of dozens of
archives around the world (please see note about archives, page 691) thousands
of letters written by Willa Cather are now available to us. The attitudes, emotions, and voice of Cather's letters are as diverse as one would expect from
any human being over the course of sixty years. Yet in another way, there is a
consistency of personality throughout all of them, a tang of Cather's character
that one can sense in all of her prose. It is difficult and perhaps fruitless to try
to define this quality, but one might call it frankness or self-possession. Cather
is always vitally herself, even when she confesses anxious self-consciousness,
and in spite of her habit of writing falsehoods about trivial matters. Her voice

in her letters, as in her fiction, emerges from an emotional and intellectual commitment to what it is she has to say. Her writing is not pretentious and does not seem, as Cather said about the work of another writer, "as if she were packing a trunk for someone else, and trying conscientiously to put everything in."* Instead, when reading Cather's letters one can feel the force of a vibrant, individual personality deeply interested in things.

Cather herself identified this ability to be interested as the source of her strength as a writer. In a 1938 letter to her brother Roscoe, she wrote, "As for me, I have cared too much, about people and places—cared too hard. It made me, as a writer."† What she called in the same letter "the heat under the simple words" is present throughout her correspondence, from the funny reports of Red Cloud life she wrote when she was a teenager in the 1880s to the painful letters of the 1940s when she despaired at her own worn-down body and the heartbreaking destruction of a world at war.

The voice of Cather's correspondence is in many ways strikingly consistent with the voice of her fiction: it is confident, elegant, detailed, openhearted, and concerned with profound ideas without relying on heavily philosophical language. In other ways, the style of her voice in the correspondence is significantly different than the polished voice of her fiction: one senses that the letters are Cather's voice without the refinement of the revision process. The letters sometimes reveal Cather as a rather histrionic character. Her correspondents get regular tirades about poor health, challenges of work and housekeeping, and exhaustion. She can be, in modern parlance, a drama queen. This results in claims that are not measured or deliberate, but instead made for dramatic rhetorical effect. For example, in a 1916 letter to her brother Douglass, she discusses some conflict she had with him and the rest of her family and huffs, "I think I've had my belting, and it has taken the fizz out of me all right—and I'll tell you this, it's positively shipwreck for work. I doubt whether I'll ever write anything worth while again. To write well you have to be all wrapped up in your game and think it awfully worth while. I only hope I'm not so spiritless I won't be able to make a living."‡ But Cather's hyperbole, though it can be misleading—another letter written on the same day to a different brother reveals excitement about an idea for a new novel—is not exactly dishonest. Rather, it is consistent with her straightforward emotional experience of the world.

---

* See page 517.
† See page 561.
‡ See page 225.

"I am sure you realize," she wrote Carrie Miner Sherwood in 1945, "that things have always hit me very hard. I suppose that is why I never run out of material to write about. The inside of me is so full of dents and scars, where pleasant and unpleasant things have hit me in the past. . . . Faces, situations, things people said long ago simply come up from my mind as if they were written down there. They would not be there if they hadn't hit me hard."* She felt things keenly, and her letters are one of the chief records she left of that feeling. In some respects, that is what makes Cather's letters such a pleasure to read. She is wrapped up in whatever emotion she wished to communicate: when she is angry, she lets fly with specific, strongly worded scoldings that almost make one wince; when she is ill, one practically feels the pain and lethargy with her; and when she is excited, when she is consumed with the pleasure of creative work, or when she wants to let someone know that she cares deeply for them, the glow of that emotion is felt, even across all these years. That is, in the end, why Cather's letters should be published. She was a great writer, and these words of hers deserve readers.

*See page 647.

Note on Editorial Procedures

➤⬅

IN THIS VOLUME, a generous selection of the correspondence of one of America's foremost writers is made available for the first time. In selecting letters for inclusion we have given preference to those that particularly relate to the creation of Willa Cather's fiction, her career in journalism, her perspectives on issues of the day, and her relationships with key people in her life. A few seemingly trivial letters are included in order to give a sense of how she handled routine business or social obligations, her sense of humor, and her enjoyment of daily life. We hope that together these chosen letters present the complex humanity of Willa Cather.

The organization of the volume is strictly chronological. Reading through these selected letters in order provides a kind of autobiography: Cather's own words sketching the episodes that constituted her life.

All of the letters are presented in their entirety. We have made the utmost effort to present the original letters with meticulously accurate transcriptions while also providing a reading experience that is unencumbered by superficial errors. Our procedures in attempting to accomplish this goal have been as follows:

1. We have retained the spelling in the original letters, even when it was in error. These misspellings are most frequent in Cather's early letters, and keeping them allows the reader to sense the vital messiness of those youthful writings. However, in other letters, particularly in typewritten correspondence, there are frequent minor errors that are not necessarily reflective of a style or of weak spelling skills, but are mere typographical mistakes. These obvious errors (like "graoned" for "groaned") have been silently corrected. If we have

inserted whole missing words—or parts of words—because we believe they were intended, we have used brackets to indicate our insertions. In choosing which passages could be silently corrected and which ought to be left alone, we had to use our editorial judgment, and we were guided throughout by the goal of providing accurate transcriptions without the clutter of trivial errors.

2. When Cather has made revisions (additions, deletions, etc.) in the text of a letter, we have presented the text as Cather revised it. Cather's deleted words are not present in our transcriptions.

3. In many handwritten letters, Cather's punctuation is more than a little ambiguous. To resolve such ambiguities, we have relied on punctuation patterns that are discernible throughout the letters and have assumed Cather was being consistent rather than inconsistent. For example, when a title in double quotation marks is at the end of a sentence, Cather usually put the period outside of the quotation marks, like this: "Title". In many of her handwritten letters, however, it is difficult to determine whether the double quotation mark or the period is further to the right, and we have decided to follow the pattern as illustrated above. We have not altered Cather's punctuation when, for example, her use of commas challenges our sense of stylistic propriety. We assume her frequent insertions of "unnecessary" commas is a stylistic choice, and we have honored it. In cases where the distinction between a comma and a period is ambiguous, we have chosen the punctuation that makes the most sense to us within the context.

4. In some typewritten letters, Cather (or her secretary Sarah Bloom) has rendered the titles of books in all capital letters. We have altered the all-capital titles to underscored titles. Words that remain in all capitals in our transcriptions are words that seem to have been capitalized for emphasis, or, in some cases, to make the spelling of a difficult or foreign word plain to her reader.

5. Whenever Cather underlined text in a letter, we have rendered that as underscored text in the transcription. Very rarely Cather used multiple lines under a word or phrase, but we have rendered all underlines with just one line.

6. Cather often used extended or multiple dashes in her correspondence, and we have represented them as close to the original as possible, for example using "———" to indicate when Cather wrote three dashes in the original document. When we have used only the standard em-dash (—), it indicates that, in the original, Cather used a single dash or, in the case of typewritten letters, two hyphens to indicate a single dash.

7. Occasionally, Cather inserted something into the text of a letter above the main line or in the margin that did not fit grammatically into the sentence she was composing, a sort of note on the main sentence. We have represented

these insertions in parentheses. Parentheses in this text, however, do not exclusively indicate such notes. When Cather used parentheses in her letters, these too are represented with parentheses in this book.

8. Rarely, we have followed a word in the text with a bracketed question mark: [?]. This indicates that we have real doubt about the word or words transcribed in that particular spot.

Throughout, readers will notice insertions of dates, names, and other bits of information in square brackets. Dates and words in square brackets were not written by Cather in the original letters but were supplied by us in an effort to provide helpful identifications and explanations that are integrated into the text as seamlessly as possible, without unduly cluttering the reading experience. For recurring names in the book, readers may wish to consult the biographical directory at the back, as it provides thumbnail sketches of most of the important people whose names fill Cather's correspondence.

Acknowledgments

⇥⇤

A BOOK LIKE THIS ONE is the result of cooperative work on the part of many people and institutions, and we have many to thank and acknowledge.

We first must thank the Willa Cather Trust, the entity that controls the intellectual property rights to Cather's work, for allowing this selection from her letters to be published at last. The Willa Cather Trust is a partnership between the Willa Cather Foundation, the University of Nebraska Foundation, and a member of the Cather family. The Willa Cather Foundation and the University of Nebraska have long been committed to the study and appreciation of the work and life of Willa Cather; for those of us within the Cather scholarly community, there is an incredibly deep appreciation for the breakthrough made possible by their giving permission for publication of letters. For more information about the Willa Cather Trust, please see http://www.willacather.org/permissions.

We would also like to thank the Willa Cather Foundation, its staff, and its board of governors, for the support given to this project and to Cather scholarship generally. The foundation's work during its nearly sixty years of existence has resulted in a greater understanding and appreciation for Cather through educational outreach such as international seminars, conferences, and other events, and publications such as the *Willa Cather Newsletter and Review*. Through its stewardship, the foundation has also preserved many historical properties in Red Cloud, Nebraska. Thus, the foundation is responsible for the persistence of something of the world Cather knew in the crucial years of her youth. For readers moved by Cather's work, a trip to Red Cloud is a profound and delightful experience.

The University of Nebraska–Lincoln has supported this project in very explicit and meaningful ways. As the steward of the world's largest and richest collection of original Cather materials and the home of the Cather Project, *Cather Studies*, The Willa Cather Scholarly Edition, and the online Willa Cather Archive, the University of Nebraska–Lincoln is a primary presence behind virtually all Cather scholarship. More specifically, UNL, as Andrew Jewell's employer, has supported his Cather scholarship in numerous ways, particularly by granting him a faculty development leave in order to complete the manuscript for this book. Jewell would especially like to thank the administration of the University Libraries and the staff of Archives and Special Collections for its support. Thank you to Mary Ellen Ducey, Peterson Brink, Josh Caster, Traci Robison, Maggie Van Diest, Joanie Barnes, Nancy Busch, and Joan Giesecke. Special thanks goes to Katherine Walter, a simply wonderful department chair, who has been a steadfast supporter of Cather scholarship and who has done more than anyone else to make Jewell's career at UNL a pleasure and an honor.

The Cather scholarly community is known for its collegiality, and we would like to thank several scholars who have brought information to our attention, provided us with materials, or otherwise demonstrated support. Though so many have helped in small ways (the applause and encouragement we received when we announced the project at the 2011 International Cather Seminar in Northampton, Massachusetts, should not be underestimated), we would like to single out several colleagues in this community who have assisted in larger and more specific ways, especially Melissa Homestead, Robert Thacker, and Richard Harris for providing key materials; Timothy Bintrim and Matthew Rubery for bringing individual letters to our attention; Mark Madigan for assisting with a tricky transcription; and Kari Ronning, Ann Romines, and Guy Reynolds for their continual intellectual and personal support. Jewell also thanks Tom Gallagher, a Cather Foundation board member, for his great help and camaraderie while poring over the Cather-Knopf correspondence in New York.

Janis Stout adds her voice to all of these expressions of gratitude and wishes to mention, in addition, Nancy Chinn (a Cather colleague now deceased who always cheered on Stout's Cather studies) and John McDermott (not a Cather colleague, but a colleague nevertheless, who first urged the preparation of a calendar of letters).

The Cather family, with their continued generosity and enthusiasm, has been crucial both in making letters available to readers and in allowing them to be published. We would especially like to thank Jim and Angela Southwick, Trish and Jim Schreiber, Katie Shannon, Ann W. Shannon, Elizabeth A.

Shannon, Margaret Lundock, John Cather Ickis, Margaret Ickis Fernbacher, Dr. Mary Weddle, and George Brockway.

Several students and former students have given important assistance in various stages of preparation of this book. Thanks to Paul Callahan (who is responsible for the translations of Cather's French), Rosanna Dell, Molly McBride Lasco, Amanda Kuhnel Madigan, Carmen McCue, and Jeremy Wurst (who is responsible for the translation of Cather's Latin joke). Special thanks goes to Sabrina Ehmke Sergeant, who served as editorial assistant on *A Calendar of the Letters of Willa Cather: An Expanded, Digital Edition* and who has given much diligent, intelligent energy to working with us on Cather's letters in various ways.

The archivists and staff at the many institutions that hold letters deserve repeated thanks, and we would again like to acknowledge their work. Throughout our long work with multiple and varied organizations, we were impressed again and again with the professionalism and generosity of those who make research materials both safe and available. Please see our note on archives for a complete listing of institutions whose materials are represented in this volume.

At Knopf, we have been very fortunate to work with Ann Close, a terrific editor and a supporter of this project from the moment she heard about it, and we thank her and other staff members at Knopf for their fine work. Cather's admiration for the skill and quality of Knopf publishers is something we now understand on a personal level.

Personally, Jewell would like to thank and acknowledge his parents, Steve and Cheryl Jewell, for their steady love and encouragement throughout his whole life, an anchor that has made everything he has done possible. And, most profoundly, Jewell wishes to thank his wife and daughters, Becca, Emma, and Jane Jewell. All three celebrated the opportunity to make this book, even if it meant constant dinner chatter about Willa Cather, endless anecdotes from the letters shared on the ride to school, and giving up a great art area so Dad could have somewhere to work every day. Becca, thank you for saying, many times, and in many ways, that this book was worth it. As Willa Cather would say, a heartful of love to you all.

As ever, Stout thanks her husband, Loren Lutes, for being a sustainer of and an active contributor to everything she does. She also thanks, without naming them, her eight adult children, sixteen grandchildren, and numerous friends for having refrained from saying they wished she wouldn't be always talking about this Willa Cather person.

THE SELECTED LETTERS
OF WILLA CATHER

PART ONE

The School Years

1888–1896

How can I "do anything" here? I have'nt seen enough of the world or anything else.

—WILLA CATHER TO MARIEL GERE, May 2, 1896

Willa Cather about 1894, when she was a student at the University of Nebraska

T HE FIRST KNOWN LETTER by Willa Cather was written on August 31, 1888, when she was fourteen years old. This letter reveals—like the few other letters that survive from her childhood in Red Cloud, Nebraska, and her college days in Lincoln, Nebraska—how precocious, witty, and provocative Cather was as a young person. In her teenage years, she resisted most signs of conventional femininity, shearing her hair dramatically short, wearing masculine clothing, studying science and classical literature, and signing her name "William Cather" or, sometimes, "William Cather, MD." There is little sign, however, that these daring expressions of independence made her an outcast in her Red Cloud community. Just the opposite: the letters reveal a robust social life with the most elite citizens of the town. Many of her early friends mentioned here, like the Miner family (James and Julia Erickson Miner and their five children, Carrie, Charles Hugh, Mary, Margaret, and Irene), Silas and Lyra Garber, and Dr. G. E. McKeeby would one day inspire major characters in her fiction. Three of the "Miner girls"—Irene, Carrie, and Mary—were lifelong friends of Cather's, corresponding with her until her death.

In addition to friends like the Miners, in these early letters we begin to meet various members of Cather's family, notably her six siblings: Roscoe (b. 1877) was Willa Cather's next younger sibling, followed by Douglass (b. 1880), Jessica (b. 1881), James (b. 1886), Elsie, often called Bobbie (b. 1890), and John, usually called Jack (b. 1892).

In 1890 Cather went to Lincoln to attend the University of Nebraska, and most of the surviving letters from this period were written to college friends while she was home for summers in Red Cloud. These years at the university were tremendously important for her; in *My Ántonia* she wrote that the university had "an atmosphere of endeavor, of expectancy and bright hopefulness" in those days. Her five years in Lincoln helped her begin to find her mature personal identity, provoked her literary ambitions, gave her valuable writing and editorial experience, and (readers will soon be grateful for this) taught her how to spell.

❧ ❧

Willa Cather's earliest surviving letter is to a Webster County neighbor, Helen Stowell, who reportedly came to Nebraska from Boston and had a ranch house with a piano and a library, making her a sophisticated presence in Cather's childhood. Like many that follow, this letter is dotted with names as Cather shares news of her community and family.

TO HELEN LOUISE STEVENS STOWELL

August 31, 1888
Red Cloud, Nebraska

Dear Mrs. Stowell

When I recieved your letter I was much pleased for I had begun to doubt your intention to write.

Grandma [Rachel Seibert Boak] is much better now though we do not think she will ever walk again. Her son from Va. [J. S. Boak] spent six weeks with us. He, papa & Mama went to Denver Col. and had a very pleasant time.

We do so hope that you and Alice will come with Mr. Stowell, do come. You may not have the chance again, the Whites have moved here now & Mrs Sill is here and I know you would have a pleasant time.

School begins Monday & I suppose I shall go though I dont feel boyant over the prospect, I have grown so attached to my work & place in the office & to my little labratory & dissecting outfit & my stuffed animals it is hard for me to leave them. Then here I am "Miss Cather" & govern, there I am a child & am governed. That makes a great difference with frail humanity.

I had quite an adventure yesterday. A man came in & tried to sell papa a bogus paper on some poor farmer. Papa could have made $50 on it but he thought perhaps the man was a snide & did not like to in any way help defraud an honest man so he told him to return in an hour. Then when we were alone told me he was going to hitch up the buggy & go see the farmer & when the agent returned to hold him at all costs.

In an hour the man returned & I never had such a time. Of course I had to talk the fellow to death to keep him. His buggy was ready & if he got away goodbye. Papa & the farmer returned & tackled him, he made for his buggy & escaped. the sherif caught him at Amboy.

Carry Miner has gone to college. The Metzcars [Metzgers] from Beatrice are visiting Anson [Higby], the[y] will live here & run the new paper. Anson & his wife live where Mrs Roe used to live so you see we are near neighbors. I do not think they are very happy togather (but happy is a word few of us realize or are) nothing he can do seems to pleas her & she is cross as two sticks.

Fred [Winifred Richardson Garber] & Suard [William Seward Garber] are still happy in the blissful illusion that they love each other as no one but "Ouida's" heros ever thought of. They still amuse the town by their pranks, such as gong swimming togather, takeing endless rides at night in closed hacks, acting "Princess Napraxine" [an 1884 Ouida novel] on the medow by Garbers & spending Sunday in the woods with claret & "Ouida"

I should think there would be a good deal of ennui in such romance—especelaly on $1200 per year.

Molliee, Bess [Seymour], Lillie Letson & Nellie Atdelshime [Nellie Adlesheim] had a picnic the other day.

I have been stuffing some birds lately. Tell Alice that Jess [Jessica Cather, Willa Cather's sister] often speaks of her & would love to see her again. We children have a great many picnics, parties & circus' this summer & would love to have she & Jessie Moon to help us enjoy them.

Hoping to see you <u>all with us</u> 'ere another Xmas, I remain

Your affectionate friend
Wm Cather

➢ ➣

While growing up in Red Cloud in the 1880s, Cather encountered a number of adults who perceived and appreciated her intelligence and originality. As she reports in the following letter, she was reading Latin with some proficiency by age fifteen. She studied Latin and Greek with William Ducker, a well-educated Englishman who worked in his brother's store in downtown Red Cloud and served as an important intellectual mentor for the young Cather.

TO HELEN LOUISE STEVENS STOWELL

May 31, 1889
Red Cloud

My Dear Mrs Stowell, and Gorgie

I suppose that of all the varied emotional phases of human life there is none so exhilarating as that of triumph and it is a caprice of fortune that under such I write to you. This day closes the school year and I am favored with the class honers and bare off the prize for best Latin translations, & consequently I feel rather cheerful.

My grades are as follows

Latin - - - - - - 95
Physics - - - - - 100
Astronomy - - - - - 100
Retoric - - - - 90
Ancient History - - - - 100

100 is perfect and all grades 90 or above are excellent.

On the back of my report card Prof. wrote

Friend Willa—I hope your naturaly aquired taste for the parusal of good literature—a taste through which you have been one of the most pleas-ant companions & most through students I ever knew—may continue dureing your life, that the fruits of it may, at all times, especially in your mature years render you attractive intellectually and socially.

Your respect for your teacher will, at all times be kindly remembered and your name upon his list of <u>special</u> friends.

Your Sincere Friend & Teacher

Jno F. Curran

My card was the only one he wrote apon and I can tell you [I] keep it in a safe place.

I have rigged up my room of the office anew, a regular library it is now, here I read and study. I am deep in "Caesar"—poor vetren, who are we that we should censure Brutus when in youth we do the dread dead dayly,—murder Caesar.—Translateing the Latin Bible, reading Astronomy, geology, history, Homer, Milton, Swinburne "Ouida" & Gorge Sand.

By the way have you read any of Swinburne's poetry? Some of it is fine I inclose a line or two from "Locrine."

Had good memorial exercises yesterday at the opera house. Jessie took part, forty two little girls represented states and they had good music. Two weeks ago Mrs Bloom, Padden Briggs and Johnston of Superior [Nebraska] were up. Mrs Curran had a big dinner and Mrs Platt a tea. We had a high time I assure you.

Yesterday Mrs [Fanny Meyer] Weiner, Higby, [Lyra Wheeler] Garber, Mama and their husbands and a lot of the boys went on a big picnic, they go very often but seldome take their husbands, they take Ryland, Dave, Tom, Mr Beechy and a few girls. They go to a place in the country, Mrs Smiths, where he has made a big pond filled it with fine fish and has two lovely boats, they take fine lunch and beer, have a regular "picnic" in the full sense of that expressive word. Anson declares he and papa and Mr Miner, Mr Curran & Garber will get the girls and have a picnic as well as their better halfs.

I had a big card party last week, all the younger "set" of girls & boys.

I see a goo[d] deal of [music teacher] Mrs [Peorianna Bogardus] Sill for she is at least a imatation of the things I most lack. She is as self satisfied as ever and her <u>narrations</u> are pretty much the same as they were some four years ago when I met her first. I am, to say the least, familiar with them—say, some things look better at a distance, dont they?—A continental tour is a test of character, some men it makes, some it mars. I am very egar to "press with my profane pedals the native soil of heros and poets," but when I return I dont want my whole life to be "a European Souvenir."

Mary Miner is really doing splendidly at her music, she play Listzs "Spinning Song" adapted I beleive, from Wagner's "Flying Dutchman" beautifuly her expression is unusual for a girl who has heard so little. But Mrs S— has actualy given the child of 16 Listzs 14th <u>Hungarian Rhapsody</u>!! the idea. What next I wonder? [Beethoven's] "Moonlight Sonata" or Mozarts "Requiem" perhaps. say, that is <u>profanity</u>, the old masters will turn in their graves.—I dont mean they will turn the music for her.—If Rubenstine [virtuoso pianist Anton Rubinstein] comes to Omaha Mrs S— will take Mary & Lo Bellow [Loua Bellows] her best pupils an go up. She has told me her plan. They will purchase the music he will play and when he to whom the crowned heads of Europe bow in reverence strike the keyboard. Pythagaras and her disciples will follow him

> "with a critical eye,
> "Nor pass his imperfections by"

nodding approval when he does well and frowning when he blunders. Truly they burn strange fire apon the alter of the Gods in these dgenerite days.

I may go but not with that intellectual crowd, I shall go as a pilgrim to worship in a far country. I have a lot of musical book and try to kee[p] abrest with music & muscal things and any one who can feel can tell when one play well. Poor "Richard" how tired and sick he must be of it all, what a fortunate thing he is not brillint, for himself. But Heaven and earth "talk of the Angels"—you know the rest—here he coms himslf to see about some loans & chattels and I dont want him to see this. In Haste

Yours Truly

Wm Cather Jr.

P.S. Mama send love to you & Gorge. Bess and all the girls join in the latter. The children send many message to Alice but I am in a hury. How is Gorgie's health now? I think I could cure her soon.

P.P. Mrs Stowell

Our house as usual is a regular "Grenta Green" for the younge folks, they are there always and I flee every night to the office for philosophical solitude. Molly is—well—she is "Molly"—that is the only way to discribe her.—Mr Harris & Crane who take Highland's & Welch's places are "sweet young men" the girls say. I dont know much of them though they are at our house almost every night with Bess, Mollie, Nellie Weiner and Mine Johnston & Miss Benett. Gorgie must come to see us all, she would have a good time I can promise. When she tiers of green peas and chocklate cake (I beleve she like them?) and "tailor made" young men she can console herself with my chemicals, stuffed birds, bottled snakes, philosophys, shells and Latin Bibles. I mean it, though no other girl in town dare medel with my "hobbies", you know I allways thought lots of Gorgie though I seldom care for gir[l]y[?] girls.

Yours truly

Willa Cather

The spelling and penmanship of this epistel are copyright
All Rights Reserved

Wm Cather Jr.

Gretna Green was a noted destination in Scotland for young couples eloping from England beginning in the mid-eighteenth century.

TO HELEN LOUISE STEVENS STOWELL

August 28, 1889
Red Cloud

My Dear Mrs. Stowell,

We were all much alarmed by the report that dear little Alice had been bitten by a mad dog, pray is it true and how is she? We heard that you had taken her to Boston, from another quater that you went to New York, again that you were at the sea side and lastly that you had gone to Paris to see Pasturé. Which is correct and at which quater of the globe shall I next address you? I have been studying Greek this summer and have enjoyed it very much, I like it even better than Latin though it is harder for me. I have been reading a good many of [Edward] Bulwer Lyttons & [Charles] Dickens novels. Did you ever read "The Light of Asia" by Edwin Arnold? It is a masterpiece in its way. Who is "On the Hights" by? by the way have you read [H. Rider] Haggards latest work "Cleopatra"? You must for though it has some decided faults it has some acual virtues and is the best thing he has written so far.

The Firemans State Tournament that met here was a big affair. Mrs Sill had an art exhibition of which I send you a catalouge. Roscoe was foreman of the Tomlinson Juvenile Hook and Ladder Co., which called fourth so much applause. The visiting firemen made a pur[s]e of $18.00 and gave it to the little fellows, really it was a fine run, Roscoe & Douglas [Cather's brothers] pulled off the ladder (a 16 ft ladder) and held it up in the air while John Cumings mounted it. Gov [John M.] Thayer said it was the best run made and he would have come all the way from Grand Island to have seen it alone, all the papers in the county blew about it. they ran 100 yds. & mounted a 16 ft. ladder in 21½ seconds.

Do you take the Republican? I wish you did as I am on[e] of the staff reporters and gaurentee it to be the newsiest paper printed in town, you know I have a natural propensity for knowing the business of the town in general. Doctor McKeeby is editor and that insures the intellectual & political items as first class, if you want to know all the social ins & outs, <u>Take the Republican</u>, only $1.00 a year and remember that I am an agent allways ready to recieve subscriptions. Mrs. Stowell I have been to fifteen picnics in Garber grove this summer, and such fun. Mr. Harris, the man who takes Mr. Welches place at the depot looks <u>just</u> like Mr Beechey, one can hardly tell them apart, he is very soft on Nellie Wiener (I mean Nellie Adelshime [Adlesheim] you know), soft did I say? is there no word which means softer than soft? it is posatively awful, they will stand in Weiners store when any one is in there and hold each others hands and kiss, last night I went rushing into their parlor, I never knock you know, and he lay on the sofa with his head in her lap, she had her cheek laid against his, her "ivory fingers toying with his raven locks, which are rather thin on top of his head.

At the last picnic in the grove Mrs Jester lost a spoon, when she asked if I had seen it I glowered at Nell & Harris & remarked "No, but there are more "spoons" than one in this grove" he only laughed and kissed her. Bah! some women are like a wet sponge, just let a man squeeze them once and all the sense they ever had runs off. (the metaphor is more true than elegant) The late cantata "Queen Esther" was very good, Jess Roscoe & Douglas took part. Jess was Zerash's child, Bessie made her costume and it was very pretty.

The probabilities are that Mr Hougton will be married soon to the star of his amorous existance.

Carry Miner is in Chicago with her father.

I was in Superior for a week in July. Next week the Omaha & Superior Base ball teams play at Superior. Mary & Hugh Miner & I will probably go down.

But I fear you will say like a friend of mine in Florida, "My dear your letter would no doubt be delightful if one could only read them." Beside that there is a dance in Garber grove tonight & I guess we will go, they have a fine platform down under the trees. Bess & Mollie send love to Gorgie.

Yours Truly

Willa Cather

P.S. Jess said to tell Alice how we have missed her at our picnics this summer. Roscoe & Douglas had a drama in the barn this afternoon. they rendered "Robinson Crusoe" to a large and apreciative audience.

✦ ✦

In September 1890, Cather went to Lincoln and enrolled in the University of Nebraska's "Latin School," a college preparatory school designed to supplement the irregular educational experiences of students from different parts of the state. She enrolled as a freshman at the university in September 1891. The Gere family—father Charles, editor and publisher of the Nebraska State Journal, *mother Mariel Clapham, and daughters Mariel, Frances, and Ellen—were important friends of those days in Lincoln. Cather's first serious publication came*

Left to right: Mary Miner, Willa Cather, and Douglass Cather on bicycles

in March 1891 when her professor, Ebenezer Hunt, submitted her essay on Thomas Carlyle to the Nebraska State Journal *without her knowledge. Years later she remembered, "Up to that time I had planned to specialize in science; I thought I would like to study medicine. But what youthful vanity can be unaffected by the sight of itself in print! It had a kind of hypnotic effect. I still vaguely remember that essay, and it was a splendid example of the kind of writing I most dislike; very florid and full of high-flown figures of speech." She was soon hired as a columnist and reviewer for the newspaper and published dozens of articles there while a college student in Lincoln.*

TO MARIEL GERE

July 16, 1891
Red Cloud

My Dear Mariel,—

What power on earth, or rather under it, tempted you to purchase that abominible Sappho [1884 novel by Alphonse Daudet]! I had fallen into that trap myself once,—the name of the book is both innocent and classic—and honestly wished to save you the pain which it gave me. So you see you thwarted the one Christian effort of my life.

Kit [Katherine Weston] persisted in leaving Monday, and we really did not get time to write the combination letter, then you know Kit's attitude toward the Pounds is not any too amorous. Say, you should have seen Kit and Mr. Myres, they just set me in the background completely, Kit went to church <u>twice</u> on Sunday to hear him and they just had raptures over each other when he called, you may know they found each other interesting as he stayed 4 hours. If ever you meet Katherine again, you will he[a]r a learned and scholarly, not to say enthusiastic, dissertation apon Prof [Ebenezer] Hunt and Mr. Myres.

I feel awfully lonesome since all you fellows are gone, and am consoling myself with French History, Gorge Eliot, and endless rides over the prairie.

Kit and I spent Sunday evening with Mrs. Garber. James McDonald still makes night hideous by wailing for Lincoln and Louise [Pound], he has kissed the combination photo until her face is almost obliterated, he does all the caressing on <u>her</u> side, I wonder if the one at North Platte [Nebraska] is not almost in the same condition by this time. By the way you must go down and demand one of those photos. Jim never said what I was afraid he would to Kit at all, he never noticed it.

Just got a letter from Katherine stating that she had lent Sappho to a good, church going maiden in Beatrice [Nebraska]! the abandoned wretch! how could she do it, <u>I</u> at least try to warn others from those pitfalls which I have digged for mine own feet.—Now, I flatter myself that sounds very biblical.—Why on earth didn't you ask me for a book to read on the train I forgot to give you one, it was a beastly shame! You left Mr. Kenyon's Coulter [probably a college textbook] here, shall I send it or bring it up in the fall?

Kit and I drove a good deal, and I continued to punctuate my effusions with the whip apon the horses back, until the poor creature presents a most startling figure of one vast "homogeneous amalgamation of a hetrogeneous mass" of comas, periods, colons, semicolons, and—as our discussions were generally very rapturous—of many exclamation points. I know you will indeed rejoice to hear that the Cather family have a new <u>lap spread</u>!

I have been working on some frogs all morning for the purpose of getting some information concerning their circulatory systems. Both they and myself are rather tired now, so I think I shall kill the little fellows, and quit for the day. I don't know by what method to advise you to move your cruel mamma, but if she remains inexorable, could you not get on the good side of the "devils" down in the Journal office, and make a table on some friendly "hell box,"—are you "<u>on</u>" to newspaper slang, or rather technicalities?—the roar of the press would drown your victim's cries so nicely, and their blood and thunder are so appropriate in a newspaper office.

Yours
Willa Cather

→ ←

In the fall of 1891, Cather helped create a short-lived college magazine, the Lasso, *with classmates Louise Pound and James MacDonald. Soon after its demise, she began working on the well-established campus literary magazine the* Hesperian.

TO MARIEL CLAPHAM GERE

[October 1891?]

Dear Mrs Gere,—

I send you the first copy of "The Lasso", which has been issued to any one. I suppose you will be somewhat interested in this latest "lark" of mine, as it is rather a dareing one, so not having leisure to come up my self this evening, I send you my private copy of the new venture.

I would like to have told you of the plan some time ago, but it was found necessary for a time to keep the affair absolutely secret; and even now Louise and I shall keep our connection with it some what quiet. I have taken the liberty to mark my articles * in this copy I send you.

Hopeing for your approval in this "our" new hazzard, and sure of your support, I remain

Yours Truly
Willa Cather

TO MARIEL GERE

Miss Mariel Gere
is
Cordially Invited
to
Be Present
at

An Informal Feed
To be held at the Crypt of
Wm. Cather Jr.
Nov 26
1891

Seven O'clock <u>Be there</u>

✧ ✧

As evidenced in the following letters, Cather's affection for classmate Louise Pound was one of the most passionate attachments of her young life.

TO LOUISE POUND

1:30 PM [June 15, 1892]
Lincoln

My Dear Louise,

I am just about half through a nasty job of packing, and the idea has suddenly occured to me that after going up to your place tonight to see your new "Worth Costume," I did not give voice to my admiration. I dont know just why I did not, but it rather overcame me, the general effect struck me so hard that I lost track of the incidentals. I find that I have four very distinct impressions left with me; the neck, the train, the color, and what the whole affair set off. I suppose you would object to my saying that you looked very handsome last night; well it is true at any rate, and the man in the dress coat had the greenest envy that I was able to generate,—I am not sure that it is the first time he has had it.

Just a word about that Persian poem with a name which I have forgotten how to spell [*The Rubáiyát of Omar Khayyám* by Edward FitzGerald]. I wanted to get some thing that I liked awfully myself, something that I liked in its self, then it would not seem so formal, and so like carting merchandise up to your house. I thought of sets and sets, Ruskin etc. but, well, sets are sets. Then I thought of that Rubyat, I have liked it thing ever since I was a kid, and they are not so beastly common as every thing else, and I got awfully smitten with the illustrations [by Elihu Vedder], they are so queer, unlike any one else, and that swirl he brings in so often is a great idea if you take the note's explanation of it. I dont know of any thing that has the horror and mystery of the whole thing so strongly as those whirling curves. I got that instead of any other or others because I just loved the book through and through as much as it is possible to love another persons work, and because of that I felt more of a right to inflict it upon you, see?

I was rather a bore tonight, or rather last night now, wasn't I? Well, I could not help thinking that it was the last time I should see you for some time, and it affected me rather strangely. If I had known how queer it would make me feel I would not have gone up to your house. I suppose you did not feel just as I did because I was only one out of a great many who was going away while Miss [Minnie] DePue and the Deputy Governor and all the rest will be on deck so that one gone wont make much difference with you. I did feel queer, I did'nt know it had gotten such a hold on me, I shook myself after I got away, but it did'nt alter the facts of the case any. I wanted very much to ask you to go through the customary goodbye formality, but I thought it might disgust you a little so I did'nt. It was so queer that I should <u>want</u> to, when three years ago I had never seen you, and I suppose in three years more—but I dont like to think of that, three years have'nt any right to make any difference and of course they will, and I suppose we will laugh at it all some day as other women do, it make[s] me feel horribly to think of that, it will be worse than if we should hate each other. It is manifestly unfair that "feminine friendships" should be unnatural, I agree with Miss De Pue that far.

I did'nt congratulate you today because I did not know what to say, I care more for what you will do than for what you have done. I want for you in every channel just about the best that life has to give, thats all.

This epistle is infinitly sillier than one I tore up last March and did not send you, but I am tired and just have'nt physical energy enough to tear it, so you will have to pardon my "frame of mind," and lay it all to the weather.

Yours

William

I suppose you will get this in bed, for goodness sake dont let Tude [Olivia Pound] look over your shoulder.

<u>Save that Union photo, please</u>

TO MARIEL GERE

June 1, 1893
Red Cloud

Dear Mariel—

—I declare I don't know whether your name is spelled with an e or an a—I am awfully sorry that I did not get up to bid you good bye before I left, but I got a telegram asking me to hurry home as my grandma was very ill. She is much better now but is still quite weak. All the other folks are well but James who has the measels at present. Elsie is a little beauty and is as cunning as she can be. The funniest thing she has yet perpetrated is that she persists in calling Louise "WILLWESE" and talks continually about "Willie and Willwese." It is hard on poor Louise to be called a form of the name she detests. You know the fact that I lack a decent first name is a great trial to her, and strange to say she wont call me "Love"—not in public, at any rate.

It has been very dry down here, and every one has been talking about rain. Mamma told Elsie that God made the rain. Yesterday Mr. McNitt had his two lawn sprinklers going for the first time this year. Elsie came running in screaming, "O Willie! come quick and see, there are two little Gods out in McNitt's yard just raining away like everything."

Please write and tell me Mariel when you will return from Chicago and if you think you and the girls could come down and endure the solitude of semi-barbarism some time this summer. We live in rather primative style you know, but no more so than you did in the Black Hills I suppose. And the children wont bother you any more than the insects you had to contend with in camp.

Say Mariel, you have that "Elizabeth Stuart Phelps-Ward" business [book by the prolific author], have'nt you? Just send it down some time if you think of it. Louise wants to look over it once more when she comes down and see if she thinks the person who wrote it is necessarily the hardened villain she thought her two years ago.

Mrs. Wiener is very much better. Mrs. Garber as jolly as ever.

All the folks send love and Jim sends his regards to "those Gere boys" as he calls Ned [Ellen] and Frances. Tell Ned to telegraph me if she flunks in Latin.

W. Cather

I am forced to direct this Miss M— Gere, as I dont know how to spell your name

TO MARIEL GERE

August 1, 1893
Red Cloud

My Dear Mariel,

I have not written to you before because I have been away. After Louise left I was lonesome and weary of life so I went westward and sojourned some days in the country.

Well, I will begin at the beginning. The day before Louise came I bribed James for the sum of two nickles and a bottle of pop to go out in the country and stay in order that he might not bother the young lady. I was determined that she should not suffer what you girls had endured. James, being greatly in need of funds, went, but I, alas, forgot to specify how long he must remain away, and the very next evening he ran away from Papa and begged a ride of a farmer who was coming to town and dashed in on the newly arrived. They got on much better than I expected, but you know Jim is disposed to be affectionate, and the young lady is not used to children and used to positively blush under his caresses. He made brakes (or is it breaks?) as usual. Imagine my horror when one morning at breakfast he cooly said, "I say, Louise, they've got some mighty nice chocolate drops downtown, suppose you set 'em up to me, Ned did." So she set 'em up. He liked her pretty well, but he struck the same ice that I have been three years getting through. He declares that "Louise is not as good as Ned's little finger." Tell Ned I have a lasting grudge against that little finger, though I am tremendously fond of the rest of her. For me the visit was all to short, just enough to make me feel the need again and then lose her.

I wish you could have been out in the country with Roscoe and myself. When you come down next summer we will drive you all up to Bladen [Nebraska] for we find that the drive can be made in one day though it is some what tedious. We will treat you to Bladen ice cream and if you survive <u>that</u> you will be good fellows.

We spent several days at my uncle's [George Cather], who lives in a small colony of Virginians who came out here overland ages ago about the time of the creation. They are a clannish set and hang together. They have the usual country "Literary" on a somewhat better scale than it is usually carried on. My aunt [Frances Smith Cather, or Franc], who is a graduate of Smith's and Mt. Holyoak is at the head of it and surely does her share in distributing manna in the wilderness. Roscoe and I went to one of their meetings and it was really quite endurable, except a great deal of singing by a young lady who could not sing. You see the meeting was at the fair damsel's house, so it was her great and only chance to go on the programme as often as she wished, and she sang <u>twelve times</u> not counting encores. Yes, positively she sang a song or rather warbled after every number on the programme. All the while that file-like voice grated on her mother stood in the doorway gazing on her with fond pride. The twelfth song had a refrain beginning "Pray does this music charm thy heart?" which, considering the universal disgust was a some what delicate question. The programmes were all printed in the paper and the fond mother bought fifty papers and sent them to all her friends "back east" to let them know what a talented daughter she posessed. The author under discussion that night was [Ralph Waldo] Emmerson, and I think the hayseeds understand transcendentalism about as well as most university students, some of them better. By the way I must tell you about that aunt of mine some time, she is one of the ugliest, smartest, and most eccentric of human kind,—they say I am like her in ugliness and eccentricity.

One of our favorite amusements out there was sitting on top of the fifty foot wind mill tower at night. It was great on calm evenings. We could see for miles and miles, see "right off the edge of the world" as Ross said. The red harvest moon, swollen with plenty, rose over the lagoons and wheat fields, not very clear at first, but fleecy and cloud girt, as though timid of her own richness and fullness. But in an hour or so, when she felt the full zest of her race and the strength of her serenity, she left the vapors behind her. As soon as she was up, the little ponds all over the country began to glimmer, and the corn tassels in all those forests of corn looked white as silver. We could see the windmills and groves of cottonwoods all over the country as plainly as in day light. Moonlight has a peculiar effect on a country; it obliterates what is ugly, softens what is harsh,—and what is beautiful it raises almost to the divine and supernatural.

But the greatest thing we saw from that mill tower was the coming of a storm. The moon did not show herself at all, there was a long black bank of clouds in the west, and the lightening kept playing along it as steady as the fire of a battery. The world seemed to get ready for a storm; the cattle all huddled together in one end of the corall, the corn leaves got restless and began to toss their long blades up as if to reach for rain. In a moment the big wind struck us, just such a wind as struck Roscoe and the girls out by the brick kiln, and we fifty feet up in the air on a four-foot platform! Roscoe howled, "Off with your skirts, Willie or we'll never get down" you bet I peeled them off, all but a little light one. The descent was something awful, the tower shook and we shook, the wind hummed and sang and whirled all about us, if it had not been for Rosses grip on me I believe I should have fallen. My hands are still blistered from the way I hung to the rounds of the ladder.

Roscoe is out on the farm making hay now. When he comes in he and I are going to have a pull up the river and brave the horror of that accursed island again, "Ora pro nobis!" ["Pray for us!"] Poor Jack has been awfully sick. All the babys around here have been dying and Mamma has been pretty badly scared about him.

The world goes on as usual here. The elephant, Lora, still jumps the fence, "Winning Card" still paces the side walk attended by master and mistress, "Chew Spear Head Plug" still burns before us in letters of living light as a guide to our youth and innocence. We were deprived of cream for some days after you left, using it all to annoint Roscoe's back which was one large blister as a result of an unfortunate swimming expedition. The poor lad lay for two days on his stomach reading Ebar's [Georg Ebers] "Egyptian Princess" in sore travil of back and spirit.

Mother sends her regards and says she was very much pleased to get your letter, but she is too busy with Jaques to answer it at present. Roscoe sends his regards also, and James his "affectionate regards." Neddins is the one Jim singled out upon whom to bestow his worthless and oppressive affections, though he feels that he must show proper regard for Frances because of certain mysteries connected with his beehive bank.

I am afraid I must spend the rest of the summer at home and in the country. I want to get some more air and level, and write a little nonsense. I hope I can get up awhile before school begins, and if convenient I should like very much to spend part of that time with you. Give my love to all your folks, and if you meet a certain blond haired maiden gaze on her tenderly for my sake. I am eager to be back to my work, you see there has been a whole summer of DePue and it has left its mark. But DePue will marry this winter, and you know what that means, it means victory! I have won the ground from under her inch by inch, and that marriage of hers will be my coronation. You see when she is gone I will be <u>first</u>, and I will keep my place, if honor and watchfullness can keep it. Heaven help the Greek and Latin in this year's warfare; you see it is a fight in which so much time must be spent in doing nothing gracefully and patiently.

I am pretty well now, save for sundry bruises received in driving a certain fair maid over the country with one hand, sometimes, indeed, with no hand at all. But she did not seem to mind my method of driving, even when we went off banks and over hay stacks, and as for me—I drive with one hand all night in my sleep.

You can read all of this letter to Ned and Frances except the last part, as I dont wish to corrupt them by spooniness. This is a very silly epistle on the whole, what Louise would call "soulfull," she has broken me of writing this kind but once and awhile old tricks creep out.

Yours
Cather

TO MARIEL GERE

June 16, 1894
Red Cloud

My Dear Mariel;

I arrived in this substitute for Africa in due season and found the children all togged out in their new dresses in honor of my arrival. I wish you could see the little ones this summer. Jack is just as pretty as he can be. I used to think he was a decidedly homely baby, but the charge won't hold good this summer. Those big gray eyes and long black lashes make him quite a masher. Elsie is much better looking than she used to be, too. She is not so fat as she used to be and as cute as ever. The evening I arrived she asked me if I were going to stay all night and appearantly without conscious irony.

Roscoe and I are reading Virgil at lightening speed. He is still wild over botany and when we are up to your place this summer we will capture that Jack-in-the-pulpit. He is busy classing and pressing flowers most of the time.

Mr. Wiener boards over at Mrs. Garber's now. Mrs. Garber came over yesterday and asked me to dine with them Sunday. Mr. Wiener has a new trotting horse and takes me out driving almost every after noon. As a proof of my gratitude I gave him The Heavenly Twins [a provocative 1893 novel by British feminist Sarah Grand] to read!

We have had a little rain here and are hoping for more. Of course I want it to rain but I am rather disappointed in loseing such a good crop of suicides as dry weather would certainly have brought.

Smile sweetly upon Edgar for me, I like the little chap immensely. I have spent the day sending all my acquaintances photographs. I send yours by this mail. You have probably already been overwhelmed by it before reading this. They are certainly the best I ever had taken. I sent one to Ally at Rising.

Now I am writing this letter as a pretext to tell you something that I had neither nerve nor opportunity to say to you. It is not exactly a declaration of love, but of very great gratitude. I was in pretty hard straits this winter and spring. I sometimes came nearer the verge of desperation than even you knew. The fact is the thing I had been living for and in was torn away from me and it left just an aching emptiness in me. I dont think the scar will ever heal. But the fact is, if it had not been for you Mariel I never could have stuck it out in Lincoln at all. I dont believe you know quite how good and patient you were with me. I know I took an awful lot of your time, but I suppose soul-saving is a fairly respectable business, even when the soul is as worthless a one as mine, and you are certainly responsible for my pulling myself together. Of course my meeting with Miss Craigen [probably the actress Maida Craigen, who toured in Lincoln in the spring of 1894] helped me lots, but that was merely a lucky chance. It came and went like a flash and wasn't the steady light I needed. She made me forget entirely for a little while, but you made me forget a little all the while which was much better. I told Miss Jones I never felt quite sure of Kit because she just withdrew, as it were, for about two years. Miss J— responded warmly that a friendship that could be under ground three years and then come up stronger than it was at first was a thing to be proud of. Yes, but I prefer friendships that have always kept on their pins to resurrected ones. Miss J— said Katharine practically considered me dead those two years. Kind of her! Perhaps I was, so she and the Prof. did not find the company of dead folk festive and they withdrew, but you stayed by the corpse and sort of held on to it, and the corpse in its blundering way is deeply grateful. How awfully patient you have been all these years. Patient when I raved over her <u>grace</u>, her <u>beauty</u>, her <u>beautiful playing</u>, her <u>beautiful dancing</u>! Patient and sympathetic when I was in rapture because I had accidentally touched her hand, and still patient when ever the happiness of loving her was lost to me forever. Well, I can't thank you, I can only hope that you will never know such pain to need such a consoler. It is a good thing to love, but it don't pay to love that hard. It makes a fool and dupe of you while you are at it, and then it must end some time and after it is taken from you the hunger for it is terrible, terrible!

Be sure to go to Crete [Nebraska], we will have a good time there I know. Doug will come too if he can leave the farm. He is cultivating 90 acres of corn himself this year. That is pretty steep work for a little boy. I hope that old paper wont take too much of my time. I want to have leisure to knock around with the rest of you. I guess I can make time though, I generally can. Write to me if you want to. That is, dont make yourself if you dont want to.

Yours
Willa

In June 1895, Cather graduated from the University of Nebraska. She remained in Nebraska for several months while trying to decide what to do next.

TO MARIEL, ELLEN, AND FRANCES GERE; ALTHEA "ALLIE" ROBERTS; AND MARY "MAYSIE" AMES

January 2, 1896
Siberia [Red Cloud]

Mariel, Ellen, Frances, Allie, and Maysie;
My Dear Push,

I address you thus in a bunch because I dare not address Mariel singly as I do not feel equal to discussing Love and Live and Death and Alvary [Max Alvary, a German opera star] and German opera with her by mail. My spirit is willing but my pen is weak. When I see her I will consent to talk it however. I wonder if it would diminish Mariel's adoration to know that Alvary's real name is Max Achenbach and that he has nine charming little Achenbachs and a Frau who weighs three hundred.

I had a fine time in Beatrice, the fascinating Katharine is just as fascinating as ever and Bertie's charms grow apace. He and I used to sit around and quote Ella Wheeler Wilcox until we wellnigh drove Katharine crazy. He was very nice and I dont blame Katharine for liking him, I do and he is not my brother either.

Well, girls, I must tell you about a New Year's dance Douglas and I went to last night. Douglas made me go, for about sixteen girls wanted and expected him to ask them and he thought it would be nice to make them all furious. He sent to Lincoln for a lot of flowers for me and so on and I really had to go with them. And of all rough-house affairs, of all cake walks! The hall was big and the floor might have been good, but they had the floor heaped with shavings and chunks of wax, chunks which you had to leap and mount and clamber over with an alpenstock. For seats they had big rough planks resting on chairs. The boys and girls had the same dressing room. The refreshments consisted of ice water in a wooden pail, coffee and ham sandwitches which they passed in a bushel basket, a potato basket. But this is only the setting, the environment, the dance was the thing! The men caught your arm just as high as your sleeve would permit, fortunately they could not get up any <u>farther</u> than my elbow, and they hugged you like ten thousand Ourys. I had a terrible feeling that they were likely to lay hands upon my bare neck at any moment and wished for a high neck. The men fell down every now and then and you had to help them up. Yet this was a dance of the elite and bon ton of Red Cloud. Mary and Margie and Hughie and my fair cousin [Retta Ayres, who married Hugh Miner in 1896] were there. One thing was a comfort, Douglas did splendidly and he certainly was the most civilized looking object in the crowd.

Say girls, you remember our handsome preacher Putnam whose bible Marie returned two years go, well he is pastor of the First Christian Church of Denver now. He was in town yesterday and he is better looking than ever.

I suppose poor Ned and Frances are getting the best out of their vacation ere their period of servitude begins again. Smile sweetly on Mr. Oury for me, Neddy. I send him some literature on Virginia today. Have you heard any thing from John Charles or from the sister of John Charles?

Say Mariel, I am going to ask a favor of you and if you hate to do it, why just dont. Sarah Harris has a little book of mine, "Sapho", by Alphonse Daudet, which I am very fond of as it is illustrated by Rossi and every picture is a whole French novel. Now considering the existing relations it would be snippy of me to write and demand it from Sarah, and alas I know too well her habit of forgetting to return things. Would you please tell her sometime that you want to read it and I told you to ask her for it? I really want the thing awfully and I dont want to ask Mrs. Imhoff to get it for me as I am afraid the book might corrupt her morals or dispel her illusions or something, but you see I have confidence in Mariel.

I dont know when I will appear in Lincoln next, nor do I much care. One of the charms of the Province is that one gets indifferent toward everything, even suicide. "Then think of me as one already dead, and laid within the bottom of a tomb." Please let me know the university and "social" news from time to time, you know I really am interested in all those complicated matters. When you next see "all my friends" give them my love, unqualified and unmodified.

Farewell, O Maids,

> "And when like her, O Saki! you shall pass,
> Among the guests star scattered on the grass,
> And reach the spot where I myself made one,
> Forget me and turn down an empty glass."

Thats poetry, I quote it to Jack and the cats now that I have not Allie and Bert Weston anymore.

Farewell all of ye
Willa

Love to your Papa and Mamma.

The poetry quoted at the end of the letter is from FitzGerald's The Rubáiyát of Omar Khayyám.

❖ ❖

Hoping to get a temporary teaching appointment at the University of Nebraska to replace her favorite English professor, Herbert Bates, she tried to draw on her friendship with the influential Charles Gere to obtain the position. She did not get the job.

Will Owen Jones, mentioned in the following, was the managing editor of Gere's newspaper, the Nebraska State Journal, *and an important early mentor for Cather.*

TO CHARLES GERE

March 14, 1896
Red Cloud

Dear Mr. Gere;

I inclose a letter from Professor Adams which will explain its self. I have just seen regent C. W. Kaley and he tells me that the whole business of appointing the new Instructor rests with Mr. Morrill, himself and the Chancellor. I think if I could get the appointment for the remaining two months of the year that I could hold it next year. I have been in all of Bate's classes and he writes that he will recommend me to any extent I desire. If you could see the Chancellor and Mr. Morrill for me I think my chances would be good. Of course the two principal things against me are my age and sex, but I think I could over come both of those. On the other hand the university is hard pressed for funds and I would go in as an Instructor and they would pay me five hundred dollars less than the man they intended getting who would have been Adjunct Professor. Mr. Bates says that whatever is done must be done at once, and untill I can get up to Lincoln I must trust to my friends. If you could see Mr. Morrill and the Chancellor it would be a great help. Please ask Mr. Jones to send me some transportation as soon as possible so that I can go up to see to it. I telegraphed him please to send it this afternoon, but he may not understand.

Of course you know how much the appointment would mean to me if I could only get it. I have had some experience in coaching students in English and I am sure I could teach it.

Faithfully yours
Willa Cather

➳ ❦

The "Pound scrape" mentioned in the next letter probably refers to Cather's publication of a thinly veiled lampoon of Roscoe Pound (Louise's brother) in the pages of the Hesperian *in March 1894. Why she chose to ridicule him in print remains a mystery. It led to a falling out with the Pound family.*

TO MARIEL GERE

May 2, 1896
Red Cloud

My Dear Mariel,

You are a trump, and you seem to have the knack of soothing the afflicted spirits of the undersigned when no one else can quite reach them. You have sort of been a bracer to me ever since I was a shaved headed Prep with very idiotic notions about things and a sweet confidence in myself which, odious as it must have been, I wish to God I had back. I never should have got through that Pound scrape without you, as I have told you before. No matter how daffy I may seem sometimes I have never forgotten that when my father and my mother and Katharine and the Lord himself deserted me, then you took me up. Heavens Mariel, I wonder will I <u>ever</u> be done making a fool of myself? There has been another little scrap recently with some one I like that I may tell you about sometime if I can get my nerve up. It was all my fault and I am an unspeakable fool to let it hurt me, but it is not in one's power to help being hurt sometimes. Lord but I have always been a monumental idiot and I dont see how you have stood me at all. For a time I affected the scholastic and quoted Greek at you, and then I affected the Bohemian and what not. They were all honest enthusiasms at the time, but they seem terribly silly now. I think I should get so disgusted with myself that I would just quietly take a dose of Prussic acid to rid myself of my own company if it were not for this one thing, that most of my idiocy has come from liking somebody or other too well. That's a very pitiable sort of justification, but it's the best that I've got. I might say from liking things as well as people. Its a curse to be built that way. In the years I have been away I have kind of grown away from my family and their way of looking at things until they are not much comfort and I have the unpleasant feeling that they are all the time kind of waiting for me to "do something." People have joshed them about my "ability" until they sort of expect something unusual of me and the Lord only knows where its coming from for I dont. I feel all played out. How can I "do anything" here? I have'nt seen enough of the world or anything else. I am a terribly superficial person. If it were not for Jack I should get quite desperate sometimes. That little chap's big grey eyes have a power of consolation in them, he comforts me just as he comforted Katharine in her woe last summer. He is just made to love people dearly—a sweet enough thing for other people, but it will cause him suffering enough I am afraid.

Yesterday I drove overland twenty miles to Blue Hill [Nebraska] with Douglas to a dance. It sounds giddy, but I went because the kid was wild to go. I did'nt expect to have a good time but I did. In the first place I found a dandy sort of a girl, handsome as a picture and finely educated, reads and speaks French and German like a top. She is teaching for the first time and by some strange chance drifted to Blue Hill. She is boarding with an old high school Professor and his wife whom I went up to visit. Then at the dance who should I meet but old Fred Gund, once a co-editor of the Hesperian with me. He was a cigarette smoking sport of the Sawyer gang then, but now he is a sane manly business fellow and cashier of the Blue Hill bank. He was awfully nice and devoted himself to me the whole evening and it was good to see him and talk over old times. There were <u>thirty five</u> dances and I danced them all. After the dance Professor Curran had a lunch for us and Fred went with us. After lunch the Miner girls—they went up to the dance too—played on the violin and piano a long time it was half past three when the young gentlemen said good night. We had danced until two. Then the Hill Girl—Miss [Anna] Gayhardt—and I went to bed, and she was so glad to meet somebody "from civilization" that we talked books and theatre until the daylight came through the shutters. Then we slept just two hours and got up for breakfast. I came home on the train at noon. The worst about going out and having a good time is that it makes you all the more blue when you get back to your solitude and your accursed unfinished manuscripts that you haven't got the heart to work at. "Life is one d—d grind, Cather" as Prof. Hunt used to say. There is nothing to do but quietly peg along and lie low until I get out of debt, for I haven't got the nerve to ask my family to help me out any more. Besides they cant. Hang it, I've made a sweet muddle of things for a maiden of one and twenty. I'd be all right if the several fair actresses to whom I have rashly loaned money would see fit to remit, but bless you they cant live without paste diamonds and champagne and I haven't the heart to dog them about it. I suppose they would do as much for me. Anyway I have learned a lot from them—not that it's much worth knowing, but I suppose I must consider it all for the "good of the cause of art" and let it go as the price of experience. Only there have been times when I could better afford to pay for experience than just now. I cant tell this sort of thing to Katharine—you know why. Well, I have bothered you enough for this time. I want to come up to Lincoln sometime this month and I will be only too glad to stop with you a day or two—my stay in Lincoln wont be long. I get the happiest letters from poor old Bates, he is so gay now that he is in a hill county where people care about Paderewski and Swinburne. I think he has come into his kingdom. Not a big one, but he will get a sight of pleasure out of it.

Yours as Ever
Willa

PART TWO

The Pittsburgh Years

1896–1906

There is no God but one God and Art is his revealer; thats my creed and
I'll follow it to the end, to a hotter place than Pittsburgh if need be.
—WILLA CATHER TO MARIEL GERE, August 4, 1896

Willa Cather and a young fellow passenger
aboard the S.S. *Noordland* on her way to Europe,
June 1902

In the summer of 1896, when Willa Cather was twenty-two years old, she left Nebraska to become a self-supporting working woman. Building on her college experience working for student publications and the *Nebraska State Journal*—and probably with the help of the Lincoln newspapermen who had befriended her—she got a job as editor of the *Home Monthly Magazine* in Pittsburgh, Pennsylvania. Though she got homesick for her family and friends in Nebraska, this daring move east suited Cather's ambition. She went to a new community where she could re-create herself as an independent woman, spending her time and money as she saw fit. Moreover, she could do it while editing and writing: this magazine would need to fill its pages, and that was something Willa Cather—or her nom de plume "Helen Delay"—could do.

TO MARIEL GERE

Friday [July 1896]
Pittsburgh

My Dear Mariel;

I have only been a few hours in this City of Dreadful Dirt, so you must not take my first impressions seriously I feel like being funny. I began to feel good as soon as I got east of Chicago. When I got to where there were some hills and clear streams and trees the Lord planted I did'nt need any mint julip. The conductor saw my look of glee and asked if I was "gettin' back home."

Mr. [James W.] Axtell met me and timidly approached me. I did not think he could be the man and at first repulsed him with scorn. He was exceedingly cordial and brought me right out home. They live in a beautiful part of the city where the hills are all built up with big ivy-grown houses that are beautiful to see. When we entered the parlor my heart sank. It is one of the hair cloth furniture kind and its only ornament was a huge crayon portrait of Grandpă!! But the library is much better. It also contains a picture of grandpă, but there are also novelists of the milder sort and I saw Mrs. [Nellie] Axtell reading Harpers, which is encouraging. Now for the sad news, the Puritan maid [daughter Clara] is not at home. She is over in Wainsburg [Waynesburg, Pennsylvania] visiting "aunt somebody" and being coached in Greek preparatory to going to Vassar this fall—not Wellesley—So they say, but I secretly believe they sent her away to save her from my contaminating influence. I am rather glad she is not here, it will give me a better chance to get on to my new role. The room I have must be hers, I think, as it contains three bibles. Of course she took three with her, so that makes six. Alas! It also contains many a well worn copy of the trashy religious novels of E. P. Roe. I can stand the bibles, but not E. P. Roe. Now hear the joyful tidings, Grandpă is not here, he is down at Mission Ridge with Aunt Somebody and will probably remain there the rest of his natural days. They say the climate suits him, may it continue to do so! for I feel that the stern eye of Grandpă, so accustomed to detecting the follies and foibles of this world, would penetrate me thin disguise as the old sage did Lamia's, and he would cry out "I see her, the devotee of French fiction, the consort of musicians and strolling players!" Heaven save me from the Argus-eyed grandpă.

In Chicago I caught the [Paul Gustave] Doré exhibition at the gallery. Great splurges of color, theatrical effects, enormous canvases and a sort of general spectacular effect a good deal like the "Last Days of Pompeii" bill boards. There was only one I could see any lofty or even honest work in, The "Neophyte." The rest either had a flat chromo look or they were done by a trick.

When I get a good pen and some new impressions I will write a letter that you can read. For the present this must do. Love to all and especially to your mamma.

In Haste
Willa

Came from Chicago here by the B.&.O.
℅ Home Magazine, Pittsburgh, Penn.

→ ←

After arriving in Pittsburgh, Cather got right to work, managing the magazine practically by herself only weeks after starting. At least, that's what she reported to friends back in Lincoln. Eighteen ninety-six was an election year, and Nebraskan William Jennings Bryan was making his first of several failed attempts to become the U.S. president. Cather saw an opportunity to exploit her connections in Lincoln and get something good for the Home Monthly.

TO MARIEL CLAPHAM GERE

July 13 [1896]
Pittsburgh

My Dear Mrs Gere;

Why dont some of your heartless daughters write to me? If they only knew how lonely and alone I am they surely would. I can stand it very well through the day when there is plenty of work and bustle at the office, but at night my soul yearns a good deal for my own kind and for those three beloved girls of yours. I would give anything just to see Jack ten minutes. I dream about those big tender gray eyes of his every night. The Axtells are gone West now, and from days end to days end I see only the prim old maid who keeps my boarding house and my stenographer.—Dont that sound large, my stenographer!—You see the entire responsibility of the first issue devolves on me. We are of course short of manuscript on the start and I have written fully one half of the magazine. Then the foreman is not used to magazine work and I have to oversee everything that goes on in the composing room. I'll tell you my old Hesperian experience helps me out there. I was down in composing room until one oclock last night sweating over those forms and making up the pages. Then I have all the manuscript reading and purchasing for the September number, and all the correspondence with literary people, which of course demands some care. Fortunately the stenographer is an exceptionally good one and knows how to <u>spell</u>. The responsibility is something awful. I dream about that magazine every night.

Now Mrs. Gere I want to ask a big favor of you, and no one but you can do it. I want to write an article on Mrs. W. J. [Mary Baird] Bryan and Mrs. [Ida Saxton] McKinley before any of the other magazines do. Its a chance for a big "scoop" and I want to make a grand success of it. The old maid who keeps my boarding house knew Mrs. McKinley well in her youth. I have worked her for all she is worth and got lots of valuable data. Next week I go down to Canton Ohio to get early photographs of Mrs. McKinley etc. Now I cant go to Lincoln—how I wish I could—so I want you to please send me all the facts you know and can get about Mrs. Bryan. What her literary tastes are, her club standing, her house, her legal studies, how she came to take them up etc. You know what I want, personal matter that the newspapers dont give. Of course I will keep your name out of it, and mine too for that matter. I will use a pen name, I have had to use half a dozen in the first number. Now dont fail me, Mrs. Gere, for this means lots to me. Mr. Axtell will be delighted if I can work it up thoroughly. I will write to Captain Phillips and ask him to try to get me Mrs. Bryan's photograph. I must have some if they are to be had.

The magazine is not all I could desire from a literary standpoint, its policy is rather namby-pamby, but of course that is the publishers' business, not mine. I want to show you all that I can take up a thing and stick to it even if it dont just suit me. The great key of success is to work when you are not suited, I fancy. You would'nt know the lazy girl I used to be in me now. Even the stenographer has been lecturing me about working too hard. If Mr. Axtell is suited, I'll make this thing succeed. I never felt so able to work before. My own literary work I will have to keep up outside largely, its a little too heavy for whats wanted in the monthly. Of course its a little hard for me to write gentle home and fireside stuff, but I simply will do it. Its so satisfactory to be really of some importance, to have something to do that no one else can do quite as well. It takes all the ennui out of life. At first I rebelled at some things, I had to learn that every editor is not a Mr. Gere or a Mr. [Will Owen] Jones. But I have learned that now and have resigned myself to the fact. I mean to stick this thing out. Thats the size of it. Three tall, plain, stiff, prim, Presbyterian Miss Rushes called on me this evening, three of Lydas [Axtell] ten thousand cousins. I was very demure and discussed flower gardening church music.

Give my love to the three girls who have forgotten me, and much to yourself and Mr. Gere.

As ever yours
Willa

TO ELLEN GERE

Monday [July 27, 1896]
% <u>Home Monthly</u>, Pittsburgh

Dear Little Neddins;

Excuse the diminutive, but it always seems to me that Mariel and I ought to be grandmothers to you and Frances.

Well, Neddy, its not half so bad as I feared. They are not the infant damnation sort of Presbyterians at all, in fact their church split off from the other church because of its more liberal interpretation of the creed regarding pre-destination and the "summary treatment of infants" as Mr Axtell calls it. He means to be a jolly man and is an awfully nice one, but fun does'nt come natural to him. He has told me all about Lyda's over-zeal and their worry over her. He seems to look at it quite sensibly. But everything is church here. When they have parties they invite the members of their Sunday school class! I inadvertantly told Mr. Axtell that my folks were Baptists—I had to say something—and alas, the Baptist minister lives next door and in ten min-utes he had him over and upon me. Pity me! Miss Rush, one of Lyda's five thousand seven hundred cousins, was over to dinner yesterday. She is going to Vassar with Lyda this fall and was talking about the work required in various universities. I told her how many hours I usually carried at the U. of N. The dear thing looked up in sweet surprise and said innocently, "What, how did you ever find time with your newspaper work and church work?" My church work, O Neddy! Here every girl has her church work just as other girls have fans or powder boxes.

We went of an organ recital by William Archer at the great Carnegie music hall Saturday night. It was great. I never heard [Robert] Schumann's "Trau-merei" on an organ before. The music hall is in the same huge building with the Carnegie library and art gallery. I thought the U. of N. Library was nice, but this—its marble from one end to the other and the colors and frescoes are just one artistic harmony. It is only a short distance from the office and they have all the books in the world there I think. And right near it is the Casino theatre and my old friend Pauline Hall plays there all next week. I foresee alas, that I will not go to the library on matinee afternoons but will slip across to the Casino to look upon Pauline's glorious anatomy once again. The old Nick is in me Neddy, its no use talking. The Axtells are awfully nice, but they are chilly as a wine cellar and sort of formal even with each other. I cant express it, its just the old infant damnation business. Phillip is a comfort, for he is little at least. Because I come from the West he expected me to tell him Indian sto-ries, and I fulfill my role in a way that would convulse you could you hear me. When I get through going to church and telling Indian stories I will have no more sense of truth left than [university classmate] Carlyle Tucker.

I went to Church with the Axtells and their relatives, who comprise the entire population of East Liberty, last night. Opening hymn "Onward Chris-tian Soldiers", Golden text, "whosoever will, let him drink of the water of life freely." Air'nt I doing well?

As to the magazine Ned, I fear it will be great rot, home and fireside stuff, about babies and mince pies. But the financial outlook is good, so I guess I'll stay by it for a while anyway. I will be virtually managing editor, Mr. Axtell and I being the only people who have anything to do with the literary part of it. During his month of absence I am to have sole charge. The proof reading goes all right, I found four mistakes he passed over this morning. I have a nice desk etc. of my own. Write to me <u>soon</u> and tell me if Mr. Oury goes to help the Cubans or gets killed or anything. He is real nice, is'nt he?

Hurriedly
Willa

❧ ❦

In the late nineteenth century, "Bohemianism" became a popular catchword for an impoverished, idealistic, unconventional, and artistic way of life following the publication of Henri Murger's novel Scènes de la vie de Bohème *and many subsequent dramatizations, the most famous of which is probably Puccini's* La Bohème. *Cather had already distanced herself from Bohemianism in an article in the* Nebraska State Journal *months before writing the following letter: "For the business of an artist's life is not Bohemianism for or against, but ceaseless and unremitting labor." The phrase "a desert country by the sea," which she quotes below, is Shakespeare's description of Bohemia in* A Winter's Tale.

TO MARIEL GERE

August 4, 1896
Pittsburgh

[Written in the top margin:] % Home Monthly, <u>East End</u>, Pittsburgh

My Dear Mariel;

Your letter dated July 10 has just reached me after almost a month's delay because you forgot to put the sacred words <u>East End</u> on the envelope. This is the tony part of the town and the people who are so happy as to dwell here have to be particularized.

Now I am just back from an excellent rendition of Fra Diavolo [opera by Daniel Auber]—went with a little Chicago chap—and I feel the spirit of battle. Tomorrow I will write you a lot of pleasant things, but tonight I am going to scrap with you a bit. Now Mariel, did you ever think I meditated a solid course of Bohemia in all its degrees? If you did you do me rather an injustice. Of course one may think of it at times, but I used to actually think about slapping Tude Pound, yet I certainly never would have done it. Really, I never for a moment seriously contemplated becoming a citizen of that "desert country by the sea." If I have'nt any regard for myself I have just a little for my family. I may go to New York sometime, but not for the express purpose of going to the bow-wows, and certainly not until I get some money ahead. I can most effectually surprise my friends and pain my enemies by living a most conventional existence, and I intend to do it. As to T. [university classmate Tom] Wing's words, Heaven how much or how little did I tell you on that night of much morphine and little Morpheus? The less I care about T. Wing and his "words" the better, thats one reason I was so awfully glad to get away from Lincoln. I am going to quit writing to that gentleman pretty soon and then forget all about that conversation. Only yesterday I wrote him that I had never forgiven it and never could. He has one creed and I another. They are creeds that never meet in this world. There is no God but one God and Art is his revealer; thats my creed and I'll follow it to the end, to a hotter place than Pittsburgh if need be. Its not an affectation, its my whole self, not that I think I can do anything myself, but the worship of it. That is about all that life has given me: it is enough. I dont ask anything more. I think I get as much good out of it as most people do out of their religions. I love it well enough to be a failure in it myself, well enough to be unhappy. It has felt this way from the time I could like anything, and it only grows stronger as I grow older.

Just now I find it very easy to be "conventional," I never worked half so hard before. The only form of excitement I indulge in is raceing with the electric cars on my bicycle. I may get killed at that, but certainly nothing more. And as to writing, it is not likely that I will treat more delicate subjects than "The Care of Children's Teeth" for some years to come.

Then really I like the work, grind though it is. I really like it immensely. Its a great boon just to be of some absolute use somewhere, to be at the head of something and have work that you must do. It does away with the tedium of life. Then the town and the river and the hills would compensate for almost anything. And I meet so many different kinds of people. I have met a lot of New York dramatic critics, [popular novelist] Amelia E. Barr paid me a business call last week as she went through Pittsburgh, and I have talked 46 minutes with Rudyard Kipling, which alone was worth coming here for. Then my head is so thumping full of new ideas. I seem for some reason to be able to do better work than ever before. I begin a little serial story "The Count of Crow's Nest" in the September Monthly which I showed to Harold Dundy one of the mss. readers of the Cosmopolitan, and he pronounced it first class stuff, said he could use it and would give me a hundred dollars for it. Of course I was'nt at liberty to sell it as it was needed here. The artist to whom I sent it to be illustrated [Florence Pearl England] also wrote me a charming note about it, though she did'nt know it was mine. Its so good to be in a country where there is a Caesar to appeal to in these things. Since my work is improving I dont feel that I am wasting time here. O if I can only make it some day and triumph over T. Wing and the rest! I doubt if I ever do anything very good, though. I seem to lack the one thing.

I enjoy the manuscript reading and the proof reading dont bother me as I feared it would. They are very considerate of me at the office, and let me off a day to write whenever I want it. Indeed, I do pretty much as I please, I am rather at the head of things so long as I follow their policy.

I cant tell you how nice Mr. [George] Gerwig has been to me. He is my devoted slave and I can call on him for anything. I have met a lot of charming people and already belong to the "swell" Woman's Club of the town. That dont look very Bohemian, does it?

Well, I have written you a long tirade about my work. Pretty soon I will get time to tell you about the picnics and boat rides and excursions and things. I have a good deal of that sort of thing and enjoy it immensely.

Please dont forget to thank your mother—or yourself—for those photographs.

In Haste and with much love to all
Willa

P.S. I have a real live stenographer of my own, she is a dandy too. I dictate all my business letters.

W.C.

TO FLORENCE PEARL ENGLAND

September 10, 1896
The Home Monthly, Pittsburgh

My Dear Miss England:

Your drawing arrived this morning, and while we like it we do not find it as satisfactory as the others. I send it back to you by express this morning, hoping that you can make a few changes in it for us. In the first place I very much wish that you could have Mademoiselle DeKoch appear without a hat. I have been among singers a good deal, and never knew one to wear a hat to a concert. It seems to me if you could just have a wrap thrown over the back of the chair and have her hair done high that it would be a very great improvement. Some way she and Buchanan do not seem to look just as they did the last time. If you could put him in a dress coat and have him look a little more like he did last month, I think it would improve the picture. The tenor is thoroughly satisfactory, but if you will notice he seems to have a good deal more animation and intelligence in his face than either Buchanan or Mademoiselle, whereas he was supposed to be rather a silent partner.

Now we must have the picture by the 18th. If you will not have time to make the changes or do not feel as though you can do so, please send it back to us at once as it is and we will try to use it.

It has occurred to me that perhaps you may not have kept a sketch of the former drawing you made of Buchanan and Mademoiselle, so I take the liberty of sending back the scene of three figures, hoping that you can make Buchanan especially more nearly resemble his own self. Please send both of these pictures back to us, as we like to keep the original sketches from which illustrations are made.

Yours sincerely,
Willa Cather

P.S. I think the tenor is just about right, but Buchanan and Miss DeKoch should be "keyed up" a little higher, more animated etc. And dont you think Miss de Koch's gown is rather flimsy. She had such a decided air and style in the first picture last month that it perhaps makes one expect too much of her this. I hope you wont think we are chronic kickers, we were delighted with the first illustrations, but I think you will see yourself on comparing them that this last one is inferior.

Sincerely yours
Willa Cather

The illustrations in question were for Cather's own story "The Count of Crow's Nest," published in the September and October 1896 issues of the Home Monthly. *While working hard on the magazine, Cather also published pieces in the* Pittsburg Leader *and in the* Nebraska State Journal, *managed by her mentor Will Owen Jones.*

TO WILL OWEN JONES

January 15 [1897]
Pittsburgh

Dear Mr. Jones;

I may not be able to get my stuff in this week. "This is our busy week."
But I had an experience with the managing editor of the "Times" and "News"
that I thought might interest you, so I'll take time to tell you. It is W. A.
Magee [she probably means Christopher L. Magee], you know, the man who
"owns" Pittsburgh. I have known his sister in law but had not met him. He is
the political "boss" here, President and Chief stock-holder of the Consolidated
Street Car Company that owns 8000 miles of track, is a multimillionair and
is managing editor of two papers. Of course he dont do much editing. Well, I
have been thinking for a good while that it would be a good thing to be working into some solid newspaper in case the Monthly should collapse. So last
Friday with merely a note of introduction from my actress friend Miss [Maida]
Craigen I went to his office. There were more people there than I ever saw in
an office; poor women who wanted work for their husbands on the car line;
men who had been fired for drunkenness and wanted to "try again", men who
wanted to sweep the streets, and seedy looking newspaper men in last summer's tan shoes and red neckties whose appearance told plainly why they were
there. Well, we waited two hours and at last Magee came in. He was a little
ugly man carelessly almost shabbily dressed with an intensely nervous manner.
When all those people began at him I thought it was simply no use to try and
was about to go away, for here were all these hungry looking people "wanting jobs." But I stayed just for the pleasure of seeing this millionair's manner
with the poor devils. He had a kind word for every one of them and it was'nt
unctious patronizing kindness, just the simple sort that a man whose heart
was good might let drop to his less fortunate fellows as he hurried through
the thousand gigantic plans of his busy life. He knew most of the women by
name, gave them letters to the engineers, encouraged the men, & gave them
letters. At last it was my turn. Well, I had never asked a stranger for a "job"
before, so I did'nt say I knew his family; I wanted to talk business only. Like a
fool I had'nt thought just what I wanted to ask for or what I would say I could
do. But I told him what I had done and that I had only a limited amount of
time for newspaper work & that I was on the magazine. He was as nice to me
as to the rest, helped me to say what I wanted and got my whole history out of
me in five minutes by the clock. Then he said he'd look up my case and asked

me to come again today. I went back this afternoon not expecting anything but to see and wonder at this queer nervous little fellow again. Why there were ten experienced newspaper men in his office begging for a job. I just went because the fellow was a wonder to me. He asked me into his library—both of his offices were literally <u>full</u> of people—His library is a palace, though he says he seldom reads. He got to the point right away, remembered my name and said he "took to me." Told me to go ahead and do some special articles as things struck me and he'd take them. Said there was a vacancy on the evening paper and he would see that my chance was good there. Then he said, "Now there is one thing I should have asked you the other day, but I was really very much exhausted then. Some times when people strike a new town they are laid up. I've been that way myself. If you're fixed that way I'd be glad to tide you over." I cant tell you how nicely he said it, Mr. Jones, it did'nt hurt my pride a bit. Of course I told him I did'nt need anything, but I added "You're a white man sure." He goes to New York tomorrow, gets back Monday, made an engagement with me for Wednesday and Friday goes to Chicago. I'd work for the fellow just to study him, this queer fellow who controlls the politics of Pennsylvania, "owns Pittsburgh", edits two papers, rides in a carriage, lives in a palace, wears dirty collars and shoes run down at the heel, talks to street car conductor's wives like they were his friends and picks up poor lone maidens he has never seen before and does the big generous by them. How can he do it all? I should think he'd just <u>drop</u> from exhaustion. He left me to meet with the architects to examine plans for an immense new bank he is president of.

Well I did'nt mean to write you a volume, and of course nothing may come of it. But my admiration for W. A. Magee will be just the same. I thought it might interest you to hear about such a giant, we dont see much of that sort of thing in the west. Say, Mr. Jones, if you'd drop me a line about your New York adventures I'd greatly appreciate it.

Sincerely
Willa Cather

TO MARIEL GERE

April 25, 1897

My Dear Mariel;

If you dont want to write to me I'll say no more about it. What your reasons are I can't guess but I suppose you have them. I guess though you won't mind me talking to you a little while tonight? You have so often taken pity on my loneliness long ago. Dorothy Canfield has been spending a week with me you know and she is gone now and the reaction has set in. I cant tell you what a charming girl she is growing to be. Her visit was a joy and a comfort to me. All my friends rose nobly to the occasion and gave her a downright jolly time. Theatres, parties, excursions, drives in the park until we were thoroughly exhausted. The child said it "was the first time she had ever really been treated like a young lady" and the haughty offhand manner in which she received the attentions of the men was very funny and so <u>sweetly</u> young. It's tough to come back from the office now and find no one cuddled up on the divan waiting for me. Dorothy approves of the young Doctor who wants me to marry him. I have not as yet decided whether I will or not. It would be a very excellent match in every way, but I dont care for him. I suppose though that really does'nt matter much. He was very nice to Dorothy and I'm glad she carried away pleasant impressions of every one.

Business affairs are going much better than they were this winter and I am doing my work better. That is I am learning to keep still and do just what I'm told. Of course the magazine is the worst trash in the world, but it is trash they want and trash they pay me for and they shall have it.

Socially my life here is more pleasant than it ever has been or than I ever thought it could be anywhere. I want you to come like Dorothy and see how pleasant. You see here I have neither short hair nor Dr. [Julius] Tyndale nor dramatic propensities nor any other old thing to queer me. It's like beginning a new life in broad daylight away from the old mistakes. As Charles Lamb says "Gad: how we like to be liked." It's a novel experience for me and it's rather gone to my head. I tell you all this because you stood by me in the day when my friends were not many and when I owed much more to your friendship than I then knew. And by the Lord I'm going to make you glad you did it all some day Mariel! I am that! I'd rather make you and Roscoe proud of me than anything else in the world.

And now "Good night, good night Beloved!" as Nellie Griggs used to sing to Max two miles off the key.

Yours as Ever
Willa

Did you see my Brownville tale ["A Resurrection," published in the *Home Monthly* in April]? I sent you a paper.

Cather had met Dorothy Canfield while at the University of Nebraska, where Dorothy's father, James Canfield, was then chancellor. Dorothy Canfield was six years younger than Cather, so only in her early teens when they met, but her precocious intelligence and maturity made her an excellent companion. Their friendship—with some bumps along the way—lasted until Cather's death.

➤ ❖

After the Home Monthly *was sold, in 1897, Cather left the magazine. She made a visit to Nebraska before returning to Pittsburgh to work for the* Pittsburg Leader.

TO WILL OWEN JONES

Tuesday [September 7, 1897]
Red Cloud

My Dear Mr. Jones;

The Pittsburgh Leader wired me this morning to come at once to fill a position at $75.00 a month. I must get there next week. Please send me transportation to Lincoln at once so that I can tarry there a few days before going east, and get me fixed for Chicago as soon as you can.

I almost hate to go just now. Have been writing stories and getting on at it better than I have ever been able to do before. But I don't dare let this chance slip. Somehow though I can do better work in stories down here than anywhere. I do the society act too much in Pittsburgh. They don't often "take a stranger in" down there and I am as vain as all the rest of my sex and can't do the hermit act one bit. But dear me there is next summer and a lot of summers ahead, and in Pittsburgh there will be Calve [Emma Calvé] and [Sarah] Bernhardt and all the rest of "the great["], so I guess I'll go. Then I think it was awfully white of The Leader to send for me when Pittsburgh is full of unemployed reporters.

Yours Faithfully
Willa Cather

TO MARIEL GERE

Sunday [probably September 19, 1897]
Pittsburgh

My Dear Mariel;

It was just a week ago that I watched you all get further and further away from me, and that I had to overcome a mighty impulse to jump off the train and run back to Lincoln.

I am fairly settled in my work now and like it very much. My duties are those of day telegraph editor besides doing the dramatic work for which latter I receive extra pay. I edit and write the headlines for all the telegraph matter that comes in from 8 a.m. till 3. p.m. After 3 oclock I am entirely free and have all my evenings to myself except Saturday when I work until midnight.

Five gentlemen met me at the train and every one seems really glad to see me back. But Mariel, I <u>will not</u> be away from Nebraska another year. Of what use are money and success if one is not happy? And I can not be happy so far away from home. O Mariel, I am so tired of it, their gay Bohemia! I have seen enough of it. It is not so black as it's painted, but it's such a lone and loveless land and it's so many leagues from home. Sometimes I wonder if I am the same girl who looked at all these gilded lies so eagerly two years ago. I think my heart was asleep in those days, but ah it is awake now, awake and aching for one little lad [Jack Cather] who is asleep in his bed a thousand miles away. No one but God will ever know what that baby has done for me. I think he has killed every unworthy ambition in me forever. I don't want money or fame at all any more, but just my three boys always. You believe this, don't you? You see here I get a good deal of—well, of admiration, people here think I am cleverer than I am and of course that is pleasant in a way. But I'd rather have Roscoe's good opinion and Douglass' laugh than all of it. I guess Mariel, that you were the only person who ever really understood me, for you always said that I never was and never could be a "Bohemian" at heart—even when I tried to be one.

Mrs. [Elia] Peattie entertained me delightfully in Chicago, and there are a lot of nice things to tell you, but I'm not in the mood for that tonight. When I see you in mine own land I'll tell you all, or when you come Christmas. My window is open and a west wind blows in and that never makes me merry.

"The winds out of the west land blow,
My friends have breathed them there;

Warm with the breath of the lads I know
Comes east the sighing air.

Life is too short for love anyway, one is a fool to be an exile. My best love to you and yours.

Faithfully
Willa

The poem Cather quotes is the first stanza of "The winds out of the west land blow" by A. E. Housman, from A Shropshire Lad *(1896).*

TO LOUISE POUND

October 13, 1897
Pittsburgh

My Dear Louise.

I don't quite deserve that ironical thrust about not sending my address, and if you'll pardon an autobiographical paragraph I'll tell you why.

You see I came to the Leader expecting to do their dramatic work only. A few days after my arrival the day telegraph editor left for New York and I went on to help do his work until a man could be got to take his place. I liked the work and a wild idea took hold of me to demand the place for myself. I did so. Of course there were objections to my age and sex and inexperience, but I hung on, and they said I might try it for a few weeks just as an experiment. The work is not quite so thrilling as dramatic work, but it is a much more responsible and remunerative position. There is no hack work about it, simply editing and expanding or "padding" foreign telegrams. For instance, when a cable comes announcing the birth of a prospective Duke of Marlborough, to add a short history of the house etc. Then one has to judge what of all the avalanche of matter that descends upon the desk is really important. The chief requisites are discretion, some general knowledge of foreign affairs and history, and the trick of writing headlines. The latter was, and is still, hard for me. It all has to be done so quickly and a dozen telegraph boys at one's elbow rattle one somewhat. Then it's so absolutely irrevocable, when a thing once shoots up that pneumatic tube it's beyond the power of man to get it back or change it. Well, you know I am naturally slouchy and uncertain, so you will appreciate that I have been on the race track since my return. Saturday night the directors met and gave me the editorship and the boys gave me a supper and the other papers had a few headlines about me and there's an end of it. The work is stiff while you are at it, but no end exciting and the hours are only from 8 a.m. to 2 p.m. and after that I am absolutely free. It is so funny to have to hold a form half an hour because the King of Belgium is on a spree or to be almost wild because somebody in Paris shot herself just five minutes too late to get in on the dramatic page where she ought to be and maybe have to put her right next to a W. C. T. U. [Woman's Christian Temperance Union] Convention in Ohio. And it's so perplexing to think up different headlines for twelve suicides all at once. People show such a poverty of imagination in the way they kill themselves. But the political news is the stiff tangle. When you get one cable from Berlin saying this about the Emperor William's speech, and another from Vienna saying exactly the opposite, what <u>are</u> you going to do? Those Continental folks have such different points of view. But this is decidedly too autobiographical.

As to the Portrait of a Lady [probably the 1881 novel by Henry James], I will let her tell me the message I want to hear, may I do that?

I see you have resorted to designating me by my sex. Do you remember how Tucker used to wail "Alack,

> That I have worn so many winters out,
> And know not now what name to call myself"!

I had just settled down to tell you a lot of things, but the maid has just brought up Mr. [Preston] Farrar's card and I recall now that I promised to go to a reception with him this evening, so I'll just have to thank you for the picture and say good night. Let me hear from you.

Faithfully yours
Willa Cather.
309 S. Highland Ave.
East End
Pittsburgh

The quoted passage beginning "That I have" is from Shakespeare's Richard II.

TO MARIEL GERE

January 10 [1898]
Pittsburgh

My Dear Mariel;

It is with considerable fear and trepidation that I address my spidery scrawl to the proud possessor of the library hand. The reasons that I have'nt done it before are many, chiefly because I am doing more work than I ever did in my life before and just the kind of work that everyone always said I'd never be able to do—work requiring care and judgment. I don't do it perfectly by any means, but it seems to suit the publisher.

I don't need to tell you how much care and anxiety and grief Roscoe's illness has caused me. It seemed at times that I must go to him, but if ever the lad needed money he did then and my duty seemed to be to stay here and edit telegraph. I can never thank you for your kindness to him, Mariel. How strange it seems that you should be going to comfort him as you once did me. I look back upon those years now with a sort of wonder and doubt if it were really I. Golden days, Mariel, we won't see their like again. I am so deeply sorry for Allie. Poor little Allie! she was the gentlest and most easily hurt of us all and it seems as if she were having the toughest time.

I scarcely know how to tell you about my life here. It is a queer one, cut up between rather rigorous work and the craziest possible diversions. The theatre is about the only part of the old life that merges into this. Mr. Farrar broke his leg in a foot ball game several months ago, so I only see him in plaster, but now that he does'nt really suffer any more it is rather fun. Unfortunately I don't seem to be able to feel very deeply about him. His friendship is so warm and comforting and near to me that I don't want to change it for the other article in which the personal equation would be sure to make trouble. O I have grown enamoured of liberty! To be wholly free, to really be of some use somewhere, to do with one's money what one likes, to help those who have helped me, to pay the debts of one's loves and of one's hates!

Mrs. [Flavia] Canfield and Dorothy came to see me at Christmas time and I had to introduce Mrs. C to a lot of club magnates. Fancy her coming to <u>me</u> for that. O it does my wickid un-Christian heart good to get even, to pay off the old scores and make people take back the bitter things they said in those years when bitter things hurt so. But you must not take this too seriously, I'm not really such a cross sour old thing. I suspect the trouble tonight is loss of sleep. First it was [Nellie] Melba in opera, next night a supper party given by

Mrs. [Lizzie Hudson] Collier to Mr. and Mrs. Crane [actor William H. Crane and his wife Ella Chloe Myers], next night a dinner to Ethelbert Nevin the composer, and tonight I was out to dinner with a crowd at the Bishop's.

I have met some very interesting people this year. Got to know Anthony Hope Hawkins quite well, he was here several days and one of my friends here knew him at Oxford. [F.] Marion Crawford is a detestable snob. [Fridtjof] Nansen is all the Norse gods and heros in one, though he would talk nothing but [Robert] Browning and [Henrik] Ibsen. Ethelbert Nevin is prince and king of them all. He went shopping with me this afternoon and carried my bundles and got me a bunch of violets as big as a young moon. Think of it, the greatest of American composers and a fellow of thirty with the face of a boy and the laugh of a girl. You know his "Thine eyes are stars of morning" and "O that we two were maying" "Narcissus" & "Little Boy Blue".

I will do better than this when I'm not so sleepy. My love to you all

Willa

The scene Cather briefly describes above—shopping in the winter with composer Ethelbert Nevin—was likely remembered years later when, in her 1925 story "Uncle Valentine," she includes a brief description of Valentine Ramsay "hurrying about the shops" at Christmastime and buying his companion a gift of flowers.

❧ ❦

In the spring and summer of 1898, the Spanish-American War was dominating the headlines—headlines Willa Cather was writing as part of her job in Pittsburgh.

TO FRANCES GERE

June 23, 1898

[Written in at the top, upside down:] So Fritz Westermann has gone to war, nothing so good ever happened! Perhaps that is what the war is for!

My Dearest Frances;

It was awfully nice of you to remember me with a commencement invitation and it was a great disappointment to me not to be able to see you graduate. I had always counted on being present at that festal time and seeing you dressed for the Senior Prom. and all the rest of it. But the horrors of war seem to be a good deal worse in newspaper offices than in the field and I had to stay on here grilling in the heat and writing headlines about Cervera [Spanish admiral Pascual Cervera y Topete] being bottled up in Santiago harbor. I expect to start west for a two month's vacation the first of August, however, and then I will see you and hear all about the commencement festivities.

Dorothy [Canfield] will be with me for a few days week after next. Her mother has been having serious trouble with her eyes—threatened with cataracts and a total loss of sight. I believe she don't want Lincoln people to know it though. Dorothy is now in Vermont, where her grandfather died a few weeks ago. Poor child, she has been having a rocky summer of it.

I hear that all the old maids in Lincoln have been marrying off in cohorts, cant you find a widower or something for me when I am there this summer? Do try to manage it.

I spent the first two weeks of May in Washington with my cousin Dr. [Howard] Gore, a Prof. in the Columbian University, who was sent by the government with the Wellman polar expedition. He was giving farewell dinners to all his friends and going out a great deal and we had a gay time. I met no end of interesting people. The new Turkish charge d'affairs took me out to dinner one night and I have a score of funny things to tell you about him. Then we had the Norwegians ambassador out to dinner, and the secretary of the German legation, Count Alexander Finch von Finckenstein, and Herr Otto Schenfeldt, who was the tutor of Signor de Louie's sons and who is so pro-Spanish that his mail is under government survillience. My cousin married Lillian Thekla Brandthall, a famous Christiana belle and daughter of a former ambassador from Norway to America. O my child but she is glorious! l'etoile du Nord and no mistake. She is one of the hundred and one cousins of King Oscar of Sweden, and can relate no end of interesting court experiences. It is all arranged that I am to go back to Norway with her some day—perhaps I may go to the Paris Exposition with them. But I must save all those charming Washington adventures to tell you by word of mouth. Howard will write me from Siberia before he takes the final plunge into the Polar sea, which we all shudder to contemplate. If I had so lovely a wife as his, and one who could sing Grieg's songs as she can and read Ibsen like the very Tragic Muse herself, I would not go hunting the North Pole. But one is never satisfied it seems, when a man has the front of his coat covered with decorations from the various majesties and Royal Socities of the Continent, and has wedded a very Brunhilda, then forsooth, he must want the Pole, having nothing else left to wish for.

Goodness how glad I will be to see you all again this summer! I can't seem to like any other place on earth so well. There is nothing I fear so much as that I may gradually drift out of your lives until I will be—O well, just like any other stranger. You won't let that happen, my dear, will you? I think nothing in life could quite make up that loss to me. With a heart full of love for all of you

Willa

❧ ❧

During a long vacation in the summer of 1898 Cather traveled to Nebraska and, with her brother Roscoe, went on an extended hunting trip into the Black Hills of South Dakota and in Wyoming. While in Red Cloud, she worked in a family friend's office on a projected book made up of open letters to famous actors and actress, to be called The Player Letters. *It was never published, but some of the individual letters did appear as articles in the* Lincoln Courier.

Sometime in 1899, Cather developed a close friendship with a woman who was to become one of the great loves of her life: Isabelle McClung, a member of a prominent Pittsburgh family. The two met backstage in the dressing room of actress Lizzie Hudson Collier.

TO DOROTHY CANFIELD

October 10, 1899
Murray Hill, Pittsburgh

My Very Dearest Kid;

Here I am chez the Goddess and studying Greek to beat the band. Have'nt seen the Nevins yet, but they telephoned me a rousing welcome home and Ethelbert sent me a note and a copy of Shakespeares sonnets this afternoon. Say, do you know it isn't half bad to be back. I had a good trip and spent a most delightful day with the Peatties in Chicago and dined with "Misther Dooley" [Finley Peter Dunne], the irresistable Dan. Mrs. Peattie has at last arrived, so to speak, for her story "The Man at the Edge of Things" in the September Atlantic is literature, as good as most modern French things and as elusive and artistic. She wants me to go to Chicago in the spring, and I think I shall. Dooley says there is no woman doing newspaper work there now that I need be afraid of. I guess he and the Peatties will make the venture safe.

When I arrived at the union station here, on the very train on which you used to arrive, Isabelle met me, looking as though all the frieze of the Par-thenon ought to be tripping after her, and I began to have a better opinion of Pittsburgh. She's so darned good to me that she's making me positively kiddish. She'll have me playing with dolls next. We've been tramping over the hills and hearing the [Walter] Damrosch orchestra every day and having no end of a frivolous good time.

I know pretty well how you are located, but small thanks to you, my Lady. I read all Mariel's letters home and know all about your fellow voyagers, the red bear[d]ed artist and the dwarf and the woman with the marquise rings, and saw her diagram of your flat in Paris, though I suppose only a Nebraskan like myself would speak of a flat in Paris. But that all seems second hand, I want to know how things seem to <u>you</u>, won't you please write me exhaustively? As soon as I get located in my new den I'll write you young novels, I will.

Isabelle and I went down to see the Willards [Elise May and Marie Willard] last night and had a hilarious time. It was quite a reunion, Miss May from California, Miss Brooks from Europe and W. C. from <u>Red Cloud</u>!

When my train stopped at Columbus I had the queerest lonesome feelings all over me. Bridge the distance in some way, and do it quickly. <u>What</u> are you studying, with whom is your mother painting, I want to know everything. I'll keep up my end if you will yours.

Good night my dearest, I'll send my next letter by express.

Yours always

Willa

P.S. I of course know all about your father's great big hit in Bishop Potter's church and advertised it the whole length of Nebraska. Hurrah for him, which means, eventually, three cheers for you. O these haughty, prosperous, getting there Canfields.

Isabelle sends everything in the shape of regards and Alfred [McClung]—O but I'll tell you about him next time!

→ ←

Though Cather's social life in the fall of 1899 was obviously full, she was also quite active in her writing. She apparently met Leonard Charles Van Noppen, a poet and lecturer on Dutch literature born in the Netherlands, through her work at the Pittsburg Leader. Edwin P. Couse, mentioned at the end of the following letter, was her boss there.

TO LEONARD CHARLES VAN NOPPEN

January 26, 1900

Pittsburg Leader, Pittsburgh

My Dear Mr. Van Noppen;

I have delayed welcoming you back so long that now I am almost ashamed to do it, but I'll take the chance and congratulate you on your successful year.

First in answer to your question about a Dutch lecture in Pittsburgh. Surely you lived here long enough to know that the people have no interest in English literature, much less Dutch. [Israel] Zangwill can't draw a beggars dozen here, and I would'nt let my cousin Dr. Gore of Washington, try it.

No, [Arthur] Stedman did nothing with the manuscripts [of *The Player Letters*] except get them dirty and cause me a considerable loss of time. I have not placed them yet. An illustrated article of mine ["The Man Who Wrote 'Narcissus,'" about Ethelbert Nevin] appears in the May Ladies Home Journal, a story will be out in the New England Magazine sometime this winter ["El Dorado: A Kansas Recessional"], I shall have some verses in the Feb. or March Critic ["Grandmither, Think Not I Forget"], a poem in the Criterion soon, one in McClures and several in smaller publications. So you see I have not been altogether idle. The Player Letters are now with R. H. Russell & Co., of New York. Do you happen to know any of his people? If you do I'd be mightily obliged if you could speak a word for them and ask him what he thinks of them. Rupert Hughes, of the Criterion says they will surely go somewhere.

Let me know how the translations come on, and especially how you come on yourself.

Mr. Couse and all the boys join me in best wishes.

Faithfully your Friend

Willa Cather

➢ ➤

In 1900 Cather left her position at the Pittsburg Leader *and went to Washington, D.C., to work with her cousin James Howard Gore, a mathematics professor at Columbian University (now The George Washington University), as part of the United States Commission to the Paris Exposition of 1900.*

Willa Cather during the years she was a teacher in Pittsburgh

TO PRESTON COOKE FARRAR

February 4, 1901
Columbian University, Washington, D. C.

My dear Mr. Farrar:

Before I close any newspaper contracts in Pittsburgh, of which I have several pending, I want to ask your advice about a long cherished plan of mine. When I first graduated from the Nebraska State, I was not twenty, and had a record of insubordination in [Lucius A.] Sherman's classes behind me. What I wanted to do then was to begin to teach English or English literature at some other school, but I was patently too young and too undignified, so I took the nearest substitute that came to hand. Since I have been here in Washington my headquarters have been in a university, and the atmosphere has appealed to me very strongly, and made the disagreeable features of a newspaper office seem more disagreeable than ever. It seems to me to be a good time to begin to think about making the change which I have always intended to make, and my family are very anxious for me to do so. My professorial friends down here have given me warm encouragement. It may be that I can get pretty much what I want here, but for personal reasons I would a little rather be in Pittsburgh next year. I want to ask you whether you think there would be any chance for me in any of the high schools there, or if you are not much in touch with the schools now, what would be my best method of procedure to find out? I am aware of course that I should have to force my dignity by a hot house process, but I am getting to be an astonishingly serious sort of person now, so I think I am ready to take up a more staid pace.

Dorothy has written me vague and tantalizing hints of all sorts of glorious prospects for you in New York, until I confess I am consumed with curiosity, and would be grateful for more definite information.

Isabel[le] is at the hospital, and is mighty sick of it, but I think it will do the young person a world of good.

Please let me hear from you about your own affairs as well as mine.

> Very faithfully,
> Willa Cather

❧ ❦

On February 17, 1901, the composer Ethelbert Nevin died suddenly of a stroke at age thirty-eight. The following letter is to his widow.

TO ANNE PAUL NEVIN

237 R. Street N. E.
Washington
Saturday [February 23, 1901]

My Dear, Dear Mrs. Nevin:

I have begun so many letters to you this week, but the writing of them has been impossible as their message was unspeakable. I do not feel like one at a distance expressing sympathy, but as one near at hand expressing sorrow, for in an infinitely less degree I suffer of the same hurt. A shadow has come over the sun and nothing seems worth the doing. Mr. Nevin had a genius for being beloved, and for taking hold upon the minds and hearts of people. I am sure

I never wished any other human being so well, nor wanted the noblest success so much for anyone. I know that I shall never feel that youthful and genuine enthusiasm for any one or for any one's work again, and I feel as though my own youth had died with the man who, even when I did not know him, meant so very much to it. His personality was to me the very exponent of song, the embodiment of all the happy privileges of art—and all of its tragic sadness. It used to seem to me as though he were quite simply a shepherd lad strayed out of Arcady into this dreary land of dullness and uniformity and shop-keeper standards. And yet there was such a tragic vein in him, and some of the stuff of martyrdom. He used sometimes to seem like a man stripped of his skin, with every nerve quivering to the torture of the air, like that other unhappy singer Marsayas, whom jealous Apollo flayed.

Isabelle wrote me of his last silent home coming. Had I known there was a possibility of seeing his face again I should have gone on from Washington. I want to remember him always, always, just as he was. I am sure you must have arranged the services yourself, for they were so eminently fitting, but I dont think I could have stood it to hear his songs when he was in so deep a sleep. I am not one of those who learn easily to kiss the cross.

The last time I saw him he said he was going away "where people could not say unkind things any more." Oh I hope those people will suffer and suffer and <u>suffer</u>! And they will, I know it. Heaven calls the world to account for souls like his. I think you and his mother are perhaps the only two who could have nothing to regret. If ever any one had and fulfilled a commission from God you have done it, for you saved him and the wonder of him for us all as long as you could, otherwise he would have lashed himself out long ago. I do believe with all my heart and mind that your service was not only unto him but unto all men, and that he will be one of those whose tapers burn throughout the night of time.

Dear Lady, for the last week tears and I have not been strangers, but at the bottom of my grief lies the thought of the sweetness of his sleep, of the utterness of his peace. Oh lady, life is not so gay that one need dread to sleep! I have learned that already. Le sens de la vie, est ce qui est difficile pour nous autres. Le sens de la morte est facile——on la comprend comme la chanson d'une mère. ["The meaning of life is what is difficult for the rest of us. The meaning of death is easy——we understand it like a mother's lullaby."] When I think of him, and that is so many times in the day and the night, I think also of the blessed truth of the lines that Shelly wrote to Keats after the world had killed him, and that were afterward put on the Shelley tablet at Oxford.

He has outsoared the shadow of our night;
Envy and calumny, and hate and pain,
And that unrest which men miscall delight
Can touch him not, nor trouble him again.

I will return to Pittsburgh next week and then I hope you can see me. Surely you know without my saying it that if in collecting his papers or in preparing any biographical matter I can be of any service to you, it will be my happiness and pride to serve you to the very utmost capacity of my ability and my love. There are many nearer friends and longer-tried near you to sympathize with you, but I don't think there is one whose love or whose sorrow is more sincere. A master of any art holds a peculiar place in the lives of his believers. To them he is the expression of what seems most rare and precious in life, and when he dies something of themselves goes out with him. I think my sense of heaviness and loss will be less if in any way I can serve you a little. All the love of my sad heart goes to you with this letter. With a loyalty that shall last as long as I live, Dear Lady.

Willa.

The lines of poetry and the phrase "whose tapers burn throughout the night of time" are from Percy Bysshe Shelley's Adonais, *an elegy for poet John Keats published in 1821 shortly after his death (except the last line should read "Can touch him not and torture not again"). Later, Cather would write poems inspired by Nevin's death titled "Lament for Marsyas" and "Arcadian Winter," employing some of the same metaphors she uses in this letter. Much later, Cather would draw on Nevin for her character Valentine Ramsay in her 1925 short story "Uncle Valentine."*

❧ ❧

She came back to Pittsburgh and, late in the winter of 1901, took a job as a teacher of Latin and English at Central High School, filling in midyear for a teacher who was ill. She hoped a teaching job would leave her some free time for her own writing. In the spring of 1901, at the invitation of Isabelle McClung, Cather moved into the McClung family's large home at 1180 Murray Hill Avenue. Isabelle believed in Cather's potential as a writer and provided Cather with encouragement and a room in which to write: a former sewing room on the third floor of the house.

TO DOROTHY CANFIELD

[March or April 1901]
Pittsburgh

My Dearest Dorothy.

The first month of teaching is at an end and I have about decided to let some one else take up the good work for the rest of the year. I want to go home to Red Cloud and work for awhile. I know now that I can teach, and that better than I had expected, but I can't help taking the matter seriously and I doubt whether that pays in a High School where the salary means ultimate financial ruin.

Now about the letters [*The Player Letters*]. I think Mr. Carpenter was a Christian gentleman to give them his consideration, and I think his opinion on their ephemeral interest about agrees with mine. Then they seem to me to perilously approach fine writing. I had thought that Miss [Jeannette Leonard] Gilder might be able to use some of them in the "Critic" in the summer season when the theatres are closed and "copy" runs low. Have you any means of access to her? I believe she thinks rather well of me. If she were to see some half-dozen of the better ones she might consider the scheme.

"Jack-a-Boy" appeared in the Easter Sat. Eve. Post with the most satisfying illustrations and so like my little brother that they gave me a turn. I will mail you a copy. I think Miss Gilder ought to see the letters this month. If you think it would be just as well for me to send her copies from here, let me know, though I am sure that, if you could face a thankless errand of that kind, a word to her from you would give them a better chance.

Did'nt I write you about the Edouard Rod? I could not put it down after I had once begun it, and it seemed to me a wonderful piece of work and noble beyond most clever things. I want to read some more [Jules] Lemaitre whenever you can send him. I wish I knew the really wise thing to do about the school. I like to plow a furrow to the end, and yet to move, set up a room, unpack etc all for two months seems a good deal of trouble for a very little experience. Then the spring months are good ones to loaf and invite your soul, and if I went west something might come of it.

The McClungs have moved into their new house next door to the old one, and Isabelle's new room is a beautiful place to dwell in, with big windows that face on a wood and the sunset. I want to talk to you about the Pittsburgh novel, but it cant be done by letter, and an attack of cramps, several days over due is getting the better of me. Isabelle sends many messages to you, but I am being slowly drawn up into a lumpy coil and cant even write my own. With all my love to your mother and yourself, and anxiously awaiting word from you

Willie

"To loaf and invite your soul" is a reference to Walt Whitman's "Song of Myself." The "Pittsburgh novel" referenced above was never published. According to a February 11, 1950, letter from Edith Lewis to E. K. Brown held in the collections of the University of Nebraska–Lincoln, it was titled "Fanny" and focused on "stage people." Lewis told Brown that Cather kept the manuscript for some time, only destroying it after moving to 5 Bank Street in New York in 1912.

At the end of the school year, Cather went to Nebraska.

TO GEORGE SEIBEL

July 17, 1901

My Dear Mr. Sibel;

I arrived home two weeks ago very much worn out by the years hard work, and am not feeling much rested yet. I am twenty pounds thinner than when you saw me last. I dont object to that but I do object to the good for nothing feeling that comes with it.

I find my mother somewhat better than she has been for several years and Jack and Elsie grown beyond all belief. They ask me to tell them about Erna [Seibel's daughter] every few days and are never tired of hearing about the Christmas tree and the bunnies in the cellar.

I expect a story of mine will be out in the August or September Scribners; when I read the proofs it was scheduled for August but that guarantees nothing. I had a story in the June "New England Magazine" that I would like you to read if you have time. My mother has basely filched all my copies and sent them to deaf great-aunts etc, but perhaps you'll have time to look it up at the Library some day. I start for the Rockies the first of August to be gone for several weeks and I hope to hear from you before then. I thought surely I would get to see you before I left Pittsburgh, but the horrors of the High School closing examinations ought to be exposed to the public. I simply had to give up everything in order to get through the work at all. Tell Erna she must not forget me, and that I hope to help her trim her tree next Christmas. Is the heat as terrible at World's End as here I wonder? It is like to be worlds end in truth here. With my heartiest love to you all and prayers for cool weather.

Willa

→ ←

In the early summer of 1902, after another year teaching at Central High School, Cather and Isabelle McClung sailed for Europe. They spent a few months touring England and France, satisfying Cather's long-delayed desire to see something of the countries whose culture and art she adored.

TO DOROTHY CANFIELD

[Late May 1902]

[Written in the top margin:] Remember me warmly to your Aunt Helen and my very best to your mother.

My Dearest Dorothy;

I am mightily sorry to hear that your aunt Helen is so much worse, but glad you are out of the rush and riot in a cool and quiet place. The rush of examinations is about to begin and for the next two weeks I shall be dead to the world. We sail on the fourteenth on the Noordland, <u>American Line</u>, from Philadelphia. We will be in England until the middle or last of July, according to the date on which you can meet us in Paris. Let me know about that as soon as you can. I am unable to believe in it at all. It's too good. I am none to joyful these days, and need to see you sorely, sorely. To think of your reading Hesperians! What do you mean by telling me there was anything good in it? As I remember it, it was really grand-eloquent stuff enough, of the heart-on-the-sleeve order. Ipsa glorior infama, as I remember, when there was little to glory in, God wot, and enough to be ashamed of. Well, we go on making fools of ourselves just so. I grow older and tireder but very little wiser. No, I surely was not very happy then. People cut me deeper than they do now.

Please let me hear from you before we start and dont forget a steamer letter. Do you like these Marsyas verses at all? I think the Hawthorn Tree rather prettily illustrated. I've got to the point where letter writing will not answer, I must talk to you to let my heart out at all or to feel you with me. But I will do that soon, wont I? Heaven speed the day.

Shall I send your French books to you in Vermont or express them to New York? Heaven! I wish I could see you before I sail. The distance seems long and the chances of missing you many. I wonder whether, if we do meet in Paris, I can shake off this fog that has gone clear into my bones and be made anew? I almost believe I can.

All my love goes to you

Willie

Greet warmly for me your cousins Hermie and Nat and think a thought for me at Equinox and pray him to send me a little of his repose. Did I tell you that from Liverpool we are going right down to—Shropshire!? Someway I always rather link Equinox with Shropshire.

"Lament for Marsyas" and "The Hawthorn Tree" were two of Cather's own poems. Shropshire was an exciting destination because of A. E. Housman's book of poems A Shropshire Lad *(1896). As the next letter suggests, the book was one of Cather's great enthusiasms. All of the quoted verses in the letter are from Housman.*

TO DOROTHY CANFIELD

Sunday, July 6, 1902

Ludlow, Shropshire, England

My Dearest Dorothy;

> Oh come you home of Sunday
> When Ludlow streets are still,
> and Ludlow bells are calling
> To farm and lane and mill,
>
> Or come you home of Monday
> When Ludlow market hums
> And Ludlow chimes are playing
> 'The Conquoring Hero Comes.'

And they <u>do</u> play that tune every Monday in the year, and even now they are calling to farm and lane and mill. I've so much to tell you, Dorothy, that I've simply run away from the task of doing it; I never ran such a gauntlet of experiences. I draw a long sigh of relief when I think I am to tell you them in Paris.

From Liverpool we went directly to Chester, lost our hearts to the place and stayed there five days. Then we coached fifty miles to Shrewsbury and there saw how

"High the vanes of Shrewsbury gleam
Islanded in Severn stream,
The bridges, from the steepled crest,
Cross the water east and west."

We sat for two sunsets on the very spot where he must have done it and watched the red steeples in the clear green water which flows almost imperceptibly. And what do you think was going on in the wide meadows on the other shore? Why boys were playing <u>foot-ball</u>!

"<u>Is</u> foot ball playing
along the river shore?"

Well I guess yes. And we went to Shrewsbury jail. You remember

"They hang us now in Shrewsbury jail;
The whistles blow forlorn
and trains all night groan on the rail
To lads that die at morn."

Of <u>course</u> they do, for the jail, which is the most grewsome building the hand of man ever made, is on a naked hill right over the switch yard and station, so you see "forlorn" was not put there to rhyme with "morn". Somehow it makes it all the greater to have it all <u>true</u>. When we got into Shropshire we threw away our guide books and have blindly followed the trail of the Shropshire Lad and he has lead us beside still waters and in green pastures. Of course no one in Shropshire has his books or ever heard of him, but we telegraphed his publisher for his address and will see him in London. I read the old files of the county paper to where most of the verses first came out.

I dont know when we shall leave here. Ludlow Castle in itself is enough to hold me forever. It is one of the most perfect Norman-Elizabethan compounds in England and one of the least visited. The history of the place and the magnitude of its interior together are enough to turn one daft. Is'nt it nice that Sir Philip Sidney grew up and first wrote in Ludlow castle when his father held the Welsh border here for Elizabeth? We have read those two singing Shropshire Lads until our eyes are blinded and our reason distraught. They are not so unalike, either. Yesterday we bribed the keeper and climbed the circular stairway to the very top of the old Norman keep, and there, over ivy, ivy, ivy, walls and walls, the ruined splendor of a thousand years, on the topmost turrets, a thousand scarlet poppies flaunted their color and nodded and balanced themselves in the wind.

> When ages old remind me
> How much hath gone for naught,
> What wretched ghost remaineth
> Of all that flesh hath wrought,
>
> Of love and song and warring,
> Of adventure and play,
> Of art and comely building,
> Of faith and form and fray,
>
> I'll mind the flowers of pleasure,
> Of short-lived youth and sleep
> That drank the sunny weather
> A-top of Ludlow keep.

I've been madly a-doing those poppies in every metre I know ever since I saw them, and all are alike unsuccessful. We are stopping at the most beautiful old hotel in the world, which was for three hundred years the over-flow house to the Castle, all black oak and diamond windows and that. We are going to bicycle to <u>Wenlock</u> <u>Edge</u> this afternoon, "Oh tarnish late on Wenlock edge" etc. I'll not quit Shropshire till I know every name he uses. They are just making hay now, too, and I think I might almost find Maurice behind the mows somewhere. I hope to find letters in London telling me when to meet you in Paris. To meet you at last, and tell you everything!

A light heart to you from me
Willie

The lines beginning "When ages old" were later published as part of Cather's poem "Poppies on Ludlow Castle." Dorothy Canfield, then doing graduate work in French at the Sorbonne in Paris, joined Cather and McClung in London, and the three went to call on poet and classical scholar A. E. Housman. Housman received them politely, but Cather struggled to make conversation with him. He and Canfield, however, had a pleasant chat about Latin manuscripts. After the visit, Cather was so disappointed that she broke into tears.

→ ←

Evelyn Osborne, mentioned in the following letter, was a friend and classmate of Dorothy Canfield's who accompanied Cather, Isabelle McClung, and Canfield in their sightseeing. Osborne had a disfiguring scar along the left side of her face, and in every existing photograph of this trip to Europe in which Osborne is present, she stands in profile, showing only her right side. This letter to Dorothy and the following one to her father were both written on a blank postcard.

TO DOROTHY CANFIELD

August 9, 1902
Paris

My Dear Dorothy:

This morning we took the films to the photograph place and were disappointed to find that we could'nt get the prints until Monday. Then we went with Miss Osborne and purchased many foolish underclothing, called at the American Express, etc. After eating unto discomfort of Mme Sibut's delicious fish au gratin, we went to the Luxemborg, sat in the garden and put in two hours in four rooms. Then we had a royal bath and, returning, clad ourselves in white duck which fired Miss Osborne to array herself likewise. <u>Dorothy do please speak to Miss Horne about our washing</u>. The woman failed to return a new suit of union underwear that I paid much good money for. Love from us all.

Willa

Weather fine.

TO CHARLES F. CATHER

[August] 1902
Paris

[M]y Dear Father:

I have [b]een in Paris now two weeks [and] I shall remain two weeks [more]. The city is certainly the most [beau]tiful that men have ever [?] and genius to create. I find new pleasure and wonder in it every day. The tomb of

Cather and Dorothy Canfield in Europe, summer 1902

Napoleon is the only thing I have ever found in the world which did not <u>at all</u> disappoint. I think it must be quite the most impressive and awe-inspiring spot on earth. The people here are the most industrious, neat and painstaking people I have ever seen, and yet they take life comfortably. The do not wear themselves out, but whatever they do they do thoroughly and well.

Much love to momma and the children.

Willie

➵ ➴

While visiting Paris, Cather and McClung stayed at 11 rue de Cluny at the board-inghouse operated by the Sibut family.

TO MARIEL GERE

August 28 [1902]
Paris

My Dearest Mariel;

Every day since I have been here—four weeks now—I have said, "tomorrow I will write to Mariel." But you know how many things there are to do. Isabelle and I find this the most interesting family to stay with. Both the old ladies are as kind as possible and Mme. Merton certainly is an admirable and remarkable woman. Pierre [Sibut] is good for nothing but to look at and enters the army next month. Blanche is away. Dorothy and I do not agree at all about Mlle. Céline [Sibut]. Dorothy joined us in London, spent three weeks with us there and came on to Paris with us. She left some days ago to join her parents in Scotland. A New York girl who is a classmate of Dorothy's is stopping here at 11 rue Cluny, and we like her tremendously. Heaven knows its a comfort to have a sane American somewhere near, who believes in baths and self control and has no "temperament"! We three went out to Barbizon together and have a great many gay parties. We also ran across Louise Pound's friend Miss Lathrop in London and how we did like her. Why Mariel, that girl just put in her days showing us about and being nice to us. I hated mightily to say goodbye to her. We have been singularly fortunate in meeting the nicest kind of people ever since we started out, and, after all, people count more than places, do they not? We leave for a two weeks walking trip through Provence and along the Mediterranean next Monday. I have enjoyed both Paris and London, of course, but I like the country even better. We had a delightful walking trip up the Valley of the Oise, the scene of Stevenson's "Inland Voyage."

I have good news to tell you: Douglass expects to spend next winter with me in Pittsburgh. He will meet us at the docks when we return to America. Won't that be famous? I have so much to tell you that it is useless to try to write it. I will certainly see you next summer if you are at home. My warmest love to your dear mother and Frances and Ellen, and Isabelle and the Sibuts join me in a great deal to you.

Faithfully always
Willa

→ ←

All during her tour of Europe, Cather wrote travel articles and sent them back to Nebraska, where they were published by her old paper, the Nebraska State Journal. *In the fall of 1902, she returned to Pittsburgh and to another year of teaching—and writing. By this time, she had enough poetry to make up a slim volume,* April Twilights, *which was published in the spring of 1903 by Richard G. Badger. Though Cather doesn't mention this in the following letter to Will Owen Jones, her old friend at the* Nebraska State Journal, *Badger flattered aspiring poets with an offer of publication but also requested that they pay the costs of such publication themselves.*

TO WILL OWEN JONES

January 2 [1903]
Pittsburgh

My Dear Mr. Jones;

Did you ever get my letter telling you the papers I wanted, the ones containing the letters from Avignon, Hyeres, and Lavandou? Can you find them for me.

I am to have a volume of verse published this spring—March or April. Badger, of Boston is the publisher. He is putting out a lot of new verse by Clinton Scollard, Edith M. Thomas, Harriet Prescott Spofford etc. He has made me most liberal terms and if the book sells well I shall make a neat little sum from it. He wants to send circulars to a number of people who know me, and I want to ask you if you can lend me a Lincoln directory for a few days? I shall need it next week, and will express it back to you shortly. If you cant send a directory a telephone book would help me out. I shall have a review copy of the book sent you as early as possible.

Best wishes for the new year to you all.

Faithfully
Willa S. Cather

→ ←

In the spring of 1903 Cather was also working toward publication of her first book of fiction: a collection of short stories called The Troll Garden. *Though this and* April Twilights *were her first books, she was by then an experienced and well-published author. Since her college days, she had published several hundred newspaper columns and reviews, many poems, and more than thirty pieces of fic-*

tion. Nevertheless, she felt that this first book of fiction, filled mostly with stories that had not yet appeared in magazines, was crucial to her development as a writer. She would soon travel to New York, to the offices of S. S. McClure, to see if the publisher might be interested in her manuscript.

TO DOROTHY CANFIELD

Saturday [March 28, 1903]

My Dearest Dorothy;

I dont know when I have been so beaten out with mental effort and so sick with disappointment. I ought to have been more considerate of you and faced the facts and let you know yesterday, but it just seemed as though I <u>couldn't</u> give it up. I'm almost in despair for fear I cant explain clearly enough for you to really understand. You see, Dorothy, those wretched tales went back on me. When I got my Chicago mag. work off my hands and came to the pruning and fixing of that set of short stories I just fainted by the wayside. There is weeks of work to be done on them. Then I decided to throw them aside and go without them, but [Francis] Hill and several other people of some experience told me it was a great advantage to take things to the publisher ones self. I will have them ready later in the spring and will have to go on with them then, and as I have to go to Red Cloud this summer I cant afford two trips to New York. I hate to let such a consideration stand between me and what I want to do, and much worse do I hate that it should cause you disappointment. Really, Dorothy, you'll never know how cut up I am, how much I want to go and to go <u>now</u>. It's been a long time since I have wanted anything so desperately hard, I'm almost glad to find that I haven't lost the capacity. I was so <u>sure</u> about those tales, that itself is a blow under the belt, but its quite faded into nothingness at my keener chagrin at disappointing you and not seeing you. After my wretched misunderstanding of things last fall, it seemed necessary to see you before the spring days set life fairly in motion again. I can only beg you to help me bear my own disappointment and say with me "another night, another day". It really wont be long, Dear, and you will have more respect for me if I come with the work done at last. It's bitter hard to grind and grind, when I have so little time to live at all, but if I once get this volume done and done well, I'll be a more agreeable person to know. Some of it is mighty good, and in the next few weeks I'll bring the rest up or just break down trying. Do you want to know the discouraging details I wonder? Well, the last story, "Paul's Case" is just undigested, shows the haste in which I put it through, and Pilgrim Joy has fallen down completely, will have to be thrown out and another done in its place. Then I'll have my cycle, 2 painter stories, 1 actor, 1 sculptor, 1 musician, 1 musical study, 1 literary man, and one case of an artistic constitution without talent, and Fulvia. The title is to be "The Troll Garden" ([printed out:] The Troll Garden) with a sentence from Chas. Kingsley to explain its fitness. Bear with me yet a little longer, Dorothy, and then in the day of ripe fruit we'll rejoice together.

Oh if only I felt that I could make the two trips, how much we could put into the yarns together! I am so tired of things and people here that it seems as if I could not stay and grind the weeks away when you are waiting for me under brighter skies. I want to go so much more than ever I wanted to go abroad last summer. I some how need your counsel and encouragement more than ever I needed it before. But since I must fight it out alone a few weeks longer, dont <u>please</u> think unkindly of me. You know how hard it is for me to give things up. I never knew half how much I wanted to go to you until it was born in upon me that I must not. For just once I'm going to do the hard and irksome duty and hammer away with dull eyes and a heavy heart. Pray for me that it be not in vain. I am going to send Phaedra ["The Marriage of Phaedra"] on to you and I want you to ask your mother to read it for me too. Heavens! those tales ought to go after this, I feel as though I'm giving up enough for them. Please dont think I'm selfish about them if you can help it, dear,—I'm harder on myself than on you.

Will you please apologize to your mother and father for my bad manners? I shant blame them if they just quietly refuse to see me when I do come, nor you if you lose all patience with me. I remember well enough how badly I behaved when you once disappointed me about coming. My dear girl I am just all beaten out with battling with myself, and I'll not write you more now. You'll never know how hard it was to send that second telegram. I feel as though it would be many days before I will really want my dinner. Please let me hear from you that you do understand and have not left me to fight with my failures alone. If I can only get the rest of these things worked up to the proper key, I believe it will make you as happy as it does me. If you could see what I have done with Fulvia [eventually titled "Flavia and Her Artists"] you would see why I am hopeful. It seems as though I really cant say goodbye for five or six weeks longer, but if I can just go to you bringing my sheaves with me—Dear Dorothy burn a candle at some little Latin church for me.

All my love goes to you
Willie

I feel that I ought to tell you why I put off reading those things and finding out as to where I stood for so long. We have had no servants for three weeks, Mrs. McClung has been sick in bed ever since the cook left, and to cap it all one of Isabelle's cousins died last week. I cant do much to help in the house with all my school work, but I have not had an evening to myself until Thursday and Friday for about three weeks. I just could not get at my own work before, and when I finally did the blow fell. Isabelle feels dreadfully about it, both on my account and yours.

TO GEORGE SEIBEL

April 28 [1903]

My Dear Mr. Seible;

Certainly you are better at not forgetting old acquaintance than anyone I know. I could not at all tell you over the telephone how much I feel your good will in going into that review [of *April Twilights*] so heartily. Of course the appreciative tone of the notice will help the book, but it was not that which especially pleased me. There was a frank and friendly ring about it that put courage into me and made me feel equal to trying almost anything. Of course I am mighty glad that you like the verses, but I am much more pleased that you seem glad to like them, and that you blow upon me with such a friendly wind. Surely we can disprove Hesiod's epigram that,

> "Potter hates Potter,
>   and poet hates poet."

To tell you the truth, you have so often handled me severely in private apropos of some of those same verses that I rather expected chastisement and sunny clemency has quite taken my breath away.

We shall expect you on Thursday night, and please come early, as soon after seven oclock as possible.

Faithfully always
·Willa S. Cather

→ ←

In early May Cather met S. S. McClure, the owner and publisher of the very successful magazine McClure's, *at his offices in New York. The meeting was the beginning of a great change in Cather's life.*

TO WILL OWEN JONES

May 7, 1903
Pittsburgh

My Dear Mr. Jones;

I do believe you've got me fairly launched at last, at least it looks so. About a week after I sent my stories to S. S. McClure, he telegraphed me to go to New York at once. I went and our first business talk took up two hours of a fine spring morning. Life has simply been another proposition to me ever since. I go about with care because I have become so much more valuable to myself. At ten oclock last Friday I was not much afraid of street car accidents and things, but when I left the office at one I had become worth saving. He will publish the collection in book form, but will first run them in the magazine to give me the benefit of the extra revenue. [William Dean] Howells, he thinks, will use some of them in Harpers [*Harper's Monthly Magazine*]. The book will be out next winter. But the important result of our several interviews is that he has agreed to take everything I do and place it for me if he cannot use it himself; and that he has so encouraged and strengthened me that I feel as though I want to do well almost as much for him as for myself. What a genius he has for proselyting! He takes hold of you in such a personal way that business ceases to be a feature of your relations with him. He has the enthusiasm of a boy. He took me right out to his house and wanted me to stop with him, but I only stayed there one day as I had promised to go to the Canfields. Then Mrs. Robert Louis Stevenson [Frances (Fanny) Matilda Van de Grift Osbourne Stevenson] was at the house and she had read the yarns and talked very helpfully. In the end Mr. McClure took them without any changes at all. I don't think there was a circumstance of my personal life the man did'nt go into and discuss and plan for. If he were a religious propagandist he would have people going to the stake for him through sheer personal devotion.

Surely you never did such a good turn to anyone as when you gave H. H. [McClure, S. S. McClure's cousin and colleague] a strong talk about me. Several of these same stories had been sent back to me by Mr. McClure's readers without having ever reached him at all. During my first interview with him he rang for the boy and had the two readers sent in and asked them to give an account of their stewardship. Surely I sat and held me chin high and thought my hour had struck. A moment of that sort turns back the clock of time for one and makes one feel almost as important as when one was editor of the Hesperian.

There are other plans in the wind, but if I wrote them all I should write until midnight. In the meantime, here's to you here's thanks to you, for this and for Auld lang Syne, and its with a light heart I write you.

Faithfully always
Willa S. Cather

<u>Where is Sarah Harris</u>? I've written her three times and elicited no reply.

➤ ◄

The following letter is available to us through a transcription apparently made by Witter Bynner.

TO VIOLA ROSEBORO'

Sunday, June 14 [1903]

My dear Miss Roseboro:—

<u>Do</u> I know a Shropshire Lad? Do I? Isn't the internal evidence of my own verses all against me? Why I've been Housman's bond slave, mentally, since his volume first appeared some six years ago. As soon as I got to England I went straight to Shropshire, to all the places—Shrewesbury, Ludlow, Kneighton, and the rivers "Ouy and Teme and Clun". I even went to Shrewesbury jail—it stands just above the railway switch yards and that is why "Trains all night groan on the rail to men that die at morn". I saw the "Vanes of Shrewesbury gleam islanded in Severn stream" and "football playing along the river shore, and heard the Ludlow bells play "The Conquering Hero Comes" of a Monday. In short I found everything there except Housman. Of him not a legend, not a button or feather or mark. Nobody had ever heard of him or seen his book. There was a copy in the Shrewesbury public library, but the leaves were uncut. In London I battered upon the doors of his publishers until they gave me his address. He lives in an awful suburb in quite the most horrible boarding-house I ever explored. He is the most gaunt and grey and embittered individual I know. He is an instructor in Latin inscriptions in the University of London, but I believe the position pays next to nothing. The poor man's shoes and cuffs and the state of the carpet in his little hole of a study gave me a fit of dark

depression. I would like to tell you all about it sometime: I think he is making about the only English verse that will last, the only verse of this decade I mean. It is as remarkable technically as it is unique in the truth of its sentiment. That sounds rather flat, but you will know what I mean. And how intensely it does appeal, where it appeals at all. It's not every one who can care for it. I only know a dozen or so who see anything extraordinary in it.

He does it all so beautifully from the country boy's standpoint that the castle is just "Ludlow Tower" to him, as it is to the lads who walk there with their girls on Sunday afternoons. The way that man has kept all his Classical philology <u>out</u> of his verse, the way he has kept the meadow-level! I was there in haying season and I used to look for poor Maurice behind the hay-cocks. By the way did you know that the poor man's name is Albert Edward, after H. R. H? I've gone on at great length about him, but I've tracked the man the length and breadth of England and done much shameless detective work on him, that I'm glad to be able to tell a few of my discoveries to some one who agrees with me about his verse. If you ever want more information just give me an opportunity and I will play on and on like a music box.

Faithfully yours,
Willa S. Cather

TO DOROTHY CANFIELD

July 13, 1903
Cheyenne, Wyoming

My Dearest Dorothy;

I got just a line from you forwarded here from Pittsburgh and hope to find a letter from you awaiting me at Red Cloud, where I will be in a few days. It is fine and cool here and Douglass and I have been enjoying our stay together mightily, though I think we both feel [the] curse of growing older more than ever before, and it is a little harder for us to get together than it has ever been. But in some ways these things make it only the more necessary and blessed to be for awhile side by side.

The night I left Pittsburgh I was elected to the head of the English department of the Allegheny High School at a salary of $1400. There were fifteen applicants for the position so the committee declared competitive examinations on July second, and that is what kept me in Pittsburgh over time. Isabelle's father and uncle did all the going about and seeing people for me. They were just fine, I never saw the Judge so bestir himself. I wanted it chiefly because of the desirable hours—from 8:30 to one oclock only.

I did not get to stop in Lincoln at all, but will do so on my way back. It seemed awfully funny to come straight through. I'm not very well and the sudden jump into a very high altitude rather exhausts me. I am all unreconciled to losing all hope of seeing Vermont this year, but I do believe that its my duty to be here and in Red Cloud. I cant endure the thought of going clear out of Roscoe and Douglass' life, and I want to keep alive all my feeling for them, whatever else I loose.

What are you doing or studying this summer, and is your mother painting anything? My best love to you all—not forgetting your cousin Hermie

Faithfully always
Willie

TO DOROTHY CANFIELD

Friday [probably November 27, 1903]

My Dearest Dorothy:

Now by Saint Peter's Church and Peter, too, I dont know who your Childs people are, nor does Isabelle. Of course I understand how hurried your father was and it's all right, but I should have liked to see him. He will be in Lincoln about Christmas time, you say? He'll meet with a warm welcome there surely. Of course you are all anxious to see the new boy in Columbus. I'm glad he's a Canfield.

Isabelle and I have been to the theatre just once this winter—Mrs. [Minnie Maddern] Fiske in Hedda Gabler. She doesn't do it half so well as Blanche Bates did. We do go to all the Symphony concerts however, and to a good many musical things of one kind and another. I have to go to bed at ten oclock or I'm no good for teaching the next day. Edith [McClung] had her coming out party two weeks ago, and we did the heavy social for awhile, but have pretty much settled down to our monastic routine again—except Edith and her mother. We read a good deal and see a good deal of Francis Hill,—and Miss May occasionally, as often, that is, as she'll let us. I have'nt told you what I'm writing because I dont know where I'm coming out on it—looks rather discouraging lately. It's a rather long thing which I never intended to write but fell into by chance. I have no name for it yet and am not saying much about it because I dont intend to use it unless it pleases me at least moderately well.

There are about 40,000 words of the first draft done. It's good practice, if nothing else.

We had a hilarious Thanksgiving dinner last night, as the Judge was away, and I feel rather knocked out this morning as a consequence. Do you remember that first Thanksgiving dinner I ate at your house in Lincoln, when Arthur Canfield was there and you were sick? Poor Marian Smith was there, too. But I wont go into reminiscences or I shall get dismal,—in consequence of too much turkey last night. I'll hie me out and take a walk in the snow and be a little more alive next time I write. I dont mean to let letters go unanswered; I just somehow do. It's poor management.

A happy vacation to you
Willie

Cather had seen Blanche Bates star as Hedda Gabler while in Washington, D.C., in the fall of 1900. It is unclear whether the forty-thousand-word manuscript refers to any work Cather eventually published.

→ ←

In January 1904, Cather wrote to Dorothy Canfield complaining that Canfield had not written for six weeks. Cather suspected something was wrong, and sometime in the early months of 1904, Canfield responded.

TO DOROTHY CANFIELD

[Early March 1904]

My Dearest Dorothy;

This will be a hard letter to write, as yours to me must have been. We have surely got into a snarl somehow, and I think you are right that its best to admit it. The worst of it is that its nothing that one can really put ones finger on. Of course I've always been conscious that I was ill tempered and ungrateful and that I behaved very childishly abroad two years ago, and frankly, I dont see how you could over look it. There is just a terribly low streak of something both ill tempered and ill bred that comes out in me only too often. It was surely not your fault that I didn't understand French and that I felt very provincial and helpless and ignorant, and its incredible that any grown person should have behaved as I did. It makes me ill to think of it, it surely does. Ive realized what a disappointment it must have been to you, too, after you had made such an effort to be with me. Oh, the whole thing was simply beastly!—and I've no one but myself to blame. I suppose I am one of those perverse beings who get stiff and haughty when they know they are in the wrong, for I've felt a little constrained ever since, knowing all the while that the unpleasantness was all of my manufacture. That's an ugly thing to admit, but its only fair to own up to one's pettiness. It is just a grudge against myself that in some way gives me a sense of aloofness. That's one thing.

Then we have both changed. Teaching school is a quieting, settling, ageing occupation, that makes one reliable and thoughtful and consciencious, but it is not good for ones <u>disposition</u>. I think I must take it too seriously, for it seems to take out of me most of the elements that used to be most active between you and me. You ask about what verse I'm doing,—my dear girl, I have not done a line, literally not one line since I did the Provencal Legend [the name of a poem published in *April Twilights*] last December. It's simply a case of no tunes ever flitting across my tired and torpid brain. I'm really alarmed, Dorothy, at the rate at which I seem to be losing the capacity for emotion. I often wonder whether that is like other things, that one can simply spend it all and then have to go without for the rest of ones days. The Francis Hill you've heard me speak of so often, the fine lad whose companionship has meant so much to both Isabelle and me, told me only last week with a tremor in his voice, that he was not going to see me any more for a while. He said I had grown formal and cold and absent minded to the degree that he simply couldnt stand it, that he wanted at least to keep the memory of our old jovial comradeship unspoiled. I have not seen him since and dont know when I shall—he comes to see Isabelle in the morning while I am at school. He says when he sees me, the person he addresses by my name is simply not I at all. As for Isabelle, she is growing old and sad under this prolonged winter of discontent. I dont know myself, I have'nt encountered the person who used to go down to the Nevins for many months. I sometimes wonder whether there is not some physical cause for it. I went to the doctor to ask whether it might not be a case of pre-mature arrival at old age, physically. He laughed at me and gave me a tonic, but Hoffs malt [Johann Hoff's Malt Extract, a digestive aid] does not reach the spot.

Just as I cant find myself, so I cant find you. I insist that you, too, have greatly changed. I cant define it, but I feel it maddeningly. You used to complain of losing yourself, but in those good days I never really lost you. Yes, in a certain way I feel that you are always there. If I were in trouble or ill I should know where to turn. The physical person of you, the almost family tie between us, the old wish for well being, hold perfectly staunch. But the <u>spirit</u> of you eludes me. Perhaps it is because our lives are so different. I hesitate to speak of it, partially because you asked me not to, partially because it may be largely due to my own torpid and unnatural state. When Francis and Isabelle have lost me, seeing me every day, how can I expect to project myself to one at a distance, how can I believe that my own feelings and impressions concerning you are trustworthy or at all reliable. Yet I am as sure of the change in you as I can well be of anything. Now what all these psychic mysteries do not effect is my feeling for you, that is the same because the roots of it go back prior to all change, back to a time when I was prodigally rich in the one thing which makes life worth the living, and was fabulously happy, even if I didn't know it at the time. But what it does painfully effect is our intercourse. That we both feel. How is one going to shake hands, for example, i[f] ones hand has been cut off? Now I am patiently expecting that mine will grow out again, like a lobster's claw, but it seems to take a long time for it to come. If I had left Pittsburgh when my judgement told me to, four years ago, while you were in Paris, I might not be so far afield now. I believe the truth is that one simply has to pay, hour by hour, for every whit they have taken of happiness, of excitement, exaltation—call it whatever you will—that they had no right to take. I did not know it then. I flattered myself that one could do as one pleased if one respected all the written laws. But I find there are unwritten ones which, if one disregards them, one must pay for just as dearly. Even the consolation that I hurt no one but myself has failed me, for in this aftermath of apathy and dullness you and Isabelle and Francis are called upon to pay into the bank. Hard work seems to be the only escape for me. I am dull, and poor company for myself or anyone else. I suspect in years agone I overdid the romantic aspect of things generally, and my sack cloth and ashes is to be bound in chains of apathy in a Hades of dullness for a thousand days. It may be that the life I live is too monotonous for me, that I'm reflecting the greyness around me. I fell into it all when I was tired and sore and in real grief, but the real grief, oh, that was an easy thing compared to living with myself now. I lost something, or I contracted some disease of the will, or I played to myself and posed to myself until my poor spirit will never again hold up its head.—But that's all talk, it will. I'll come out of this if only you can wait for me, and elope with a tenor when I am forty. Could ye not watch with me one hour? You've already done more than that, but if you can hold out a little longer I feel sure that this period of hibernating will pass. I will cast my dead skin and emerge—and oh if it were but to find you again as you used to be! That would be another spring indeed! I hope for it, far away as it seems. I wrote you once desperately how changed you seemed to me,—I know I must seem so to you, since I am to myself. But surely, if we tell the truth to each other—we have'nt always done that lately—the fog between us will grow thin at last.

Thank you, Dorothy, for what you say of the Wagner matinee ["A Wagner Matinée"]. When you wrote me about your boy story the Outlook was not to be had here. I went twice to the Library, but their copy was in use. I've ordered one from the publisher and shall write you of it later.

I've looked over this letter and am in despair at not having put anything intelligibly. I'm having to write another meaningless explanation to Francis Hill. Isabelle told me to say to him that what he felt was just that I have lost the quality of "abandon" which I once had and which people expect to find in me. She says that if she had not seen me for three years, she would not know me now, and that it's only because she lives with me and believes that I make an honest effort that she can still care for me and believe in me. Perhaps that will help you to understand. I think its that same quality you miss in my letters. Now I've written you the introspective sort of letter I hate to write—you'll bear me witness that I seldom write much about my "feelings" now—and it takes me a whole, dreary Sunday to write it. I only hope to make you <u>feel</u> it is not only toward you that I have changed, but toward everyone, every thing, and most of all toward myself. Goodbye for this time, Dorothy. Let Auld Lang Syne count for as much as you can. The present is not worth talking about, so far as I'm concerned. I suppose living with an honest person like Isabelle has taught me what a sham I am—and always have been. I've lost a good deal. "Honest, my Lord?" Well, I'm at least trying to be that. I've given up living on various and manufactured excitement. It makes me dull and cross and uninteresting, but I'll be honest if it takes every nerve and idea. Do you know what I mean, I wonder? I hope so.

Willie

I can't, in common decency say much about the trying and complicated household in which I live, but you must realize that such conditions do not contribute to ones being oneself. There is a continual restraint necessary.

➔ ❧

Cather's story "A Wagner Matinée," about a hard-worked, discouraged Nebraska farm woman who returns to Boston for a visit and responds powerfully to an afternoon concert of Richard Wagner's music, features bleak descriptions of Red Willow County, Nebraska. Will Owen Jones did not respond to it favorably in his Nebraska State Journal *column.*

TO WILL OWEN JONES

March 6, 1904
Pittsburgh

My. Dear Mr. Jones;

That was a ringing slap you gave me in your more or less personal column. I wonder whether you really mean it, or whether it was for the benefit of the Red Willow contingent? I never even had an idea of disparaging the state. One morning last Spring I got a letter from just such a woman in Western Nebraska, that afternoon I happened to go to a Wagner matinee, and the story was all worked out before I left the hall. I simply used the farm house we used to live in and a few of my recollections of life there. It is so beastly true that my own family are quite insulted—they say it isn't nice to tell such things.

Now my good friend, how could I have explained that years of prosperity had followed the pioneer days, and didn't I take the pains to date the story back in the pioneer times? A story is but a personal impression, a sort of mood, anyhow, it isn't a real estate advertisement nor yet a "roast" for any particular locality. Perhaps it was a mistake to use the name of an actual county, I shall change that in the book proofs. This is not for publication, nor yet to protest against what you had to say—you have said so many agreeable things that I should be a very thin skinned individual if I pouted. But I should like you to know that I had no spiteful intentions and did not mean to throw any cheap slurs upon the state. I though[t] everyone admitted that those pioneer days were desolate, and I was misguided enough to think the story a sort of respectful tribute to the courage of those uncomplaining women who weathered them. Farm life in that territory when I knew it fifteen years ago was bad enough, what must it have been before?

I have about decided to delay the publication of the "Troll Garden" until next fall, as we have arranged for serial publication for a number of the stories and they will not be cleared up until then. Maybe it will relieve you to know that the one under discussion is the only Nebraska tale in the lot.

Willa S. Cather

✦ ✦

According to Edith Lewis's 1953 memoir Willa Cather Living, *she and Cather met in Lincoln, Nebraska, in the summer of 1903. Lewis worked in publishing in New*

York City, and when Cather visited New York after meeting her, Lewis graciously
hosted her. The unfinished novel mentioned in the following letter is probably the
abandoned and unpublished "Pittsburgh novel." The "ordeal" Cather refers to is
Canfield's dissertation defense at Columbia University.

TO DOROTHY CANFIELD

Saturday [probably March or early April 1904]

My Dear Dorothy;

It was good of you to write me what Miss Roseboro' told you about the
yarns. I hear from her occasionally, but she has said nothing about them. I am
surprised to hear that you heard some good ones from her own fair hand. The
only ones I have seen were ludicrous muddles of sentimentality. There was one
in Scribners that was a fright, a crazy sort of condensed novel.

You surely have my prayer for your ordeal in May. However, I cant believe
that you are really apprehensive about it. You are usually pretty cocksure about
anything before you allow yourself to go into it, arent you? You never struck
me as a person who took chances, especially in a thing of that sort. I can
understand though, how, even after the most sound preparation, you might
wish it well over. Let me hear as soon as you get a verdict, please.

I may get to Vermont this summer, for my plan is to spend the summer in
New York, down near or with Edith Lewis, in Washington Square. She has
been a regular trump about looking up rooms for me and such things. I want
to get off somewhere and make a final struggle with this accursed underdone
novel, and New York seems a good place to do it. When the thumb screws are
on so hard I can't endure it, I might be able to run up to see you for a few days
and seek for sympathy. Is there a summer course in English at Columbia? I
should like to take one, I think,—that is, if I'm not too much worn out when
summer comes. I've been up to my ears in school work, altering the course,
looking and writing for two new assistants. This is new work, for me, and I
find it a lot of worry. It's the first really hard pull I've had. Responsibility for
other people's work is certainly a cross, even when they do it pretty well. I've
not left the school building before six at night for two weeks.

What a villain you were to inflict my labored attempt at literary criticism
upon your poor father and mother. It was absurd, I know, but then I found
it hard to say just what I wanted to say, I can tell you much better than I can
write it. If I can get up to Hilhouse we can thrash it all over under the peaceful
brow of equinox, cant we?

Isabelle is still wretched, her throat is bad all the time and she does not seem to gain strength at all.

My family have moved into a big, comfortable house they have just built, and are more comfortable than they have ever been. They would like me to go home this summer to help them with the selecting of wall paper and furniture, and to admire the big lawn and fine pines and maples and locusts in which they take much pride. I'd like to go, I hate to let a year pass without seeing Elsie and Jack—I wish you could see that dear, clever, high-hearted little sister of mine—but I <u>know</u> I would'nt work there, and it does seem that the McClures will lose patience if I dont get this novel to them in some shape or other. Then dont you really think that I ought to get into a more stimulating atmosphere for a few months in the year? Something that will, as you say, waken me up. I almost think that I need that more than rest and quiet. I have food and sleep and regularity enough all year, I dont need that sort of rut. I think Miss Lewis would be a good pilot for me, she's all wrapped up in her discoveries in local color.

Let me hear what you think about it, and what your mother thinks, too. I believe New York would be next to going abroad, for me.

Here's hoping the best for the examination, and that all will go well with you. I'm pretty confident about that, though.

Willie

Dont talk about trouble until you have had to make out <u>in detail</u> a four year's course of study in such a vague endless subject as English Literature & Composition! Map out the work for eight teachers!

As Cather was preparing the final manuscript for her first book of short stories, The Troll Garden, *Dorothy Canfield learned that one of the stories, "The Profile," featured a woman with a disfiguring scar over half of her face. She was concerned that this character too closely resembled her friend Evelyn Osborne, whom Cather had met on her trip to Europe in 1902.*

TO DOROTHY CANFIELD

Sunday [December 18, 1904]

My Dear Dorothy;

I have just received your telegram, and I judge that what you wish to know about the story is in how far the woman in it resembles Miss Osbourne. I think she has nothing in common with Miss O. except that she has a scar on her face. She is addicted to loud clothes, but Miss O—'s certainly could not be put in that category. The story relates chiefly her domestic infelicities and ends with a divorce. The serious tone of your telegram rather perplexes me. A scar is not so uncommon a thing as to point directly to anyone; indeed the painter in this story marries twice and both wives have scars. They could not both be supposed to refer to Miss Osbourne, so you ought not to feel responsible—as, from your telegram I fear you may. I should be very sorry indeed to think that Miss Osbourne would take the story to herself at all, but since the women are both totally unlike her, I dont see how she reasonably could do so. If she did, I should not consider that I would be any more to blame than if I had written the story without having seen her. I surely think you have taken the thing altogether too seriously. Your telegram sounds as though you were hurt—or indignant—and for that I am concerned, and am heartily sorry to have caused you anxiety. But why, for mercy's sake, should you be anxious? One surely cant be held responsible for the sort of stuff ones friends see fit to write. We all have our own degrees of conscience or conscienclessness about that sort of thing. I'm sorry that I'm not going to be able to see you this week to talk it over with you, for I think I could set your mind at rest. At least dont be annoyed by it until you've seen it.

Hastily
Willa

➤ ◆

On New Year's Day 1905, after reading "The Profile," Canfield wrote to Cather and implored her not to publish the story, saying that it would be a cruel, cold-blooded thing to do.

TO DOROTHY CANFIELD

[About January 5, 1905]

My Dear Dorothy;

The proofs of the book were returned to the office some days before your letter came. The pages are now being made up, the story you ask me to withdraw occurs the third in the series and the whole collection is barely long enough to make a book. To withdraw the story would be to withdraw the volume. Perhaps that would not daunt you, but I scarcely know how one would proceed to withdraw a volume already in type. Even if one paid the cost of composition, there would still be the advertising arrangements, which I believe are already made.

I find that I had not really expected you to rise to the pitch of asking me to withdraw it. You write with such rapidity and facility yourself that you probably forget how slow and painful a process writing is for me. When one has spent some two months of Saturdays and Sundays on a story, one has a particular interest in it, and a rather secure sense of ownership.

Then I have another very potent reason for refusing to throw the book overboard, a reason which it is difficult to explain to anyone who does not understand it, and which may sound exceedingly fatuous. I am not the sole proprietor of this book. There are other people who have quite as deep an interest in it as I have myself. Isabelle and Francis Hill are two of them. They have both, as it were, invested capital in the venture. With Isabelle this lot of stories is the fruit of a thousand little personal sacrifices—some of them not so very little, either. To these several people, as to me, your reasons for asking what you ask seem inadequate, arbitrary and visionary in the extreme.

I very much doubt whether Miss Osbourne would take the matter half so seriously as you do, and I doubt still more that she will ever see it. And I beg to differ with you about the resemblance. The scar is, to me, the only thing the two women have in common. I do not think I am doing anything wrong or brutal in publishing the story. I have never been convinced that I have a definite moral sense myself, but I know that Isabelle has one. I have lived beside it for four years, and I have never ceased to wonder at it. I have never known her to do one thing unkind or ungenerous or ignoble. Her opinion gives me absolute conviction. If I contemplated doing anything base or ugly, she is the one who would detect it first and feel it most keenly. I cant help feeling that on such a question her feeling is trustworthy. I can see that this thing has worried and hurt you, and I think that you have fretted yourself into an exaggerated point of view and then forgotten that there may be such a thing as another opinion quite as sincere as your own.

For one thing I am heartily sorry, and that is that you should have been annoyed by it, for however mistaken your feeling may be, I know that your position seems the right one to you. It has been disagreeable enough on both sides. The whole thing, coming about as it has, has pretty effectually dampened my ardor and put a very bitter sting into what I have for several years looked forward to as a pleasure. It seems to be paying a very heavy price for a book which in itself contains many keen disappointments. It must be a jar for you, too. Yet I cannot help feeling that my brother was right when I laid the whole question before him summer before last and he said "It will all depend upon where Miss Canfield stands with regard to you." I am sorry the issue could not have been avoided until after the book was published. It would then have been too late for any discussion and your own course would have shaped itself before you. I shall not send you the lengthy letter that I wrote you when I was ill at Christmas time, as it seems to me that the less there is said on the subject now, the better.

I hope you will not think me too unreasonable—for surely your request was equally so. I should not ask such a thing of anyone, not even my brother. It seems to me tha[t] when you know how much these stories have meant to me—it's not a question of what they mean to you or to anyone who will ever read them—when you know how long they have been in coming and under what disadvantages, that your asking me to demolish has its own satiric touch of inconsiderateness. You can scarcely be surprised that I am hurt by it, even though I anticipated your displeasure. I did not, however, in my most misgiving moments, imagine that you would take it in anything like the way or to anything like the extent that you have. The story that I discussed with you in London, by the way, was quite a different story. That <u>was</u> personal.

I have read this letter over, and it sounds as though I were in a towering rage, the which I am not. But you have put the screws on rather hard and I seem to find it necessary to be savage to stand up against it. I think, of course, that you have considered me very little, and that never really flatters or pleases one. I certainly do know, however, that you must act as you feel. But you must see that I am acting in equally good faith. I dont expect other people to take the stories seriously, or to see why they should not be recalled, but you will certainly admit my right to take them seriously.

Hastily
Willa

By the way, Dorothy, I once sent you a complete list of these stories, and I remember well that I named the Profile, for I asked Isabelle whether she thought you would recognize it. I had no intention of hiding the thing, I only preferred to have it come to your eye with the others. There are at least two more which you have not seen.

→ ←

Dorothy Canfield was astonished that Cather would not budge from her position on the story, and neither Cather nor Isabelle McClung (who also wrote Canfield defending the story) could convince her that publication was morally acceptable. Canfield decided to use her connections to pursue the matter directly with Cather's publisher, McClure, Phillips, and Co. The Canfield contingent apparently persuaded McClure that "The Profile" should not appear in The Troll Garden, *for it is not among the stories in that volume. Nevertheless, the story appeared in* McClure's Magazine *in June 1907. Writer Viola Roseboro' was on the staff of* McClure's *during the "Profile" conflict.*

TO VIOLA ROSEBORO'

Sunday [winter 1905]

My Dear Lady;

You were the most tactful as well as the most generous of people when you gave us that picture of yourself. It has been a singularly actual comfort in a rather gloomy and disheartening period. As I told you before, it's to me what country folk call a speaking likeness. And as I'd been feeling eternally disgraced in the eyes of everyone connected with the firm, it brought me to my feet with a start. The whole affair, you see, has been the nearest approach I've ever made to a personal disgrace, and the whole row has been so incomprehensible to me,—I seem to have done something so horrid and am so utterly in the dark as to what it is,—that I've been seriously questioning as to whether I have any moral sense at all. If Isabelle didn't feel just as I do, and if I had not such entire confidence not only in her very vigorous sense of right and wrong but in her admirable taste in matters of conduct generally, I should certainly think I must be deficient in the finer kind of moral rectitude. I'm sure that some day the humor of the whole complication will stand out above everything else, but so far I've been rather too sore to laugh much.

I have a week's vacation the last of March and I am hoping to go to New

York then. One gets so terribly in the rut here in the winter, though, that one's rather timid about venturing out. I don't know whether you've ever been in a grind long enough to realize what that feeling is, and how stupid and flat and dull it makes people. You get to wanting to stay at home just to hide your own dullness—you're so afraid you'll be found out and your shameful nakedness exposed. Isabelle frequently threatens to drug me and put me in a Pullman and ship me off for parts unknown, so that I'll have to waken up and use my wits. So I may arrive in New York in a semi-conscious state sometime in the last week of March.

The exceeding heaviness of my mind accounts for my not having written to you before. I've been really too dead to address so living a person as yourself. You may remember the shadows who came up and accosted Ulysses in Hades and tried to communicate, but only succeeded in troubling the air with a sigh or two and then drifted back into the myrtle wood. Well, I'm not reclining under the myrtles, and outwardly I'm pretty active, but I feel something of the impotence and timidity of the aforesaid ghosts. I went to hear [pianist Ignacy Jan] Paderewski the other night and I verily felt so much a ghost that I wanted to quit the hall. My silence, you see, has been gracious. It was almost like seeing you myself, to have Isabelle there, and I was particularly glad to have you see her again.

Faithfully
Willa S.C.

➔ ←

When The Troll Garden *was published in March 1905, the* New York Times Book Review *critic effectively summarized the critical response with the comment that the stories in the book "seem to be more the work of promise than of fulfillment." Nevertheless, it was an important moment in Cather's career, and the stories in the book—"Flavia and Her Artists," "The Sculptor's Funeral," "The Garden Lodge," " 'A Death in the Desert,' " "The Marriage of Phaedra," "A Wagner Matinée," and "Paul's Case"—contained themes and settings that filled her fiction the rest of her career.*

TO WITTER BYNNER

June 7, 1905

My Dear Mr. Bynner;

In regard to Mr. Slosson's question as to where I got my information about Western life, you know I lived there for ten years. When I was not quite nine years old [actually, not quite ten], my father moved from the Shenandoah valley to a ranch in the South-western part of Nebraska, about ten miles north of the Kansas line. There was a word in Mrs. [Margaret Wade Campbell] Deland's letter, you remember, about a "curious lack of a sense of beauty in the tales" which I suspect is true enough. I had never thought of it before, but I suppose one's early experiences rather cling to one, and the years when I first began to note my surroundings at all were pretty much devoted to discovering ugliness. If you've never been about in that part of the West, you simply can't imagine anything so bleak and desolate as a Nebraska ranch of eighteen or nineteen years ago. In "A Wagner Matinee" I used some of the features that I best remember of the one on which I lived. Up to the time of our going there I had always lived in the most beautiful part of that very beautiful valley, and during the first year that we spent in the West I came about as near dying from homesickness as a healthy child well could. There was one miserable little sluggish stream about eighteen miles from our ranch. It was perhaps ten feet wide in the Spring, and in the late Summer it was no more than a series of black mud holes at the bottom of a ravine, with a few cottonwoods and dwarf elms growing along its banks. I remember that my little brothers and I would do almost anything to get to this creek.

The country was then almost absolutely treeless. About half way between our ranch and the town where we bought our supplies, or, in the local parlance, "did our trading", there was a row of Lombard poplars which had been planted for a wind break, and when we children went to town the sight of those poplars was the joy of the occasion. From the moment their tips came into view we began to shout,—and as the town was twenty miles from the ranch, we were generally pretty tired before we got to the trees.

I shall never forget the first Christmas I spent in the West. Most of our neighbors were Swedes and Norwegians, and my brothers and I were taken to a Christmas entertainment at the Norwegian church. The Christmas tree was a poor little naked box-elder—you probably don't know that travesty of a tree—all wrapped in green tissue paper, cut in fringes to look like foliage.

During the four years in which I attended the State University at Lincoln, from 1890 to 1894 [in fact, she graduated in 1895], all that country was burned up by a continuous drouth. Our old neighbors, the Norsemen, began to go insane and to commit suicide in the most heartrending fashion. They were all deeply in debt and heavily mortgaged, and of course the credit of the country went all to pieces during those years. Those who lived through it are men of some means today, and it's a delight to go back there now and be shown their brussels carpets and bath tubs and shiny oak furniture, and to hear their daughters do runs on parlor organs. Nevertheless, those four years were a rather grim chapter of human history to have lived through. I knew one little Norwegian girl whose sister committed suicide by drinking carbolic acid. The girl herself thought that was wrong, but she was always praying to die. I don't believe you could imagine how sincerely she wished to die. She was so uniformly sunk in depression that, when they happened to have a half crop one year, her father sent her to Iowa to visit his cousins. She went in a day coach, but when she came back she told my little sister and me that she would never want to die again because she "had found out how beautiful the world was."

Things are a good deal better out there now, you understand, but, whenever I go back, I see the old tragedies that I knew so intimately in the background. I suppose the wild soil has to be reclaimed and subdued in that way, and always at pretty much the same cost,—but it must be less grim in countries where the mere external aspect of nature is something gentler.

I'm apt to be somewhat unrestrained and sentimental upon this subject; that's why I avoided it when you wrote me before. But this you have brought upon your own head.

Sincerely
Willa Sibert Cather

TO MARIEL GERE

[Probably September 30, 1905]
Pittsburgh

My Dear Mariel;

Thank you many times over for the long letter you wrote me this summer. You told me just the things I wanted so much to know and yet had not the courage to ask your mother about. I think I missed your father every moment of the time that I spent in Lincoln this summer. He was one of the people whom I had always so wanted Isabelle to meet.

I had a very happy and very busy two months in the West this summer [accompanied by Isabelle McClung]. In Wyoming we spent a week with Douglass in Cheyenne and a week camping and fishing in the Black Hills with Roscoe. After that we were in Red Cloud four weeks, helping father fix up his new house, which is the pride of his heart. Jessie [Cather Auld] has a dear little house of her own and is as happy as the day is long in making preparations for my small niece or nephew that is to be. We saw a good deal of Mrs. Garber, who is as charming as ever, though greatly aged and saddened. I think she misses the Governor [Silas Garber] sadly, care though he was. Jack and Elsie are big children now, but they keep many of their childish ways and still seem little to me. I think, more than ever, that the West is the only place I want to live, and I am planning to get home to Red Cloud for a year before very long. There are many people there of whom I am very fond.

After leaving Nebraska I went right on to New York to see Mr. McClure and was there for a week.

I stayed with Edith Lewis, and had luncheon with Mrs. [Emma Tyndale] Westermann on her fifty-fifth birthday.

I expect you are, like me, in the thick of your school work again. I am just beginning to get settled in mine. I like it better every year and feel that I do it better. I have such pleasant assistants now; Miss Wilson of Hastings, Neb. and a Wellsley girl.

Please give my love to your mother and to Ellen and Frances, Mariel, and remember me warmly to Mr. and Mrs. Jones, also to Miss Harris and Mrs. Phillips.

Faithfully always
Willa

→ ←

Upon publication of The Troll Garden, *Witter Bynner sent a copy (along with some of his own poetry) to Henry James, who responded that he found it difficult to read new novels, especially those written by American women, but nevertheless would make an effort for Miss Cather.*

TO WITTER BYNNER

February 24 [1906]

Dear Mr. Bynner;

Thank you for sending me the story, which I think I have been able to improve somewhat. You ask me about the novel—indeed, you asked me about it once before and I neglected to answer your question. The truth is that I had not taken it out of the wrapper in which you sent it back to me, nor even opened it, until some weeks ago when I needed a piece of string and used the one which had been put around it in your office. So you see that I have done absolutely nothing with it. It seems to me not quite bad enough to throw away, and not quite good enough to wrestle with again, therefore it reposes in my old hat box.

I do think it was most awfully zealous of you to put in a word to Mr. James and definitely call his attention to the book, but I know that you must think his reply worth your pains. It's such a strikingly personal communication, although it's about something toward which he declares himself dead. The letter has given me a very keen kind of satisfaction, for the attitude he admits is so exactly that which one would wish him to have. I've always known that he must feel just so, but it's comforting, all the same, to have it from him in black and white. If Mr. James and one or two other men did not feel just as he affirms about our whole amazing scheme of production,———well, it would really break one's spirit, you know. It would be a very deep personal hurt. It's the unshrinking positiveness of his statement as to his estimation of the value of what he terms "promiscuous fiction" that makes Mr. James' letter a kind of moral stimulant. You shall see with what good grace I can stand up to whatever punishment he metes out to me in his second letter, to have had the satisfaction of the first. In anticipation of a second letter, however, I certainly do ask your sympathy, even though he should refine upon his treatment in the light of the presupposed youth and innocence of the subject. I feel a good deal as if I were about to undergo a searching physical examination from which I should come away with my former unsuspecting confidence in the ordinary reputableness and dependableness of my organs forever shaken. Or, worse still, with my doubts horribly confirmed. The prospect of his doing what he calls "his best" by me,———well, wouldn't you, now, were you actually facing the prospect of such an attention, have to whistle to keep up your courage?

So I'll ask your sympathy and beg you, when you get his diagnosis, to let me have it faithfully and soon.

Faithfully
Willa Sibert Cather

Henry James never made any further comment on the stories.

❧ ❧

In the spring of 1906 Cather's decade in Pittsburgh came to an end. Anticipating a major shake-up in his staff, S. S. McClure came to Pittsburgh and asked Cather to join McClure's Magazine *in New York. In May 1906 she began her work at one of the most influential editorial offices in the country.*

The following letter was printed in Wah Hoo, *the Allegheny High School newspaper.*

TO HER HOMEROOM CLASS
at Allegheny High School, Pittsburgh

June 6, 1906

Dear Boys and Girls;

Now that I find that I shall not return to the High School next fall, I have a word to say to you. A number of my pupils in various classes, and especially in my Reporting Class, asked me, when I came away, whether I should be with you next year. At that time I fully expected to be. The changes in my plans which will prevent my doing so have been sudden and unforeseen. I should hate to have you think that I had not answered you squarely when you were good enough to ask whether I should return, or to have you think that I put you off with an excuse.

I had made many plans for your Senior work next year and had hoped that we should enjoy that work together. I must now leave you to enjoy it alone. One always has to choose between good things it seems. So I turn to a work I love with very real regret that I must leave behind, for the time at least, a work I had come to love almost as well. But I much more regret having to take leave of so many students whom I feel are good friends of mine. As long as I stay in New York, I shall always be glad to see any of my students when they come to the city.

I wish you every success in your coming examinations and in your senior work next year.

Faithfully yours,
Willa Cather

PART THREE

The *McClure's* Years

1906–1912

Mr. McClure tells me that he does not think I will ever be able to do much at writing stories, that I am a good executive and I had better let it go at that. I sometimes, indeed I very often think that he is right. If I have been going forward at all in the last five years, [it] has been progress of the head and not of the hand. At thirty-four one ought to have some sureness in their pen point and some facility in turning out a story.

—WILLA CATHER TO SARAH ORNE JEWETT, December 19, 1908

Willa Cather, about 1910

CATHER'S EXPERIENCE IN JOURNALISM and magazine publication stood her in good stead when, in 1906, she left teaching and joined the staff of *McClure's Magazine.* At that time, no other magazine was as successful and respected as *McClure's.* The magazine created sensations with its investigative reporting on corporations and municipalities and also published fiction by some of the best-known writers in English, including Rudyard Kipling, Robert Louis Stevenson, and Jack London. S. S. McClure himself was celebrated as a kind of genius of journalism, but he was also notoriously erratic and difficult to work for. He hired Willa Cather, in fact, because he had just lost the bulk of his staff after an office uprising, including well-known writers like Lincoln Steffens and Ida Tarbell. Cather began as a fiction editor but within months was given the onerous writing assignment of pulling together into publishable form a set of research notes about Mary Baker Eddy, the founder of Christian Science. She spent much of 1907 and 1908 in Boston rechecking and extending the research. The results first appeared as a series of articles in *McClure's* (published under the name of the original researcher, Georgine Milmine) and then as a book, *The Life of Mary Baker G. Eddy and the History of Christian Science* (Doubleday, Page, and Co., 1909), still showing authorship by Milmine. Although seven stories and a number of poems written by Cather would appear in *McClure's* between 1906 and 1916, her main energies during the six years she actually worked for the magazine (much of that time as managing editor) went into editorial work—to the point that she became convinced it was draining her creative energy.

✦ ✦

When Cather moved to New York in 1906, she took an apartment at 60 Washington Square South, in the same building as her friend Edith Lewis. The apartment was in the heart of Greenwich Village, right next door to the "House of Genius" at 61 Washington Square South, where over the years rooms had been rented by various artists and writers, including Stephen Crane and Frank Norris.

The following letter to a McClure's *contributor provides a glimpse into Cather's editorial work in her early days at the magazine.*

TO HARRISON G. DWIGHT

October 9, 1906
New York City

Dear Mr. Dwight:

We took "The Valley of the Mills" because we liked it in spite of the fact that we felt it lacked something; at least Mr. McClure and I both liked it very, very much. I always hold out in argument that a feeling can be a story just as much as an incident, or rather that a story can be made out of a feeling as naturally as it can be made out of an incident.

Still, I do think there are certain ways of arrangement which are as necessary in the management of a story made out of a feeling as they are in the management of a story made out of an incident, but this is futile talk, because you know the weak side of your own work better than anyone else knows it. It really seems such a trivial weakness that I cannot believe you will find it very hard to get over.

If you are going back to hallowed and wholesome lands, I feel that you ought to be able to find stories there for us. As long as I am here your work shall always have an ardent advocate. There is nobody here who would not like the "outlandishness" and picturesqueness, provided that you can make the story run a little hotter and swifter through your atmosphere.

I want to see you before you go away because I have long been thinking about the possibility of a series of descriptive articles which would have to do with Mediterranean countries and I want to talk this matter over with you. I am going to Pittsburg on Friday night of this week to be gone until the first of November. After I return I shall be at #60 South Washington Square. Please telephone or drop me a note before you come so that I may be sure to be at home.

In case you are going away before I come back, I hope you will try to drop into the office some day this week. I shall be there every day until Saturday.

Very sincerely yours,

Willa Sibert Cather

You do so nearly press the button in the story we took. Of course we all think it's world's better than plenty of stories that "get there" admirably—but if this story arrived with both its feet it would be a really valuable thing—a stem winder!

TO CHARLES F. CATHER

Monday [December 17, 1906]

My Dear Father;

I feel so badly about not getting home to spend Christmas with my sick daddy. Until today I have thought that I might be able to make it, and I have shed a good many bitter tears over giving it up. For eight years it has been my dream to have a Christmas at home, and this year I thought I would make it. But if you were here, my father, you'd tell me to stand by my job and not to desert Mr. McClure in this crisis. It would mean such a serious loss to him in money and influence not to have the March article come out—Everyone would think he was beaten and scared out, for the articles are under such a glare of publicity and such a fire of criticism. I had nothing to do with the January article [on Mary Baker Eddy] remember, my work begins to appear in February. Mr. McClure is ill from worry and anxiety, and though he wants to let me go home and knows how homesick I am, he begs me to stay here until after Xmas.

I am working night and day to buy my freedom and get to you, father, and it helps me to think that in staying I'm doing just what you would do in my place and what you always taught me to do. I feel like a poor excuse of a daughter to be away from you when you are so ill, but my heart is with you and mother now, and the rest of me will be there before New Year's day.

Lovingly

Willie

➔ ←

Ida Tarbell, a famous "muckraking" writer of McClure's, *left the magazine with many others in 1906 to run the* American Magazine. *Tarbell's series of articles* The Tariff in Our Times *began there in the December 1906 issue.*

TO IDA TARBELL

Friday [probably January 4 or 11, 1907]
New York City

Dear Miss Tarbell;

Being house-bound with a cold I have been compelled to take a short vacation from Xtian Science. In this breathing space I have turned to the Tariff for consolation, and, almost against my will, have found it. I hadn't the least notion that a frivolous person like myself could find it interesting, but I read it with growing enthusiasm and the second article quite vanquished me. I simply would not have believed that anyone, not even you, could give that subject such vigorous and picturesque treatment. I wish I had read more political history. I feel so sure that this is not only very different from but greatly superior to any other historical writing of this kind we may have, that I'd like to be able to say so with authority. You see I know very little about these things, but these tariff articles seem to me very much the most important things happening in magazines just now.

Faithfully
Willa Cather

➤ ◄

In late January 1907, Cather went to Boston to continue her work on the Mary Baker Eddy series, which had already started running in the magazine.

TO HARRISON G. DWIGHT

January 12 [1907]
New York City

Dear Mr. Dwight:

I don't believe God owed you Italy. You just went and took it. And I am sitting here this tepid rainy day envying you. I'm sure you're working and happy—but perhaps it will make you even more satisfied with your destiny to hear what I am doing. Perhaps you dont know it, but we are publishing a series of articles on Christian Science and Mrs. Eddy which have made a great sensation and run our circulation up into incredible thousands. They are the work of a thorough investigator but a very untrained writer and it is necessary to work them over very thoroughly in the office. Mr. McClure tried three men at this disagreeable task, but none of them did it very well, so a month ago it was thrust upon me. You may imagine me wandering about the country grubbing among newspaper files and court records for the next five months. It is the most laborious and sordid work I have ever come upon, and it takes every hour of my time and as much vitality as I can put into it. When it is over I am promised six months abroad on full salary, but I doubt whether what is left of me by that time will be worth taking across the Atlantic. You cant know, never having done it, how such work does sap your poor brain and wring it dry of anything you'd like to pretend was there. I jump about like a squirrel in a cage and wonder how I got here and why I am doing it. I never in my life wanted to do this sort of thing. I have a clean conscience on that score. Then why am I hammering away at it, I'd like to know? I often wonder whether I shall ever write another line of anything I care to. It seems rather improbable that I shall. I do not believe people often get out of this sort of coil, once they are in it. My mind is so full of other things that notions have simply stopped coming my way. I don't feel any impulse to work—or to do anything except grind and "edit." All this should make you feel that cheerful sense of being alive that we have when we hear that someone we know is dead. I hope you'll go for a walk and have a gay dinner after you read this—I want you to appreciate your good luck.

Tell me, <u>why</u> do you so scorn [Pierre] Loti? If anyone told me they saw a trace of Loti in anything I had done, I'd swoon with joy. And here you are indignant at such a suggestion. I don't know the new one you read but "Le Pecheur d'Island", "Le Desert", "Le Roman d'un Spahi" and a dozen more are surely among the most beautiful things in the world. They stir one up like music and steal your senses away in the same fashion. Why do you scorn him? I cant make you out. Why are you afraid to touch the poetic aspect of things when you all the time want to. Take that story "Mortemain". If you'd thrown away what smelt of slang and Kipling and kept what was really your own story—which happens to be like Loti's own—I dont see why it might not have been a very perfect thing. But it seemed like a compromise—a purely imaginative and poetic conception tricked out with a little slang and a few colloquial phrases to disguise it from the eyes of the scoffer. Are you afraid of being called serious and imaginative? Why do you have to make friends with the college boy and the cub reporter by throwing in a good-fellow phraseology? Why do you go in for any disguise, whether smart or jaunty? Why are you such a mortal coward about fine writing? I wish you'd try hitting out squarely—give an imaginative subject a treatment in the tone of the conception, build up your mystery and illusion instead of hinting at it in a curt colloquial remark. I doubt whether the colloquial ever really suggests your kind of thing anyway. It may serve in stories of violent action, but I dont believe it is effective where the point of the story is a perception, or a feeling. I have it now! You are afraid of being sentimental. Yes, I believe that is the solution. So you try to compromise by being slangy. I wish you'd try the other way—Loti's way, and not try to crawl out through Kipling's expedient.

Now I have something to tell you which I hope will please you—supercilious though you are. We sent "The Valley of the Mills" to London to Frank Brangwyn (the best painter of oriental subjects alive) and have squandered five hundred dollars on him, for which sum he is to lavish colored pictures upon you in his best manner. Of course our color reproductions are usually very poor because we have to print 500,000 copies while Scribners, for instance print only 80,000. Hurried printing is ruinous to color work. Still, we shall do our very best with these. We are planning to use the story in the August fiction number. It would fair turn my head if Brangwyn were to illustrate a thing of mine. I think he does the most glorious work of the decorative sort that appears now-a-days.

I was in Pittsburgh two months ago and had a delightful glimpse or two of the Willards.

Of New York there is little to say. It is as big and raw and relentless as ever and grinds one up into little bits every day. Hideous literature is produced as fast as the presses can grind it out. [Wassily] Safonoff, the new conductor of the Philharmonic, and the opera are the only things that save my soul from death.

Here's hoping all the good in the world for you, and do let me know about what you are doing. I'm eager to see some work from you. Please ask Mr [Paul Revere] Reynolds to send it to me personally, as otherwise it might be merely ground in the mill and never get to me at all.

Faithfully always
Willa S. Cather

The Loti works Cather mentions above have been translated into English as An Iceland Fisherman, The Desert, *and* The Romance of a Spahi.

TO WILLIAM E. CHANDLER

July 16, 1907
Boston

My Dear Mr. Chandler;

In the last chapter of our "History of Christian Science" it will be necessary to take up the litigation now in progress, and I fervently hope that by that time we shall be able to set down in our chronicle the result of the action. The most human and interesting way to treat this episode, I think, will be to approach it through a review of George Glover's relations with his mother. I am going to Nebraska to visit my family in about ten days, and I should like to go on further west and see Mr. Glover. Could you give me a letter to Mr. Glover or to his daughter? If you would feel at liberty to suggest that they talk freely to me, I shall be very glad indeed to submit to you the proofs of the article making use of the information they furnish me. This article would not be published before February, and in submitting the proofs to you I shall ask you to cut out any statement of Mr. Glover's which might be detrimental to his interests.

I should like, if possible, to get a full and detailed story from Mr. Glover in the first place, and then cut out whatever you wish me to cut.—Of course the article will not be written in the form of an interview—Even if I use very little of his information, I can, of course, write much better from a full knowledge than from a superficial one. If you feel that you can conscienciously recommend my discretion to the Glover's, you would be giving very material assistance to Mr. McClure and to me.

Mr. Peabody says you have been unable to find a copy of the 1881 edition of "Science and Health". I have one of my own which I should be very glad to lend you for the next few weeks if it will be of any service to you. If you would like to have it, I can mail it to Waterloo at once. If we have anything else that could be of use to you, please do not hesitate to command us.

Very sincerely yours
Willa Sibert Cather

➜ ❧

Cather spent her time in Boston not only working on the Eddy articles, but also getting to know something of Boston's social world, notably celebrated hostess Annie Adams Fields and her companion, author Sarah Orne Jewett.

TO ANNIE ADAMS FIELDS

Wednesday [probably early 1908]
Parker House, Boston

Dear Mrs. Fields

I shall be so glad to see you this afternoon at five. You will not think me importunate for having telephoned so often, will you? You see I have wanted to know you and Miss Jewett for so many years, and as my time is short now I cannot bear to go away without having seen more of you.

Sincerely
Willa Sibert Cather

✢ ✢

Included in Cather's letter to her brother Roscoe, below, was a receipt from Melvin W. Kenney, 65 Bromfield Street, Boston.

TO ROSCOE CATHER

March 2 [1908]

My Dear Roscoe;

Is it too late to thank you for the nice l[e]tter you wrote me at Christmas time? I came back to Boston in January, had a delightful two weeks with Mrs. Deland and the[n] came back to my old happy home at the Parker House—the best hotel for dignity and solid comfort that I know in America—hasn't changed a bit since [William Makepeace] Thackeray stayed here many years ago. I have been meeting a great many delightful people here, the most cultivated and brilliant people I ever met anywhere. One of the particularly attractive men in Boston is Winthrop Ames, grandson of Otis Ames. He is a patron of the arts, especially of the drama, rather given to Ibsen, handsome, young, and somewhat tired of life. When you sit at dinner with him talking about [Frédéric] Mistral and the tendencies of the modern drama, your mind harks back to that windy mountain top with its red granite boulders and the monument to Oakes and Otis [near Laramie, Wyoming]—no world-weariness or Ibsen for them I trow! So it goes. The sons of the barbarians do have to pay a heavy price for their enlightenment. Perhaps in future years, when our part of the world has found itself, sophistication wont hit so hard, but now the men first acquainted with the tree of Knowledge are apt to have the colic. You remember the gentleman's speech about the Northmen and the Troll Garden [from Charles Kingsley's *The Roman and the Teuton: A Series of Lectures*] .

Isabelle and I are going to sail for Naples either on the Carpathia (April 8th) or on the Freiderich der Grosse (April 11). We shall spend a week at Naples, Capri and Pompeii, then go to Rome for a time, and then walk about three hundred miles along the Mediterranean shore from Monte Carlo to Marseilles. After a few weeks at Arles and Avignon we shall go to Paris and settle down. We hope to be gone for six months. I got my guide book for Rome the other day. Seems queer to be really on the way to Rome; for of course Rome has always existed for one, it was a central fact in one's life in Red Cloud and was always the Capital of one's imagination. Rome, London, and Paris were serious matters when I went to the South ward school—they were the three principal cities in Nebraska, so to speak.

I don't know whether I shall come home by way of London or not—seems too bad to miss the chance, for I have letters to Kipling and Maurice Hewlitt and Barry [probably means J. M. Barrie] and [Arthur] Conan Doyle and a lot of people. Just now I am so tired that I do not feel much like people, I want to poke around among vineyards and olive trees and what's left of the Roman Empire. When you come to study Roman colonization and Roman government and Roman manners seriously, it's all very different from the simple schoolbook tale—it's so much the biggest thing that all the centuries have produced and makes our own civilization look a very temporary and tawdry affair. In the south of France, since it is a rather desert country, no big new civilization has come up and effaced Rome—there it all is, theatres, baths, aquaducts; most of the best vineyards were planted under Augustus, and people live just as they do in Virgil's Georgics. It is just as if that whole Roman worl[d] had been preserved in some clear wine. I'm keen to be there again.

Now my boy, I can get you stunning pictures here very cheaply, but the framing is more expensive than it was a few years ago when I last got any pictures. However, I have been to nearly every picture shop in Boston this morning, and have done the best I could for you. I got seven, and I hope you won't think they are too expensive. You asked me to get something for myself when I got them. Thank you, my boy, but I'd rather you would have some nice pictures in your house, so my present goes into the chromos, please. Now here is the list of them, and you must keep it. I also send you the framer's list to be business like, but mine is more full.

Van Dyck's portrait of himself-------------------------------- $2.25
The Windmill (Old Dutch School)--------------------------- $2.25
Song of the Lark (Jules Breton)-------------------------------$3.00
Calling the Moose ([N. C.] Wyeth)------------------------- $1.75
Indian Hunter (Wyeth)--$2.25
"The Dinkey Bird is singing in the amfalulu tree"
     (Maxfield Parish)--$2.85 (In gold)
Caught in the Circle ([Frederic] Remmington)-------------$1.98

                                                    $16.23

The last on[e] is not on the framer's ticket because I got it at another shop.
I will send them by freight, collect at your end, for they will reach you more
promptly if the freight is unpaid, I fancy, and even then you will probably not
get them for weeks. But they will leave Boston Friday, I can assure you of that.
I have paid for them, so you owe me $16.23. I do hope you will like them, and
that they will please Meta [Schaper Cather, Roscoe's wife]. It is hard to select
pictures for other people, but I think I know pretty well what you like. If
you don't like the [Anthony] Van Dyck I shall hate you. I have one like it,
and I think it has given me more delight than any other picture I possess. I
got the Song of the Lark because Jessie said you liked it. Personally, I would
rather have sent you all brown photogravures of French and Dutch pictures
that I like, but I thought you might like some of the real modern fellows better. They are all mighty good reproductions and I am sure they will add to
your nice new house and help you to rest and moon sometimes wh[e]n you
are tired.

How did you like The Queen's Quaire [1904 novel by Maurice Hewlett]?

With lots and lots of love too you, my Boy, and hoping that "The Dinkey
Bird is singing in your Amfalulu Tree",

Lovingly
Willie

TO ANNIE ADAMS FIELDS

                                        Wednesday night [probably April 1908]
My Dear Mrs. Fields:

This is to bid you good morning and to tell you how much I hope that you
are quite yourself again. I had the most delightful afternoon going through

Mrs. Gardener's house last week. The day was fine, you remember, and there were thousands of daffodils in the court and much yellow sunshine. But I am a haunted creature, I begin to think. In the Dutch room there is a portrait of Mary Tudor which looks so much like Mrs. Eddy that I positively fled. I seem in a fair way to become a kind of terrible modern Midas.

I took some books back to the Public Library tonight, and instead of tearing up my card I asked them to keep it for me until I came back. That made me feel that I really am to come back. I first came to Boston last January and arrived at the Parker House at midnight with Mrs. Eddy for my guiding star. I had to get to work that very first morning, and as soon as I had breakfasted I humbly asked the clerk to tell me where the Common was. He informed me with great consideration for my feelings, and I went out and succeeded in finding the Common! Since that morning I have liked Boston better and better every day. It is the only city I have ever lived in that I have cared about, and I am downright homesick at leaving it. New York always seems to me like a beleaguered mediaeval city, with all sorts of atrocities going on in the streets, and one has to go about armed, so to speak. I shall always come back here every time I can, and I shall hope to see you every time I come.

I cant help groaning a good deal that Mr. McClure did not come up and take me to see you a year ago. But I should think, instead, of my good fortune in coming to know you at all. Mrs. Eddy has been a hard mistress, but hereafter I shall always think that, in some mysterious way, she and her affairs brought me to know you and Miss Jewett, and that you are, in a manner, the rewards of my servitude. This may sound like empirical reasoning, but I shall stick to it, for it is the one course of reasoning which makes the year's work seem worth while to me.

So, if you and Miss Jewett do not object to being considered as the Rewards of Industry, then I can write as do the contributors to the <u>Christian Science Journal</u>, "To our Beloved Leader, Mrs. Eddy, I owe a great happiness etc."

If I do not see you again before I go, I shall look forward to the autumn, and I beg you to let me send you a note now and then this summer.

Faithfully
Willa Sibert Cather

The home of collector and philanthropist Isabella Stewart Gardner is now a distinctive art museum in Boston, and the wonderful collection remains as Gardner eccentrically arranged it. Flowers continue to bloom in the glass-topped garden courtyard. The Mary Baker Eddy look-alike is a mid-sixteenth-century portrait of Mary I, Queen of England, by Dutch artist Antonis Mor.

→ ←

In April 1908, Cather and Isabelle McClung left on their second trip to Europe, this time to Italy. "If Blood be the price of admiralty," below, is a line from Rudyard Kipling's poem "Song of the Dead."

TO ROSCOE CATHER

April 18 [1908]
Royal Mail Steamship "Carpathia"

My Dear Boy;

At three oclock this afternoon we sighted Portugal, Cape St. Vincent, and ever since we have been sailing very softly along this shore which is pretty nearly holy ground to them as speak the English tongue. In a few hours we will be in Trafalgar Bay, where [Horatio] Nelson broke Napoleon's fleet for good. He chased the French fleet all up and down this coast as far as Cape St. Vincent, and the bottom all along here is strewn with the bones of Frenchmen and Spaniards and Italians that went down. Our English captain confessed to me this afternoon that he never steams down this coast without thinking of it and setting his heels tighter on his bridge. I keep seeing Nelson on his great column in Trafalgar Square in London, and thinking of the letter he wrote Lady Hamilton [Nelson's mistress] the night before the battle, which I saw in the British Museum. All up and down here Nelson chased them. "If Blood be the price of admiralty." I love to think of all those bones along the bottom here. I love to think of the little admiral chasing them up and down. I love to think how here the English navy was exalted above all the navies of the earth. And when he had chased 'em up and down and cleared the waters of 'em, the little admiral up and died. And they put him up on his column in London and [Edwin Henry] Landseer made his bronze lions to guard him, and the English people loved Lady Hamilton better than the queen because Lord Nelson had loved her.

I wish you could see these soft gray waters, and the wild bleak Portugal coast, and could sit here with me and think about all their bones down below.

[Unsigned]

→ ←

The following was written on a postcard with a view of the Santa Lucia Hotel and Mount Vesuvius in Naples, Italy. The hotel is circled, and next to it Cather wrote, "our hotel."

TO ELSIE CATHER

[Late April or early May 1908]
Naples

Dear Elsie—

Here we are and it is like this only a thousand times more beautiful. We have a balcony facing on the sea, which is much <u>much</u> bluer than in this picture. The most beautiful gardens are only two squares away, and all the world seems like fairy land.

Willie

TO ALICE E. D. GOUDY

May 3 [1908]
Santa Lucia Hotel, Naples

My Dear Mrs. Goudy

My friend and I have just come back from a week up in the Apennines where we have had some wonderful long walks visiting some old forgotten monasteries where there are only one or two monks left. In one splendid old building we found but one lonely monk. It is high on a mountain top and very few people ever take that terrific climb over a ruined mountain road. We found some wonderful latin manuscripts in his crumbling library. In another monastery, the famous Benedictine abbey of La Trinitá della Cava, we found the original code of the Lombard League. The place was founded by a Lombard king in 1030. It is a great rambling white building built against the side of a perpendicular cliff and below it is a dreadfully deep wooded ravine to which you can descend by flights of steps cut in the cliff. Down there the angry little river Bornea leaps along under its stone arches and turns the wheels of half-a-dozen little stone flour-mills set here and there down the narrow, winding valley.

I spent two long days in Pompeii, which is so much more wonderful than anyone can imagine, and have returned here [to] spend some time looking over the great Pompeiian collection in the Naples Museum. I love Naples and am living in a most delightful hotel situated right on the Bay of Naples which, I am convinced, is the most enchantingly beautiful body of water in the world. I have marked my balcony in the picture at the head of this hotel paper. I sit there every afternoon and watch Vesuvius change from violet to lilac and then to purple. I could almost throw a stone over to the tiny island of Megares [Megaride] where Lucullus had his gardens and where Brutus met Cicero after the murder of Caesar. The street singers sing all the old Neapolitan airs under my window every night, and every morning I go out and buy roses and camelias on the Spanish Stairs. The gardens in Naples are beautiful, and the Royal Museum is the richest in portrait sculpture I have ever seen—the British Museum seems quite poor in comparison. The portrait sculpture of the Roman Emperors, particularly of the Antoinine house, leave nothing to be desired. The royal families appear in youth and age, and I feel as if I had known every member personally. I have rubbed up my Latin enough to get through Tacitus and Suetonius quite carefully. This is the place to read those detailed historians, for details cannot mean much unless you are in the place where it has a physical and concrete reality.

There was a photograph of the wonderful head of Caesar at the Naples museum in the copy of Allen & Greenough's "Gallic War" which I read in Red Cloud under Mr. [Alexander K.] Goudy. I always knew I should see the original some day, and I thought of Mr. Goudy when I came across that great head the other day in its lofty marble gallery. Of all the statues of Caesar I have seen it is the most wonderful. Such a head! Napoleons is a wooden block compared to it. I go back and back to it and I doubt whether the world has produced another such head in all the centuries since.

We spent a good deal of time in the vineyards and fields last week. The oranges and lemons are ripe in their orchards and the peach and cherry trees are in bloom. The vines are in little new leaf and the olive groves all along the Mediterranean are so soft and gray. All the country folk are in the fields digging and planting the fall crop, and they do it just as Virgil describes in the Georgics: the same heavy hoes, the same white saplings for the vines, the same old songs as the husbandmen toil along the furrows and work this old, old earth which has produced most of the beautiful things in the world.

Next week we go to Rome, but I shall leave Naples and the soft Companian country with tears, I am afraid. Such a ravishing world and such a short life to see it in!

Lovingly
Willa

TO SARAH ORNE JEWETT

May 10, 1908
Hotel & Pension Palumbo, Ravello, Gulf of Salerno

Dear Miss Jewett,

Do you, I wonder remember what an extravagantly beautiful place this is? The camelias are all in blossom in the Rufolo gardens and our hotel is over run by yellow roses. I have one of the rooms on the terrace which hangs above Minori and the sea. You probably remember what a magical aspect the sea presents from that terrace—very much like hot green porcelain whose flow has been chalked by those jagged cliffs along which runs the Salerno road. From here it is certainly the sea of legend—nothing else, and it glimmers centuries away from you, like the opaque blue water that [Pierre] Puvis de Chavannes painted. When I was little I knew a funny old lady in Nebraska who had some water from the Mediterranean corked up in a bottle, and when you looked at the bottle for a long time and suddenly shut your eyes you saw the sea itself for a moment, and this was the way it looked—a color and a remoteness that exist in legends and nowhere else. But the color one does find elsewhere, after all. I have seen this turquoise kind of green in Japanese porcelain, haven't you?

Seven hundred years ago yesterday a galley from the Holy Land first brought St. Andrew's skull to Amalfi, in Amalfi's time of sea-sovereignty. Every hundred years the arrival of the skull is celebrated. On Wednesday the skull was taken up from the crypt and sent down to Sorrento. It was brought back to Amalfi yesterday by a fleet of forty-seven vessels, and the cardinal from Rome was down at the marina to receive it. The bells in Ravello rang all day long and the whole countryside trooped down to Amalfi. I fell in with a priest and a lot of old people who were hurrying down the footpath that outruns the carriage road. We were all feeling gay and tramping hard, and all wore our best things—except the priest who wore his old cassock and carried his best one in a handkerchief. But just as we were hurrying over the one place where the wood path winds out a hundred feet above the carriage road, yes, just at that identical instant, some people from Nebraska, whom I had not seen for years and years, swung into the carriage road, and by some diabolical pres-byopy recognized me and shouted and gesticulated and haled me from that glad company. I shall probably not see those good people for a dozen years to come, but I had to go back to Ravello with them and lose the festa and my pleased companions. I have felt as if I were being put through the world by some awfully complicated kind of clock-work ever since.

The volume of Mrs. [Alice] Meynell's essays [*The Rhythm of Life and Other Essays*] you gave me has been an inexhaustible delight. Do you remember the one which she calls "The Lesson of Landscape"? It seems to me about the only truthful writing I have ever read about Italy—in English. I cannot, alas, feel that Vernon Lee is altogether, or even measurably, truthful. Surely she is capricious and self-conscious and she takes liberties with things and places to get her effects. But Miss Meynell tells the truth—How beautifully truthful she is about all this pale-colored lovely earth, and how her words show the frugality and temperance that it ought to teach one. What a coarse and stupid conception of Italy we have all been reared upon! A tufted Monte Carlo palm garden sort of country.

But Mrs. Meynell has a fellow in the truth. Housman—A.E.—did a little poem which rings in my ears all day when I tramp about the gray terraced mountain sides and go in and out among the fields, so little and precious and dear-bought. It is not in "The Shropshire Lad", but he gave me a copy of it, and I must quote it to you here, at the risk of misquoting it. My copy is in Pittsburgh, and I have never seen it (the verse) anywhere else. I never cared about it much until I left Naples three weeks ago, and then it rose out of the limbo of forgotten things and smote me full in the face.

THE OLIVE

The olive in its orchard,
If man could plant it sure,
The olive in its orchard
Should flourish and endure.

So deep among the trenches
Its dressers digged and died,
The olive in its orchard
Should prosper and abide.

Thick should the fruit be clustered
And light the leaf should wave,
So deep the roots are planted
In the corrupting grave.

That's the Italy I have found—just about all of it. And how miraculously true the truth is! This morning when the Cardinal visited the church here and all the children for miles about came up the hill before his carriage carrying big olive branches, what incredible lightness and spring it had, that hard, dry, sharp, little leaf that is so tempered to dust and wind and sun and damp and drought.

Betsy Lane has gone spiriting on to Rome in my other trunk, but the "White Heron" and the Dulham Ladies abide with me always. Ah <u>they</u> are like the olive leaf—"si triste, si gai [so sad, so gay]."

Faithfully
Willa Cather

Cather's memory of the Housman verse, which was published The Outlook *in June 1902, is not accurate in all details, but well remembered in general. "Betsy Lane," "the 'White Heron,' " and "the Dulham Ladies" are references to Jewett's works: the short stories "The Flight of Betsy Lane," "A White Heron," and "The Dulham Ladies."*

➔ ←

The following was written on a postcard showing the view from Villa Doria Pamphili, Rome, Italy.

TO ROSCOE CATHER

June 10 [1908]
Rome

My Dear Roscoe: This is the dome of St. Peter's from where I first saw it—one of the wonderful Roman gardens. It looms up from the east wherever one turns, and after you stay about the church and the Vatican and the catacombs for a time it is borne in upon one that there is where the modern world was born. From the day Charlemagne was crowned there and before, the Vatican was fashioning modern Europe. Next in wonder to the Rome of the Empire is the Catholic Rome of the middle ages.

Willa

➔ ←

The following was written on a postcard showing a view of Castel Sant'Angelo, Rome, Italy.

TO ELSIE CATHER

June 16 [1908]
Rome

My Dear Bobbie: This is the Tiber with St. Peter's and Hadrian's tomb. It is such a lifeless, discouraged little river. Yesterday we spent all the morning in the old Palace of the Caesars—such millions of poppies as do grow over them. All the rooms are taller than the Stand Pipe (Red Cloud measure) and there is an enormous race track inside the palace. Last week I walked so long in Caesar's home one day that I had to stay in bed the next.

W.S.C.

→ ←

The following was written on a postcard showing canals in Venice, Italy.

TO ELSIE CATHER

July 8 [1908]
Venice

My Dear Elsie

Isabelle left me yesterday and she sails for home from Genoa tomorrow. I follow her two weeks from today and sail on the Königin Louise, arriving in New York August 6th. I wanted two weeks more of Venice, but I am so lonely that I scarcely know whether it will pay.

Willie

→ ←

The following, on a postcard with a view of the Hotel Royal Danieli in Venice, is one of only two pieces of correspondence from Cather to Isabelle McClung known still to exist.

TO ISABELLE MCCLUNG

July 14 [1908]
Venice

I have been to Santa Maria della Salute this morning to see another Titian and a beautiful Tintoretto. <u>Please</u> do not give away the Bacchus and Ariadne to <u>anyone</u>. I want us to have that for ourselves. I have bought some other pictures but not that, and I love that best of all. You are in the Atlantic now!

W.S.C.

➤ ❤

Upon returning to New York, Cather resumed editorial duties at McClure's and moved to a new apartment at 82 Washington Place, only a couple of blocks from her first Greenwich Village apartment. She shared this new apartment with Edith Lewis, an arrangement the two would maintain until the end of Cather's life.

TO SARAH ORNE JEWETT

October 24 [1908]
New York City

Dear Miss Jewett;

Your letter reached me on a gloomy and tired day and such a new heart as it gave me. It is so true that "great worries make little frets", and that worried people become sour and disposed to find faults. Let me take that as a rebuke, whether you meant it so or not, for it is a rebuke that will do me good. The fact that both you and Mrs. [Annie Adams] Fields felt vitality in the first chapters of Mrs. [Mary Augusta] Ward's story has cheered me mightily. I am sending you a letter from her in which she outlines the rest of the story. I am now ransacking libraries to find material on divorce for her. I sent her off a bundle of pamphlets yesterday.

I knew Mr. [Charles Eliot] Norton's death would be a sorrow to both you and Mrs. Fields, and I thought of you both when I saw the headlines announcing it. Mrs. Fields is the only one left who can evoke that vanished time that was so much nobler than this. How she does evoke it! I think it never had much reality for me until that afternoon when I first went to her house on Charles Street, and she sat in the window with the fine broad river and a quiet sunset behind her. It was the first time in my life that I ever felt that we had any past—of that kind—of our very own, and I went out with an exultant feeling of acquisition. I dont think she said anything about those old chapters of her life, but one got the feeling of them almost more than if she had. That is one reason why I love her verses to the Charles River. The moment my eye fell on them they brought back that first meeting with you both—a thing so long waited for.

What joy I have had from "The Singing Shepherd," which you marked and tied up for me with your own hands. I love "Blue Succory" and "An Autumn Bird" [actually, "The Bird of Autumn"] and "Winter Lilacs." But I think "Still in Thy Love I Trust" is perhaps the most beautiful. That is one of the complete things that give one such complete and utter satisfaction. And then there is dear "Little Guinever," that is so like a song in some Elizabethan play. How really gay that is, and how it sings.

I feel sure that you are both back in Charles Street by this, and I am hopeful that Mrs. Fields is getting joy out of these soft warm autumn days. "The Gloucester Mother" was copied in the N. Y. Times, and when I was on the train going up to New Haven to spend Saturday and Sunday of last week, I saw a dear old lady cut the verses out of the paper with a hair pin!

Miss Lewis and I are enjoying our apartment more every day, although we lead so dreary, idle lives in it. Mrs. Fields, I know, will exclaim when you tell her that so far we have largely fended for ourselves and have managed to get our own breakfast and luncheon and, about three days a week, our dinner. We dine at the Brevoort [Hotel] on other nights and have a maid come in to clean two days a week. There are good reasons why we should each of us practise reasonable economy this winter, and cooking does take one's mind away from office troubles. These latter cares will, we hope, be somewhat lighter after the middle of November. Meanwhile, we shall have a pretty thorny path to tread until then. The sales for October were 10,000 more copies than last October, and November has started well.

I have just finished the page proofs of my story ["On the Gulls' Road"] in the December number. I am afraid you wont like it, dear Lady. The scent of the tube-rose seems to cling to it still. It rather screams, and I cant feel that stories like that matter much. But there is a little one ["The Enchanted Bluff"], which Mr. McClure and Mr. [Edward L.] Burlingame [editor of Scribner's] sniff at, which I somehow think might interest you a little—because it is different from the things you knew when you were a child. In the West we had a kind of Latin influence, as you had an English one. We had so many Spanish words, just as you had words left over from Chaucer. Even the cow-boy saddle, you know, is an old Spanish model. There was something heady in the wind that blew up from Mexico. I make bold to send this scorned tale (Mr. McClure says it is <u>all introduction</u>) and I pray you cast your eye upon it in some empty half hour. It is about a place a weary long way from South Berwick.

I hope the size of this packet will not frighten you. A thousand good wishes and much love goes with it to you and to Mrs. Fields. Are you rested by this, I wonder, and is your anxiety for Mrs. Fields quite over? I hope so. Good night, Dear Lady.

Devotedly
Willa

The Singing Shepherd *was a volume of poems published by Annie Fields in 1895.* *"The Gloucester Mother" was a poem by Jewett published in* McClure's *in October 1908 with an elaborate decoration designed by W. T. Benda, who would later illustrate* My Ántonia *for Willa Cather.*

➤ ❖

Cather received encouraging responses from Jewett to the two stories she had sent. In a remarkable letter of December 13, 1908, full of sincere concern and good wishes, Jewett also gave Cather important advice that would permanently influence her writing: "your vivid, exciting companionship in the office must not be your audience, you must find your own quiet centre of life, and write from that to the world that holds offices, and all society, all Bohemia; the city, the country—in short, you must write to the human heart, the great consciousness that all humanity goes to make up. Otherwise what might be strength in a writer is only crudeness, and what might be insight is only observation; sentiment falls to sentimentality—you can write about life, but never write life itself. And to write and work on this level, we must live on it—we must at least recognize it and defer to it at every step. We must be ourselves, but we must be our best selves." Cather's response follows.

TO SARAH ORNE JEWETT

Saturday, December 19 [1908]
New York City

My Dear, Dear Miss Jewett;

Such a kind and earnest and friendly letter as you sent me! I have read it over many times. I have been in deep perplexity these last few years, and troubles that concern only one's habits of mind are such personal things that they are hard to talk about. You see I was not made to have to do with affairs—what Mr. McClure calls "men and measures." If I get on at that kind of work it is by going at it with the sort of energy most people have to exert only on rare occasions. Consequently I live just about as much during the day as a trapeze performer does when he is on the bars—it's catch the right bar at the right minute, or into the net you go. I feel all the time so dispossessed and bereft of myself. My mind is off doing trapeze work all day long and only comes back to me when it is dog tired and wants to creep into my body and sleep. I really do stand and look at it sometimes and threaten not to take it in at all—I get to hating it so for not being any more good to me. Then reading so much poorly written matter as I have to read has a kind of deadening effect on me somehow. I know that many great and wise people have been able to do that, but I am neither large enough nor wise enough to do it without getting a kind of dread of everything that is made out of words. I feel diluted and weakened by it all the time—relaxed, as if I had lived in a tepid bath until I shrink from either heat or cold.

I have often thought of trying to get three or four months of freedom a year, but you see when the planning of articles is pretty much in one person's head it is difficult to hand these many little details over to another person. Your mind becomes a card-catalogue of notes that are meaningless except as related to their proper subject. What Mr. McClure wants is to make me into as good an imitation of Miss Tarbell as he can. He wants me to write articles on popular science, so called, (and other things) for half of each week, and attend to the office work in the other half. That combination would be quite possible—and, I fear perfectly deadening. He wants, above all things, good, clear-cut journalism. The which I do not despise, but I get nothing to breathe out of it and no satisfaction.

Mr. McClure tells me that he does not think I will ever be able to do much at writing stories, that I am a good executive and I had better let it go at that. I sometimes, indeed I very often think that he is right. If I have been going forward at all in the last five years, [i]t has been progress of the head and not of the hand. At thirty-four [actually, she had just turned thirty-five] one ought to have some sureness in their pen point and some facility in turning out a story. In other matters—things about the office—I can usually do what I set out to do and I can learn by experience, but when it comes to writing I'm a new-born baby every time—always come into it naked and shivery and without any bones. I never learn anything about it at all. I sometimes wonder whether one can possibly be meant to do the thing at which they are more blind and inept and blundering than at anything else in the world.

But the question of work aside, one has a right to live and reflect and feel a little. When I was teaching I did. I learned more or less all the time. But now I have the feeling of standing still except for a certain kind of facility in getting the sort of material Mr. McClure wants. It's stiff mental exercise, but it is about as much food to live by as elaborate mental arithmetic would be.—Of course there are interesting people and interesting things in the day's work, but it's all like going round the world in a railway train and never getting off to see anything closer. I have not a reportorial mind—I can't get things in fleeting glimpses and I can't get any pleasure out of them. And the excitement of it doesn't stimulate me, it only wears me out.

Now the kind of life that makes one feel empty and shallow and superficial, that makes one dread to read and dread to think, can't be good for one, can it? It can't be the kind of life one was meant to live. I do think that kind of excitement does to my brain exactly what I have seen alcohol do to men's. It seems to spread one's very brain cells apart so that they don't touch. Everything leaks out as the power does in a broken circuit.

So whether or not the chief is right about my never doing much writing, I think one's immortal soul is to be considered a little. He thrives on this perpetual debauch, but five years more of it will make me a fat, sour, ill-tempered lady—and fussy, worst of all! And assertive; all people who do feats on the flying trapeze and never think are as cocky as terriers after rats, you know.

I have to lend a hand at home now and then, and a good salary _is_ a good thing. Still, if I stopped working next summer I would have money enough to live very simply for three or four years. That would give me time to pull myself together. I doubt whether I would ever write very much—though that is hard to tell about for sure; since I was fifteen I have not had a patch of leisure six months long. When I was on a newspaper I had one month vacation a year, and when I was teaching I had two. Still, I don't think that my pen would ever travel very fast, even along smooth roads. But I would write a little—"and save the soul besides [from Robert Browning's *The Ring and the Book*]." It's so foolish to live (which is always trouble enough) and not to save your soul. It's so foolish to lose your real pleasures for the supposed pleasures of the chase—or of the stock exchange. You remember poor [Oliver] Goldsmith [from "The Deserted Village"]

> "And as an hare whom horns and hounds pursue,
> Pants for the place from which at first she flew"

It is really like that. I do feel like such an rabbit most of the time. I dont mean that I get panic-stricken. I believe I am still called "executive" at the office. But inside I feel like that. Isn't there a new disease, beloved by psychologists, called "split personality"?

Of all these things and many others I long to talk to you. In lieu of so doing I have been reading again this evening [Jewett's story] "Martha's Lady." I do think it is almost the saddest and loveliest of stories. It humbles and desolates me every time I read it—and somehow makes me willing to begin all over and try to be good; like a whipping used to do when I was little. Perhaps after Christmas I can slip up to Boston for a day. Until then a world of love to you and all the well wishes of this season, an hundred fold warmer and more heartfelt than they are wont to be. I shall think of you and of Mrs. Fields often on Christmas Day.

Devotedly
Willa

[written in the top margin of the last page:] As I pick up the sheets of this letter I am horrified—but I claim indulgence because I have left wide margins.

→ ←

Cather met Zoë Akins, the writer to whom the following letter is addressed, through her work at McClure's. *The two remained friends until the end of Cather's life.*

TO ZOË AKINS

January 27, 1909
New York City

My dear Miss Akins:—

I was so glad to hear from you and delighted to hear about the funny negro family. What a rich sort of people they are in imagination, after all!

I am sending the verse back to you. None of it is adapted for magazine publication. The short one, "The Road", is not quite up to the standard we try to follow, and the good ones are much too long. One of the long ones, "L'empire de l'amour", has real merit —feeling and melody. In some places it falls to a rather childish form of expression—the first five lines in part II, for instance,—but I think there is real poetic feeling in it.

I wonder if you will ever settle down and do something with all your might and main, and whether it will be verse, or playwriting, or what? And whether you will ever cease to coquette with the stage. Perhaps it will be better if you don't. Playwriting, if one has a gift that way and if one cares about the stage, must surely be a most delightful occupation as it is a most remunerative kind of work. About these things I know very little and can give you no suggestions.

The older I grow the less interest I have in the theater. I used to care a good deal about Miss [Ellen] Terry and was interested in Mr. [Richard] Mansfield. I still feel a good deal of interest in George Arliss, but for the most part the work that is being done on the stage just now does not happen to be the sort that I can get any satisfaction from. I have a sort of feeling that your real gift lies toward playwriting; some of the verses that you have sent me have, I think, fancy and melody in them.

Whatever your work may be I wish you every success in it. If you can once get away from "people",—the "interesting" followers of this art and that,—and get settled to the work itself, I shall look for something from you.

Faithfully always,
Willa Sibert Cather

TO ZOË AKINS

Tuesday [February 1909?]
New York City

Dear Miss Akins:

It is I who should apologize, and I do with all my heart. That was a harsh blunt-sounding letter, one of thirty or forty dictated in a hurry. Sending things back, when I like them at all, is always a hard business for me—I never get used to it. And I am afraid I am often curt when I honestly feel only regret. I am truly pleased that you like the verses from "April Twilight", and I like young writers to care for my things—who would not like that? I wonder if you noticed "The Palatine" [poem by Cather], published in McClure's sometime last summer? I thought it rather better than the "April Twilight" things. I had noticed that one of yours in <u>Harpers</u> and was so glad to see it there. I like the Sapphic verses, too. Please send us some more verse when you feel inclined to do so, and I shall understand that you will not misunderstand if it does not seem to be what we need.————Do you know Miss [Louise Imogen] Guiney's work well? Do study "A Wayside Harp" [actually titled *A Roadside Harp*]. There is a richness and delicacy and restraint there that ought to help all of us.

Faithfully
Willa Sibert Cather

→ ←

The following was read at the Red Cloud, Nebraska, high school commencement in 1909 and published in the Red Cloud Chief *on May 27, 1909.*

TO EDWIN JAMES OVERING JR.
President of the Board of Education, Red Cloud, Nebraska

April 30, 1909

My Dear Mr. Overing:

As I wrote you sometime ago, I had very much hoped to be present at the Red Cloud commencement exercises this year. I had made all my plans to go west about the first of May, and until a few days ago, confidently expected to be at home by the time the school year closed.

Within the last two or three days, however, I have seen that instead of turning westward I must face in the opposite direction, and that very soon. I am sailing immediately for London to attend to some business matters there.

Since you asked me to go on the commencement program, I had expected to get something ready for you on my way west, but my hurried departure will not leave me time to prepare any sort of paper to send you. I would be glad to write something on the way over and send it back to you, but the time would be so short that in all probability anything mailed from England would not reach you before the 19th. Let me thank you for the invitation and ask you to express to the Board of Education my regret at being unable to accept it.

Since I cannot be present, therefore, I will ask you to let this letter represent me, if you see fit.

I have been interested in the Red Cloud schools for many years, and have kept in touch with them through so many brothers and sisters, that to think about them and wish them well has become a mental habit. I could not forget the schools if I tried; they play a part in many of my happiest memories, and some of my truest friends have been closely connected with them. If I had no other reason to love the schools of my own town—and I have many others—I should always love them because of Mr. and Mrs. A. K. Goudy and Mr. and Mrs. O. C. Case. When my father first moved into Red Cloud from his ranch, and I was taken to the old high school building to be entered as a pupil in the Red Cloud schools, Mrs. Case—then Miss King—was principal, and she was the first person who interviewed the new county pupil. She had a talk with me up in the old bell room. I remember her well as a stalwart young woman with a great deal of mirth in her eyes and a very sympathetic, kind voice.

I was placed in a class in Miss Gertrude Sherer's room. I do not remember much about what went on during my first day in school, but that afternoon I brought away three distinct impressions that Trix Mizer was the prettiest little girl I had ever seen, that Margie Miner was so jolly I wanted awfully to know her, and that Eddie Emigh never looked at his book because he was always looking at Trix.

The next year Miss King was made principal of the South Ward School, and I was a pupil in her A. grade. I am very sure that Miss King was the first person whom I ever cared a great deal for outside of my own family. I had been in her class only a few weeks when I wanted more than any thing else in the world to please her. During the rest of that year, when I succeeded in pleasing her I was quite happy; when I failed to please her there was only one thing I cared about and that was to try again and make her forget my mistakes. I have always looked back on that year as one of the happiest I ever spent.

After I left Miss King's room she became County Superintendent. As I went on through the high school she always helped and advised me; she even tried very hard to teach me algebra at night, but not even Miss King—who could do almost anything—could do that.

After I went away to the State University there came a year or two when I was so taken up with new things and people, and so much excited about my work in Lincoln, that I saw comparatively little of my old friends. Just before I went away to school Miss King had married Mr. Case and when I began to see a good deal of my old friends again, I learned to care for Mr. Case almost as much as for his wife.

I believe I am not the only graduate of the Red Cloud schools whose courage Mr. and Mrs. Case revived time and again. I believe that all the boys and girls whom they helped will agree with me that one of the things best worth while in life is to keep faith with those two friends of ours who gave us their confidence. In the long summer evenings Mr. Case and his wife used to sit on the front porch behind the vines and the little maple trees and plan out useful and honorable futures for the Red Cloud boys and girls. There is nothing for us to do now but to try to realize those generous dreams of theirs.

I can scarcely realize that it has been nineteen years since I stood on the stage in the Red Cloud opera house with two little boys—if I remember rightly we all three looked like little boys—and made my Commencement speech. Let me warn the graduates of 1909 that the next nineteen years will go so quickly that they won't have time to turn around in them.

The thing I best remember about my own graduation is the class tree. It was a little crooked-backed honey locust that Alec Bentley and John Tulleys dug out of a row of locusts on my Grandmother Cather's land. I don't know why I was more interested in the tree than in anything else about graduating, but I was. My brothers and I carried water from the High School pump and watered it ever so many times that summer. The tree wilted and peaked and pined and languished all summer. But look out for what it would do next summer, we thought. But next summer it was no better, nor yet the next. The thing simply would not grow. For years it seemed to stand still. For the matter of that we all stood still; John didn't grow, and Alec didn't grow. But the tree, at least was getting ready to grow. I went home one summer to find that after having been a crooked bush for years and years it had really shot up to a considerable height. The tree stands in the south east corner of the High School yard, and I hope the Red Cloud boys and girls will be good to it.

I hope none of your graduates tonight are as much frightened as I was when I got up to deliver my important oration. When Mr. Goudy read my name and I rose and went to the front of the platform, the room looked as if it were full of smoke and the people seemed to have run together. I looked at this blur and made out three faces looking intently at me. Mr. Henry Cook in the front part of the house, and further back Mr. William Ducker and Mrs. Case. These three friendly faces gave me courage, and I am sure they always will.

With a world of good wishes for your graduates, Mr. Overing, and greetings to my old schoolmates, I am

Faithfully
Willa Cather

Evangeline King Case was indeed remembered long and warmly by Cather; she served as the model for Evangeline Knightly in "The Best Years," one of Cather's very last stories.

The scouting trip that Cather mentioned in her public letter to Mr. Overing became a two-month stay in England. She met a great many interesting people—such as critic William Archer, and writers H. G. Wells, Edmund Gosse, and Katharine Tynan—and attended such diverse events as the funeral of writer George Meredith and the London premiere of John Millington Synge's Playboy of the Western World. *Another writer she met was British novelist Ford Madox Ford (then Hueffer), with the following unhappy results.*

TO ELSIE MARTINDALE HUEFFER

May 20, 1909
Thackeray Hotel, London

Dear Mrs. Hueffer;

I am so sorry to have let you in for a sharp note from Mr. [Joseph] Conrad. You see the whole matter was, in a manner, accidental. I was telling Mr. Hueffer how much I hoped that we might be able to get some of Conrad's works for the magazine, and he said "Why don't you go down and see him?" Before that I had not the remotest intention of trying to see Mr. Conrad because I had not the slightest excuse for doing so beyond the wish to get some of his work if possible. Mr. Hueffer, who has been helping me to several good things for McClures, said he thought Mr. Conrad would not resent an interview on these general terms, and added that if I went down to Smeeth I would have a few hours with you. I do regret missing you altogether like this, and I hope I have not made a lot of bother for you. Surely you had nothing to do with with my projected invasion. You were the helpless victim of a letter and a telegram, and I can't see that you were at all "drawn in" as Mr. Conrad says, to any attempt. I should say that you were quite guiltless.

I am leaving for Paris on Saturday, to return to London in about two weeks. Surely by that time you will have come to town, and I hope you can come to see me. I shall be stopping at this same hotel.

With greetings and many good wishes to you, I am

Faithfully
Willa Sibert Cather

➤ ❧

In February 1909, Sarah Orne Jewett suffered a paralytic stroke at Annie Adams Fields's home in Boston. She was moved that spring to her family home in South Berwick, Maine, where on June 24, 1909, she had a second stroke and died.

TO ANNIE ADAMS FIELDS

June 27, 1909
London

Dear Mrs. Fields;

Yesterday at noon I learned of the bitter loss that has come to us all and to you more than to anyone else. I think you will know better than I can tell you how constantly my thoughts have been with you since then. This city, and my walking about the streets of it, seem very much like a dream when my heart is straining over-sea to you and to her who loved you so well through so many years. For I cannot bring myself to feel but that somehow she is there near you, and that if I could go to you today I would feel her presence even if I could not see her, as I felt it when I went to see you when she was first ill in the winter. When one is far away like this one cannot realize death. Other things become shadowy and unreal, but Miss Jewett herself remains so real that I cannot get past the vivid image of her to any other realization. I know that something has happened only by the numbness and inertia that have come over me. I find that everything I have been doing and undertaking over here I have done with a hope that it might interest her—even to some clothes I was having made. And now all the wheels stand still and the ways of life seem very dark and purposeless. There is only one thing that seems worth hoping or wishing for, and that is that you and Miss Mary [Jewett] are finding strength and comfort from some source I do not know of, for I know that Miss Jewett's first care and anxiety would have been for you. She was always so afraid of losing you, so afraid, as she told me at Manchester last summer, "that her life might be blown away from her without warning."

I shall sail for home some time next week, as soon as I can get a boat, and I can hardly expect to hear news of you from anyone until then. I shall let you know as soon as I land in New York. If there is anything, little or big, that I can do, if there should be anything which I could attend to for you, or any way in which I could lighten your loneliness, it would help me more than anything else in the world could and give me deeper pleasure.

Dear Mrs. Fields, one cant speak or write what I want to say to you, for nobody's heart can ever speak. Let me love and sorrow with you, and think of me sometimes when you are thinking of Miss Jewett. I could never tell you, I cannot ever tell myself, how dear you both are to me.

Willa

➤ ✦

Cather returned to the United States in July, made a trip to Nebraska to see her family, and then returned to New York and magazine work. Though it is unclear what official title she held at McClure's, *she was (like other senior editors) at times practically in charge of the whole operation as S. S. McClure bounded around the world.*

TO FRANCES SMITH CATHER

January 5, 1910
New York City

Dear Aunt Franc;

Is it too late to wish you a happy New Year? I have been wanting to write to you for a long time. But as soon as I got back to New York this fall Mr. McClure went South, and then went to Europe, so I have been getting out the magazine alone. As I have not been very well any of the time, my editorial work has not left me with much time or strength for other things. During the Christmas holidays I went to bed for a rest of several days, and since then I have been feeling much better. Miss McClung, whom you met six years ago, came on from Pittsburgh and spent November and December with me. She did a lot of shopping for me and trained a new maid, and my apartment is really a very comfortable little place. I was so glad to have Isabelle with me at Christmas time, for that is usually a homesick season for me. New York is so full of homesick people then that there is a kind of wistfulness in the air. Last year, on the day before Christmas, I went down to Old Trinity Church to hear the children's service—a glorious service, <u>truly</u> glorious, but most of the people who sat near me were crying, and I surmised that they were all think-ing of little towns far away, just as I was. Jack and Elsie always go down to [the] grave yard at home on Christmas eve for me, and put holly and evergreens on Mr. and Mrs. Case's graves. I always like to think of their doing it, and it will make them always remember those two dear friends. I get great comfort out of Jack and Elsie—they are dear children. And when Elsie is a little older she will not be so "sure" about things.

I have not heard from Bessie [Elizabeth Seymour] or Auntie [Sarah Andrews] lately, but I like to think that they are both together and comparatively free from care. I used to be so worried and distressed about both of them and it was pretty hard to know what I ought to do. That trouble was the only bitter, breaking trouble I have ever had, and everything I did about it seemed a wrong to someone. There was simply nothing to do, it seemed. And now it has all fallen out so fortunately, and everybody is so much happier that things are as they are. It makes every day of every week easier for me. I get up in the morning feeling better. And as for Auntie, there are more untroubled times than she has known for many years, I am sure.

I have the most cheerful letters from home. I have not known mother so well and contented for years, and Elsie is enjoying her work at school.

I remember that I spoke to you about an article on Mme. Vera Figner I got in London ["The Secrets of Schluesselburg," about a Russian prison and former prisoner Vera Nikolaevna Figner]? I wonder whether you saw it in the December number? I have just been working very hard upon an article on the Cherry Mine disaster ["Heroes of the Cherry Mine," about the 259 men and boys who died in a coal mine fire in Cherry, Illinois] which I got Edith Wyatt, of Chicago, to write. It will be in the March number, and I think it is a very strong and simple piece of work. There is to be a Grand Jury investigation as a result of our article on Tammany and the white slave trade ["The Daughters of the Poor," by George Kibbe Turner, which appeared in November 1909], but the Tammany people are playing their cards so well that I am afraid the investigation will be a very superficial affair.

I expect I shall have to go to London again in the spring, but I am hoping to get home next summer, and to run out for a little visit with you. The one this summer was such a satisfactory visit. It was the first time I've really seen you for years. Mother was so willing about my going into the country this time, and I went with a light heart and enjoyed every minute of it. There is no place in the world where I can be so happy or rest so well. I am so glad that Bess and Auntie are near enough so that you can keep an eye on them. And whenever you see that they need anything, you will let me know, won't you? And I will be so grateful to you. The pleasure of doing things for them is one of the most real I have.

A great deal of love goes to you with this letter, dear Aunt Franc, and many, many good wishes for you and yours.

Lovingly
Willie

TO ROSCOE CATHER

February 13, 1910

My Dear Boy;

What a wild winter you have had. Mine has been wild, too, but weather has had little to do with it. Mr. McClure has been abroad all winter and I have been in a seething whirlpool of work. Before Christmas I had a dismal bronchitis and was in bed for two weeks and Isabelle came on and took care of me. I was pretty sick for two months, but I had to dictate dozens of letters and read manuscripts and see people in bed. You see a magazine is like a sick baby—you've always got to be stuffing something into its blessed insides or it dies. The stuff I got in England last summer—the Russian stuff and the [Xavier] Paoli articles [the "Recollections of the Shah of Persia" and "Recollections of the Kings and Queens of Europe" series] helped me out. I am about again now and much better, but I still have to lie down every day and drink lots of milk and behave like a baby generally. However, its been a very successful winter. From Sept. 1908 to Sept 1909, the first year that I have had charge of the magazine, we made sixty thousand dollars more than the year before. I say "we"; I dont get any of the money, but I get a good deal of credit.

Watch for the March number, I've taken such pains with it, and read "A Joint in the Harness" [by "Ole Luk-Oie," pseudonym of Sir Ernest Dunlop Swinton]. I got that in England. You know, my boy, if you would tell me what stories you like (and don't like) it would help me a lot. I am so thankful when people do tell me. You see when they know you are responsible they are shy about telling you. Of course I dont like everything that goes into the magazine, by a long shot.

I have just been writing to Mrs. [Alice] Goudy, who is very ill in a sanatorium, and to poor old Mrs. [Adelaide Hazen] Fulton. She is quite blind, you know, and now she has broken her hip.

You were a nice boy to send me silk stockings at Christmas time. I love silk stockings and I was especially pleased with these, for I spent Christmas in bed and my presents meant a lot to me.

Have you ever seen Mary Virginia [Auld, daughter of sister Jessica Cather Auld] since she could talk? She is the dearest baby. I sent her a lot of jolly things at Christmas time.

I got a nice long letter from Aunt Franc this week. I had such a good visit with her this summer, and with Bess and Auntie, too. I really love the "Far

Country." I get there so seldom that it seems about the farest and most restful country in the world.

I shall have to go to England in May if I am well enough. I wish you could run away with me on one of these long trips. What wouldn't I give for a long talk with you! If I could, I'd start for Lander [Wyoming] tomorrow. But to do a job one has to stay on it, I suppose, and this is a harder job to boss than Sandy Point. Poor little Jim Yeiser, where is he now, I wonder? I'm afraid he's fallen on hard times. Goodnight, my boy. I could write to you better if I could see you once again. This long stretch of time and distance takes the starch out of one. I think you'd be interested in a lot of the people and things I have to do with, but its hard to write about them. Some day I shall get desperate and take a west-bound train and let the office do the best it can.

Lovingly
Willie

"Sandy Point," which Cather would frequently mention in her letters to her brother, was a play town made of packing boxes that she and her brothers and friends (including Jim Yeiser) created when they were children in Red Cloud, Nebraska. Cather was elected mayor of Sandy Point.

→ ←

The next letter both demonstrates Cather's ongoing editorial work at McClure's and marks the beginning of a warm friendship with the young writer Elizabeth Sergeant.

TO ELIZABETH SHEPLEY SERGEANT

April 5, 1910
New York City

Dear Miss Sargent:—

We feel that there is very little about your article ["Toilers of the Tenements," published July 1910] that will have to be changed; it will be mostly a matter of cutting and condensing. You realized yourself that the article would have to be cut, and we are going to use so many pictures that this will be even more necessary than I thought. It will be hard for me to write you about these cuts, so if you are willing, I will go over the article indicating the cuts and suggesting some changes here and there. I will send you the revised article by next Monday, April eleventh, and if you object to any of the cuts or changes, we can take that question up then. I don't think there is the slightest need of your putting off your sailing date.

I will ask the business department to get your check for two hundred dollars to you within a few days, as I have always found it convenient to have all my checks come in before going abroad. I think there is no more than several hours' work to be done on the article, and it is almost wholly a matter of condensation.

I am a little puzzled about a title; I wish you could suggest one—or several.

Very cordially yours,
Willa Sibert Cather

TO ELIZABETH SHEPLEY SERGEANT

May 31, 1910
New York City

Dear Miss Sergeant:

The proofs of the article went to Brookline merely in the course of routine, they are always sent by the proof reader to the last address, etc., etc. But I read the proofs of the article myself and hope you will not find much amiss in it.

About the Labor Congress articles, I do not believe we could use more than one. Of course, what we want is not so much a report of what is generally done by the Congress, but a sort of summing up of the interesting things that have been done abroad for the protection of the laborer. We would pay $150. for the article and such photographs as you could send to accompany it.

I forget whether you intend to go to Germany at all. Do you know the Permanent Exposition for the Welfare of Workingmen at Charlottenburg, Berlin? I understand it is a museum where one finds practically everything that has been invented to protect the lives of workingmen, builders, firemen, divers, factory workers, miners, etc. It seems to me that an article on this museum, illustrated by many photographs of the apparatus would be tremendously effective. In short, it would be a new way of writing on the old and fascinating subject of "dangerous trades." It might even be that under such a concrete guise you could best present your information about what is done at the Congresses.

Would it, do you think, be feasible to write an article professedly on the interesting exhibits in this museum (describing the most interesting apparatus and the dangers it is made to circumvent and overcome) and incidentally, to pack in the best of what you get at the Labor Congress?

Of course, I do not know how much you will get at the Labor Congress, or what ground it will cover, or in what shape it could be best presented. But I can see an article on that museum as a very good magazine feature, with a lot of very useful information and suggestions about labor conditions in other countries behind it.

If you think this sort of an article feasible will you write me at once. I wrote Mr. McClure about the idea the other day, and I am afraid he may put some one in Berlin on it. If you see the thing as a practical undertaking, I would much rather have you do it. For such an article, we would be willing to pay $200.

Miss [Edith] Wyatt is here at work on the Working Girl material. Whether we would be able to use an article on the French working girl depends a little, I think, on how long Miss Wyatt's series runs. I wish you would give me a chance at the article, anyway.

No, I shouldn't think you would mind being in Paris in the spring. I am afraid I am not able to read your letter with the properly unselfish spirit. So far as mere weather is concerned, I have nothing to complain of. I am wearing winter clothes to-day with great comfort. We have scarcely had a hot day. But weather does not go very far. Most of the buildings which were standing when you were last here [the *McClure's* offices were at 44–60 East Twenty-third Street] are in the process of demolition. You cannot go a block in any direction without encountering a steam hammer and an iron drill. All the pavements are being repaired and all the sewer pipes are being changed. The place couldn't be more smelly and noisy so we shall be in a pitiable state when it does get hot.

Very sincerely yours,
Willa Sibert Cather

TO NORMAN FOERSTER

July 20, 1910
New York City

My dear Norman:—

I am genuinely and heartily delighted to hear how splendidly you have been getting on in English, both as regards the scholarly side of it and the practical side. The Monthly [the *Harvard Monthly*, which Foerster co-edited and contributed to], which you say you have sent me, has not turned up yet, but will doubtless do so, and I shall read it with the greatest interest. I am starting away for a week in the mountains, tomorrow, and that is why I am acknowledging your letter today before I have read the article on Gilbert White.

I always felt that you would learn to write well some day, if you cared to and had the patience. And now, your real work has just begun. The distance between excellent writing and good writing that has a commercial value because it is unique and individual, is the longest distance in the world. I am not speaking now of bad writing that has a commercial value, because there are millions of reasons why bad writing should have a commercial value. But there is only one reason why good writing should have it. A man must have experienced things pretty keenly and must have got pretty close to things before his experiences or the degree of his nearness can matter to many people in this frenzied workshop of a country.

When you were a young lad, I always thought you were well equipped and that the only thing that might tell against you was a certain mild self-sureness that almost approached self-satisfaction. This was quite inoffensive to other people, but I used to wonder whether it might not become a habit of mind and settle into a sort of philosophic self-content, which is apt to keep people from experiencing things very keenly and genuinely, and, as people grow older, to result in a sort [of] constitutional mental phlegm. When you tell me that your writing tends toward the manner of both [Walter] Pater and [Matthew] Arnold, I would be a little bit alarmed, if it were not true that every writer I know, at some time thought he wrote like Pater.

Now as to the practical aspects of the case: As to a book of essays; we have no book publishing business. We sold our book publishing business to Doubleday Page and Company two years ago. They publish a good many nature books, however, and if you have anything you want to try there, I shall be glad to give you an introduction. I should think, though, that your kind of nature book might be much more in Houghton Mifflin Co.'s line. The head of the book publishing department there, Ferris Greenslet, is an old and dear friend of mine, and I should be glad to give you a letter to him, if you ever wish to approach them. As to magazine work, the McClure motto is "A great deal of matter and as little manner as may be." We like scientific subjects handled in a style rather scientific than literary. But I am not sure that it might not be good drill for you to try, at some time or other, some popular science articles in which the information end was uppermost. For instance, I thought about you a long time in connection with an article which I have just had written on John Brashear, of Pittsburg ["John A. Brashear of Pittsburgh" by Edwin Tenney Brewster appeared in the April 1911 issue]. I remembered some themes that you did once on the Allegheny river valley as one saw it from the hilltops, and I thought you would be able to get the feeling of the place into the background—and Professor Brashear and his background do so belong together. But I thought you were probably busy with commencement matters and, when I mentioned you in writing to Mr. McClure, he replied: "Aren't recent graduates often apt to be mannered and to be averse to giving information?" We wanted the facts about Mr. Brashear told pretty plainly, for the facts' sake, so I sent Mr. Edwin T. Brewster of Andover, who has done a good deal of scientific writing for us, out to Pittsburg. Now, if you want to try a practical commission of this sort for us sometime, I shall be more than glad to give you a chance. Nature articles in the nature of essays, of course, go more properly to the Atlantic Monthly, as the interest of such essays is primarily literary rather than scientific. The popular scientific article must be done mainly for the sake of conveying certain information. In short, the scientific theme must not be used as a hook on which to hang a certain kind of writing. [Thomas Henry] Huxley, I think, is one of the best of scientific writers. He was never in the least too technical or too obscure or too literary.

This is, of course, random advice that occurs to me as I read your letter over. The commercial scientific article and the literary essay are two wholly different things. Of course, an ideal article on Mr. Brashear would have just as much feeling and just as much literary depth as the writer could put into it, but instead of being brought to the front it would be so restrained and crushed into the background as to be scarcely noticeable and all the more potent for that fact.

This seems to have become a long gossipy letter of the kind that I do not often have time to write and, even if you do not agree with me, I hope you will take it as a proof of my pleasure in your collegiate success and my interest in your future.

Faithfully

Willa Sibert Cather

Mr. McClure has been ill in Europe for six months and I have been running the magazine alone. I shall not get away for more than a week or two until he returns in October. So come to see me if you are in N.Y. I go abroad this winter.

→ ←

During these times when Cather was "running the magazine alone," she still managed to write and publish some fiction. The story mentioned in the next letter appeared in the October 1911 Century Illustrated Monthly Magazine *as "The Joy of Nellie Dean."*

TO ROBERT UNDERWOOD JOHNSON

August 30, 1910
New York City

Dear Mr. Johnson:—

Would you be kind enough to change the title of the story which I recently shortened for you? The story never really had a name, and I think it was called "Nellie Deane", or "The Story of Nellie Dean" provisionally. I think "The Flower in the Grass" would be a good title for it. That is really the idea of the story; a beautiful girl hidden away in the prairie country where nobody ever saw her. If you will ask one of your assistants to make the change on the manuscript, I shall be very grateful to you.

Very sincerely yours,
Willa Sibert Cather

TO FRANCES SMITH CATHER

February 22, 1911

My Dear Aunt Franc;

How many times I have wanted to write to you this winter! But life drives us all pretty fast. Elsie came down from Northampton and spent two weeks with me at Christmas time, and we had such a happy Christmas. It was her first visit to a big city and she seemed to enjoy the stir and excitement of it. We were a good deal worried about mother, who had had a fall and was very miserable at Christmas time, but we began to get good news from her before Elsie left me. Elsie seemed to like my little apartment and my way of housekeeping and my excellent colored maid. This last named person is my chiefest treasure. She has been with me for more than a year now and my flat goes like clockwork and I have very little bother about it beyond doing the marketing. I have been ever so much better in health this winter than last, and I think it is partly due to getting the bother of housekeeping off my mind. Mr. McClure was ill and abroad all last summer and I had to stay in the city until late in

September. It was a terrible summer, and I was pretty well fagged when it was over, but I went away in the fall and by the middle of December I had got my energy back again. Then Mr. McClure went abroad again, and since then I have been keeping the shop alone.

Several weeks ago I went to dine with Mr. Charles Wiener and his [second] wife. They have lately come back from a long stay in Europe and they have a beautiful house up on 124th street, where they own a great deal of real estate. Mr. Wiener looks very little older than he did twenty years ago, and a great deal of money has not made him hard-hearted or changed his simple manners. He had been ill with grippe, and his wife telephoned me that he wanted to see me. I had a great many things on hand that week and it was hard for me to go, but I was so glad that I did manage it for he seemed to enjoy having me there. He is very fond of his old friends. He asked about all of my family and enquired about you and your health and about Uncle George and the boys. Yesterday his wife wrote me that he is still confined to the house and I am going to see them again soon. She is a good woman, and I like her very much.

You remember my friend Isabelle McClung who went out to your house with me once? She is here making me a month's visit, and she begs to be remembered to you. We are enjoying every day of these weeks together.

I had a letter from Howard Gore this morning and he tells me that he and Lillian [Thekla Brandthall Gore] are going to see the new king of Siam crowned. Howard went about the country with the new king when he was crown prince some years ago. I love Howard, but I wish my family wouldn't strive to get mixed up with kings and move in the highest society. But really, all Washington people are like that more or less. It seems to be in the air. A little vanity can undo a really big man.

Bessie writes me a good long letter every few months, and keeps me informed as to what goes on in the neighborhood. She and Auntie seem very happy and contented. You are well this winter, she tells me, and Uncle George had wonderful crops last year. Sometime when you have an empty hour—I know you don't have many—and are not tired, please write me all about yourself and the children. I may have to go to London in April, and I'd love to hear from you before I go if you have time. I send a world of love to you, my dear aunt.

                                                                              Willie

Elsie Cather was in Northampton, Massachusetts, as a student at Smith College, which was also Aunt Franc's alma mater.

❧ ❧

When the following letter was written, Cather's old college crush, Louise Pound, was a professor of literature and philology at the University of Nebraska and a highly respected folklorist.

TO LOUISE POUND

May 9, 1911
New York City

Dear Louise:

Elsie spent her Christmas and Easter vacations with me. She is in excellent condition and seems to enjoy her work at Northampton. She does not get nearly so much out of the English Literature, however, as she did under you, and she is really very appreciative of the help you gave her. I am so glad that she had enough work under you to get well started, and I only wish she could have had more. Perhaps she can do some postgraduate work under you. She would love that. I do think we had a pretty sane attitude about the immortals when we went to school.

Are you coming east this summer I wonder? Please let me know if you do. I shall probably be here until the first of August. I'll love to see you. Of course you like Arnold Bennet[t], don't you? He's too fond of "symptoms" maybe, but at least he seems to have some goods to sell, which most of 'em emphatically have not, even when their salesmanship is most impressive and their floor-walking manners very grand.

Faithfully
Willa Cather

[Written on the back:] Does Miss Lathrop ever come to New York? Please tell her I want to see her.

TO LOUISE IMOGEN GUINEY

May 25, 1911
Parker House, Boston

My Very Dear Miss Guiney;

I have come over to this pleasant hostelry to transact some editorial business, after a whole week with our dear lady on Charles Street. I meant to write to you from there, but Mrs. Fields had a good deal of company and there were some funny bits of shopping to do preparatory to her departure for Manchester next week. I think I have never seen her so well. She actually came to the station to meet me! John fell upon me as I descended from the train and said "Miss' Fields herself is out there waitin' in the carriage, an' it's the first time she's been to the South Station in years." You may well believe I hurried!

We had beautiful days and evenings, and the magic of that magically haunted house was never so potent for me. That other rare spirit whom we all loved so well [Sarah Orne Jewett] seemed not far away, and one kept stumbling upon things that were hers. We talked much of you (I had brought your last letter with me for Mrs. Fields to read) and last night, the last night of my stay, Mrs. Fields read aloud from the "Wayside Harp" for a long while. "The Cherry Bough" she read especially well, with her old-time fervor, and she wiped her eyes when she finished it and then read it through again.

Some friend of hers has had a little lift put in the house for her, and I learned to be an expert elevator boy. So if I fail as managing editor, I can still hope to get a job with the company. The lift saves Mrs. Field's strength greatly, and I bless the friend.

Don't speak to me of ears! I've had them—mastoid. Doesn't [John] Milton say something about "trembling ears?" Well, mine tremble when I hear of anyone going to an aurist. I am so sorry, so sorry that you've had bother with yours. I hope the specialist has given you an honorable discharge by this.

Mr. McClure stays abroad for months and months, and won't be home until July, so I am afraid I won't get over this summer. But when I come I'll run you down. All luck and love to you!

Affectionately
Willa S. C.

❖ ❖

In the early part of the twentieth century, many well-educated women were deeply engaged in reform efforts across a wide spectrum of issues. Hull House, mentioned in the next letter, was a settlement house established by Jane Addams and Ellen Gates Starr in Chicago, Illinois, in 1889 to help recent immigrant communities adapt to urban American life. Sisters Josephine and Pauline Goldmark, friends of both Cather's and Elizabeth Sergeant's, were two of the leading reformers in New York at this time. It is unclear which sister is referred to here.

TO ELIZABETH SHEPLEY SERGEANT

[June 4, 1911]

Dear Miss Sergeant;

This time the candy came straight to the mark, and I've now been nibbling at it for three days with the greatest possible comfort. And there is still lots and lots of it left, you sent such a big box. I have had a great deal of fun out of that box.

One of the Hull House women came to the office yesterday. She said that Miss Wyatt has given herself over wholly to the cause of the White Slave; that she never talks or thinks about anything else, and feels pretty bitterly toward those of us here who didn't sympathize with her. I'm sorry. I've seldome been more disappointed than I was when I found that we had no possible point of contact. She seems to me to be maddened by having lived to long in the company of a horrible idea—like Electra. She used to frighten me. Her eyes seemed to burn with a rage to destroy the germ which replenishes the race. I cant chat comfortably with people who are panting for the destruction of anything. Would that she could forget it all, and begin to be touched by the amusing traits of human nature again! Oh I <u>must</u> tell you; she says that the ones who go back to it are the most wronged slaves of all for <u>they</u> have been made the slaves of an appetite! Aren't we all? Even Miss Wyatt and Cassandra, the slaves of some taste or other?

Miss McClung arrives Tuesday, and I hope we shall be seeing Miss Goldmark within the next week. I wish you could be here. I awfully want Isabelle to know you, and you'd like her. She's so fond of lovely things and so full of them, and so <u>frightened</u> of reformers.

Thanks a million million times for everything. And I'm so glad you got in to have tea with me!

Faithfully
Willa Cather

✧ ✦

Cather's mention of "those stories of mine" in the letter below was likely referring to The Troll Garden, *and the "little western story" was probably "The Enchanted Bluff," published in* Harper's *in April 1909.*

TO ELIZABETH SHEPLEY SERGEANT

June 27, 1911
South Berwick, Maine

Dear Miss Sergeant:

Some day I am going to answer your nice letter, and tell you how glad I am that you found anything to like in those stories of mine. They were written a long while ago and seem very far away from me. I can't see much in them now but the raging bad temper of a young person kept away from the things she wanted. The note of personal discomfort does distort, even in the Western ones. Not very long ago I published a little western story which I think is candid and not chesty. If I can find a copy someday I will send it to you.

But this note is only to thank you for your good letter and to let you know that I am in the place of all places where I can rest most perfectly, and that I am saluting you from the little desk where it all happened. In this garden I can forget the facts that do confront us—Rex Beach and the White Slave and all such cheerful things; all the overwhelming vulgarity in which we live. It's good to come here where the very young woman seems always to be moving about over the smooth garden paths—always a little disdainful, and a little, little self-conscious then—and to brood upon it that we had once that flash of elegance. Never was a house so permeated by a presence [Sarah Orne Jewett] as this one is.

Miss Goldmark delivered your message—we had a splendid evening with her—and you may be sure that if I can go to Dublin [New Hampshire], I'll at least telegraph and give you the chance to say that you are or are not otherwise engaged. I would love to go. I'll be going down to New York, alas, tomorrow.

Faithfully
Willa Cather

TO ELSIE CATHER

August 30 [1911]

My Dear Little Sister

Of <u>course</u> I want you to come for a week or eight days before you go to Northampton. We wont begin to tear up the place much before the 20th. I want you to see the last of the apartment. We have a good maid so you can really be comfortable.

Ask Margie [Anderson] if she has ever found the pictures of Willow Shade [the Cather family home in Virginia] she said she would hunt for. I do awfully want one. I wonder where Grandma Cather's pictures of the place are?

I'm so <u>glad</u>, so awfully glad you all like the Swedish Mother [a poem of Cather's published in the September 1911 issue of *McClure's*], and that Mary Virginia knows who the people are. Tell her her "Nanypaw" ought to remember one special night when he left me by the barn of the field we called "the mountain field" when I actually saw the <u>nose</u> of the bear between the bushes, only the nose, and it looked a good deal like a pig's, but it made me very unhappy. I used generally to wait under a hawthorne tree that grew by the barn and was very lovely in the spring, but I didn't know what the Swede woman would call a hawthorne tree. Mr. McClure says the poem has been a good deal talked about wherever he has gone and that "he is as proud of it as if he had done it himself". I'm glad people like it, and everyone says "what a dear little girl". "Red-haired" doesn't seem to me a very specific adjective, but it seems to make a picture to everyone.

I'll be so, so glad to see you, Bobbie, and I want to ask you so much and tell you so much. You must tell Mary about the little girl I rescued in the Park when the dog attacked her crow. Tell her she must take her crow to call on Irene [Miner], I know Irene would appreciate it. Just think, you'll be here at 82 in ten days or so now!

Very lovingly
Willie

Get up on a <u>chair</u> and kiss Toby for me before you leave.

➵ ➴

In September 1911 Cather made another decisive change in her life: she left her position as editor at McClure's *when the company went through another financial restructuring, one that removed S. S. McClure from control. She intended to take only a temporary leave of absence and then return to the magazine as a staff writer. During that leave, however, she completed her first novel, and from then on her career was solely that of a professional writer.*

Set in Boston and London and centering on a love triangle involving a bridge engineer, his wife, and an actress, Cather's first novel was serialized as Alexander's Masquerade *in the February, March, and April 1912 issues of* McClure's. *It was published in book form by Houghton Mifflin in April 1912 with the title* Alexander's Bridge. *Cather later wrote that the book "was the result of meeting some interesting people in London. Like most young writers, I thought a book should be made out of 'interesting material,' and at the time I found the new more exciting than the familiar. The impressions I tried to communicate on paper were genuine, but they were very shallow."*

TO S. S. MCCLURE

November 5, 1911
Cherry Valley, New York

Dear Mr. McClure:

I cannot tell you how glad I was to get your two kind letters. I wish you could have stayed longer when you were here. You could not get an idea from those few hours of how really well off we are here. The weather is about the only thing that happens, but when one is resting that is quite enough. I am working on another story about the length of the Bridge Builder one, and enjoying it greatly. It is a great relief to get back to writing again. I shall try not even to think about magazine work for awhile, so I won't write you anything about it this time. We have been much more cheerful since your visit. A talk with you straightened me out more than anything else could have done, and I can tell you that I was much more delighted to see anyone.

Your photographs came on Isabelle's birthday. We had a grand birthday dinner and wished that you could have been with us. I hope that you are still feeling as well as you were when I saw you.

Faithfully
Willa Cather

The other story she was working on was "The Bohemian Girl," set in Nebraska and published in the August 1912 issue of McClure's.

TO ELIZABETH SHEPLEY SERGEANT

[Postmarked March 1, 1912]
New York City

Dear Elsie Sergeant;

No! You communicated no germ to me unless it was the coy germ of selling things; for I have actually sold the Bohemian Girl. Isn't that a jolt? On
that sodden Monday when you were taking trains for Boston and when I was
lunching with the business manager, he asked me if I had nothing to show for
my stay in the country. When I told him that I had a story too long, to "highbrow", too remote etc, he said he guessed he'd like to see it that night if I'd
send it up by the office boy. The next day I had tea with him at the Brevoort
and he offered me seven hundred and fifty dollars for it. I laughed him to
scorn; he doesn't know how much a story is worth to his magazine half so well
as I do, and I told him so. By no sort of figuring can such a story possibly be
worth more than five hundred to McClures, so we finally agreed on that price.
But he said I was a silly, and I promised to take $750 for the next one. Everyone
in the office was enthusiastic about the story—in the name of goodness why,
I wonder? They will publish it this summer, all in one number, though I shall
have to cut it some. But isn't this too amazing? And how can I ever leave the
faithful McClure's? Mr. [Cameron] Mackenzie wrung the plot of the opera
singer one out of me and went to the office and told it to everyone, and one
of the article writers came to Miss Lewis and asked her which character she
thought more interesting, the mother or the daughter! They say they would
like the copy July 1, and I have not even a plan for it as yet, and I know it will
be distant and sentimental and terribly hard to write. All this, of course, is
because the business office has been getting a good many letters and notices
about Alexander, so they come after the Harp that Once [song sung by character Hilda Burgoyne in *Alexander's Bridge*] with a football tackle. This morning a note comes from Mr. Mackenzie asking for an outline of the unwritten
story to advertise in the prospectus! I'll never be able to write it at all if the
advertising man is loosed to snap at my heels. I shall need the imperturbable
nerves of Rex Beach himself. Really, I've got such a case of stage fright about it
that I dont see how I can ever put pen to paper. The brazen immodesty of having your unwritten plot discussed about the office, anyhow!————However,
despite these disadvantages, if this was the germ you handed on, I'll keep it
thank you, until you do the sanatorium novel and want it back again.

I wonder whether you'll be reading this scrawl between gargles; I do hope not. But <u>why</u> didn't you send for me on Sunday if you were down and out and not doing things? I call that a chill omission. And that Boston train, with a bad throat—! I know all its dismalness: I am really somewhat better and am staying over for the Howells dinner. I keep wishing you could have stayed a little longer, though it was better luck than one usually has to have you here at all. I did get such delight and satisfaction out of seeing you here. As to feeling a drop after you departed—well, one does not so often miss people that one can't afford a little loneliness. What joyful things we can do the next time we make the same port! I think it will always be easier to catch step again now. My metaphors seem to be a little mixed, but my feelings are quite clear and simple, and its very jolly to care about you so much. Admiration is always a pleasant thing to feel, and I've always felt a great deal of that for you, since the first few times I saw you. But you probably know that, without my telling you.

Now I must dress in three square feet of room. I wish the fourth dimension were in practice!

Faithfully always
W.S.C.

Am I becoming cleverer, or is your handwriting plainer than of yore?

It is unclear if the "opera singer one" mentioned above was ever written or published, though later in her career Cather published many works of fiction with opera singers as central characters. The "Howells dinner" was a gala held in honor of writer William Dean Howells's seventy-fifth birthday. Among those in attendance were Howells's fellow Ohioan President William Howard Taft.

TO ELIZABETH SHEPLEY SERGEANT

Tuesday [March 12, 1912]
Pittsburgh

Dear Elsie

So many things have happened since I got your long letter: Getting away from New York was difficult because the Chief, Mr. McClure arrived and sought me out several days before I came away. When I got here I found Miss McClung's mother much worse. On Saturday she had a stroke of some sort (no one could know less about <u>what</u> sort than the doctors seem to know) and has been unconscious ever since, though there is no paralysis. Something has happened in her brain, but no one knows more than that. You will be wondering what I am doing, I expect. But really I am doing very well. I am something languid as the result of a bad fright, but really I have managed to get the proper amount of food and sleep and to keep from being excited. The latter has been difficult, but I really have done it. The moment I feel myself getting strung up, I go for a long walk in this wet somber air, and it quiets me like a soporific. Of course when the whole household is waiting rather than living, one cannot lead a normal life, but I do the best I can.

Oh I'd be more than glad to have you in Arizona, highbrow though you are, but you see I am even more plan-less than usual, and more at the bidding of chance. I don't know when I can leave here, to begin with. Not, of course, until Mrs. McClung begins to pull up a little. Then I dont know whether I shall have to stop a few weeks or only a few days with my mother, and I dont know the least little thing about Winslow [Arizona], the town in which my brother [Douglass] lives. Sometime in April I shall arrive there; if it seems to me a good place, I shall at once let you know; then if you are still unfettered and not already sold into summer slavery, you might take your chance with me and try the desert country. But you see there are so many family complications that I have to be thus casual. All I know is that I shall alight at Winslow sometime this spring.

I was just called to Mrs. McClung's room to find her for the moment quite conscious. She soon dropped off again but this may be the beginning of a turn for the better. We all feel as if a tight string had snapped and the snapping thereof will bring this dull note to a close. O tea for me, and slumber: The rain without and the fire within have brought me to a state of cat-like drowsiness. Perhaps I shan't even wait for tea but, like Harry Greene on The Birth Night, sink to sleep on the hearth rug. It's so good to have people get better. And this gray, sullen weather of itself puts one to sleep. Forgive me that this letter is one week late and empty and drowsy. Many good wishes go with it.

Faithfully yours
Willa Sibert Cather

PART FOUR

Finding Herself as a Writer

1912–1916

I feel as if my mind had been freshly washed and ironed, and were ready for a new life.

—WILLA CATHER TO S. S. MCCLURE, June 12, 1912

Willa Cather at "Cliff Palace" on Mesa Verde, 1915

IN THE SPRING OF 1912, Willa Cather was at a turning point in her life. She had succeeded completely in her editorial job at *McClure's Magazine*, but what she really wanted to do was write fiction. As her first novel was being serialized in the magazine, she took a leave from her job at *McClure's* and planned a trip west. Her brother Douglass worked for the Santa Fe railroad in Winslow, Arizona, and she boarded a train in Pittsburgh and went to see him.

This 1912 trip to Arizona and New Mexico changed Willa Cather and the way she wrote. As she reflected later in "My First Novels (There Were Two)," "The longer I stayed in a country I really did care about, and among people who were a part of the country, the more unnecessary and superficial a book like *Alexander's Bridge* seemed to me. I did no writing down there, but I recovered from the conventional editorial point of view." What she saw and did there, and the intensity of emotion that the Southwest evoked in her, gave her the confidence to try a different kind of writing. The story she wrote before she left on her trip, "The Bohemian Girl," with its Nebraska setting and immigrant characters, presaged the novels to come. When she came back east after several months, she was ready to produce what she called her second "first" novel: *O Pioneers!* A book about farming people set in Nebraska, it was published in 1913. It was followed in 1915 by *The Song of the Lark*, a longer novel about a talented western woman's emergence as a great singer. The psychological high point of that novel—when the heroine, Thea Kronborg, begins to understand what will transform her from a gifted singer into a fine artist—is set in Walnut Canyon, Arizona. Cather knew Walnut Canyon and its power from her visit there in 1912.

TO ELIZABETH SHEPLEY SERGEANT

April 20 [1912]
Winslow, Arizona

Dear Elsie:

I've been tramping about the West for two weeks now and have just reached my mail, which was all forwarded to Winslow. Your letter has made me feel that I would like nothing quite so well as to run over to North Carolina and see how you do. I feel pretty dismal about your being knocked out like this. There are so many people who could better afford to be ill—who would not be restive or impatient under it, and who would not use up their good brain-stuff in the dismal game of being sick, as I am afraid you do yours. Everything that happens is apt to set a good many wheels going, and wheels that do not in the least take the place of iron pills. Isn't that so? It makes one rage to have wheels of that sort spinning in empty air. And when one is ill they do just spin on without registering. But you have got so much done in the last two years that perhaps all these things, even Polk County, will register in time. But I know you will be too wise to feel discouraged about being divorced for awhile from the manual labor of using a pen. It's when you come to banking your fires that I'm doubtful about you. If one has the habit of living keenly they're apt to go on doing, I've observed, in a desert, a cell, a pallet—in the dust, if the poppies that blaze on the Palatine Hill mean what they seem to. But I hope you can turn the lamp low for a little while. I would run over to see you if we had not the misfortune to be born in such a big country.

But "Bigness" is the subject of my story. The West always paralyzes me a little. When I am away from it I remember only the tang on the tongue. But when I come back [I] always feel a little of the fright I felt when I was a child. I always feel afraid of losing something, and I don't in the least know what it is. It's real enough to make a tightness in my chest even now, and when I was little it was even stronger. I never can entirely let myself go with the current; I always fight it just a little, just as people who can't swim fight it when they are dropped into water. It is partly the feeling that there are so many miles—wait till you travel 'em!—between you and anything, and partly the fear that the everlasting wind may make you contented and put you to sleep. I used always to be sure that I'd never get out, that I would die in a cornfield. Now I know I will get out again, but I still get attacks of fright. I wish I didn't. I somehow feel that [if] one were really a fit person to write about a country they wouldn't feel that.

But really, the Bohemian Girl <u>is</u> in the right key, like that country, I mean. I went out into the Bohemian country when I was in Red Cloud and it seemed just like that to me. By the way, while I was in Pittsburgh I gave that story a good "going over" and I wrote in a new scene which I think helps it very much. I am grateful to you for backing me on that story, for it really is like the people, gets the undulation of the ground.

Now about Arizona: it's good, but New Mexico is better. Winslow is an ugly little western town. I send you a picture of it. Only railroad people here, but a good hotel. The Santa Fe road carries no dining cars and all the through trains stop here for one meal or another. The homes are little egg shell affairs. My brother has a whole one—the "casa" the Mexican wash woman calls it, and what a "casa"—and I don't believe the whole home is big enough for me to write in. But the real thing is that the air of the place is "off" for that sort of work. My brother, poor chap, couldn't understand that, but it is. So I don't think I shall stay here very long. I'll run about the country with him a good deal for awhile and see a lot, and then fade away in search of that seemingly simple but really utterly unattainable thing, four walls in which one can write. After you cross two miles of tin cans and old shoes the desert is very fine—bright red sand, like brick dust, and the eternal sage and rabbit-brush. But the sand storms! They often stop the trains. I am almost sure I could work at Albuquerque, New Mexico. It is in the most beautiful country I have ever seen anywhere, like the country between Marseilles and Niece only much more brilliant. All around it lie the most wonderful Indian villages—not show places, real places, each one built close about its church. There are dead villages, too, that were Spanish missions in Elizabeth's time. My brother and I are going there next week to spend a few days, and I'll see whether you could find a room easily. After that I'll know more about the place, too. But I <u>think</u> it would give you—well, just that something that one needs. If I were still here I could go over to see you. It's only a night away, and when people live by and on the railroad that is nothing. I feel pretty sure that Winslow would depress you terribly—the wind, the sand storms, the tin cans, the stolid humanity. But Albuquerque is another story. There is a strong pull about the place, and something Spanish in the air that teases you. Such color! The Lord set the stage so splendidly there. It can't have been all for nothing, for motors and phonographs and our damned good <u>plumming</u>! There really must be a new hope yet to come—a new tragedy or a new religion, some crusades or something. It is too utterly splendid, from Trinidad to Albuquerque, to go to pot. The valley of the Rhone is nothing to it. From Trinidad to Las Vegas there is a continuous purple mountain that does tune one up.

Now please write to me, and write <u>plain</u> script, because I want so much to hear from you, and not to be in any doubt as to what you say. (This is slightly facetious, for I can really read you very well now.) But I do most particularly and definitely and acutely want word of you; of how you do and of what you are thinking and feeling—though I do sincerely hope you aren't feeling anything but sleepiness and laziness. It is because I really want word of you so much that I have prolonged this letter so unduly, and keep on writing. You know that absurd and interesting habit of mind—which always acts on the principle that if one bullies an idea long enough the idea will give back. And now, as the poor Mexicans say to their sweethearts, "May all the gold I have ever dreamed of be yours."

Yours
Willa S.C.

TO MARIEL GERE

April 24, 1912
Winslow

Dear Mariel

I have been travelling and missing my letters and have only just heard of your dear mother's death [Mariel Clapham Gere]. It is very hard for me to believe that she is not with you anymore. I cannot realize that she is not there, just the same as she used to be, with all her force and kindness and dignity and keen understanding of life, that was tempered by so much charity and such a rich sense of humor. I can hear her little laugh now, the one she was so apt to laugh when young people were talking large or taking themselves too seriously. How much more good that laugh did one than any amount of scolding. It was so wise and kind that for the moment it made one wiser too. How much I owe her; and I am only one of many. I always loved her very dearly, even when I was too young to be willing to show that I did. And I always really wanted to please her, even when I was too silly to want to show that, either. I don't believe anyone but your mother could ever have persuaded me to let my hair grow or to try to learn to spell. I remember, as distinctly as if it were yesterday, the first time you took me home to dinner, when I was a preparatory student, and how your mother knew just what tack to take with me, and how kind your father's eyes were when he looked me over and said I looked like

"Sadie Harris." I can't believe it was so long ago. I hope you and I can keep half the gallant spirit your mother did, and the splendid love of life and pleasure in people. I cannot think of her except as living as richly and vigorously as she did in the years when she was so kind to me—when she did so much for a clumsy country child simply by being her lovely and gracious self. It was like reading a fine story to be with her, I used to think. Her kind of charm and vivacity were such a new thing to me.

I wish I were to see her again, Mariel. I had counted upon stopping to see you on my way East, whenever I am called back to New York. I had a sharp illness and an exhausting little surgical operation in February, so Mr. McClure is going to let me stay away as long as possible.

Please let me send my love, useless as it is, to Frances and Ellen and to you. Letters do not help one, I know, and the ache of another heart does not ease one's own. But I want you to know that I do not forget.

Very lovingly
Willa Cather

I am ever so much better in health now, and am here visiting Douglas.

→ ←

While she was on leave, S. S. McClure wrote to ask if she would ghostwrite his autobiography when she returned.

TO S. S. MCCLURE

April 22 [1912]
Winslow

Dear Mr. McClure;

I will certainly be glad to help in any way I can with the autobiography. You have, indeed, wonderful material. I am having the most interesting adventures with my brother here, exploring the Pueblo towns and re-discovering the cliff-dwellers. We are planning to go to the Moki [Hopi] snake dance, and we are going over to old Mexico.

I can imagine how shocked and horrified everyone in New York must feel because of the Titanic disaster. Even here in the desert it shakes me up a little. I am so sorry about poor Mr. Stead.

The one book everybody is talking about in Nebraska, Colorado, New Mexico and Arizona is "The Iron Woman." They are piled up in the Santa Fe "Harvey Houses" and every brakeman owns a copy.

How splendid this part of the world is!

Faithfully
Willa Cather

Influential British investigative journalist William T. Stead died when the Titanic *sank in April 1912.* The Iron Woman *(1911), by Cather's Boston friend Margaret Deland, was one of the biggest best sellers of the era.*

TO ELIZABETH SHEPLEY SERGEANT

April 26, 1912
Winslow

Dear Elsie—

People are the only interesting things there are in the world, but one has to come to the desert to find it out, and until you are in the desert, you never know how un-interesting you are yourself. When it's too windy to walk or ride, I am a punctured balloon. My brother is out with the construction gang most of the time. He shares this casa with a well-informed brakeman named Tooker. Douglass has been away for three days now, and Tooker and I have been living on together, which is quite in accord with the proprieties of Winslow. Tooker has been off on his "run" two of the nights, and then I've been quite alone. (The tipsy London cockney whom my brother picked up overcome by thirst in the desert, and who does the housekeeping! would afford small protection) But dear me! I don't mind being here alone at night. I'm so glad to get the well-improved Tooker out of the house that I'd gladly get up at any hour of the night and make cocktails for any wandering Mexican who would come in to relieve the boredom of life. Tooker reads Emerson—in full morocco—all the time. He is one of Nature's Noblemen and looks just like [actor] Henry Miller in "The Great Divide" [play by William Vaughn Moody]. Also dresses as such. Don't tell me that life is anything but a poor imitation of art—and of mighty poor art, always. I've been doing target practice with a pistol, and I know the day will come when I shall let drive at Tooker. I cannot stand either his information or his nobleness much longer. He has done a lot of prospecting in South America and worked in mines in Mexico and he really can tell one a good deal. But the square jaw and the bold carriage of the head make him useless to me.

I would perish if it were not for the Mexicans. We have an inferior lot, of course, but it's a lovely speech, and they have such nice manners and go their own way. They all live "south of the tracks" and their village is a delight after this hideous little railroad town.

I do want to hear from you. I shall hope to get a letter by Saturday or Sunday. I suppose I really am very lonely. But you would die here; you are at least one thousand years more civilized than I. You'd simply go up in smoke. I can see you getting on the train in your little nightie; you wouldn't stop to dress. Maybe you could save your soul by studying Spanish with the priest. I can't even do that. But my brother returns tomorrow and then we are off for Flagstaff and the Cliff Dwellers.

Tooker never permits himself an action in one syllable. He "arrives", and he "removes" his hat, and he reflects. When the wind blows the sand it "retards" his freight train and he is late on his runs.

The cockney housekeeper <u>is</u> good fun, but he is reeling drunk <u>all</u> the time, and has to be sat upon and sent away. He once worked in a stable in Paris and speaks an awfully funny kind of French very fluently. When he is at his worst he recites his poem "The Widenin' Foam" and weeps bitterly. Every verse ends:

> "Where'ere I look, on sea or skies,
> I see them fair, deceivin' eyes."

But really, with the best will in the world, one tires of freaks. Please write to me. I've been thinking a great deal about you.

Buenas noches
W.S.C.

Tooker, the brakeman, contributed to the brakeman Ray Kennedy in The Song of the Lark. *The "tipsy London cockney" who keeps house shows up in the character of Henry Atkins in* The Professor's House. *But Cather felt that the wealth of material in the country she was experiencing extended beyond these unusual characters. She would feature the Southwest and its history in multiple novels, including* The Song of the Lark, The Professor's House, *and* Death Comes for the Archbishop.

→ ←

The following was written on a postcard showing an adobe "Mexican home" in New Mexico.

TO HELEN SEIBEL

May 12 [1912]
Winslow

Tell Mr. S— to revise his idea of a Cliff-Dweller house, and to come down here and do it. There is <u>lots</u> of material and I am saving it all for him. The old Spanish Mission churches are wonderful.

Willa Sibert Cather

→ ←

The following was written on a postcard with a view of the corner of pueblo of Mishongnovi, Arizona.

TO ELIZABETH SHEPLEY SERGEANT

May 12 [1912]
Winslow

Dear Elsie:

I've been hard bit by new ideas of late and am as happy as possible. I've caught step <u>at last</u>. Am just back from a long overland trip with the priest out to his Indian missions. A string trio of Mexicans come often to play for me—one a bartender, two are section hands. They play divinely, and there is a boy of unearthly beauty who sings. He is simply Antinous come to earth again!

W.

Antinous, a frequent subject of classical sculpture, was a beautiful youth beloved by the Roman emperor Hadrian.

TO ELIZABETH SHEPLEY SERGEANT

May 21 [1912]
Grand Canyon, Arizona

[Written above a picture of El Tovar, Grand Canyon, in the top margin:] I've been walking with such nice English people here—went down to the Half Way House—an awful pull!

My Dear Elsie:

For the first two weeks <u>nothing</u> happened to me. Then things began to happen so fast that I've had no time to write letters and I wanted to write to you too much to send postcards. I wrote you about the trip with the Priest over to his Indian missions? The[n] came Julio—pronounce Hulio, please—and he came and came, too beautiful to be true and so different from anyone else in the world. He is the handsome one who sings; from Vera Cruz; knows such <u>won</u>derful Mexican and Spanish songs: But there, if I began on Julio you would have to like me very much to be patient, and I don't wish to put you to any such test as yet. But he is won-der-ful!

Then came three days in the upper Canyons—Clear Creek, Jack's Canyon, and Chevelin. It had all the advantages of a camping trip and yet we got home every night and had hot baths and beds to sleep in. We started every morning at day light, light wagon and light camp outfit, canteens, coffee, bacon, fruit, cream etc. Tooker is a different man in the Hills. All his miserable information, the encrustation of a wash of millions of magazines, drops away, just as a boy drops his clothes when he goes swimming, and there emerged the real Tooker, the man the sheep camps and the hills made, a very decent sort, strong and active and lots of nerve. We did some really good stunts in climbing. Went down one cliff 150 feet by hand-holds, and it was no joke. I have some white canvas shoes with red rubber soles that I got in Boston, and they are fine for rock climbing; you can walk right up a slant of 45 degrees on sandstone or granite. And Tooker told me <u>lots</u> of stories; he's a perfect mine of them when you get through the sediment deposited by magazine articles.

Then came a day in the Painted Desert with Julio. It took several days to get over that; and I have already been five days at the Grand Canyon. It is really the most attractive place I have found in this country. Wonderful walking and riding. The whole place is interesting aside from the "wonder", which, indeed is wonderful enough. Of course a "wonder" that has only a geological history can be interesting for only a limited space of time. But the place is so "let alone". Not one shop, you can't buy an orange, even; Not one amusement. Two hotels—one magnificent and the other excellent—set down in an immense pine forest; these, and silence and the "wonder", nothing else.

I don't know what to tell you about New Mexico. It's all so big and bright and consuming. And it's expensive everywhere. The old Bright Angel Camp house where I am staying is comfortable but very simple. It costs me three dollars a day and is the very cheapest place I have found. Then all the places most worth seeing are off the railway, and you pay about $2.50 a day for a riding horse and five dollars for a team and open wagon. Then it takes time and strength to find ways and routes. Then you would certainly pick up a Mexican sweetheart—don't laugh scornfully, for you couldn't help it, and he certainly couldn't—and wouldn't; and he would take just as much time and strength as you would give, and he would be so attractive that you wouldn't be tight-fisted, and so it would go.

I have a feeling that about Albuquerque and Old Santa Fe things are closer together, simpler, cheaper, and I'll certainly let you know. I meet my brother in Flagstaff Friday to find some Cliff Dwellers along the Little Colorado. Then I shall be in Winslow a few days, for I have to go to a Mexican dance I've been asked to; and then if I can really sever Julio's strong Egyptian fetters, I am going to Albuquerque with my brother and from there trail about over pretty much all of New Mexico. Write to me at Winslow, please, the faithful Tooker will forward all mail. But will you go to Mexico with me some day? My brother and Julio have told me of such splendid places to go as soon as the fighting is over—buried cities and Aztec ruins and gold mines—perfect Arabian Nights stories. Julio knows one such lovely story about an Aztec Cleopatra, and it is called "The Forty Lovers of the Queen" and I am going to write it when I can go to the place where it happened. There are some very sharply cut figures in it, not at all the type-figures. [Historian William] Prescott has a dim account of it, I remember, but Julio's version is much more alive. He's never read anything but the prayer-book, so he has no stale ideas—not many ideas at all, indeed, but a good many fancies and feelings, and a grace of expression that simply catches you up. It's like hearing a new language spoken, because he speaks so directly. He will drive any number of miles to see flowers or running water, but Cliff Dwellers bore him awfully. "Why," he says raising his brows "do you care for Los Muertos? We are living." For him, as for Mrs. Bell, there are only the quick and the dead; it is fitting to say masses for the dead, but that ends our business with them; any further attention is a waste of time. It annoys him to be pressed about certain dim details connected with the "forty lovers". "No me importa. They die so long ago. Pobrecitos! (poor fellows)."

Well, I broke into Julio after all! I was afraid I would, and that's the real reason I have not written before. <u>Next</u> to "travel" letters, I hate to get letters that rave about the beauty of untutored youths of Latin extraction. People always do one to death with such letters when they go to Italy. But Julio is not soft and sunny. He's indifferent and opaque and has the long strong upper lip that is so conspicuous in the Aztec sculpture, and somber eyes with lots of old trouble in them, and his skin is the pale, bright yellow of very old gold and old races. I really think I must get him to New York. He'd make an easy living as an artist's model. They'd fight for him. Pardon!

W.S.C.

Cather used the story Julio shared, "The Forty Lovers of the Queen," in her 1920 short story "Coming, Aphrodite!"

⇀ ↽

The following was written on a postcard with a view of the pueblo of Isleta, New Mexico. On the front of the postcard Cather wrote, "Such a lovely place! My brother and I have spent two days here. Behind the church the priest has wonderful gardens, full of parrots and snow-white doves." Written over the church on the front image are the words "church 1680."

TO ELIZABETH SHEPLEY SERGEANT

June 2 [1912]
Albuquerque, New Mexico

Dear Elsie:

Oh I <u>did</u> hope you would never run across that book of bum verse! It seemed quite probable that you never would. I've bought up and sunk in a "tarn" all the copies I could get. I thought it entirely dead. I really was very young and had never been—anywhere. But, even for a Cliff Dweller, it was pretty bad. I seem to remember one that began "Stark as a <u>Burne-Jones</u> vision of despair!" I hope you appreciated <u>that</u> fully! But please don't ever try to buy one. If you dislike me enough to want one, I'd rather give it [to] you than have you pay out money to scorn me.

She is speaking of her 1903 book of poetry, April Twilights. *Her poem "White Birch in Wyoming" does indeed begin "Stark as a Burne-Jones vision of despair," a reference to the work of the English artist Edward Burne-Jones.*

TO S. S. MCCLURE

June 12 [1912]
Red Cloud, Nebraska

Dear Mr. McClure;

I sent two letters to you in Paris while I was in New Mexico, but your letters missed me when I was off in the desert on my horseback trip. I reached home yesterday and sent you a telegram explaining. I am distressed to hear of Mrs. McClure's condition and of all the business troubles which awaited you in New York. You have always been so generous with other people that it seems terribly unjust that you should be harassed and tormented about money in this way. I can not believe that there is not some way out. I can not believe that your career is over. As I told you in New York I never felt the power to do things so strong in you as now. If this were the end of your work, that would be much more remarkable than your original success—quite too remarkable to happen, it seems to me. But I don't wonder that you are tired. The original contract has undergone so many changes and modifications that I cannot make just what the state of your affairs is now, or what your actual holdings in the stocks of the company are. What ever else I am doing this fall I could certainly give you some help on the Autobiography. Going to London would, I should think, increase the cost of producing it, both for you and for me. I think I ought to be able to do it along with other work, so that I would not have to "charge" you at all for my own work on it. You would have the expense of a good stenographer anyway. My interest in the work would be an interest of friendship, a purely personal interest, and I think I could do it better and would feel more zest in the doing of it, if there were no question [of] payment at all. You have done more favors for me than a few, (more than I could count!) and I should like to have the opportunity to do a small one for you. If I had money or influence, believe me, they should be yours to command. These, alas! I have not. But if my wits can help you out any, that will be a pleasure to me indeed. Of course, I may not be able to write the articles in the way you wish them written; the _way_ in which one writes a thing, you know, is not altogether under one's control. There were chapters of Christian Science, for instance, which I simply could not write in the way you would have liked best.

And so it might be with these autobiographical articles; the events that sing one tune to you might sing another to me; I might not be able to catch step with you. As to all that, we can but try. But if, as the old song says "a willing heart goes all the way," we shall make out very well; for I was never more willing about a piece of work.

I have not written a line since I left New York, but I have such a head-full of stories that I dream about them at night. I've ridden and driven hundreds of miles. You would not know me, I'm so dark-skinned and <u>good humored</u>. Oh please forget how cranky I used to be when I was tired! I hope Miss Roseboro' will forget, too. I can't <u>bear</u> to have either of you remember me like that. It will seem so foolish now; such an ado about nothing. But I'm never going to get fussy like that again. I've never been so happy since I was a youngster as I have been this summer, back in my own country with my own people. Those weeks off in the desert with my big handsome brother—six feet four, he is—and his wild pals, are weeks that I shall never forget. They took all the kinks and crumples out. I feel as if my mind had been freshly washed and ironed, and were ready for a new life. I feel, somehow, confident; feel as if I had got my second wind and would never torture my self about little things (like the ART DEPARTMENT!) again. A thousand, thousand good wishes to you, and loyalty and hope:

Faithfully
Willa Cather

TO ELIZABETH SHEPLEY SERGEANT

June 15 [1912]
Red Cloud

Dear Elsie—

I did escape, some of me, you see. I wasn't utterly drunk up by the sand of the desert. But when you are there you do feel as if you might very easily be drunk up. I may still go back for Julio. He would be lovely at Mrs. Fields'. A mimosa tree is nothing to him. But Mrs. Gardener [art collector Isabella Stewart Gardner] would snap him up and take him to Fenway Court and he would like that better than my apartment. The only cloud on my joyful horizon at present is the news that you are no better, or not much better. Oh I wish, I wish you were! Perhaps, after all, Julio would have done you more good than Tryon [North Carolina]. I wish I could simply say "yes" about Paris. But I fear I wont be able to get away. But as to Provence. I know you can work at

Avignon, and if the mistral blows there go to Lavendou. A tiny fishing [village] down on the Mediterranean about forty or fifty miles east of Hyères—it may even be nearer. Sea, fine woods, a good hotel, nothing else. No cottages. It is on the coast road to Italy, and motors may have made a difference. The hotel may be more expensive now, but eight years ago it was something less than nothing a day. Trust me, the place is just right for work. And I know you could work in Avignon. The Rhone does put it into one; and the Rhone is your whole life at Avignon—the Rhone and the sun. The place is at its best in September. Oh I wish I were to be with you! But perhaps you can go to Madre Mejicana with me sometime. Julio has a song about "Oh bright-eyed Mexico, oh golden Mexico!" I went to a Mexican dance with Julio the night before I left Winslow, but that was a dance. They have a curious pantomime waltz which a man dances with two women. It is certainly the prettiest dance I've ever seen. I was the only "white" at the ball; such music and such dancing. How can I write you about Julio? He is without beginning and without end, and there is no place to begin. He really was like all the things in the Naples museum, and having him about was like living in that civilization. He had a personal elegance of which I've never known the like. You see I use the past tense; I did get away. I made a sort of translation of one of his songs which may give you some idea of his music, except that it is sultry and he is not at all sultry, anymore than lightning is. And aside from his lightning aspects he is a very cool and graceful young man who carries his great beauty as lightly as one could ask. This serenade, he explained carefully, is to be sung only by a "married lady", but she may with perfect propriety sing it to either her husband or lover.

I'm so glad to hear of Mrs. [Elia] Peattie's daughter, and trust she is happy. Her mother was so kind to me long ago. Do let me hear more from you soon. I wish I could give you Julio's serenade in the Spanish, with the stars and the desert and the dead Indian cities on the mesa behind it. The English is clumsy. But don't mind the accent on "but"; they have a trick of accenting unimportant words with the guitar and voice, as if, after all, the words were a mere convention, and the undertow was as apt to break through at the wrong place as the right.

SERENATA MEJICANA

(Voz Contralto)

The flowers of day are dead—
Come thou to me!

The rose of night instead
Shall bloom for thee.
Stars by day entombed
In darkness wake;
The rose of night has bloomed—
Beloved, take!

The wine of day is spent,
The springs are dry;
So long above them bent
The ardent sky.
A thirsty lip since dawn
Hath pressed the fountain's brink—
The wine of night is drawn,
Beloved, drink!

The eyes of night are shut,
So thine should be;
The tired stars fade but
To dream of thee.
Dew-drenched blossoms spill
Their odors deep;
The heart of night is still—
Beloved, sleep!

[Unsigned]

TO ANNIE ADAMS FIELDS

June 27, 1912
Red Cloud

Dear Mrs. Fields:

I am at home again with my family, and we are all having a very happy visit together. My mother had to go to Omaha for a surgical operation two months ago, but she recovered very rapidly and is now in splendid health. And so am I! Tomorrow I am going up into the Bohemian country for a week to see the wheat-harvest. That is always a splendid sight, and there is much merry-making among the people. They are a wild, fierce people, but very energetic and intelligent. I have known but one really dull Bohemian, and I have known a great many clever ones. You know [Richard] Wagner said that whenever he got dull he went to Prague. "There I renew my youth," he wrote, "in that magical and volcanic soil of Bohemia."

You can scarcely imagine, in the cool shade of the home at Manchester, looking above the tree-tops at the ocean, what torrid weather I am tasting here. The whole great wheat country fairly glows, and you can smell the ripe wheat as if it were bread baking. But the nights are cool, and just now the full moon makes an enchantment over everything. I have been motoring about the country with my father almost every day, but when I go up into the Bohemian township I shall drive, and saunter about from farm to farm in the old-fashioned way.

Please send a card to me here and tell me how the summer has gone with you so far. I long to tell you about wonderful Arizona. I really learned there what [Honoré de] Balzac meant when he said "In the desert there is everything and nothing—God without mankind."

My heart to you, my dearest Lady, and many, many loving thoughts.

Willa

I expect to spend August in Pittsburgh with Miss McClung.

→ ←

Her buoyant frame of mind helped Cather see literary possibilities in the lives of the Nebraskans with whom she grew up. The next letter references "The White Mulberry Tree," a story that would become part of O Pioneers! *The poem included in the letter, later titled "Prairie Spring," was printed at the beginning of the novel, almost exactly as it appears here.*

TO ELIZABETH SHEPLEY SERGEANT

July 5 [1912]
Red Cloud

I'm hoping for a line from you that will tell me you are better and at work. I have just come back from the Bohemian country, and next week I go up there again to see the wheat harvest. It is a great sight and I have not beheld it for years. All the prosperous Bohemians have gone back to Prague to a great musical festival. Six hundred left Omaha a few weeks ago. I shall start for Pittsburgh about two weeks from now. There I shall fall to work. I've a new story in mind that will terrify Mr. Greenslet. I think I'll call it "The White Mulberry Tree."

W.S.C.

[Typewritten on a separate sheet of paper:]

> Evening and the flat land,
> Rich and somber and always silent;
> The miles of fresh-plowed soil,
> Heavy and black, full of strength and harshness;
> The growing wheat, the growing weeds,
> The toiling horses, the tired men,
> The long, empty roads,
> The sullen fires of sunset fading,
> The eternal, unresponsive sky.
> Against all this, Youth,
> Flaming like the wild roses,
> Singing like the larks over the plowed fields,
> Flashing like a star out of the twilight;
> Youth, with its insupportable sweetness,
> Its fierce necessity,
> Its sharp desire;
> Singing and singing,
> Out of the lips of silence,
> Out of the earthy dusk.

[Handwritten at the bottom of the page:] This is how the wheat country seemed to me three weeks ago when I first came back from the Southwest. There's another note in it now.

TO ELIZABETH SHEPLEY SERGEANT

August 14 [1912]
Pittsburgh

Dear Elsie

What a splendid long letter from you did await me here—and full of such interesting plans. And if you are sleeping again you won't sail all worn out, and if this cool weather holds it will be a help to you. Then, from the equestrian photo—art department phrase—I don't gather that you are far gone in emaciation. Surely when you are at sea, with such a calm companion as [Henri] Bergson, you'll get the rest that awaits one on the water.

Last night Isabelle and I read the Scribners paper aloud with such enjoyment. The way you shortened the Burgundian part seems to me most successful and satisfactory, and the whole paper has such lightness and go about it. Mr. [Edward L.] Burlingame [editor of *Scribner's*] wrote me such a pleasant and friendly note about a piece of verse he took while I was in the West. I'll send you a copy when it is published. Sometime, when you are comfortably settled again, I shall beg you to look over the other "foreign" story I did in Cherry Valley. It's a cold, chilly sort of thing and would be a dull chore on an eventful day. Besides, it has to be worked over, when I can get round to it. I am delighted that the Bohemian Girl did not disappoint you. The Mulberry Tree is about Bohemians, too.

Do you know, I'm glad, glad to be back out of the west—for the first time in years and years I've had enough of it. It <u>is</u> too big and consuming. I'm glad to lie down among a few books and slowly come to myself again, with all that swift yellow excitement to think of. That pace did tire me out after awhile. Slowly the real meaning came upon me out there of a sentence that I once read carelessly enough somewhere in Balzac: "dans le desert, voyez-vous, il y a tout et il n'y rien; Dieu, sans les hommes." [Cather's translation, from the letter above: "In the desert there is everything and nothing—God without mankind."] That sentence really means a great deal. I was sitting mournfully beside the Rio Grande one day, just outside a most beautiful Indian village—Santo Domingo—when I looked up and saw that sentence written in the sand, and it explained what was the matter with me. Julio <u>was</u> a wonder, but he couldn't, for very long, take the place of a whole civilization. That's a stupid thing to say and I'm not really so calculating as that sounds; but you see you can play with the desert and love it and go hard night and day and be full of it and quite tipsy with it; and then there comes a moment when you must kiss it goodbye and go! Go bleeding, but go, go, go! It's a sudden change, like a norther, and when it comes you have to trek.

Isabelle and I are having the most peaceful and satisfying days—[Jules] Michelet, tome 9 [of *History of France*]—and enjoying the emptiness of the city and the freedom it gives us. I had such interesting days in the Bohemian town. There is a chair of Bohemian in the University of Nebraska; a woman holds it, a very unusual person [Šárka B. Hrbková]. I can tell you a thrilling story about her sometime. Such a clever chap committed suicide on her account last winter.

You shall have the letter to Pinker within a very few days, as soon as I get his address from the office. Don't think of writing to me again until you are on the boat. I shall love to have word of you from there. I'd like so much to see you before you go. It's a thousand years since March, and so many things have happened to each of us. What a lot of things lie before you just now! I'm so g-l-a-d!

W.

The "cold, chilly" and "foreign" story is "Alexandra," the story Cather combined with "The White Mulberry Tree" to make O Pioneers!

TO ELIZABETH SHEPLEY SERGEANT

September 12 [1912]
Pittsburgh

Dear Elsie;

I am just back from two very busy weeks in New York, where I made satisfactory arrangements for my winter's work. I am to stay here and write until January first, then go back to the office for five or six months. I've agreed to deliver two stories to the magazine between now and Christmas. I'm afraid, in the nature of the case, they can't be very good ones, but I shall give only part of my time to them. I did not send you the Swedish story because I have been moved to do her over and lengthen her by half, thus making a two-part "pastoral",—the most hopeless proposition under Heaven—quite enough to offset my doing two stories to order. So much for plans—you asked about 'em.

I went to see Mr. Burlingame last week and told him how much I had enjoyed your paper in the July number. But words of mine weren't needed. I found him a Captive, bound hand and foot. As Tooker would say, you "have him buffaloed." He said he was so sorry not to be in town when you sailed, which, for Mr. B.— I thought going some. He asked if you had done anything for McClures and listened with great interest when I told him. He ended by saying "Besides being a brilliant woman, she seems to have all the mark of being a really first-rate person," from which I infer that he has not always found that he could safely postulate the latter in the former.

I saw almost no one in New York, and was really out of the office. The Arlisses [actors George and Florence Arliss] were there, very happy over the success of "Disraeli," rich and prosperous and flaunting a motor car. I spent several evenings with them.

If you happen to think of it when you are in the marts of trade, do take a look at the English edition of Alexander—Heinemann—it's so much better looking than the Houghton Mifflin. And do, in mercy, tell me whether there is any new French worth reading. I've gone back to Balzac in sheer desperation and have just run through "Histoire des Treize" and a French translation of Dostoiefsky's "L'Idiot", a dreary and disgusting thing enough. If you don't have any new French books to recommend, pray suggest some old ones. You named one of Flaubert's once that I've not read; what was it?

Yes, I think the first two chapters—or books?—of "Creative Evolution" [by Henri Bergson] glorious. But the last one, the historical one, I did not like nearly so well.

I wouldn't have thought Sedgwick's letter possible if you hadn't sent it. The real truth is this, my friend—you probably know it—you are not flat enough for Ellery. He doesn't know but your laugh may be dangerous; he doesn't know just where you stand; you won't give him the one solid paragraph that would make him feel safe about you. He's afraid that if he follows your giddy pen about he may suddenly find himself laughing at something he shouldn't laugh at. Didn't I tell you how he once said sadly to me "Isn't it strange that with such good actors the French have never been able to originate a drama or to write a comedy!" When I remonstrated he said "Irreverence is not humor"! That's your trouble. Mr. Burlingame said you were a first rater because only they could see the humor of their own enthusiasms, but that does not go down with E. S. Bear yourself more seemingly, Audrey [paraphrase from Shakespeare's *As You Like It*].

Why don't you send me the article you sent Sedgwick? I've plenty of time now and should love to read it. My surplus of time, my release from office bondage is really due to the strange way that "The Bohemian Girl" has "gone"; at least the business office has heard a lot about it and we've had a lot of letters. One lady did write and quote Tennyson to say that I was in danger of becoming "Procuress to the Lords of Hell", but I am sure she was prejudiced by Miss Wyatt. Everyone seems to like it much better than Alexander, which upsets all my theories about what people like and all Mr. Mackenzie's.

I'm being very lazy, working only three hours a day and walking a lot. Let me hear very particularly about your health, please, and whether you can sleep and work. I can't see how you can do either if you visit!

Affectionately
W.S.C.

The "two-part pastoral" would become O Pioneers! *Cather never delivered the two stories to* McClure's *that she promised by Christmas.*

⇀ ↼

In the fall of 1912, Cather and Edith Lewis moved to 5 Bank Street in New York, the comfortable apartment where the two would live for fifteen years, regularly hosting "Friday teas" for friends and colleagues.

TO ELIZABETH SHEPLEY SERGEANT

October 6 [1912]
Pittsburgh

Post cards are enough—I understand the rush and the number of notes and telegrams that "meeting" Londoners entails. Since I wrote you I've been in New York twice—have leased and moved my effects into the ideal, the perfect apartment, large old-fashioned, roomy, one flight up; good fireplace, good windows, good woodwork, wide stairs up, <u>and</u>, if you please, number 5 Bank Street, off Greenwich Ave., two blocks from Jefferson Market. I hope to be here <u>now</u> until January. Everything going well, work <u>pretty</u> well. These calls to the New York office <u>do</u> interrupt. Your card makes me restless. I want to <u>be</u> in London. There's no place like it!

Hastily
W.S.C.

TO ZOË AKINS

October 31 [1912]
Pittsburgh

My Dear Zoë

I turn again to your beautiful long letter and again hope that you are quietly settled, with some fine person to keep you from shopping when you have a temperature. Working, writing, at least, is not apt to hurt you if you do a little at a time and try not to get excited about it. I believe one works better when one is reasonably calm, after all. Don't you?

I <u>am</u> so glad you liked "The Bohemian Girl." Yes, I really think it's pretty good myself. I'm doing another about three times as long about the same country. In this new one the country itself is frankly the hero—or the heroine—though I think the people, Swedes and Bohemians, are rather interesting, too. There'll be a little verse about that country in the December <u>McClure's</u>.

I've been on to New York twice since I wrote you, and saw one excellent play there—Arnold Bennett's "Milestones." Quite a new sort of thing, strong as a steel spring. Of course I'd get on faster with my new story if the office would let me sit tight for awhile.

I loved your letter about California and the strange people you found there, especially Mrs. Oliver. She must have been a delightful person. What you said about liking to "impress" people amused me greatly.

I had such awfully hard training in the corn fields that I don't think I had that joyful stage—no "effects" could be made there by any stunts I could do, except, maybe, horseback riding. You can't get any rise out of a cow with a sonnet, none whatsoever. Still, the desire to shine a little to people we admire, we all have, and in you its a thing to which I find myself soft-hearted. I'm hoping for a line, with good news of you, when you have time.

Affectionately
W.S.C.

The "little verse" in the December McClure's *was "Prairie Spring," the poem she had sent Sergeant a few months earlier.*

TO ELIZABETH SHEPLEY SERGEANT

December 7 [1912]
Pittsburgh

Dear Elsie—

Such a splen-<u>did</u> letter as you did write me! I've been over it until I've deciphered every pencil stroke. Thanks for the tip about Harrison. I have nothing but work to talk about, as I'm on the home stretch with the new story. It is running about the same length as "Alexander" and is certainly a great deal better than The Bohemian Girl. It has been rather a pull because it's knit so much closer than anything I have ever done before. No, I don't think one can write much when one is getting the material—at least I, for one, can't. But, do you know, I think getting the material, coming up against the surfaces of things, is the exhausting part of it. The mere working it off one's pen is on the whole a peaceful chore. I don't believe you can write over there unless you have a flat of your own and insulate yourself! One has to sleep to work, and one has to be dull to sleep.

Have you read Tchekov? "The Cherry Orchard" etc? Do! I've been reading such lots of things that I never have time to read in New York. I assume the office chains again January 1st, but not for long! There are too many things I want to write. I say, it's great sport when you get down to it—get down and see! Do you know that rhyme

> "Oh London, London, my Delight!
> The flower that blossoms but by night;
> Oh bloom and bloom I see them stand,
> The iron lilies of the Strand!"

I want to write many things to you, but Christmas—people—a bloody murder in my story—(I've been three mortal days a-killing them!) all these have reduced me to a state where I can only make a few scratches and wish you well and well and well. Christmas in Paris seems good luck enough to wish any mortal—only I should go to Provence to meet the Three Holy Kings! Oh I hope I can be there where you are, sometime!

Yours
W.S.C.

TO ELIZABETH SHEPLEY SERGEANT

[Early 1913]
New York City

No, my dear Elsie, I honestly don't think I'm so bad as that! I can miss people even when I am happily and gainfully employed. But there are times when I am very little of an individual and when everything about me is rather pale. In Pittsburgh I was working in a house over hung with the shadow of a distressing and hopeless illness. Life and the world and the weather were pale, and if one got enough blood to pump into one's daily stint of work, one did well. There were many days when I didn't get it, and went out and kept the pale weather company. But when I got back and began to go to the opera twice a week and feel the world go round again, then I began to want things—and people. I never get much satisfaction out of seeing the people I care for under the wrong conditions, and the last time you were in New York conditions were bad enough—I hated the place where I was staying, and I hated myself for a piece of damaged goods. But if you can stop here in June, we'll better it. I'll be here through June, though I may go to the Blue Ridge for a few weeks in May.

Please stop here in Bank street with me. If its Hellish hot I won't keep you, I'll be strong minded and send you away, so you'll be taking no risk.

The Pioneers are on their way to you—must have gone out on yesterday's boat. For the love of Gawrd tell me the truth about it. I know how hard it is to tell people the truth, but one can do it. And I promise you I can take it. I'm not sentimental about things just because I've made them. I've a notion there may be some flossy writing in this, too emotional, I mean. And if so, please hit it a swat. I can use the blue-pencil with a light heart. Shall I have Mr. Greenslet include "The Bohemian Girl" in the same volume with this, or do you think it will go better alone? It's long enough to make a good sized book. I await your verdict—with terror!

W.S.C.

→ ←

Edith Lewis's presence at 5 Bank Street is conspicuously missing from Cather's following report to her aunt about her new apartment. The March article for McClure's *she mentions working on was "Plays of Real Life," about the New York theatrical scene.*

TO FRANCES SMITH CATHER

February 23, 1913
New York City

Dear Aunt Franc:

It has been a long while since I got your good letter, but this has been a busy fall and winter for me. I have just finished a new novel which will be published in the fall, and I have been doing a great deal of magazine work. Besides these things, I have had the care of getting settled in a new apartment in New York. I did not move in to my new flat until the first of January, but I came on in October from Pittsburgh and leased the place and moved my furniture in. Then I went back to Pittsburgh to work on my story in peace and quiet. At last I have an apartment that is roomy, quiet, and that suits me perfectly. When I came back in January the first month was given over to paperers and painters and furniture dealers. I actually had to write an article for the March number of McClures while the floors were being painted under my feet. But I have taken a good deal of pleasure in fixing the place up, for it is exactly the kind of apartment I have always wanted, and I had almost despaired of ever being able to find one that would suit me for a reasonable rental. I have the competent colored girl who has been my maid for four years, and she tyrannizes over me—and makes me very comfortable. I have never before been so happy and comfortable as I am this winter. Probably one reason is that, for the first time in several years, I am perfectly well—well enough to enjoy everything, work and play alike. My office work I have cut exactly in half, and this gives me much more time to write—and to live, for that matter. I wish you and Bessie and Auntie Sister could see my new flat. What do you think of two open fires, one in the dining room and one in the sittingroom? I have a snug little study off the sittingroom and a comfortable bedroom and bath, a large dining room and a good kitchen. Plenty of sunlight in the two front rooms. I now own four very beautiful Persian rugs, of which I am very proud.

Yes, my dear Aunt, I know there was a sort of moral flimsiness about "Alexander." But writing is a queer business. If one does anything that is sharp and keen enough to go over the line, to get itself with the work that is taken seriously, one has to have had either an unusual knowledge of or a peculiar sympathy with the characters one handles. One can't write about what one most admires always—you must, by some accident, have seen into your character very deeply, and it is this accident of intense realization of him that gives your writing about him tone and distinction, that lifts it above the commonplace, in other words. Now there are three people, two men and one woman, whom I admire more than I do any other people, and about whom I feel very strongly. More than once I have tried to put these people, about whom I feel so keenly, into stories. I assure you, the result was a blow to pride—the stories, when I had finished them, sounded as if A. C. Hosmer [*Red Cloud Chief* publisher] might have written them, they were that commonplace. They were just like hundreds of other stories. Why, you ask? My dear Aunt, I don't know. I only wish I did! But, to be worth anything, a story must have a flavor entirely its own. And often one can't reach that point of differentiation with the subjects one would most love to handle. Maybe there's a weakness in me that makes me able to handle the weak people better—I don't know. Alexander has already gone through two editions in England, and the royalties are coming up to a nice little figure. The new novel is twice as long as Alexander and is much, much better. I'm almost sure you will like the heroine.

Bessie wrote me about G. P.'s [Franc's son, G. P. Cather] hunting trip. Please congratulate him for me. Elsie [Cather] is so happy in her teaching. She loves the place and the work and the people. I am so glad. You were well when Bessie last wrote, and I hope you are now, my dear Aunt. Your niece would like to drop down for a day with you before this short month is over. I found such satisfaction in the time we had together last summer. One of the pleasures of getting older is that one can get so much nearer to one's own people, and that the dear ones of them become dearer all the time. I always used to be a little afraid of my grown-up relatives as a child. I felt as if all of them, even father, wanted to make me over, and I didn't <u>want</u> to be made over—oh, not a bit! It's worth nearing forty to have got rid of all those queer fears and shynesses that I used to feel with my own people—less with you and father, I think, than with any of the others, but still I was always a little nervous. For the last five or six years it has been such a pleasure to me to go back and find that all gone, to feel not a bit afraid, and to feel sure that where you did not agree with me you would give me the benefit of the doubt, and that people can be very fond of each other even if they cannot always think alike.

With a great, great deal of love to you,
Willie

❧ ❧

In the spring of 1913, Cather was beginning to get personally acquainted with a woman she had long admired on the stage: Wagnerian soprano Olive Fremstad. For the next two years, Fremstad was an enormous presence in Cather's life, first as a central subject of her article "Three American Singers," which appeared in the December 1913 McClure's, *and second as a major influence on the development of Thea Kronborg, the central character in Cather's 1915 novel* The Song of the Lark.

TO ELIZABETH SHEPLEY SERGEANT

April 14 [1913]
New York City

Dear Elsie:

Your glorious letter from Avignon makes me happy and rebellious. I am a fool not to have managed to be there when you are there. I've seldom been so happy as I was there. I knew you'd love it. Isn't the Rhone the most splendid river in the world, anyway? I suppose all the little poplars along the shore were knee-deep in water when you wrote. I hope you'll manage to get back to the "Rocher" to work, even if you go to Arles and Orange now. Are the gardens on tops of the Rocher as beautiful as they used to be, I wonder, and does a little ferry boat still come across on a trolley—always in danger of being swept off its wire and sent spinning down the current? And the terrific way in which the river sweeps about that elbow of the rock! It's the most satisfying exhibition of force I've ever seen. You'll be amazed when I tell you that I didn't go [to] St. Rémy. I don't know why, except that we kept putting it off and bad weather came on. You say you had mud in Arles—don't I know how muddy it can be! But fair days there are never-to-be-forgotten. I hope the wild mustard will be in bloom about the tragic theatre.

The proofs of "Pioneers" have begun to come—I haven't looked at them yet, not read a sentence, though there are a pile of them on my desk. As I wrote you before I am somehow "down" about it—I don't know why. And this after being so well pleased with it at first. I'm more than glad you let Mrs. Muirhead see it, and that she liked it. NO! It made no difference, getting the ms. off a few days later or earlier to Harrison. I don't think it interested him in the least, for he returned it nearly a week ago with the enclosed, and upon the cover six one-penny stamps. About the latter I won't be punctilious—too much bother for too few stamps. It was the irony of fate that you should have to lug all Nebraska sod into Provence, probably paying excess baggage on it all the way! But I'm more than ever glad I sent it to you, now that I seem to have got separated from the story myself in some mysterious way. It isnt that I feel anything definitely wrong with it—I simply don't get a thrill out of it anymore. But there, no more whining! I'm too dull to write any but a very dull letter today; and I should have waited, only I want to thank you for your splendid one from Avignon. Lord! I wish I were there this minute!

Yes, "discovering" is the verb that expresses intercourse with Fremstad—the poor dear calls herself "Olluv", or "Oluv", but neither she nor I can help the fact that we grew up in the middle west. But be not misled by an "Oluv" or two—take my word for it that its an intelligence that batters you up as the Rhone would if you fell into it. And this not because her talk is so emotional but because under its vivid imagery it's so complex and tightly packed and elliptical. Suddenly she stops "you know what I mean? Then say it." If you can't "say it" she throws you out the window without a qualm. I shall like to tell you about her when I see you. And may that be soon! I'm more grateful than I can tell you for this good letter on a blue day. And I've no reason to be blue: where I caught it, found it, or came by it, I am to learn. But that's only one more reason to be thankful to you that you won't demand that I "show sufficient cause why, etc". Anyhow, if I could sit for an afternoon on the Villeneuve shore and watch the gold virgin on top of the Rocher des Doms, or if I could have a cup of tea with you in Place de la République and see a <u>soldat</u> lift the corner of his mustache ever so little at me, I should and would be cured!

A great many thoughts to you, and I wish I could go with them.

W.S.C

If you get stranded, cable me for nine francs!

↛ ↚

In the opening paragraph of the following letter, Cather is trying to help her friend negotiate with Outlook *magazine, which had published an article of Sergeant's in October 1912.*

TO ELIZABETH SHEPLEY SERGEANT

April 22 [1913]

My Dear Elsie:

The Outlook people simply say that they do not know when they can publish the second article. I told them that I wanted to know to arrange for book rights, but they replied coldly that they were sorry, but they could give me no date. You should certainly write to whoever said the articles would be published in successive numbers. If this was said in a letter from the Outlook, so much the better. I would not write in wrath, but I would speak firmly. They have not behaved well and they ought to explain their conduct. I know no one on the staff there, so my conversation with them was by telephone from our office. They would be more likely to tell the truth to another publishing house, and the interest of one publishing house always stimulates another. But these people are a dead lot.

I cabled you to send the story along to Harrison because I thought he could get an idea of it even with one page gone, and since the book is to come out early in the fall there would be no chance of his running it except in the summer numbers. I shall write to him at once explaining this, and telling him that I will send a postal note for the postage. That will be simple. I'll be forever grateful to you if you corrected the French. I tried to use the queer sort they speak out there, but I felt that I was unsuccessful, so it will be better to have it simply correct. I wrote it down by ear, so to speak, phrases I heard out there last summer. They are inconsistent—always spell the church "Sainte Anne", the town "Saint Anne." etc.

I feel such a sense of relief that you do like it [*O Pioneers!*]. You put your finger exactly on the weak spot when you say that the skeleton does not stand out enough. The modelling is not bold. But the country itself has no skeleton—no rocks or ridges. It's a fluid black soil that runs through your fingers, composed not by the decay of big vegetation but of the light ashes of grass. It's all soft, and somehow that influences the mood in which one writes of it—and so the very structure of the story. Oh I would like to do one with nice sharp lines, like the mountains you now have behind you! That I would!

Mr. Greenslet rose to the occasion like a gentleman. He was delightfully enthusiastic about the story, and they are rushing it into type without delay. He is very strong for Marie, like the other gentlemen. I believe Frank satisfies me more than any of the people in it. Just now I'm in the trough of the wave about it. Having got it through and arranged for, I can be honest with myself and admit that I really want to do a very different sort of thing. I went up to see Fremstad last week and ever since I've been choked by things unutterable. If one could write all that that battered Swede makes one <u>know</u>, that would be worth while. Lord, but she is like the women on the Divide! The suspicious, defiant, far-seeing pioneer eyes. Yesterday, after she sang <u>Kundry</u> in the Good Friday "Parsifal," I ran into her as she was getting into her motor. I wanted to shout "Pretty good for you, Mrs. Ericson!" But instead I bowed to her charming secretary. Fremstad's eyes were empty glass. She had spent her charge. Hurrah for Mrs. Ericson!

And Oh, Elsie Sergeant, her apartment is just like Alexandra's house! The mixture of "mission" and gold legs, <u>and</u> the chairs! The poor thing's ideas of comfort have never had a chance to develop. I learned from her secretary that she had had some twenty "sets" of furniture sent up before she selected the agonizing objects I saw about me.

Miss McClung has been with me for three weeks. She says please remember her in that land where you now are. I've been thinking of you there with a kind of mournful pleasure. It wont be very long until you come now, will it? That will be good indeed! Thank you for everything: for reading the story and for liking it and for wanting to like it—this last most of all. It gives me great pleasure to please you; but more pleasure to feel that you care about the whole thing,—aside from stories, aside from me or yourself or anybody else. As I've told you, I dont know as many as six people who know or care anything about writing. You've read Mérimee's "Lettres a une Inconnue"? If not, do! I love that dry, proud old chap! I like his pride, and his contemptuousness. Thank you, and thank you.

Goodbye
W.

TO ELIZABETH SHEPLEY SERGEANT

April 28 [1913]

Dear Elsie:

I am running off to Boston for a week with Mrs. Fields, and before I start for the train I must again remind you that I am counting on your stopping with me a few days—as long as you can—when you land. And I want to add that although I am counting on it a whole lot, more and more every week, I shant be snippy or "feminine" if, when I meet you at the boat, you tell me that you are going to chuck me and go right through to Boston. So you must not feel that you "ought" to stop in New York with W.S.C. etc., and that that is one thing more between you and getting settled. Don't, please, let me be an ought. I am writing this <u>now</u> because, as I turn toward Boston, the number of people I've promised to visit, stare me in the face. And I'm not going to visit them. It's outrageous in one to let people they like become a tax. So I write to beg you not to let me be a "tax"; to tell you that I am tremendously hoping that you can stay awhile with me, and that if you can't you are not to fidget one second. You won't have to "get past" me to the 42nd St. station. You know what I mean.

Houghton Mifflin changed their plans five days ago and decided to bring "Pioneers" out in June. I read the whole lot of proofs in three days, and this time it seemed pretty good again. I must tell you about the Swede girl who posed for the frontispiece. And Fremstad, wonderful Fremstad! New countries are easy to reach; but to find a new kind of human creature, to get inside a new skin—that's always [the] finest sport there is, isn't it? [Geraldine] Farrar is good fun, too—Manon after Isolde. So, you see, I've much to tell you.

A gay goodbye to you
W.S.C.

O Pioneers! *was published in the summer of 1913, and though it did not have an enormous popular success, it was received warmly. Floyd Dell, in the* Chicago Evening Post, *called it "worthy of being recognized as the most vital, subtle and artistic piece of the year's fiction." The response reinforced Cather's confidence about the subjects and style she called her "home pasture."*

TO ELIZABETH SHEPLEY SERGEANT

Sunday [late August 1913]

Dear Elsie

Damn this paper? Yes, but I got a lot by mistake and I have to use it up on people who know the worst of me. As soon as I really care about people, I begin to give 'em my worst—always. Please send the correspondence school novel along when it's ready. I'm glad to read, but I'm not up to writing much these days. Long ago I promised McClure's an article on the Metropolitan ballet someday—not that I know anything about it—now they are in a rush and I have to stay over in this cursed heat another week and write it—or break my word, which I ought never to have given. However, I guess I can stand punishment for a week. Of course no dancers, no trainers in town whatever; result a shockingly shabby article. But it can't be helped now. "Enough of that", as Fremstad said when wrote that the moonlight was shimmering on the sea.

Elsie, the notices are simply too good to be true. The Western ones all say its just like that. Did you see the Transcript one? May I send you some of the best? It's not what they say about me that I want you to see, but what they say about <u>the country</u>.

I do hope I can come to you in October, but do not refrain from asking anyone else because I hope, for a dozen things may turn up to keep me away. I go to Virginia with Isabelle for September, that is certain.

I'm <u>so happy</u> that the West likes the book. I'd love to have you see the reviews. They're so hearty, and have such a note of personal enthusiasm in them.

Everything good to you!

As always
W.

⇥ ⇤

In September 1913 Cather made a two-week trip to Frederick County, Virginia, where she was born.

TO ELIZABETH SHEPLEY SERGEANT

September 12, 1913
Ye Winchester Inn, Winchester, Virginia

My Dear Elsie:

Life has been rather a mess since I last wrote you; Pittsburgh, Lake Erie, Virginia. Winchester I find too, too dull. I can't care anymore about the holy and sacred peculiarities of the people I knew when I was little. Isabelle is with me. Tomorrow we start on a driving trip through the North Mountains, and that will be better, except for food----I am sure that there is no remote province of Russia in which the food of commerce is so abominable. And I won't visit, not I! All the people I really loved here are dead. I love the mountains still, but I have not the courage to bury myself in them for very long. If one had a house here, then everything would be simple.

I wish I were going to Chocorua [New Hampshire], but I'm afraid I'm not. A few weeks in Pittsburgh after this jaunt is over, and then Bank Street again. I'm impatient to lead an industrious life once more. Vacations always tire one more than work, anyway. They have enslaved us. I believe we really dread them at heart. You will have a more satisfactory note from me when I've got away from the romantic "Southern" attitude, and all the oppressively budding and lonely "gills"—the male of the species is almost extinct hereabouts, and so cowed and house-broken that he can do nothing but carry wraps and dance and touch his hat. I hope you are enjoying work as much as I'm bored with loafing.

By the way, why did you never send the correspondence novel? Do read it to me in Pittsburgh—I'll be back there in ten days.

Yours always
Willa

TO ELIZABETH SHEPLEY SERGEANT

September 22 [1913]
Valley Home Inn, Gore, Virginia

Dear Elsie:

It's been a great success after all; glorious from the moment we took our plunge into the mountains. Five days of steady rain and I walked not less than six miles on any one of them. These woods are particularly fine in the rain. We go back to Pittsburgh on Sept 25th, alas. There is really nowhere here to stay after that. I'm sure now that I can't join you in the country, though perhaps I can get up to spend a few days with you. There are weddings and all sort of things to break up my schedule. The Opera Singer article was finished before I left Pittsburgh, but I've got to fall to work next week. Fremstad writes me from Munich that she arrives this week and goes up to her camp for several weeks and that she would like to have me stay with her there. Such a terrifying proposition I absolutely pass up! In the safe paths of civilization I'm not afraid of her, but I decline to risk her uncertain temper in the Wilds of Maine. I also decline to take the risk of boring her—for after all the only thing she really cares about is music. Her letter reached me here in the mountains and quite stumped me. She begins "I am sailing for home, (i.e. America) on the 17th" etc. I love that i.e.! How can anyone be so consistent?

Thank you very much for writing me about what the Flexners said of "Alexandra". I am greatly interested and pleased. What's the matter with "globules"? I could not say drop because a drop may be flat, or pear-shaped, whereas a globule means to me something round and firm, and that's the way the dew is on the short grass. The English notices are a perfect delight, every one of them.

We have had nine wonderful days here, and there are still two more.

Yours
Willa S. C.

✦ ✦

While in Virginia, Cather saw many members of her extended family, and in the following she dutifully reports on them to her father.

TO CHARLES F. CATHER

September 25 [1913]
On the train.

My Dear Father

I spent most of yesterday afternoon with Mary Smith, and then Isabelle and I called again in the evening and I took her some roses. She was terribly bruised and is still suffering a good deal, but was keen and chatty as ever. She has aged a good deal, but I would have known her anywhere. She was delighted to see me and sent you and mother many affectionate messages. I went to the Bank to see Walter Gore. He was polite but not very cordial. He lives only a block from the bank but he did not ask me to go to see his wife. You remember when Lillian Gore came back from Europe a few months after Walter's marriage, she came up to Winchester with a lot of silver she had bought for them in Holland. She sent up her card to Mrs. Walter, who sent back word that she was not feeling well and could not see Lillian. After she left the house Lillian met Walter on the street. He said very cordially "Hello, Aunt Lillian, I didn't know you were in town!" but he said no more. Lillian went back to Washington in a rage and has never been back since. Walter seems a nice lad, but he does not find his relatives interesting, and is sensible enough not to pretend.

I had such a nice long visit with Miss Jennie Smith, now Mrs. Garvin, before I left Gore. She is almost as large as her mother and has only two teeth, but there is something fine and dignified about her face all the same. How many relatives she has nursed and buried! The last was the aunt Mary (or Liza) Trone who used to keep house for Captain Murl. I met the old Captain on horseback, still a fine upright figure of a man, I declare; with wonderful white beard and hair.

One beautiful day we walked up to Anderson's Cove. I had never been there before. It is one of the finest views I have ever seen in any country. We stopped and had a chat with Miss Ellen Anderson; such a dear little house as she has away up there, with lovely flowers and a grand "balm o' Gilead" tree, and everything whitewashed like snow. She seemed so lonely and glad of company. "Yes ladies," she said, "the view's grand; but ladies, I prefer city life!" She was so earnest one could not even smile. It was a glorious walk up and down, and we saw only one small copperhead. That afternoon Miss Ellen rode down the mountain on her cavalry saddle in a flowing skirt to get another look at us.

We saw Giles and Dorothy set out for the North River in their "jagger" that looked as if Noah had built it instead of Mr. Potts. They went up in summer clothes and came back in winter clothes, Giles in a fur cap and Dorothy veiled like an ancient priestess. They drove a mouse colored horse, as round as a barrel. I never saw such a fat, sleepy horse. They are dear people, and I love them dearly. They brought back watermelons for us to eat, but our stay was over and we could not go over to their house again, we left the morning after they got back. Giles will be delighted to get the seeds and your letter. They were in the post office when I left Gore, but he checks for his mail only twice a week.

Tell mother I will write to her soon, and that I send much love to you both.

Willie

TO ELSIE CATHER

[October 1913]

Dear Bobbie

This is from the "Nation", which seldom reviews and about never praises a novel. I am very proud of it. I used to meet [David Graham] Phillips about the Waldorf and talk to him and I used to think "you big stuffed-shirt-and-checked-pants, I know more about the real west than you do, but I could never make anybody believe it, because I wear skirts and don't shave." But you see people do believe it, after all, and I call that very jolly. Please show this notice to Roscoe and send it back to me.

Willie

The Nation *review of* O Pioneers!*, published on September 4, 1913, was very strong. It begins "Few American novels of recent years have impressed us so strongly as this," and favorably compares Cather's novel to the work of Frank Norris and David Graham Phillips.*

➤ ❦

In the following, Cather's remarks about telephone directories are a coy way of referring to her efforts to find the perfect name for her heroine in her new novel, The Song of the Lark.

TO ELIZABETH SHEPLEY SERGEANT

October 11, 1913
Pittsburgh

Dear Elsie:

I was in hard luck to miss sharing the little house with you. I don't know whether I shall be able to get into the country again even for a few days. I have to go to New York on business next week, then hurry back. I've been busy, but the result of my activities does not seem to be very thrilling. I've been thrilled by a new line of reading, however. I've been reading the directories of American cities. New Orleans, St. Louis, St. Paul, Minneapolis. They seem to me about the best literature we have produced. They leave Walt Whitman away behind. Try "L" and "K" and "O" in Minneapolis sometime; they stir ones imagination more than all the works of the New England school. Rather! When I am old and gray and full of sleep I shall read nothing but directories.

The wedding comes off tonight, Isabelle's sister, Edith. Mr. McClure, by ill chance, arrives tomorrow.

You shall see all the notices someday. Here is one from the "Post" and "Nation" which pleased me. The Athenaeum had a good one, and Clement Shorter wrote a most enthusiastic one in his paper [the *Tatler*].

These ought to be grand days for work—I'm wishing power of hand to you!

Yours
W.S.C.

"When I am old and gray and full of sleep" is an allusion to the William Butler Yeats poem "When You Are Old."

→ ←

By the late autumn of 1913, Cather was deeply into her work on her new novel, and her article about Fremstad, Geraldine Farrar, and Louise Homer, "Three American Singers," had appeared in McClure's.

TO ELIZABETH SHEPLEY SERGEANT

November 19 [1913]
New York City

Dear Elsie:

Life and death and the things pertaining to both have kept me from writing. My Swedish cousin [Lillian Thekla Brandthall Gore, wife of Cather's cousin James Howard Gore], of whom I was very fond, died in Paris under an operation. Her husband made two terrible trips across the ocean and brought her body back on the "France", the boat on which I saw her off in June! I went to Washington soon after he got back and spent some days with him. I've been home a few days, and of course find a great deal to do, settling the apartment and making business arrangements. I'll be glad when its over, for I am tortured by the temporary stop in work. "Tortured" is rather strong, come to think of it; It's a bore to have to mark time, but I guess I'll live through it.

The new novel took a bound before I left Pittsburgh, and I did about 28,000 words in four jolly weeks; did it twice, which means that it's in almost final form. That was going some! As the wind blows now I could keep that pace up for some months to come. If only I could nail up the front door and live in a mess, I could simply become a fountain pen and have done with it—a conduit for ink to run through. And I like that well enough, too. I'm less trouble to myself than I am at any other time.

Have you seen the Singer article in the December McClures? Fremstad's "perfectly" delighted with it. Really, she says the most rewarding things about it—about the Farrar part, too, and she has not the <u>least</u> small quibble about my having gone into her Minnesota past. I do think that large minded of her. "Mind?" says she "what's the use of minding, when its the truth." That's the attitude for a perfect lady to take toward her biographer.

For goodness sake write and tell me all about yourself. Mrs. Fields begs me to come to Boston; says she is pretty frail and tired these days. I do long to go, but I don't see how I can until after Christmas. The world is certainly too much with me these days. I had the telephone disconnected, but all I got out of that was Fremstad wearing down her two-thousand-dollar Isolde vocal cords trying to get 2036 Chelsea, and always getting a Brewery! But send a poor sinner a line, do! I know I'm the lost chord myself, but I'll come to the surface very soon now. Wasn't it compromising to have Mr. [Hamilton Wright] Mabie [of *Outlook*] say all those kind things about "O Pioneers"! Him, of all folks!

I wish you were going to the Russian Dancers with me tonight. I'd give a good deal for a bit of an evening with you. Sometime you must let me tell you about my Swedish cousin. We were really and truly friends.

Yours very much
W.S.C.

Mrs. Fields writes of the last naked woman—they are all alike—on the McClure cover, "But Oh, this undesirable cover!" <u>Undesirable</u>! Nothing has pleased me so much for years! And [Cameron] Mackenzie feeling so happy and wicked all the time because he thought she was so lusciously desirable! Can't you hear her say it "un-de<u>sir</u>able" !

➔ ❖

Cather regularly exchanged work with other literary friends, and often they encouraged one another and celebrated each other's successes, but Cather could not be noncommittal and polite about something she found unworthy.

TO ZOË AKINS

Friday [January 1914]

[Written in at the top, above the letterhead:] I've kept this three days, thinking I'd write a milder one. But if I say what I think, it would always be more or less like this. You ought to know that heartless kind of story is not in my kind, Zoë!

Dear Z.A.

Your exile is by this [time] nearly over, I hope? I've been in Boston—and in shops, which accounts for my not writing. This story, my dear Zoe is written to be smart. You can't make me believe it was written for anything else. Now lots and lots of people are interested in cleverness and liveliness and the airy touch. I am not. So what can I say that's worthwhile about such a story as this, which seems to me to have nothing to do with human folk as I know them. Neither of the people seem to me individuals at all and the episode—you can't expect one to take that seriously. It is phrased in a sprightly way, but that counts for nothing to me. I'm one-sided, so you may take that into account in reading what I say. Seems to me you are talking to hear yourself here—through your hat. Now when people talk through their hats, it's all one to me what they talk <u>about</u>: murder and mistresses or tea and toast—they're merely names and no more; the toast is no warmer than the lady, or the lady than the toast. You go in too much for the far-fetched and queer <u>because</u> it's queer, to suit my farmer mind. There's either got to be real feeling in a story, or an intellectual interest of a high order. You can't dodge both issues and come it off over one by being <u>queer</u>. Now this is meant to be a scolding because I think you ought to be more in earnest and less interested in yourself and the part you make in the picture, and in what people think of you. I'm afraid you've been "spoiled" by fond parents. Can't you pull yourself out of it? Or don't you want to? You'll never do anything worth while as long as you flutter so. No, that's too strong; but you'll never work up to your best in that state of mind. A serious New Years to you!

Hastily
W.S.C.

→ ←

The following, written while she was hospitalized for a blood infection caused by a hatpin scratch, reveals Cather's peculiar aversion to deformity or illness, though she was still able to make puns.

TO ELIZABETH SHEPLEY SERGEANT

February 24, 1914
Roosevelt Hospital, New York City

My Dear Elsie:

Not much to say. I've been here a week and shall be here one or two more. Operation went very well, I believe; back of my head shaved and most of the scalp seems to be missing. Dressings very painful and are to continue five weeks if all goes well, three months if it goes not so well. Seems it takes scalp a long while to grow back. These details are enough, are they not? There are others but they are just as unpleasant. As Fremstad says "if it had been a railroad wreck one might endure it; but when it's a pin scratch, it's simply silly." And it simply is.

There's no place in my scheme of life for the unlucky. I'll have to think it over. People who go and have grotesque accidents are clowns, and I feel toward them exactly as the people who used to go from London to Bedlam felt toward the sport they went to behold. I can't share the tender feeling of our time toward the abbreviated. People minus their leg or their hair are roaringly funny and ought to be laughed at and exhibited, not coddled.

It's very little coddling I'm giving myself these days. Don't expect to hear from me. If anything worse turns up I'll let you know. But for the present I'm in hiding—trying to grow hide. I have not, I'm sorry to say, begun to grow any yet. I'll have to wait a week or two more before I begin to heal, and then it's slower than time. Very well, once I get out of this place I'll work, and curse! Can't help about five weeks dead loss of time, and plenty of losses in other directions, especially self-respect.

Yours
W.S.C.

TO ELIZABETH SHEPLEY SERGEANT

[March 2, 1914]
New York City

Dear Elsie:

I'm home again, came yesterday, and am perfectly happy. I can't understand now how I ever felt as I did at the hospital. But really, it was an ugly and agonizing business. Somehow, when you have blood-poisoning, you feel so unclean. You pulled me out of a bad situation in Boston two years ago and brought me to New York on your back. (I seem to be a mollusk when I'm ill.) This time Fremstad pulled me out. Singing only three times last week,—once in Brooklyn—she came down to the hospital unannounced and unheralded, with a motor-load of every kind of spring flower, pulled me out of the mud-shallows and got me into current again. She showed me how to do my hair in two braids above my forehead, German fashion, and to make a chiffon thing over the bandage like <u>Elizabeth</u> wears in the last act. She showed so much interest in and so little horror of my ugly head, that I lost my own horror of it. It had taken a sharp turn for the better the night before she came, and now it's going ahead by leaps and bounds. The moment the destruction of tissue stopped, which was not until Wednesday night, the world turned a different color, and I was sorry I'd sent you such a disgusting letter. But while one is making poison, there's a cloud of madness over one's brain. I never put in any three weeks like those before. A high temperature, and consistently unrelenting pain in such an inconvenient place—well, they make a mollusk of one, that['s] all. But now—oh everything's so jolly. Forget the invertebrate, please, and consider me draped in chiffon, like Louise of Prussia!

Yours
W.

TO ELIZABETH SHEPLEY SERGEANT

Tuesday [April 28, 1914]
New York City

Dear Elsie:

I certainly do not deserve the splendid heartening letter I got from you last night, but I enjoyed it as much as if I merited it. And I have laughed all these weeks about the story you wrote me about the Outlook. If that isn't the skimpy old maid among magazines!

I've been out of bandages for five weeks now, and after I first got to work everything went swimmingly. I went to Atlantic City for a few days, and to visit Mrs. [Clara] Davidge-Taylor on Staten Island. Then I got off my trolley and couldn't get on with the story for two dismal weeks. Now I seem to be on my wire again and I hope for consequent peace of mind. But there have been singing-teachers, more young singers, Fremstad's last performances, all the petty politics of an opera fight—disgusting enough, but interesting when it's new to you. All these things—except the Fremstad ones—would have been cut out if I'd been working, but since I could not figure out my next move, or rather how to make the next move, they kept me from getting sullen and taught me a good deal. I've been perfectly well for more than a month, but I had three months of unanswered letters to take up; and work going in jumps, like the weather; now all tension, now all sag. Very unsatisfactory way to have your brains behave.

Elsie I so l-i-k-e (like) the Hoyts [artists Alice and Henry Hoyt]! They are about the only married people I know in New York who are both nice. Before I was ill I had a string of endurance tests, enduring stupid wives for clever husbands and vice versa, until I was a-weary of the world. One is so pleasantly sure with the Hoyts that one won't suddenly become conscious of a strain between them. I went to their exhibit, and there was so much freshness and charm about the out-of-door things. The portraits I did not care for so much.

I expect to leave for Pittsburgh on the fifth of May. But if my time is extended beyond that, I shall certainly stay until the tenth to see you. Is Mr. Greenslet writing novels, I wish to ask, and many other things. But also I would like to show you a fat and grinning face and to convince you that I am no longer of the Caliban mood. But when I'm hurt like a beast I'll always become a beast, NOT a saint! Cum Lupibus Vivens, Lupus Sum ["When living with wolves, I am a wolf"]. I invented that in the hospital, so I'm not sure about the participle. I have not quite got back my drive for the story yet, but otherwise I think I am as well as I was before.

I've ordered "The Romance on the Riviera" but it's not come yet. I'm eager to see it.

I don't think there will be much trouble with Mexico. Yes, I wish they would take a nerve tonic and repose themselves and let me go and explore the buried cities. I've found some lovely cliff-dweller things in the Natural History Museum here—a really rich find. If we meet on the 10th I may drag you to see them. Please send me some more Provence things when I get settled in Pittsburgh. I have such peaceful hours of reading there. I hope you've been going at a more even pace than I have. With joyful thanks to you for yesterday's good letter.

Yours
W

Fremstad flees on Friday to the inclement wood of Maine.

➜ ✦

The ghostwritten autobiography of S. S. McClure was published serially in McClure's *from October 1913 to May 1914 and in book form later in 1914. McClure was listed as the author of the book, but included a note: "I wish to express my indebtedness to Miss Willa Sibert Cather for her invaluable assistance in the preparation of these memoirs." Her personal copy of the book, now at the University of Nebraska–Lincoln, is inscribed to her by McClure: "With affectionate regard for the real author."*

TO WILL OWEN JONES

May 29 [1914]
Pittsburgh

Dear Mr. Jones;

Yes, I enjoyed writing Mr. McClure's biography; mainly because he was so honest about it and was not for dressing up the truth any. If he had wanted it ornamented or softened, or had wished to put all the emphasis on the pleasant side of farm life in Indiana, the story would have been dull to write and dull to read. He told me the facts exactly as he remembered them, and wanted them put down that way.

Yes, the newspapers have gone down a lot in the last few years———and so have the magazines. The news-stand public prefers yellow fiction to anything else. All the flashy young business men in this part of the world want to be gay dogs and to be thought worse than they have time to be. It's a curious phase; probably comes from too much prosperity.

No, I don't hold any grudges about those early stories. They were warped, but they were so frankly so that I wonder that anyone should have misunderstood them. If a young man—or young woman—sits down in the cornfield and howls because he can't hear any music-dramas, it does not mean that he has fallen out with the corn-fields. Give him all the music he wants and take him about the world a little until his mind finds what it's hunting for, and he will come out all right with the corn. His was a case of mental dietetics; he hadn't found the right food and went about half-nourished.

When I was working on the Journal you were always more than kind to me, and I cannot think without amazement of the amount of rhetorical wild oats you stood for. I don't believe anybody ever made such hideous sounds in trying to learn to play an instrument as I did. When I've had to wrestle with young writers on McClure's, I've often remembered your patience.

I am away on a long piece of work now and shall not return to New York until the late fall. I am going to Wyoming this summer and may see you in Lincoln, as I shall of course go to Red Cloud.

Faithfully always
Willa Cather

TO ROSCOE CATHER

June 5 [1914]

My Dear Roscoe:

Thank you, my boy, for your nice hearty letters. I wish I could go out to see you at once, but I must do one more lap on this story or it will get away from me. I am turning a hard corner in it just now and must get it turned before I quit. I am never afraid to leave a story when it is going well, but it is bad policy to leave it when it is hardening up on one—takes too much energy to make it loosen up later. I do think I will get to you in July, but you must never kill any fatted calf for me—unless you have plenty of cold storage! If one will have an uncertain job like writing, one has to be governed a good deal by its uncertainties. On Sunday I am going up to Maine to spend a week with Mme. Fremstad, the opera singer, in her camp. I had not expected to do this, but it is the first summer that she has spent in this country in many years, and goodness knows when she will be here again. So I had better get her while I can. She is a combination that the Lord must have made to interest me even more than she does the rest of the world. The greatest artist of her time—which interests everyone—and a Swede off the Divide, "all same yense", which interests me most of all. When I was ten years old I knew that a great artist, a new kind of artist, would come out of "the old peoples in a new world", and it has been a fine adventure to see that belief realized. But I will tell you about all these things when I see you. I am perfectly well again. Indeed I do want to see Meta and the little Virginia. Now I'm off on "the long trail, the trail that is always new"—human people—most interesting things God made—beat the Grand Canyon!

With a heartfull of love
Willa

"The long trail, the trail that is always new" is a reference to Rudyard Kipling's poem "A Long Trail."

TO ELIZABETH SHEPLEY SERGEANT

Tuesday [June 23, 1914]
Pittsburgh

My Dear Elsie:

I went to wildest Maine June 7th and got home only yesterday. My letters awaited me here, so you had no word from me. As I went direct to Portland via New York, I didn't go near you. I had a glorious time with Fremstad and when I left her dropped down in Mary Jewett's garden for a few days to recover and get rested. While I was in Fremstad's camp we did things every mortal minute except when we were asleep, and even then I dreamed hard. She fished as if she had no other means of getting food; cleaned all the fish, swam like a walrus, rowed, tramped, cooked, watered her garden. I was not much more than an audience—very little help, but it was the grandest show of human vigor and grace I've ever watched. I feel as if I'd lived for a long while with the wife of the Dying Gladiator in her husky prime, in deep German forests.

I think Thornton Oakley [American artist and illustrator] is a really big man. He once did some wonderful things of Pittsburgh and the mills. He's never commonplace. An illustrated book on Provence would have more "drive" in the market of a motor-mad world, than a book of essays; surely. And Scribners are the best people to handle such a book. I should think you could have an absolute unity of treatment throughout the book, and at the end insert several historical studies for such as would care for them,—among whom I am one.

The new review sounds promising. I wish we <u>had</u> something of that sort.

I am struggling to clear my desk and cannot more than salute you now. I shall be starting for the west soon, I fancy. I stayed in Maine longer than I meant to and now must begin to move rapidly. Miss McClung sends her greetings. She will probably go to Italy when I go to Wyoming. I'll let you know when I go and where. I've got to have a run out there before I do much more work. In haste, yours

W.

Sergeant's unillustrated book on France, titled French Perspectives, *was published by Houghton Mifflin in 1916.*

→ ←

She did go west soon, and she wrote to her brother Roscoe from their parents' home in Red Cloud. Her brother James was thirteen years younger than she, and Jack nineteen years younger. She and the two brothers closest to her in age, Douglass and Roscoe, often felt an almost generational distance from their younger siblings.

TO ROSCOE CATHER

July 14 [1914]
Red Cloud

Dear Roscoe

I had a thrilling and delightful time in Maine, then stopped in Chicago a few days to attend to some work, and came on home. I will get out to see you sometime this summer, but I can't tell just when. Things here are in a rather confused maze. I'm afraid James has got father in for a good deal. Houses and farms are going up, wells and windmills being dug and reared, horses and wagons being bought,—and nobody has any heart for farming! James, to be sure, wants to be thus established, but he seems to do no work except to give Jack orders. I feel sorry for a chap who is not strong, but James is surely on the grab, and he does not care how much trouble he makes for other people. All the worry and fret and farm-provisioning of 1893 are being repeated on a costlier scale, and mother and father are 20 years older. Father looks sick and tortured with worry all the time because he has to spend so much money, and he seems unable to say "no". Jim has the key of the situation; he simply worries father down. You know father would do anything—forge a check—if you nagged him <u>enough</u>. Douglass is here and is doing all the work on Jim's property, and he keeps things from getting altogether away from father. For years father has lived so pleasantly here, and now its 1893 over again. I'll write you again when I learn the run of things better. It's not quite clear now just which things <u>are</u> Jim's, and which he thinks are his.

Yours
Willa

TO ELIZABETH SHEPLEY SERGEANT

August 10 [1914]
Red Cloud

Dear Elsie:

I am just back from a two weeks driving trip up in the French and Bohemian country—all day on the road or in the thrashing fields with the thermometer often up to 110 and never lower than 90. It was all very fine, but one had to go a stiff pace. I saw many old friends and many places that I often get hungry for. Only the intense heat drove me home at last. I would like to have gone on for two weeks more. All those people are like characters in a book to me. I began their story when I was little and it goes on like "War and Peace", always rich and various, always so much stranger than any invention of man. Whenever I go back there there is so much to catch up with. I have some friends up there who save all the details for me, of all that happens in my absence.

I suppose it's been hot any where, and you seem not to have escaped. I'm not working at all. It was not my plan to work any out here. It's a waste of time to write when there's so much doing. If you go abroad in September—but you can't, now, certainly, with the Kaiser in this high Napoleonic mood. You'll simply have to stay at home, and maybe that will be good for you!

I'm not much interested in "letters" just now, but I suppose I shall be when I go back in the fall. Let me hear what you are going to do in case you cannot go abroad. I expect to fall to work in Pittsburgh about a month from now. Fremstad is working hard and firing one cook after another. What a woman she is to look for trouble. Peace is where she is not, and yet it is peace that she's always looking for. May you have cool weather by this time, and good energy.

With my heartiest greetings
W.S.C.

→ ←

The following was written as World War I was breaking out in Europe and is one
of the very few extant pieces of correspondence between Cather and her beloved
friend Isabelle McClung. It was written on a postcard with a view of the Spanish
Peaks as seen between La Junta and Hoehne, Colorado.

TO ISABELLE MCCLUNG

Saturday [September 12, 1914]
Spanish Peaks, Near Trinidad, Colorado

You won't hear from me for two days after this card, but don't worry, because
I shall be well and happy. Such wonderful country.

W.

TO ELIZABETH SHEPLEY SERGEANT

Sunday [September 27, 1914]
Pittsburgh

Dear Elsie:

I'm back again after an adventurous but not very restful summer. As I
seemed to need adventure more than repose, I'm not complaining. I have
brought with me my kid brother [Jack] and put him in the Carnegie Technical School, and it is great fun to get him started. He is just off the farm and
has never before been out of Nebraska, but as he is candid and honest and
has not a particle of vanity, his initiation is very jolly and not at all painful.
He <u>will</u> tell people the names and <u>weight</u> of his big work horses, and all about
his Bohemian neighbors, and he never tries to talk about things of which he
knows nothing, so there are no difficulties. He's over six feet, rather good looking and twenty years old. I think you would like him, though he <u>will</u> say "yes
mam" to older women—older than twenty.

The war broke in on things a good deal. Even when I was up in the Sangree
de Cristo mountains I felt rather restless. One can't get away from the pull of it
because somehow everything one most cares about seems in danger and under
test. Before this no one knew how much they cared. I don't believe we'll hear
much about suffrage and tea-party legislation for awhile. Now, as always, the
power to take determines the extent of possession, and that is as far as we've
got.—Have you see the last six or eight numbers of <u>Punch</u>? Don't miss them.

It's like going back to Henry Esmond after reading [John] Galsworthy. You feel that the old rock is still under your feet, the rock that is different from any other. Lord, they are a game people, and so orderly in their habits of banking and war. Wasn't Kipling's Breighton [Brighton] speech a fine one?

I shall go to New York for a week in October, but after that I hope to be here until January 1st, working on my story and playing with my brother. I did no work while I was in the west, but now I am taking it up easily and have done a lot in the three days since we reached Pittsburgh. How and where are you? Have you any friends in the French army? You must be kept busy writing to France these days—not that many letters reach their destination—but send me a word, I beg of you.

Yours
Willa

The History of Henry Esmond *(1852), by William Makepeace Thackeray, was one of Cather's early favorites. She once called it "my old friend."*

TO FRANCES SMITH CATHER

November 17, 1914
Pittsburgh

Dearest Aunt Franc:

I have been getting through with a great deal of work in the long weeks since your good letter came to me. I am so glad that the flowers reached you at last if they were, like Gilpin's hat in the old ballad, a long while on the way. I have heard of you since I got your letter from Auntie Sister, and from Mother, who saw Carrie [Cather, Willa Cather's cousin] at the Bladen Fair. I spent two weeks of October in New York, but I hope to be in Pittsburgh until Christmas.

Jack is doing well at his school, and I see a great deal of him and often drop in at his rooms when I am out walking. My friends here have been very cordial to him, and he is with older people a great deal, which is very good for him. He has grown much more manly and serious since he has been here, and it is a great pleasure to me to watch him. He says he was never so happy before.

We talk and think of little but the war. My friend Mrs. Flahant, a Belgian woman, has just landed in New York. She writes me that her brothers and sisters are starving in Brussels. She can get no word or money to them, their houses have been destroyed and they cannot get out. Last night I went to hear an address by Mrs. Vandervelde, wife of the Belgian Minister of State. She speaks English fluently and is in this country soliciting money to feed her starving countrymen. She spoke for more than an hour, and I think I never heard such a good address by either a man or woman. It must be a great joy to be able to do such good work for one's country. She is not more than thirty, and is a very beautiful as well as a very intelligent woman.

I have a letter from one of the Belgian Relief Committee in London. He tells me that unless Americans can carry Belgium through this winter, the civilian population must starve to death. Neither England or France can spare anything, and the Germans will allow no food bought in France or England to be shipped into Belgium. The United States is the only power which has official assurance that the food stuffs it sends may go unmolested to the Belgian people. There are now actually four million people there on the point of starvation, more than a million are living on three ounces of flour a day, doled out by the relief committee. There was never such famine before in the history of Europe, and now the hardships of winter are being added. I mean to give no Christmas presents this year, but to give what I can to that fund instead.

I wish there were some way of arousing the little towns of Nebraska. If every family in Red Cloud gave a dollar or half a dollar, and other towns did the same, think what a stream of money that would soon make. We are the only nation not suffering, and I do think History will be ashamed of us if we are niggardly.

I am well and hard at work, dear Aunt Franc, and happy to have Jack here. Write me a line when you can, but do not put a tax on your poor eyes. Call Bessie up on the telephone and give her my love and tell her she must write and tell me how you are. Take the best care of yourself that you can, and do not forget that you have a niece who loves you very dearly.

Goodbye for today
Willie

TO FERRIS GREENSLET

December 13 [1914]
Pittsburgh

Dear Mr. Greenslet:

The novel will be done by mid-summer at latest—perhaps by April—and ought to come out next autumn. It will be fully twice as long as "O Pioneers." The title is still uncertain. What would you think of "The Song of the Lark"? with apologies to the author of "The Nightingale." It is, I think, as a story, much more interesting and color-ful than "O Pioneers"—so many more peo-ple and places, and I think you will like the heroine. I shall be glad when it is in shape for you to read.

Faithfully yours
Willa Cather

TO FERRIS GREENSLET

December 21 [1914]
Pittsburgh

Dear Mr. Greenslet;

I am pulling off the story at record rate, and enjoying this spree of work so much that I have decided not to go to New York until February 1st. I shall have a large chunk of the book done for you in April.

Please do stop the war. There will be nothing agreeable in the world until it is stopped. I suppose they will patch up a temporary peace and then, in twenty-five years, beat it again with a new crop of men. I hope to see you in New York when you sail, if not before.

Honor bright, the new novel is a good one!

Faithfully
Willa Cather

TO FERRIS GREENSLET

March 28, 1915
New York City

Dear Mr. Greenslet;

I am sending you by far the greater part of the novel. The remainder, which is nearly all done, will not run more than twenty thousand words. I think so well of this book that I had probably better not confide to you my own opinion of it. I will say, however, that I don't believe you publish a story like this every day. I beg you to put it by for a reading until you can take it up with some sense of leisure, for I am hoping that, although you have to read so much, you will have a good time with this manuscript. The manuscript is untidy, but the story is not. I have not had it copied by a stenographer because I did not want to take the time to go over it again and correct the copyist's mistakes, but I apologize for sending you such messy pages.

My old friend Mr. [Burton] Hendrick, who is now with Doubleday, came to see me several weeks ago and told me such attractive things about their book-selling methods that I feel rather wistful. They are getting such astonishing results from even "high-brow" slow sellers———a lot that they took over from McClure's, of which I know the history.

I was well satisfied with the advertising you gave "O Pioneers!," but I think this book ought to be pushed a good deal harder, because I think it has more momentum in it and will go further. I want to sell a good many copies. The next novel will be a New York story, will be long and hard to do. I don't think it will be as fine as this is at its best; certainly not so lyrical. But if I can write it under good conditions it ought to be very interesting. I shall need money and time, and after I once get it under way, I do not want to stop to write articles and short stories to replenish my bank account. I did not expect a large sale for "O Pioneers!," but I think this one ought to go thirty thousand. As to length, it will run something over two hundred thousand words, but not much over, I think; say two hundred and ten thousand. It has been a long job, and I am eager to know what you think of the result. I have never had such a good time with any piece of work before. Goodness knows this ought to be cheerful enough for you, happy ending and all! It seems, as I go over it this last time, better than cheerful to me. It seems to have a lot of the kind of warmth and kindliness that can't be made to order, and that you can only get into a story when the places and the people lie near your heart; when you write of things that, under all the thousand things you like or think you like, have the most persistent and unquenchable reality. The death of the noble brakeman was the original germ of the story, I suppose. It happened when I was about thirteen, and I was "on the spot" as the Red Cloud paper used to say. Ever since then this story has been in the back of my head in one form or another. It has gone through many incarnations, but the germ of it, the feeling of it, has never changed. Long before I knew any singers except the kind described in Bowers' studio in Chicago, the heroine was a singer. Unless you had lived all over the West, I don't believe you could possibly know how much of the West this story has in it. I can't work over it so much that I ever blunt the "My country, 'tis of thee" feeling that it always gives me. When I am old and can't run about the desert anymore, it will always be here in this book for me; I'll only have to lift the lid.

Did you ever hear me talk like a travelling salesman about my own works before? I tell you I've <u>got it</u>, this time!

Faithfully

Willa Cather

→ ←

On April 5, Greenslet wrote Cather that he enjoyed reading the manuscript but thought the beginning and the ending were incongruent, both in tone and in length; he noted that part one was 162 pages, whereas part five was only 35 pages. He also criticized as too conventional Cather's choice to make one of her characters, Dr. Archie, the governor of Colorado. And, he noted, Dr. Archie ought not to have been described as playing "billiards" in the opening of the novel, but, instead, "pool," as billiards is almost never played four-handed.

TO FERRIS GREENSLET

Tuesday [April 6, 1915]
New York City

Dear Mr. Greenslet;

Yes, pool, of course. The man this was done from always played billiards and the word came automatically, the moment I began to think of him. I think I would be willing to deprive Dr. Archie of the Governorship and make him a political dictator and the head of a big mining company. But the diminishing scale you noted, after the end of Part II, is really a part of the plan of the book. The latter part of the manuscript explains that plan somewhat, but I would like to talk with you about it. Can't you come to see me on Saturday or Sunday? Send me a line giving me a hint as to when to expect you, as I have no telephone—and shan't have until this story is done and off my mind.

Perhaps the peculiar structure of the story would be better explained if I used a sub-title and called the book; "The Song of the Lark: The Story of an Artist's Youth."

Faithfully
Willa Cather

→ ←

Greenslet claimed to be satisfied at her justification of the "diminishing scale" of the novel, and he sent contracts as well as requests to see the final chapters of the book. When Cather mentioned that there would be an epilogue, he cautioned that it would be important—and difficult—to get it right. Though his words and tone were positive and encouraging overall, Cather was sensitive to the few criticisms he offered.

TO FERRIS GREENSLET

April 28, 1915
New York City

Dear Mr. Greenslet;

Here is a hasty first cast at the Epilogue, which will be rather casual and not more conclusive than this first draft. I begin to feel as [Robert Louis] Stevenson did about his wife and The Black Arrow, when he waited in vain for it to take hold of her. I have a mournful conviction that you do not get what you look for from this book, and that you find it eccentric and unsatisfying. I would do almost anything to please you, except change the story, which I can't do. If you feel reluctant about publishing it, there is still time to call it off. I am sure that if you can give it an approving push at the start, it will make its way to a good many people. If it doesn't, and I am mistaken, then you will have a right to be severe with me. I hate to feel that I am not living up to your expectations, but I feel so much more confidence in this book than I did in the other.

Faithfully
Willa Cather

If you go ahead with this, will you please make a note that I am to have <u>three</u> pulls of each galley proof? I always use two in correcting, and one is to go to a musical expert.

→ ←

On April 29 Greenslet reassured her that he did truly feel enthusiastic about the novel, and though he still believed the structure was unusual, he wasn't the kind of inexperienced publisher who thought every book had to conform to his specific expectations. He did think the three-foot Venetian tide mentioned in a metaphor in the very last sentences of the epilogue was perhaps, hydrologically, an exaggeration.

TO FERRIS GREENSLET

[After April 29, 1915]
New York City

Dear Mr. Greenslet:

I am much cheered by your letter. If you feel that way, we'll pull out with a creditable showing, I am sure. Yes, the tide in the Veneto is only 1 1/2 feet. I was merely guessing. You had best send the Epilogue back to me, as I hope to bring it out a little more sharply.

I wish you could have been here at a little dinner and theatre party I gave for Fremstad last Wednesday night. It was really a wonderful party. [Pitts] Sanborn, musical critic of the Globe was here. He has written the most penetrating and appreciative notices about Fremstad for ten years, and it was the first time they had ever met. It was like Turgenev's story of introducing Charity and Gratitude in Heaven.

Faithfully
W.S.C.

TO MISS VAN TUYLL, HOUGHTON MIFFLIN

May 24 [1915]
New York City

Dear Miss Van Tuyll;

In the first place, let me tell you how delighted I am that you get a thrill out of the story, and in the second, let me tell you how I lament the custom of publishing photographs of authorines. I meant to read "Men of Iron." The publishers sent me a photograph of the author; fat woman with no neck, big stupid face set on her shoulders. I'll never read it. Now, if I have a prejudice against her type of face, mayn't hundreds of people perfectly well have a prejudice against mine? I can see it, for actresses and singers; but authorines, for the most part, possess countenances that do but discourage one with their wares.

If I had some good pictures taken down in the Cliff Dweller cities, I could see that they might suggest a breeze to the onlooker. But I have only those you saw. The one you have reproduced fairly well. I'm going to the big cliff ruins down at Durango, Colorado, late this summer, and could have some taken, but that would be rather late for you, wouldn't it?

Now, in the meantime, do you want me to go to Dupont and strive for as good a conventional picture as possible, or do you wish me to have Underwood and Underwood sleuth me to the Park and take me feeding squirrels or doing folk-dances? How can an informal picture be interesting, unless it is taken in an interesting place? I have some rather good ones of me and Fremstad, that were taken up in the woods last summer; but those, of course, I couldn't let you have, unless I died; then you could come and take them.

Tell me what you want me to do, and I'll be as compliant as possible. Myself, I think the public prefers to think that authorines are tall, slender, and nineteen years of age.

Cordially yours,
Willa S. Cather

I hope you will put something like the enclosed slip on the jacket of the book. I think a jacket ought to announce interesting subject matter, where there is any to be announced. I thought the jacket of "Sinister Street" interesting—it promised a long sight more than the book delivered, but it made me buy the volume.

The book Cather mentions, Men of Iron, *was actually a Howard Pyle book from 1891. She may have been thinking of the recent success* The Iron Woman, *which she referenced in 1912. However, the "authorine" who wrote it was Cather's friend Margaret Deland, a woman who had nursed her through an illness in her Boston home, hardly someone we would expect Cather to think of as having a "big stupid face." At any rate, she made her point to Miss Van Tuyll.*

TO ELIZABETH SHEPLEY SERGEANT

June 27 [1915]
New York City

Dear Elsie:

I have just read the mistral article in the Century with the greatest delight! I think it the best of those Provencal studies I have seen and quite wonderful in the way it rolls up so much of the soil and air and breath of the place. It's lovely and warm and <u>most</u> satisfying.

I'm still here, bound by proofs which dribble along slowly. Wonderful weather for New York; either green and gray like London, or blue and breezy like Denver. Never knew anything like it here.

Jack is Morris dancing at Eliot Maine, with Cecil Sharp. He got some sort of scholarship and was sent up from Pittsburgh with five other lads to Sharp's summer school. I believe they are to help teach it in the public schools next winter in return for their month at Eliot. Jack is simply dizzy with joy. He writes that he's so happy he wakes up at night and has a terrible moment of fear that it may not be true. He's shockingly poor, so I sent him some "sport shirts" Saturday.

When I get a big fat wad of page proofs, I'll joyfully send them along to you. But the first part ought to be read with no long waits.

The best and most musicianly musical critic I know is reading the galleys with me, and his enthusiasm is the greatest possible reassurance. We are two-thirds through and so far we have not differed on anything, except that he has urged me to keep in some musical details of her student life which I had decided to cut. In the singing lessons he says that the points are not only correct, but very telling ones to anyone who has worked with voices, in his own phrase "eloquent." That pleases me, because I got such pleasure out of all the singing lessons I heard. If I'd gone wrong I'd have hated myself! Then, too, the musical part of it is so much disguised as to be very unobtrusive to anyone who isn't interested in voices. The critic, knowing nothing about the story, was able to tell from her early lessons, just what characteristics I meant her voice to have in later life, and yet nowhere in the early lessons is her voice described or defined.

This sounds laughably boastful, doesn't it? But you see it was a very real difficulty, and I'm still panting with relief at having got over it without disaster—until Mr. [Glendinning] Keeble [of the *Pittsburgh Gazette-Times*] agreed to read the galley proofs for me, not one musician had seen a line of it. It was a risky method of procedure, but I wanted to work it out my own way.

Mary Jewett was so pleased by the article on S.O.J [Sarah Orne Jewett] in the New Republic, and so was I. I sent it [to] her at once. Have you seen article on Mrs. Fields by H. James in June Atlantic? Weren't you disappointed in Owen Wister's "Quack Novels"? Oh <u>why</u> is he a rough-neck? When he is really so clever! Well, "Litracher" (I mean lit'ra'cher) is a skin game, and no mistake.

Yours
Willa

<u>Oh</u> my new kakis for the Cliff Dwellers—Just like Kurt's in Fidelio

Henry James's article "Mr. and Mrs. James Fields" appeared in the July 1915 issue of the Atlantic Monthly *(actually published in June). Owen Wister's "Quack-Novels and Democracy" appeared a month earlier in the June 1915 issue of the same magazine.*

TO FERRIS GREENSLET

June 30 [1915]
New York City

Dear Mr. Greenslet;

I think the jacket a delight to the eye, and I think the description pasted inside the cover exceedingly good. Better say the heroine grew up in Moonstone, <u>Colorado</u>, however, not Arizona. Colorado has a considerable reading public, interested in local color, and Arizona has not. Also, Thea and Fred run away to Old Mexico, not New Mexico, which would not be much of a run, from Arizona. I wish, perhaps, that a word more could be said about her struggles in Chicago, and a word to the effect that it was the Cliff Dweller ruins that first awoke her historic imagination—so necessary to a great Wagnerian singer—and that there, away from drudgery for the first time in her life, she really grew, all at once, into a powerful and wilful young creature, got her courage, began to find herself.

I am not wholly happy about the cover, but I shan't be stubborn about it. You've never given me a cover I've liked. I've only borne them patiently. Have you a copy of the English edition of "Pioneers"? I think that a de-<u>light</u>ful cover, both as to color and composition. Couldn't you copy that cover for this book? If you have no copy of it, I'll send you mine. I'm afraid this cover will pain me as long as the book exists. I most <u>heartily</u> dislike it!

On the chance that [you] haven't one of the Heinemann books at hand, I am sending you one, along with the dummy. Please send it back to me.

I think Mr. James entirely too patronizing in his paper on the Fieldses. Mr. Fields was the collector, anyhow. The habit of gathering eagle feathers was superimposed upon Mrs. Fields. She would never have begun it of her own volition, or gone farther than keeping by her charming things that reminded her of charming people. The place was a reliquary, not a museum, and the relics were attuned to each other and had been lived with so unceremoniously and intimately that they had lost their unique quality; they had become, and were, simply Mrs. Fieldses things, and one never felt they were there to be looked at or referred to. I always thought that Jamie, himself, probably made his treasures stand out from the walls a little more, during his lifetime. But Mrs Fields enjoyed their companionship and associations, not their uniqueness. I think H. J. owes 148 Charles street a "solatium"!

Yours
Willa Cather

Please tell Mr. Scaife I will send him the screed he wants for the Boston Herald.

TO ELIZABETH SHEPLEY SERGEANT

July 28 [1915]
Pittsburgh

Dear Elsie:

I was all ready to sail for Germany this week for Mr. McClure, but at the last moment Judge McClung got nervous about the uncertain situation and would not let Isabelle go, and I did not want to go alone. So I start for Durango August 6th to air my new kakis and things. The proofs are all done. Even the page proofs were somewhat messy, and I thought I'd rather you read the book between covers. I'd like you to think as well of it as may be, and I think it will be more interesting as a book than as a mass of proofs.

Isn't "North of Boston" [by Robert Frost] a real thriller? Such individual verse, and all made out of the cold twilight-zone stuff that one has always thought pale matter for poetry. (I don't, of course, mean the avowed subject matter but the unavowed—Mr Frost's own mental reactions.) The book is so important and so devoid of splendor. Out of this shabby, ungrammatical new bunch it's so amazing to find some one who can write verse, and such real,

Achsah Brewster (left) and Edith Lewis in Italy, 1914

tight, tough verse as it is! Individual syncopation, individual intervals, queer swell in the middle of the line, and then a dreary flattening out of words to off-set it. The atmosphere (the mental atmosphere, I mean, not New England) is a little like Tchekoff, don't you think? Awfully damp, marshy mind, with June bugs. Lots of cheerfuler things, too. But he's a really, truly poet, with something fresh to say, and it's fine that he has come along. I can be more patient now even with the Witter Bynners.

You'll soon be getting hideous postcards from the West. Let me know when you and Miss Goldmark start. We may manage to meet out there.

Yours
W.S.C.

➤ ❖

In the late summer, Cather took another trip to the Southwest, this time with Edith Lewis and featuring a tour of Mesa Verde in Colorado. This tour, and especially her discussions with Richard Wetherill, who had "discovered" the cliff dwellings of Mesa Verde, were deeply influential on the "Tom Outland's Story" section of her 1925 novel The Professor's House. *Cather and Lewis got lost while touring the canyons and spent several hours waiting for their inexperienced guide to return with help from the camp of Smithsonian archaeologist Dr. Jesse Walter Fewkes. Lewis remembered that those hours waiting were Cather's "most reward-ing" of the trip, and the* New York Times *published an article about it on August 26 headed "Lost in Colorado Canon: Women Editors Suffer as Result of Trip with Inexperienced Guide."*

Throughout the summer of 1915, Cather continued her discussions of promo-tional efforts for The Song of the Lark *with Ferris Greenslet. She felt that Hough-ton Mifflin ought to play up the cliff dweller aspect of the novel, as cliff dwellers were getting quite fashionable. When the press decided to produce a booklet on Cather herself as part of their advertising campaign, she cooperated by writing a brief autobiographical sketch.*

As a result of her second trip to the Southwest, she considered writing a nonfic-tion book about the region.

TO FERRIS GREENSLET

September 13 [1915]
Red Cloud

Dear Mr. Greenslet:

I think you did a grand job on me in the booklet, and the poster delights me. Thank you for the copy of the book. I am <u>thoroughly</u> pleased with all the mechanical detail of it; cover, jacket, and typography. And I think the text looks interesting.

I have the most wonderful and glorious photographs of the Cliff Dweller ruins on the Mesa Verde, the jewels of the Denver and Rio Grande Railroad Collection, furnished me by the general Traffic Manager, who was of great assistance to me in many ways. I also have a hundred splendid photographs of the wonderful Taos region and all the Rio Grande pueblos about Espanola, near Santa Fé. Do you still want a book on the Southwest? I think I could do a good one now. Next summer we might induce the Santa Fé railroad to furnish some transportation, in which case I could run about to some of the more distant places in Arizona and finish the whole thing off, giving the story of the Santa Fé Trail along with the rest. It would be the only reasonably good book on that country ever done. Earnest Pixiotto [author and illustrator Ernest Peixotto] was down there doing a book for Scribners, and he stayed <u>one day</u> at the richest places and merely rode through the others in a motor. He's a charming man, but he knows nothing at all about the country. Miss Lewis and I met several old friends in the artist colony at Taos, among them Herbert Dunton and [Ernest L.] Blumenschein.

Please send the copies of "The Song of the Lark" due me to me at 1180 Murray Hill Ave. Pittsburgh.

If you can send me thirty copies of the booklet and fifteen of the posters, I can place them to good advantage, and please send them to me at Red Cloud.

In spite of constant climbing and horseback riding in New Mexico and Colorado, I gained six pounds which are a great grief to me, while Miss Lewis lost a few that she could ill afford to spare!

With great satisfaction in your letter and its enclosure, yours

W.S.C.

TO ELIZABETH SHEPLEY SERGEANT

September 21 [1915]
Red Cloud

Dear Elsie:

Your letter has just reached me, after countless forwardings. Five chunky pounds were the worst misfortune I got out of the Mesa Verde. We had a rough twenty-four hours, certainly, but I never learned so much in any other twenty-four hours, and most of it was glorious. Of course one would never knowingly go in for anything so difficult, no matter what the possible rewards, so it was good luck to have it thrust upon one, since we didn't break any bones. If we had had such a mischance I don't see how the men would have got us out in a week's time. It is the worst canyon in Colorado—I believe there are some in Utah even worse. I was on my horse again four days afterward, and I want to go right back into that canyon and be mauled about by its big brutality, though all my bruises are not gone yet. It's a country that drives you crazy with delight, and that's all there is to it. I can't say anything more intelligible about it.

Mr. G. has sent me an advance copy of my book; an example of the worst proof-reading I've ever seen. Mostly my fault, of course, but the Riverside Press is surely not blameless. "The beauty born of murmuring sound" appears "the music born of etc." I don't doubt it was so in the copy, but a proofreader ought to justify quotations [the phrase is a quotation from William Wordsworth]. There are a lot of others, quite as amusing. I am going to adopt a more sober method of composition, and I'll never hurry a book again. The result is too untidy. All Mr. Greenslet's work—cover type, etc.—is very satisfactory. The carelessness is mostly up to me.

I got a lot of glorious photographs in the Southwest—most of them belong to the President of the Denver & Rio Grande, but I hope I can show them to you before I send them back to him. They are the pick of hundreds of attempts; in that light, and before such heights and depths the camera becomes inarticulate—it stutters and it raves. What that country waits for is a painter, but he'll have to be a big one, with an egotism as big as the Cliff Dwellers' was. Otherwise he'll only do colored photographs.

Have you seen [Robert Frost's] "A Boy's Will" Elsie? I like it better than "North of Boston", a good deal better. Let me hear how my messy book strikes you when it comes along. I'm not a little anxious! Now as I read it over, I wonder <u>why</u> it was so much work!

With joyful greetings—joyful because the Mesa Verde exists!—

Yours
W.

❖ ❖

When The Song of the Lark *was published, in October, Houghton Mifflin produced a special "Cather" issue of their* Book News Monthly *to promote it and asked if she would supply an article, and also if perhaps S. S. McClure might write a little something. Cather dutifully supplied him with an essay about Mesa Verde.*

TO FERRIS GREENSLET

November 17 [1915]
Pittsburgh

Dear Mr. Greenslet

Here is the belated copy for the Book News. I have not written it before because Miss McClung's father grew much worse a week ago. He died on Friday and the funeral was on Sunday. So you will understand that my hands have been full. I have even had to give up going to Chicago tonight with Fremstad who has to sing some opera engagements there. I had, however, a glorious day with her in Nebraska, where our trails once more crossed. She had with her a dirty rumpled book which had once been "The Song of the Lark", and which she said had "not been read but eaten". I believe Fremstad likes the book better than anyone else does, because she knows just how much of it is her and how much is not, and the why of pretty much everything that is in the book and everything that isn't in it. I had thought she might be angry, but she only said with a shrug that there was nothing about her that was "too good to be used for an idea—when there was a <u>real</u> idea." Her enthusiasm was all the more gratifying because she liked the first three books best—especially the first one and the Arizona canyon.

I am glad, though, that none of the reviews have mentioned Fremstad. It rather belittles a book to tie it up to a personality, I think. Have you seen the notice that says the book is "the story of Geraldine Farrar"?!

I've not heard from Mr. McClure, so I fear he is not to be counted upon, though the enclosed letter will tell you that he is very much excited about the book. I also enclose a nice note from Mr. Ellsworth—who has the worst <u>possible</u> taste in books!

Yours
W.S.C.

➔ ⬅

Cather closely followed the reviews of the book, which were generally good, if not enthusiastic. Henry Walcott Boynton of the New York Evening Post *celebrated it, though, titling his review "The Great Novel Is Only a Dream but a Chapter in It Is Willa Sibert Cather's* The Song of the Lark.*"*

TO H. W. BOYNTON

December 6, 1915
New York City

My Dear Mr Boynton:

It seems impertinent to thank a critic whose opinion one values; but I hope it is not amiss for me to say that your sympathetic understanding of what I tried to do in my last book, and of some of the difficulties that made it hard for me to carry out my intentions, gives me very deep gratification and encouragement. I would also like to tell you that your review of "O Pioneers!" was a very real help to me in undertaking the longer book. In that review you suggested some feeling on your part that the cow-puncher's experience of the West was not the only experience possible there, and you seemed to feel that one might give some truthful account of life in a new country without pretending to a jovial brutality which, however much one might like to have it, cannot be successfully affected—at least, not by women.

Very sincerely yours
Willa Sibert Cather

TO ELIZABETH SHEPLEY SERGEANT

December 7 [1915]
Pittsburgh

Dear Elsie:

Miss McClung's father died three weeks ago, a week after my arrival here, and since then we have been in a half-awake state, which is why you have had no answer to your hearty and cheering letter. I do wish you might have reviewed the book. I'm especially glad you like the Mexican ball—which means the flowering of whatever is feminine in her, really—for before that she is not much more than a struggling mind. I miss the companionship of the character in a degree that is really laughable. In spite of the fact that I had given her a good many of my own external experiences—because they were handy to get at—she remained so objective that I had grown to depend on her companionship more than I realized. So often she set the pace herself, and she pulled at me until I was hers more than she was mine. I would like to feel her stretching herself inside my skin again. Another story that I have in hand seems spineless—a thing I can bully at my pleasure.

I had the good luck to meet Fremstad in Lincoln just after she had finished the book—she had seen it in Brentanos on her way to the train before leaving N.Y. and had snatched it up. I felt rather as if I had received a decoration after our first interview about it. I had thought she might be furious, but she was glowing with excitement. She declared that even the latter part had the right "stimmung" and said "you might think that it's all old stuff to me, and yet I know what she was up against and I wanted her to pull it off." But she said a great many things, which you can hear if you wish; among them was the gratifying remark that it was the only book about an artist she'd ever read in which she felt that there was "something doing in the artist."

I always regretted the rather coarse necessity of crowding her out before the footlights, but since the people interested in her were all like Dr. Archie and Johnny, it had to be done. I felt that it was up to me to give her the kind of success that even Tillie could understand, to meet the issue and do it poorly if I couldn't do it well. I dreaded it from the first chapter on, and spent many more hours in trying to shirk it than I spent in doing it at last. At any rate, I kept within the range of the Moonstone comprehension, and gave them a triumph that they could get their hands on.

I'll be in N.Y. after the Holidays. If I run down for a few days before, I'll let you know. Just now I'm finishing off a lot of small jobs. For this time, goodbye. Take warning: It's a great mistake to get in too deep with your heroine and set your watch by her; you miss her too drearily when she's gone.

Yours
W.

I enclose a notice you may not have seen.

⇢ ⇠

While receiving her own accolades for The Song of the Lark, *Cather made time to write a fan letter to Robert Frost, still very early in his writing career.*

TO ROBERT FROST

December 17, 1915
New York City

My Dear Mr. Frost:

Will you pardon an expression of gratitude from one who is very willing but utterly unable to derive much pleasure from the crackling little fire of poetical activity which is being fanned, so to speak, by a wind off Spoon River? Your two books contain the only American verse printed since I began to read verse, in which I have been able to feel much interest—the only verse of highly individual quality. The appearance of such verse seems to me a very important event, and the warmth of appreciation which it kindles in one is a pleasure to feel. I would like to believe in the whole army of poets catalogued by Mr. [Witter] Bynner and Miss [Jessie] Rittenhouse; but if Ezra Pound and Mr. Masters are poets, clearly you are none. One comes to feel ashamed of being unable to share any of this enthusiasm about "new poets", and ashamed of one's desire to ridicule. So let me thank you for the pleasure of admiring your verse,—which is "new" enough and which yet contains so many of the oldest elements of poetry.

Very sincerely yours
Willa Sibert Cather

"Spoon River" is a reference to Edgar Lee Masters's popular 1915 book of poems Spoon River Anthology.

TO ROBERT FROST

January 20 [1916]
Pittsburgh

My Dear Mr. Frost:

I am so sorry that I shall not be in New York on the date of the Poetry Society dinner. It would give me great pleasure to meet Mrs. [Elinor Miriam White] Frost and yourself. I want, among other things, to ask you if you ever happened to meet Miss Jewett. I cannot help regretting that your two volumes of verse came along too late for her to see them. They would have meant more to her than to most people, and would have helped to lighten a deep discouragement. She knew a piece of verse from a piece of Ivory Soap, and she died when none save Witter Bynner and the Phoebe Snow poets smote the lyre.

Of course, the very worst feature in your case is that most of your confreres of the Poetry Society are so fuddled by the democratic idea of "free verse" that they do not know the difference between the best line you ever made and a line from the social paragraphs of the country newspaper. For what can you hope from an audience of people who have no ear to be hurt by the screech of Florence Earle Coates (the worst old war-horse among them!) and no taste to be offended by the "congenial verse" of Ella Wheeler Wilcox? I believe that most of the young offenders are "poets" simply to oblige Miss Rittenhouse. Like every other book of worthless stuff, the Poetry Society hurts the real values temporarily. I've never yet dared go to a meeting for fear that I might be tempted to hint at something of the sort. So I shall ask you to regard these remarks as confidential. Publicity is good for poets as well as for breakfast foods—Miss Rittenhouse and her staff may be of some use to you, after all. And their methods do not silence quieter ones. In an un-evangelical way, I've put The Mountain, Mowing, Going for Water, The Tuft of Flowers [poems by Frost] and many others, before a good many people who did not have to be told anything about them after they read them, and whose ideas of—well, of anything!—have not changed because, as Mr. Masters writes "the hammock fell [/] Into the dust with Milton's poems." (Anthology p188) We can't all regard that event as symbolic!

Very cordially yours
Willa S. Cather

The Poetry Society of America was founded in 1910 to promote the reading and appreciation of poetry in the United States. "Phoebe Snow" was a character created at the turn of the twentieth century by the Lackawanna Railroad for advertising its cleaner-burning coal-powered locomotives; the ads were accompanied by short poems, like, "A cosey seat / A dainty treat / Make Phoebe's / Happiness complete / With linen white / And silver bright / Upon the Road / Of Anthracite." Cather quotes—with minor errors—"Many Soldiers" from Edgar Lee Masters's Spoon River Anthology.

TO HELEN SEIBEL

January 31 [1916]

Dear Mrs. Seibel:

I put your letter by for a rainy day; first because it is a nice sort of letter to read on a rainy day, and second because I wanted to answer it when I was not rushed and in a hurry. I have seldom got a letter about a book that pleased me more than this one of yours. You seem to have liked the book [*The Song of the Lark*] in the way in which I wanted it liked and to have read it in the spirit in which I wrote it. If I had written a preface to the book, I would have said "I for one am tired of ideas and 'great notions' for stories. I don't want to be 'literary'. Here are a lot of people I used to know and love; sit down and let me tell you about them."

From your letter, I judge that you took the book up with just such an open mind, and I am pleased to the heart of me if it gave you that sense of real people and real feelings and places which I seem to gather from your words that it did. I am just answering a letter from an American artist in Italy of whom I've never heard who wants to know if there ever was such a "piece-picture" as Mr. Kohler's or if I made it up. That's the kind of question I like to answer. I didn't play any sentimental tricks about that picture, but I cared about it, and so he cared. (Perhaps you know it hung in the fitting room of a German 'Ladies Tailor' in the East End, long and long ago. I always felt injured that I could not have had it to look at when I was a child, and this was my revenge on Fortune. It looked <u>just</u> as I say.)

It was a joyful book to write, I assure you; never a dull day while I was at it and only one long interruption—a month in Roosevelt Hospital from blood poisoning resulting from an infected scratch. That knocked me out four months altogether, but at other times all went well. It was while I was in the hospital that Mr. Seibel's mother died. I heard of it afterwards.

You are good to say you have believed in me. I haven't always in myself. But if I've made this little town full of people quite live and real to you, why then I have in a manner made good to you, have I not, though I have been absent for so long in body. I'm glad you still like those old simple things we used to laugh about and enjoy. If you did not like them, you would not like this book. Thea herself is a little different, and yet she is made up out of those same things,—plus one other big thing.

Please come to see me when you are in New York. I am afraid I shall not be in Pittsburgh very soon again, but I shall hope to see you here in my own place sometime.

Faithfully always
Willa S. C.

TO KATHARINE FOOTE

February 17 [1916]
New York City

Dear Miss Foote:

Your letter gave me great pleasure—the more because you talk in it of friends bitterly missed. You could hardly say anything that would please me more than to tell me that you think Miss Jewett would like my new book. That was a kind word for you to say, and it goes to my heart. I am so glad that you have taken pleasure in the book and that it has not offended you as a musician. I put off writing the story for years because the woman had to be a singer, and because I hate most musical novels—a compound of a story and a lot of musical criticism which never blend. Even [George Moore's 1898 novel] Evelynne Innes is such a failure as a novel. I am not a musician and I know about it only what who cares greatly for it may pick up in the course of very busy years. I never heard any music at all until I was sixteen, that means really none, and when I was seventeen I heard an orchestra and a symphony for the first time;—Theodore Thomas and the New World Symphony, in Lincoln, Nebraska. He happens to mention that day and that performance in his published letters to his wife. It was a great day for me.

So I naturally felt timid about trying to present, or even to indicate, a character and a gift like Thea's. What I tried to do was to tell the human side of her story, of course, to present it as it looked to and as it affected her friends. My theme was always her "Moonstone-ness", and what she gave back to Moonstone in the end.

Please let me know when you come to New York, I do not want to miss seeing you. If you can, send me a line before you come. I shall so love to talk to you of Mrs. Fields. I sometimes think that only one who grew up in the rawest part of what she used to call "our great west" could feel all the complete completeness of her atmosphere.

Faithfully yours
Willa Sibert Cather

I hope to see more of Miss Nielsen

Antonín Dvořák's Symphony No. 9 in E Minor "From the New World," popularly known as the "New World Symphony," was played by Theodore Thomas and the Chicago Orchestra when they were in Lincoln during their 1894–1895 season. In The Song of the Lark, *Thea Kronborg hears the orchestra play the Dvořák symphony in Chicago, and has something like a revelation: "She was too much excited to know anything except that she wanted something desperately, and when the English horns gave out the theme of the Largo, she knew that what she wanted was exactly that."*

➤ ⬅

Since their dispute over "The Profile" in 1905, Cather and Dorothy Canfield (who married John Redwood Fisher in 1907) apparently had little to do with one another. They occasionally exchanged courteous letters, however, and the one below hints at the hope Cather had for rekindling their old friendship. The review she references is an unsigned one titled "Diminuendo" published in the New Republic *on December 11, 1915, which has been identified as Randolph Bourne's. The singers mentioned in this letter are a list of many of the most celebrated female opera stars of the nineteenth and early twentieth century.*

TO DOROTHY CANFIELD FISHER

March 15 [1916]
New York City

Dear Dorothy:

I'm so glad you had <u>fun</u> with it, and so grateful to you for telling me so. It is a carelessly written book because I had so much fun writing it I could <u>not</u> be careful. Even in the proofs I fooled myself into my own fairy tale and raced ahead. The year and a half I spent writing it—about six months of the time vacation but with the story more or less in mind—went by like a dream. I never had a dull hour with her—if I'd had to work harder I'd have taken more pains and the book would be a better one. I had a lot of the chapters of the German part written, but they seemed to destroy the composition; for of course it's all really done from the Moonstone point of view. The German part had to be so different in tone, even in language, that it destroyed my point, though it made a more consistent book. For, of course, my point was not the development of a genius—my point is always Moonstone, what she got from it, what she gave back to it. It is really written in the speech of Moonstone, and when a very cultivated Russian-Jew tells me the English is loose and lacks distinction, he is right. It's not the purest Ritz-Carlton English that a Continentalized Russian would know <u>at all</u>. The whole book is practically in indirect discourse, quotation once removed. I used single quotes and double quotes until I was ashamed and gave it up.

Yes, most of the reviews have been sympathetic, but a few high, alabaster brows have clouded with pain. They say they wanted her to lose her voice, or "do something exquisite", not by any means to go through with her job successfully. I send you the best of these adverse reviews, the only interesting one. He is quite right about the title—its trashy and poor. He puts his finger on another thing. The book is done in two manners—one intimate, one remote. She goes on, but I stand still in Moonstone with Tillie, and I write from Moonstone. That change in presentation was in the very germ of the idea, and my doubt as to whether it would be convincing kept me back from writing the book for several years. But it's not because the early experience is more real than the later. It's because the heroine's life became less and less personal. The early years are the most interesting—they were to her, too. The personal life of singers like [Milka] Ternina and Fremstad arrives at the vanishing point. There is just about as much left of them as Dr. Archie saw when Thea got home after singing <u>Elsa</u>. Of course if you're doing a gay Geraldine [Farrar], that's another story. I think the book rather 'peters out', but it's because all in Thea that is proper material for fiction 'peters out', not, Heaven knows, because my interest is any less. I think that is a flaw; but I think almost any novel about an artist must have that flaw, for the order of their development is from the personal to the impersonal, when they cease to be proper material for a human story. The last chapters were written not so much for Thea as for Moonstone and Dr. Archie. She had to make good to them. And a singer is the only artist who makes good to Moonstone. Red Cloud people go to Kansas City to hear Farrar and Mary Garden. It's half art and half natural phenomenon; it's personal, concrete, a living woman, a living voice there before them. Anyhow, it's the combination that "gets" them. [Adelina] Patti, Jenny Lind, [Maria] Malibran.

Then in Red Cloud they truly love, as they say "the voice." It fills them with pleasure and content. She had to be a singer <u>for them</u>, not because I happen to go to the Opera a great deal. I wasn't trying to put something over on Red Cloud. I was writing it from their point of view. And they did like it very much. I was out there when the book came out, and the way they talked it over was a great satisfaction.

No, Dorothy, I've been unable to start a new book this winter. Judge McClung died in November, and the breaking-up of my old home there was a sad thing to live through. On April 3d Isabelle is to marry Jan Hambourg, violinist, younger brother of Mark Hambourg—but very much nicer. I am glad, for she is very happy, but the final closing up of that long Pittsburgh chapter is very hard, all the same. May Willard is coming on to stay with me for the wedding reception, which will be at Sherry's. Jan and I are not very congenial. He's a strong personality—one likes him or one doesn't. So, although Isabelle will be in New York a good deal, things can't, of course, be as they were. It's an amazing change in one's life, you see, and on the best terms one can figure out, a devastating loss to me. My old friend Mrs. Fields, of Boston, died last winter. A good many doors have been closing. The next book is there, ready to be begun, but I've felt indifferently toward it. When my interest is out of commission, I have very little wit to work with.

Are you never coming to New York? There are such a lot of things I'd love to talk over with you. Don't you think the general misery let loose in the world gets to one? I believe that when nations war the milk and cream go sour and the hens refuse to lay. Of course the pursuit of happiness is not the reality it's supposed to be. The pursuit of pain seems to be just as irradicable a human instinct, and it breaks out in spite of all the wisdom in the world. There were three Poles dining with me last night. Why do the Poles always have to bleed, no matter who cuts? I wish you were coming down, and that I could put these things up to you.

Please return this New Republic notice. It presents the other side which it's only reasonable to consider. The book moves about, and yet all hangs on the Moonstone relation—which latter fact this Mr. Bourne did not get. Anyhow, I'm glad the story gave you the same kind of "let-ones self go" feeling it gave me. Send me another note.

Yours
Willa

PART FIVE

Becoming Well Known

1916–1918

As long as one says "will people stand this, or that?" one gets nowhere. You either have to be utterly common place or else do the thing people <u>don't</u> want, because it has not yet been invented. No really new and original thing is <u>wanted</u>: people have to learn to like new things.

—WILLA CATHER TO ROSCOE CATHER, November 28, 1918

Willa Cather in front of her tent in a pasture on High Mowing farm, near Jaffrey, New Hampshire, where she wrote part of *My Ántonia*, 1917

I N THE FIRST MONTHS of 1916 the McClung home in Pittsburgh where
Cather had spent so much time so comfortably for nearly twenty years
was sold, and in April her close friend Isabelle McClung was married to violinist Jan Hambourg. An important era in Cather's life was over. No longer
would she have the kind of companionship with Isabelle that she had cherished. But after these bitter personal disappointments she turned her energies
to writing the novel by which she has been most widely known, *My Ántonia*, a story of affectionate memory set against a narrative of Czech immigrants and transplanted Virginians in the farming country and small towns of
nineteenth-century Nebraska. It was—and is—a greatly beloved book, to the
point that in Cather's later years readers were sometimes disappointed because
she didn't go on producing others in the same mode, one after another. *My
Ántonia* was also heralded by critics and fellow writers. It established her reputation and marked her arrival, after a long apprenticeship, at the status of true
literary artist. Letters written during this period show how involved Cather
was in every phase of the production of a book not only as a piece of fiction
but also as a physical object: a total work of art.

*The following two letters to Cather's brothers are a rare example of two pieces of
correspondence written on the very same day, but revealing quite different moods.*

TO DOUGLASS CATHER

July 8 [1916]
Columbian Hotel, Taos, New Mexico

My Dear Douglass:

Edith [Lewis] and I are here again after five gritting hot days in Denver. The nights are cool here and the days are hot for only a few hours. We can get excellent horses. Edith is a showy rider, and I can at least manage to get about on a horse and don't much mind a rough trail.

You said you were coming north in July. I wonder how far north? As far as Albuquerque, for instance? Unless there is some good chance of meeting you we shall probably not stir far from here. Perhaps we may take another driving trip among the Rio Grande pueblos about Española, if Edith is well enough. Edith must be in New York on the 25th of July, and I am afraid her vacation so far has been more interesting than restful. After she leaves me I may go to Lander [Wyoming, Roscoe's home]. Eventually I will reach Red Cloud, and then I hope I can persuade mother to go to Denver for a couple weeks, as Elsie writes that she is not well. I want to stay at home for a month or two, if it is agreeable to everybody, but I won't stay after I begin to get on anybody's nerves. I shall always be sorry that I went home last summer, because I seemed to get in wrong at every turn. It seems not to be anything that I do, in particular, but my personality in general, what I am and think and like and dislike, that you all find exasperating after a little while. I'm not so well pleased with myself, my dear boy, as you sometimes seem to think. Only in my business one has to advertise a little or drop out—I surely do not advertise or talk about myself as much as most people who write for a living—or one has to drop out. I can't see how it would help any of my family any if I lay down on my oars and quit that rough-and-tumble game. It would be easy enough to do that. I've had a very hard winter and have got no work done except two short stories—one very poor. Judge McClung's death and Isabelle's marriage have made a tremendous difference in my life. The loss of a home like that leaves one pretty lonely and miserable. I can fight it out, but I've not as much heart for anything as I had a year ago. I suppose the test of one's decency is how much of a fight one can put up after one has stopped caring, and after one has found out that one can never please the people they wanted to please. I suppose it's playing the game after that, that counts.

However, the truth is usually gloomy, and one doesn't have to talk about it all the time, thank goodness. I don't see why you and I can't meet and do things together, even if you find my sort trying. I know I'm "trying". Most women who have been able to make over a hundred dollars a month in office work, have been spoiled by it in one way or another. It is bad for all of them and it was bad for me. But even so, I don't see why we can't make it go better, and have lots of good times together. I enjoyed every minute that I was with you in Denver last year. I can have a better time with you than with almost anybody, when you are not grouchy. And when you are grouchy, after this, I'll simply flit. I won't sit around and weep. I can't be hurt again as badly as I was last summer. After this I'll be more philosophical; I won't expect too much, and I mean to enjoy any goodwill or friendship I get from any of my family. I enjoy every single member of my family when they are half-way friendly toward me. I enjoy them a great deal more now than I did in my younger days when I kept trying to make everybody over. My first impulse, of course, is to think that my own way of seeing things is the right way. But my second thought is always to admit that this is wrong and that I have been often mistaken. I even think I've grown a good deal milder in the last year—I've had trouble enough and losses enough. Three friends died during the winter whom it seemed to me I could not get on without. And perhaps the disapproval I got at home last summer has been good for me. I am quite a meek proposition now, I can tell you. I think I've had my belting, and it has taken the fizz out of me all right—and I'll tell you this, it's positively shipwreck for work. I doubt whether I'll ever write anything worth while again. To write well you have to be all wrapped up in your game and think it awfully worth while. I only hope I'm not so spiritless I won't be able to make a living. I had two stories turned down this winter because they had no "pep" in them. The editors said they hadn't and I knew they hadn't.

Be sure to meet me somewhere if you can. I think you'll find me easier to get on with. Time is good for violent people.

Yours with much love
Willie

TO ROSCOE CATHER

July 8 [1916]
Taos, New Mexico

I got your letter just as Miss Lewis and I were leaving Denver for Taos. I would have preferred Lander, but Edith wanted very much to return here, where we had a delightful week last summer. Probably we shall be here for about two weeks now. I hope I can go up to Lander on our return trip. Eventually I shall get to Red Cloud. I hope I can get Mother to go to Denver for two weeks, as Elsie writes that she is not at all well. I am impatient to see the little West Virginia [Roscoe's daughter Virginia]. Perhaps I shall stay at home until the late fall. The last winter has been a sort of Waterloo for me; my best and oldest friends dying or marrying all winter long. I got nothing done the whole winter long and spring long but two short stories. You probably saw the Century one—bad enough!—the other, sold to McClure's, is much better. I have a new idea for a novel which I'd like to talk over with you—not very new, none of my ideas ever are. I don't seem to have acquired a single new idea since Sandy Point [the make-believe town of their childhood]. The trouble about this story is that the central figure must be a man, and that is where all women writers fall down. I get a great many bouquets about my men, but if they are good it is because I'm careful to have a woman for the central figure and to commit myself only through her. I give as much of the men as she sees and has to do with—and I can do that much with absolute authority. But I hate to try more than that. And yet, in this new-old idea, the chief figure must be a boy and man. I'd like to talk it over with you. You might help me a good deal. I wish you'd kept a diary on your Yellowstone trip of long ago—It's a little that kind of story.

Pardon this spidery scrawl: Five Jewish travelling men waiting for the one ink bottle in this adobe hotel. It's kept by a Mexican woman and a parrot that speaks french—property of her late husband, who was a Frenchman. Taos is a beautiful place, you know, forty dreadful miles across canyons from the railroad; all Mexicans, no whites, wonderful Indian pueblo near the Spanish town. I like the Mexican woman and her cool clean hotel and her grand manner. I wish you could do some of these things with me. But life is so awfully one-sided; if you keep free you're too damned free, and if you tie up—why, there you are.

Isabelle has married a very brilliant and perfectly poisonous Jew. Not one of her old Pittsburgh friends can endure him. Nice situation for me. I think I shall travel rather light after this.

Goodnight, my boy. I want awfully to see you and Meta.

Lovingly
Willie

The "bad enough" story was "The Bookkeeper's Wife"; the "much better" one was "The Diamond Mine." Cather called Roscoe's daughter "West Virginia" because she lived in the West, to distinguish her from Jessica's daughter, also named (Mary)

Virginia. The new story resembling Roscoe's trip to the Yellowstone may be My Ántonia, *which is told from the perspective of a boy and a man, but might possibly be "The Blue Mesa," which finally became the central section of* The Professor's House.

❧ ❧

After traveling in New Mexico, Cather went to Lander, Wyoming, in July to visit Roscoe and his family, including his infant twin daughters, Margaret and Elizabeth. By August, she returned home to Red Cloud.

TO ROSCOE CATHER

Sunday [August 20, 1916]

My Dear Boy;

This is the first moment I've had alone. The day after I got here I had to make a speech to Gertie Coon's Institute. West Virginia is such fun that I fool a lot of time playing with her. She's a totally new kind of child to me and mighty interesting. I love her pretty little voice and cunning face. Her grandmother makes a brave show of discipline, but she babies her in secret and I fear the strong hand has relaxed a good deal. I don't think Virginia has ever been homesick except on the one sad day when she saw her grandfather with his teeth out and cried all day, wailing "I am so ashamed of my grandfather." She will be a hard child to bring up, I suspect, because she is very individual and because she seems to have no eye to the main chance. She will spoil a whole picnic about which she really cares a great deal because she can't wear a certain hair ribbon, when she does not really care which ribbon she wears. Compromises seem foreign to her, and I suppose she will have to learn to yield in trifles to get the big thing about which she really cares. After she and her grandmother have a strong difference of opinion as to whether one should play in the rain-water tub with one's white dress on, she never holds a grudge but comes up smiling. Her uncle Doug and I both think she has about the sweetest little voice in the world. You must be stern with her when she is fussy about which seat she will sit in or which ribbon she will wear, brother, for it will make her life simpler and stronger. People's lives always get messy if they don't acquire a sense of proportion. It's about the only direction in which I think she needs improving. All her personal habits are charming. I want to see her learn good business, and not spoil the party for some little personal quirk—it will smooth the next ten years out for her so. I think she's intelligent enough to see these things even now if you talk to her. Her dear grandmother can't help her much there, for the ribbon or the jelly we forgot to bring home spoiled so many hours for grandmother herself. Mary Virginia and Tom [Auld] have learned not to fuss because they like to do things with their grown up aunts and uncles who won't be bored with it—and this in spite of the fact that their mother [Jessica] encourages them to fuss.

I don't know what Jim [Cather] is going to do—no mortal could tell!—but if you have to come for V—, don't come too soon. We all get so much pleasure of her and would miss her terribly. She and her grandmother have lovely times and I like to see them together. It's quite touching the way mother loves her and keeps coming in at night to look at her—and mother is sure no sentimentalist.

Do you know, I miss Margaret and Elizabeth as if they were real persons, and I wish they were old enough to write letters to. Please ask Mr. Sproul to make four prints of each of the three pictures of me and the twins in the back yard. I am very proud of them and want to send them to several people, Jack [Cather] and Isabelle among them. Ask him to mail the pictures to me, with the bill, just as soon as he can.

When I went to Lander I was certainly sick in my mind. I was morbid and saw everything darkly. I came away another person. I am happy and well, and everything looks good to me. The twins really smoothed out my troubles with their sweet good little ways, and our long horseback rides just set me up in spirit. Then it was such a pleasure to get to know Meta and to find that we could be such congenial companions. You know how I am—I don't mean to be difficult, but if I can't like, I can't. I've always been just a little timid about going to Lander, for fear that Meta and I couldn't catch step, and I knew it would make me very sad, and you, too. Now I feel as if Meta and I could travel about and take the twins along and not get bored with each other. And travelling is that high-pressure test of congeniality. I hope we three can run about together a little someday. I wish I'd gone to Lander five or six years ago, but it never could have done me more good than it has this summer. I miss the twins aw-ful-ly! I find myself talking about them all the time. Did they like the bear Isabelle sent?

With a whole heart-ful of love to you and Meta

Willie

Don't forget to order the photographs of me and twins!

➤ ❖

In August, Cather's editor at Houghton Mifflin, Ferris Greenslet, wrote asking if she might have another book ready for them for their 1917 list. The Song of the Lark, *he noted, was selling strong.*

TO FERRIS GREENSLET

August 22 [1916]
Red Cloud

Dear Mr. Greenslet:

I have been up in the Wind River Mountains in northern Wyoming for a month, and reached home today. Your letter greets me with cheering news. Have you seen Alice Maynell's review of the book in the Manchester Guardian? The Westminster Gazette is also excellent. Indeed all the English reviews are very gratifying.

Oh yes, I will certainly have another book ready by the end of next year. It will probably be a story of the Southwest, and the title will probably be "The Blue Mesa" or something of that sort, and it will be full of love and hate. I've not written a word of it yet, but I shall get to work the first of September, after our family-reunion house-party here is over. I shall try to work here, and if things go well I shall not go to New York before November or December. I ought to be able to pull copy out pretty fast after I do settle down to work. Last winter was a hellish winter, but I've forgotten it. I left the last memory of it above [the] timber line in the Wind River mountains.

Yes, I think the book on the Southwest will come along right after the novel—out of the leavings. But the novel first.

Please, when you next write to England, order eight copies of the English edition of The Lark for me. I hope I can get them before Christmas.

Thank you for your good cheerful letter. I'm keen to fall to.

Faithfully
W.S.C.

TO DOROTHY CANFIELD FISHER

September 2 [1916]
Red Cloud

My Dear Dorothy:

I have just dropped down in Red Cloud after three glorious months in New Mexico and Wyoming. My brother Roscoe lives up in the Wind River mountains in Wyoming, and he has an interesting German wife and a little girl of five and cunning girl twins with whom I had the most fun. Here is a picture of them playing with me in their lovely back yard which has a mountain river rushing through it. We rode home—back from over the wildest mountain trails, and I was "requested to speak" on [Canfield Fisher's novel] "The Bent Twig" to a bridge club! If I could remember my remarks, I'd write them to you. I think it's funny that we both hit on rather the same method of treatment for such very different characters. And I think in both books the early part, and the American small town, came out the best, though you do it rather from the standpoint of the law-maker and I from that of the law-breaker, or at least of the rebel who bootlessly kicks against the pricks. I feel rather like poor Molly, who bolted out of the moral law in her car. That's the best use for a car I've ever discovered. If the Army of Unalterable Law closes in on me too hard, I'd escape like Molly, so I would. I do like the naughty ones, Molly and Aunt Victoria, better than the 90 and 9 obedient—except the mother; on the whole I think she is the dominating figure of the book. I don't feel that she particularly enjoyed her own scheme of life, Dorothy, only that her intelligence was too good to deceive herself. Here's a recast: There was just such a Maine woman who used to come to spend the afternoon with Fremstad once when I was visiting O.F. in Maine. What a beautiful, noble, sad—and humorous—face she had. She knew all about O. F. (how she was made) God knows how, but she did. Two of her sons had just had their eyes blown out dynamiting orchards, and her dignity and graciousness under such a misfortune was beyond anything. It was so interesting to see the two women together—so much wisdom in one and so much force in the other. I used to go about thanking God that Fremstad didn't know as much as the farm woman, for if she had she would not have been any good,—See? If she had seen what the other woman saw she positively couldn't have lifted a leg to sing a part, ever. Great wisdom is like Nirvana—it takes the "pep" out of people. You know I always liked the Romans because they were so non-wise and so full of "pep". It's blooming, full-blooded ignorance that makes the bright show, after all. And, my dear, whether it's a wheat-thrashing or an opera, it's the Bright Show that I love. I can't help it. It's like hearing the band play when you are little; my feet begin to move, and <u>nothing else makes them move</u>, alas!

Do you know that in Lincoln my readers and your readers—please don't be insulted if I tell you that yours outnumber mine 20 to 1—<u>always</u> fight whenever our names come up? Yours say insulting things about me, and mine say drastic things about you. Yours say they can't read me because it's all rot and most immoral, and mine (only about six) say they can't read you because you are dull. You have the Geres, and the Westermanns, alas for me, and the university people, and <u>Will Owen Jones</u>—you're welcome to him, madame—and I have five German brewers and Sarah Harris, who still cries out to a deaf world that Bessie Tuttle and I are Geniuses. But they never do discuss us like ladies, their eyes begin to snap and they begin to buzz like hornets. Mariel [Gere] is especially bitter agin poor me; she says that just because my bad morals are not <u>very</u> vulgar they are the more insidious and that there is a flavor about me she simply can't stand. I like the Geres and dearly love the Westermanns, and I was a good deal hurt at first, but there's nothing to do but get what fun I can out of their loyalty to you. Old father Westermann you never got away from me, for he was really a brewer at heart, and old Dr. [Julius] Tyndale's life is one long warfare agin your admirers. I wish you could go to Lincoln. My Public tactfully tell me all that your Public say about me, and cry imploringly "She didn't live with him in Mexico anyhow, did she?"

Father and Mother are both well, all the nieces and nephews handsome and happy, and grown brothers and sisters coming and going, checking baggage in and checking out like a hotel. It's very jolly to be here.

Lovingly
Willa

TO FERRIS GREENSLET

December 16 [1916]
New York City

Dear Mr. Greenslet;

Miss [Hanna Astrup] Larsen, one of the editors of the Scandinavian Review, and Ann Erika Fries, a Swedish writer and a lecturer on Scandinavian literature, have both suggested to me that there is a strong probability that we can have a Swedish and perhaps a Norwegian translation of "The Song of the Lark" and "O Pioneers!" if we bring them to the attention of the proper persons. Nielsen, the Danish poet made the same suggestion about the earlier book when he was here two years ago. He advised me, however, not to take it up through any American-Swedes, like [Edwin] Bjorkman, who all have irons of their own in the fire. Lacking addresses of the right people abroad, I thought no more about it then. Miss Larsen and Mrs. Fries, however, have given me the names and addresses of several publishers and critics to whom they think review copies should be sent. They feel quite confident that I would get good results from approaching these gentlemen, and perhaps get a fine translation which would have a considerable career in the Scandinavian countries.

It seems to me that you could take this matter up with the foreign publishers and the critics who read for them, more gracefully than I could. If you wrote each gentleman a letter, enclosing a copy of Edward Garnett's article in the Atlantic of last February (?) and sent to each copies of the two books, it would be much better than anything I could do. This, I know, would be a good deal of trouble, and I don't know that there would be any direct return to the house from a Scandinavian translation, but there would be a great deal of satisfaction and stimulus in it for me. I have been wanting to ask you whether you could attend to it for me, for six weeks or more now, but I've hesitated to come to the point. If you hate to write letters as much as I do, it is asking a good deal of you, especially as you will probably have to write letters long enough to give reasonable pretext for asking these gentlemen to examine the books. I think the Garnett article will help. They will all know him, in any case.

I enclose a list of the men most approachable and influential. If, in your letter to [Carl Joachim] Hambro, you mention the fact that the reviews in the Musical Courier and in Musical America said that the character of Kronborg was drawn after Olive Fremstad, it would engage his attention. He himself translated my McClure article on Fremstad and published it in the Morgenbladet with fine illustrations.

Now, another request. If you have any of those booklets you wrote about me to advertise the "Lark", will you send me three dozen! I have sent every one of those you gave me to women's clubs and people who write to me asking for "a short biography." Those books have saved me time and misery, and I want a lot of them. I am saving three requests for biographical matter until I can get some of those booklets from you, and I hope you have a supply still on hand.

Just now I am finishing up some short stories for [literary agent] Paul Reynolds. By the first of the year he will have made me so rich that I can afford to bone down on my long story, which will probably come rather slowly at first. I have promised to do an article for the American, but I think I can wriggle out of that. When are you coming to New York? I would have liked to talk this attack on the Scandinavian publishers over with you. I have it very much on my mind and want to go at it in the proper way. I think it ought to be done through my American publisher, and your exposition of the two books in the booklet for which I am now begging, makes me think that you could write to this group of highbrows more effectively than anyone else, if you are willing to undertake such a chore. As soon as my telephone is in, I will send you my number. I wish you were going to be in town on Thursday night and could dine here at seven with Isabelle and her husband. Let me know if by any chance you are to be here. S. S. Mc.[Clure] will be here, and will tell you all about the war. He is really very interesting about it. Harry Dwight will be here. Do you know him?

Faithfully
Willa S.C.

TO ELSIE CATHER

December 30 [1916]

Dear Bobbie:

How clever you were to go to Chicago and have your party just as you planned! I am so glad you did. Those things do one a lot of good. Jack could not come. We had a quiet Xmas for Edith's eye was bad again. Xmas Eve I went to the Hambourgs for dinner, and Xmas night we had Joe Charter, our young widower and [Pitts] Sanborn the musical critic of the Globe here for dinner and sent them away at 9 oclock because of the game eye (Edith's).

Yesterday we were in health and had a very gay Friday afternoon, about 30 people came, many of them friends from Pittsburgh here for the holidays, among them Alfred McClung. After tea I had to dash up to the Biltmore to dine with some friends from Boston. Today I'm quite tired, but I had to go to a concert with the Hambourgs this afternoon. On Wednesday I lunched at their home with Harold Bauer, the pianist, and his wife, and [Fritz] Kreisler the violinist. Isabelle makes a charming hostess for artists and celebrities.

Isabelle and Jan gave me two beautiful Russian candelabra for Christmas, beautiful design and each one holds five candles. They make a lovely light for tea. We have also a new tea table, but our grandest possessions are three wonderful new paintings—scenes along the Mediterranean and the Ionian sea by her artist friend, Earl Brewster, who lives in Italy. They are so large and handsome that it will positively impoverish us to frame them. His pictures bring from $200 to $500 each now, and these are very fine ones. They are not a gift outright, but he says he wants us to keep them for years and years.

I have a trifling little story ["A Gold Slipper"] in Harper's Monthly this month. It might amuse you if you happen on it. It is so bad that I got $450 for it. I quite needed the money. The 'high cost of living' makes our expenses here about a third more than they were last year. It takes 25¢ worth of apples to make one pie, and chickens are 42¢ a pound. A five pound chicken costs $2.10! Beef is 36¢, nearly as bad.

Well, we'll probably manage to keep the wolf off Bank street somehow, and meanwhile I positively rejoice in your Chicago adventures, my dear Bobbie.

With much love
Willie

TO MARY VIRGINIA BOAK CATHER

Saturday [early 1917?]

My Dearest Mother;

The napkins are simply lovely—much the nicest ones I have, and I thank you so much for remembering Isabelle. She was so pleased. She is going to use hers as table-doylies, as she always has her little table set with doylies and without a table-cloth. It is less work for her and better suited to studio dinners. Isn't it funny; Isabelle, who always lived in such a substantial, well-ordered house with such solidity and regularity about it, really likes this studio sort of life. And I, who had to knock about for so long, love to run my apartment as methodically and regularly as a well kept-house. It really means "success in life" to me to be able to do that. If I had to live in a studio apartment and eat in my parlor, it would just mean failure and wretchedness to me. Isabelle is poor this winter—Jan has lost his grand job tutoring the millionaire's children, for the children have been put in schools—so perhaps Isabelle pretends to like living in three rooms better than she does. Of course they are lovely rooms, with lovely things in them, and beautifully kept.

I took her napkins up to her on Xmas eve, as I was dining there. She had me and my friend Pitts Sanborn the musical critic, and Mr. Goehghan [Harold Geoghegan] of Pittsburgh, Jack's favorite teacher, you remember. She had cooked all the dinner herself right there in the tiny closet-kitchen opening off the parlor, and it was delicious; <u>real terrapin soup</u>, a leg of mutton beautifully cooked, plain boiled potatoes in their skins, grapefruit salad, good wine, and for dessert a chocolate cake bought at an excellent bakery. Very little, everything the best of its kind. After dinner she looked so tired that my heart ached for her.

She and Jan were here at the dinner we gave for Fremstad, also Mr. Sanborn. There was a blizzard that night, all the guests were late, and I had to carry coal all day and stoke the fires to get the house warm. I almost never had such a nice party. I got the flowers for the table fixed just right—one can't always get them <u>just</u> right—pale yellow roses and white narcissus in a white Japanese bowl. Your long tablecloth did service again. We had oysters on the half shell, soup, roast turkey and cranberries and canned peas, salad, and caramel ice-cream with freshly-made maringues. Everybody was so gay and jolly. Fremstad insisted on singing a little although I have no piano. If I had a piano here, what wonderful music I could have sometimes!

Both last Friday and yesterday we had lots of people for tea—all we could make comfortable. So many old Pittsburgh friends are in town for the holidays I have had a rushing week of it—have really neglected my work in a way that I don't often do. The Hambourgs and Jack's professor and Sanborn are to dine here New Year's eve. The first of this week Edith had a dinner for some of her friends, and she was feeling so badly I had to manage it and help Josephine [Bourda] with the table, and do the marketing. I always do the marketing and all the housekeeping when I am here. I like it, but it <u>does</u> take time, and now I've got behind with my book and am getting nervous. I'm going to cut out parties for the first two months of the New year.

Now, mother dear I must stop. But don't discourage Father in his Red Cross and Home Guards, mother. Such work is very good for him and wakens him up. He won't be rash with contributions. If he is more interested than his sons it is to his credit, not to theirs, I am sure. But Jack is not interested in anything but the war, and I think Ross [Roscoe] would be full of it if he was not kept pegging away pretty hard by his little family. But it is a splendid time for father, and I'd be awfully ashamed if he did not help all he can.

Goodbye now, dear mother. The struggle to get coal and sugar here now is awful. I spend whole afternoons trying to get a few bushels of coal. I hope you are warm and comfy down there, and that you get some comfort out of all your children for they all love you very dearly, and I know we grow closer together as we grow older, and will understand each other better every year. I send you a heartful of love, dear mother, and I am so pleased with the napkins.

Willie

This is a piece of the new dinner dress I am having made.

TO MARY VIRGINIA BOOK CATHER

February 2, 1917

Dearest Mother:

I am so worried to hear that you have a cold. Please go to Yuma if it does not get better. Surely it will improve before long when you are out of doors so much every day. I am glad you have found congenial people at your boarding house, as I know that one cannot get on without people. I think that sometimes pleasant, friendly strangers are more of a rest to one than one's own family or than one's old friends. One makes more of an effort for them, and the effort does one good. I am writing in bed, as I am taking a few days off with my "friend". I think the specialist, Dr. Van Etten, whom Dr. Wilner sent me to is doing me good, and I hope he will gradually regulate that trouble until I wont lose so much strength every month. He says my nerves and general health will be ever so much better if he can reduce that waste to normal.

We are all terribly upset here by the turn the war has taken. I have written father about how it affects us in many ways, and have asked him to send you the letter.

I have got such a nice black silk bag, with gay beads on it, to send Auntie Sister for Easter. I got it for one dollar at Wanamaker's sale as I was hurrying through the store to buy sash-curtains. I am so pleased, for I believe she will like it very much. It is very "genteel" for an old lady.

It is costing us fifty dollars a month more to live than it did last winter, and we have cut out the opera altogether, and most concerts. We get free tickets to a good many theaters. Mrs. Deland wrote me for ten dollars for the Belgians last week. As I had been ill in her house for three weeks after that operation in Boston, I could not well refuse.

Jack is back in Pittsburgh again doing some temporary work, but I am afraid his job can't last long now that all trade with England will have to stop. His letters have been rather braggy lately, and I wrote him a long lecture about it yesterday. I don't want him to be boastful with our friends in Pittsburgh. It would make him look too ridiculous. He has always been nice and modest and I hope he is not going to lose it. I expect this is only a passing moment of large-heartedness.

I will send you the February magazines, dear mother, as soon as they are all in, and I want to send West Virginia a valentine if I get out in time. I will also send Mrs. Letson a book I think she will like.

This is Friday, and I still have to get up for awhile this afternoon to see the people who come in for tea. I hope not many will come. I use the lunch cloth you gave me every Friday for tea. I have some of Isabelle's silver here while she is away, and it makes the tea table look very pretty.

With much love, dear Mother
Willie

➙ ⬏

Though Cather had been talking about "The Blue Mesa" as her next novel through-out 1916, the next letter makes it clear that she has now put that manuscript aside and moved on to My Ántonia. *The "set of six stories" she mentions below is* Office Wives, *a never-published collection to be made up of stories about women in the world of office work.*

TO R. L. SCAIFE

March 8, 1917
New York City

My Dear Mr. Scaife;

As soon as I returned to New York at the end of November, I put aside the notes of "The Blue Mesa" to take up another novel,—a Western story which will run about the same length as "O Pioneers!" and which has a somewhat similar background. I am now about half-way through with the first writing of this story.

Please tell me, what is the latest date on which I could turn in the manu-script for fall publication? I know that I will not have finished it by the end of April. By the end of May, or the middle of June, it may be quite ready for the printer.

In case you give me a date so early that I feel I cannot make it, I shall prob-ably put the long story aside and take up a set of six short stories which I have arranged to do for Reynolds. He can get me $700 apiece for them, so of course it would be better business than completing the novel. If it is possible to get the novel ready for fall publication without rushing it too hard, however, I would rather finish it, now that I am so far along in it.

I think Mr. Greenslet is rather to be envied for having an enforced holiday in an interesting part of the world [England].

Very sincerely yours
Willa Sibert Cather

→ ←

Scaife replied that Houghton Mifflin would like the manuscript by June 1 for fall publication, but might be able to accept it as late as August. Cather's response below suggests how invested she was in the physical design of this book from the very beginning.

TO R. L. SCAIFE

March 13 [1917]

Dear Mr. Scaife;

Since you can give me such good lee-way, I think I ought to be able to get the story done in time for fall publication. I can get you some sort of prospectus done when you need it, and, if you think best give you the first few chapters in time to have them set for your July program.

Unless I can find just the right person to do some head and tailpieces, I had rather not have illustrations. As for the cover design, I rather wish you could reproduce the "Song of the Lark" cover in a darker blue, a strong navy blue, with, of course, quite a different jacket. I wish you could have a bright yellow jacket, with very heavy black type, if that paper would not be too expensive. However, we can take up these things later. For the present I will push ahead with the manuscript, and I shall try to give you some more definite idea of its length and character very soon——by the middle of April.

Faithfully yours
Willa Cather

→ ←

On Cather's suggestion, Scaife spoke with dance trainer Luigi Albertieri (whom Cather had written about in her 1913 article in McClure's *"Training for the Ballet") about a proposed book on the dance, and he checked out the sales history of* Green Mansions *by William Henry Hudson, one of the young publisher Alfred A. Knopf's first successes. He also suggested a couple of potential artists should Cather want illustrations for her new western book.*

TO R. L. SCAIFE

April 7 [1917]
New York City

Dear Mr. Scaife;

I will be glad to help in any way about Albertieri's book. I don't suppose he will want to split it, as from his point of view it seems a complete and logical presentation of the subject.

With regard to the decoration of my book, I think [Wladyslaw T.] Benda might be able to do it. His half-tone illustrations are rather too mannered, but he used to do good head and tailpieces, and he knows the material. I will try to have a talk with him and let you know about it later. The samples of binding I will return soon, naming a first and second choice. Within the next four weeks I shall know whether this story is going to come together in time for fall publication or not. I think it will.

I hear from a bookseller in Oxford Junction, Iowa, that he has had several orders for "O Pioneers!" and has been utterly unable to fill them. Will you please have a notice to the effect that there is a new printing of the book to; Mr. Arthur Grimwood, Oxford Junction, Iowa.

Isn't there a statement of sales due me sometime in April?

If I can't get better reports of "Green Mansions" than you did, I am afraid I shall have to send you some candy.

Faithfully
Willa S. Cather

→ ←

Despite her intentions, Cather was unable to get the manuscript for My Ántonia *done in time for publication in 1917. She was also, like most Americans, distracted by the United States's declaration of war on Germany in early April.*

TO ELSIE CATHER

May 4 [1917]

My Dear Bobbie;

I have simply been ashamed to write you, because I had neglected it for so long. I've tried to write mother often this winter, and while Jack was sick I tried to get a few notes off to him because he seemed blue and hated Detroit, but I've neglected everyone else. I kept putting off writing to Mrs. Deland though I knew Mr. [Lorin F.] Deland was very ill, and yesterday he died, and I do feel more than ashamed. The war has made everything so much more difficult, housekeeping and meeting ones bills,—and it has taken all the fun of work away, somehow. One can't feel that writing books is very important. I am fairly stuck on the novel I wrote you about, and will either have to give it up or try it over again a new way. Two Houghton Mifflin men were here last night and I had to make the sad admission to them that I couldn't get a new book out this fall. They are disappointed, and so am I. There is a great deal that's good in the new story, but I have not gone at it right, somehow, and I'm going to quit it for awhile and do some short stories to build up my bank account.

Did you know that Kipling's only son, John, who was the Dan of the Puck [of Pook's Hill] stories, was lost in the war, and they don't even know how or where. They have not heard of him for over a year and have given up hoping. Mr. Greenslet, of Houghton Mifflin, just back from England, told me last night that the old man is all broken up and sees nobody. Life has gone pretty hard with him, and he has given so much pleasure in this world.

Edith has been pretty well this winter. I blue-stone her eyes for her every week, which saves occulists' bills, and time, too. We are going down to Washington tonight for a few days. But the magazine business is cramped and made harder by the war. High cost of ink and paper take all the profits and shut down advertising.

I have been to a lot of very gay musical parties with the Hambourgs, and I had such a joyful dinner party for Fremstad and her new husband [Harry L. Brainard]. Everything went just right and I never saw her enjoy herself so much. I wrote mother all about it, and she probably sent you my letter.

People connected with the British war office tell me that they don't hope to end the war under two years. Even at the best London hotels Greenslet could get only two courses for each meal, and a miserable bit of boiled beef three days a week, no other meat at all. He was uncomfortabl[y] hungry for the two months he was there, and hotels and public buildings were unheated all winter. The papers give no idea of what the submarines have really done. If America had not gone in, the allies would have been beaten, that is the grim truth. The submarines have cut off all chance of feeding the army. The food situation is much worse in England and northern France than it is in Germany. If we can build boats fast enough to keep the Allied armies going, and if we can reinforce their numbers with men, it may be over in two years. If we don't do this, we will have to be Prussians in the end. Russia is helpless. Unless the allies can keep the whole German army busy on the French front, the Germans will take St. Petersburg, and enough Russian grain and farm land to enable them to go forever. The United States has never had such a chance before; no country ever has. We can literally save Democracy————or lose it————for the whole world. And [m]y nice guide on the Mesa Verde writes me that the war is "considered a joke" out there. We are a good deal like Russia; so big and unorganized. Take it from me, Bobbie, the next year is going to be a black one.

Now I must stop for this time, dear girl. I'll try to do better hereafter, if you forgive me.

With heaps of love to you
Willie

TO ROSCOE CATHER

June 23 [1917]
Red Cloud

My Dear Roscoe;

I have never answered the nice letter you wrote me about Virginia's tooth, though all my friends in New York had to hear the story. I came west suddenly because the University of Nebraska wrote me that they wanted to give me an honorary degree on their Semi-Centennial Commencement. They gave me and Edith Abbott (she is Jane Addams' assistant and some wonder in sociology) Doctor of Letters, the first honorary degrees ever granted to women. They gave John Neihardt the poet Lit.D. also, and Doctor of Laws to [Theodore] Roosevelt, Roscoe Pound and Gen. [John] Pershing. Elsie was in Lincoln visiting, and Daddy came up from Red Cloud. I think it was so nice of him! Barnard McNeny was there and he seemed no end pleased. I was pleased because all my old teachers seemed pleased with me. There have been very few honorary degrees given to women in this country; not more than a dozen all told, and most of them to great educators like Alice Freeman Palmer and Jane Addams.

Tell me, Roscoe, do you think there would be a furnished house for rent in Lander from July 15 to August 15? Edith Lewis comes west then, and we may go up into your part of the world. Don't bid us come to you, for Edith wont visit anyone, she won't even stop here, I'm afraid. Let me know soon if you have heard of a house to let for that month. The Amoretti ranch at five dollars a day seems rather expensive for war times. Do they make a better rate by the month?

Poor twin-ies! Their aunt's degree cost them some dear little dresses. I had to close apartment and leave New York on three days' notice and all my summer shopping and theirs went by the board. But someday they shall have some dresses from New York.

Lovingly
Willie

Daddy and Elsie are both fine.

→ ←

Cather wrote about the same events to her friend Elizabeth Sergeant and to her editor Ferris Greenslet, providing us rare examples of the way the tone and content of letters vary with different addressees.

TO ELIZABETH SHEPLEY SERGEANT

June 23 [1917]
Red Cloud

Dear Elsie:

Even if I could have answered your letter within a decent time, I could not have given you the least help. Your own book is the only new one I have read with any pleasure. Most of the ones I've tried have been thick slices of commonness. The New Republic would point you to Mrs. [Katharine Fullerton] Gerould would it not? Have you tried Mary Austin's new novel "The Ford"—unfortunate title for anyone but the Williamsons!

I came west unexpectedly and unprepared because the faculty of the University of Nebraska wanted to give me an honorary degree—Doctor of Letters—on their semi-centennial commencement. Edith Abbott, Miss Addams' assistant was given the same degree. They were the first honorary degrees that university has given to women. I was pleased because it came from that institution and this state.

After Commencement came ten days of intensive visiting. Lord, how many people I saw, and at how many parties did I try to be merry! I enjoyed the first few, but there is an innocent sameness about these festivities on green lawns with oldish girls in white dresses and stranded professors from "Maine, N.H., Rhd. I., VT".

Red Cloud is patriotic and bubbling hot—the amorous sinners of Dante were no more persistently singed by fire than are the corn-country dwellers in

July and latter June. Corn-germination takes a terrific degree of heat, and we pant under a kind of magnificent fire all day, with the air full of sweet, hot smells.

I go to Wyoming soon. This address will reach me, however.

Yours.
WSC

TO FERRIS GREENSLET

June 25 [1917]
Red Cloud

Dear Mr. Greenslet;

I came West rather suddenly to receive an honorary degree from the University of Nebraska at its Semi-Centennial Commencement. Roosevelt, Dean Pound of Harvard Law School, and Gen. Pershing were given Doctor of Civil Laws—the latter in absentia, of course. John S. Neihardt, Edith Abbott, who is Jane Addams' assistant at Hull House, and I were given Doctor of Letters. It was a rather joyful occasion because so many old friends from this town and other friendly little towns were there.

I am now at home and will let you know when I flit away to Wyoming. I may join Isabelle at Dublin N.H. instead of going further west. Nebraska is bubbling hot for war!

Yours
Willa S.C.

→ ←

In September 1917 Cather's cousin G. P. Cather, son of her uncle George and aunt Franc, sailed to France with the American Expeditionary Force.

TO FRANCES SMITH CATHER

September 9, 1917
Shattuck Inn, Jaffrey, New Hampshire

My Dear Aunt Franc:

I don't wonder that your patriotism does not always reach as far as France! But G. P. has always hankered after military life, and this is the day when the fellows with that hankering have their chance. And we've got back to first principles, it seems; everything goes back to the man who can carry a gun. I know it's pretty hard on you to have him go, but I am glad he can go, and go as an officer. I'm ever so proud of him. I wish Jack were going, I really do, though I think he is very useful where he is.

I was so disappointed not to get out into the country again, for a visit with you. But the hot weather used me up shockingly, and my friend [Edith Lewis] was more worn out by it than I. We had to give up and flee. I was exhausted when I got back to New York, and had to come up here to cool, green New Hampshire to recover from Red Cloud. I was too worn out to work. Unless I have a great deal of vitality, I simply do bad work, which is much worse than doing none.

Douglass writes discouraging reports about mother. I don't know whether I ought to go to California or not. I hate to break in on my work. I live at a comfortable hotel and have a little tent a mile away in the woods, where I go to work every morning. My friend Mrs Hambourg, (Miss McClung when you met her) was here with me for three weeks, and she asked about you and was disappointed that I had not seen you.

Elsie is so fortunate in her schools—I expect a cheerful disposition is largely responsible for the fact that she finds each place lovelier than the last. She is delighted with Albuquerque and is so happy there. I will send you her letter when Jack returns it. Both she and Jack are a great deal of satisfaction to me.

I would feel very cheerful and happy if only mother were better.

Mother's address is

> Hotel Garfield
> 354 O'Farrell St.
> San Francisco

Do send the letter that was returned from Los Angeles to her there. Now I must write her a little note. Elsie got to like Frank's wife [wife of Frank Cather, Franc's son] so much. I wished I could have seen her again, too. Families are pretty good things to have, after all, aren't they?

With a great deal of love to you, dear Aunt Franc,

Yours always
Willa

I shall be at home on Bank Street after October 1st.

➤ ⬅

In a letter in mid-October encouraging Cather to have her book ready for spring 1918 publication, Ferris Greenslet also passed along a contract from French publisher M. Conard for the "Continental rights" to Cather's next book.

TO FERRIS GREENSLET

October 18, 1917

Dear Mr. Greenslet:

I return M. Conard's contract herewith and think it a good proposition.

Surely, I'll be glad to take the reduced royalties on "O Pioneers!" sold to Soldiers Libraries.

I'm so sorry I was fussy about the date of the statement from the business office. I'll try to make your date for spring publication, but I can't tell you surely for about a month from now.

The Century people begin the series "Office Wives" in January. They want the book rights also. I don't imagine you will mind, as there is not much money in a book of short stories, and this series would not be ready for book publication until next fall. I told [*Century* editor Douglas Zabriskie] Doty I thought they could have the book all right, but I did not absolutely promise. At least, I don't think I did.

Do let me know when you come to New York. I want very much to talk to you about the physical make-up of the next book. I want to try something a trifle new in color of the binding and jacket. I am going to ask Benda to dinner and talk to him about head and tail-pieces. If he doesn't get the idea, no one else would, and I'd rather go un-illustrated.

The truth is, I've tried to make my own head and tail-pieces in the text itself, and unless the artist can echo them, I'd rather not.

Faithfully yours
Willa Cather

Only three stories for the proposed book Office Wives *were ever completed and published:* "The Bookkeeper's Wife" *(Century, May 1916),* "Ardessa" *(Century, May 1918), and* "Her Boss" *(Smart Set, October 1919).*

TO CARRIE MINER SHERWOOD

October 29, 1917

My Dear Carrie;

I have been up in New Hampshire all fall, and did not know of your dear mother's death until a few days ago, when I was looking over a pile of Red Cloud papers that had accumulated in my absence. Father does not write to me very often, and he always hates to write bad news.

You said last summer that your mother was so changed by her illness that you felt that she got very little satisfaction out of life, and for that reason I feel that her going may have been a release for her. But I know you must all feel heavy without her. Even after her memory failed and her mind wandered a good deal, there was still something fine and forceful in her, and last fall she seemed to me as much "Mama Miner" as ever she was.

While I was in New Hampshire I was working on a part of my new novel in which a character very much like your mother appears, and all during September I was thinking about her about every day, trying to recall certain tricks of voice and gesture. I have had a little of Mrs. Miner in almost every mother I have ever done, but this character in this new story is quite a clear little snap-shot of her as I first remember her, and I hope you will like it. I want, by the way, to dedicate this next book to you and Irene, and I hope you wont [mind] appearing in print along with me. It will give me a great deal of pleasure to have your names in a book of mine that will in some places recall to you places and people that have interested you as well as me. The older one grows, the dearer, and the clearer, one's early impressions somehow become.

Please give my love and sympathy to Mary and Margie, and to Irene [all Carrie's sisters] when you write to her.

Always affectionately yours
Willie Cather

Carrie's mother, Julia Erickson Miner, appeared in My Ántonia *as Mrs. Harling.*

TO FERRIS GREENSLET

November 24 [1917]
New York City

Dear Mr. Greenslet;

Mr. Scaife put me in an awkward position when he was here, and as I have not been able to get any work done since, and the first of December approaches, I think I had better write and tell you my troubles.

You will remember that illustration was not my idea at all. When Mr. Scaife was here last spring, he urged it very strongly. I told him then I didn't want a mere conventional frontispiece; unless I could get a set of decorations done that would have some character and interpret and embellish the text, I didn't want anything. He distinctly said that I could go ahead and see what I could do.

I selected Benda as a man who knew both Bohemia and the West; and because he has imagination. He has already given me a great deal of time, making preliminary sketches and trying to get exactly what I want. Our plan was for twelve line drawings, which would print on text paper, to be scattered through the book where there were blank half-pages at the ends of chapters. Three of the completed drawings are already in; they are admirable and give the tone of the text better than I could have hoped for.

For the price Mr. Scaife named when he was here, I can't let Benda do more than these three. Now three tailpieces, scattered in a book would look hap-hazard and mean. These three were meant to be a part of a developing scheme of decoration. One can't ask a man to do twelve difficult compositions in an exacting medium, for $150.

Mr. Scaife told Benda over the telephone that he was indifferent to this scheme of illustration, anyway, and would much prefer one full page picture which he could use in advertisements.

Of course, it would be much easier for Benda to do one conventional wash drawing, wash is his usual medium, than to work out sympathetic compositions in pen and ink which require a careful study of the text and some work from models. I am clearly the one who is making the trouble.

I know, now, that I should have got a definite figure of expenditure from you[r] office before I proceeded at all. But I knew Benda would do the work more cheaply than anyone else for me—for one thing I knew he would like the story—and a figure like $150 did not occur to me. We seldom had an art editor at McClures, and when we hadn't, I usually arranged for the use of the illustrations made for our serials and sets of stories by book publishers. We always asked one third of the original cost of the drawings, and got it without any trouble.

The misunderstanding, apparently, has come on the meaning of the word "illustration." But I told Mr. Scaife last spring that if I had any pictures at all, I wanted real illustrations, not a conventional frontispiece. He also said that illustrations "enriched" a book, which I think, since he had only a frontispiece in mind, was misleading. The scheme of decoration which Benda and I have worked out does, I think, enrich the book, but three tailpieces won't do anything but make it look shabby.

This is my position: If Benda's first drawings had been unsatisfactory, I could say so, and get out of the whole thing. That was my understanding with him. But they are more satisfactory tha[n] I could reasonably have hoped, and he has put a great deal of conscientious work on them, besides special knowledge. I can't throw them back at him and say they are not good. He must be paid for them.

These three drawings, however, three lone tailpieces, would make the book look patchy————would be worse than no pictures. But I can't ask Benda to do twelve difficult compositions in line for $150!

It's a misunderstanding, and I am willing to admit that I am to blame for it. I absolutely misunderstood Mr. Scaife's language and his meaning.

If you can see your way to write Benda a polite letter, offering him $200 and telling him you know it is very little for his work, I will try to get him to do eight, or perhaps even ten of the decorations as originally planned.—These decorations, you understand, are pictures, like old woodcuts in effect, and evolved out of close study of the text and western photographs which I have been at great pains to get.————That, it seems to me, would only be evidence of good will on the part of the publishers. It wouldn't by any means pay for the work Benda began at my solicitation, but it would somewhat cover my retreat.

If this is impossible, then we will have to pay Benda for three drawings and not use them. I don't see anything else to do, unless Mr. Scaife wishes to withdraw entirely from the responsibility of this book, for which I am now, as always, perfectly ready. In any case, please do not go ahead with the dummy until you have told me what you can do. I don't think it was quite fair play of Mr. Scaife to repudiate, without examination, a scheme of decoration which I had worked out with so much pains, or to destroy the zeal of the artist. He said something to me over the telephone about "little pictures" not being worth as much as big ones! Why, doesn't he know that I know that [Frederic Dorr] Steele gets more for one pen drawing than artists usually get for several wash drawings?

Faithfully
Willa Cather

An inquiry from Philadelphia says the bookseller there cannot get "Song of the Lark." Is it out of stock with you?

→ ←

R. L. Scaife, to whom Greenslet showed the letter above, wrote Cather to justify the price he was offering to Benda—$150 for ten drawings—as a standard rate artists received for book work. Magazines, he said, had "spoiled artists" by inflating their fees.

TO R. L. SCAIFE

December 1 [1917]
New York City

My Dear Mr. Scaife;

The series of pen-and-ink drawings I had in mind, and Mr. Benda's fitness to do them, was suggested by a similar set of pen drawings he made to illustrate Jacob Riis' book, "The Old Town." I knew that Macmillans paid him nine hundred dollars for these drawings, which were not used in any periodical, but in the book only. I had planned to have only about a third as many pictures as were in the Riis book.

Mr. Benda telephoned me after your conversation with him. He was very polite and considerate, as he always is, but he said that Doubleday had paid him $150 and $200 for one or two wash drawings to illustrate novels, and that had he known how little he was to receive for these pen pictures he would not have felt that he could undertake them. He also said he could not do the drawings we had blocked out, as they would require a great deal of work and some of them would have to be done from models. On the other hand, he had already spent a good deal of time in studying the manuscript, collecting material, and making preliminary sketches, and he thought perhaps we might be able to substitute a set of drawings more conventional and less exacting.

These drawings, however, would have to be done at odd moments of his time, and he could not promise to deliver them before the first of March, as he could not afford to put more remunerative work aside for them. On this point he was very firm.

I am going out to his studio on Monday night, to see what we can do toward planning new compositions, and after that I can write you more fully.

I am cutting the story a good deal in revision, and I can now say positively that it will run very little, if at all, longer than "O Pioneers!" I hope you can use the same type as in that book, and give the text pages the same look. I have broken it up into chapters as much as I can, and liberal page-margins and spaces at chapter-ends will make the decorations look better. Would your foreman be willing to let the artist and me size the cuts and decide on the reduction of the drawings, provided we do not ask for cuts more than a third of a page in size? If you could give me the exact size of the page and send me a sheet of the paper you will use, it would be helpful.

Benda asked me not to send away the three drawings I already have until we had come to some decision about those that were or were not to follow. I will send them to you as soon as I have his permission to do so. Meantime, please let me know whether I may size the cuts.

Very sincerely yours
Willa S. Cather

→ ←

Scaife didn't immediately change his mind about Benda's fees, but he did tell Cather to work with Benda to get the kind of illustrations she desired and they would work it out.

TO R. L. SCAIFE

[December 9, 1917]
New York City

Dear Mr. Scaife;

The dummy will reach you Tuesday morning, also two Benda drawings, with the size marked on the margins. Mr. Greenslet and I agreed when he was here that it would be better to give each of these drawings a full page, with plenty of margin about it, than to use them as tail-pieces. They are illustrations, in reality, not tailpieces, but should be printed small on a liberal page, to give the effect of old woodcuts, and without captions.

The drawings will be more effective if they all occur on right-hand pages. That, I think, is rather important.

They should be printed in the same black ink as the text.

Please use the accent mark over the initial A in Ántonia in the running title. Even if many of the accents break, the majority will remain and give character to the title.

Please send me proofs of the drawings as soon as they are printed. They will be a help to me and to the artist in future compositions.

One of the two drawings I send you is sized a little wider than the text measure, but I think that will make no trouble in printing. The other is slightly narrower.

Sincerely yours
Willa S. Cather

→ ←

In the early months of 1918 Cather was nearly, but not quite, finished with the book. After reading the first few chapters, Ferris Greenslet told her he thought the story was "going very soundly" but he suspected a "strong dramatic thrill" should be coming in the next batch since it wasn't in those early pages.

TO FERRIS GREENSLET

Friday [February 1, 1918]

Dear Mr. Greenslet:

I am afraid the Introduction will be almost the last thing I write. I shall have to wait to see how far the story tells itself before I know how much to put in the introduction. But I will do it as soon as I can.

Tomorrow I shall send back to you the dummy Miss [Helen] Bishop left with me. I like the look of it very much. My name on the cover is "Willa S. Cather"; if it is not too much trouble I wish you would ask them to cut out the S and solder the plate, leaving it simply "Willa Cather." I think the S looks too business-like for the queer title above it. Cutting out the S., you have a bunch of queer enough proper names!

I shall have another bunch of copy to send you in two weeks.

Faithfully yours
W.S.C.

Please send Miss Bishop over soon again!

✦ ✦

After she wrote a letter to Greenslet bemoaning her inability to complete the book as quickly as she wished, Greenslet wrote back to say that they should abandon publishing it in the spring and would just bring it out whenever Cather was done.

TO FERRIS GREENSLET

March 7, 1918

Dear Mr. Greenslet;

Thank you most heartily for your kind and consoling letter. Don't you think it would be better to get the book out among the first of the autumn books, say late in September, than to get it out in the summer when people are out of town?

Will you please ask your printing house to save enough of the cream-tinted, rough-finished paper used in the dummy to print the full edition in the summer?

I will send you three Benda drawings tomorrow; the two full figure ones, of Antonia and Lena Lingard—the latter fairly busting out of her clothes—I think extremely good. I wouldn't ask for better. That will make eight drawings I have sent you. I have still two more which do not quite suit me. Unless I can get Benda to re-draw them for me someday, I won't use them. But will you please ask Mr. Scaife to send Benda his check as soon as you receive the three drawings I am sending you by express? His work is all done. If there is any business office formality which prevents your paying an artist in the middle of the month or the dark of the moon, won't you please send him the check and charge it to me until such time as it becomes proper to transfer it to manufacturing charges.

Will you also please have one copy of "O Pioneers" and one of "The Song of the Lark" mailed to W. T. Benda, 140 Wadsworth ave. New York, and charge to me.

If you like I will send another bunch of copy to you in two or three weeks, and you can return it to me, as I may want it by me until the end, which I devoutly hope will not be very far off. I'd like to have you see the next installment before I begin the last round, if you will have time to look it over. I am

Benda illustration from *My Ántonia* of Lena Lingard
"busting out of her clothes"

well again, and what is more important as regards the production of copy, the maid is now well enough to keep the kettle boiling.

Faithfully yours
W.S. Cather

TO CARRIE MINER SHERWOOD

March 13, 1918
New York City

My Dear Carrie;

   It has been a long while since I received the letter from you which gave me so much pleasure. I still have it and shall always keep it. I like to know that you, too, feel that our friendship is simply one of those which last for life. How few of those friendships one has, in the long run, and how precious they become as time goes on. One has to live about forty years to find out which things are the temporary excitements, and which are the lasting affections. In every letter I get from Father I hear something of you, and of what valuable work you have done this winter for the Red Cross.

I have had a rather hard winter, though many pleasant things have happened and I have never enjoyed living more. The fuel shortage was inconvenient for me. My study is heated by a coal grate, and during the terribly bitter weather, which lasted over a month, I had to vacate my study and work in the dining-room, where we managed to keep one coal grate going. The change was disturbing. Then Josephine, my good French maid, was ill and not able to come for a month; and scrub women and ice-men and laundry-men frittered away my time. The net result is, that my new book, which was scheduled for spring publication, cannot come out until early fall. It is a disappointment, but the book may be all the better for not being hurried. At least, I hope so.

Several weeks ago I had a nasty bronchitis for about two weeks, before my maid was well enough to come back to work. When I was recovering my old friend, Olive Fremstad, the singer, came to my rescue and made life more cheerful. Every evening she sent her car down for me and hauled me up to her apartment on 86th street—about three miles from Bank street—gave me a good dinner and a little music, and then sent me home again in her car. Since no German operas are being given this winter, she had had more leisure than ever before, and we have done many pleasant things together.

I have also done many pleasant things with the Hambourgs. I get on well with Isabelle's husband now; have really learned to like him. Like most people, he has many good qualities when you come to know him well. We have gone to concerts and to the opera often together. We heard [soprano Amelita] Galli-Curci several times during her season here. That is certainly one of the loveliest voices that have come along in my time. She had an overwhelming success here.

Before Mr. [Charles] Wiener died, during his illness of four months, I was at their house often. I usually dined there Sunday night, and after he grew too weak to come to the table I used to see him in his room after dinner. His death is a great loss to me. He was the oldest friend I had in this part of the world. All his family here have always been cordial and friendly to me. At the funeral I was put in the first carriage, with the widow and the only remaining brother, and all the troop of nieces and nephews came after. I would not have thought it would ever make much difference to me in which carriage I was put at a funeral, but somehow this pleased and touched me very much. I thought it an appreciative recognition of a long friendship. The brother, Dr. Richard

Wiener, telephoned me often during Mr. Wiener's illness. He comes to see me sometimes. He is a very interesting and cultivated man, and fond of music. He is [pianist Ignacy] Paderewski's physician, and [soprano Marcella] Sembrich's and [violinist Eugène] Ysaye's. His wife, too, is such a cordial, human sort of person. I have a warm feeling for the whole family. They are not clannish and selfish like many big rich Jewish families.

Edith Lewis sends her warmest regards to you and Walter [Sherwood]. She had a hard winter, but kept pretty well. While we managed to keep part of this apartment comfortable, in spite of the fact that the gas and water froze, many of the office buildings were almost entirely without heat, and Edith's office so cold she had to work in her coat and furs for weeks. The suffering in the poor quarter to the south of us was disheartening and discouraging. But it's been, on the whole, a happy winter. Every Friday afternoon there have been pleasant and interesting people here for tea, and we have given some jolly little dinner parties. When Josephine is well, she is a splendid cook and a good manager, and makes us very comfortable. How I would love it if you could drop in on us sometime. There have been a lot of Lincoln people here this winter, at one time and another.

Now I must close a long letter. Please give my love to Mary and Margie, and keep a great deal for yourself and your household.

Affectionately always
Willie

➔ ◄

On June 8, 1918, the New York Times *printed Grosvenor P. Cather's name among the list of Americans killed in battle in France.*

TO FRANCES SMITH CATHER

June 12 [1918]

My Dearest Aunt:

Each time I try to write to you I feel helpless to do so, but a line must go to you today to tell you that you and your loss are in my thoughts always. Everything seemed strange and unreal to me on the day I saw G. P.'s name in the New York paper, under that glorious title "killed in action" which sets men off from their fellows. I feel proud and humble to be one of those bearing the name that your son put in a place of such honor. After watching the casualty lists closely for weeks, I had not opened the paper that morning when Isabelle came to me and said "Who is Myrtle Cather?" [Myrtle Bartlett Cather was G.P.'s wife.] I told her, and then she said "What is G. P.'s full name?" Then I turned around and asked, "Has anything happened to G. P.?" She nodded and took the morning paper out from under her jacket. I had thought that, out of so many thousand, harm would not come to G.P.

I know how terrible it must be for you that it all happened so far away. But I feel sure that you are glad G. P. lived through his illness the time he was burned, lived to find the work he loved and seemed to be made for, and to give his life to the greatest cause men ever fought for.

You remember, I was staying at your house the week in August, 1914, when this terrible war began. I drove over to Campbell one day, and G. P. took a load of wheat over. I was coming back and met him just on the edge of town, and we stopped to chat about the war news. I believe he always wanted to be a soldier. I can see him sitting on his wagon as plainly as if it were yesterday, in the middle of a peaceful country, with thousands of miles of land and sea between him and those far-away armies we were talking about. What would have seemed more improbable than that he should fall, an officer, in France, in one of the greatest battles the world has ever seen. He was restless on a farm; perhaps he was born to throw all his energy into this crisis, and to die among the first and bravest of his country.

I know your heart will ache none the less, but you have always looked up to high things through faith, and it seems to me that now you must feel that your son is among those high things. Some people rise by faith, and some people by prayer. But there come critical times in this world when a man can rise in action to all that he could ever be. I believe G. P. was one of the men who can do that, and he found his opportunity.

Goodbye, dear Aunt Franc. I keep thinking how lonely you and Uncle George must be feeling; yet, surely, you have cause to be proud and thankful, too, to have been able to help this country at a time of such need. There were so few men ready to take hold and help as G. P. did. Most of the willing ones were only a burden.

My heart is full of love and sympathy for you.

Willie

→ ←

Cather got the entire manuscript of My Ántonia *to Houghton Mifflin in June, and they quickly got the rest of it into type and sent her the proofs for review.*

TO FERRIS GREENSLET

July 2 [1918]

The Shattuck Inn, Jaffrey, New Hampshire

Dear Mr. Greenslet:

Please give the enclosed proofs of cuts and instructions relating to them to the right person.

The proofs are going well, except that the Riverside copy reader changed the spelling of Mama to Mamma—too sophisticated a form for these country people—and I have to change it back in every case. Also I have to insist on an occasional use of the subjunctive mood, and the copy-reader belongs to that ferocious band who are out to exterminate it along with the brown-tailed moth. I hope the Riverside Press won't charge me for such corrections. I've enough changes on my own head, mercy knows!

Please tell me if you have read the last part of the story, and please get the proofs to me as soon as you can.

Don't you ever motor out in this direction? It's a pretty country.

Did you see what a splendid citation was given my cousin, Lieut. Grosvenor Cather, who was killed in action May 28th? He led the list of American officers in the first citations published.

Faithfully

W.S.C.

P.S. Most of the copy-reader's changes were good, by the way.

TO FERRIS GREENSLET

July 11, 1918

The Shattuck Inn, Jaffrey, New Hampshire

Dear Mr. Greenslet:

A lot of page proofs have come, but I am perplexed at finding that no blank pages have been left for the cuts. Wouldn't it be much cheaper to print them in the four-page forms with the text than to bind them in as inserts?

You know I am particularly anxious that the cuts should be printed on the same paper as the text, and not on coated paper.

I wrote asking for page proofs of the cuts, so that I can see how they are set on the page. (In the dummy the cuts were set too high in each case.) Also I asked for information about the cut of the old woman gathering mushrooms, no proof of which was sent in the envelope which was supposed to contain proofs of all cuts.

I have not yet had any light on either of these points. I would not be perturbed except for the fact that the make-up seems to be going ahead without regard for the cuts.

Hastily
W.S.C.

P.S. Had you rather I wrote directly to the department in charge of these details, and, if so, whom shall I address?

W.S.C.

→ ←

Cather's cousin G. P. Cather was awarded a Distinguished Service Cross for bravely climbing a parapet and directing fire.

TO ROSCOE CATHER

July 19 [1918]
Shattuck Inn, Jaffrey, New Hampshire

My Dear Brother:

Some Twins, those pictures! please thank Meta for me.

The horrible increase in railroad and Pullman fares made Wyoming out of the question for both Miss Lewis and me. But mother says you may be in Red Cloud this summer with West Virginia. I will be there by the 15th (fifteenth) of August to stay a month. Do try to get there while I am at home if you can.

Isn't the news from France glorious? I was so proud of G.P.'s citation. It was published in all the New York papers and dozens of people called me up to ask if he were any kin of mine. It seemed to me such a useful sort of bravery that he was cited for—so much more useful than if [he] had brought in a wounded comrade.

I am here in this quiet hotel in the woods reading the proofs of my new book, and hope to finish them by the 6th of August. It's a queer sort of book. It's at least not like either of the others. Did you know that both the others are studied in a good many colleges now, for "style"?

Goodnight and love to you and Meta. Didn't Jack surprise you? I don't know her, but if she's nice and <u>can spell</u>, it may be a splendid thing for him [marriage to Irma Wells]. I think your marriage was a splendid thing for you, and I'm going to hope that Jack's will be just as fortunate.

Goodnight
Willie

Aren't the American boys <u>some soldiers</u>! (I can't write with this horrid "hotel ink".)

TO FERRIS GREENSLET

[Probably late August 1918]
Scarsdale, New York

Dear Mr. Greenslet:

I go West via New York and came here last Friday to spend a week with the Hambourgs, who are here for the summer. Ysaye and [violinist] Maurice Dambois are staying with them and [violinist Jacques] Thibaud has a house across the street. We have Beethoven quartettes and Motzart every night. Last night the Tenth Beethoven and Schubert's Death and the Maiden. The gods on Olympus' hill do not have such music. One might travel the world around and not hear its equal. My right to be in this Heavenly choir is mainly that I loaned the bunch my cook, Josephine, for the summer. They are so fond of her good french food, and so afraid I'll take her away that they will even play 'request' programs for me. It is a glorious party, but the silence of the cornfields will be almost welcome after so much of it. As Josephine says; "Les sonat', les quatuores à deux heures le matin—c'n'est pas raisonable, vous-savez, mademoiselle!" ["Sonatas and quartets at two in morning—come now, this is outrageous, Miss!"]

So this is why I won't have the pleasure of lunching with you in Boston. After Sunday my address will be Red Cloud, Nebraska.

Faithfully
W.S.C.

→ ←

My Ántonia was published in October 1918, featuring eight drawings by W. T. Benda. The critics loved it right away. An early review in the Nation *(November 2, 1918) said the novel was "among the best of our recent interpretations of American life."*

TO IRENE MINER WEISZ

October 26 [1918]
Toronto

Dear Irene:

This review will answer your question as to whether strangers get the little things in a book like this. Apparently, this man got every least little thing. A stranger, if he has an eye trained for literary values, is apt to get the whole picture more <u>as a whole</u> than anyone who knew the people from whom the characters were sketched, and who must be more or less preoccupied with the question of where the characters are like the model, and where they are wholly unlike. The further you stand away from a picture of this kind, the more you get the painter's intention.

Please send this review to Carrie as soon as you have finished with it. I will send you a bunch of reviews after they come in. <u>This one you need not return</u> to me—you or Carrie may keep it. I like it because it is not so much a literary appreciation as it is an expression of honest personal enjoyment on the part of the reviewer.

I have told Isabelle many times about my happy day with you in Chicago [Cather was in Toronto to see Isabelle McClung Hambourg]. I go on to New York and Bank Street on Tuesday, Oct 30th.

Affectionately always
Willie

TO FRANCES SMITH CATHER

November 11, 1918
New York City

[Written under the date in the top margin:] (an immortal day!)

My Dear Aunt Franc:

On this first day of the greater Peace, when this city is mad with joy and all the church bells are ringing, my heart turns to you who have helped to pay the dear price for all that this world has gained. Think of it, for the first time since human society has existed on this planet, the sun rose this morning upon a world in which not one great monarchy or tyranny existed. You remember [Ralph Waldo] Emerson once wrote that one day God would say, "I am tired of Kings." I know you will wish that G. P. had lived to see this glorious day, and to help in the reconstruction work which must follow. But when I think of him I think of the last act of Macbeth, when they bring old Siward word that his son is slain in his first battle, and the old man says, "Why then, God's soldier be he!"

I like to feel that G. P. and the brave boys who fell with him, who went so far to fight for an ideal and for that only, became and are God's soldiers. Whatever the after life may be, I know they have a glorious part in it.

This is not meant to be a letter—I have so many letters to write to friends who have been bereaved by this terrible scourge of Influenza—but I must send you a greeting on this great day when old things are passing away forever. It is a day when we think of all the people we love, and I must send a word to mother and father, too. Goodbye now, and let us be thankful that we have both lived to see this day, and to know that our countrymen and kindred have done such noble things to bring it about. I love to see our flag in the churches. It seems to me to belong there more than it ever has before.

Very lovingly
Willie

I enclose a letter from Elsie. Do not return it.

The influenza epidemic of 1918 killed an estimated 50 million people worldwide, far more than died in World War I. Twenty-five percent of the U.S. population was affected by it.

TO ROSCOE CATHER

Thanksgiving Day [November 28, 1918]
New York City

My Dear Roscoe:

Your nice letter deserved a speedy answer. I am so glad that you and father and mother liked this book. Most of the critics, too, seem to find this the best book I have done. I got quite a wonderful letter about it from France today, and it will be published in France very soon. Personally, I like the book before this one better, because there is more warmth and struggle in it. All the critics find "Antonia" more artistic. A man in the Nation writes that "it exists in an atmosphere of its own—an atmosphere of pure beauty." Nonsense, its the atmosphere of my grandmother's kitchen, and nothing else. Booth Tarkington writes that it is as "simple as a country prayer meeting or a Greek temple—and as beautiful." There [are] lots of these people who can't write anything true themselves who yet recognize it when they see it. And whatever is really true is true for all people. As long as one says "will people stand this, or that?" one gets nowhere. You either have to be utterly common place or else do the thing people <u>don't</u> want, because it has not yet been invented. No really new and original thing is <u>wanted</u>: people have to learn to like new things.

[Unsigned]

Cather's quotations in the letter above are a bit of a mystery. The passage she claims to quote from the Nation *does not appear in the review published there on November 2, 1918, and no published or unpublished remarks about* My Ántonia *by Booth Tarkington have been located. However, Tarkington does use the comparison "as simple as a country church—or a Greek statue" in a letter to S. S. McClure praising McClure's* Autobiography *(see Lyon, p. 347).*

→ ←

Shortly after turning in the manuscript for My Ántonia, *Cather began corresponding with Greenslet about a possible book of short stories focusing on writers and artists.*

TO FERRIS GREENSLET

December 2 [1918]
New York City

Dear Mr. Greenslet:

I don't seem to feel much interest in getting the short stories together just now. I haven't time to write enough new ones to make a volume. I've begun a new book—in fact I've begun <u>two</u> new books, and they are rather chewing me up just at the present writing. One is company, but two are a crowd. When you are next in town I would like to talk them over with you.

Meantime, please telephone the Atlantic Monthly and get Edward Garnett's present address for me.

And please have four (4) copies of "Ántonia" sent to me here. How is the book selling now?

Hastily
W.S.C.

Isn't it terrible about poor Elsie Sergeant being so badly hurt? I had no idea it was anything serious until I heard from her the other day.

Please for mercy's sake send a copy of "Antonia" to the N.Y. "Globe"! I've just had a piteous note from the editor saying that they would rather review my books than most, but that they had never received a copy. I've long bought the Globe for its book reviews—they are the only ones I read and I think they are much the most intelligent and interesting that appear in any New York paper.

Won't you please rush off a copy yourself to

N. P. Dawson
Literary Editor N.Y. Globe

Sergeant had been injured while touring a deserted battlefield in France as a correspondent for the New Republic. *Her official guide picked up a "souvenir" from battle and it exploded, killing the guide and seriously injuring others who were nearby. Sergeant had shrapnel embedded in her legs and ankles and had to spend several months in the American Hospital in Paris, where Cather directed the following letter.*

TO ELIZABETH SHEPLEY SERGEANT

December 3 [1918]
New York City

My Dear Elsie:

What you write me about yourself simply amazes me! I was in the west at the time the paper announced the accident. They had your name entirely wrong at first, and later said you "got off with slight injuries". Got off somehow conveyed to my mind—well, that you had "got off"—certainly not that you had most woefully got in! F.G. [Ferris Greenslet] didn't write me about it. I got back to town just a few days before the Armistice was signed, saw very few people, and did not hear a word about you. Your letter simply struck me dumb, therefore. I wonder you had to come in for a share of the unjust suffering of this unjust war. Why did that poor foolish woman go and pick up something? I thought the French were always gaily guying the Americans because they pick up souvenirs—I didn't know they practiced such countrified habits.

My shaved head seems a trivial thing to compare to cruelly shattered bones, but when I remember how sort of degraded it made me feel, it makes me groan to think of you—being knocked about in dressing-tents and railways when you were in such pain. The mere shock of the explosion and the suddenness of the way in which you were hurt must have broken up your nerves terribly, and the long "getting well" process is about the worst of all. Do you know, it seems as if you were fated to have this war get through your skin. I know it had already tortured your mind and heart.------The Mauretania got in yesterday with five thousand of her sister's avengers—the first big landing of troops. But one meets lots of them about now, in theaters and hotels, and oh Elsie they are so jolly and modest and amused at everything—so just all that one could want them to be. They are not conceited as I heard a very clever and very nasty Frenchman say the other night, and they don't think they won the war. The newspapers put on swag, and the Tammany mayor does, but not the soldiers. A funny little marine is coming here for dinner tomorrow night who never wears his croix de guerre except indoors because people look at him so. At the French theatre last night I saw a few of "ours" among a lot of nice French soldiers and sailors—but my gracious "ours" were nicer! So different—the French boys were awfully fine fellows—but ours were so wonderfully, so unsuspectedly picturesque and they seemed so more alive than anything one had ever seen before! You could see their eyes and teeth flash when the lights were down. Oh, my dear Elsie, the flood of french that has broken loose on Broadway! All the shop girls speak it now when they dine at Monquin's, and one is always hearing "vive le France" and "Je suis amoureuse de cette robe" I could give you a hundred joyful phrases from the stenographer world. It's going to make quite a new Broadway language—like the Norman Conquest!

I'm glad F.G. sent you "Antonia" because I'm so pleased and happy at what you say about it. I didn't send you one because when I finished it the waters of bitterness simply closed over my head. When I finished the proofs it seemed to me that nothing—simply nothing had got across. When I wrote you I wasn't on speaking terms with the book, and I was trying to forget it. Now when people like you like it, I feel better about it. You see I liked it at first, while I was writing it, and then in the proofs it seemed a gray waste of dullness. It came out while I was at home and my father said it was all so exactly the way he remembered it, that I began to feel encouraged. If it lightened up a few hours in the hospital for you, that is an especially nice association for me to have with it.

It's cruel how many boys have died in our training camps here. Before I left Red Cloud we had seven funerals in one week for boys who were sent home from Camp Dodge, Iowa. The rumor is that more of our boys have died in camp at home than have been killed in France.

I've talked over the telephone with Mrs. Boas, who had not heard of your illness and who will write you at once. She is nice, but somehow so <u>German</u>! I like outright pro-German better than Pacifists, with their wise talk. I suppose you've heard all about the high cost of living. The monthly meat rise is a thing to weep over. New York was never so gaudy and extravagant. What you say about things abroad is discouraging. Come home as soon as you can and recover from it all—then go back to France and finish your work. Maybe you'll find that this terrible thing you've had to go through will bring good things to you as well as bad—that is bromidic, but so many bromides are true. It's a queer world we look out upon, isn't it? With Germany howling to be fed first and most! But at any rate, come home and rest. I wish I could send you all sorts of nice things from my very loving and admiring self, and from all the people who love and admire you. You are very rich in friends, you know.

Yours always
Willa S. C.

TO ROSCOE CATHER

December 8 [1918]

[Possibly a continuation of the unsigned November 28 letter above]

My Dear Roscoe;

It has been a long time since I began this letter to you. The town is full of newly returned soldiers now; I have been seeing as much of them as I can. They like to talk to almost anyone who will talk to them about France.

I am sending you a copy of one of the best reviews, from the Sunday "Sun," a full page with a large photograph of me. I had some copies made because in these paperless days one can't get extra copies of Sunday papers. This man surely had a good time with the book. It amazes me how many people feel that way. I thought nearly everybody in this country had to have a story. I never did like stories much, and the older I grow the less they interest me. I see and feel only the carpenter work in them. In this book the pitch of life as it was lived isn't raised half a tone, and yet, you see, how many people do like it. Professor Geoghegan writes me that it is certainly the best novel that has come out of America. "We know," he says, "that perfect art returns to nature, bu[t] only a very great artist can so return, or can make the nakedness of nature beautiful in art." Yet Father likes it "as well as any book he ever read." I feel well content to have touched two extremes. If only I can do as well with the next!

I am so happy that Virginia's coat is a success. Mother sent me part of Meta's letter that told about it and also about your family whooping cough. I was at Trix Mizer's this summer when her six began to whoop their heads off.

Now goodbye, my boy, forgive this scrappy letter and write me when you have time. I am always glad to hear about everything that goes on in your pretty little house. Tell Meta to write me when she can. I am wrestling with the Blue Mesa story a little; but the commonplace way to do it is so utterly manufactured, and the only way worth while is so alarmingly difficult. Wish me luck!

Lovingly
Willie

→ ←

Cather took a keen interest in the American soldiers returning home from the war. According to Edith Lewis, her old student Albert Donovan, who was in the army and in New York, would bring a few servicemen with him when he came to visit, and she also visited wounded soldiers at the Polyclinic Hospital.

TO META SCHAPER CATHER

December 27, 1918

My Dear Meta:

The box of jams and jellies that you and Roscoe sent me is perfect for afternoon tea—all done up in cunning little jars, and such strange and interesting varieties! So far I have tried only the Citrus Jam, and it is delicious! They came in such a lovely box, too. I shall use it for ribbons after I've eaten all the jam. I feel that I have cut myself off from a great pleasure this year in not sending anything for Santa Claus to give Virginia and my cunning twins. I've sworn that I won't let the chance escape me next Christmas. You see, to get things there on time, one has to buy and send before the Christmas feeling is really in the air here. About December 20th I began to wish I'd sent some funny little things for your babies. Then it was too late. I've put "toys for twins" down on my 1919 calendar, and I'll write you for a list of their desires in November.

I don't do much now but run about to see wounded soldiers. They are nearly all fine fellows—I don't see how one country can have so many nice ones and so few rottens. A marine dined here last week, hung with medals a king might envy, and as he said "There's one subject you can always pull the U.S. Marines together on———La Belle France." They were in France long enough to learn to love it, and they had the Blue Devils [a nickname for French soldiers during World War I] for their first teachers and drill-masters. And the brave always love the brave. I've always loved France so much that I can't help getting tearful when the lads talk about her. They don't care a damn for her intellect or her art; they've learned to love her industry, her sobriety, her courage. And what it has done for them———! Street-boys, farmer boys, any old boys———they have a kind of gracious grace. A one armed lad who was here on Xmas eve could eat, and seat his hostess at the table, so deftly with one strong, warm, brown hand. After dinner I went to the theatre with six of them who had landed that morning—six western boys alone in New York on Christmas Eve. We had some time, I can tell you! No, I don't do anything but run about with soldiers. They come in from Europe now at an average of five thousand a day, and to most of them this city is stranger and more confusing than Paris. On Christmas Eve there were 30,000 soldiers and sailors, on leave from camp, tramping the streets of New York hunting a good time. I wanted to go to the theatre with them all!

May you all have a Wonderful New Year

Affectionately
Willie

→ ←

With the end of World War I, Cather's attention was turning away from My Ántonia *and toward a new novel. It was to be a Nebraska story again, at least partly, but would have its action in the thriving, established farms of the early twentieth century, just before—and during—the great war whose conclusion all were now celebrating.*

TO CHARLES F. CATHER

December 28, 1918

My Dear Father:

Have you succeeded in loaning any more of my money yet? I hope Mr. [Joseph] Topham will pay his interest promptly this year. Don't forget, when you send it to me, to take out the money I borrowed from you when I left home this summer. The royalties on my new book are not due until April. I have had to ask for an advance of two hundred dollars from the publisher, but I don't want to ask for more if I can help it.

Please tell me, father, is it a binder or a reaper that has a big wheel at one side with wooden slats across it? That's a poor enough description, but I think you will know what I mean. Maybe it isn't a wheel, but it looks like one, and its much taller than the rest of the machine.

I am fairly well, and am at last getting down to work on my new book—but it is a long hard road ahead, this time.

Lovingly,
Willie

PART SIX

A Change of Publishers and *One of Ours*

1919–1922

The discouraging thing I get from your letter is that Houghton Mifflin, having already handled my books in the way they think adequate, would probably do not more for them in the future than in the past. I think, on the other hand, that among the people who form opinion, I have a very different position from that which I had five years ago, and that this fact, for a publicity department interested in such things, makes me a very different business proposition. I am also writing better than I was then, considerably better, which at least is a feature in the case.

—WILLA CATHER TO FERRIS GREENSLET, May 30, 1919

Willa Cather in Cavalière, Provence, France, with "Claude" under her arm, 1920

WITH THE GREAT ACCLAIM evoked by *My Ántonia*, Willa Cather's literary reputation was made. She was not convinced that her financial return on the book was what it ought to have been, however, and for that she blamed Houghton Mifflin's ineffective (so she believed) publicity campaign. Her conception for her next book, *One of Ours*, which she always called "Claude" after its central character, came to her even before *My Ántonia* was published, when the death of her cousin G. P. Cather in battle brought her passionate distress about the war to a focus. As she neared completion of the long manuscript, a series of minor irritations with Houghton Mifflin fueled her interest in choosing another publisher. When the young Alfred A. Knopf proposed bringing out a volume of her short stories, retaining some of the stories in *The Troll Garden* and adding several new ones, she agreed. Pleased by the quality of Knopf's work on that volume, *Youth and the Bright Medusa* (1920), and his belief in her as an artist, she then granted him the contract for *One of Ours* (1922). The reviews were mixed, with some of her former critical champions actually dismissing the novel, but she was awarded the Pulitzer Prize for it. Under the savvy guidance of Alfred Knopf, it became the best-selling novel of her career thus far and established the financial security that would support her creative work for years to come.

→ ←

In his review of My Ántonia *in the December 14, 1918,* Dial, *shortly before his death from influenza, Randolph Bourne wrote, "Here at last is an American novel, redolent of the Western prairie, that our most irritated and exacting preconceptions*

can be content with." Foreshadowing Cather's own statements about the art of the
novel, he praised her book for having "all the artistic simplicity of material that has
been patiently shaped until everything irrelevant has been scraped away."

TO ROSCOE CATHER

Sunday [January 5, 1919]

Dear Roscoe;

The other day I sent you an important notice of Antonia by a critic who has since died of influenza. He was the ablest of our critics, and I had rather dreaded his review. He gave me some sharp knocks on the Song of the Lark, though he liked the first part of it very much. I like his comparison of the book with [William Allen] White's. Long before I began to write anything worth while, I hated White and [David] Grahame Phillips for the way they wrote about the West. I knew that there was a common way of presenting common life, which is worthless, and a finer way of presenting it which would be much more true. Of course Antonia's story could be told in exactly the same jocular, familiar, grapenutsy way that Mr. White thinks is so American. He thinks he is presenting things as they are, but what he really presents is his own essentially vulgar personality. I don't deny that Mr. White sells a thousand to my hundred, but nobody can really reach both audiences, so I don't bother about that, so long as I have some of the savings of my old McClure salary left to live on.

Weeks ago I got such a heart-warming letter from a former president of the Missouri Pacific, Edwin Winter, who as a young man helped to carry the U.P. [Union Pacific] across Nebraska, and who built the bridge over Dale Creek canyon———the first bridge, which was of timber! He asked if he could come to see me, and on Friday he came. Such a man! all that one's proudest of in one's country. He picked the book up in his club and sat right down and wrote me the most beautiful of letters. I'd rather have the admiration of one man like that than sell a thousand books. He said that reading the story was a stirring adventure to him, that he felt as if he must get at me at once somehow, and he wondered if I were a Swede, because, he said, "the book looked to me too much like literature to be American." I feel that I've made a new friend who is going to teach me a lot and give me a great deal of pleasure. He has the most brilliant mind I've come up with in a long while, and such a vast and varied experience. I think I must copy his letter for you, sometime.

Please send the copy of the Dial and the notice about poor Bourne back to me when you've done with it. Tell Meta I am still eating that delicious jam on my toast at tea every afternoon when I have tea at home. I have finished the <u>scuppernong</u> jam, and am now on the pineapple. I wish I could have been with you for the Holidays.

[Unsigned]

TO FERRIS GREENSLET

January 6 [1919]

Dear Mr. Greenslet:

Thank you for the check on account.

The "Globe" telephoned me this morning to say that they had not yet received a copy of my book. I am sending them my own and only copy. Will you please <u>send me</u> a book and charge it to advertising?

Have you tried any of the English publishers, now that the war is over? I think this book would get an audience in England. I suppose you have seen poor Mr. Bourne's very gratifying review in the "Dial."

I have written four chapters of the soldier story. To be truthful, it writes itself. I don't believe I contribute any more than the ordinary "writing medium."

Faithfully
Willa Cather

➤ ◄

Throughout the winter, Cather continued to correspond with her family, friends, and publisher about the positive response My Ántonia *was getting. Edith Lewis got the flu, but recovered; Cather, luckily, did not catch it. Greenslet continued to give Cather unenthusiastic reports about the sales of the novel: they were having trouble getting an English publisher to accept it and the sales were "steady" but not "strong." Then, in May 1919, he wrote her about the debit against her royalties due to the excess corrections that she asked for after reading proofs.*

TO FERRIS GREENSLET

May 19 [1919]
New York City

Dear Mr. Greenslet;

I have waited to answer your letter because there are several things I want to take up seriously with you, and yet I do not exactly want to risk a talk with you, because you can frequently persuade me against my own judgement.—

While you were away MacMillan's sent for me to see whether I would let them have a Western story to go in a series of American novels they are bringing out. I said, unwisely, that I was not free to do so. During the last few years I have met several propositions from other publishers in the same way. I hate the bother of changes, and business transactions are never a pleasure to me. I have avoided talking to publishers because it made me restless and discontented, and because my relations with you, personally have always been so pleasant, even in business. But this bill for proof corrections has brought things to a head with me. I do not think it a just charge. I kept duplicate proofs, with the corrections, until after your first statement came in; then, as there was no charge entered, I threw them away. I do not think it is the custom of publishers to make these charges in the case of painstaking writers in whom the publisher, so to speak, "believes". I have just seen some of Mr. [Theodore] Dreiser's proofs; his books are practically re-written in proof, and he is never charged a cent for corrections. Do not Houghton Mifflin make this charge as a sort of luxury tax on a carefully written book? I don't mean I doubt that there is some charge from the printer, but it seems that a publisher usually pays this charge for a book he wants and is glad to handle.

MacMillans, whose books are well printed, tell me that the cost of composition on a long novel at the present time, is about $600.00, and that author's proof corrections cost about a dollar an hour. If my book cost $500.00 for composition, then by the 20% quoted in the contract, you would give me a hundred dollars' worth of proof corrections without charge, would you not? Add to that the amount you take out of my royalties, and we have author's corrections amounting to $244.00. Is it possible that it took one man thirty working days to make my corrections? You may tell me that the Riverside compositors charge more per hour, but why, after all, should your authors be charged more than MacMillans'?

Within the last few weeks, three New York publishers have made me definite propositions for my next book, offering better terms than my present publishers make me; in addition to increase in royalties and $1000.00 to $1500.00 cash advance on delivery of copy, they offer to give the book and me much better advertising than I have hitherto had. One firm has outlined an advertising scheme which seems to me excellent. They believe that the aim of advertising is not so much to sell one particular book, or to be careful to come out even on one book, as to give the author a certain standing which would insure his future and interest in his future books. Houghton Mifflin's policy may work out well for them as a business policy, but I do not think it works out well for me. I think the recognition of the public and reviewers has outstripped that of my publishers. This has been borne in upon me by a hundred little and big things until it has become a conviction. The publishers have made no use of this growing appreciation, and take no account of any evidence of it except the evidence of sales, which, with work like mine, is not indicative of the real interest.

I want to say a word about reviews. I know it is your theory that reviews do not sell a book. But some publishers do make them sell books. Several men have told me here that they believed the review of "Java Head" [by Joseph Hergesheimer] in the New Republic sold several thousand copies of the book. I know a number of people who bought the book after reading that review,—I did so, at once,—and they are all people who help to make opinion. I believe the New Republic never received copy of my last book, and Mr. [Francis] Hackett protests, not to me but to people to whom he would speak more frankly than to me, that his attention was never called to it by the publishers as being an unusual book. You remember that after writing you twice, asking you to send a copy to the editor of the Globe, I had to take a copy to Mr. [N. P.] Dawson's house myself.

One of the cleverest reviewers in New York telephoned me not long ago to discuss [H. L.] Mencken's review, and remarked that nobody had been afraid to come out and say that this book was unique in American fiction, except the publishers! That is certainly true; glance, if you will, at the jacket on that book; if ever there was a timid, perfunctory endorsement! "We unhesitatingly recommend etc"! No use has been made of the very unusual reviews the book has had. One of the best was lost in a special publication, The Dial; but couldn't the publishers of the book have got that notice to the part of the public who would be interested? MacMillans thought so, and the same notice was a roast of their book. That excellent appreciation of Brunius, instead of being quoted in some advertisement devoted to the best foreign and American notices of my books, was printed in The Piper (!) with the strongest sentences of commendation and such expressions as "a new and great writer" <u>carefully</u>

omitted. Now I don't want Houghton Mifflin to call me a "great writer", but why are they so shy about quoting anything of that sort when other people say it? If it were from a delicate literary conscience, I would admire the firm for it, but they do not feel this timidity in advertising frankly meretricious work.

I think "Java Head" has been splendidly advertised, with real enthusiasm and fire. You may tell me that it has not done a great deal for the sale of this particular book, but I know it has done a great deal for Hergesheimer.

This brings me to the real point of my dissatisfaction about advertising. My present publishers print my books and give them a formal introduction to the public. At least one of the publishers with whom I have been talking here believes in my books, and he wants my kind of work enough to spend money in pushing it, to lose money for the first year or two in pushing it. You know that has to be done to place an author of any marked originality. You know that even Conrad was a man absolutely recognized but almost unsold until Doubleday, urged by Kipling, took some real interest and pride in selling his books.

I know that you like to publish my books, but I am not assured that the other members of your firm do. If they do not, they will never do more than print them (the books) and let them take care of themselves. You know the real temper of your colleagues. This is not a business letter, but an appeal to you for personal advice, which will be absolutely confidential.

Do Houghton Mifflin want to publish me enough to put some money into my books, and to give my next novel as many inches of advertising as have been given to "Java Head", for instance. That book is still being advertised, by the way, while Antonia was long ago dropped out of Houghton Mifflin's ads.

Is not the Houghton Mifflin mind and heart entirely fixed upon a different sort of novel?

Frankly, I despair of any future with them. I see they have now on hand eight copies of "The Song of the Lark" and four of "O Pioneers". That seems to me indicative of the cautious spirit in which they have always handled my work. They don't believe they can make much on me, but they will be very careful not to lose much.

Books like mine require a special kind of publicity work. The New York publisher with whom I have talked most will give them that, and he will let me cooperate with his publicity department. I must give him his answer very soon.

I don't like to have my books come out in two groups, from two publishers; and I suppose if I go to another publisher Houghton Mifflin won't keep even four copies of any of my books on hand! But as it is, they never take advantage of the fact that every review of Antonia was a review of my three novels and discussed them all as things forming a group by themselves. The three books are never advertised together as a presentation of special features of American life, as Knopf advertises all of Hergesheimer's books, even those that are out of print. I don't care about the cash advance and that sort of thing, but I know I can work better for a firm that can give me some of its ingenuity and enthusiasm.

Faithfully yours,
Willa Cather

Though Cather's language above rather vaguely refers to "New York publishers" throughout most of the letter, she was thinking, as she reveals at the end, of Alfred A. Knopf.

TO WILL OWEN JONES

May 20, 1919
New York City

My Dear Mr. Jones;

As to the introductory chapter of "Antonia": such a device is very often employed by Russian and French authors, when they wish their narrative to be colored by a certain mood and certain personal feelings throughout. It is a device, and since it is, the more frankly it is presented as such, the better. I wished here to present the chief character through a man's memory, because the most interesting things I knew about the several women of whom she was made, were told me by men. I also wanted it written in the first person, since it was so entirely a story of feeling and not of action. I felt competent to handle a man's narrative in the first person—a very hard thing for a woman to do—mainly because of the severe training I had in writing Mr. McClure's autobiography, where I tried so very hard to give his exact impressions in his most characteristic language and with his nicest feeling. In that I succeeded so well that Mrs. McClure and Mr. [John S.] Phillips, his partner and school-mate, wrote me that it seemed to them a perfectly convincing presentation of him as a boy and young man, and that the sentences themselves had the abruptness and suddenness characteristic of him. From my success in that piece of work, I believed that I could interpret the youth of another man, of a different sort, whom I also knew very well.

The method employed in this story is, in itself, dangerous, and usually fakey; but it was the only one to convey the shades of feeling I wished to convey, and my work on that autobiography gave me the courage to try it. At first I found it awfully hampering to try to be Mr. McClure all the time, but in the end it got to have a kind of fascination to work within the limits and color of that personality I knew so well. Ever since I have had a sort of nagging wish to try the experiment again. In this case the introduction had to state the facts that the narrator of the story is a man of worldly experience,—for only those who know the world can see the parish as it is—,that he has no children to plan for and is not particularly fortunate in his domestic life. If he were, he would not dwell upon the years of his first youth either so minutely or so sympathetically. This, I take it, answers your question.

I am very sincerely glad you like the book. I suppose every serious writer goes through the experience of disappointing and estranging his early friends, and everyone develops as he must and can, not as he would. The enclosed notice from a Chicago paper seems to give a pretty clear statement of what I have been trying to do from the first. My aim has never changed, but in the early twenties one simply does not know enough about life to make real people; one feels them, but one has neither calm insight nor a practised ease of hand. As one grows older one cares less about clever writing and more about a simple and faithful presentation. But to reach this, one must have gone through the period where one would die, so to speak, for the fine phrase; that is essential to learning one's business.

Yes, I want to stop in Lincoln again and see everybody.

> Faithfully yours,
> Willa Cather

> ✦ ✦

On May 23, after looking into the matters Cather brought to his attention in her long letter, Ferris Greenslet responded patiently to each point, even including copies of interoffice memos and bills he called, jocularly, "Exhibit A," "Exhibit B," and so on. He agreed to split the cost of proof corrections fifty-fifty, and addressed the issues of reviews, advertising, and Houghton Mifflin's ability to produce and market Cather's work properly. He explained, with humor and grace, his feeling that Cather would not be so hard on Houghton Mifflin if she more properly understood all of the details, and he offered to follow his letter with a trip to New York to speak with her in person about these matters.

TO FERRIS GREENSLET

May 30, 1919

Dear Mr. Greenslet;

Excuse my delay in replying to your kind and friendly letter. For ten days now the town has been full of returned Nebraska boys, and, quite aside from the fact that it is a great and exhausting pleasure for me to be with them, they are just now rather distinctly <u>mon affair</u>.

I now feel quite satisfied about the charge for proof corrections. I am perfectly willing to stand half of it, as I think that is an entirely fair distribution. I was right about Dreiser, however, for I have since inquired of his publisher.

Yes, on the whole, I think we had better have a talk about some of these details when it is possible. I have decided not to sign up with anybody until the fall. I am leaving for Toronto tomorrow to spend a month or more with the Hambourgs. Later I may be in Jaffrey for a few weeks later in the summer before I go West. I expect to spend September and October in Red Cloud.

The discouraging thing I get from your letter is that Houghton Mifflin, having already handled my books in the way they think adequate, would probably do not more for them in the future than in the past. I think, on the other hand, that among the people who form opinion, I have a very different position from that which I had five years ago, and that this fact, for a publicity department interested in such things, makes me a very different business proposition. I am also writing better than I was then, considerably better, which at least is a feature in the case. The publisher here of whom I have been thinking favorably, told me frankly that it was a deciding fact in the case with him, and that he wanted "somebody who could do that kind of work and keep it up", and that my three books, read one after another, had convinced him that I could keep it up. In other words, he wants my "distinction" enough to take risk and trouble for it, while Houghton Mifflin have plenty of distinction, past and inherited, and for the last six years they have been out for quite another sort of bird, in fiction, at least.

By the way, have you read [Grant] Overton's amusing book on authorines [*The Women Who Make Our Novels*]? Voila ces dames! He wriggles and lies like a gentleman, and the Worst of the Virtuous Tribe he lets speak for themselves–––don't they do it, though!

I am returning some of the documents you sent me. Do you know what Swedish firm are translating "O Pioneers!"? Wonderful punctuation! I hope you'll have a fine fishing trip. Nobody shall see Claude [the manuscript for

One of Ours] until fall. He is getting big enough to look after himself. Frankly, I won't hand him over to anybody who won't do a good deal for him.

Faithfully yours
W.S.C.

→ ←

Cather's humorous mention of Grant Overton's 1918 book was not incidental: he begins his chapter titled "Willa Sibert Cather" with the claim that Cather is one of the "very few" authors who show "steady and rapid growth" in each of their books. It was just the point she was trying to make to Houghton Mifflin.

That point was, apparently, already made to the publisher Alfred A. Knopf. In the spring of 1919, Knopf was a young man, only twenty-six years old, and his publishing house had only been in existence for four years. This stood in stark relief to the venerable Boston publishing house of Houghton Mifflin, which could trace its history back to the esteemed Ticknor and Fields, publishers of classic works of American literature since the mid-nineteenth century. The following is the earliest known letter from Cather to Alfred Knopf.

TO ALFRED A. KNOPF

July 2 [1919]
Toronto

Dear Mr. Knopf:

Thank you for letting me know that you are still interested. The Japanese novel has not reached me yet. It is probably held up in customs, like everything else that comes into Canada. No, you don't owe me any candy, but perhaps you will owe me a half-hour's conversation when I get back to New York next fall.

Very cordially yours
Willa Cather

→ ←

Throughout the summer and fall of 1919, Cather continued to work on "Claude" and to correspond with her friends and publisher. Whether she was feeling unusually confident with the success of My Ántonia *or was just testing the loyalty of her publishers, Cather demanded quite a lot of Ferris Greenslet and Houghton Mifflin*

at this time, even asking Greenslet to get her a tent and to help her with a tele-
phone hookup. She complained that she had to keep writing short stories in order
to make a living, and thought "Scandal," published in the August 1919 Century,
an inferior product. She was very pleased about the positive response she continued
to receive for My Ántonia, *though, and enjoyed learning that well-known writers*
like Mary Austin and William Allen White were paying her compliments. She
wrote the following letter to her mother in the knowledge that it would be shared
with her sister Elsie, nicknamed "Bobbie."

TO MARY VIRGINIA BOAK CATHER

December 6 [1919]

My Dearest Mother;

I know I've not written for a long time, but I did not mean to be neglectful.
I thought Daddy would tell you about me and about how torn up my apartment was. It has taken so much work to get it even a little in order and the
way I want it. You know I have no maid this year, and as Edith is away from
eight-thirty in the morning until six-thirty at night, most of the housekeeping
falls on me. Father will tell you how we are boarding out for our dinners, and
you know I don't like that. Josephine now gets $80 a month; any good maid
would now cost us $60 a month, and we would have to send the washing out!
With eggs at $1.00 a dozen, and butter $1.04 a pound, we simply can't afford
to entertain any more, and what a servant would eat would be a very considerable item. Mrs. Winn, that noble widow, of whom father will tell you, comes
three half-days a week and keeps us clean, but there are so many, many other
things to do, and I have been far from well.

I am ashamed not to have written Elsie, when she wrote me such a nice
letter, and sent me Marguerite's letter, too. But I have simply been too tired,
Bobby,—the rush of the world has been too hard. But I am coming home this
winter, in February or March. I have waited to write until I could tell you that.
You see the expense of the trip is something one has to think about, when
the cost of living has increased here so enormously, and when I have to go to
France in the spring in order to finish my book at all. I expect, Mother, that I
have a brother or two who would xxxxxxxxxxx There, I had a burst of temper
at the bottom of the page, but I've cut it out. It seems extravagant for me to go
abroad now, but you know, Mother, that I always have known what was necessary for my work, and that I have been right not to take advice or reprimand
from any source about that.

I have thought you were doing pleasant things with Douglass, and would not need letters so much as last winter, and I didn't want to write Elsie until I could write her a long letter, and tell her how much I rejoice to hear of Marguerite's [Richardson] interesting life in California. She deserved it, and I'm so glad she has it. Dear Bobbie, I don't see how you did get on when you were teaching and cooking and taking care of Margie [Anderson]. Lord, my child, it's a blessing I DID NOT go home then, for you'd simply have had another Margie on your hands.

In addition to painting the bathroom and doing the house work and trying to write a novel, I have been becoming rather "famous" lately, and that is an added care. In other years, when I was living like a lady, with an impressive French maid, I could have been famous quite conveniently, but then I had only to receive a few high-brows. Now the man in the street seems to have "got onto" me, and it's very inconvenient. The enclosed, on the editorial page of the Tribune, is only one of a dozen articles that have come out in all the New York papers in the last two weeks. People write furious letters to the Sun to ask why their editor has not stated that I am the "greatest living American author"; the Sun editor replies, give him time, maybe he will say that. I have had nothing to do with this little whirlwind of publicity, God knows! My publishers have had nothing to do with it. They are the most astonished people you ever saw. One of them came racing down from Boston to see me, and he kept holding his head and saying, "but why should this book, this one catch on? Anybody would have said it could never be a popular book." You see they advertised it hardly at all, and I didn't urge them. I thought it was a book for the very few. And now they are quite stunned.

I'm like Roscoe when he said, if only his twins had waited till next year to come. This is such an awkward time to be famous; the stage is not set for it. Reporters come running to the house all the time and [keep] finding me doing housework. They demand new photographs, and I have no new clothes and no time to get any. Yesterday, when I was washing dishes at the sink with one of Mother's long gingham aprons tied round my neck—I've never had time to shorten it—I heard a knock at the front door and didn't stir. Then a knock at the kitchen door; such a very dapper young man asked if Miss Cather the Author lived here that I hesitated. He said, "Tell her I'm from the N.Y. Sun, and want to see her on very important business." I told him that Miss Cather had gone to Atlantic City for a rest! I simply couldn't live up to the part, do you see? He left saying there was to be a big article about her on Sunday.

Now, at least, Elsie, you don't have to wash dishes and be famous at the same time. Now, in other years, Josephine and I with our haughty French, thrown lightly back and forth when a visitor was brought in, could have made a great impression on reporters. We made a great impression last winter on the editor of the Chicago [Daily] News [Henry Blackman Sell], who has been my passionate press agent ever since.

By the way, Elsie, you must write the Chicago News for translations of the Swedish review. They are fine. The new Swedish edition of "O Pioneers" is one of the handsomest books I have ever seen. I have ordered several from Stockholm, and when they come I will send Mother one. The Swedish looks so funny to me, Mother; like the Petersons' newspapers I used to bring home from Mr. Cowley's in a flour sack, on horseback. You remember? A very fine French translation is being made of Antonia, some of the chapters have been sent over to me for suggestions, and it is simply beautiful French, clear as Latin. Miss Herbek [probably Šárka B. Hrbková] was here for dinner last week—I got the dinner—to see about getting the rights for translation into Bohemian. You see the tide seems to be coming in for me pretty strong. It won't make me any richer, but it makes me a great deal happier, dear Mother.

We have not been able to have our dear Fridays at home yet, but will begin next week, and on our cards we have written that it is only December and January that we will be at home. That is because I want to go West later,—I mean home, of course. The reason I could not go home for Christmas was that my Publisher came up to Jaffrey to see me and begged me to get as far along with the novel as I could before I broke off, for he is going to England in March, and if he can take about one-half or two thirds of the story in its final shape, he hopes to be able to make good terms for it there. You see Hugh Walpole, author of "The Dark Forest", is lecturing in this country now, and he talks about my books everywhere he goes, even at dinner parties, "raves" about them the newspaper men tell me, and he says the younger men in England are getting very much stirred up about me. So my publishers think this is the time to try for good contracts in England. I have got about two-thirds of my book written through for the first time; next week I begin to write it through from the first again. Some of it will have to be done over four or five, or even six times, but there is good life and movement through it. I hope I will be at home when it comes out, for it was almost the greatest pleasure I ever had to be at home when Antonia came out, and you and Father were reading it, both of you at once, and I could see how much you really did enjoy it. Yes, I think that was about the most satisfactory experience I ever had. It made me happy the way I used to be when I was a little girl and felt that you were both pleased with me.

I was at home when "The Song of the Lark" came out, too, but you and father were in Lander, and Douglass was at home, and he was cross about the laundry bill and the book, and sore at Mr. Cotting because he put the book in his window. That was an awful time, and I cried every day and was afraid to meet people. And, anyhow, I had paid the laundry bill!

Evening

Why, Mother, your letter has just come, and I had completely forgotten that tomorrow is my birthday! You were so nice to write me. Please thank father for the interest check he sent me.

Mother, I am so sorry, so sorry, to hear about your eye. Do, do, be careful of the other one! Oh, I am sure it's come from reading lying down so much,—and I do just the same thing. Don't do that any more. Don't read much; get Father to read to you. Don't fret about being a care to people. The last two summers I have had at home with you and Father, were among the happiest I ever had in my life. I wouldn't give them up for anything. And I'll always be glad to come and be with you. You ought to believe that, after the good times we had last summer. I will come in February or March to see you, and then I'll come again as soon as I get back from France, and I will always be glad to come. Of course, I almost have to have a place here, and if you have a place you have responsibilities, and must keep up to them, but I will always be glad to go home to be with you, and then Elsie can go away for a change. For didn't we get on nicely last summer, when we had nobody else to help us? It seems to me I can't remember a single unpleasant moment, except when I got cross about Mrs. Bradbrooks pan! You tell her for me, that I'll never forget her pan again.

Dear Mother, I send you such heaps of love. I think daughters understand and love their mothers so much more as they grow older themselves. I find myself loving to do things with you now, just as I did when I was a little girl, and I used to ride up to Aunt Rhuie's on the horse behind you and feel so proud that I had such a handsome young mother. Oh, I don't forget those things! They are all there, deep down in my mind, and the older I grow, the more they come to light. Of course, there was a time when I was "All for books" as Mrs. Grice says, and didn't think much about people. I suppose that had to be; but, thank God, I got over it!

Oh mother, I would do anything if I could help your dear eye! If you'll only be good to the other one I'll come and help you any time.

So lovingly,
Willie

Dear Mother, if you love your daughter, send her some of Margie's dish towels for Christmas, and a WHITE APRON to meet reporters in!

I can't send any presents to anyone this year, but I will try to find something nice for you. I have no time at all, and not nearly strength enough to keep all my engagements. You see, while this little flurry of excitement about my books is on, I must see a great many people, and I must answer their nice letters. I wish, sure enough, that it had waited, like the twins!

➤ ❤

Though Cather still planned to let Houghton Mifflin publish her new novel—or at least she was undecided about it—she did agree to a proposal from Alfred Knopf to publish a book of short stories. The book, titled Youth and the Bright Medusa, *came out in the fall of 1920 with four stories that had already been published in* The Troll Garden *("Paul's Case," "A Wagner Matinée," " 'A Death in the Desert,' " and "The Sculptor's Funeral") and four new ones ("Coming, Aphrodite!," "Scandal," "A Gold Slipper," and "The Diamond Mine").*

TO FERRIS GREENSLET

December 28, 1919
New York City

Dear Mr. Greenslet;

You have probably not followed the controversy in the Tribune about Antonia. The enclosed is an extract. I will tell you what I think about Mr. [Arnold] Mulder's book [*The Outbound Road*] when I see you. When, by the way, shall I see you? Is there any chance of your being in town before January 7th? I would like to have a session with you before that date if possible.

Within a few days I have had to autograph four copies of "O Pioneers!" three of them for publishers, it is true, but they had price marks on the front page, so I think they were honestly bought. The ugliness of that mustard-plaster binding has begun to get on my nerves. I have always hoped that if the book kept alive you would, of your own accord, give it a new binding. Now, won't you please tell me how many are left bound up in this ugly cloth, and whether you will be willing to give it a new binding in the cloth I sent you sometime ago. The typography is good, and you used to print it on good paper; why not drop the incongruous colored frontispiece, give it a decent binding, and let it look like the book that it has proved itself to be. Please let me hear from you definitely about this. If your people do not want to bother about the book, and would like to get rid of it, tell me upon what terms.

I have promised Mr. Knopf that he can bring out a new edition of the "Troll Garden" stories, as he has made me very generous terms. This, I am sure will not displease you, as Houghton Mifflin have never shown even a momentary interest in reviving this volume. The plates were destroyed, so it will have to be set anew.

Mr. Knopf would like, of course, to bring it out in the early spring. However, if you are to bring out "Claude", there might be some unfairness to you, and incidentally to myself, in letting the impetus of "Antonia" be transferred to this book or earlier work instead of passing it on directly to "Claude". If you advise, I will stipulate that the volume, which will have a discriminating introduction by an interested person, does not come out until six weeks or two months after Claude. I suppose he will be dashed when I make this condition about the date of publication, but I expect you will agree with me that I had better make it. Knopf will make a handsome book for me, and the introduction will state clearly that the stories are early work. I think it a sporting proposition in him, and I shall be interested to see what he can do with such a slight book.

Faithfully yours
Willa Cather

P.S. There is a phrase in Miss Birtwell's letter that ought to direct the advertising of the books mentioned; that the fine thing is rare, very. But your publicity man will never, never be bold enough to use that phrase. What he says is, "All our books are the fine thing, our great country is full of them, genuine interpreters of American life." With one exception, the page ad in the Bookman, the copy he prepares for me would do just as well for [prolific American novelist] Clara Louise Burnham. Please show your publicity man this post script, and ask him if all books read just alike to him.

Greenslet was cordial and even optimistic about Cather's deal with Knopf for the reissue of old material; he thought keeping her name in the public eye would benefit sales of all her books. The staff at Houghton Mifflin, including "publicity man" Robert Newton Linscott, did not much like Cather's characterization of him in her letter to Greenslet, though. Linscott wrote Cather a cordial defense of the copy he had written on her behalf, though he admitted in his letter that he didn't like the

last half of Song of the Lark *and so put off reading* My Ántonia. *He said he loved* My Ántonia *after he finally read it, of course.*

TO FERRIS GREENSLET

January 7, 1920

Dear Mr. Greenslet;

[Thomas] Capek's book on the Cechs [*Czechs in America*] arrived today. The idea of advertising Antonia so conspicuously on the back cover is a splendid one, so good that I hate to see it spoiled for many people by a stupid mistake. The Bohemian who wrote that letter is a prominent man among his people in Nebraska, as you say; he is well known all over the state; but his name is SADILEK, and your advertising people have printed it Sadiler! Now, I very much doubt if Sadiler could be a Bohemian name at all. Such a needless mistake destroys part of the authenticity and force of the letter. I have several perfectly needless mistakes of that sort against your publicity department.

Have you forgotten that when you were here you definitely promised me that every line of copy to advertise any of my books should be submitted to me in proof? With a stroke of the pen I could have caught up this foolish mistake. Besides, that was an agreement.

I am looking forward to seeing you soon. There are a number of things I want to take up with you as soon as I can, not least among them is Mr. Linscott's remarkable letter. You had better read it before you come, to be prepared, knowing me as you do, for my state of mind. Are there no diplomatic posts vacant?

I've just finished a really fine 15,000 word story that I did for a Christmas treat and to rest my hand from the long book. New York 'studio episode', and it's turned out very well; and it's opened up a mine of untouched material, a long account in another bank,—on which I can draw pretty heavily when I want to. Attendez-moi!

Hastily
W.S.C.

The 15,000-word story was "Coming, Aphrodite!," which was first published, in an expurgated form, in the Smart Set *in 1920.*

➔ ←

Cather took delight in her nieces and nephews throughout her life, taking time to write them entertaining letters like the one below to her niece about the German American puppeteer and artist Tony Sarg.

TO MARY VIRGINIA AULD

[Probably February 21, 1920]

Dear Mary Virginia;

Some day when you go over to see Grandmother, you will find this note for a surprise. Several weeks ago Tony Sarg came for tea, and brought one of his marionettes, carried him over in a large paper sack. He was Prince Bo-Bo, from Thackeray's "Romance of the Rose." He walked in beside Tony, just like a real man, only very tiny. Tony introduced him to me, and he bowed very politely, and I introduced him to everyone else. I asked him if he would have some tea, but he shook his head and picked up a cigarette out of a tortise shell box someone brought me from Italy. I told him he was too young to smoke, and he tossed it into the fire and fell down upon his face and sobbed piteously, his back just heaved up and down as if he were choking with grief. I told him I was sorry if I had hurt his feelings. Then he wiped his eyes, snuffled a little—Tony does the snuffling—and sat down on my foot, where he sat for half an hour in an attitude of deep dejection, while I poured tea for people. He did not forget his manners, however, and whenever a lady came in, or got up to take her leave, he rose instantly to his feet. When Tony came to take him away, the little Prince took up his feathered hat and kissed my hand very gallantly, and bowed his way out. He really was a wonder; few live men are as entertaining at a tea,—though of course, here, men go to teas, not for the tea but because they want to see the hostess. I do love to live in a world where everybody is polite. Everybody is so much happier. It is merely a habit, anyway, whether people get into the way of saying agreeable things all the time, or disagreeable ones. Never, my dear, get into the habit of knocking! It disfigures people for the company of nice people as much as a hare-lip or a hump nose. Verily, verily, I say unto you!

I go to the Opera a great deal this winter. My old friend Zoë Akins, who made a lot of money on her successful play, "Declaseé" has season tickets for every Thursday night, splendid seats, near the front, and she comes down in her car for me, and brings me home in her car, so it's little effort, even if I'm tired.

I wish you could have seen my little house on Valentine's day, it was like a conservatory, so full of flowers. I hope you will have a splendid winter, dear. Please give my love to our little neighbor, Helen.

With heaps of love from
Your Aunt Willie

➤ ❬

Though Cather seemed to rely on anecdotes from friends for her evidence, she was convinced that Houghton Mifflin was failing to fill orders for My Ántonia *correctly and, thus, hurting its sales. Houghton Mifflin claimed that the orders were being filled properly.*

TO R. L. SCAIFE

February 21 [1920]

Dear Mr. Scaife;

Your letter about the supply of "Antonia" in Chicago is a distinct shock. The three people who wrote to me before Christmas were not "investigators", but bone fide buyers who wanted the book, were unable to get it, and two of them sent me checks, begging me to send a copy if I had one. I am convinced that they had made an honest effort to get the book at home before they took that trouble. It must be, as you say, that they applied to a green salesman, or to several green salesmen. Could the fact that the buyers called my name rightly, and that clerks in bookstores usually call it "Kay-thur" have anything to do with it. It is all nonsense that an unusual name is an advantage in authorship. One had much better be named Jones. Salesmen in New York and Chicago always correct me when I pronounce my own name. Mr. Sell published a paragraph telling people that the name rhymed with 'rather,' but if it convinced others, it did not convince the bookstores.

I will read Miss [Elsie] Singmaster's book [*John Baring's House*] as soon as I have time, but I'm not very hopeful. Like everybody who has ever done editorial work on a magazine, I've read scores of her manuscripts. Sometimes they served a useful purpose and we bought them; but there was no more surprise in them than in Kirkman's laundry soap. Even her faults were not interesting. She not only hadn't a voice, she seemingly had no ear; she droned along. However, I'll read her book, since you've been kind enough to send it.

Sincerely yours
Willa Cather

→ ←

In May 1920, Cather left for her fourth trip to Europe. This time she was going to France as part of her research for her new novel.

TO MARY VIRGINIA BOAK CATHER AND ELSIE CATHER

May 27 [1920]
aboard the R.M.S. "Royal George"

My Dearest Mother and Elsie:

A week today since we left land, and we land in three days more. I have never had such a restful, peaceful crossing before. The weather has been beautiful, cold but not too rough, and I have felt exceptionally well all the time. Edith is always seasick and has been miserable—had to stay in her cabin most of the time. I don't see how she can be so patient. We left New York with our cabin full of fruit and flowers, six baskets of fruit in all and three boxes of flowers; from both my publishers, from Madame Fremstad and other friends. I sent a lot of the fruit down to the children in the steerage and gave one basket of it to Miss Pfeiffer, of Lincoln. As Edith can't eat any fruit, I am not equal to it alone.

I saved your letter and Elsie's to open and read on the steamer. Yes, Elsie, the novelette in my book is the one Mencken bought for the "Smart Set." ["Coming, Eden Bower," August 1920, later retitled "Coming, Aphrodite!"] It had to be cut and changed so for the magazine that I don't see why they wanted it—I really think they wanted me to have the $450 they paid me for it to help me on my travels. They never pay anybody else more than $100, so they make good their faith with works, which is more than most admirers do.

I liked Miss Pfeiffer when I was a kid, and still like her, but that hard grind has surely worn her out. The suffragettes don't bother much—some of them are nice and some dreadful. But there are many nice English and French people on board. I do very little but eat and sleep and look at the sea and look at the water, and sometimes think about the new novel that will be so good or so bad. I've not many ideas about it, but I've a great deal of love and a good deal of faith. Goodbye, now, dearest ones, I will write again from France.

Willa

TO MARY VIRGINIA BOAK CATHER

[May or June 1920]
Paris

[Written in the top margin:] address % Thomas Cook & Son, 1 Place de l'Opera

Dearest mother:

We have safely arrived in Paris. When we got here Edith was very sick after two weeks of sea-sickness, and we drove about hunting rooms, found everything crowded, and had to go to a very grand and expensive hotel for two days until she got better. Yesterday we moved to a small old-fashioned hotel, where we pay only three dollars a day and are fairly comfortable. That would have been very dear for a small hotel in Paris before the war, but everything has doubled or trebled in price. We find the French people kind and cordial, though of course they distrust Americans because after making such friendly protestations, we behaved so badly about the Peace treaty.

I never felt better than I did at sea, but I am always let down for a few days after I land. It is rather hard to travel with anyone as frail and sick as Edith, though she is so patient and asks so little. If only she gets well over here, we will have a beautiful stay in Paris.

With much love,
Willa

TO BLANCHE KNOPF

June 12 [1920]
Hotel du Quai Voltaire, Paris

Dear Mrs. Knopf;

The wonderful basket of fruit you sent me lasted nearly all the way across the ocean and did a great deal to help out the monotonous Cunard table. The weather was fine and I never felt better than during those eleven days at sea. I got a complete rest and reached Paris full of "pep". After a few days of costly magnificence at the Palaise d'Orsay I settled in this quiet hotel, just across the river from the Louvre. I have two small rooms, four flights up, facing on a quiet court; a bedroom, and a writing room in which I do not write one word! I write even my letters in the Luxembourg Gardens. The weather is gold and gray all mixed up—anybody would be a fool to shut themselves up with their own ideas with the city, this rather particular city, swimming in light outside. However, in the hours between sleeping and waking, in the hour before lunch and the idleness in the gardens after tea, I'm gradually getting the things I came for.

I live very comfortably for fifty francs a day—food and lodging, that is—which is not much if you consider exchange. Food is not so dear as in New York, and is of course ten times better, from the soup to the wonderful desserts. Theatre and music as cheap as ever, excellent seats for two dollars. But all the things in shops are twice as expensive as in New York,—hats, gloves, everything. The city itself never seemed to me so beautiful, and I find it a great advantage to live on the Seine. The streets are lovelier than anything in the art galleries. The Hambourgs will join me in two weeks and after lingering here for a time we will go South together.

With greetings and good wishes to you and Mr. Knopf

Faithfully yours
Willa Cather

TO FERRIS GREENSLET

June 20, 1920
Hotel Continental, Paris

[Written in above the hotel letterhead:] Do you know the rue du Chat qui Pêche?

Dear Mr. Greenslet:

I still live at the Hotel du Quai Voltaire, but am for the nonce visiting friends at this rich hostelry.

Last week Miss Lewis and I had an excellent dinner, with a good champagne, at Lapérouse for a hundred francs. I liked the place itself almost as much as the food, and it is not extravagant in price as Paris restaurants go now. At small hotels, like the Voltaire and the Hotel des Saintes Peres, one can still dine excellently, though somewhat slenderly, for ten francs. I am not going to shop any more than I have to, however. Everything in shops is costly, and the great change is that now all the less expensive things look cheap and shabby, as cheap things used to look in London. You can still get a beautiful hat for 500 francs, but a 150 franc hat looks like 14th street in New York. Silk gloves at 18 francs come to pieces the first time you put them on.

When we first arrived we spent a week in costly splendour at the Palais d'Orsay, and we still go there for dinner when neither of us is dining with friends. Miss Lewis goes on to Italy next week. The Hambourgs arrive on Saturday. I shall be here with them for several weeks, then go for a trip about the south of France with them. We will all meet at Sorrento about the end of July. Then I hope to fall to work in a lemon house in the garden of my friends there. The garden runs down into the sea—or the bathing beach which terminates it does.

I have not planned any new paragraphs for Claude yet, as a result of being here,—but I <u>have</u> planned to cut out several that otherwise would have gone in—so I feel I've not spent my francs in vain, especially those I have seen disappear in liquids ruddy and golden, lively and still, thin and sharp, thick and yellow as machine oil. The fruit and street flowers are not to be despised at this season. But the wines of France are really the supreme expression of its moods. I wish you were here. I could tell you a great many things that would sound absurd on either Bank or Park streets!

Faithfully
Willa Cather

TO FRANCES SMITH CATHER

July 4 [1920]
Paris

Dear Aunt Franc:

This morning I saw 20,000 French war orphans, who are supported by Americans, march down the Champ Èlysèes past our Ambassador and the President of France, each carrying a little American flag, and many carried a second flag with the name of the state in which their protector lives. They seemed nice, healthy children, not forlorn orphans, and very proud of they flag they carried. Certainly that flag never looked so beautiful to me before. Twenty thousand children are a great many, and surely that is a fine thing to do with money! All those children will grow up loving our country and our people. After the parade I stopped a number of the children and greeted them and one little boy would point to himself and say "I am Michigan", and a little girl would say "I am Tex-ass". The French always make the best of things, and these youngsters are so proud of being protected by the citizen of a great State, they regard it as a distinction as well as a charity, and they try so hard to speak a few English words. One tiny boy said he had to come so early, at eight oclock, tried to count the hours to me in English, got to six and had to finish in french!

Today the American flag is flying on all the old palaces of the Kings of France, and on all the public buildings. I find all the french people kind and friendly. The American soldiers are much beloved, though [Woodrow] Wilson is not. [Theodore] Roosevelt is still the great American name here. Next week I hope to get to Cantigny [where Franc's son, G. P., died]. I have made several efforts to go, but it is a difficult spot to reach as the trains in that section are few and irregular. Cantigny itself is not on any railroad line, and the railroads in that region are very much disorganized. In that demolished district there are now no hotels and no places to spend the night. I want to get there if possible in order to see it for you and to tell you about it when I get home.

When I last heard from home you were much better in health, and I pray that by this time you are almost well again. I had a hard winter with two attacks of Influenza, but the sea voyage did me a world of good and now I feel quite like myself again. After a few more weeks in France I am going to Italy to spend the rest of the summer with some friends [Earl and Achsah Barlow Brewster] who have a house on the sea near Naples. I rather dread the long trip, as travelling over here now is difficult, with waits and delays and poor service. Goodnight, my very dear Aunt. I wish you could have seen the thousands of war orphans with their little flags. I like to think of them and thousands more in the remote parts of France, growing up with the feeling that that flag is their friend.

With a heartful of love to you.

Willa

This Fourth of July in Paris is the most American "Fourth" I have ever spent—no noise or row, but real feeling about something real, all the ceremonies solemn and beautiful.

TO CHARLES F. CATHER

July 7 [1920]

Paris

My Dearest Father:

If the weather is good I wish you would go out and tell Aunt Franc that I have at last succeeded in finding where G. P. is buried. I have talked to a woman who has seen the cross on his grave with his name upon it, and his grave is properly and clearly registered here in Paris in the books of "The Society for the Care of the American Dead."

He is registered:

2nd Lieut Grosvenor P. Cather
(Inf.) I.R.C. Att. Co. A. 26th Inf.

Location of Grave

Villiers Tournelle
Grave No. 2. Plot B.

I copy the above exactly. He is therefore buried in the American Military Cemetery of

VILLERS TOURNELLE,

which is about ten miles from Cantigny, and is in plot B, among the very first who fell. The bodies of the men who fell at Cantigny were taken up within a few weeks after they were first buried, placed in coffins and taken to Villiers Tournelle while that section was still under fire. The bodies had been wrapped in tarpaulin and blankets, each marked with his name and company, and the coffins were marked from that data, and each was simply registered,—so there can be no mistake. G. P. is unquestionably buried in grave 2, plot B.

I shall go to the cemetery next week and take a photograph of the grave for Aunt Franc. I had made all arrangements to go yesterday, but the heavy rains in that part of the country have made the roads impassable. Isabelle is going with me, as it is a hard trip. I leave Paris at 6 oclock in the morning and go to Montdidier (MONTDIDIER). It is not far, but there are two changes of cars and long waits, before one gets there and only one train a day. At Montdidier I will have to hire an automobile to take me to Cantigny and from there on to the Cemetary at Villiers Tournelle. There are no hotels in that devastated region, but a French woman belonging to the Society of French Homes will keep us over night. This beautiful Society tries to help Americans hunting for dead soldiers in every possible way. I enclose their letter which you will please give to Aunt Franc. After I have been to the cemetery and photographed the grave I will write to her. I know she will be glad to know that G. P. is lying in a cemetery, with a cross on his grave and his name on the cross. When I last saw her she thought he must be lying somewhere out in No Man's Land. In the registry here in Paris, under the number of his grave and his name and rank, there is added "Killed in action at Cantigny." His name on his cross is printed "Cacher," but it is correct in the registry, and I will have the spelling corrected on the cross when I go up there. "The Society for American Dead" have given me authorization to do so, in order to make the name on the grave as it is in the Register. I want to do this because I feel it would be some satisfaction to Aunt Franc, and because it is all one can do to show one's appreciation of a kinsman who was a brave soldier. If I were buried in France, I would want my relatives to come to see me if they were in this part of the world.

Goodbye now, dearest Father. I am well and am very happy to have Isabelle and Jan here. I am beginning to be a little homesick from time to time, and I shall not be sorry to turn away from all this beauty and from this wonderful people and face the West, toward the people and the country that are my own.

With a great deal of love to you and Mother and to Aunt Franc,

Willie

→ ←

Though Cather went to the south of France with the Hambourgs, she never made it to Italy to visit the Brewsters as she planned. Edith Lewis found food scarce in Italy, so the two of them retreated to Paris, where they could stay comfortably. By November of 1920, they were back in New York.

That fall, while she was in France, Alfred Knopf published Youth and the Bright Medusa, *and the critical response to the book of stories reaffirmed her reputation. The* New York Times Book Review *said, "If Willa Cather had written nothing except 'Coming, Aphrodite!' . . . there could be no doubt of her right to rank beside the greatest creative artists of the day." The book, though a minor one compared to* My Ántonia, *made her as much money in its first six months as* My Ántonia *had made her in a year, according to her biographer James Woodress. Cather was impressed with Knopf's work and the attention he lavished on her.*

TO FERRIS GREENSLET

January 12, 1921
New York City

Dear Mr. Greenslet;

After our last talk at the Brevoort I did not see Mr. Knopf for three weeks or more, but during this time I watched his advertising pretty carefully and decided that I would let him publish "Claude." My decision is based entirely upon the conviction that his publicity work is, for me, much more spirited and effective than Houghton Mifflin's has been. The publicity work he has done on this volume of short stories has helped me along very much indeed. The influence of the 'strong talk' on the jacket was perceptible in nearly all the reviews, and in his advertisements he did not hesitate to express an enthusiasm about my books which he says he quite genuinely feels. I have always believed that you have a strong liking for them, but your publicity department does not express this liking very convincingly.

I think you know that the publicity work is the only feature of the Houghton Mifflin handling of my books that I have seriously found fault with. Perhaps in a few years I will not feel that an enthusiastic publicity department is so vital to me. At any rate, I hope you won't feel that you must consider this departure a final break. I don't want to consider it as such. It is only a break with your publicity man or men. I would like still to call you my publisher, if you don't mind, and maybe the next novel will be the Pittsburgh story you have always wanted. That you published my first novel, and that you used to urge me to try my hand at long stories, long before that, I do not forget. Just now I am really going away from your firm for Claude's health; because I feel so sure that he particularly needs 'presentation', a certain kind of publicity work. But, unless you see it otherwise, I shall refuse to say that I have 'left' you. I would like to say that I have by no means left you, but that it is true that Knopf is going to publish this next book.

Mr. Knopf, by the way, has not heard these glad tidings, though I think I will try to see him tomorrow. No, I remember no[w] that I shall be seeing him on Saturday evening at a party, and I'll tell him then that I'm going to let him try it out with this book.

You've always groaned a little at the War—as do I!—and a great deal about the West, and this novel is so wholly West and War that maybe you will feel a little relief as well as, I hope, some decent regret, at not having to be responsible for it. Anyhow, please don't lose interest in my humble affairs, please keep those of my books you have now on the market, and please don't reject the next novel I send you.

Always faithfully yours
[Signature cut out of original]

When do you go to England? I want to write you a personal letter before you go—that is, unless I can see you. Please let me know if you are to be in N.Y.

❖ ❖

Greenslet wished Cather the best with "Claude," and then said he was going to go and read the Book of Job and lament his situation. He claimed that Houghton Mifflin would always welcome her back.

TO FERRIS GREENSLET

January 21 [1921]

Dear Mr. Greenslet;

I remain your everlasting debtor for the nice letter you wrote me a week ago. I often tell Mr. McClure that he and I never began to be the best possible friends until our business relations were over. I already begin to feel that poor Mr. Knopf is the day's work and you are the vacation. Knopf, by the way, seems willing to print the name of my other publishers in the list of books facing the title page as you suggest. I have just had a statement from him of the sales of the "Bright Medusa" up to December 31st; 3385 copies sold up to that date, and my royalty amounts to eleven hundred and eighty some dollars. Surely, that's very good indeed for a book of unrelated short stories, half of which were taken from an old book. I am sure he will always try to push the books you publish as well as the new one.

The Hambourg Trio has been here for ten days, giving concerts, and I have been terribly rushed. Drop me a line to let me know when you are going to be in town, and tell me when I can telephone you. No, I have no telephone: I am going to have a rubber stamp made of that phrase! But I want to see you when you are here, without fail, and this time we won't have any troubles to discuss. I wonder if you can manage to send me my March check before you go?

I seem to be needing a great deal of money this winter. When you come I'll tell you how I was kidnapped about two weeks ago,—if Elsie Sergeant doesn't see you and tell you first.

Faithfully yours
WSC

❖ ❖

In April 1921, Dorothy Canfield Fisher published a review of Youth and the Bright Medusa *in the* Yale Review. *It must have given Cather great satisfaction to read the ungrudging opening line of her old friend's review: "There is no writer living in whose excellence Americans feel a warmer, prouder pleasure than we all feel in the success of Willa Cather."*

TO DOROTHY CANFIELD FISHER

March 21 [1921]

Dear Dorothy:

Mr. Knopf brought in a copy of the <u>Yale Review</u> yesterday and showed me what a fine generous thing you had done for me in that number. I am the more pleased because the commendation of no other person would mean as much in Red Cloud, where you and your work are much beloved, and where I am always eager to give satisfaction. They have no opinion of 'critics' in general there, but they have confidence in you, and an expression like that from you will please them more than anything else could. The Red Cloud public is ready now to hear a good word, for after "Antonia" they really came round, and said "yes, it was exactly like that; that is the way we remember it."

Are we never, I wonder, to come together for a talk again? There are so many, many things I would like to ask you about and tell you about. I have such a far-flung family that I am kept rushing about in the West when I am not at my desk on Bank Street. But won't you write me before you come to New York next time, so that I can get at you? If we could get an afternoon away from the rest of the world, I think we'd both get a good deal out of it. Lucy Allen came in here one day and said she'd get me in touch with your mother sometime. I was pleased to see Lucy, but she brought along an up-and-coming club woman who spoiled the fun.

I'm always wonderfully glad to please you, Dorothy. The first letter you wrote me about "O Pioneers!" long ago was the most helpful "hand-up" I had had, and I've always kept it and the other generous letters you've written me about my books. You know, better than anyone else what a long way I had to go to get—anywhere. And you know, too, the difficulties of the road. It is strange to come at last to write with calm enjoyment and a certain ease, after such storm and struggle and shrieking forever off the key. I am able to keep the pitch now, usually, and that is the thing I'm really thankful for. But Lord—what a lot of life one uses up chasing 'bright Medusas', doesn't one? I think we might get together and compare our scars, like doughboys. I'm not at all fierce anymore—unless you bring a <u>clubwoman</u>!

Your pleased and grateful friend

Willa

TO DOROTHY CANFIELD FISHER

Friday [April 8, 1921]

Dear Dorothy:

It's foolish for people who have so much to say to each other not to get into communication with each other, don't you think? Can't we manage better in the future? You do come to town sometimes, and I'll manage to get at you if you'll let me know. I believe we could quite come together again now—and oh how good that would be for me! I know I was sullen and defiant for a good many years—like Paul in "Paul's Case", all mixed up—but getting started at my own job has straightened me out inside. Try me on again, and you'll find I'm reasonable now!

After you left the other night I was thinking about that very time in Pittsburgh, while I was undressing, and wondering how people who had that basic understanding and affection could ever drift apart. But that person who made such a fuss about a story ["The Profile"]—a rotten bad one, of course—was not I, "it was the fool of me", as the Diamond Mine's husband remarked,—the wrong-headed and tormented fool of me. Discouraging years those were, you know; teaching all day, writing at night, never getting on. They are over—let's forget them.

I've always kept the letters you wrote me about each of my books. If you had, for instance, written me a discouraging one about "O Pioneers!" it would have frightened me a great deal—and the one you did write helped me a great deal. I suppose its because you know me so well—and so much—that it means so much to me to please you—and because you know "the fool of me" also! I think you over-estimate my "success", both the inner and the outer. I've really a very small public, and, of course, I'm a rather one-sided writer. But those things don't trouble me if I can have the fun of doing what I like and only that, and can manage to please you and half-a-dozen others.

But what I started out to say was, why can't we see each other sometimes? We own a considerable bit of "past" in common—nearly all of it delightful to remember. The people with whom one has that grow always fewer. There are years when life is a frenzy—a crazy affair, you know. But now, jamais plus [never again]! I can take as much or as little as I like of several kinds of insanity. A new kind of freedom for me, when the trees grow thin enough so that one can see the wood! And dear Dorothy, let's see some of the rest of the wood together! There were long years when I loved you very, very dearly, you know—and when one is older that comes back, with a difference, and the new people can't mean as much. I feel very happy in my heart about you, as if we were going to have a great many lovely hours together.

With my love and gratitude

Willa

I'm off for Toronto tonight
℅ Jan Hambourg
38 St. Vincent St
Toronto, Canada

➔ ←

In 1921, the novelist Sinclair Lewis was getting a lot of attention from the huge success of his 1920 novel Main Street *and was lecturing around the country. During a stop in Omaha, Nebraska, he told the audience, according to the* Omaha World-Herald, *"Willa Cather is greater than General Pershing; she is incomparably greater than William Jennings Bryan. She is Nebraska's foremost citizen because through her stories she has made the outside world know Nebraska as no one else has done."*

TO SINCLAIR LEWIS

April 14, 1921

Toronto

Dear Mr. Lewis:

My father has sent me an Omaha paper quoting some very fine and generous things you said about me in your lecture there. That you have read me and like me would in itself be good news enough,—but this downright friendly push from your strong hand, is something that touches and pleases me more than I can say. I would not be at all surprised if your vigorous talk did more to make Nebraska people read me than my own books have done. So I've to thank you for helping me to get the attention of my own folks out there. But I've to thank you much more for letting me know that you like my books yourself. I would rather have the respect of a few (about three) strong, straight-hitting young writers like yourself than anything else that can come out of the writing business. That's the truth, and I am therefore very gratefully yours,

Willa Cather

→ ←

In the July 27, 1921, issue of the Nation, *influential critic Carl Van Doren wrote about Cather in the seventh part of his series called "Contemporary American Novelists." Like many critics after him, Van Doren saw the connection between the pioneers and the artists that populate Cather fiction, noting the peculiar kind of "heroism" in both.*

TO CARL VAN DOREN

July 30 [1921]
Toronto

My Dear Mr. Van Doren;

I have been watching with the keenest interest your hair-raising feat of writing about a group of most dissimilar writers, each in his own manner; from the lumpy mountain range of Mr. Dreiser to my own comparatively calm vegetable garden. I am naturally most interested in the article on myself, and I think you have done well and generously by me. I had never tried to puzzle out why my bow had two such dissimilar strings; except that when one lives in the cornfields the people in The Musical Courier look very dazzling, and after one has lived a good deal among the dazzling, the cornfields have their distinct merits. Since you have managed to find some sort of logical connection between these two obsessions, I am very glad to accept it.

The new novel which I am just bringing toward the close is better than the others for several reasons, but I wonder whether you will find much improvement in form. As Mrs. [Edith] Wharton once said; even among good things one must choose, and one must renounce. I chose what I cared for most, and I had to renounce 'form'———in any very sound and gratifying sense. Probably, like so many modern composers, I shall always be weak on that side.

Please don't return my copy of "The Troll Garden" until the autumn. I won't be home until late in October, and at this season things get lost in the mail.

With my heartiest thanks and warm appreciation,

Faithfully yours,
Willa Cather

TO ALFRED A. KNOPF

August 26 [1921]
Toronto

[Card attached to top:] It may help you in selection of type to know that the novel will run just about one hundred and fifty thousand words. W.S.C.

Dear Mr. Knopf:

Greetings to you and your lady, and welcome home.

Miss Lewis will see you today, and will deliver a bunch of manuscript to you with explanations. I am hoping that by throwing the first part of the story into type you can manage to get serial publication for it.

I have been able to finish this story much better than I dared to hope. The latter part is now quite as close-knit and as personal as the first part. In other words, I have at last brought it across. I have stayed here and boned away at it all summer, but now it is done.

The press this summer has been extremely good. I hope your people have saved the clippings for you, including the well-placed <u>Nation</u> article.

Now, a sad blow for you. The novel will have to be called "Claude". I did the best I could by the other title—I lived with it for months,—and I hate it vehemently. It sounds like an Alice Brown title—an evasion, an apology. "Claude" is the <u>only</u> title for this story—any other title would spoil the book for me, and this book is a present I am making to myself. I won't have it spoiled. Trust me, this story will make its own title. No title could have seemed more unpromising than "Antonia" seemed at first. Scaife said bitterly, "Couldn't you manage to call it something that people could at least pronounce?" Yet the story has made the title go. This title won't offend so many people as you think.

1. For low-brows "Claude" is as good a name as any.
2. The high-brows ought to give me the benefit of the doubt.

If Mr. [Joseph] Hergesheimer, for instance, called a story "Myrtle" or "Elaine", I should of course know he had a reason for doing so. Nobody has objected to "Sir Claude" in "What Maisie Knew"—in fact, it is one of H. James' most successful names. If he had called the book "Sir Claude", that would have been nothing against it. It is not a sissy name like "Reggie"—it is clumsily romantic—and that is just what this boy is.

"Claude" is the title, and by that we must sink or swim.

I am leaving for Red Cloud, Nebraska on Tuesday the 30th. I must get to work at once on an article on "Nebraska" the Nation has asked me to do for their Portraits-of-the-States series. On October 29 I will lecture for the Omaha Society of Fine Arts. I hate lecturing, but they made their case very strong, and this lecture opens their season.

Faithfully
Willa Cather

P.S.

1. I have decided to let you use two names (Willa Cather) for me on this novel, and to drop out the "Sibert" for good,—except in signing checks.

2. Since "Claude" is to be the title, perhaps you would like me to name each of the several parts of the story, and thus give variety to the title of right-hand pages. If so, you may use the following:

Book I   Lovely Creek
Book II   Old Falsehoods
Book III Sunrise on the Prairie
Book IV   The Voyage of the Anchises
Book V   "Bidding the Eagles of the West Fly On."

W.S.C.

→ ←

On her way west, Cather stopped in Chicago and talked with her friend Fanny Butcher, writer, critic, editor at the Chicago Tribune, *and owner of Fanny Butcher Books.*

TO ALFRED A. KNOPF

September 1 [1921]
Hotel Clarke, Hastings, Nebraska

Dear Mr. Knopf,

O.K. to every thing in your letter. I had a long talk with Fanny Butcher about the title, and am again shaken—not as to the rightness of Claude, but as to the wisdom of using it. She begs and implores me not to!

Now, I will be quite satisfied with "One of Ours" [then printed out] "One of Ours," if you like it. It has merits; it has plenty of "O"s, is euphonious and mystifying—and it is "easy to say".

Please let me hear from you as soon as you have read the manuscript, as I am very eager to know how it strikes you when you read it altogether—the relation of one part to another and the corresponding changes in tempo were the things I was most interested in throughout this story, and I have never regarded them at all in any book I've done hitherto. I can say without boasting that the French part of the story took more self control and more kinds of skill than—well, than most things that are written now-a-days. And the tone does not break once! I do not once "show off" or write gaudily————and there were so many places where I could have done it.

Cordially yours
W.S.C.

The story is nearer 150,000 than 160,000, I think.

TO MARY VIRGINIA BOAK CATHER

November 26 [1921]

My Dearest Mother;

I was so pleased to get a card from you and Father on Thanksgiving morning. I hope you went to Retta's [Ayres Miner], or had a good Thanksgiving dinner somewhere. I had mine at home, with Josephine to cook it for me! You tell Margie that now I have that nice Frenchwoman back, that always took good care of me. Her two little girls from France have come over, one eight and one ten, and she has her own house to keep. Her husband works, and the three children are going to school. But she gives me half-time; on Monday she comes for the whole day and does the washing, but on every other day she comes at two oclock and works for the rest of the day, and gets dinner at night.

So far, it seems too good to be true. She did not have to be told one thing about the house; she walked in after two years' absence and knew where every napkin and doylie was kept. She was much annoyed because I had put the oyster forks in another drawer, and had put the ice-cream freezer on the top shelf of the kitchen cupboard instead of the bottom. She told me when she came that if she found she would have to neglect her own house, or if the children or her father got sick, she would have to give it up, so it may be too good to last. I'll enjoy it while it does last, for nobody can take care of me and the house as well as she can. She knows just how I like things done,—and she, too, is an artist in her way; most French people are. She respects my work, and I respect hers.

Of course we still have to get our own breakfast, and I make my bed and tidy my room. The only really hard thing is that the ice comes up every other day on the dumb-waiter, and it always comes at eleven, so I have to lift it off and carry it through the hall into the dining room and put it in the box. There is really no other way, though it is hard on my back. You see it takes a quarter of an hour's fussing to get the janitor to come up from the basement and do it, and cuts into my working time.

Do tell Carrie that I have Josephine back; I know she will be glad. And tell Carrie please to send me Irene's address, as I'm getting nearly frantic because she does not send me my bill. I hurried away from Omaha, leaving her to pay everything.

How nice you were to slip the baby's picture into the box, mother! It's such a nice picture.

Dear Mother, if you have one of those big shopping bags like Douglas sent you that you <u>do not need</u> yourself, I'd be delighted to have it for Christmas. And please send me two kitchen aprons, old ones will do just as well as new, one dark gingham and one white one, for Josephine.

No word from Isabelle yet, but their boat got to France all right. Now Goodbye for this time, dear Mother. I think about you so much, and about how kind and patient you and Father both were with me this summer. I was sick and worried too, most of the time. A sick grandchild and a celebrated daughter both in one summer made a pretty heavy dose for you! I'll do so much better next time: I somehow know that then I'll be calm and peaceful, because I know I'll be better in health.

With so much love to you both,
Willie

TO DOROTHY CANFIELD FISHER

January 26, 1922

My Dear Dorothy;

I did indeed get a long letter from you in November, but the general crush of things has delayed my reply to it. Even if I don't write often, its the realest sort of pleasure to me to be in correspondence with you again, and to be intending to write you. Things never should have been any different, and I always felt that sometime we would just naturally touch again. I often dreamed of it, and I think the things I dream of are those I really believe in.

My plans for next summer are vague, but I shall probably go West sometime. I wouldn't be able to tie myself up to a six weeks engagement, but I might be able to give three or four lectures for the Middlebury school [the Bread Loaf School], which, God help me, I've never heard of before! When does it begin? I imagine I am more likely to be free in the early part of the summer than later.

Yes, the novel is finished, and I'm reading the proofs. The last part balances the first, I think, and that is all I hoped for. It won't be as satisfying as the first, either to me or to other people. Are our endings, in life, I mean, ever as satisfactory or as glowing as our beginnings? I will see that you get one of the first copies, next fall—I don't favor a spring market—and you'll agree that I set myself an impossible task, but I think you'll also see that if there is any "victory" at all in it, it's a kind of moral one. "Aphrodite" was one of the parties by which I rested myself from the long strain of being so unnaturally good—a perfect saint for three years!

Have you seen the two volumes of hitherto untranslated [Ivan] Turgenev stories [*The Two Friends and Other Stories*]? There's a perfect beauty in one, called "A Quiet Backwater"[.] I remember he speaks of it in one of his letters to [Pauline] Viardot.

I'm so glad for the good news from your family, and that you are well enough to skate. My dear father and mother are well, Isabelle and Jan are having a glorious winter in Paris. I am sulking with a hatred of my kind, just at present; as a result of having broken over my rule and gone to a string of 'literary' dinners in New York. My God, the faces of them are as terrible as those in the Musical Courier! Writers don't have to grin for a living, if they only knew it. It makes me want to hibernate at Five Bank street and wear a never-lifting frown.

With love always, dear Dorothy
Willa

✦ ✦

Edith Lewis, a professional advertising copy writer, often used her skills to help Cather with the book jacket text.

TO ALFRED A. KNOPF

Saturday [February 5, 1922]

Dear Mr. Knopf;

Here is the text for the Jacket. I am sending it to your house, as I am utterly unable to get your office by telephone—you seem almost as telephoneless as I am!—and I am sure you will be at home this evening. Perhaps you will have more time to regarder it there than you would at your desk.

Miss Lewis says that it's very difficult to write an ad for a story when the author insists that the theme of the story must not be whispered in the ad! Please ask Mr. Spier to have a proof made of this and send it to me, as she may be able to better the text in the proof. And if you yourself have any suggestions to make, please let me have the benefit of them.

Faithfully yours
W.S.C.

All the galley proofs of the novel are now in my hands. About when would you like to have them done?

I look forward to hearing Miss [Myra] Hess on Monday.

✦ ✦

By explaining One of Ours *to the critic and fellow writer H. L. Mencken, Cather was trying to influence one of the most important reviewers of the book.*

TO HENRY LOUIS MENCKEN

February 6 [1922]

Dear Mr. Mencken;

The article in the Sun on "Our National Letters" gave me much joy. That's just it, when we're at all true to facts and existing conditions, when we get away from "Old Chester Tales" and Booth Tarkington platitudes, we seem foreign! I've often had a deep inner toothache of the soul, wondering whether I was unconsciously copying some "foreign" writer. When "O Pioneers" was written, it was a terrible lonesome book; I couldn't find any other that left out our usual story machinery. I wondered then, and still sometimes wonder, whether my mind had got a kink put in it by the four shorter novels of Tolstoi, "Anna Karenina", "The Cossacks", "Ivan Ilyitch", and "The Kreutzer Sonata", which, in paper bindings and indifferent English, fell into my hands when I was fourteen. For about three years I read them all the time, backward and forward; and I used to wonder whether they had so "marked" me that I could not see the American scene as it looked to other Americans————as it, presumably, really was. I tried to get over all that by a long apprenticeship to Henry James and Mrs. Wharton, and to make an entrance in good society (I mean in, not into) in good company, with ["]Alexander's Bridge". "The Bohemian Girl" and the first draft of "O Pioneers", the nucleus from which it was made, were written before that first artificial novel, but I did not even send them, or show them to a publisher. Because their pattern was different, I thought they must be the artificial ones—real only to me, because I had a romantic and lyric attachment for the country about which they were written. I thought Alexander'[s] Bridge the natural and un-exaggerated book, because it used all the conventional machinery in the conventional way, and so, with pride, I published it. This lengthy confession is apropos of your article, but you may put it in your graveyard as handy for an explanatory obituary.

May I ask you to read a copy of the new novel in June or July, an advance copy? It's so very different from the others that I'd like to know what you think of it. I might be hit by a taxi-cab or something before you got round to reading it in the regular course of things. It may be a complete mistake, and you would be a good man to smell out falsity, if it's there, for you are just a little prejudiced against the subject matter, and against the sentiment on which the latter part of it is built————or, rather, the sentiment by which it moves and draws the next breath. If Claude's emotion seems real to you,—scoffer that you are!—if his release makes something expand the least bit behind your ribs or under your larynx; then, I shall know that in spite of the <u>damnable</u> nature of the material I've got to port before the perishible cargo spoiled. Remember: this one boy's feeling is true. This one boy I knew as one can only know one's own blood. I knew the ugliness of his life and the beauty—to him—of his release. He can't help what went over this country, any more than you or I can. His own feeling was fine; and by an utter miracle one so disinherited of hope, so hopelessly at odds with all his life could ever be,————such an one found his kingdom; found conditions, activities, thoughts that made him glad he had lived. You see I absolutely <u>know</u> this; some of him still lives in me, and some of me is buried in France with him.————But the presentation, of course, can make any truth false as Hell, as Mr. Othello said; and the pity of a true knowledge and a true desire is always that it should be so at the mercy [of] the feeble hand,—the hand that very fullness of truth makes unsteady.

But presentation is always a gamble; the road is so rutted with old tracks, we can't go as we would.

Please save this lengthy epistle and read it over when you read the book. I may be guilty of special pleading, but I want to give this boy every chance with you. And if I've done a sickly, sentimental, old-maid job on him, tell me so loudly, like a man, rub it in, pound it down; I'll deserve it and I'll need it for my soul's salvation.

Faithfully yours
Willa Cather

→ ←

In addition to being eager to rekindle her friendship with Canfield Fisher, Cather also felt that Dorothy's deep knowledge of France and French culture could help her with the difficult final parts of "Claude."

TO DOROTHY CANFIELD FISHER

February 6 [1922]
New York City

Dear Dorothy;

I hate to bother you so often about this, but I have had a letter from Mr. [Wilfred] Davidson, and the delicate gentleman does not say anything about terms; neither does he tell me <u>which</u> six weeks of the summer his school [Bread Loaf] is in operation. The date would be an important consideration for me. Of course one wouldn't expect lecture prices for talks to a small number of specially interested students, but I think before writing him I would like to know whether the school would pay my traveling expenses and cover the week or so I would be there. A slow-selling author, who pays little attention to in-come, has to pay attention to out-go, or be in the hole at the end of the year. Now, I am NOT, with tightly compressed lips, throwing your magnificent sales in your face! I'm not a bit sore about being a slow proposition on the market; but I have to cut my plans according to my cloth in order to avoid worrying. Hence, I ask you for light about terms before replying to the Dean.

And now, a counter proposition, in which I really am asking something for nothing:

When the page proofs of my new novel are ready, sometime in May or June, would you be willing to read them over, not carefully and under any strain, but merely as a general reader, and report me if you notice anything that seems to you misleading as to facts, or false as to taste. The last third of the story, unfortunately, takes place in France, under conditions of which my knowledge is not great. I have tried not to pretend to know more than I do. If it got by you, that would mean a good deal. The one character that matters is all right there, I am sure; I would certainly know it if he wasn't. But some of the things that touch him may be wrong, and at a word from you I could drop an indiscreet phrase or incident.

Tell me quite honestly and unhesitatingly if it would be inconvenient or embarrassing to you in any way.

Yours
Willa

➤ ⬱

Fisher agreed to read One of Ours *in proof, and Cather began sending the pages to her.*

TO DOROTHY CANFIELD FISHER

Wednesday [probably March 8, 1922]

Dear Dorothy;

Yes, it will be classed as a "war story", which means it will sell about twelve thousand. And God knows I never wanted to write a war story. I lost six months, refraining from putting pen to paper on this one. But it stood between me and anything else.

It was like this: My cousin, Grosvenor, was born on the farm next my father's. I helped to take care of him when he was little. We were very much alike———and very different. He never could escape from the misery of being himself except in action, and whatever he put his hand to turned out either ugly or ridiculous. There were years when we avoided each other. He had a contempt for my way of escape, and his own ways led to absurdities. I was staying on his father's farm when the war broke out. We spent the first week hauling wheat to town. On those long rides on the wheat, we talked for the first time in years; and I saw some of the things that were really in the back of his mind. I went away and forgot. I no more thought of writing a story about him than of writing about my own nose; it was all too painfully familiar. It was just to escape from him and his kind that I wrote at all.

He went over in July, 1917. He was killed at Cantigny, May 27, of the next year. That anything so glorious could have happened to anyone so disinherited of hope! Timidly, angrily, he used to ask me about the geography of France on the wheat wagon. Well, he learned it, you see. I send you his citation. I first came on it in the morning paper when I was having my hair shampooed in a hairdresser's shop. From that on he was in my mind. The too-personalness, the embarrassment of kinship, was gone. But he was in my mind so much that I couldn't get through him to other things. It wasn't affection, but realization so acute that I could not get away from it. I never meant to write a story with a man for the central figure, but with this boy I was all mixed up by accident of birth. Some of me was buried with him in France, and some of him was left alive in me.

It's a misfortune for me and my publisher that anything so cruelly personal, so subjective, as this story, should be mixed up with journalism and public events with which the world is weary and of which I know so little. But that's the way things come about in this mixed-up world. You'll admit I've not been very sentimental, I've held the rein tight on him. I've cut out all the pictures—I believe it's 'pictures' that I am suppose to do best,—because he wasn't much the picture-seeing kind. I've allowed myself very few accessories to work with. If the reader doesn't get him, he gets nothing————not one pretty phrase, not one 'description' the old ladies on hotel piazzas can comment upon.

I tried to keep the French part vague, seen from a distance, and only what he sees.

Well, he's given me three lovely, tormented years. He has been in my blood so long that it seems to me I'll never be quite myself again.

I am sending you the rest of the story by this mail. I will write you and tell you where to mail(#) it to me. I'm too shaky and worn to go a-visiting, my dear. I want to go to see you when I am a little bit, if not all, there. I will probably leave for Wernersville, Delaware Water Gap, on Monday.

Yours
Willa

#The last part. The part that you now have you will send back to me here, as you say in your letter. The proofs should have reached you last Monday, with my letter.

TO DOROTHY CANFIELD FISHER

Monday [probably March 13, 1922]
Galen Hall, Wernersville, Pennsylvania

Dear Dorothy:

I don't see how you managed to get the proofs back to me before I left on Saturday afternoon, but you did. They arrived at eleven A.M. and I left at four p.m. I wish so much that I could talk to you about them. I know that a lot of people, perhaps everybody, will feel as you do about Enid [character in *One of Ours*]—and yet there I am just as sure! Of course it happened—it's the sort of thing one wouldn't have the courage to invent—and it happened somewhat differently, but it was a part of the original conception of the story. Perhaps it got in because this story was worked out in about half an hour on the train, and this depressing adventure which happened to a Pittsburgh boy I knew got worked into it. But it <u>got</u> worked in because my poor real Claude's real wife [Myrtle Bartlett Cather] had a gentle habit of locking him out, when she wasn't going away from him to spend the winter in Florida. She was a lot more Enid-y than Enid, truly!

I know it's raw—it gave my poor publisher a shock—but it saves an awful lot of writing of the kind I hate to do, that episode. I hate writing about people's feelings, or their lack of them. And that episode seems conclusive.

Don't hurry to get the second lot of proofs back to me—anytime next week will do. And just make your comments on the margins of the proofs themselves—that will really be easier for you, and that set will not go back to the printer, anyhow.

By now you know the most of poor Claude—I expect the last part runs pretty thin—not that I didn't try. <u>I tried just awfully hard</u>. But that's the fascinating thing about art, anyhow; that good intentions and praiseworthy industry <u>don't count a damn</u>. If they did, it wouldn't be much more interesting than bookkeeping. I knew when I began this story that it was, in a manner, doomed. External events made it, pulled it out of utter unconsciousness, and external events mar it—they run through it ugly and gray and cheap, like the stone flaws in a turquoise matrix. It had to be that mixed up sort of thing, or not be at all. If it wasn't strangled by those external dates and facts and feelings, it would be a good book. But it's a "my only love sprung from my only hate" sort of thing; it's the one I love best and can do least for. But do you know; listen: I came off here to this sanitorium in the mountains with those proofs you sent back, feeling so aggrieved that I had to read them now when I am so weak and miserable [from a tonsillectomy], and today I took them out and mournfully began, and read 30 pages. And as truly as I sit here tonight, Dorothy, <u>he got me again</u>! After all this work and worry for these years, after the last wearing six weeks, <u>he got me again</u>, he was real to me again! So you see he must be true.

This gigantic prison is set in beautiful country, just coming green, lovely soft warm air, so that I can work out of doors in a cedar wood. I'm getting better already, though I was pretty sick when I got here. As I read your letter with the proofs in hand today, I felt what a lot I had asked in asking you to read them and to read them so quickly. But I'm glad I asked it, anyhow. It lets a lot of light in when another person reads a story. I've kept this one in a dungeon all this while, hoping I could hide the dark secret that it gets into the war. But that won't matter so much ten years from now—perhaps. Anyhow, I couldn't help it. The war gave him to me. I never knew him till then. And it gave him to himself. He never knew himself till then. He was—not there! How foolish to keep defending my hero! If I couldn't do it in three years, I'll hardly do it now. The queer thing is that someway I care about him more than I did about the others. Even if the book falls down, I'd somehow like Claude himself to win through in spite of that—I'd like to save him outside the book; have him jump from it as from a burning building and catch him in a blanket, perhaps! You see, he "got me going", indeed!

Goodnight, dear Dorothy, and thank you a thousand, thousand times for the trouble you've taken and the heart you have given to it. I'm still not up to writing a long letter, and with hotel pens I can never write at all. When I'm better you'll hear from me. I go back to New York on Monday, so you'll mail the proofs to me there. Thank you so, so much.

Willa

I remember tonight—I suppose because the rustic orchestra is trying some <u>Tannhauser</u>, a letter of Wagner to Wesendonck in which he said "Tristan— Tristan—he lags behind, and yet to him, to save him, I would sacrifice <u>all the unborn</u>!"

TO DOROTHY CANFIELD FISHER

Tuesday [probably March 21, 1922]

I can never in this world thank you enough for you letter, or for giving poor Claude so much feeling and sympathy. You say you find just what I tried so hard to make; a narrative that is always Claude, and not me writing about either France or doughboys. No, I wasn't in France during the war. I went afterward, after most of the french part was written, to see whether, when I read it there, it would seem 'descriptive' or impressionistic or knowing. After all, it's hard to write about a country without description; and I didn't always keep to the narrow way; the Beaufort part is still too fussy, too 'picturesque'. But there, you know all the difficulties as well as I do. I am sure you find it better than it is. Someday I want to tell you how I got the material for the last part———not easily. A great deal of living went into it. But for that matter, there wasn't any other life for at least two of those three years. There was only one question, ever; "How is Claude this morning? For nothing can be ill if he be well." And that's just what one gets out of it; that's the disease and the cure. But how it drains one———afterward, you don't notice it at the time, thank God, you somehow always have enough to feed him till he's done. But now, life does seem a casual affair. The new one? Oh, it's an external affair. It's not Claude.

When the proofs come, I'll write you again; and thank you, thank you, thank you. It's now, when I can do nothing more on him, that I need to feel that he matters to someone else, that he can come into the room and make you care about him.

You'll never know how glad, how relieved, I am that you feel it's solid work, under so much excitement. I've hammered away whole chapters, and there are still some that ought to go, like that one about the shell bursting under Claude.

You've made me very happy about it.

Willa

➵ ➴

The following letter may be a fragment, or it may have been included with the letter immediately above; it bears no salutation and no signature.

TO DOROTHY CANFIELD FISHER

[Probably late March 1922]

The proofs have come, dear Dorothy, and God reward you for your comments, for I can't. There is so much I want to tell you about. So many of your queries will help me to better it.

Yes, the English had independent guns that wandered about, I know the captain of one of them. I could never tell you what work I put in on these details. I got a great deal of it in the hospital here, winter of 1918, when a lot of Western boys lay here in the Polyclinic all winter with no one to talk to and were so glad to talk to me. Such clear, vivid memories come back to sick men. The young captain who killed the degenerate German officer didn't know what it meant, that was why I used it, it seemed so sweet. He had his wonderful rings etc. I spent a large part of that winter listening to quiet memories,—like that about the terrible little girl and the horrid baby.

For the transport part I had the diary of a New Hampshire doctor who was on one of the worst influenza transports. How that diary came into my hands is a story that would thrill you as a writer. Every one of those episodes is chosen from many, many, which all reinforced it. They nearly all cost somebody's blood, and they cost a good deal of mine. You have to give out a whole lot to make people remember aloud to you. I saw many, many well ones, too, here and in Canada; but the sick ones often talked like men in a dream, softly remembering dead lives.

No, Dorothy, our men went into action at Chateau Thierry on the 31st of May, 1918, and the Marines marched in Paris on the Fourth of July.

There are a hundred things I'd like to tell you the how and why of, and as I'm going over these proofs I'll write again.

But how I laughed when you lighted upon Claude and David's violin. That, my dear, I didn't get from any soldier boy. That was the way you made me feel when we were in France together that time; and that was the way that I made my poor cousin feel. You never meant to, you couldn't know it? Neither could David! neither could I, when Grosvenor's lips used to twitch and curl. It's the way helpless ignorance always feels, and so many of the best of ours felt it in France. This book gathered up everything; even you did not escape, you see.

All the same, it's a war book, and most of my few readers, even, won't give it a chance.

But of all these things, much more hereafter.

TO DOROTHY CANFIELD FISHER

Friday [probably April 7, 1922]

Dear Dorothy:

Of course I'd rather have you write a review of Claude than anybody else. You know all the factors; you know me, and It, and Claude—the West, the War, the doughboy. It's such a thankless task that I would surely never be the one to suggest it, but since you suggest it, I'm selfish enough to grab. Knopf is out of town. When he returns I'll consult him. If you undertake it, I'd like it to be the authoritative review, and to be where it would count most.

Of course the fact that my cousin was the germ of the book is between you and me—that's not the public's business, I've never even mentioned it to Knopf. I don't know myself how much the character is Grosvenor. It's a good deal me, a good deal one of my brothers—a sort of composite family portrait. And when I saw so much of the wounded men in the Polyclinic, so many of them seemed to me more or less like Claude, that he gradually came to mean for me————well, young America in the war, especially the American country boy. That was why I tried not to make the latter part <u>too</u> individual, and tried to keep it within the consciousness of such a mind; a mind so intelligent, so sympathetic, so uncultivated, so jealously honest. It's rather hard to say anything about France through such a medium—that's why I did things like using "enragé" for the baby—I always tried to use french words enough like English so that the women in Red Cloud—where there is not one french dictionary!—could tell what they meant by the look of them. But I suppose the laws of the french language won't relax—even for Red Cloud!

Victor's [Victor Morse, character] elderly charmer wrote on her photograph <u>à mon aigle</u>—being as he was an air-man and she very subtle.

Well, I've accomplished something if after twenty years I've got across to you what the roughneck, the sensitive roughneck, really does feel when he's plunged into the midst of————everything. It's not only his vanity that suffers—though that very much—; he feels as if he has been cheated out of everything, the whole treasure of the ages, just because he doesn't know some language or play some instrument or something. Those experiences are very terrible—they have even effected the history of the world ("The Dying Goth"). I found so many of the sick men I got to know had suffered that chagrin, and had brought back with them another wound than the one on their leg or breast—a wound that would ache at odd times all their lives, and that wound made them wiser, always. You see we had no colonies; for the first time our uncultivated thousands were brought up against older civilization—it really was like the Crusades—but why tell this to you, who know it all better than I? But when you hit on Claude and David as enlightening, that revealed to me instantly where I really got Claude and David. David is David Hochstein—all the same, the emotional picture is you and I, in France, twenty years ago. And now, after so long a time, it "gets" you. I have my revenge! In a very joyful form, too. And that's the way old suffering and old chagrins ought to work out in the end. But its a long journey between being burned at the stake and being able to write about it agreeably. No ray of hope gets across to one then.

But it was because I happened to be there on the farm with Grosvenor when the war began and saw its effect on him, and because I had a blood-identity with him—a Siegmund und Siegelinde bond, the woes of the Volsungs—that I had the courage to try to write a young man's story. Life became a series of assignations, of stolen interviews with Claude. He met me when I walked in the park; in the middle of a symphony concert he was suddenly at my shoulder. I always had tea alone that first winter, hither and yon, for I never knew when he would appear and sit opposite me and let me feel his strong shoulders and stubborn head. Oh that was life at its best, that first winter—life and complete possession. I was always frightened and nervous about the last part, but even that shadow couldn't kill the joy of that perfect companionship. I envied no man his adventure in those days.

And now——well now its pretty bleak, and that is where you help me. Now when I can do nothing more for him, what is there to do? I feel as if he had drained my very power to care for things. At least, that part of me must have a long rest. I paid out everything I had. The pile of rejected chapters would make a book. Yes, I have to thank him for these wonderful years. He will never bring back what he cost in mere money—he was an expensive boy to keep, I had to travel with him and cut off any source of income to give him a perfectly undistracted mind. But it was worth going into debt for—a fortune could not buy such excitement and pleasure.

I wonder whether in your secret heart, you will think it worth all this? Well, it was to me: and that's the only answer to the question of what anything's worth. For days and days together I was somebody better than myself. Three intense hours with him every morning, and the rest was wreckage——sleep, and that queer physical feeling of resting myself in his stronger, younger body. Like Mrs. Wheeler [character] I used to say to him "rest, rest, perturbéd spirit."

After all, isn't a game so vivid, so long sustained, worth anything, everything to the player. "Game" is a disgusting word—it was companionship with a human soul.

I'm in bed—still very flabby—so excuse lead pencil. Thank you for listening.

Willa

TO DOROTHY CANFIELD FISHER

Saturday [probably June 17, 1922]

Dear Dorothy;

Sometime when you come back from Rome won't you let me come to talk to you about a few things that I want to talk of with you more than with anybody else? Futurist painting, and 'wide open' art, and the vanishing conception of Sin, which is going to leave people of our profession bankrupt. I'd give a great deal to have a long session with you about these things. We knew one world and how we both felt about it. We now find ourselves in quite another. I wish I knew how it all strikes you.

Anyhow, it's a great pleasure to me to see you looking so well as you did yesterday. You were much too thin when I saw you a year ago, but now you look absolutely yourself, as if your life had made you more and more yourself instead of different and strange, as it does so many of one's old friends. I've rushed at you for Claude as if he were a sick child and you were the doctor, but when that is over I don't see why we shouldn't have something for ourselves.

I sent the proofs to Arlington this morning. There is no need for you to send them back, so don't add that to the chores of departure. You can cut them if you wish to quote. I forgot to tell you that I'd rather you didn't hint it was about anybody of my own name and blood,—otherwise there are no restrictions of any kind. No use my trying to tell you how grateful I feel to you for undertaking this review in the hurry of departure, when you of course ought to be hoarding every bit of your strength for your own book. If I were very noble, I'd have snapped [Sinclair] Lewis up last night and taken this task off your shoulders. But I'm not noble enough for that. Long before you came to see me last year I'd been wishing I could get your impression of this story. I felt that nobody I knew had both ends of [it] in hand like you. And I felt that like me, you knew that I was almost the last person to do such a story; therefore, <u>if</u> it got across, you would instantly recognize it.

I did enjoy the party last night. Harcourt is fine. He's a new type of publisher to me, and a very engaging one. I felt less of the hopeless constraint that I always feel with publishers with him than with any other man of his profession I've ever met; as if I had some common language with him. You see vellum and hand-laid paper mean nothing to me, anymore than they would to "Claude's folks," as you happily termed them. I know they are meant as a compliment, and try to look pleased, but they leave me cold. I have my own kind of fastidiousness, but the idea of twenty-five dollar books for collectors is repulsive to me———it's making a lot of dead books. I should think it would make even booksellers feel that this is a sort of George Moore affair. I had not heard of this lovely plan before, and it rather floored me when he sprung it on us. Lord, what did vellum mean to Claude, or his dear, dear Mother? And sure this book was written to them, if ever one human being did a thing for and to another. All I got out of it was to be close to their noble selves as I could get in no other way. I forwent all splendor, went without adjectives like going without sugar, and Italian paper is wasted on Claude, ought to be used for other books, with other lips and other hearts. But enough———I know you understand perfectly, and it's a world of comfort that you do.

Yours
Willa

TO DOROTHY CANFIELD FISHER

Wednesday [probably June 21, 1922]

Dear Dorothy

The amount of ground you got over on Claude's account when you were in town (to say nothing of all the other things you did) writing ads and signing slogans! The "slogan", by the way, was an invention of Knopf's. He blushed very red when he said he thought I said you'd said something of that sort in a letter. When I declared you never did, he murmured "Oh, never mind!" I'm doing my best to get the price reduced—the difficulty is that it will, he argues, make trouble about his other $2.50 novels, "Cytherea" [by Joseph Hergesheimer] in particular, if he cuts the price on this one. But of course my future relations with him depend on what he can do with this book, and he is fully aware of that.

It does seem a shame that you will have to bother about that review on a sea voyage that ought to give you nothing but rest and relaxation for your own work in Rome. You probably won't have a typewriter and will have to worry it out by hand. I only hope you won't have to take those heavy proof sheets along with your cabin luggage,—that you remember it well enough and won't have to carry pounds of Claude out to sea! How that to-me-unknown man, Mr. [John Redwood] Fisher, will hate me if he has Claude stuffed into his steamer trunk!

Well, I'm looking forward to your return and for the day with you you've promised me, when we can begin to talk about everything that has happened in the world, and to us, since the years when we used to talk. So far, I can see in you only the things I always knew in you—there must be some changes, but I suppose its the person one knew that one looks for first. As I think I wrote you last spring, I've always dreamed about you, and I don't dream a great deal—at least not the kind of convincing, sane dream that one remembers after one wakes up. And in dreams there was never a shadow of change or misunderstanding. I remember once, away back when I was in England for McClure's, I had such an extraordinarily strong and living dream that when I awoke I resolved to write you and tell you I thought there must be something in it, when a feeling like that, a sense of perfect accord and harmony, with such happy affection, persisted on underneath life, in spite of changed conditions. But there was really, then, no way to say such a thing without blubbering. Think of it, that was actually before Freud had escaped into the English tongue, at least, and there <u>was</u> no sub-conscious—except that which everybody always <u>knew</u> there was—from personal experience. But I can remember half-a-dozen or more dreams like that, years apart, and they always pleased me. I never wakened with the bitter feeling that I had been fooled, with that a delightful feeling and a delightful part of my life had been revived for a little while. Now I suppose a Freudian would explain all this quite glibly, but I prefer my own explanation. I always knew that sometime I would be in touch, in some actual relation with you again. There were certain feelings connected with you that never changed a particle. And isn't it funny; when one is ancient enough to begin to <u>look back</u> on one's own youth as an ended thing, then the people who were the lovely and precious figures acquire a sudden clearness, our minds turn and clutch at them, it is almost as if we saw them clearly for the first time. I came to the reflective stage later than most people—until four or five years ago it was impossible for me, like abstract reasoning. My mind couldn't be made to do it. Then quite naturally I found myself drifting into it. And that process brings one close to the figures in that world behind. And what a dear figure you were in it, absolutely the only younger person for whom I had any deep affection. The people I liked were always years older, if not hoary with age! The young ones were blank sheets of paper. The only trouble with you was that you always had so many engagements which I considered trivial!—like taking a fencing lesson with Jessie Lansing. I could not see why you would not rather translate Victor Hugo for me. (I shall give out an interview someday on you as I first remember you. I can do a nice picture of you.)

If you are to live on the road to Versailles and I am to live on the same road, I should think we might meet up whenever you didn't have to fence with Jessie Lansing or go to a faculty party. I suppose now you fence with Sally [Fisher], though! But as for you and me, that was <u>always</u> one of the things which ought to have come out right, and it will, if we give it half a chance. I am just as sure of it as I am that everything was all right once. And what a deep pleasure it can be to both of us,—if for no other reason than to remember what tremendous excitement we used to find in each others society, the times when you came to Pittsburgh for instance, and the time I went to Vermont.

I feel as if you'd sort of rescued Claude, Dorothy, as if you'd snatched him up when he fell and born him off through the fray. When I was reading proofs alone up at that sanitorium, I surely learned how black defeat can look. The book seemed dead. Then I got home and found your letter and that he was alive to you. You'd caught him like a ball, and the world has looked cheerfuller to me ever since.

So lovingly
Willa

TO SINCLAIR LEWIS

June 27 [1922]

Dear Mr. Lewis:

Dorothy wrote me that you are going to review "One of Ours" for the Post, and that's a great satisfaction. At either a funeral or a wedding one wants one's friends and not hired men to act as ushers—and this will be either a funeral or a wedding! I'm sure I'm not noted for bragging or over self-confidence, but nobody ever does a book as much beyond their normal best as this is beyond mine, and then repeats. You can only do it once. That's honestly the way I feel about it. I will never expect as much of myself again. When you read it, I'm sure you'll understand why.

I'm joyful to have met the Lewises at last, and I'm sure you'll let me know when you're in town (what a silly idiom, as if we had but one) in New York next winter, and we can each talk about our new books! With heartiest regards to you both,

Willa Cather

TO CARRIE MINER SHERWOOD

September 1 [1922]
Grand Manan Island, New Brunswick, Canada

Dear Carrie:

Nothing that "Claude" can do for me will give me more pleasure than your dear letter—few things can give me as much. I woke very early this morning and watched the dawn come over the sea, feeling so glad and grateful that my book had gone home to you like that. Long ago, in my lonely struggling years when I was learning to write and nobody understood what I was trying to do, and I didn't understand myself,—I used to think bitterly, (oh so bitterly!) that no matter how well I got on, I could somehow never write the kind of thing that would seem interesting or true to my own people, and they would never know how much I loved them. I had to live among writers and musicians to learn my trade, but I do think my heart never got across the Missouri river. And now you do all know, after all—at least those of you I love best know. Claude and his mother are the best compliment I can pay Nebraska.

I am sending your letter to Isabelle in Paris, for she will know how much it means to me to have touched my old friend's heart like that, and she will share in my thankfulness and will send it back to me—to keep in my writing desk forever, along with the one you wrote me after your mother's death. I am so grateful to have been able to get my story and my boy to you so entirely. Things have turned out very well for me at last, you see.

Lovingly always
Willa

I go back to New York next week.

→ ←

Knopf released One of Ours *in September of 1922. Dorothy Canfield Fisher's glowing review appeared in the* New York Times Book Review *on September 10. H. L. Mencken's and Sinclair Lewis's reviews both found the last half of the novel unsuccessful. Mencken began his review, "Miss Willa Cather's* One of Ours *divides itself very neatly into two halves, one of which deserves to rank almost with* My Antonia *and the other of which drops precipitately to the level of a serial in the* Ladies' Home Journal.*" Though the novel was praised by many reviewers, many of the most prominent panned it and said that Cather had particularly failed in her representation of the war.*

TO ELSIE CATHER

[Probably September 16, 1922]

Dear Elsie:

Poor Claude seems to have kicked up the devil of a row. He is not regarded as a story at all, but as an argument, as everything he is not. Lots of my old best-friends don't like it; Mencken thinks it a failure, Fanny Butcher wails forth her disappointment. They all expected it "would be just like Antonia" they say! It's hard to part with old friends, but one can't be a trick-dog and go on repeating even to please one's friends. It's a parting of the ways, I'm afraid, and here I lose friends I'm sick to lose. They insist that I could not resist the temptation to be a big bow-wow about the War. "The other books were personal, this is external" they say!! Of course the people who are for it are just as hot, but they are rather a new crowd, not the old friends I liked to please. I always hate to lose old friends. Well, we never get anything for nothing, in life or in art. I gained a great deal in mere technique in that book—and I lose my friends.

Please take the enclosed notices to Dr. Tyndale. He is so old and full of dope, poor dear, he can't take in much, but if you read them to him, he'll understand. He deserves to get any wedding cake there is coming. The truth is, everything in his life has failed—but me.

These facts are for you alone. So far Knopf has sold 15,000 copies. He has 18,000 more ready at the factory in case booksellers re-order. If they do not re-order, he'll be badly stung. He spared no expense to make a handsome book. He was here yesterday and is as plucky as can be; says he's willing to go bust on it. I get 37¢ on each copy sold. Sinclair reviews it—as a failure—in tonight's Post. "Why the devil should a woman write a war book?" Well, why should she? This one was "put upon me" I didn't choose it. Don't try to read Lewis's review to Dr. Tyndale—he couldn't understand it, but do read him Zoe's and the two by Burton Rascoe. I'll send you Heywood Broun's roast as soon as I can get a copy—I'm in bed with my friend, superintending the housecleaning, and not in a very "literary" mood. I got back only yesterday and am not even unpacked. Have seen no one but Knopf, but find a host of letters and telegrams, expressing either the warmest congratulations or the saddest regret!

Write soon, Bobbie, to your loving sister,
Willie

→ ←

The following was written to an acquaintance from Cather's days in Pittsburgh.

TO ELIZABETH MOORHEAD VERMORCKEN

Tuesday [September 19, 1922]
New York City

[Written in above salutation:] Josephine is back and we are struggling to get the house clean and to keep the Pacifists from eating us up!

Dear Elizabeth:

I returned from New Brunswick only yesterday, to find that you had been in town again and that I had missed you. I am delighted that you like "Claude," however. I've never tried to do anything that took so much out of me; nor anything that was so absorbing and exciting to do. I miss it terribly—terribly! It determined almost every action in my life for so long that now I hardly know where to turn. The Pacifists have come at me like a swarm of hornets. It's disconcerting to have Claude regarded as a sentimental glorification of War, when he's so clearly a farmer boy, neither very old nor very wise. I tried to treat the War without any attempt at literalness—as if it were some war away back in history, and I was only concerned with its effect upon one boy. Very few people seem able to regard it as a story—it's friends as well as its foes will have it a presentation of "the American soldier", whereas its only the story of one. I wanted to call it merely "Claude" but the publisher and everyone else was against me. However, I do think its a good book and that it will live through the controversy as an imaginative work and not a piece of reporting.

Hastily
W.S.C .

[Included with letter above:]

Tuesday

I wrote this note yesterday, lost it in the mass of things on my desk, and have just found it. So you get two! W—

Monday

Dear Elizabeth:

I got home from New Brunswick only last night, so I've missed you altogether. But it was a delight to find your letter. I am so glad you liked it—Claude, I mean. For the present he seems to have no existence as a story, but as an expression of opinion about <u>war</u>! My desk is filled with letters from Pacifists: one tells me that I will be forever-more "a woman stained with Crime"! Apparently, if a story touches the political opinion of people, they can't see it as an imaginative thing at all. It's as if a pianist, in the middle of a sonata, began to play "The Watch on the Rhine"—in war time! Everyone forgets he <u>was</u> playing a sonata!

Hastily and affectionately
Willa

TO ELIZABETH SHEPLEY SERGEANT

October 4, 1922
Central Park, New York City

[Written in the top margin:] I've telephoned the office to send you a copy of Claude anyhow!

Dear Elsie:

It's certainly a disgrace to me if you've had to send to Brentano for Claude! But I've been driven to death—and only knew your whereabouts from your letter. The day it came I had tea with the Will Whites—aren't they <u>nice</u>, and jolly? And both of them are such good friends of yours. We had a friendly time and he teased me a lot about being kicked out by my highbrow friends: "When thy [George Jean] Nathan and thy Mencken forsake thee, then the Lord Will take thee up."

I told him Claude didn't mind—he likes a row, always did! Almost every day there's a letter for or agin in some paper. Mencken—Freeman—Liberator—Dial etc all say that now I write <u>exactly</u> like the Ladies Home Journal, and that's the place for me anyhow. The New Republic lives up to my impression, I think. They give me a paragraph at the end of a lengthy review of—Kathleen Norris!

The book is selling quite amazingly. For the last week it has sold ahead of "Babbitt" [by Sinclair Lewis] and "This Freedom" [by A. S. M. Hutchinson] in Chicago and Minneapolis. I don't know about other cities, but I have official returns from those two.

You seem to have a great deal more literary news in N.M. than there is in N.Y. Here there is none—except Galsworthy's new Jew play, "Loyalties". So interesting and well acted—no emotion in it, but so well-made and well-bred.

Why is he such a gentleman in his plays and such an—an old maid in his novels! I sat and looked at his handsome head all evening and wondered. He was penned in between two <u>very</u> fat Jewesses, and it was a <u>boiling</u> hot night. At the end of it, I wondered whether he would like to touch the text up a little!

It looks as if Claude might do something handsome for his Ma. And then the critics will be quite sure! The Dial-Freeman-Liberator say its a change in the brain tissue that has come quite suddenly; I simply can't write anymore—it is now mere cataloguing and without life or thrill of emotion in it. Well, now I know where I get off—and I surely know where they do!

They simply can't recognize writing unless it has all the <u>usual</u> emotional signs—H. [Heywood] Broun says there's <u>not</u> five minutes of interesting reading in the book. I've just begun to learn how to write in this book, and I'm going right on!

Yours

W. S. C.

➤ ←

In November 1922 Cather wrote a review of M. A. DeWolfe Howe's Memories of a Hostess, *about Annie Adams Fields, for the December* Atlantic Monthly. *In the four years since she wrote her aunt Franc a letter trumpeting the end of the war and "a world in which not one great monarchy or tyranny existed," Cather's sense of the war's legacy had changed dramatically.*

TO ELLERY SEDGWICK, *THE ATLANTIC MONTHLY*

November 17, 1922
New York City

My dear Mr. Sedgwick:

I am delighted that you liked the article about Mrs. Fields. It was hastily done, but I think that no one who knew her could touch that subject at all without trying to remember her as she was.

I am so sorry you have been ill. I think these last few years have been hard on everyone. It seems to me that everything has gone wrong since the Armistice. Why they celebrate that day with anything but fasts and sack-cloth and ashes, I don't know.

Thank you most heartily for your letter. I shall be so pleased if all Mrs.

Fields' friends feel about the article as you do. Perhaps some day when you are quite well and I have a little leisure, you will want me to do something about Mrs. Fields and Miss Jewett for the Atlantic.

Very cordially yours,
Willa Cather

TO MR. JOHNS

November 17, 1922
New York City

My dear Mr. Johns:

How splendid of you to write me that nice letter! And I can't tell you how glad I am that you like <u>Antonia</u> and <u>Claude</u>. You wouldn't have made a bad Sherlock Holmes. You are the first sleuth who has dug the Parsifal theme out of Claude Wheeler—and I thought I had buried it so deep—deep! Yet, all through the first part of the book, I kept promising myself that I would put "The Blameless Fool, by Pity Enlightened" on the title page, where I eventually put a line from Vachel Lindsay. Now, either you or I did pretty well, when the theme got through to you out of absolute and consistent reticence.

I am going West next week to be gone until about the middle of January, but then I shall be home on Friday afternoons until I sail for France in March. Won't you and Mrs. Johns please try to come in often on Fridays? You are such near neighbors now that it ought to be easy, and I enjoyed seeing you so much when you were here before.

Very cordially yours,
Willa Cather

Parsifal, *an opera by Richard Wagner, was first performed in 1882.*

→ ←

Throughout 1922, while Cather was preparing for the publication of One of Ours, *she was also writing her next novel,* A Lost Lady. *Shortly before she wrote the following letter, she received one from Knopf telling her that his "enthusiasm" for* A Lost Lady, *which he had read in manuscript, was "limitless" and that, though the novel was short, it should be published alone. He commented wryly, "You ought to be restrained by law, if necessary, from publishing this book with anything else."*

TO ALFRED A. KNOPF

Tuesday [November 21, 1922]

Dear Mr. Knopf:

It surely does help one along to publish with people who can like a thing for what it <u>has</u> got, and not just feel nervous and anxious because it hasn't the Rex Beach quality—as nice Ferris Greenslet <u>always</u> felt. If it was "Western" then it ought to be Rex Beachy and rough-house. He never saw what <u>was</u> there, only what wasn't, and whistled to keep up his courage. What I want to do is to find a few qualities, a few perfumes, that haven't been exactly named and defined yet. And if I have a publisher who is interested in new tastes and smells, I can go a good way toward finding them. This story [*A Lost Lady*] is an example of what I mean; it's a little, lawless un-machine made thing—not very good construction, but the woman lives—that's all I want. I don't care about the frame work—I'll make any kind of net that will get, and hold, her alive.

Of course, if you can get serial publication, I would like it because of the money. The more expert personal service I can afford to pay for, the more I can write. If I can find and afford a really competent secretary, that will help a great deal. On the other hand, I don't want to delay publication too long. I am beginning to be awfully weary of the hoot-owl legend that it takes me three years to write a book. I've no drive to do stunts, but I don't wish to get into a three-year habit. It depends on the kind of book. I think you had better use your best judgment about serialization. Why not offer it to someone who will pay well and see if he'll make an offer? If we had an offer, we could decide. I confess to a shudder where the magazines are concerned. But serialization is supposed to be good advertising, isn't it, as well as good pay? You will be leaving tomorrow, but perhaps I can manage to talk this over with Mrs. Knopf before I go.

Faithfully yours
Willa Cather

The news about "One of Ours" is simply splendid!

➔ ←

The following is a reply to the head of the New York Public Library, who had inquired about the long-ago book The Life of Mary Baker G. Eddy and the History of Christian Science. *Throughout her life, Cather received many inquiries about her work on the book, which bore Georgine Milmine's name as author.*

TO E. H. ANDERSON

November 24, 1922
New York City

My dear Mr. Anderson:

I am just hurrying off for the West to spend Thanksgiving with my mother and father, but I will try to answer your questions briefly.

1. There was a Georgine Milmine, now Mrs. Benjamin Wells, of Aubrey, New York, a Canadian newspaper woman, who spent years in getting together a great deal of material relating to Mrs. Eddy's life and the history of Christian Science.

2. Mr. McClure bought her material and notes. There was an enormous amount of it; cuttings from newspapers of forty years ago, court records, early editions of "Science and Health" now absolutely unobtainable. It was a splendid collection of material and after Mr. McClure sold the magazine to a perfectly irresponsible young man named [Frederick] Collins, this was all scattered and lost—a first edition of "Science and Health" thrown away with junk.

3. From the first, Miss Milmine admitted that she hadn't sufficient technical ability to combine all her evidence and produce a biography. Mr. McClure tried out three or four people at writing the story. It was a sort of competition. He liked my version the best chiefly because it was unprejudiced—I haven't the slightest bone to pick with Christian Science. This was when I first came to New York, and that piece of writing was the first important piece of work I did for magazines. After I finished it, I became Managing Editor.

4. A great deal of time and money were spent on authenticating all the material, and with the exception of the first chapter, I think the whole history is as authentic and accurate as human performances ever are. All the letters and documents quoted are absolutely authentic, and in every case, we either had or personally copied the original documents———the first chapter, however, I did not write. It was written by Burton J. Hendrick, who has now an important position with Doubleday. Mr. Hendrick was very much annoyed at being called off the job and never forgave Mr. McClure. Hendrick is an accurate writer, but much of the first chapter—especially the first part of it—frankly deals with legend—with what envious people and jealous relatives remember of Mrs. Eddy's early youth. It was given for what it was worth, but I always consider such sources dubious.

5. Undoubtedly, Doubleday has perfectly good business reasons for keeping the book out of print. There has been a great demand for it to which he has been consistently blank. You see nobody took any interest in its fate. I wrote it myself as a sort of discipline, an exercise. I wouldn't fight for it; it's not the least in my line. Miss Milmine, now Mrs. Wells, is in the awkward position of having her name attached to a book, of which she didn't write a word. I am only sorry that the splendid collection of material, from which the story was written, was lost and destroyed.

Now this is absolutely confidential, Mr. Anderson. I have never made a statement about it before, in writing or otherwise. I suppose somebody ought to know the actual truth of the matter and so long as I am writing to you about it, I might as well ask you to be the repository of these facts. I know, of course, that you want them for some perfectly good use, and will keep my name out of it.

With my heartiest greetings to Mrs. Anderson and yourself, I am

Faithfully yours
Willa Cather

TO ALFRED A. AND BLANCHE KNOPF

Sunday night [1922?]

My Dear Friends;

A wine for princes, simply that! And one I had never tasted, though I've been in the South a lot. I have been laying the foundation of a long friendship with it tonight. It's soft as a purple butterfly wing.

The case arrived on Friday. For the first time in history Josephine came bursting into my room and into my afternoon nap, like a joyful elephant. Her husband had been in that Rothschild vineyard many times, because two of his friends worked there. I had the size and history of the vineyard pretty well ground into me before I could get to the invaluable Martin Strand. It is a superb wine, and shall be reserved for special occasions when I feel a little hard and want to have a glow put into things, a kind of stained glass treatment of pallid daylight.

Gratefully, your fortunate
Willa Cather

TO BLANCHE KNOPF

December 4 [1922]

Dear Mrs. Knopf:

How good you are to me! The beautiful basket of fruit kept me company all the way home, and I hadn't eaten it all at the end of the journey. I had a splendid trip, beautiful golden weather, and I am writing this on the front porch in a blaze of sunlight under a fierce blue sky. Tomorrow is my Father's and Mother's golden wedding day; all my sisters and brothers are at home and we are having a very jolly time. Both my parents are simply incredibly young to be having such a celebration. They drive a hundred miles in their car any day and are not tired the next. I have to take a nap after lunch, but neither of them ever do, not much!

It's always a joy to be back here—I get more thrills to the square mile out of this cornfield country than I can out of any other country in the world.

A thousand thanks and my loyal friendship to you both.

Yours always
Willa Cather

PART SEVEN

Years of Mastery

1923–1927

I do hope you'll like my Archbishop, Fanny. . . . It's an altogether new kind for me, but how I loved doing it! It was as if one had always played modern composers, and at last had the time and control to practice Bach awhile. Modest comparison!

—WILLA CATHER TO FANNY BUTCHER, October 27, 1926

Willa Cather with Léon Bakst in his studio, Paris, 1923.
Photograph by Henri Manuel

C ATHER WAS NOW at the height of her powers and the pinnacle of her career. After a bout with the flu in early 1923, she went to France for a long visit with Jan and Isabelle McClung Hambourg, who had settled in a house near Paris. Soon after her arrival she received word that she had been awarded the Pulitzer Prize for *One of Ours*. The year 1923 also saw the publication of *A Lost Lady*, sometimes considered Cather's masterwork. Three more of her finest books—*The Professor's House*, *My Mortal Enemy*, and *Death Comes for the Archbishop*—followed in 1925, 1926, and 1927. She often said that the writing of *Archbishop* was such a pleasure that it was like a vacation. In the same otherwise satisfying year as its publication, however, Cather was forced to leave her comfortable apartment on Bank Street.

In February of 1923, on the heels of One of Ours, *Knopf published a special edition of Cather's poetry, titled* April Twilights and Other Poems. *The volume included several poems from her 1903 book, plus several new poems that had previously been published only in periodicals. Elmer Adler of Pynson Printers designed and printed the first limited edition.*

TO ELMER ADLER

Sunday [probably January or early February 1923]
New York City

Dear Mr. Adler:

What a beautiful book you sent me yesterday—and what beautiful roses! We will set a new standard of relations between writer and printer. The pains you have taken with this volume and the absolutely satisfying result you have achieved have quite revived my interest in the text. I hope you can do another book for me sometime. I am very proud of this one, I assure you.

I will come to your office Wednesday afternoon a little after four, and you can take me to your place, as I have forgotten your house number.

Please accept my warmest thanks for the flowers, and my heartiest congratulations upon such a fine piece of work as this book.

Cordially yours
Willa Cather

→ ←

With the success of One of Ours, *Cather got her wish: a publisher who would know how to market her books and stimulate good sales. As she soon realized, such success had its obligations. Cather became acquainted with painters and writers Earl and Achsah Brewster, to whom the next letter is addressed, by way of Edith Lewis, with whom Achsah had attended Smith College.*

TO EARL AND ACHSAH BARLOW BREWSTER

February 21 [1923]

Dear Earl and Achsah:

How often I've wanted to answer your dear letters about "One of Ours". But I went home to my parents' Golden Wedding, and life caught me up and carried me furiously away. I understood exactly what you meant about Howard Pyle. This book has been a new experience for me. The people who don't like it detest it, most of the critics find it maudlin sentimentality and rage about it in print. But the ex-service men like it and actually buy it. It has sold over forty thousand now and is still selling. I've had to take on a secretary to answer the hundreds of letters I get about it. The truth is, this sort of success does not mean much but bother and fatigue to me—I'm glad I never had it before.

I am so glad the Hambourgs chose the "Blue Nigger" [painting by Earl Brewster] and that I shall soon see him again. The photograph you so kindly sent me has just come and is a great pleasure, but it makes me long for the splendid color of that painting. We have had the greatest happiness from the picture we brought home with us, and do you know, I have come to like the "Three Scallops" [another painting by Brewster] best of all of them!

I will sail for France about the first of April. Ah how lovely it will be if I can meet you in Paris! That seems about too good to happen in this pesky world. I beg you both to write often to Edith while I am gone. I must tell you a secret that is a little difficult to tell: Edith does not like the Hambourgs at all—never has. They irritate her, rub her the wrong way; Isabelle even more than Jan. I think it's been hard for her to face that they were seeing you this winter when she was not. We are like that about the people we love best sometimes, we have a kind of loving jealousy about them. It has always been difficult about the Hambourgs, because they are old and dear friends of mine, and yet they do darken the scene for Edith whenever they appear—put rancours in the vessel of her peace, as Macbeth said. I think the way that likes and dislikes interweave is the most disheartening thing about life anyway. It's nothing Edith can help; their personalities simply hurt her. She feels that their attitude toward her is rather patronizing, but there I feel sure she is mistaken.

I hope Edith can see a great deal of you if you are in America this summer. Your being here will make up to her for my absence. As you know, she does not care for a great many people, and for them she cares very much. This has been a hard winter for her—her family has made such heavy demands upon her and she has not been very well. Before a great while I am going to get her away from all these hard and wearing things.

If you come to America this summer you will have an exhibition here in the fall, will you not? There would be time to give one here in the early fall, before you return to Paris. We thought the notices of your exhibit in Paris this fall were splendid.

I do hope you have got Edith's box by now—she took such pleasure in arranging it. She sent a beautiful one to me in Red Cloud, too. Dear friends, there are so many things I wish to say to you—about painting, about writing, about ourselves and this queer business of living. I can only recall some lovely hours we spent together in the twilight at Naples and hope that they will come again. This has been a hard winter for everyone I know in this part of the world. The Golden Wedding and my Christmas at home was the one thing worth while for me. But since then a thousand stupid interruptions have kept me from work—and when my work is interrupted nothing compensates.

We both send you our dearest love and wish you happy working-days with all the deep satisfactions they bring. I wish Edith and I could be with you next year. I believe we could all help each other.

With love and happy memories
Willa Cather

TO DOROTHY CANFIELD FISHER

Sunday [probably April 1, 1923]

Dear Dorothy;

It was heartbreaking to miss you, when if I'd known the day before, or Thursday morning, I could have arranged it so easily. Josephine was ill, so I sent her home and told her to go to bed, and I decided to devote the day to dismal chores. I left the house at ten, had lunch and dinner up town, and didn't come home until nine at night. At that hour I was too beat out to go over to the pay station to telephone your mother's apartment,—and by that time you were probably gone, or just getting ready for the train. It was an utterly wasted day, and the afternoon of it might have been so nice! Well, things have been going rather that way lately; the mechanics of life have been grinding hard since I got back from my wonderful time in the West. However, it's silly to get discouraged; my cold is gradually departing, I've been hearing some glorious music, and behind the music a few comfortable ideas are stirring to make me feel that there is something worth—to me—carrying on the routine for. The funny thing is that one can never make publishers and editors and friends see that with a story just forming you have to be alone like a thief hiding from the police,—alone with just the precious, cursed stuff you have stolen and are hiding from everybody. How much I owe to the non-success of those early books! I dropped them into the void and there was no come-back, no fuss, nothing to get in the way of the next one.

No lectures for me till I come back from France, my dear! I've had to take on a secretary [Sarah Bloom] to take the people who want lectures off my back. She told me last week that she'd written nearly a hundred letters declining lectures for me in the last four months. People don't in the least want one to write—perhaps what they really want is a vacation from having to bother about one's books at all. Well, Dorothy, they are not going to spoil things for me, so there! Be witness to my bold boast. I don't really mind not being read, (not a whoop, really———some times a little fussed, but nothing deep.) But if they devil me so I can't write, they destroy my game, my fun, my reward, the whole splendour and glow of life,—all there is for me. And they shant do it, damn them! You'll stand by me, won't you, and understand that I'm not being disobliging?

Yours always
Willa

→ ←

On May 14, 1923, shortly after Cather arrived at the Hambourgs' home near Paris, Alfred Knopf sent the cable that announced her Pulitzer: "Claude wins Pulitzer prize. Hearty congratulations affectionate regards."

TO ALFRED AND BLANCHE KNOPF

May 16 [1923]
Ville d'Avray, France

Dear Mr. and Mrs. Knopf:

I nee[d] hardly say I was delighted to get your cable! So many cablegrams arrived that day that Ferruccio, the Italian man-of-all-work, thought another war had broken out. I hope the publicity will stimulate sales and will be good for you as well as for me. Those High-Brows, Heywood Broun & Co., will storm worse than ever and say it's but one step more to Mary Rinehart.

I have a gratifying statement from Houghton Mifflin; Antonia sold 3,000 in the last six months and The Song of the Lark 600.

The Oliver typewriter which Mr. Samuel Knopf ordered sent to me has not arrived, and after a gay week in Paris I want to get to work and need a machine. Will you please find when it was shipped? If through some mistake it was not sent at all, I may have to buy one here, though they charge twice what Olivers sell for at home. If the machine was sent and is on the way, will you please cable me to that effect as soon as you get this letter?

I had a wonderful week in Paris all alone. I am much better in health and am feeling very jolly over the Pulitzer prize. Please write me who the judges were. I couldn't have got it if [William Lyon] Phelps was still one of the judges.

With warmest greetings from the Hambourgs and myself

Yours
Willa Cather

Willa Cather and Isabelle McClung Hambourg in Ville d'Avray, France, 1923

In the spring of 1923, Judge Duncan Vinsonhaler of Omaha, Nebraska, contacted Cather to express the desire of the Omaha Society of Fine Arts to commission a portrait of her to hang in the Omaha Public Library.

TO DUNCAN M. VINSONHALER

May 23 [1923]
Paris

My Dear Judge Vinsonhaler:

I am greatly flattered and deeply pleased by your letter. Sooner or later I will see that my Omaha friends get a portrait if they want one. I ought to be able to get a good one made here in Paris—perhaps I can find some gifted young American artist—if not, a french one. Just now I am so beset by photographers and interviewers, french and American, that I haven't time for anything. This is apropos of the Pulitzer Prize, of course. Unfortunately the cable announcing the award to the Paris papers said that it was a "war novel", so the French journals keep sending men to get my opinion on the present political crisis in France.

Please accept my friendliest wishes, and greet the [Harvey] Newbranch family for me. I will go ahead and hunt a painter in the near future, and send you a report of what progress I make with him.

Cordially yours
Willa Cather

TO ALFRED A. KNOPF

June 6 [1923]

Dear Mr. Knopf:

Please give the enclosed to Mr. Oppenheimer for publicity. Isn't it a joke, with those two numerical titles? "One of Ours and Three Soldiers by two Americans", as one of the french papers puts it! The dinner was to have been given for me and your Spaniard, [Pío] Baroja, but he characteristically didn't get here, so the Secretary snatched up [John] Dos Passos.

It has been black winter here for one month, with rain every day. I am daily awaiting the typewriter. Is Claude still selling, by the way?

With best regards from all of us

Yours
Willa Cather

➜ ⬅

The following postcard to Edith Lewis—showing Bartolomé Esteban Murillo's La Naissance de la Vierge *from the Louvre Museum—is one of only two surviving pieces of correspondence from Cather to Lewis.*

TO EDITH LEWIS

Sunday [summer 1923]
Paris

A whole morning alone in the Louvre. This will recall to you that lovely group of Spanish pictures at the far end of the long hall. I still think the Murillo Virgin the prettiest woman in the world, and I still love the [Jusepe de] Ribera Nativity [*Adoration of the Shepherds*] and its homely shepherds.

W.S.C.

TO IRENE MINER WEISZ

August 11 [1923]
Ville d'Avray, France

My Dearest Irene:

I have wanted to write you ever since I first arrived in France, but this has been a hectic summer. You probably know that the city of Omaha raised a fund and asked me to have a portrait painted for them—your own idea, you see! I was terribly puzzled about choosing a painter, and I at last decided on Léon Bakst, who did all the costumes and settings for the Russian Ballet, you know. He happened to be in Paris just now, and he was the most interesting man in sight. He seldom does portraits, but some french friends of his like my books and told him about them, and he said he'd like to paint me. It's a long story, how I came to meet him, and someday I'll tell you all about it.

I will certainly be at home for Christmas this year, and I hope to go out to Red Cloud the first week in December. I hope you can go then, too. I'll have so much to tell you about this lovely house of Isabelle's and all the delightful people I've met.

Bakst is distinctly "modern" in his painting, you know, and rather fanciful. He won't do a photographical likeness for anybody. Yet I think this picture will look like me in the end. Of course the Omaha people won't be satisfied—people never are with a portrait, but they ought to know his name well enough to be glad to have a picture by him.

With my love to you and Mr. [Charles William] Weisz

Yours always
Willie

→ ←

Fastened at the top of the second page of the following letter is a clipping with horse race entries and the name "Red Cloud" marked with a note written beside it: "See! A horse named Red Cloud has been winning some races in Paris!"

TO ELSIE CATHER

August 11 [1923]

Dearest Sister:

Yesterday I had my first sitting with Leon Bakst. He pronounces his name just like the past tense of the English verb "to box"; that is just as if it were spelled Boxed [in cursive writing], Boxed [printed]. But if you prefer to give the one and only vowel in his name a middle-West sound, why then you can pronounce his name so that it rhymes with WAXED, as in "the floor was waxed." You must instruct father and mother and the two Virginias how to call his name, as it will be much mixed up with mine for awhile.

His studio has three enormous rooms, and they are full of beautiful things from all over Europe and Asia. To sit there for two hours in the afternoon is like going to church—a church where all the religions of mankind come together in one great religion. He is just one of the simple people I have always loved—like Annie Sadelik and Joe Pavelik Sr. and all the friends of my childhood. He is reading "One of Ours" with the help of a dictionary, but he speaks little English. He speaks to me in French and I reply in English. He began by telling me Russian fairy tales, and is going to tell me stories every sitting, he says. He is doing only my head and shoulders, and thank Heaven did not want me to "dress up". He selected a green georgette waist I happened to have, with a little gold in it, loose and plain, like a Russian smock or a middy-blouse.

Not since the days when old Mr. Ducker used to talk to me in the store and spit tobacco juice all round me, have I had such an experience as this, or been so much the pupil sitting at the feet of the teacher. I think the hours will fly by in those great quiet rooms. You wouldn't believe the neatness and order of them—never a pen crooked on his many desks, all that marble and bronze and porcelain dusted every day. You can touch a hundred objects, even the portfolios of drawings and never have a particle of dust left on your fingers.

Now goodbye, I'll write you when Bakst and I are further along.

Lovingly
Willa

TO DUNCAN M. VINSONHALER

August 27 [1923]
Ville d'Avray, France

My Dear Judge Vinsonhaler:

(1) First let me acknowledge receiving from you a check for one thousand dollars, which shall be endorsed to Mr. Bakst as soon as the portrait is completed. The work has taken much longer than he thought at first, and both he and I need a rest from it. I had no idea that sitting for a picture was such hard work. I have not been in the best of health this summer, and now I am going down to Aix-les-Bains for three weeks. When I return I will have three more sittings with Bakst for details of the figure—he eventually did a half-figure, seated, with the hands. The face will be practically completed in tomorrow's sitting, and I think the likeness very unusual.

(2) I know that my parents will want to go up to Omaha to see the picture, but I don't know about asking them to unveil it. You know old people are sometimes very much fretted and wearied of doing something a little unusual, and both my father and mother are rather nervous people. Won't you let me put the question to them and then follow their wish in the matter? I know you would not want to put any sort of strain on them. I think it likely that they would much rather sit quietly by, with no responsibility, and let my little niece, Virginia Auld, unveil the picture. (By the way, Judge Vinsonhaler, I wish pictures didn't have to be unveiled! And won't you do what must be done just as quietly and simply as possible. I like to feel that you want my picture because of a feeling of friendliness, because I've pictured truthfully the life you know. Don't, please, let people like Mrs. [Margaret Badollet] Shotwell [of the *Omaha Daily News*] turn all this nice feeling into cheap newspaper copy and make me heartsick about it.)

To return to my little niece, she is a great pal of mine, and I think her grandmother would love to have her for an understudy. She's a charming young girl, and not a bit cocky.

(3) Bakst is to have an exhibition of his work in Philadelphia, in November, and in Boston in December, and he asks permission to exhibit this portrait among his other pictures. I don't feel that I can grant him this without the consent of your committee, but it is customary to extend this courtesy to painters and I hope to hear from you that your committee is willing. In that case, he will select the frame—a very important matter—though the frame would probably have to be made in New York.

(4) As to the date of my return: I will probably sail late in October, but I don't know how early in the winter I can go west. I am afraid unless the importunate Mrs. Shotwell can be subdued I shall never go to Omaha again! She wrote a letter to Bakst which passes description, asking him what he had to say about my eyes and my nose, how he would define my personality, what <u>flower</u> he thought appropriate for me, etc. As if any painter would give an interview on the physical characteristics of his sitter. Why, the woman must be mad! I'm confident that you and your friends didn't want this picture in Omaha to give an opportunity for columns of cheap, noisy publicity, and I'm sure I did not sit for it for that purpose. Won't you be a hero, a very heroic hero, and try to tell this lady that I hate such methods, that I don't want to be "boosted" in any way, and I don't like being made ridiculous. The less publicity, the better. When Mr. Newbranch and Miss [Eva] Mahoney [both of the *Omaha World Herald*] do me the honor to write about me, I am always pleased, pleased and proud. But this sort of vulgar horn-blowing really hurts me, and I know that it offends all people of good taste. It offends my own Father <u>very deeply</u>, and I care a great deal about that. If you will be noble and kind enough to use your influence in my behalf, you might prevent what the diplomats call future unpleasantness.

I dine with the Hitchcocks tonight. I am staying in Paris now, but all my letters still go to my permanent address at Ville d'Avray. Senator [Gilbert Hitchcock of Nebraska] and Mrs. [Jessie Crounse] Hitchcock went out there for tea with me on Sunday afternoon.

Forgive me for my rhetoric regarding Mrs. Shotwell, but do put the soft pedal on her if you can.

Faithfully yours
Willa Cather

TO ELSIE CATHER

August 27 and September 4 [1923]
Aix-les-Bains, France
August 27

Dear Sister:

<u>Don't let these people worry mother!</u> The portrait won't reach Omaha before January, or later, as it will be exhibited with other Bakst paintings in Philadelphia and Boston before it goes west.

I know how Mother frets about such things, and I won't let them put any strain on her. Why, she might worry herself sick over it! She's no brassy club-woman. So tell her in the beginning, I think it nonsense. If she <u>wants</u> to do it, all right, but there's no sense in going to any strain about it. If the picture has to be "unveiled", Mary Virginia can do it, it won't hurt her nerves one bit! And mother I am afraid would worry about what she should wear, and thus make it a hardship. So, if she begins to look forward to it and worry, <u>just stop her</u>, and tell her M.V. can do this silly business more gracefully than <u>any</u> <u>mature</u> person. It's <u>so</u> silly, anyway!

Aix-les-Bains
Sept 4

Here I am, my dear, "taking the waters" as the English say. My back had been getting worse all summer, and when Dr. [Lawrence] Litchfield was in Paris for his daughter's wedding he gave me a going over and urged me to come here and take the baths, which he said are the best in the world for rheumatism. He had been here with rich patients from Pittsburgh. Mr. McClure has been trying for five years to get me to come here, as Mrs. [Hattie] McClure was cured of terrible rheumatism here. Finally Bakst begged me to come and said he would change all his engagements and give me five more sittings when I got back to Paris. (The picture will take 15 sittings instead of 10; they always take more than one expects.)

Well, the doctor to whom Dr. Litchfield directed me here says all my back-ache is from intercostal rheumatism, and that a course of baths every day for three weeks will cure me. Of course if my friend comes along in the middle of the treatments, then it will delay them and I'll have to stay longer. It's hard to be away from Paris, which is so lovely in the fall, but if I can get rid of this continual backache it will be worth a few weeks of exile. The gay, fashionable season at Aix is over now. I tried to come in August but all the hotels were full.

I have a nice room in a very clean and comfortable hotel—no running water in the rooms, but I don't need it when I'm in a hot sulfur bath for an hour every morning. I get my room and three <u>delicious</u> meals for 35 francs a day, about two dollars! And at Lakewood N.J. last winter I paid $8 a day for a poor room and dreary, messy food! Of course the doctor and the baths will be expensive. All the time one is in the bath, two fine big women gently massage one's sore back and shoulders <u>under water</u>. Then they play a hot sulfur hose on you for half an hour.

I came down here on the grandest train in France, the Paris-Rome Express, with a private state-room, and it all cost nine dollars, the present fare from N.Y. to Boston! Of course this is all because of exchange; all these things are expensive enough for the poor French. I wonder they don't hate us, when we can come with our dollars and buy all the nice things they love and have to go without. And there wouldn't <u>be</u> any nice things if all their sons and brothers hadn't died to save them.

I just love Helen Louise [Cather] and the baby's pictures, dear. So does Isabelle, and the Italian cook, who is expecting a baby of her own any day now, looked and looked at it and said she hoped her baby would be like that one. She and her husband have been getting ready for their baby all summer, and a sister came on from Italy to do the cook's work while she is in bed. Jan is to be godfather and it is to be named after him, if a girl, why then Giovanna.

Goodnight dear, with much, much love. I want to get this off on a fast boat.

Willa

[In the top margin of the last page:] <u>Address me always Ville D'Avray.</u>

➤ ⟵

Cather's sixth novel, A Lost Lady, *was published by Knopf in September 1923, while she was in France. The critics who dismissed* One of Ours—*"Heywood Broun & Co.," Cather called them—now again sang her praises. Broun himself said it was "truly a great book."*

TO CHARLES F. AND MARY VIRGINIA BOAK CATHER

[September 1923]

Dear Mother and Father:

If you look Aix-les-Bains up on the map, you will find it around a hundred miles south of Lake Geneva, beside a little lake—Lake Bourget. Long ago, when I used to complain of a sore arm, Mr. McClure used to beg me to come here—I suppose it's the most famous resort for rheumatic people in the world. The first week of my stay I did not see much improvement, and my writing arm was so badly crippled with neuritis I could hardly write at all. But all through the second week my arms and back have got much better, and I hope the third week will almost cure me. It's the same old backache I've been having for years, and Dr. Litchfield and the doctors here say it is intercostal rheumatism. You tell Carrie Sherwood, and she'll get Dr. Creighton to explain it to her.

I take a bath every morning at nine oclock—it takes about an hour. Two husky women massage me under a stream of hot water. Then I go back to my hotel, all bundled up, and stay in bed until noon. That's part of the treatment. But after lunch I am quite gay. I take motor rides or go up the mountains in a little narrow-guage. The French Alps are so beautiful I never tire of them. I love to see the cottonwoods and chestnut trees growing side by side—like Virginia and Nebraska being married! I have found an eager little man with an eager little car who will take me about the country all afternoon for about two dollars. I don't see how he buys the gasoline for that. I wrote Elsie how comfortably, even luxuriously I live at this hotel for about $2.50 a day.

Splendid news comes from my publisher about the large advance sales of "A Lost Lady". But I can quite truthfully say that this does not please me half so much as Mother's liking for the story pleases me. I do love to have my own folks like my stories—I hope the granddaughters will all like them when they are older, too.

I expect to sail the first week of November. Both Dr. Litchfield and my doctor here at Aix advise me not to try a winter in France until my rheumatism is better. The house[s] are all so much colder than ours. Even Isabelle's house, though she has a furnace, is very draughty and cold in the halls, and there is no heat in the bedrooms. In the spring I felt the cold there very much, and coal is so dreadfully expensive that one hates to keep asking for more heat.

Now I have just got such a nice letter from Elsie that I must say goodbye to you, dear daddy and mother, and reply to her. She has been such a dear good girl to write me so much this summer and tell me everything I want to know. I know how precious vacation hours are, and I do appreciate Bobby's kindness to me. You will probably see my letter to her, too, so it's the same as writing another letter to you.

Now I have written on my manuscript paper, because I can write more plainly on a hard paper,—and all the note-paper Isabelle ordered for me is soft, and I can't write plainly on it even if I try. I hope you will find this easy to read, dear parents!

Your very loving daughter
Willie

TO ELSIE CATHER

Dear Sister Elsie:

Both "sat" and "mine" are simply typographical errors, both wrong, of course. They got by Edith and me both, evidently. I ought to have read the book after the first printing for errors, but I really haven't been half-way well since it came out, and I never dreamed it was going to sell so many thousand before I'd have a chance at it again.

I pondered about the telephone—you see there are no dates given, only the story covers a considerable period of time. I meant the last part to be about 1900, but it might be 1903 or 1904, and I'm sure there were through telephones as early as that. The time element in that story was hard to manage—it has to account for about 15 years before it (the story) actually begins, and about 15 years after it actually ends. The episodes in the story extend over about ten years, actually, but you must be made to feel the changes of about 30 years. So you see one can't be too definite.

I don't believe anything I have ever written has given you more pleasure than your letters have given me this summer, dear sister.

Have you seen the full-page ad in the Atlantic? And the nice editorials in the Bee and World-Herald? Judge Vinsonhaler writes me that if mother doesn't want to unveil that portrait Mary Virginia can do it for her. He is a nice kind man, it's that vulgar Shotwell woman, friend of Nell McNeny's! who makes all the troubles.

Bakst has had some quite lovely photographs made of me and him in his studio. Would you like one? They're quite expensive, but if you'd like one I'll make you a present. I think I ought to get one for Carrie, she'd treasure it so.

I took a chance on pneumonia yesterday, and went up on Mt. Revard, after being kept away from it for ten days by rain. It was chilly up there, but how magnificent! There had been a new fall of snow on Mt. Blanc, and with the purple clouds driving over it, it was simply overwhelming.

Bobbie, the Paris papers have had such stunning articles about me lately. On my way down to Aix I bought two papers to read on the train, and they both had such nice articles about me. I sent them to my publisher. This is a secret: the editor of Figaro came to see me before I left and told me that I very nearly got the Legion of Honor for Claude—all the committee who had read it were eager to give it to me, but the majority can't read a long English book.

It's to be translated now, and brought out by one of the best French publishers, and this publisher says I'll be given the Legion of Honor on it eventually, he thinks [she did not]. All this writing in French papers has been by people I've never heard of. Whenever a frenchman reads that book something seems to happen inside him—he becomes my press agent. I wish I could send you some of the articles, but I only see them by chance, as I did those on the train. If I could just get really well again, I'd have so much fun out of all this.

No, I never used Margie's knife for an ice-pick! I broke it cutting the bones of father's soup meat, so there! I'm glad Sambo's alligator died. The Mathenys are getting to be too silly!

I've just heard from Isabelle that her nice Italian cook gave birth to a dead girl baby, after a terrible delivery—the doctor thought she would die. I'm so sorry. Bagina and her husband had bought it's clothes, and bed, and cloak and everything, and were looking forward to it with such happiness. I send you a letter of Isabelle's about Giotto and things.

No, I never saw the interview about Hochstein at all! It was published in the N.Y. Herald while I was in Red Cloud at Christmas and the entire edition was sold out. Now <u>where</u> do you suppose the Hastings paper got it? Even Isabelle never got a copy.

Goodnight dear sister. Remember, we are going to have a trip in the Alps.

Lovingly
Willa

The article about David Hochstein, the violinist who inspired Cather's character David Gerhardt in One of Ours, *was entitled "Fiction Recalls Violinist Lost in War: An Interview with Willa Cather." It appeared in the* New York Herald *on December 24, 1922, and was reprinted in Red Cloud's* Commercial Advertiser *on September 3, 1923.*

TO ACHSAH BARLOW BREWSTER

November 29 [1923]

Dearest Achsah:

I had a dream-like crossing over a blue sea. There were many nice people on board, the very nicest was Frank Swimmerton, the English novelist, who was my table companion and of whose really charming personality I never tired. He's so honest and kind.

Since I smoke very little at sea, Edith is getting her share of Earl's cigarettes, and I saved all your chocolates for her because she likes french candy so much. I've told her lots about your exhibition, but I find it impossible to make her understand about your Ceylon pictures, or to tell her what Earl did to the Sailors. Dorothy Canfield dashed in to the boat train to see us off, and I was delighted to see how deeply stirred she had been by that exhibit. She thought your triptych the most beautiful and uplifting of them all.

My love to you both—happy working days to you, and peace of soul.

Lovingly
Willa

A big hug to [daughter] Harwood [Brewster], please, from me.

In January of 1924, Cather received a telegram from the Omaha Daily News *saying that people were criticizing the Bakst portrait as "mediocre, valueless, crude, a poor likeness, outrageous coloring, etc." and asking Cather's personal opinion. She replied in a telegram saying that she would not make a public statement unless it was to the committee that commissioned the portrait.*

TO DUNCAN M. VINSONHALER

Sunday [January 13, 1924]

Dear Judge Vinsonhaler:

I enclose a telegram I received this morning and a copy of my reply. I have been meaning to write you more fully about this matter, but I wanted to wait until after Bakst's visit to Omaha, as that would give him a chance to explain his picture in his own way.

Of course I am not satisfied with the picture as a portrait of myself; but I think one is not likely to be a good judge in the matter of one's own likeness. If I didn't like it, why did I accept it?

Before I accepted it I took two American painters to the studio when Bakst was not there, and they discussed it at length. They assured me that it was a conscientious piece of work—too much so, that he had tried until the result was labored and stiff. They thought all the accessories, even the dress, were beautifully painted, as only a distinguished painter could paint them, but that the face and hands were too labored. They agreed with me that one could not refuse to accept an honest piece of work, even if the likeness was unsatisfactory. When we employ an eminent physician and the patient dies, we pay him, just the same. When we employ an eminent painter, it is just the same. I know several people who have had to take much worse portraits than this one from [John Singer] Sargent, at much higher prices. We know great portrait painters by their successes; we do not take into account the many pictures that almost arrived or utterly failed. A portrait is always a gamble, as we agreed in the beginning. I think this time our luck was bad, but I can at least comfort myself by believing that the result is a little harder on me than on any one of my friends in Omaha who did me the honor to want a painting of me. Surely they won't accuse me of having accepted the picture out of personal vanity!

I gave Bakst sixteen sittings, and several long afternoons in the country. The sittings were usually three hours long. I never saw anybody work harder, and I never worked harder myself. If he failed to make a good likeness, it was not because he was careless. If I had felt that he slighted the commission in any way, I would certainly have refused to take it, but under the circumstances, I did not feel that I could do so.

Now, on the other hand, had I been Bakst, I would have refused to let a commission go out that fell so far short of being a satisfactory likeness. That he might have done, but he did not. I have resolved never again to have anything to do with a work of art which I can not destroy if it does not suit me. I have a large and commodious grate in my apartment for that purpose. My friends in Omaha ought not to feel about this matter as they might feel if I had painted the picture, or if I had just published a book that had the faults of this likeness. I set out to do a portrait in "A Lost Lady" and I had, I think, better luck than Bakst,—though I am sure I didn't work much harder. But often an artist <u>does not know</u> when he has failed to get a likeness.

I hope that some time in the near future I can get the time to sit to another painter and get a picture for which you will give me the Bakst picture in exchange. Or if it would seem better, I will so gladly send a check for the price of the picture and cease to worry about it.

May I tell you in confidence, Judge Vinsonhaler, that this unhappy painting has cost me more downright worry and anxiety and distress than any book I ever wrote? I never spent sleepless nights over any work of my own as I did over this. It wasn't poor enough to refuse, it wasn't a good likeness and therefore did disappoint. My only hope was that I was really worse looking than I had hereto thought, and that perhaps it looked like me after all.

Now I want you to show this letter to such interested persons as you may see fit; to such as have bowels of compassion and some imagination, and who know how difficult it sometimes is to divine the right line of conduct. Your people meant so well, and I meant so well,—and I insist that Bakst meant so well! Mercy, how hard he and I did work, those grilling-hot summer days! Beg all your committee to sit for portraits, quickly, and then they will judge me mercifully!

Mournfully but faithfully yours
Willa Cather

TO ACHSAH BARLOW BREWSTER

February 16 [1924]

Dearest Achsah;

We are having such an interesting and happy winter—lots of nice people, and music, and flowers, and Montana's turning out to be a splendid maid. I'm working hard and with great joy, and I'm well and not anguished and perplexed as I was nearly all the time in Paris. Did Edith tell you that her company [the J. Walter Thompson advertising firm] gave her a check for a thousand dollars for a Christmas present, <u>and</u> a month later raised her salary again! You have to deliver goods to make a New York business firm treat you like that, I assure you. Both Claude and a Lost Lady keep right on selling, so we're indulging ourselves in lots of little luxuries and <u>not</u> splurging. It's so good to be at home again Achsah, and I know you are saying the same thing in your heart every day. I use your wonderful vaporizor for my nose every day, and bless you for it—it's as useful in a New York climate as in that of Paris.

Give my love to Earl and Harwood and tell her we love the cards she sent up. How fine life is, when one does not fret about silly things, dear Achsah!

Lovingly
W.S.C.

→ ←

In early 1924 Ferris Greenslet asked Cather if she would be interested in compiling a collection of Sarah Orne Jewett's stories with a "critical and appreciative" preface. He intimated that Jewett's sister, Mary, was also enthusiastic about the idea.

TO FERRIS GREENSLET

February 17 [1924]

Dear Mr. Greenslet;

Yes, I'd much rather do this than make my fortune at the various lucrative commissions that are constantly pressed upon me.

In the first place I must ask you send me down a complete set of the books, the original edition. The safest way is for me to cut them up myself and bind them up into volumes in the sequence that seems best.

The first volume, of course, would take in all the Pointed Fir sketches, including "The Queen's Twin", "A Dunnet Shepherdess", and "William's Wedding". The second volume, if one took only the very best, would be an equally fat one. "Deephaven" is charming, but I don't think it belongs with Miss Jewett's best mature work.

The librarian at the branch library round the corner tells me that the young intellectuals of Greenwich Village sometimes ask vaguely for "some of Sarah Jewett's books", but when she produces volumes like "The White Heron" they finger them, say they look like children's books, and leave them on the desk. She thinks their physical appearance is much against them with this generation. I rather love those dumpy little books myself, but if you are going to make an appeal to the reading public of today I think the stories ought to have a fresh envelope and be issued in standard-size volumes with good clear type,—(I would suggest type like that you used in "Antonia")—some type that does not look like text-book type. I don't mean that I think the books ought to look loud, naturally, but modern.

If you send me down the books at once I will get to work in any spare moments I have. You can be setting the new volumes while I do the introduction. And, by the way, I do wish you would come to see me sometime when you are in town.

Faithfully yours
Willa Cather

Mrs. Knopf has just sold the movie rights of "A Lost Lady" for me for twelve thousand.

Jewett's The Country of the Pointed Firs *(1896) is set in the fictional Maine village of Dunnet Landing. The other stories mentioned share the same setting.*

TO DOROTHY CANFIELD FISHER

February 27 [1924]

My Dear Dorothy:

Your letter came at the happiest time for enjoying letters—I was, and still am, in bed: partly because of a stiff neck, and partly because I saw that a stiff neck would let me out of three dreaded pleasures; a song recital by an old friend, the first night of an old friend's play, and a literary dinner. Your letter came just when my splendid darkey maid was bringing in my tea, and it made a tea-party for me. How I have enjoyed these days in bed! You remember when I was a youngster I couldn't bear solitude at all—and now I can bear about nothing else: Isabelle has written me all about your mother, and I rejoice in her activity. I've written my mother all about her. By this boat I'm sending Isabelle an account of how they crowned my photograph with a "laurel wreath" in Red Cloud! I'm just childish enough to be awfully pleased. It means I've kept their affection, really.

I'm so glad you remember our walk and our morning in Paris with pleasure—I do, with deep pleasure and gratitude. I wish I could have been with you all in Switzerland. I'd love that.

Oh, I've read [Joseph Collins's] "The Doctor Looks at Literature," and I delight in it—especially the chapters on [D. H.] Lawrence and [Marcel] Proust. Do read Mme. [Marie] Curie's life of her husband [*Pierre Curie*], and the admirable sketch of her own life, Dorothy.

All winter I've been getting the nicest love letters from young boys. I've begun to save them—they are quite different from other admiring-reader-letters. I suppose actresses get a great many such, but I don't believe writers often do. In my college days it was the girls, not boys who wrote to authors.

No, Bakst doesn't spoil my life anymore—though he did cloud a good many months of it. Mother is the one worst hit, poor dear! She goes on moaning as if I'd done something disgraceful myself! Sure, it's like the Purple Cow—I'd rather see than be one. But she won't consider it that way.

I'm beginning to select material for a new collection of Miss Jewett, in accordance with a promise made years ago. Houghton Mifflin are so anxious to prevent me from producing copy for Knopf that they are even willing to spend a little money on Miss Jewett, if they can distract me from other activity!

Poor Knopf, anyhow! Just when he has got his booksellers where they can sell most any old book I do about the West, I refuse to have anything to do with the West, but have gone charging off on certain stories of embarrassing length—or shortness—that have nothing to do with locality—or geography whatever! My familiar spirit is like an old wild turkey that forsakes a feeding ground as soon as it sees tracks of people—especially if the people are readers, book-buyers. It's a crafty bird and it wants to go where there aint no readers. That's the truth: they go and paw a place all up and spoil it for me. It isn't my secret any more.

Write me again, dear Dorothy. It gives me so much pleasure. Now my stiff neck—I really have one—rebels at a writing posture, and I must stop. With my love to you and my blessing on you all.

With my love
Willa

Is your yellow cat a Tom or a lady? I took a great fancy to her—or him, and I'd like to know.

The novel Cather published after A Lost Lady, *the new writing she seems to be referring to in the penultimate paragraph, was* The Professor's House.

❧ ❦

In the spring of 1924, Burton Rascoe, a sort of literary gossip columnist, published a column about Cather in which he quoted Cather as saying, "Sarah Orne Jewett was too much cuddled by her family. They'd have kept her in cotton wool and smothered her if they'd had entirely their own way about it. She was a very uneven writer. A good portion of her work is not worth preserving." Jewett's family read this when it was republished in the Boston Transcript *and were quite angry, but Greenslet and Cather demonstrated that it was a case of inaccurate, careless journalism, and the Jewett family was mollified.*

TO FERRIS GREENSLET

April 15 [1924]

Dear Mr. Greenslet;

These are rather frantic days for me. An old friend has been very ill. Now my maid is ill, and I swing like a pendulum between my desk and the kitchen, and taxi (what a verb!) about New York for food. None the less, I have begun the Introduction. When it is finished I shall send it to Miss [Mary] Jewett for her approval. If there is anything in it she does not like, I will do all I can to mend it. I do not want her to have any more care or worry; I want to please her in this undertaking if it is within my power.

No, we have not been too hard on Burton Rascoe. He has caused both me and Miss Jewett the kind of heartache that is very hard to bear. It took more out of me than many an illness has. I understand that a garbled version of the same luncheon party was written by him for a small magazine [*Arts and Decoration*], with many offensive statements about me, supposed to be complimentary. I have not seen it, and do not want to.

Did the Transcript ever publish Thomas Beer's letter? Or a letter written them by Professor [Herbert] Bates, one of the men who heard my talk at Columbia? If not, it was very dishonest of that paper.

I inclose a list of the stories which I think would be the best ones to use in the second volume,—which I beg you to send Miss Jewett, along with this letter. I would write to her if I were not so driven.

As I told you, I think the last edition of the "Pointed Fir" stories can stand as it is, for the first volume, with a slight change of paging; I would strongly suggest that "The Queen's Twin" be placed <u>between</u> "A Dunnet Shepherdess" and "William's Wedding," both to suggest the passage of time, and to make less obvious the difference in treatment of William and Esther in the two stories,—the latter, of course, is something paler than the former, as it did not have that final clarifying touch by the writer's hand.

If Miss Jewett will only trust me, <u>I will do my best</u>.

Faithfully yours
Willa Cather

Stories suggested for volume II
  1. The White Heron
  2. The Flight of Betsey Lane
  3. The Dulham Ladies
  4. Going to Shrewsbury
  5. The Only Rose
  6. Miss Tempy's Watchers
  7. Martha's Lady
  8. The Guests of Mrs. Timms
  9. The Town Poor
  10. The Hiltons' Holiday
  11. Aunt Cynthia Dallet

Mr. Greenslet;

What about a title, a collective title, for the two volumes? How would something like "The Riverside Collection of Sarah Orne Jewett's Stories" do? Some title like that, but better.

TO FERRIS GREENSLET

May 10 [1924]

Dear Mr. Greenslet;

I do beg you not to use the [Elizabeth] Fairchild sonnet! As the tribute of a friend, even, it is not convincing, because it is so full of artificial, colorless phrases. Many a college undergraduate could do better. The sonnet is distinctly third rate as poetry. I had hoped that this would be an edition of Miss Jewett for writers. If Mme. [Olga Knipper] Tchekova, or [D. H.] Lawrence, or [John] Middleton Murry picked up these volumes and ran them over, the first thing their eye would light upon would be a tiresome piece of "old-lady-poetry." Why put a piece of feeble, foolish verse into a volume whose avowed excuse for being is its literary excellence?

I wish you would read "Decoration Day." It's simply one of the times when Miss Jewett didn't accomplish what she longed to do. It scarcely belongs in the second grade of her work, much less the first.

However, if Miss Mary is set upon it, and you feel that you must concede to her, put it in; and I will, in that part of the preface where I say that the stories in Volume II are of unequal merit, simply say that I do not consider that one among her best, but include it at the request of friends. I'll try to word it nicely. But do not take out "The Hiltons' Holiday"! I don't greatly love it, but one of the longest talks I ever had with Miss Jewett was about that story, and she felt strongly about it. I wonder what was the date of her letter to Mrs. Richards? To me she spoke differently. When I told her that "Decoration Day" to me seemed more like other people's stories, she said with a sigh that it was one of the ones that had grown old-fashioned.

You see, in the preface I've made a very high claim for these stories, and I can defend it with any really first rate writer of any country; but no critic, no writer, could make such a claim for a conventional magazine story like "Decoration Day." If you have to include it, I must say that it is done by request (which sounds foolish); otherwise that one story would quite invalidate the preface.

About this story you must do as you think best. I <u>wish</u> you could omit it. But about the Fairchild sonnet I can't compromise———what has an "occasional" sonnet to do with a literary work, even if it were a good sonnet? If you use the sonnet, I must withdraw the Preface altogether. I won't be one bit disagreeable about it, you understand,—but I shall be firm.

Faithfully yours
Willa Cather

Won't you take this up with Miss Mary? As an editor, with a publishing interest, you will have more influence than I.

⇥ ⇤

Typically affable, Greenslet met Cather's demands. Neither the sonnet nor "Decoration Day" appeared in the volume.

TO ZOË AKINS

September 7 [probably 1924]
Whale Cove Cottage, Grand Manan Island

Dear Zoë

I started to write you a birch bark letter, kid-fashion, but my pen is too stiff for it. We've had every kind of weather <u>but</u> heat; sun and and wind and splendid stunning fogs, and the tempest that beat the "Arabic" up so heavy carried our whole island out to sea. I've enjoyed every day of it and have been working hard and with great zest. Also walking lots, and cruising round among lighthouse and bell-buoys. Miss Lewis and I have a lovely little cottage all to ourselves—the house at which we eat not far away. I have literally lived in the tan-colored hunters suit you gave me two years ago, as it sheds the water from grass and trunk better than anything else I have. For really bad weather I wear knickerbockers. There are no roads—or very few—mostly trails through the woods and along the cliffs.

Love and greetings to you, dear Zoë, and I'll have a few interesting things to show you when I get back about October 15.

Devotedly
W.S.C.

Willa Cather with her brother Roscoe's daughters:
Virginia and twins Margaret and Elizabeth, July 1924

[Enclosed, written on birch bark:]

Dear Zoe:

Here I am in wild woods and wild weather. I've been working awfully hard on a quite new novel [*The Professor's House*], and have got nearly half way through the first writing of it. It's not very sweet or "appealing"—any diabetic patient could take it with safety! But it is, to me, fascinating in form—not intensely satisfying, but I can't get away from it, and so I'll have to see it through.

I've often thought with delight of the romantic costume with which you honored me that day you came to see me on Bank Street. It is really lovely for you.

TO FRANK ARTHUR SWINNERTON

September 18 [1924]
Grand Manan Island

Dear Mr. Swinnerton:

First let me set your mind at rest about the Proust book: I got the American edition of "Within a Budding Grove" [translation of Proust's *À l'ombre des jeunes filles en fleurs*] some weeks before I received your letter. You were most kind to remember my impatience to get it, and far from having been neglectful, you've been over-punctilious in remembering your promise.

I am so glad you had a pleasant stay in Rome, and found the region of the Pincian gardens especially attractive. I always feel as if that were more all the many Romes of many ages heaped up together than any other part of the city. I'm sure it's a Roman habit to pick up trifles: I once saw a lean priest appropriate a loaf of bread from a cart [and] tuck it into his gown.

You know something about American geography: June 10th I went out to Ann Arbor, Michigan, to receive a doctorate degree from the University. Then I went home to Red Cloud Nebraska (named for an Indian chief) and stayed six weeks with my father and mother. Early in August raced back three days and three nights on trains and then a day by boat, out to this Island in the Bay of Fundy, off the coast of New Brunswick, where I had rented a cottage for the summer months. My little house is in an apple orchard that drops off into the sea about thirty yards from my study window. I have been working very hard, and happily, after six months of idleness. I hope you are happily at work by now. Working periods come and go like the tides in this treacherous Bay of Fundy—there's no controlling them or prognosticating them. The Autumn fogs have come on now, and in three days I am leaving by our one and only twice-a-week-boat, for the mainland. I go for a week in Boston and then return to 5 Bank Street. You may be sure that when I go to England I shall call upon you and Mrs. Swinnerton, and shall hope to see a lot of you, in American idiom. With heartiest good wishes to you both,

Willa Cather

TO MR. MILLER

October 24, 1924

My dear Mr. Miller:

I am so sorry my writing vexes you, and it will continue to vex you! I do not in the least agree with your assumption that one kind of writing is right and another kind is wrong. I write at all because it pleases and amuses me—and I write in the way that pleases and amuses me. I had a perfectly good reason for writing "Antonia" in the first person, masculine—and I did not for one minute try to "talk like a man". Such a thing as humbugging any one never occurred to me. It does not matter who tells a story. It is merely a point of view, a position which the writer takes in regard to his material; just as a painter must first decide what his position is to be in regard to whatever he is going to sketch.

Again, there is one kind of story that ought to tell itself—the story of action. There is another kind of story that ought to be told—I mean the emotional story, which tries to be much more like music than it tries to be like drama—the story that tries to evoke and leave merely a picture—a mood. That was what [Joseph] Conrad tried to do, and he did it well. I wholly disagree with you regarding Jean Christophe [multivolume novel by Romain Rolland] and Pelle the Conqueror [multivolume novel by Martin Andersen Nexø]. Do either of these books tell themselves? Not for a minute! I should say that Jean is one of the most subjective books written in the last twenty-five years. Where do you find any steady flow of action in that, my good man? Do you mean to say that Rolland is not Christophe, and that he is not explaining and diagraming his emotions every minute? What is that kind of "description" but explaining—explaining under a very thin disguise. I think I shall begin every story hereafter with; "We will begin our story on a winter evening in the late seventies" or something of that sort. That is a frank, honest way to begin. It is a story, and "we" are doing it, and we might as well admit it. I think the two greatest writers of fiction in modern times were Count Tolstoi and Ivan Turgenev, and I think they were equally magnificent in their achievement. Their methods were absolutely opposite, and I think both methods are entirely admirable.

You see, I pay you the compliment of coming back at you with some spirit. I should like to have a chance to argue it out with you. I admire Nexö just as much as you do, but that is only one of the dozen fine ways of writing.

Cordially yours,
Willa Cather

TO MARY VIRGINIA BOAK CATHER

Sunday [probably November 1924]

My Dearest Mother;

I hope you will be charitable with me for not having written you for so long. The first few weeks in town after a long absence are terribly wearing. Edith came down two weeks ahead of me, and with the help of the faithful Mrs. Winn got the apartment beautifully clean. We have never been so clean before. This summer the landlord painted and papered the apartment throughout for us, and we sent all our window curtains to the cleaners, and had every rug we own dry-cleaned by a most reliable old carpet-cleaning house that dear Mr. Wiener first told me about years ago. They cleaned our rugs like new, and kept them in moth-proof storage for us all summer while we were away. So I came back to clean, bright, pleasant rooms. The first thing was to get a good maid, Montana having gone south.

We have now a pretty little Baltimore mulatto girl, named Mattie. Have had her one week and are greatly pleased with her. She is a splendid cook, is pretty, and has sweet manners. The only trouble about these nice little darkies is that they get tired of working and "go South." This one is nice; I spent a good deal of last week working with her and showing her how we like things done, and I got to like her ever so much. On Friday she and I put up five quarts of quince preserves, and I think I never tasted such delicious preserves. They are the color of old amber, only redder, and I wish I could send you a jar of them. So I feel that I am fairly started at housekeeping once again.

I am troubled about you and father, for this winter. It is a hard loss to lose a faithful servant [Marjorie Anderson], even if she cannot cook much. Even if Elsie were to come home she ought to have a woman to help her, and they are hard to get. I wrote her about a delightful place in Winchester where friends of mine spent last winter. I almost wish you and Father felt like going there for the winter.

I am trying to work on my new book every day, but it is hard to get the house to running and to write at the same time. I have great hopes of Mattie. I will write you again soon, dear Mother, and I hope you are getting rested at Mrs. Wolfe's. Mary Virginia's school has invited me to spend Thanksgiving there with her, but I do not know if I can leave my desk.

Very lovingly to you both,

Willie

➤ ✦

In an interview published by Rose Caroline Feld in the New York Times Book Review *on December 21, 1924, Cather was quoted as having complained that immigrants from the "Old World" are "hound[ed]" and "pursue[d]" day and night by social workers or "missionaries" of Americanism for the purpose of "turning them into stupid replicas of smug American citizens." She referred to this urge for "Americanizing everything and everybody" as a "deadly disease with us."*

TO MISS TELLER

January 21, 1925

My dear Miss Teller:

Whenever I get time to write it, I am going to make Miss Feld print an interview on her interview. She did not misquote me exactly, but she placed all the accents wrongly, and the words she attributes to me are, of course, hers, not mine. The only kind of social workers I object to are those who shamelessly say that they are "going into social work for a time, to get material for fiction". This whole silly attitude of regarding immigrants, or any other of God's creatures, as merely subject matter for "fiction" is so false,—it certainly never produces any good writing, and I do not think it can produce any social service worth the name.

As I say, when I have time, I hope I can get Miss Feld to revise her interview, and explain that my remarks applied to a very limited and feeble kind of social worker.

Very sincerely yours,
Willa Cather

➤ ✦

In 1918, Tomáš Masaryk, a philosopher, sociologist, and activist, became president of the newly formed independent republic of Czechoslovakia. Reelected several times, he served as president until 1935.

TO "HIS EXCELLENCY THE PRESIDENT OF THE
CZECHOSLOVAK REPUBLIC," THOMAS MASARYK

February 2, 1925
New York City

Honored Sir;

Your letter, transmitted to me through your Legation at Washington, confers upon me great honor and gives me great pleasure. I am glad to have carried a message from the Bohemian neighbors, whom I loved as a child, to their home country.

I have just returned to New York from Red Cloud, Nebraska, where my father and mother still live. I spent the Christmas holidays with them, and while there I had the pleasure of taking the living "Antonia" and six of her many fine children to the first moving picture production of "A Lost Lady." I have the good fortune to preserve friendly relations with most of my characters, even after I have put them in books. "Antonia" and her twelve splendid children are flesh and blood realities. Every time I go back to them I feel how much more interesting and lovable they are than my picture of them. I wish I could present them to you in person.

The life of our Middle West is so big and various, so ugly and so beautiful, that one cannot generalize about it. All one can do is to write of what came against one's own door-step, so to speak.

I regret that I cannot satisfactorily comply with your kind request for biographical material. I avoid biographers, asking them to wait until I get my work further along. My first novel was published in 1912, and a period of twelve years is scarcely long enough for a writer to find the form best suited to what he has to say. I was not young when I began to write, and though living is a good preparation for writing, it takes some time to acquire a simple and unobtrusive manner of presentation, however well one may know what one wishes to present.

I am able to send you a very good photograph, taken recently. I enclose a short biographical account which my publisher uses for publicity purposes, and some casual reviews. Biographies usually begin to come along just about the time a writer has no more to say, and I do not feel that that time has yet come to me.

I beg you, President Masaryk, to believe in my grateful appreciation of your letter.

Respectfully yours
Willa Cather

TO IRENE MINER WEISZ

Tuesday [February 17, 1925]

My Darling Irene:

If you knew how much joy those glorious roses gave me! They came like a climax to a debauch of work and music—red <u>enough</u>, and big enough. On Sunday I sent Edith and Mattie both away for the day, and I stayed alone with my ever-becoming-more-beautiful roses and drank koumiss and rested my mind and my heart. I don't know anyone who is quite as hard hit by flowers as I am. Even the most every-day young rose gives me pleasure, but superb ones like these delight me like splendid personalities. I say "these" because at least half of them are still red and full, in a big Spanish pitcher on the mantle, and they have already given the place three days of splendour. Edith has loved them too and begs me to tell you so. Mattie admired them so much that I gave her one to wear to a colored ball Saturday night!

It was such a satisfaction to me to have you read the story [*The Professor's House*], dear Irene, and to see that you got at once the really fierce feeling that lies behind the rather dry and impersonal manner of the telling. You shall see more of it before a great while.

With a heartful of love to you
Willie

→ ←

The mention of the "publicity about Margie" in the following letter refers to rumors in the local Red Cloud newspaper in the fall of 1924 that the Cathers were hiding Marjorie Anderson. The rumors emerged from Marjorie's unwillingness to venture outside their home for fear of the return of her former husband, a man named O'Leary who had deserted her soon after their marriage.

TO MARY VIRGINIA BOAK CATHER

March 2 [1925?]

My Dearest Mother;

Now what can I possibly have done to upset you so? I have not written to Bess or Auntie since I came back to New York, nor sent them anything, but a book,—and a very poor one it was. I told you when I was at home that I had sent Auntie my old wadded dressing gown, it was in rags and I thought they could patch it up for her. Oh, yes, I sent Auntie some paper flowers for a valentine,—you always told me to send her such little things, and I haven't sent her anything for years. Why, Elsie scolded me, and sent her something at Thanksgiving for me and paid for it, she was so ashamed of me.

I haven't written you since I got back because I knew Douglass was with you and you would not be lonely, and I have been so terribly busy. I wrote Elsie once and thought she would send you the letter.

As for making trouble between you and father, I've certainly not tried to do that. Really, it's very unjust to accuse me of it. You must know, Mother, without my telling you, that all that newspaper publicity about Margie was harder on me than on any of the rest of you, and it was needless. If you hadn't been so foolish about never letting anyone see her, there would have been no "mystery." But that is past and gone. I wasn't angry about it. I thought you had been unwise, and the result of your mistaken judgement made a good deal of ugly talk about me. But I never felt in the least angry toward you, and I took my medicine and kept quiet about it. I wouldn't speak of it now, if you didn't come at me so. How foolish, Mother, for us to quarrel! I can't quarrel, because I have not a particle of hard feeling. I couldn't be angry with you now if I tried. I think one of the consolations of growing older is that one comes to understand one's parents better. I am too much like you in many ways to criticise you; I sometimes get impatient, just as I lose patience with myself, but I have never felt cross toward you, even for a moment, for years and years. I think the last time was about poor Mrs. Garber; and you see now, don't you, that I understood her better than you thought I did, and that though I admired certain things, I was never taken in by her.

Now you and I have been growing closer together for many years, don't let us spoil it. If I have done anything amiss, I am eager to make it right. But if I have done anything, it was through stupidity. I certainly did not go home to make trouble, but because I love you very tenderly and am happy in your company. Surely, you can't be seriously annoyed at my sending a few old things to the Andrews'. Elsie is always telling me that I am not very nice to Auntie.

I had meant to write you today to ask you if you want me to send you a small check for your birthday so that you can send it on to Jack, as Roscoe did. It is my hope that father will let me buy the house as I proposed, and use the money to pay Elsie a salary and let her come home to make the place a bright and happy home for both of you. I believe she would put her whole heart into it, and that you would take more comfort in being there than you ever have before. I know that Retta [Ayres Miner] has been kind, but you can hardly go on living that way.

> With my dearest love to you, dear mother
> Willa

→ ←

Collier's serialized *Cather's seventh novel,* The Professor's House, *beginning June 6, 1925, and featured the book—"A NEW NOVEL by WILLA CATHER"—on the cover.*

TO IRENE MINER WEISZ

[March 16, 1925]

Dearest Irene;

I think I ought to send this letter to you before I send it to Isabelle, because you saw my Professor in his early stages and took such a tender interest in him. Now you will know where and when to look for it. I could not sell it to a monthly, as they could not use it fast enough to eat it all up before the book date, Sept. 1st. The first editor my agent sent it to bought it within a few hours after it was sent to him, as you see. He paid ten thousand dollars for the serial rights, of which one thousand goes to my agent as commission, and nine to me. The price is confidential between you and Mr. Wise [Weisz] and me. If ones family knows about one's prices, they expect one to do such absurd things. You know how it is,—they think it's such "easy money"! But I want you to know, because I know you like to hear of any good luck I have.

Dear Irene, do you think you could send me some of those tablets to wash ecru curtains by next Monday? I'm cleaning house for Virginia's coming for Easter vacation.

A world of love to you, dear.
Willie

TO CARRIE MINER SHERWOOD

[April 22, 1925]
New York City

Dear Carrie;

[Thomas Masaryk] sent me a lot of lovely views of Bohemia. I am sending you some for you and Irene, and a bunch fastened together for Annie Pavelka. Will you please have the ones marked for Annie framed in narrow, inexpensive black frames, allowing about as much margin as I have indicated with lead pencil, and sent out to her? Please send the bill to me, as I don't want her to have the expense of framing them.

And, dear Carrie, will you also please give this check to Mrs. Diedrich and ask her to send Mother some tulips? It will save me one letter, and this time of year my mail box is like a task-master.

We had such a gay time for the two weeks Virginia was here! My friends were so nice to her, and I cut work altogether. I don't regret that one bit, though I'm having to make up for it now.

With love to you and yours
Willie

→ ←

F. Scott Fitzgerald wrote Cather in the spring of 1925 expressing both his admiration for her work and a fear that in his new novel, The Great Gatsby, *it might appear that he had borrowed too closely from Cather's description of Marian Forrester (in lines near the end of her novel) in a description early in his. To demonstrate that he had not plagiarized from her, he sent her the pertinent pages of his first draft of the novel, which he had written before* A Lost Lady *was published. He also sent her a copy of the newly published novel.*

TO F. SCOTT FITZGERALD

April 28, 1925

My dear Mr. Fitzgerald:

I had read and hugely enjoyed your book before I got your letter, and I honestly had not thought of "A Lost Lady" when I read that passage to which you now call my attention. So many people have tried to say that same thing before either you or I tried it, and nobody has said it yet. I suppose everybody who has ever been swept away by personal charm tries in some way to express his wonder that the effect is so much greater than the cause,—and in the end we all fall back upon an old device and write about the effect and not the lovely creature who produced it. After all, the only thing one can tell about beauty, is just how hard one was hit by it. Isn't that so?

Very cordially yours,
Willa Cather

✦ ✦

In the summer of 1925, Cather and Lewis made another trip to New Mexico. According to Edith Lewis, Cather had finished the short novel My Mortal Enemy *(published in 1926) before they left on the trip.*

TO ELIZABETH SHEPLEY SERGEANT

June 23 [1925]
Hotel La Fonda, Santa Fe, New Mexico

Dear Elsie:

I want to tell you again that I think you got through a hard job mighty well. I'd hate to attack such a chore myself. You surely gave me all I deserve—maybe more, but I suppose we always think ourselves deserving!

I've been loafing here in this comfortable hotel, and have met a really nice Mrs. Barker (she knows you) and a nice Mrs. Hughey. Mrs. [Mary] Austin is here, and settles all questions of human conduct and natural history with a word.

Miss Lewis an[d] I go down to San Gabriel tomorrow. It's been awfully hot down there lately.

Thank you for a painless operation!

Yours

W. S. C.

TO ROBERT JOSEPHY, ALFRED A. KNOPF, INC.

June 26 [1925]

Alcalde, New Mexico

I am sending you the first half of the page proofs [of *The Professor's House*] today, the rest will follow in a few days.

Please send me the proof of the <u>dedication page</u> as soon as possible. You remember this text is:

<u>For Jan, because he likes narrative.</u>

I've never seen a proof of it yet.

I like this jacket design <u>fairly</u> well, but I agree with you that it's too fussy—too much like an illustration. I had hoped for something simple in design and brilliant in color. The blue behind the lettering seems to me rather dark and heavy for a jacket. I enclose a little sketch which might give a suggestion—I have no crayons here to indicate the colors.

If you've no time to experiment further, I will be satisfied with this sketch of Mr. Fall's, however. Don't hold anything up in order to send me proofs of the jacket. If you are satisfied I think I will be.

Faithfully

Willa Cather

After many invitations, Cather and Lewis went to Taos to stay with Mabel Dodge Luhan in the Pink House at her large estate, Los Gallos. Luhan, married to Taos Pueblo Indian Tony Luhan, loved to surround herself with artists and intellectuals, and her large estate could offer creative people the space and comfort they needed to complete their work. After leaving Luhan's and returning to Santa Fe, Cather found and read The Life of the Right Reverend Joseph P. Machebeuf, *by William Howlett. As Edith Lewis wrote later, "There, in a single evening, as [Cather] often said, the idea of* Death Comes for the Archbishop *came to her, essentially as she afterwards wrote it."*

TO MABEL DODGE LUHAN

Monday [July 6, 1925?]
Hotel La Fonda, Santa Fe, New Mexico

Dear Mrs. Luhon:

The only ugly things we saw in Taos, the Meyers family, followed us straight to Santa Fé and the Fonda—faced us at dinner the first night! I was pleased to see Mr. [Andrew] Dasburg at breakfast this morning. I strove to get his attention for one half-hour, and then had to go up to him and hit him to get so much as a "Good-morning" out of him.

I'm sending you some bum cigarettes because the tobacconist was just opening a fresh case and I thought they might be fresh. No Salisburys in tins here, but I'll send you some from Denver. My lovely bracelet is with Mr. Yantz, and he took the turquoise out in my presence. I love it, and I think your giving it to me was a good omen for the book, for I find quite an astonishing collection of letters here awaiting me. Letters from old hard-boiled publishers and solemn professors, telling me that Tom Outland [the middle section of *The Professor's House*], in Collier's, gave them a pulse. It seems to have struck "other publishers" hard. I'm still hard on the trail of my old priests. I found a lot of interesting things this morning which I'll tell you some day.

On Wednesday we go to Laguna—though of course we'd like to start right back to Taos! Please give my warm regards to Miss [Mary] Foote and Tony. I'm afraid I'll always be one of your "hangers-on" hereafter!

Admiringly yours
Willa Cather

TO MABEL DODGE LUHAN

August 7 [1925]
Hotel Olin, Denver

Dear Mabel:

How obliging of Clarence to make a natural climax to the article! We were held up three days at Lamy because of the washout at Trinidad—nothing running except over the Belen cut-off. At New Laguna we had to wait three days before the bold Indian boy, Sarissino, would even try to get us through eighteen miles of lake and mud to Acoma. There was a cloud-burst every afternoon: But we met very interesting people and didn't mind the delay a bit.

We joined my mother and sister here July 31st. We have a very comfortable apartment in this new and very good hotel. Mother is well enough to go to the theatre and take walks and motor rides. We will go home to Red Cloud about August 12th. Then I will hurry on to my island in the Bay of Fundy to get to work.

August 8th

Your letter sent to Bank Street, on to La Fonda, and finally here, has just arrived. The quotation from Plotinus is superb—who on earth is he?—and Background is exactly the right title for the first volume [of Luhan's autobiography, *Intimate Memories*]. Don't be discouraged if the latter part is harder to do, it's bound to be harder. Very early memories are always the richest to work with. But that first part is glorious—it's full of life and vigor and reality.

My weeks with you in Taos stand out as the fine reality of the summer. I keep telling my little nieces about them. Yesterday my brother [Roscoe Cather] motored down from northern Wyoming and brought his three adorable little girls to us; the twins [Margaret and Elizabeth Cather], aged 10, and their sister [Virginia Cather] who is 13.

With my warmest greetings
Willa Cather

Miss Lewis went on to New York last Monday.

TO ALFRED A. KNOPF

Tuesday [October 6, 1925]
The Shattuck Inn, Jaffrey, New Hampshire

Dear Mr. Knopf:

Isn't the "Professor" behaving splendidly? Neither you nor I foresaw anything like this last spring—though I had a certain hope in <u>Tom Outland</u>. "The Bishop", too, is behaving well up in this part of the woods.

Please ask one of your office people to go down to Ditson's (or any other music store) and get a copy of the piano score of "Patience" and send it up to me. There's a nice boy who will drum it for me in the evenings.

And please send me a copy of the book with its new jacket, I've not seen one yet, and I did hate the text of the first jacket enormously.

On the whole, it seems to me we can so far congratulate each other on the "Professor's" account.

Faithfully yours
Willa Cather

✦ ✦

Cather had become acquainted with professors George and Harriet Whicher at the Bread Loaf School in 1922. Harriet Whicher taught at Mount Holyoke College, which is quite near Smith College.

TO HARRIET FOX WHICHER

October 16 [1925]
Shattuck Inn, Jaffrey, New Hampshire

Dear Mrs. Whicher:

I have a little niece, aged 18, in the freshman class in Smith this year. Will you look her up at sometime when it's convenient to you? Her name is Mary Virginia Auld—she pleases me, both as an Aunt and as Author. I believe you'll think she's rather charming. She'd love your boys—awfully handy with brothers.

I'm hard at work here, after a glorious summer riding horseback in New Mexico—sage brush plains and aspen woods in high mountains. I wanted to go to Paris awfully in the spring, but somehow I wanted the sagebrush more. I have a regular Zane Gray mind; roughneck and low-brow is [the] name for me.

I <u>wished</u> you could have been at the [Robert] Frost birthday dinner.

Faithfully always
Willa Cather

TO DOROTHY CANFIELD FISHER

October 22 [1925]
Shattuck Inn, Jaffrey, New Hampshire

My Dearest Dorothy:

Since June first I've only been in New York 3 days, in September, on my way here. I was in New Mexico horse-back riding and doing camping trips until August 6th, then my mother and sister joined me in Denver and spent several weeks at a hotel there to escape Nebraska heat. Then home to Red Cloud for two weeks, then here, by way of New York.

I've often spent the fall here, and love it. I'm having such a happy solitude,—after so many many people all summer. I walk in the morning and walk in the afternoon—and sleep at night, you can believe! I have to go back to Bank Street Oct. 30—but not for long, I am going to leave that hideous town for good very soon.

Now why do you suppose "The Professor" is going better than any other book of mine? Knopf didn't expect it, and I surely didn't. I thought it a nasty, grim little tale, but the reviewers seem to think it's a cross-word puzzle. It's certainly not my "favorite" of my own books.

Oh Dorothy, I love the story of your mother's class-mate going to Italy. I wish I could see the Frosts again. But life does take me by the throat—no time for anything. I come up here to play with a nice little story, and a dozen things turn up to prevent me. But I'm not "prevented", and I love this country so much.

As to that "middle-aged" novel doesn't everyone have it sometimes? I think one feels "age" more in seeing one's friends grow older than in growing older oneself. And it's [a] sad business. But the new story is "sunny" and so I've forgotten all that.

Thank you for the French notice of "Antonia", I liked it. I wish you could motor down here [from Vermont] for a day—is it very far, I wonder? I do want to live in the country all the year around!

Lovingly, my dear
Willa

TO IRENE MINER WEISZ

Monday [January 11, 1926]

Dearest Irene;

Professor St. Peter [character in *The Professor's House*] has just gone and bought me a grand mink coat! Isn't he extravagant? I want you please to telegraph Mr. Weisz's office here to send a man up to the house to insure it for me, on Friday or Saturday of this week at noon (12 oclock) if possible. I'm afraid I'll lose it just because it's the first "valuable" I've ever had.

I'm working like a beaver, Dear, and I love my Bishop!

Yours always
Willa

➤ ✦

Cather's eighth novel, a short one, was My Mortal Enemy, *published by Knopf in the fall of 1926.*

TO ALFRED A. KNOPF

Thursday [probably January 14, 1926]

Dear Mr. Knopf:

Your letter about "My Mortal Enemy" gives me great encouragement. It is an exceptional story; not many people will see that, possibly. But it means a great deal to me that you do. I want to be a "good investment" for you financially, but I want very much more to be able to interest you as a reader. I hope to be able to interest you for many years to come. I value your respect and would like to keep it. I think when you see the Archbishop you'll find a new kind of flavor.

I look forward to seeing you and Blanche on Tuesday evening.

Faithfully
Willa Cather

➤ ✦

In early 1926 Ferris Greenslet asked if she would be willing to make some change to the Introduction to My Ántonia *so Houghton Mifflin could sell it as a new edition—and raise the price a little.*

TO FERRIS GREENSLET

February 15, 1926

My dear Mr. Greenslet:

Mr. Knopf told me of your decision with regard to the question of transferring my books to him. If the company is not willing to sell the books to him, then I think it ought to be willing to make some effort to sell them as if they were live property—not merely "creditable" books on the list, by Charles Egbert Craddock or Celia Thaxter, or somebody long deceased.

Now, I come to the question of "Antonia." Of course, I do not think that in pushing "Antonia" or "O Pioneers," it is quite fair for you to disparage a book I published last year or the book I will publish next year. As I told you, I do not like the attitude that "A Lost Lady" was in any sense a repetition of

"Antonia," though Mrs. Forrester was one of the women who employed the "hired girls" to whom Antonia belonged. (Confidentially, let me tell you that the real Antonia [Anna Pavelka] actually did work for the real Mrs. Forrester [Lyra Garber].) The stories are studies of the same society, but they are studies of two very different elements in it, and they are written in a very, very different way.

Now, as to the preface. The preface is not very good; I had a kind of complex about it. I wrote and rewrote it, and it was the only thing about the story that was laborious. But I still think that a preface is necessary, even if it is not good in itself. Let me take a trial at shortening the preface. The later part of the book, I am sure, would be vague if the reader did not know something about the rather unsuccessful personal life of the narrator.

I am terribly busy just now and shrink from breaking in at all on the story I have in hand. When do you want to bring out this new edition and when would you need the copy of the revised preface?

Regarding the Benda illustrations: you would, of course, retain those. It is one of the few cases where I think the pictures really help the story, and I would not be willing to leave them out.

Cordially yours,
Willa Cather

→ ←

Carroll Atwood Wilson, another in the line of people interested in Cather's work on the Mary Baker Eddy book, was an attorney and book collector.

TO CARROLL ATWOOD WILSON

March 18, 1926

My dear Mr. Wilson:

Since my return your letter of inquiry has been brought to my attention. I do not wish to be ungracious, but the subject is really one upon which I do not care to make a statement. The idea that Georgine Milmine is a myth amuses me very much. She is a very lively and husky person who lives in the western part of this State, and who collected the great mass of material from which the McClure history was written. She did not write much of it herself. That was done mostly in the office by McClures editorial staff. I took my turn at it, as did several other persons. It was not a subject I would have chosen to work upon, or a subject in which I had any particular interest. My interest was a purely editorial one; to arrange the mass of notes and documents in a form that would be clear and effective for serial publication. You can readily understand why I do not wish to have my name connected in any way with a piece of work which was not of my own choosing, and in which I had only a partial responsibility—a responsibility shared with four or five other persons.

If I remember rightly, Mr. Smith's connection with the magazine did not begin until some time after the publication of this series of articles. His information, therefore, must have been second-hand.

I beg you, dear Mr. Wilson, to consider this confidential. I have been asked this question many times and have always before refused to make any reply whatsoever, but your profession seems to me a guarantee of discretion, and I feel sure you will keep this statement for your personal information and let it go no further. A shaping hand over the form, arrangement, and presentation of the facts in that series of articles, I did have.

Very sincerely yours,
Willa Cather

→ ←

The following letter survives only in a transcription made by literary agent Paul Revere Reynolds or, more likely, a member of his staff. According to a note on the transcription, Reynolds sent the original to the Forum *in July 1926 when he was trying to sell the serial rights to* Death Comes for the Archbishop. *The* Forum *bought the rights.*

TO PAUL REVERE REYNOLDS

[Probably April 25, 1926]

Dear Mr. Reynolds:

This story is not a love story, any more than "Robinson Crusoe" is; it is simply not that sort of story at all. It is concerned with the picturesque conditions of life in the Southwest, just at the time that New Mexico was taken over from Old Mexico, and with the experiences of two Catholic missionaries who were sent there to bring order out of the mixture of Indian and Spanish and Mexican superstitions. The real hero of the story is Father Latour (his real name was Lamy) the young Frenchman who was made Bishop of New Mexico at the age of 37, a man of an old and noble family in Puy de Dom, a man of wide culture, an idealist, and from his youth hungry for the world's frontiers. He was finally made an archbishop, and died in Santa Fe in 1886. In other words, he went there in the days of the buffalo and Indian massacres, and he lived to see the Santa Fe railroad cross New Mexico.

As I told you, I had the good fortune to come upon a great many letters written by the Bishop and his Vicar to their families in France, so that I have not had to depend upon my own invention for the reactions of these two French priests to the conditions they met there. Many of the incidents are invention, some of them are used almost literally as they happened, such as the chapter called "The White Mules."

There will be five more chapters in Part I,—they are written but not typed. Part II will be much shorter than Part I, but in a much deeper tone and with a deeper, graver color.

Willa Cather

→ ←

Cather did revise the introduction to My Ántonia, *and a new edition was released by Houghton Mifflin in 1926.*

TO FERRIS GREENSLET

[Early May 1926]

Dear Mr. Greenslet;

Here is the revised introduction. For Heaven's sake don't lose it! I'd never be able to patch it up again. Please send me proofs before the 15th of May if possible, if not you'll have to send them out to New Mexico, where I will be rather hard to reach.

Hastily
W.S.C.

Please mail me a copy of Antonia on the day you receive this,—I've had to cut into my only copy to make the Introduction.

→ ←

Cather and Lewis returned to New Mexico and Arizona in 1926 to continue research for Death Comes for the Archbishop. *While there, they were joined by Cather's brother Roscoe and his family: wife Meta and daughters Margaret, Elizabeth, and Virginia.*

TO MABEL DODGE LUHAN

May 26 [1926]
El Navajo, Gallup, New Mexico

Dear Mabel:

I don't know whether you are East or West—but I have a feeling you are west, or on the way.

We left N.Y. on the 15th, stopped a few days with my mother and father in Nebraska, and after a day's pause at Lamy came out here. Isn't Gallup the Hell of a place? I never saw so many low types in one town. We were both awfully tired and have not been doing much. Edith got a nasty cold coming out of Nebraska in a prairie heat wave, and we've been curing that. Tomorrow we go to Zuni, and we hope to make Canyon de Chelly later. We can't do it unless Edith gets over her cough, for the drivers tell me it's a harder trip than it's advertised to be. We have very comfortable rooms here, and Edith has been very happy and relaxed in bed for two days, while I've made several strange and terrible acquaintances.

My brother and his peerless twins (also his wife and another daughter aged 13) meet me at Santa Fé June 14. They will have only a week, so I expect to lead a busy life until they're gone.

July 1st I get to work again, but I've not made up my mind as to just where. Miss Lewis starts for N.Y. June 28th. She will take another vacation of a month in August and will probably join me in New Hampshire or New Brunswick.

If you're still in New York I may see you as you go through Santa Fe. Oh Mabel, we rode from Lamy to Gallup on the same train with Rin-Tin-Tin, and had the pleasure of meeting him during the half-hour at Albuquerque. I never was so excited about any celebrity before!

Yours
W.S.C.

Address LaFonda, Santa Fe after June 1st.

TO MABEL DODGE LUHAN

Saturday [probably June 5, 1926]
Hotel La Fonda, Santa Fe, New Mexico

Dear Mabel:

Here we are, after a thrilling trip to Canyon de Chelly. I am wondering if you could rent us the pink house (the one we were in last summer) for two weeks. Edith has to start for New York on the 23rd of June, but if I found I could work in the pink house I would stay on through July, coming back to Santa Fe for the last week of June to join my brother. He would be here for five or six days only.

Of course I don't know whether you are settled yet, or whether you are in the mood for wanting people about. I wish I could talk to you by telephone but this line is out of order and they won't give me a connection.

Since I can't talk to you I see no way but to thus abruptly enquire whether you would take us for boarders—whether you could make us a flat rate of twenty-five or thirty dollars each per week, as our friends at Grand Manan do. If this wouldn't suit you, simply drop me a line to that effect. I know that renting your guest houses is one thing, and feeding people quite another and much more inconvenient. On the other hand there would hardly be time for us to rig up a kitchen in the pink house if I'm going to be working.

All this is a suggestion which needn't bother you if it's impractical—merely dismiss it with a word.

We are most comfortable here, but the Indian Detourists [participants in tours offered by the Fred Harvey Company] abound and the motor horn is the worm that dieth not. The de Vargas might be quieter, but they are <u>building</u>, as you doubtless know. We got in only yesterday and have seen nobody as yet. I won't make any further plans until I hear from you. Somehow, I'm awful glad to be back in this country.

Devotedly
W.S.C

TO ROSCOE CATHER

Saturday [June 26, 1926]
Hotel La Fonda, Santa Fe, New Mexico

My Dear Roscoe:

Last night I went to sleep thinking cheerfully of the twins and surely should have had pleasant dreams. But not so at all—I dreamed that Margaret was eaten by a lion! We all saw her sitting in a lion's cage in a circus parade, and felt very proud of her, and after the cage passed word travelled back through the crowd that the lion had eaten her! And her grandmother & grandfather Cather both fainted and had to be carried out of the crowd, and then I wakened up.

Tell them I went right up to Mrs. Austin's house to work that morning as soon as you left, and found my Bishop there waiting for me. I have worked every day since then. Tony [Luhan] is still in the hospital with a high temperature, and his wife is terrified. I talked to her by long distance yesterday. I shall go back to my little house in Taos about July 4 or 5, as Mabel has a housekeeper there in her absence and a friend I like from New York is coming there at that date. I am so glad you did go home by way of Taos. Maybe I'll have a little house there some day, where the children can visit me. I hope you and Meta and Elsie enjoyed your stay here one half as much as I did, and I do wish I could see you all and the children soon again. I love your little girls very dearly, all three of them.

With much love
Willie

No sign of Douglass!

Ask the twins and Virginia to write me, and tell me what they liked best down here.

TO MARY AUSTIN

June 26 [1926]
Hotel La Fonda, Sante Fe, New Mexico

Dear Mrs. Austin;

A week ago today I first went up to your lovely house to see whether I could settle down to work there—and I have not missed a morning since then! It is the most restful, quiet, sympathetic place to work in. I do not use your little study, but sit in your dear little blue plush chair in that corner of the library—I hope I won't wear that chair out—open the screened portion of your big window, and there I sit and write on my knee. I like being in that fine big room, with so much space about me, and the breeze comes in comfortingly at that window.

The girl who waters your flowers is as punctual as a clock, and so far the house has not got at all dusty. What a satisfying, <u>real</u> sort of house it is,—and what a generous friend you were to give me permission to work there. If you hadn't had that kind thought for me, I would be up in the air now. I meant to go back to Taos soon after my brother and his family left Santa Fe, but long before that Tony, who had been ailing all the time we were there, got suddenly worse, and Mabel eloped with him to this hospital at Albuquerque. They will be there for ten days or two weeks longer, for Tony still has a temperature. For some days it was 104, and Mabel was terribly frightened. She said she'd never seen him sick before, and she didn't take it cooly at all. She has a new housekeeper in Taos, and begged me to go and stay, but I thought that would be dismal. Mary Foote arrives in Taos July 3d, and I will go down (or is it up?) soon afterward. Miss Foote is good company and I'm very fond of her.

When Mabel fled from Taos and the pink house there suddenly assumed a deserted and forbidding look, [here] appears Mrs. Huey with the key to your house, like a coincidence on the stage!

I hope your surgeon will hurry the time of your operation along. I've had several, and I always hate waiting for them much more than having them.

My love and good wishes to you, dear Mrs. Austin, and my gratitude for the happy peaceful hours I have spent in your library.

Faithfully yours
Willa Cather

→ ←

In 1932, Mary Austin wrote negatively of Death Comes for the Archbishop *and its focus on French missionaries in her autobiography* Earth Horizon, *and she reportedly showed friends the chair in her house that Cather sat in while writing the novel. Annoyed at Austin's remarks and violation of her privacy, Cather later denied that any part of the book was written in Austin's house. However, the copy given to Austin at the time of publication bore this inscription: "For Mary Austin, in whose lovely study I wrote the last chapters of this book. She will be my sternest critic and she has the right to be."*

TO LOUISE GUERBER BURROUGHS

Sunday [August 22, 1926]
The MacDowell Colony, Peterboro, New Hampshire

My Dear Louise;

Funny place for me to be? Perhaps. I found myself in New York in the first dreadful week of August, my chore at the printers' done (250 signatures [of *My Mortal Enemy*] on 100 percent linen-rag paper brought from Italy) and no place to work. So I telegraphed Mrs. [Marian] MacDowell and asked her if she could take me in and give me a studio. I have a beautiful studio in a fine wood, looking out on Monadnock. At first I didn't like the "colonists", but now I like them nearly all—some of them very much. As people they're mostly nice, if only they wouldn't talk about their damned professions and call them "arts"! Some of them are <u>very</u> nice. I'm enjoying the Bishop again, after weeks of separation—its like a ball where you have to dance for hours with other partners and then come back to the real one. When I was in N.Y. I sold the serial rights to the "Forum", to begin in December. That will crowd me just a little. September 8 I go to Jaffrey, Miss Lewis will join me for the month. I'll be there until late in October.

My dear, I found a letter from you in Red Cloud which my naughty parents had not forwarded—but no offense meant, there were dozens of letters there. My parents are Southern and don't get agitated. Don't miss "Iolanthe", if it's still going. If you hear of anything good to read, tell me. Don't get impatient, but I hope we can do some things together when I do go back to town.

Yours
W.S.C.

→ ←

Alfred Knopf wrote Cather in the summer of 1926 to ask if she would appear at a book fair to oblige the Joseph Horne Company, one of Knopf's large accounts.

TO ALFRED A. KNOPF

September 8 [1926]
Peterboro, New Hampshire

Dear Mr. Knopf;

I'd like to oblige the Joseph Horne people, but if I once began that kind of thing, there'd be no end to it. One has to do that sort of thing <u>thoroughly</u>, as Edna Ferber does it, or not do it at all. In these days, NOT doing it is a kind of publicity in itself,—though that's not the reason I refrain.

Please tell them that I will be in Canada then, finishing my new novel, and that as the serialization of that novel begins in December, I can't interrupt my work so near to publication date; The Forum has to have the copy for the first two installments November 1st.

That is all true, except, possibly Canada, and [that] is certainly a plausible escape. Please tell them I'd love to make an exception in their case, as I have old friends in Pittsburgh.

Please ask your secretary to have one copy of "A Lost Lady" mailed to me at Jaffrey, whither I go in a few days, and to send me two copies of the new book as soon as it's out. But ask your mailing department to <u>hold </u>the ten complimentary copies that come to me <u>in the office</u> until my return.

My warmest welcome to Blanche and Alfred.

Yours
Willa Cather

TO MISS CHAPIN, *THE FORUM*

September 24 [1926]
Shattuck Inn, Jaffrey, New Hampshire

Dear Miss Chapin;

I think it's rather a mistake to emphasize the landscape—to me that suggests ornamental descriptive writing, which I hate. There really is a good deal of movement in this narrative. In future announcements won't you, with Dr. [Henry Goddard] Leach's approval, use something like the enclosed, putting the stress more on the people than the scene?

Sincerely
Willa Cather

Miss Cather's new narrative, Death Comes etc, recounts the adventures of two missionary priests in the old Southwest. Two hardy French priests find themselves set down in the strange world at the end of the Santa Fé trail, among scouts and trappers and cut-throats, old Mexican settlements and ancient Indian pueblos. The period is that immediately following the Mexican War, and the story is a rich, moving panorama of life on that wild frontier.

❧ ❧

On October 2, 1926, Blanche Colton Williams, chair of the O. Henry Memorial Committee, wrote Cather offering to publish My Mortal Enemy *in the volume* O. Henry Memorial Award Prize Stories. *Cather and Knopf had no intention of presenting in an anthology of short stories a work they were soon to publish as a book of its own.*

TO BLANCHE KNOPF

Wednesday [October 6, 1926]
Shattuck Inn, Jaffrey, New Hampshire

My Dear Blanche;

Why do these <u>nuts</u> keep trying to separate us from our Mortal Enemy? Please write this lady telling her it can't be done. I have sent her a line to that effect also.

The copies of the books have arrived—I think Mr. Adler has done himself and me proud. It's a lovely book. I only hope the public will be as eager to get away with it as these short story cranks seem to be.

You'll have the rest of the Archbishop about October twenty-ninth, when I'll return to Bank street.

Please, kind friend, have somebody send me Virginia Wolfe's "The Voyage Out"—I'm in an awful plight for something to read and don't know what to order, but I want to try that.

Hastily
W.S.C.

TO LOUISE GUERBER BURROUGHS

October 15 [1926]
The Shattuck Inn, Jaffrey, New Hampshire

My Dear Louise;

I won't be back in town before November 4th or 5th, probably. I'm flirting a little with a story that's been knocking round in my head for sometime. Title "Blue Eyes on the Platte"—PLATTE, <u>not plate</u>. Rather frivolous and decidedly sentimental, love's-young-dream sort of thing. The natural result of a year of celibacy with the Archbishop. Yes, he's done and gone—at his head a copyreader's smirch, at his feet a stone.

Now <u>how</u> did I prejudice you against Rebecca West? Am I that sort of [person] who manages to give someone a black eye while pretending to praise them?

Oh <u>tell</u> me this name, the Chinese or Japanese name of that wonderful candy Bauer makes, which is butterscotch, chocolate and almond flakes, all in little squares. Almond <u>what</u>? I want to order some. It's lovely here now— everyone gone, weather wild and tragic with brilliant intervals. I have the hotel and the mountain to myself.

Yours
W.S.C.

"Blue Eyes on the Platte" probably refers to the novel that became Lucy Gayheart, *though it was not published until 1935.*

⤳ ⤶

In a review of My Mortal Enemy *in the* New York Times Book Review *on October 24, 1926, titled "Willa Cather Fumbles for Another Lost Lady," Louis Kronenberger questioned whether the book really ought to be called a "novel."*

TO BLANCHE KNOPF

Sunday [October 24, 1926]

My Dear Blanche;

I haven't seen the Times notice, and I shall avoid seeing it—just as well, as it's by someone whose opinion one needn't regard. Don't you think it is perhaps a mistake to advertise that book as a "novel," Blanche? It's not really that. Couldn't the ad writer call it a "Story," merely? That would arouse less antagonism.

I'll be leaving Jaffrey in a few days now, as I'll stop to make some short visits on the way home. So after this send all mail to 5 Bank Street.

Please thank Alfred for the Chorleys [*Thirty Years' Musical Recollections*, by Henry F. Chorley]. They are beautifully printed, and I hope they will do well. Very soon I'll be seeing you both, until then, Good Luck.

Yours
W.S.C.

After the publication of My Mortal Enemy *in late October of 1926, reviewers speculated on the meaning of its title. Fanny Butcher, in her glowing notice in the* Chicago Tribune, *stated that the book deals with "the fundamental hatred of the sexes one for the other and their irresistible attraction one for the other." Harriet Monroe, editor of* Poetry Magazine, *brought the notice to Cather's attention.*

TO HARRIET MONROE

October 27 [1926]
Shattuck Inn, Jaffrey, New Hampshire

Dear Miss Monroe;

Thank you so much for Miss Butcher's review. It's so agreeable to have someone see what the story was <u>about</u>! Not one of the other reviews I've seen but said "Ah yes, we are all our own worst Enemy!" Sad and true—but in this instance not the point!

My eyes are all right again, thanks.

Cordially yours
Willa Cather

TO FANNY BUTCHER

October 27 [1926]
Jaffrey, New Hampshire

Dear Fanny Butcher;

It's worth writing a book to have somebody get the point of it <u>absolutely</u>. I'm willing to bet you're the only one who does—no other review that I've seen comes anywhere near getting it. Of course the thing I was writing about was just that fundamental attraction and antagonism—that the more complete and intense the pleasure of being two is, the more fiercely the individual self in one resents it, sooner or later. Not a question of pale loves at all, this; but of the fierce and brilliant ones—which are rare.

Harriet Munro[e] was kind enough to send me your review. Will you please send me two more copies? I want to send them to dear friends in France.

I've had a glorious autumn up here, and have done some mountain climbing I'm very shirty about—for I have short legs, and a good many pounds to carry up to the summit! I go back to N.Y. tomorrow. Please let me know if you come to town. I do hope you'll like my Archbishop, Fanny. Begins in the Forum in January, but I'm omitting about one-fourth for the serial. It's an altogether new kind for me, but how I loved doing it! It was as if one had always played modern composers, and at last had the time and control to practice Bach awhile. Modest comparison!

Thank you, dear Fanny, for taking the trouble to get the point of a story so devilish hard to tell as my "Mortal Enemy."

Yours
Willa Cather

TO MARY VIRGINIA AULD

Saturday [February 19, 1927]

Dearest M.V.

How nice of you to send me an edible valentine! I'd been rather low in mind for a few days, and a bunch of Valentines, mostly flowers, quite cheered me up. Nothing in particular to make me feel blue, except that I don't see my way to beginning a new story as exciting as the Archbishop right now, and reading proofs is dull work after writing,—it's like trying to have a gorgeous party over again———can't be done. You can have a new adventure, but you can never have the same one over.

[Albert] Donovan was here for dinner last night and we went to see my crush, Rin-tin-tin. [Edward] Steichen, the photographer of the Rich and Great, is coming to dinner tonight. I have a new dinner dress, and a rather gorgeous new afternoon dress,—that's about all the news. When the proofs get further along, I want you to come down some week-end; you see Edith reads them with me, and we can only work at them on week-ends. By the way, how did you come out in the examinations?

With heaps of love
W.S.C.

TO META SCHAPER CATHER

March 19 [probably 1927]

My Dearest Meta:

If you want to get Virginia in at Smith in a few years, you must write an application to the Registrar at once and send the ten dollar registration fee. Mary Virginia spent last weekend with us and we were talking it over. She said a letter of introduction from me would help,—everything there is booked up for years to come.

I have time for a word only. Edith has been in the hospital two weeks, following a rush operation for a very nasty appendix. She was brought home today and will be in bed for two weeks more at least. Then I must try to get her away somewhere. The city is building a new subway down our poor little street and under our very house, so it's like living in a bombarded city———bad place for a recovery! We have the same nice colored maid we had when Roscoe was here, and she has been a tower of strength and kindness in these troublesome times.

I am so glad you all like my Archbishop. I had a lovely time working on him, and I think pretty well of him myself. But this has been a dreary, wasted winter; all broken up by trivial things.

My dearest love to you all
Willa Cather

→ ←

The following letter was published in the Nebraska State Journal *on July 24, 1927.*

TO WILL OWEN JONES

March 22 [1927]

My Dear Mr. Jones;

Certainly I wish to send my congratulations to the Journal on it's sixtieth birthday. I have many pleasant memories connected with it,—with the Journal, I mean, not with its birthday. You see I still write as badly as ever.

The first time I was ever confronted by myself in print was one Sunday morning (please don't append an editorial note here, stating just how many years ago it was) when I opened the Sunday Journal and saw, stretching out through a column or two, an essay on "Some Personal Characteristics of Thomas Carlyle" which Professor [Ebenezer] Hunt had given you to publish, quite without my knowledge. That was the beginning of many troubles for me. Up to that time I had planned to specialize in science; I thought I would like to study medicine. But what youthful vanity can be unaffected by the sight of itself in print! It has a kind of hypnotic effect. I still vaguely remember that essay, and it was a splendid example of the kind of writing I most dislike; very florid and full of high-flown figures of speech,—and, if I recall aright, not a single 'Personal Characteristic' of the gentleman was mentioned! I wrote that title at the top of the page, because it was the assigned subject, and then poured out, as best I could, the feelings that a fervid reading of "The French Revolution" and "Sartor Resartus" had stirred up in me. Come to think of it, that flowery effusion had one merit,—it was honest. Florid as it was, it didn't over color the pleasure and delightful bitterness that Carlyle can arouse in a very young person. It makes one feel so grown up to be bitter!

A few years after this, I began to write regularly for the Sunday Journal, you remember, and I was paid one dollar a column,—which was certainly quite all my high-stepping rhetoric was worth. Those out-pourings were pretty dreadful, but I feel indebted to the Managing Editor of that time [Jones] that he let me step as high as I wished. It was rather hard on his readers, perhaps, but it was good for me, because it enabled me to riot in fine writing until I got to hate it, and began slowly to recover. I remember that sometimes a bright twinkle in Mr. [Charles] Gere's fine eyes used to make me feel a little distrustful of my rhetorical magnificence. He never corrected me, he was much too wise for that; he knew that you can't hurry nature. But I think his kindness, his easy wit, the ease and charm of his personality, helped me all the time. When he was listening, with such lively sympathy and understanding, to one's youthful troubles, he would sometimes sit stroking his dark beard with his hand. No one who ever saw Mr. Gere's hands could ever forget them, surely. Even in those days, when I was sitting in his library, it more than once came over me, that if one could ever write anything that was like Mr. Gere's hands in character, it would be the greatest happiness that could befall one. They were dark and sinewy and so much alive; in a whole world-full of hands I've not seen any others that seemed to me to have such a singular elegance. None in the least like them, indeed. You see, even very stupid young people addicted to cheap rhetoric, are yet capable of perceiving fineness, of feeling it very poignantly. I was very fortunate in my first editor. He let me alone, knowing that I must work out my own salvation; and he was himself all that I was not and that I most admired. Isn't it too bad that after we are much older, and a little wiser, we cannot go back to those few vivid persons of our early youth and tell them how they have always remained with us, how much pleasure their fine personalities gave us, and give us to this very day. But, after all, it's a good fortune to have Mr. Gere alive in one's memory,—not one but a thousand characteristic pictures of him, and I congratulate the <u>Nebraska State Journal</u> and myself that we both had such an editor in our early activities.

You told me in your letter, dear Mr. Jones, that you did not wish me to make yourself the subject of my letter, but I am sure you will have no objection to my recalling Mr. Gere to the many friends who felt his quality as much or more than I.

With pleasant memories of the past and good wishes for the future of the Nebraska State Journal, I am

Most Cordially yours
Willa Cather

TO STEPHEN TENNANT

March 28, 1927
New York City

Dear M. Tennant;

Anne Douglas Sedgwick has been kind enough to send me, through a mutual friend, a note you wrote her about "My Mortal Enemy." It gives me a great deal of pleasure, and I wish to tell you so. In form that story is faulty enough, certainly, but one has to choose the thing one wants most, and try for it at the cost of everything else. Nearly all my books are made out of old experiences that have had time to season. Memory keeps what is essential and lets the rest go. I am always afraid of writing too much—of making stories that are like rooms full of things and people, with not enough air in them. If writing is easy for you, it's very hard not to over-write. I am now reading the proofs of a book which I've had great joy in writing, and in which I've succeeded better than ever before in holding the tone—in making detail do what I wished it to do. I've been turning it over in my mind in my long journeys in the South West for fifteen years, so that when I came to write it, it took only about six months—no work at all, like a sail on a fine summer morning. I didn't have to use <u>any</u> of the old machinery, had things all my own way. I'm becoming extremely confidential, am I not? But I think you'll like "Death Comes for the Archbishop." It will be out next fall, and if you'd be good enough to write me how it strikes you, I'd be so pleased! Send me a line in care of my publishers, for I shall probably be somewhere in Old Mexico by then.

I see I've written a long letter, mostly in praise of my own new book,—how like an author!

Most cordially yours
Willa Cather

TO VIRGINIA CATHER

Palm Sunday [April 10, 1927]
Haddon Hall, Atlantic City, New Jersey

Dearest Virginia;

There are many opinions about what was in the cave—but <u>I</u> think it was a rattlesnake den. Jacinto [character in *Death Comes for the Archbishop*] thought there might be some around loose under the faggots. He was afraid the heat would warm the dry fellows up and bring them out. An Indian <u>always</u> knows the rattlesnake smell, but this Bishop hadn't enough experience.

We enjoyed M.V.'s [Mary Virginia Auld] visit (Easter vacation), though we saw little of her. But we enjoyed that little, and I think she did. I took her to one very grand party. Miss Lewis is down here getting well by the sea. She joins me in love to you.

Willa Cather

TO MARY VIRGINIA AULD

Wednesday [June 8, 1927]

Dearest M.V.

Aren't we a funny family! I have got my ticket for Casper, Wyo., starting this Sunday! The subway has become very intense, and goes on every night until midnight. We have put some things into storage, and I will come back in August to help Edith empty the apartment and go into storage. The noise and confusion here is beyond words—that is why I flee. I wrote Aunt Elsie at Lincoln the day before I got your letter.

In Washington I advise you to stay at the New Willard, and to eat in the coffee shop in the basement of the hotel. The food is <u>excellent</u> and not expensive.

I did <u>not</u> go to Winchester—told the club women I would be in Wyoming May 31st, to avoid being a guest at a banquet.

I'll probably drop down in Red Cloud about four weeks from now, and Douglass will be there before that, he writes me. Tell Aunt Elsie that we will all meet up eventually to Charleston on the new carpet!

With my dearest love to you both
Willa

How wonderful for Tom [Auld, Mary Virginia's brother]!

I do not know if Howard Gore has gone away for the summer yet. His address is 2210 R. St. If he is there [rest of line cut off]

➤ ❮

Cather and Lewis's apartment at 5 Bank Street in New York had to be vacated, since the building was scheduled to be torn down to make way for new subway construction.

TO DOROTHY CANFIELD FISHER

August 17 [1927]

Dear Dorothy;

After much wandering your letter did reach me up in the Big Horn mountains. I took it back to Red Cloud to answer it, but there, just when we were all so happy, Father had a terrible attack of angina, the first serious illness of his life. For the present he is better, and I hurried back to New York to give up this apartment, where I have been for fifteen years, and to put all my books and goods into storage. I am in the midst of that doleful process now, having got back only the day before yesterday. I had taken passage for France on the 30th, but I can't go when Father has an illness which can only terminate in one way. Probably I shall trail West again as soon as this packing ordeal is over. You can always reach me through the Knopf office, however. I honestly don't know where I am going to be. My unmarried brother, Douglass, will take Father and Mother to California for the winter if Father is well enough to go.

I can't properly answer your letter, dear Dorothy, because I've almost forgotten I ever wrote the Archbishop,—so much has happened since then. I suppose some of the pleasure I had in following those two noble churchmen will go on to others,—though I can't see many people in a moving-picture-world caring much about a book with no woman in it but the Virgin Mary. I wanted to save something of those remote places before they are gone for ever. Tomorrow, the movie cameras will be at Acoma. Forgive me that I have no spirit to thank you. Deep in my heart I am happy that I was able to make you see a little of what has bewitched me down there for so long.

With my love, dear Dorothy
Willa

Death Comes for the Archbishop *was published in September of 1927.*

TO FANNY BUTCHER

Thursday [probably early September 1927]
Hotel Webster, New York City

Dear Fanny Butcher;

Five Bank street is now a thing of the past. Everything that used to be there is in storage—including myself! You see all last winter the new sub-way was building right under the house, and it will go on for two years more. The noise is maddening, the neighborhood become a sham. I hate being in storage, but I want to be free of responsibility for awhile.

I know how busy you are—but will you send me a line telling me if you got any pleasure out of the "Archbishop"? And please send me your review. (Send notes in care of Knopf, as I have no address of my own at present.) The morning <u>World</u> tells me that judged as a novel, it's a very poor performance. Just what is a novel, I wonder? I've always wanted to try something in the style of legend, with a sort of New Testament calm, and I think I succeeded fairly well. A story with no woman in it but the Virgin Mary has very definite limitations; it's a very special kind of thing, and you like it, or you don't. I had a glorious year doing it, and working in that new form with no solid drama. I found in it a lovely kind of poverty—and richness; a deep content.

You and Grant Overton were the only two reviewers in America who liked "Antonia" when it first came out. The "Archbishop" is even farther from the conventional novel. It's a narrative, like Robinson Crusoe, and it's a kind of writing that is colored by a kind of country, like a folk-song.

Let me hear from you, if you have a spare moment. I was to have sailed on the "Barengaria" yesterday, but had to give up my passage. Was detained in Nebraska by the serious illness of my father. He suddenly came down with angina—the first serious illness he has ever had. I shall probably go to the White Mountains for a few weeks, then either to France or Arizona.

With my love, always
Willa Cather

TO FANNY BUTCHER

September 17 [1927]
Shattuck Inn, Jaffrey, New Hampshire

Dear Fanny Butcher;

I said legend, didn't I, not folk-lore? There's such a difference. Folk-lore is unarticulated—detached. But legend is a sort of interpretation of life by Faith. It was that background of order and discipline that gave the lives of those missionaries proportion and measure and accent, like a work of art.

Yes, of course you may use anything I said, provided that it doesn't sound as if I were defending the book.

I'm so sorry you['re] tired and used up—I'm a wreck myself, trying to get rested enough to start for Arizona. Of course I'll let you know when I go through Chicago. Rush your Archbishop for autograph along to me here—you can have it bound afterward. I'm not likely to have an address for some months. Awful way to live!

You did nobly by me in your review—but sometimes in the country, you must run over that book just the way you read "Swiss Family Robinson" when you were little, not as writing at all, but sort of living along with the priests and their mules in a world where miracles really come into the day's work, or into one's experience of it, which is the same thing.

> With my love
> Willa Cather

> ❖ ❖

Death Comes for the Archbishop was widely reviewed. Cather refers to the following reviews in the next couple of letters: Rebecca West, "Miss Cather's Business as an Artist," New York Herald Tribune Books, *September 11, 1927; Frances Newman, "A Reservationist's Impressions of Willa Cather's New Mexican Catholic Missionaries of 1850,"* New York Evening Post, Literary Review, *September 3, 1927; and Michael Williams, "Willa Cather's Masterpiece,"* Commonweal, *September 28, 1927.*

TO LOUISE GUERBER BURROUGHS

> [September 21, 1927]

Dear Louise

I'm really desperate. I have nothing on earth to read. Won't you please see if you can get me Jane Austen's "Sense & Sensibility" in a fairly good type— not the European edition, that's to[o] small type—and rush it to me "special handling"? Then I'll get it about Monday, maybe. Knopf keeps wanting to send me new books—but there is not <u>one</u> in his fall list that I want.

I'm walking a good deal, and it's glorious weather. Yes, I've just glanced at Miss [Rebecca] West's review again. I think the question she brings up really interesting, and she says a lot about it that's interesting to me. [D. H.] Lawrence <u>is</u> the Puritan reformer, for all he's habitually indecent, and I am the Pagan, for all I'm stupidly decent!

> Hastily
> W.S.C.

TO LOUISE GUERBER BURROUGHS

Monday [September 26, 1927]
Jaffrey, New Hampshire

Dear Louise, you must have got Jane Austen here by air mail! No, I've not bobbed, but Miss Lewis has, with <u>great</u> success—very becoming. The weather is wonderful—one sun-soaked day after another. I'm not working, though, so I'm a little restless. I enclose Miss [Frances] Newman's review—but you must send it back to me—I wouldn't lose it. There is a review in the highbrow Catholic weekly, "The Commonweal" Sept. 28, which gives me great satisfaction. I feared nothing so much as seeming a sort of stage Catholic. I'm living in the woods every day, but I'm always a little bored when I'm not working. That's a grave deficit of character, and I'm sorry to admit it.

With my love
W.S.C.

TO IDA TARBELL

Friday [probably October 1927]
Shattuck Inn, Jaffrey, New Hampshire

Dear Miss Tarbell;

How happy your letter made me! The writing of that book was the most unalloyed pleasure of my life—and it keeps on bringing pleasures,—letters from priests in remote deserts and mountains that melt my heart. The rector of the Cathedral in Denver writes me that he <u>still</u> uses father Joseph's chalice and the vestments made by Philomène and her nuns! He knows every inch of the ground and he really loves the book. He is an old man, and he wrote me a letter like a school boy's.

These letters do help me to bear the trials of this hour. Of course I miss my "Archbishop" awfully, working on him was almost like working <u>with</u> him, it was so happy and serene a mood. Then I'm homeless for the present—all my goods in storage. I had to leave Bank street because a sub-way station is being built almost under the very house in which I lived. I now expect to spend the winter in Arizona and with my parents, and go abroad in the early spring.

If I am in New York at all, I do so want to see you. Nothing makes me quite so happy as pleasing my old friends, and I do like to feel that you are one of those.

Affectionately always
Willa Cather

TO MARY AUSTIN

November 9 [1927]
New York City

My Dear Mrs. Austin:

I did not mean to put the burden of a letter upon you, but I can't help being glad that you wrote me. I am staying at the Grosvenor, 35 Fifth Avenue for a few weeks, as just now I am utterly homeless! I had to give up the apartment on Bank street, which I loved and where I had been for fifteen years, because the new subway was (and is!) building a station almost under the very house I lived in. Last winter was wrecked by the noise, for both Miss Lewis and me, and the construction will go on for years. Nothing for it but to get out,—and all our goods are now in storage. We have not taken a new place because we want to go abroad for a few months early in the spring, while we are <u>not</u> paying rent. I am going out to Nebraska to spend Thanksgiving with my father and mother, but I shall be here when you come on in January. I hate these wasted, broken-up interludes in life. I never manage to have much fun in them. You're awfully mistaken if you think life doesn't get all messed up for me, too! There are just occasional intervals when I can make things run smoothly and snatch a piece of work out of the temporary calm.

I shall look forward eagerly to your article in The World Tomorrow. This book is just one too many for the poor reviewers. They complain about it, and say "it is almost impossible to classify this book", as if I had put over something unfair on them. They feel so bitterly because Knopf calls it a novel; I, myself, wanted merely to call it a narrative. I'm not sure that I know just what a novel is, and I'm not sure that the reviewers do. However, none of these things really matter. Enthusiastic reviewers may help a book along at the start; but after the first year or so, a book, like an individual, has nothing but its own vitality to carry it.

Dear Mrs. Austin, I do believe that a few months in New York will benefit you more than all the doctors in the world. You are the sort of person who needs solitude, but for that very reason you need to be lost among people and crowds for a part of every year. If only because you'll be so glad to find yourself again!

If ardent good wishes could help you over this trying time, mine would do so. But I've a feeling that hideous, resounding New York will help you.

Devotedly always
Willa Cather

TO BLANCHE KNOPF

December 31 [1927]
Red Cloud, Nebraska

My Dear Blanche;

What an amazing and magnificent Christmas Box you sent me. The children of the family were all so excited about the box and so thrilled by its contents—so many kinds of food they had never seen before. They all vociferously join me in thanks to you. It has been a fine country Christmas; zero weather, snow, the house full of nieces and nephews, my brothers from Wyoming and California dashing in for a few days. Mother and father are both very well, and all the townspeople have been unusually jolly. I really am a farmer, and this kind of life suits me better than any other. I've got loose from Bank street, and I think the next step will be to get away from New York altogether.

I shall be here for two or three weeks yet, and then start for Arizona. I'll telegraph you when I leave Red Cloud, so until you hear from me please have my letters sent on here[.]

The river is frozen over, and I'm going skating with a lot of youngsters this afternoon—they still do such things here. Altogether, it's like stepping back about twenty years. It's refreshing to find that one can still get so much excitement out of weather and wind and ice and snow.

A Happy New Year to you, dear Blanche, and to Alfred and his father, and my deepest thanks for all the many nice personal things you have done for me in this year of confusion and up-rooting.

Yours
W. S. C.

PART EIGHT

Years of Loss

1928–1931

But these vanishings, that come one after another, have such an impoverishing effect upon those of us who are left—our world suddenly becomes
so diminished—the landmarks disappear and all the splendid distances
behind us close up. These losses, one after another, make one feel as if one
were going on in a play after most of the principal characters are dead.
—WILLA CATHER TO DOROTHY CANFIELD FISHER, September 30, 1930

Mary Virginia and Charles F. Cather

AFTER THE PLEASURE OF spending the holidays at home in Red Cloud while being celebrated for the triumph of *Death Comes for the Archbishop*, 1928 started poorly for Cather. Her father, with whom she always had a tender relationship, died rather suddenly from heart problems. Her mother took temporary refuge in California with Cather's second younger brother, Douglass, but while there suffered a debilitating stroke and had to be moved to a care facility. Nearing fifty-five, Cather was becoming part of the older generation. Her home at 5 Bank Street in New York had also been lost; she and Edith Lewis had moved into a hotel, the Grosvenor, intending only a brief stay there until more suitable arrangements could be found. But for the next five years Cather would have no permanent address aside from the Grosvenor, and most of her things stayed packed away in storage. She traveled constantly—to Nebraska, to California, to Canada, to France—to attend to family and professional matters. During this time of loss, however, she did have some solace. The cottage she shared with Lewis on Grand Manan Island was a refuge. More important, she continued to write. In 1928, while on their way to Grand Manan, she and Lewis stopped in Quebec City, and when Lewis fell ill Cather had unexpected time to wander around the old French settlement. What she saw stirred her, and she set to work on a new novel. *Shadows on the Rock*, concerned with the day-to-day life of a handful of citizens in 1697 Quebec, was published by Knopf in 1931 and became one of the top-selling books of the year.

TO ALFRED A. KNOPF

February 10 [1928]
Red Cloud

Dear Alfred;

I have not written you, as I expected to be in New York at this date. My father has been very ill for the last two weeks, his second attack of angina, and that has kept me here. The things I want to discuss with you are hard to take up by letter.

The demand for the Archbishop seems a mixed blessing, as even now there seems to be no very adequate method of satisfying it. As I telegraphed you last night, the dealers here and in all the little towns about have been trying [to] get books from McClurg, Chicago, to fill the orders of a few patient friends who were not able to get the book for Christmas. Finally McClurg wrote the dealers here that they have ordered the books to be sent direct from the publisher to Grice & Grimes, Red Cloud. So far, they have not come. If all these little town dealers in Nebraska, Kansas, Colorado, Iowa, who always order from McClurg, can't get books, isn't there something wrong with the method of distribution? They tell me all their orders for "Antonia" are filled quickly and without trouble.

I have been here nearly three months, and in all that time the book has not had a fair chance in this little town, or in this part of the state. I don't know about Omaha, but it has been impossible to get the book in Lincoln part of the time. I've had so many complaints from Catholics all over the country that I'm afraid there has been the same difficulty in getting books, East and West.

When you decided not to give the "Archbishop" any individual advertising, then I understood that it was up to the book to sell itself if it could. But how can it sell itself if it is not printed, and if the jobbers don't carry it? It was out of print for a week or ten days at the most critical part of the selling season. Only ten days, but they were the ten days before Christmas. However, that's over. The point I raise is, why is it still so hard to get books?

I shall start east in a week or ten days, as soon as I feel that it's quite safe to leave my father. I'm your personal friend and admirer, now and always, but I don't think you've given the Archbishop a flattering share of your interest and attention. With any personal enthusiasm behind it, I feel sure the book would have done much better. But we can talk of these things much better than we can write of them. I write a devilish hand at best and I've been under a considerable strain since father fell ill.

Faithfully
Willa Cather

The Knopf offices, upon getting this letter, responded quickly with a promise to investigate. Internally, they suspected that Cather was exaggerating the problem.

➢ ⟜

In February, Cather returned to New York, since her father seemed to be recovering. On March 3, however, Charles F. Cather had a heart attack and died. She immediately took a train back to Nebraska, arriving very early in the morning the day after his death.

TO DOROTHY CANFIELD FISHER

April 3 [1928]
Red Cloud

My Dearest Dorothy:

My father died on March 3d, just seven days after I had left home for New York. He was ill only a few hours—angina. He was happy and gay to the very end. I'd like to show you his picture sometime, he kept such an extraordinarily youthful color and young eyes and figure. He was very handsome, in a boyish Southern way. I have lost people I loved terribly, young people, but this is the first death there has ever been in our family—never a child or grandchild. I did not know death could be so beautiful. I got home to him a little after five, just as the dawn was breaking over him. He lay on a little stretcher in the big bay window of his own room, in one of his long silk shirts, and all the rest of the tired family were asleep. He looked so happy, so contented, so at home—his smooth fair face shaved—everything as it always was. He was such a sweet southern boy and he never hurt anybody's feelings, not even in death.

Think of it, my dear, this winter of all winters, I had here with them, simply because I felt we could never be so happy again. I stayed because they were both so well, not because they were ailing. Having had those three months as by a miracle, I'll stand a good deal of punishment at the hands of fate.

Dear, I never knew any Preston in Pittsburgh. I knew a Preston Cooke Farrar but no Preston.

Mother went to California with my bachelor brother two weeks ago. I've been staying on alone to have a lot of papering and repairing done. Such a nice wise, kind Bohemian paper-hanger to do everything. And just silence in the old house and in father's room has done so much for me. I feel so rested and strong it is as if father himself had restored my soul.

I suppose after Easter I must go back to the world—but not for long.

Lovingly
Willa

→ ←

Though Cather and her parents had been lifelong Baptists, they were confirmed as Episcopalian in 1922. Charles Cather's memorial service was held in Red Cloud's Grace Episcopal Church.

TO MARY VIRGINIA BOAK CATHER

Monday after Easter [April 9, 1928]
Red Cloud

My Dearest Mother;

After two weeks of spring we had a bitter cold Easter. Elsie and I decorated the altar in memory of father. The church was nearly full of people. After the service I gave one of the Easter Lily plants to Molly [Ferris], and one to Hazel Powell, and the daffodils I took down to father's grave—you know he loved the "Easter flowers" as we used to call them, and they are the very first flowers I can remember in Virginia.

I had dinner with Will [Auld] and Charles [Auld] at the hotel. Later I made a call on Mrs. [Alta] Turmore and Clifford—she had asked me to dinner, but I could not go. Then I went over to Molly's and had a delicious little supper with her. It was lucky Elsie did not try to come down, as the weather turned so bitter.

Isn't it funny for me to be getting a card from the Peggs? When that bashful blond boy in the butcher shop lost his wife and baby I went down to Carolina and ordered a lot of those beautiful snapdragons such as were sent to father. Everyone felt so sorry. She had a tumor inside her which grew along with the baby and strangled it. A proper examination and operation would have saved her. She had been carrying a dead baby for several days. Dr. [James W.] Stockman only called [Dr. E. A.] Creighton when she was dying. Poor Albert walks about like a dead man.

Lizzie [Huffmann] has been at the Macs [McNenys'] for a week now, but she still dashes in in the morning to make the kitchen fire for me, and I dine over there occasionally. Helen [McNeny] is home sick with grippe.

I've got such lovely silk curtains up in the big dining room. My little old bed is painted primrose color like the washstand,—I mean the wooden bed that was in the west room. And the table in [the] downstairs back hall, which proved to be not walnut at all, I had mended and painted and it's very pretty.

Molly had dinner with me here on Good Friday and Saturday nights, and says I'm a good cook. She helped me wash the dishes.

I had all father's oak furniture gone over with furniture polish for you and it looks <u>so much</u> better. If ever you want it painted I'll have it done.

Please write to me, dear mother.

With much love,
Willie

TO ROSCOE CATHER

April 11 [1928]

Dear Roscoe;

Yes, indeed, I've been staying on in the old house and finding it such a comfort. I've had all the downstairs re-papered, except the parlor—thought mother might like one room just the same. They had to scrape off <u>four</u> layers of paper so it was a mess for days. Then I had father's room papered in a lovely gray English chintz paper for mother. I've had the yard cleaned and new shrubs set out, and lovely drapery curtains put up in the front dining room. The back dining room really looks lovely. Ondrals, the nice old Bohemian painter will do the bath room over after I go. We had to do a good deal of plastering, as most of the sitting room ceiling fell down. These messy repairs could never have been made with mother here—it would have fretted her to death. I'm awfully pleased with the results, and I've seldom spent money that I've enjoyed so much.

Your draft I've registered in the one account book I carry about with me—a complete list of checks received,—and I'll credit it on your note when I reach

New York. I'll stay on here a few days, then go to the Mayo's for awhile, and on to New York. Edith's poor mother is still dying—it is surely a long, hard way.

My love to you, dear brother and to all the ladies of your house. They are <u>all</u> grown up now!

Yours,
Willie

TO MARY VIRGINIA BOAK CATHER

Sunday [April 1928?]
The Kahler Hotel, Rochester, Minnesota

My Dearest Mother;

I got here this morning, and will register at the clinic in the morning. This hotel has been made over and is now better than the Zumbro.

I spent about four hours with Elsie in Lincoln, and we had a long talk about you and your future. We are agreed that whenever you want to go home one of us will be there with you and we will do <u>everything</u> we can to make you happy there. We will put our whole heart into it. Elsie can get a year's leave of absence next winter, she says. If she can't, I will be there, I promise you.

I bought a sprinkler for the lawn at last, and before I left Mac [Bernard McNeny] and I were rivals in getting the grass green. The new shrubs Will and Amos set out are coming on well. I am paying Amos five dollars a month regularly to water and cut the lawn, and May 1st he and Floyd Turner [?] will set out big red zenias in the bare patch where father used to have various little flowers. I chose zenias because they are so hardy and will make their way alone.

There will be nothing desolate <u>inside</u> or <u>outside</u> the house if you want to come back to it, and everyone wants you to come. Elsie's school is out the first day of June, so if you want to come back with Will Auld the first of June, Elsie can meet you there. The last word Lizzie said to me was, "Oh just let me know a few days before your mother comes, and I'll make the house look like a palace for her." You have your own house—the Bishop [George Allen Beecher] and Mrs. [Florence George] Beecher think it a very attractive one, and I'll make it more and more so. And you have your <u>own friends</u>, and they miss you terribly and you will enjoy them more than you ever did before. Indeed, I love them so much for their loyalty to you that I feel I can never keep away from Red Cloud long again. <u>That's true!</u>

So don't be blue, Mother. You seem to me almost the most fortunate old person I know. You have Doug to travel with, and several of us to hang about you when you want to be at home. Of course if Elsie is with you next winter you will keep Lizzie, and I think we ought to pay Elsie, too.

Now cheer up; you are getting older, and that's hard luck—but your children and all our old, faithful friends, and the young friends, too, are determined to make you happy.

With a heart very full of love for you
Willie

➜ ❦

Characteristically, she fended off attempted inroads on her time, including a suggestion by Ferris Greenslet in late April that she write a biography of the poet Amy Lowell.

TO MARY AUSTIN

May 9, 1928
Grosvenor Hotel, New York City

My dear Mrs. Austin:

I wish the suggestion made by Mr. Greenslet and Dr. [Henry Goddard] Leach had come a year ago, when I had a good deal more time and energy than I have now. Just because I never write biographical or critical studies, editors bother me to death trying to make me do them. They simply want them because I resist their persuasions. Greenslet has just been trying to crowd on me a biography of Amy Lowell—I would be as likely to undertake a history of the Chinese Empire! I wouldn't do it for the whole amount of the Lowell Estate,—simply because that sort of writing is an agony to me. I need very little money, and my life and liberty are very precious to me.

One of the pleasures of having an absolute rule is that once or twice in a lifetime one may break it, and if things were at all well with me, I would be tempted to break it on your account! [B]ut this has been a very bad winter for me, and I'm not going to do any writing at all for at least six months. My father died in March, and I have just come back to New York after several weeks at the Mayo Clinic. This is the first time in my life that I have ever felt absolutely tired, through and through, and I am simply going to rest for a while. I don't know where yet, but I may go on to my mother, who is in California with my brother. For this year, my family concerns, father's death and mother's consequent breakdown have simply wiped out everything else. I know you will understand that I speak to you with a frank and open heart. Sometimes the difficulties of life are just too much for one, and then it is best to keep away from the desk.

Faithfully yours,
Willa Cather

→ ←

In early June, after weeks battling influenza, Cather received an honorary degree at Columbia University.

TO MARY VIRGINIA BOAK CATHER

June 7 [1928]
New York City

My Darling Mother;

No, no, no, I'm not cross! But I'm still very wobbly from that influenza, and people have been unusually merciless in pursuit of me. I am not accepting any invitations, but even writing notes of polite refusal becomes a heavy task.

The Commencement at Columbia was really quite thrilling and splendid; I wish some of you could have seen it. I was the only woman among the seven recipients of honorary degrees, the rest were all old men, as you will see by their pictures. I sat between the French Ambassador [Paul Claudel] and the President of the University of California [William Wallace Campbell]. We were all in caps and gowns, of course. I really got a great deal more applause than any one else; Edith was there and she says the roar for me lasted twice as long. I rose when my name was called, walked up to the President [Nicholas Murray Butler] and stood there until the applause was over; then he made a speech at me and gave me a diploma, two Deans of the University put a gorgeous collar about my neck and fastened it on my shoulders, and conducted me back to my seat on the platform. The other six were applauded only after the degree was bestowed, but I was applauded like a ball game, both before and after.

The great old Cuban patriot, [Antonio Sánchez] du Bustamante [y Sirvén], seemed to be second in popularity, and he is a wonder. I was never so patted and embraced by so many old men at once.

After the exercise I went straight to the President's supper party, not a dinner, as no one had time to put on evening clothes. I had to meet and talk to all the Trustees and their wives, and the Professors and their wives, and a lot of Cubans and Spaniards and attachées of the French embassy and <u>their</u> wives. They are many of them wonderful people, and it's all very delightful, and exciting,———and exhausting. I was a tired creature when I came home in President Butler's car. If I'd realized it would be such [a] spectacular affair, I'd have sent for Mary Virginia to come down.

I am sending the silk-and-velvet collar of Columbia and the one I got at Michigan, home to Carrie Sherwood to keep for me. They are very large, I've no room for them now, and she has made a special place in her spare room to keep such things for me. You can see them, if you wish, when you go home.

I hope and pray you will like your beads, and <u>do not</u> say they are too young, for they are not. Everybody trusts my taste but my family!

In a few days I will send you some envelopes addressed to Grand Manan, where I think we shall go from here. All mail sent to this hotel will be forwarded, however.

With a heart-ful of love to you.
Willie

TO COLONEL BUTLER

June 14, 1928
New York City

My dear Colonel Butler:

I have to admit that I am a woman, and I must also admit that I can make no reasonable explanation of my name. I was born in Virginia, however, and in those southern states it used to be, and still is, very common for a girl to be given the first name of one of her male relatives; sometimes the parents tried feebly to give the name a feminine ending, as in my own case. If I had to be William, I would have preferred to be William without modification. This is a rather long explanation, but you seemed really curious on this point.

Thank you for your appreciative words about the book. It follows very closely the real story of the first Archbishop of Santa Fé and his vicar, and the scene, of course, is laid in a country that I know very well.

Very cordially yours,
Willa Cather

TO HENRY GOODMAN

October 13, 1928
Grosvenor Hotel, New York City

Dear Prof. Goodman:

One of my friends who did hear your radio talk tells me that she liked it very much, but that she was a good deal distressed at hearing my name mispronounced throughout. My name should be pronounced so as to exactly rhyme with "gather" and "rather". I think the name "Kayther" about the ugliest on earth, and I do consider it a hardship that people so often attach it to me. My friend Mr. Mather's name is always pronounced correctly. Nobody ever thinks of calling him Mayther.

I hope you will pardon my calling your attention to this, but next to being called dishonest, I think I would rather be called anything than Kayther!

Very cordially yours,
Willa Cather

⇥ ⇤

It was in June, on their way to Grand Manan, that Cather and Lewis first visited Quebec City. Lewis writes in her memoir that when Cather saw the city, she was struck by "the sense of its extraordinarily French character, isolated and kept intact through hundreds of years, as if by a miracle, on this great un-French continent." In November, Cather went back to Quebec, this time alone. She was at work on Shadows on the Rock. *During this same period she also wrote "Double Birthday," a short story set in Pittsburgh. Fritz Westermann, mentioned below, was a friend from Cather's university days and a nephew of Julius Tyndale.*

TO ELSIE CATHER

Tuesday [November or December 1928]

Dear Elsie:

Just back from Quebec. I long-distanced M.V. [Mary Virginia] last night to find when her father would be here, and invited the Auld family to dine with me Sunday night.

I enclose letter from Fritz Westermann. You see I took no chances this time! The story "Double-Birthday" has a sketch of Dr. Tyndale in it, so I simply <u>sent</u> it to Fritz and asked him whether I should publish it or not—told him I wouldn't think of doing it if it would annoy him or the Doctor.

It will be out in the February Forum [then written out more clearly:] (Forum). Dr. Leach says it is the best short story he ever published, but it's really not much. I can't work without a house to work in, and I can't work where I hate my surroundings. I've always felt in my bones that Long Beach [California] would be just as you say it is. One has only to reason it out from the people who go there!

With love to you
W.

I think Fritz is real nice and un-grudging, don't you?

Dr. Tyndale wrote Cather a note saying he was flattered to find any of his characteristics in one of her stories.

TO STRINGFELLOW BARR

December 5, 1928
Grosvenor Hotel, New York City

My dear Mr. Barr:

I get, of course, a great many invitations to lecture, but very few of them are as tempting as the one you wrote some weeks ago when I was in Quebec. All my letters were held for me here, as I went away to escape from interruptions. My answer, therefore, is very tardy, and I apologize.

I always feel very deeply that I am a Virginian. My mother and father, though they went West long ago, were always Winchester people—not Nebraskans. Nothing would give me more pleasure than to talk for an hour or so to your students, and I hope that at some future time you will renew this invitation when I can accept it. This winter I can not make any engagements of that nature. The last year has been very much broken up, and I have got behind in my work and my life. My father died last spring, and since then my mother's health has been uncertain. She is now in California with my brother, but I may have to go to her at any time. I always find lecturing tiring, and indulge in it but seldom. At some more fortunate time, however, I assure you I would like to go to Charlottesville and spend an hour with your young men [at the University of Virginia].

Very cordially yours,
Willa Cather

✦ ✦

Early in 1929, Cather broke away from her work on Shadows on the Rock *to go to her mother in California.*

TO GEORGE AND HARRIET FOX WHICHER

New Year's Day [January 1, 1929]
New York City

Dear Friends:

I meant to go up to the Lord Jeffrey to work for a few weeks soon after the Holidays. But now my mother has had a stroke in California, where she is staying with my bachelor brother [Douglass]. I shall have to go out there now in a few weeks and give up working altogether for the present. I'd made a pleasant start and hate to leave it. If only mother were in San Francisco! But Long Beach, near Los Angeles, is the most hideous and vulgar place in the whole world. Well, this last year was a bad one, and this doesn't promise much better. But only a part of last year was bad—all the winter in Red Cloud, where your fruit cake found me, was lovely, lovely,—like a winter flower garden, opening more and more———It was the sort of thing one has to pay for, and pay dear. I suppose I mustn't squirm now.

Virginia and Tom [Auld] gave me good word of you all at Thanksgiving time, and I send you all the good wishes in the world for 1929. I got a shopful of handkerchiefs last week, and have given them all away but yours and two others—the only one's I liked. I'm fussy about handkerchiefs.

With love to you all.
Willa Cather

TO DOROTHY CANFIELD FISHER

[Probably April or May 1929]
Long Beach, California

My Dear Dorothy:

About Christmas time mother had a stroke here where she was spending the winter with my bachelor brother. At that time I was ill with bronchitis in the Grosvenor hotel, New York and could not come. I got away in February and have been here ever since, first hunting a little home with a porch and yard to move mother to, then moving her, then spending days and days shopping for hardware, linen, furniture, dishes, mattresses—everything a home requires. Mother is completely paralyzed on the right side, and speechless. Yet behind the wrenched machinery her mind and strong will, her whole personality is just the same. She can moan[?] some times—oh so seldom!—we can understand. My sister Elsie has been here from the first. We have excellent nurses, thank God, but a tall, strong woman paralyzed is the most helpless thing in the world. She has to be fed with a spoon like a baby. Constant changes of position give her the only ease she can have. My brother carries her from bed to bed to rest her, and takes her out on the porch in a wheel chair for a couple of hours. Your letter came while I was rubbing her yesterday. I read part of it to her and she remembered you perfectly, and the time she met you at the door. She made me understand that she had seen you much oftener than that once.

This is the most horrible, unreal place in the world, on a dreary curve of the coast, I have rheumatism dreadfully here, and never felt so down-and-out anywhere. My mail is a horror—all the greedy, grasping, intrusive people who want things from writers have never been so merciless. I live at a hotel and taxi-cab out to see mother in the afternoon at the above address. The mornings I spend shopping—the thing that was always the hardest of all things for me to do. Elsie stays at the house to regulate the nurses and the servant.

Oh if only this dreadful thing had happened at home, in a human land, where mother would have had her lovely grandchildren to watch and work[?], where there were dear old friends, kind neighbors, memories, God. There is no God in California, no real life. Hollywood is the flower of all the flowers, the complete expression of it.

I stayed at home two months last spring, after mother came to California, having the old home made more comfortable for her—worked awfully hard, took as much out of me as a book—now she will never see it. Well, there is nothing to write, nothing to say or do, my dear, except to stand until one breaks, and the quicker that happens the better, if only one can break clear in two, and not just half-way. This is why I've not written, because I've lost my bearings and can't write except as bitterly and desperately as I feel. Father's death was swift and gay—he was laughing two hours before he died. Goodbye, God bless you, and don't remember this letter after you read it. There are enough people crushed under this poor sick woman who defied time so long. Goodbye, dear—nothing to say.

Willa

➔ ❮

By late May, the family had moved Virginia Cather to Las Encinas Sanitarium in Pasadena, California.

TO ROSCOE CATHER

[June 1929]
aboard Santa Fe train

Dear Brother;

I am on my way East—will be at the Grosvenor Hotel 35 Fifth Ave. for the next ten days, then go to New Haven, at Hotel Taft. On June 19 I receive a doctorate degree from Yale—the second they have ever given a woman writer. The first was given to Mrs. Wharton eight years ago. She came over from Paris and stayed in New York one week to take it.

I hope you can skip out to see mother for a week this summer, and soon. Better come alone—its bad for her to have several about, she tries even in her feeble state to arrange, direct. I went North when Will Auld was here. Better come now than to her funeral—she will know you now and her mind is still unclouded, though often tired. She is losing ground a little all the time: now up, now down, but on the whole a good deal weaker and lower than when I first came three months ago. She tries, poor dear, but the odds are so terribly against her that I hope it won't be very long, for her sake. Will Auld felt the same way. She is still herself, and can understand what you say to her. The trip would not be a very long one for you if you came by train. I had a round-trip ticket over this road, or I would have gone back by way of Rawlins. The Sanitarium is a <u>really</u> beautiful place—you could have quiet hours there alone with mother, the nurse in the other room within call. She may live like this a long while—several years, but is almost sure to deteriorate mentally and be less herself. It's a cruel and pitiful thing, but you'll be glad to have seen her, as I am. I'm wondering whether I will ever feel much enthusiasm for things again, though. I guess I will—for young people,—and young Art.

I had <u>lovely</u> visits with Jim Yeiser and Marguerite [Richardson] in San Francisco.

Willa

➤ ❬

In the fall of 1929, Knopf was preparing to release a special edition of Death Comes for the Archbishop *with illustrations by Harold Von Schmidt. Though Cather at first balked at the idea of an illustrated version, she was so pleased with the results that she later asked Knopf if they could print the illustrated version exclusively.*

On the outside of the following letter was written:

Dear Miss [Manley] Aaron:
Please get all this to Mr. Stimson, as I have telegraphed him about it.

W.S.C.

TO GEORGE L. STIMSON, ALFRED A. KNOPF, INC.

October 17, 1929

Dear Mr. Stimson;

You are a violinist, put the mute on the biography—no the extinguisher! Anything more deadly dull than this jacket text, I can't imagine. It's all too foolish, and I really don't think it's up to the office to hand out these dull facts. They tell absolutely nothing about the book, <u>or about me</u>, nothing that the public wants to know.

Now, I want you to let me decide on this jacket text. Tell the public something they <u>do</u> want [to] know, something they write me letters about until my hand is fairly crippled with answering them; <u>tell them something about how and why the book was written!</u> That is what they want to know. Instead of this wooden stuff about my grandfathers and Von Schmidt's (who in thunder cares about our grandfathers?) use this condensation I enclose of my letter to the Commonweal about the book. The English publisher had that letter printed in pamphlet form and gave it wide circulation—wrote me it was singularly effective as advertising. I have cut the article to just about the number of words in the two dreary sketches of Von Schmidt and me now on the jacket.

Please telegraph me that you will use the copy I'm sending you, and <u>not</u> that which is now in the proof of the jacket; and please write me the name of the person who wrote the copy, as I want to talk with her—or him—when I get back to town.

Now as to the copy I send you—very ragged, but I'm lucky to have even that with me.

1. Use quotes before every paragraph
2. When the long cuts occur, please end the paragraphs with asterisks.
3. Please read the proofs yourself and telephone me if you're in doubt about anything.

Hastily, to catch the mail,

Yours
Willa Cather

Please note the change in the newspaper comment quoted. I beg you to use this one from the New Republic instead of that from the Baltimore Sun.

TO BLANCHE KNOPF

October 17 [1929]
Jaffrey, New Hampshire

My Dear Blanche;

Unless there is some very important reason why you must see me before you sail, I would like to stay up here about three weeks longer. This poor book has been jumped about so much—all it needs is sitting still. It's going along smoothly now, and I don't want to interrupt it just at this point. The working conditions are good, the country lovely, I am out of doors a great deal and feel awfully well—sprint up the mountain with a crowd of boys and don't get used up. When I go back to New York I shall probably have bronchitis at once! Besides I can't get my old quiet room at the Grosvenor for several weeks. So I really think I better stay on here for the present. When you come back I hope to be pretty well on my way with this book. It's no world-beater, but I want it to be good of its kind—very quaint and dry, as I told you; mostly Quebec weather and Quebec legends. But of course the subject matter is a secret between us.

I hope you will have a splendid trip, and that you'll see the Hambourgs. They've both been ill, and I'm very much worried about Isabelle, and I'd like to hear from you how she seems.

Of course as soon as I do get to New York I'll report at the office.

With love and good wishes for a good journey

Yours

Willa Cather

Please send me Zona Gale's new book [*Borgia*], and a book on Greek Domestic Life, or Greek Family Life in the time of the early church, that you published long ago. I remember an excellent sketch of the Empress Theodora in it, but have forgotten the title [probably *The Byzantine Achievement*, by Robert Byron].

W. S. C.

❧ ❧

Yale French professor Albert G. Feuillerat apparently wrote Cather with questions as part of his work on an article about her books. On May 16, 1930, he published "Romancières américaines: Miss Willa Cather" in Figaro.

TO ALBERT G. FEUILLERAT

November 6, 1929

My dear Mr. Feuillerat:

I am sending you a pamphlet which my publisher sends to colleges and clubs that write to him for information about my books. At the back of this pamphlet there is a list of books which give such information, and I have marked the two which I think might be most helpful to you. The book "Spokesmen" by Professor [T. K.] Whipple, contains the latest and most comprehensive study of my books. The biographical sketch at the beginning of this pamphlet will answer one of your questions at least.

Your inquiry regarding a possible French influence is hard to answer. I began to read French when I was fifteen or sixteen, and for a great many years enjoyed the French prose writers from Victor Hugo down to [Guy de] Maupassant much more than I did English writers of the same periods. I never cared so much for French poetry as for English poetry; but almost any French prose seemed to me a little better than English prose, quite apart from the quality of the writer. Before I was twenty I had read all of the novels of Balzac a good many times. Now I do not read him very often. I don't think I ever longed to "imitate" one French writer more than another, but in all the great French writers I have felt a greater freedom than in English writers of the same period; they experimented more often and had a wider range of variety—usually seemed a little more direct and sincere. About nearly all the fine old English novelists (before Thomas Hardy) there is a curiously professional tone toward the reader, a joviality a good deal like that of the landlord welcoming guests at an inn. When I was much younger this tone irritated me, I remember. I do not mind it so much now; it seems a manner like other manners, but perhaps the absence of this conventional geniality in French novelists pleased me, beside their range of interest was so much wider—their theme was not always the same story of how some one got settled in life.

I have written a long letter and yet I have told you very little of what I mean. I think I must always have cared for something nervous and direct and supple in French prose itself, when I was too young to think about it or reason about it. It excited me more than English prose, just as the air in high altitudes always makes me feel better and stronger than the air at sea level.

I may say that of all the French writers I have cared so much for at one time and another, I think I now enjoy Prosper Merimée perhaps more than any of the others. I feel as if the qualities which give me so much pleasure in other French prose are particularly present in him. I believe he is not fashionable in France at present, but he has almost everything I like in a writer—along with a proud reserve that makes me respect him.

Very sincerely yours,
Willa Cather

P.S. I think an essay I once wrote, called "The Novel Démeublé" will give you exactly the information you want. You will find a convenient edition of it listed on the last page of the pamphlet I am enclosing with this letter.

Sincerely
Willa Cather

→ ←

Cather had reached the point in her career where honors began to pile up. In addition to the growing number of honorary degrees, she was notified in November 1929 of her election to the National Institute of Arts and Letters.

TO ZONA GALE

November 25, 1929

My dear Miss Gale:

As I feared, I won't be able to accept the invitation from you [to come to Gale's home town of Portage, Wisconsin] which pleased and tempted me so much. I shall have to go to my mother in Pasadena just as soon as possible after Christmas—which means that work is pretty much out of the question for this winter. But it is a lovely thing for me to remember that you did want to have me there, and I am not going to give up hoping for a sojourn near you at some future time. Things have been hitting me pretty hard of late, you know. You remember when Kent is in the stocks waiting for Lear, and says "Fortune turn thy wheel."

On the long, slow train ride down from New Hampshire I read your new book [*Borgia*] with such delight and amusement—amusement that was rather grim. Of course we are all Borgias—especially when we really get interested in other people and have kind intentions. I nearly ruined the life of a young brother by bringing him off the farm and giving him what I thought were "advantages". But one cannot live isolated in a test tube—and most contacts are pernicious.

If you come to New York before Christmas, or soon afterward, please let me know. I want very much to tell you about something that I wished to speak of when I saw you last fall, and didn't. And I want to hear how things have turned out for the nice daughter you had with you—I did like that girl so much.

Always faithfully yours,
Willa Cather

➔ ←

Warner Brothers had produced a silent film of A Lost Lady *in 1924, starring Irene Rich and George Fawcett, and now, with the emergence of sound films, sought to remake the movie. Talking actors introduced new considerations for Cather.*

TO MANLEY AARON, ALFRED A. KNOPF, INC.

November 29, 1929

My dear Miss Aaron:

My hesitation about letting Warner Brothers have the sound rights of "A Lost Lady" has been due partly to the fact that they offered me a very low price and partly to the fact that I do not want my name attached to dialogue written by some person whose name and ability I do not know.

Of course, if they would agree to make no further use of my name than to say at the beginning of the film "Adapted from the novel of that name by Willa Cather," I believe I would feel no further hesitation in the matter and would let them have it at the price they offer. I would however want a signed statement from them that they would, in all the advertising, use that phrase— "Adapted from the novel of that name by Willa Cather" or "Adapted from Willa Cather's novel." In case they are not willing to confine themselves to this limited use of my name, I would certainly want to have something to say about the person who should write the dialogue for a sound picture. I am writing you this letter because I have just heard that an old friend of mine, Zoë Akins, who writes for the movies is still in Hollywood. She is under contract at the Fox studio, I think; but the Warners might be able to make some arrangement to get her for the job, if they wished to take the trouble. Zoe Akins knows the period in which my story is laid, the part of the country in which it occurs and the kind of people who appear in it. Moreover, I feel pretty sure that she would do the best she could for me. You might send Warner Brothers a copy of this letter or extracts from it, and they could give you an answer. What they do not seem to realize is that I am absolutely unwilling to have the dialogue of the sound production written by some one I don't know, and then have my own name used in connection with it.

Very sincerely yours,
Willa Cather

TO DOROTHY CANFIELD FISHER

December 20 [1929]
Grosvenor Hotel, New York City

Dear Dorothy:

I feel as if I must manage to reach you at Christmas time, though I've no idea where you are. Forgive this dreary letter-paper—could anything be a better index of the dreary way in which I now live? I can't take an apartment, you see, when I have to make two trips a year to California. I'm going there again in January.

Dear Dorothy, I can't thank you enough for the letter you wrote me from Spain this summer. I still have it by me. It reached me in my little house at Grand Manan, an island about thirty-five miles out from the New Brunswick shore. I went up there immediately after the Yale Commencement and stayed until late in September—really got rested and began to like life again. Then I went to a place I often stay in New Hampshire and came back to town in November, because I had to see my dentist, oculist, lawyer, etc. One does have to come back to cities for some things, and it's easiest where one has connections all ready made (I mean all ready, not already.) But as soon as I get back here, I get rather used up. The old New York of ten years ago wouldn't tire me, but the <u>present</u> New York—words fail me!

Yes, that actress in Pittsburgh was Lizzie Hudson Collier, cousin of Willie Collier. I wonder where she is now? She was as kind and good as new milk, or fresh bread. The worst of living fast and hard is that one can't keep in touch with all the people one cared for. But the first little circle, I've always kept close to them. I yesterday sent off eight Christmas boxes, (very carefully chosen and bought, the contents) to as many old women on farms within 25 miles of Red Cloud. There used to be fourteen of them (not so old, then) Swedish, Danish, German, Bohemian, Irish. In all these years, since the early Pittsburgh days, I've never been too poor or too busy or too sick to send them something at Christmas time. I've had some true lovers among them.—You see, I'd loved them first. "<u>In her last illness she talked of you so often</u>," the daughters write me afterward. I live only to get back to those old friends again—as I have kept going back, winter and summer, whenever I could, for half a life-time. But you see I can't go now, with mother so ill. She's terribly jealous—it will hurt her if I even stop there.

Mother's condition changes little—has improved a trifle, they tell me.

Please give my love to your mother if you are with her. If you and I <u>have</u> to become the older generation, why in mercy's name can't it be done without so much pain? It's like dying twice.

Well, I honestly set out to write you a cheerful letter—things are not so bad with me; I'm quite well, for instance. Instead of a chatty letter, it's turned out a homesick wail. I suppose my heart is always out there at Christmas time (it is so bleak, you know; and if one can love the bleak and bare at all—why one loves it <u>more than other things</u>. If I take up a pen at all, I'm very apt to write what I'm thinking hardest about, so you get this queer letter, my poor Dorothy!

However, I do wish you a Merry Christmas, and a Happy New Year, God knows! If you are in town before the end of January, won't you please let me know at this hotel?

Lovingly
Willa

TO ZOË AKINS

December 31 [1929]

My Dearest Zoë;

Your wonderful crucifix has made me so homesick for the Southwest! What a touching and powerful thing it is—just the color of the poor believers in their little tawny houses. It's a precious thing to have in New York. Thank you, with all my heart. I'll be in California in February. Tonight I am leaving for Quebec to spend the New Year week. It will be lovely up there now—Miss Lewis goes with me and we're taking a trunk full of coats and sweaters. There are mountains of snow over all this country now. I'll drink your health in very good champagne tomorrow night, dear Zoë.

With love
Willa

TO FERRIS GREENSLET

[January 1930]
Hotel Grosvenor, New York City

Dear Mr. Greenslet:

Will you please ask your business office to send me a statement of all royalties paid me in 1929. I must leave for Pasadena in a few weeks and must make my income tax report early.

Hastily
Willa Cather

P.S. I like [Oliver La Farge's] "Laughing Boy" <u>very</u> much!

TO FERRIS GREENSLET

February 6, 1930
Hotel Grosvenor, New York City

Dear Mr. Greenslet:

You have emptied a pretty kettle of fish upon my head! Wasn't it faithless of you (and, incidently, most illegal) to use my name, without my permission, in your ad. for <u>Laughing Boy</u>? Two old and intimate friends of mine published new books this fall, and their respective publishers asked me to let them use my name in exactly the way you used it. I refused in both cases, because if one begins that sort of thing there is simply no end to it. Sometimes the best possible friends write the worst possible books, and if they come to you and say, "you allowed your name to be used for this book or that book," what is one going to say in reply? The only way to keep out of embarrassing situations is consistently, and in every case, to keep one's name out of blurbs and advertisements. It's quite right that reviewers and people who write professionally about books should be quoted, that is their job and their judgment ought to count for something, but a friendly expression of interest in a book surely ought not to be used in print without one's consent.

Now that I have got this off my chest, please have someone send me a copy of the new edition of <u>Antonia</u>. Living thus in a hotel, I have none of my own books, and I want to make some corrections in <u>Antonia</u> for the English edition (and for you, if you will make the corrections.)

Also, since I am leaving for California about the 20th, would it be convenient for you to send me my royalty check sometime next week instead of

March 1st? I want to get my business affairs all straightened up before I go, if possible.

Very sincerely yours,
Willa Cather

TO DOROTHY CANFIELD FISHER

March 10 [1930]
Las Encinas Sanitarium, Pasadena, California

My Dear Dorothy;

Mother had a little chuckle over the Mark Twain dinner picture you sent me. She is a little stronger than last spring but just as helpless,—and her state is just as hopeless.

Sometimes I wonder why they build up a little more strength for people to suffer with. My sister is off for a few days rest and I am kept pretty busy trying to divert mother a little. We have a charming English nurse who has been with her a year now and never fails us. I have a nice little cottage of my own near

Willa Cather at the celebration of Mark Twain's seventieth-birthday dinner. Cather is third from the right.

mother's cottage, the food here is excellent and I am very comfortable in body. The trouble is one can't think of much but the general futility of existence.

My love to you and your mother. I envy you a New England spring.

Yours always
Willa

The picture was of Cather wearing an uncharacteristically frilly dress when she attended a lavish dinner at Delmonico's in celebration of Mark Twain's seventieth birthday in 1905. Harper's *magazine devoted its December 23, 1905, issue to Twain, the dinner, and photographs of the guests in their finery.*

➔ ←

In the spring of 1930, Woman's Home Companion *published Cather's short story "Neighbor Rosicky."*

TO MARGARET AND ELIZABETH CATHER

March 19 [1930]
Las Encinas Sanitarium, Pasadena, California

Dear Twinnies;

Perhaps you've seen the first part of "Neighbor Rosicky" in the ["]Woman's Home Companion"—but I am sending you the first <u>and</u> second parts in another envelope, in case you have not seen it. Your daddy will read it aloud very well, as he knows the characters.

Your grandmother is about the same,—comfortable, and most of the time cheerful. I am hoping to see you in a couple weeks, my dears. I will try to make my stay in Rawlins [Wyoming] on April 12th and 13th. I will let your father know later.

With love from all of us
Aunt Willie

➔ ←

In May, Cather and Lewis sailed for France. Cather needed to make this trip in order to complete Shadows on the Rock, *but she also wanted to see her old friends Isabelle and Jan Hambourg.*

TO MARY VIRGINIA BOAK CATHER

May 24 [1930]
Paris

My Darling mother;

Yesterday Isabelle and I were walking in a park full of grandmothers and children and she, paying attention to the children, turned her ankle and fell forward and cut a deep gash in her knee on a stone. It bled a good deal. We took a taxi home, where I washed it with iodine and bound it up, but I found the flesh was badly torn, and as soon as Jan came home I sent him for a doctor. He said she must stay in bed for several days, as a tear is worse than a cut and may suppurate. Isabelle had a very serious illness in the winter and will have to be an invalid for a long while. It is very sad for me that the two people I love best in the world get sick thousands of miles apart, and I such a poor traveller! I have seen very little of the gay side of Paris as yet, we have been here only a week today, and for the first three days Edith was sick and had to stay in bed, and now Isabelle is laid low with this cut on her knee, and for part of the time I have had a rather queer "tummy" from strange water and worry and being tired. Tell Doctor [Stephen] Smith for me that living-conditions are much pleasanter at Las Encinas than in any Paris hotel I have yet found—even the food there is more to my taste, though French food is always good. In spite of every-one's being below par physically, I have made two trips over to the queer old part of Paris where part of my new story lies, and have been well rewarded. That part of the city has changed very little, many of the same houses were there when my story-people lived there two hundred and fifty years ago. I went to church at the church they always attended. Many, many things are still the same.

Now I am going over to see Isabelle and be there when the Doctor comes to dress her knee—we will talk of you as we always do. She always wants to hear every little thing about you and the place you are in.

Lovingly
Willa

→ ←

The next three notes were written on postcards of the Notre Dame Cathedral, Paris. Around the picture on the front of the first, Cather wrote, with an arrow to the bell tower, "The bells are in here,—still the same ones," and, with another arrow and a reference to Victor Hugo's Notre-Dame de Paris, *"This is the parapet from which Quasimodo threw the wicked priest." The second and third postcards feature images of Notre Dame gargoyles.*

TO MARGARET AND ELIZABETH CATHER

May 28 [1930]
Paris

Dear Twinnies:

This is the glorious church of which you have read so much. It always looks to me <u>much</u> bigger than any New York sky-scraper. I have often walked about the high parapet from which Quasimodo threw the priest.

TO MARGARET CATHER

May 30 [1930]

Isn't she a dreadful old bird? Awful to think she has been so full of spite for seven hundred years! I am sure all the figures were Quasimodo's playfellows, and that he had special friends among them.

W.S.C.

TO MARGARET AND ELIZABETH CATHER

[June 1930]

Dear Margaret & Elizabeth;

There are countless figures like these perched all over the many roofs of Notre Dame. You have to climb all over the roofs and tower to see them all. They have been there since the year 1200, some before.

W.S.C.

TO BLANCHE KNOPF

June 30 [1930]
Paris

My Dear Blanche,

I have been very busy doing nothing for five weeks now and am beginning to get a little bored with it. I may go on to Vienna in a few weeks, or I may go home and up to Grand Manan, which seems to be the quietest spot in the world for work. It has been lovely to be so near Isabelle and Jan, we have done lots of nice things together, but I hate to be in a city in summer, even when the city is Paris, and if there is any really wild country in Europe I have never found it. The automobile has spoiled all that. When I first arrived everyone was having influenza, and I had it, too, for a week. I am very well now but I begin to long for green, quiet country. I've seen the Hambourgs and checked up on all my historical background, and I came over for those two things. If I decide to go home in August I'll let you know.

With love to you and greetings to everyone in the office.

Yours
Willa Cather

TO MABEL DODGE LUHAN

July 1 [1930]
Paris

Dear Mabel:

I've been wanting this long while to write you that your article on [D. H.] Lawrence is the only thing I've seen which has <u>any</u> of him in it. Everyone else who put in an oar wrote about <u>themselves</u>, as people usually do, but you really wrote about Lawrence, and I got a thrill out of it.

Awfully nice of you to tell me that [Robinson] Jeffers liked the "Archbishop." "Roan Stallion" is such a glorious poem. I read it in San Francisco and about went to see the man. The short one called "Night" seems to me one of the finest things done in English in many years.

Paris is almost as noisy and crowded as New York. It has changed woefully in seven years. I came only to see a dear friend who has been very ill. Both Edith and I are often homesick for New Mexico, in spite of the many gay things we are doing. I'm darned tired of being gay, to tell the truth. I'd like just to be a vegetable for a few months.

With heartiest love from us both
Willa

➤ ◄

Through Jan Hambourg, Cather met the Menuhin family in Paris. The Menuhins—parents Marutha and Moshe, children Yehudi, Hephzibah, and Yaltah—were a gifted musical family who would become some of the most treasured companions of Cather's later years. Yehudi, considered one of the greatest violinists of the twentieth century, began playing publicly at age seven. When Cather met him, he was fourteen years old.

TO MARGARET AND ELIZABETH CATHER

July 14 [1930]

My Dear Twinnies;

Naughty Elizabeth, who has not written to me! Nice Margaret who did! Yesterday I climbed up to the tower of Notre Dame again and spent the morning among my old friends, the gargoyles. The stairway is a circular one of white stone, and winds round and round a central column of white stone. It is very dark, lit only here and there by a slit in walls, and only then can one realize the great strength and thickness of the walls of Notre Dame and the huge blocks of cut stone of which they are built, stone fitted into stone with no cement.

Today is the anniversary of the taking of the Bastille in the Revolution, the greatest holiday of the year, and the people are dancing in the street before every little cafe. Late last night Jan and Isabelle drove us about in a taxi to see the dancers in all the little streets in the poor part of the city. Tonight we are all going to dine together at a gay restaurant—a lovely place where I went to lunch three days ago with Yehudi Menuhin the wonderful boy-violinist from San Francisco, and his family. He has two little sisters aged nine and seven who are almost as gifted and quite as handsome as he. They were in Paris only one day and we had a very exciting [time]. The one aged 7½ last winter wrote me a dear little letter about the "Archbishop"! All three have golden hair and skin like cream and roses—simply fairy-tale children. Their parents are nice, too, especially the mother.

I am enclosing a check for Virginia, to help with her college expenses, and I'm awfully pleased that she got the scholarship.

With my dearest love to you all
Willa Cather

How awful that they translate "Notre Dame de Paris" the <u>Hunchback</u> of Notre Dame!

TO BLANCHE KNOPF

August 21 [1930]
Grand Hôtel d'Aix, Aix-les-Bains, France

My Dear Blanche;

I have been gloriously doing nothing here for three weeks, after very interesting but rather tiring travelling in Provençe. I love Aix, and this year it is not at all crowded. I've always thought the cooking and pastry of Savoie the best in France, and, alas, I have picked up a couple pounds! I expect to sail on the Empress of Scotland, September 20, landing at Quebec and going straight down to Jaffrey, New Hampshire, to the old hotel where I always work in comfort and quiet. I dont want to go to New York until I have finished the last part of the book. I've been too lazy to work over here, and seeing too many old friends. I had two thrilling weeks motoring through the wild coast and mountains about Marseille—I've wanted for years to explore it.

The Hambourgs are now in Salzburg, at the Mozart festival, but they will meet me in Paris September 4th.

My love to you and Alfred and best wishes to everyone in the office.

Yours
Willa Cather

TO DOROTHY CANFIELD FISHER

September 30 [1930]
aboard the Canadian Pacific S. S. Empress of France

My Dearest Dorothy:

Your letter, telling me of your mother's death, reached me in Paris on the day before I sailed for home. Isabelle and I happened to have been talking of her the night before. I am sorry on your account, but almost glad on your dear mother's. She was too keen and alert to linger in a clouded state—when she had a good day she must have felt that something had broken or given way, and that would have distressed her. When I last saw her, after her trip 'round the world, she was entirely and vigorously herself, all her colors flying. I thought she had not changed in the least. I am glad I can remember her like that. But these vanishings, that come one after another, have such an impoverishing effect upon those of us who are left—our world suddenly becomes so diminished—the landmarks disappear and all the splendid distances behind us close up. These losses, one after another, make one feel as if one were going on in a play after most of the principal characters are dead.

I have been in France since the middle of May and am now on my way to Quebec. From the middle of October I shall be in Jaffrey N.H. for some weeks and perhaps I can run up to see you some day.

My mother's condition is unchanged. The doctors tell me she is so strong that she may live for five or six years in this state. Goodbye, dear Dorothy. I'm so sorry that you've had this break to face, but oh I'm glad for your mother and for you too that she was not punished by a long and helpless and utterly hopeless illness.

My love to you, from a full heart.
Willa

TO ALFRED AND BLANCHE KNOPF

Sunday [October 5, 1930]
Chateau Frontenac, Quebec City

Dear Blanche and Alfred;

I was so glad to get your message at sea, and your good wishes for me were fully realized. I had a fine crossing, and anything more lovely than the approach to this continent by way of the St. Lawrence, when all the wild forests of its shores and islands are blazing with autumn color, I have never seen. I meant to go on immediately to Boston and Jaffrey, but I got rather a thrill out of journeying straight from Paris to Quebec, and as the weather is glorious I shall stay on here until Tuesday. My story comes to life as soon as I get back here and I get a good deal of pleasure out of playing with it. Books, alas, are like children,—never so much fun after they grow up and are finished as they are when they are merely things to play with and all your own. I've learned to get my fun before publication. I'll write you soon from Jaffrey.

Affectionately
Willa Cather

➤ ❖

In 1930, the American Academy of Arts and Letters awarded Cather the William Dean Howells Medal for Death Comes for the Archbishop. *The medal is given every five years to honor the best book by an American writer published during the previous half decade. That same year, Sinclair Lewis became the first American to win the Nobel Prize in Literature. Upon receiving her letter of congratulation, Lewis responded that he thought Cather ought to have been the recipient, and said that he considered* A Lost Lady *one of the very best books in American literary history.*

TO ROSCOE CATHER

November 6 [1930]
Grosvenor Hotel, New York City

Dear Roscoe;

Gold medal very large and handsome—weighs several pounds—gold with no alloy at all—handy for a paperweight. I'm going to take it to [the] bank to have it weighed and valued. It's <u>one</u> thing you can turn into money—one flattering phrase that's worth something!

I send you a very good editorial from the N.Y. Times, and I think that is <u>just</u> why Lewis got the Nobel award. We look like that to Europe, and all those Swedish chore boys we kicked around are telling us what they think of us. I expect we really <u>are</u> like that. Anyhow, I like Lewis and I wrote him that though I couldn't honestly say I'd rather he got the award than I, I'd rather he had it than anyone else. The newspaper discussed the award so much that thousands of good people think I <u>did</u> get it, and my mail is full of dozens of begging letters from preachers and widows and orphans; "please help me with just a little of that $47,000"!

I send you a copy of Judge [Robert] Grant's speech made in conferring the medal. You might send it and the newspaper clippings to Elsie. She might be interested to see them and I have over two hundred letters to dictate before I can begin to work, or even have my tooth filled, so I've not much time for family correspondence.

Mr. [George] Whicher of Amherst was to bring Virginia and Tom up to dine with me in Jaffrey on the first Sunday in December, but this medal affair called me away before my appointed time, and now I won't get back. I'm going to Philadelphia for Thanksgiving, to some old friends who will give me some dinner and a bedroom and study—and let me alone.

With much love to you and yours
Willie

Send the checks to me at this address, please

➜ ⬅

At the ceremony where she received her Howells medal, Cather met the American sculptor and writer Lorado Taft.

TO LORADO TAFT

November 17, 1930
New York City

My dear Mr. Taft:

As I had to leave the platform before the exercises were over last Friday, in order to catch a train, I did not have an opportunity for a short conversation with you. Though I was alone with you for a few moments before the program began, you were then occupied with the address you were soon to deliver. I simply wanted to tell you how much pleasure your fountain near the Art Institute in Chicago has given me for many years. I have to go West two or three times every year and I never go through Chicago, even when the interval between trains in short, without taking a cab and driving over to the Art Institute for another glimpse at that fountain. It always delights me. There is in it everything that I feel about the Great Lakes, and it always puts me in a hopeful, holiday mood. I do not know whether you yourself think it an especially fine thing, but I do. I do not know why I like it so much, because I know very little about sculpture. But it seems to me that the pleasure one feels in a work of art is just one thing that one does not have to explain.

Very cordially yours,
Willa Cather

TO READ BAIN

January 14, 1931

My dear Mr. Bain:

Yes, of course I get a great many "fan" letters as you call them—but most of them are pretty thin wind, I assure you. It is very easy to pick out the real ones. Of course, as you intimate, it is a very distinct disadvantage to be a Lady Author—anybody who says it isn't, is foolish. Virginia Woolf makes a pretty fair statement of the disadvantages [in *A Room of One's Own*]. But young children are neither very male nor very female, and I find that the impressions and memories that hang on from those early days of having no particular sex, are the safest ones to trust to—and the pleasantest ones to play with. I am glad you liked the two particular books you mention—but myself I always feel that "A Lost Lady" is, artistically, more successful than either of them.

Cordially yours,
Willa Cather

TO NORMAN FOERSTER

January 14, 1931

Dear Norman Foerster:

No, I cannot accept your kind invitation. I simply never give lectures or talks of the kind you suggest. I used to, very occasionally, but since my mother has been an invalid I have had no time for these things.

I have not written you before because I have wanted to write you a long letter about your book [*Toward Standards: A Study of the Present Critical Movement in American Letters*], and Heaven only knows when I will have time to do so. I am just finishing a new book of my own and will soon go to my mother in California. I read your book very carefully and with great interest. I am awfully glad you wrote it, and I agree with you in the main—in your opinions on the history of criticism and the critical mind, but I do feel that you take a little group of American critics, I might say of New York critics, too seriously. This of course is entirely confidential, but I think of the men you mention, Randolph Bourne and, in a less degree, [Henry Seidel] Canby, were the only ones who had that instantaneous perception and absolute conviction about quality which a good critic must have. You understand me; it is a thing like an ear for music. You can tell when a singer flats, or you cannot tell. You cannot be taught to distinguish that error.

Take, for example, an intelligent and serious man like Stuart Sherman. (And please don't think there is anything personal in this—he always treated me very generously indeed.) I knew him quite well. He was absolutely lacking in the quality I speak of. He could take a writer as a subject; talk about him and read about him and worry his brain over the matter, and say a great many interesting things about this writer—many of them true. But it was all from the outside. It was a thing worked up, studied out.

What I mean is this: suppose that Sherman had read all the novels of Joseph Conrad except the "Nigger of the Narcissus", that he had written about them and read what other critics had to say about them until he knew a great deal about these books and their quality. If all this were true, and I had taken a dozen pages from the "Nigger of the Narcissus" and mixed them up with a dozen pages written by Conrad's fairly intelligent imitators (people like Francis Brett Young for example), it would have been utterly impossible for Stuart Sherman to pick out the Conrad pages from the second rate stuff.

A fine critic must have something more than a studious nature and high ideals, and the very best criticism I happen to know was not written by professional critics at all. Henry James was a very fine critic I think; and so was Walter Pater. And so was Prosper Mérimée (Do you know his essay on Gogol? That's what I call criticism!).

I don't mean that all fine artists in prose have been good critics. Of course Turgenev was a very poor critic.

But on the whole, composers are the best judges of new musical compositions and writers are the best judges of new kinds of writing. I mean they are better judges than either musical scholars or literary scholars. But this is only a little of a great deal that I would like to say to you about your book, which does exactly what a book of that sort ought to do—makes me want to come back at you and have it out with you, both where I agree and where I disagree.

Always cordially yours,
Willa Cather

January 20

P.S. This letter was written some days ago—but my secretary [Sarah Bloom] begged me not to send it. "Just the sort of indiscreet letter that falls into the wrong hands and makes you a lot of enemies for nothing," says she. However, as she has gone to Cuba for her vacation, I think I'll send it anyhow. I feel that it won't fall into the wrong hands, and that you won't quote me—even to your publisher, who is rather a chatter-box.

Yours,
Willa Cather

TO MRS. FRANK L. GRIPPEN

January 14, 1931
The Grosvenor Hotel, New York City

Dear Mrs. Grippen:

Excuse delay in replying to your letter. I have been travelling. I think I can enlighten your perplexity. Myra Henshaw [in *My Mortal Enemy*] before her death came to consider Oswald as her "mortal enemy";—she came to believe that anything loved selfishly and fiercely and extravagantly became the enemy of one's soul's peace. Please tell your ladies that that simple fact is the subject of the story.

Very cordially yours,
Willa Cather

→ ←

Knopf published Mabel Dodge Luhan's memoir of D. H. Lawrence, Lorenzo in Taos, *in 1932. Cather read the book before it was published, the same way she read Luhan's personal memoir,* Intimate Memories.

TO MABEL DODGE LUHAN

January 17 [1931]
35 Fifth Avenue, New York City

Dear Mabel;

I've just finished "Lorenzo in Taos" with great admiration. It's as good as the Buffalo part of "Intimate Memories". It's like a big canvas full of gorgeous color and thrilling people—and motion. It's the constant changes in the personal equations and in the emotional climate that make the book so exciting. Everything that goes on between the people is unexpected and unforeseen, as things usually are in life and so seldom are in the pages of a novelist. I don't always agree with you in your interpretation of your people and their motives, but I always agree with the way it's done—with your presentation of your own interpretation, I mean. Everybody in the story is alive and full of behaviour—except a few colorless people whom you have the good sense to let alone. Perhaps you're a little hard on Frieda [Lawrence], a little hard on [Dorothy] Brett—but you've made 'em as you saw 'em and they and all the rest keep the ball rolling. You've done Tony [Luhan] magnificently! I wouldn't have thought anybody could do him so well. It's splendid, and not over-done. And you've done yourself better than anywhere except in the early Buffalo volumes. In the Italian part of the memories I always felt that a stream of interesting people went across the page but that you as a person disappeared. Here you re-appear with a bang! I imagine that it's because your eye is fixed on Lawrence and you do yourself rather incidentally that you succeed so well. It's amazingly spontaneous and amazingly true. I'm sure it's the best portrait there ever will be of Lawrence himself. I'm amused at your struggle with his giggle. Was it a giggle? Wasn't it more like a snicker? Not snigger, but snicker? To me giggle is always fat and jolly.

I simply love the way you do the Taos country and the weather. When I was writing about it in a very formal and severe manner, as befits the eye of a priest and the pen of a stranger, I kept thinking that I would love to see it done intimately, as part and parcel of somebody's personal life—not a background! (about once a week I get a letter from some puppy who tells me he has done a story of sophisticated easterners in a New Mexican background, or some other kind of simper with a New Mexican background.) I wish to God I could have put the Archbishop in Kansas or Nebraska—not many sensitive artistic natures have the grit to follow you there. It's a great advantage to work in a part of the country that is distinctly déclassé—it rids you [of] superficial writers and superficial readers. But this is a long departure. When a country like the Taos country is really a part of your life, and when your life is a form of living and not a little camera,—well, then it all works up very stunningly together. Few things have ever given me more joy than the night you all spent chasing about in [the] alfalfa field. Why Tony's car becomes a positive god of vengeance, a frightful threat to the foolishness of all of you, and to a whole school of thinking that has upset the old balance of things, where personal desires and emotions were masked under a National consciousness or a tribe will, or the particular false-front of any ones social period.

Edith is in Boston for a week, or she would probably be writing you at the same time. She read Lorenzo through before she left.

I'll be leaving for California in a few weeks, to join my mother. Her condition is about the same. The doctors tell me it may go on five or six years like this. She seems to get pleasure out of being with us, even in such a wretchedly helpless state. I have to stop off in San Francisco, so I'll probably go over the northern route. But my next long trip will be to Mexico City. I'm envious that you've beat me to it.

With heartiest congratulations
Willa Cather

TO MARY VIRGINIA BOAK CATHER

February 19 [1931]
The Parkside, New York City

My dearest mother:

Just a word to you from this hotel where I am waiting for Mary Virginia to come to dinner with me. Thank Douglass for his reassuring telegrams. Indeed I will get to you just as soon as possible—that will be very soon now.

My book is done! My publisher went to Paris soon after Christmas when the book was only about two thirds done. We rushed copies of the manuscript on to him some weeks ago, and he read it in Paris and sent me this cable for a Valentine. Everyone at the office likes it better than "The Archbishop." I do not like it better, but I think it as good a piece of work.

I am now reading the proofs—Douglass will explain to you what that means, and I am correcting many mistakes—some are the fault of the printers, and some are my own fault. It is so easy to make a little slip in a book so full of dates and historical happenings. One simply has to get them <u>right</u>.

But it won't be long now until you get a telegram telling you by what train I am coming. I expect to leave New York on the fourth of March, and will go straight through, stopping one night in Chicago to rest.

Here comes M.V. so goodbye with much love from us both

[Unsigned]

TO JOSEPHINE GOLDMARK

March 3, 1931

My dear Miss Goldmark:

I had so counted upon having a long evening's talk with you about your book [*Pilgrims of '48: One Man's Part in the Austrian Revolution of 1848, and a Family Migration to America*], but the serious illness of two of my friends has cut my winter all to pieces, and now I am hurrying off to California because my mother's condition has changed for the worse.

It is very difficult to tell you in a letter about the things which delighted me in your book—not this chapter or that, but the whole thing, moving along with such a refreshing calm and such an absence of that nervous tendency to force things up. I read it slowly evening after evening, and it was like taking a long voyage with a group of people who have become one's friends by the time one reaches port. I enjoyed the Brandeis family as much as the Goldmarks, and Frederika is surely charming enough to give a perfume to any book. What a charm and distinction there is about the personality of your mother as she appears in this book—I wish I could have met her. I am so interested in the daguerreotype picture of her—I think your sister Pauline looks very much like her.

You see, I have known a great many of those German and Bohemian families myself, in the West, three generations of them living together in little towns. I have watched the original pioneers growing old and the third generation growing up, all getting rooted into the soil and interweaving and becoming a part of the very ground. I began to watch it as a young child—it delighted me even then, and keeping in touch with those communities and watching the slow flowering of life has been one of my greatest pleasures. Your book brought it all back to me; the slow working out of fate in people of allied sentiments and allied blood. These many characters influencing each other by chance give a book a greater unity than any plan you could have made. As I have already said, reading it was like taking a long voyage with a group of people whom one likes so well that one is sorry to come into port. They have everything that was nicest about the old world and the old time, and I put your book down with a sense that even if I do not like the present very well, we have had a beautiful past.

With very deep gratitude for the happy evenings I spent with your Pilgrims of '48, for the memories they awoke and for the hope they give me for the future, I am

Your very true friend,
Willa Cather

TO IRENE MINER WEISZ

[March 12, 1931]
Santa Fe California Limited
Crossing Kansas

Dearest Irene;

This morning I wakened wondering if you were awake—I had been dreaming that you and I were on the Burlington, going out to the Golden Wedding together! At first I felt sad—then very happy. I did not really deserve that happy time. I had never been a very thoughtful daughter. My mind and heart were always too full of my one all-absorbing passion. I took my parents for granted. But, deserving or not, I had it, and there is no one in the round world whom I would have chosen before you to share it with me. You were just the right one, and I shall always be thankful for that trip we had together back to our own little town. I'm glad nobody met us at Hastings. I remember every mile of the way home, don't you? And the bitter cold in which we left Chicago? You see you are the only person who reaches back into the very beginning who has kept on being a part of my life in the world where, for some reason I have to go on and on, from one change to another. The other friends, Isabelle and Edith and Mr. McClure and many others, don't go so far back. And the dear Red Cloud friends (Carrie and Mary dearest of all) have not been so much in my later life as you have. With you I can speak both my languages; you know the names of all the people dear to me in childhood, and the names of most of those who have grown into my life as I go along. I suppose that is why I crowd so much information about the MENUHINS and the new friends on you. I want somebody from Sandy Point to go along with me to the end. My brothers are loyal and kind but they <u>are not</u> interested in these things. I feel so grateful to you for having kept your interest. Carrie and Mary are so loyal to our old ideals, but they have not been in my later life so much as you, geography, long distances have been against us. I am always so glad Mary and Doctor [E. A. Creighton] were in New York that winter, and of course came to tea and met my friends.

When I go back to Red Cloud to stay for a few months sometime, you must come; Mr. Weisz must surely spare you to me for a little while.

So lovingly
Willie

This train jumps about so—I'm afraid you won't be able to read this scrawl at all.

TO ELSIE CATHER

March 17 [1931]
Las Encinas Sanitarium, Pasadena, California

Dear Sister;

I won't write you a letter until I return from San Francisco and am more settled in mind. Mother has failed so much since I last saw her, but she does have some hours of restful quiet each day, I think. She is not in pain—just the weariness and discomfort of every physical act growing harder and harder. Sometimes she is quite cheerful for an hour, and she goes out in her chair every day and wants to go.

I am going up to San Francisco to take a Doctor of Laws at Berkeley, and devoutly hope that someone here will move out of a cottage while I am away. I am in the main building, next the dining room, and don't get much rest.

I don't think you could help much if you were here, dear. Mother is conscious, but her perceptions are so dim—with occasional hours when she seems to understand.

Mrs. Bates is so good to her, and so consciencious, and Douglass I think does more for her than any man ever did for any woman since the world began.

With love
Willa

TO ALFRED A. KNOPF

April 2 [1931]
Fairmont Hotel, San Francisco, California

Dear Alfred;

I've written Mr. Levinson that I cannot speak for him. I'd never get away from here without making a lecture tour if I did!

I agree with you that a type jacket with distinction and style would be best, and I shall be very honored if you see fit to add to it any words over your signature.

Yehudi's arrival was splendid; it brought all the clans together, as it were. <u>Do</u> you know the Ehrmans and the Helmans? They are the most enchanting people. Sidney Ehrman started Yehudi, long ago (five years, to be accurate!) and they are, through the Jacobys, distantly related to a Mrs. Charles Wiener who lives here now, and who started me on my road in Red Cloud Nebraska, when I was ten years old. I suppose I got a kind of Hebrew complex at that age, and the grand Jews still seem to me the most magnificent people on earth. They simply get me, I'm theirs, I can't refuse anything.

Hastily

W.S.C.

TO GEORGE L. STIMSON, ALFRED A. KNOPF, INC.

April 18, 1931

Pasadena, California

Dear Mr. Stimson;

A Catholic attorney [Garret McEnerney], the most celebrated lawyer on this coast, has found some bothersome "errors in Catholicism" in our page proofs. I can get out of them with safety, but it will hold the works up a couple of weeks, and will mean another set of proofs for Miss Lewis to go over after the corrections are made. I feel awfully apologetic to all the office, and especially to you.

To call a Bishop an Archbishop is unpardonable carelessness—but the french sources I read, of course use the same word, Monsiegneur, for both Bishop and Archbishop. And who on earth (but a Catholic) could guess that until about 1900 it was not permitted to say a mass for individual souls on All Souls' day! One could only have masses for the dead in general, it seems.

With this book I bid adieu to Rome—otherwise you and Alfred Knopf would have to become converts in order to keep me out of trouble.

I'm terribly sorry to make you all so much trouble, and I do feel rather an idiot. However, thank God for the San Francisco lawyer who will at least have enabled me to conceal my blunders from the Catholic world in general.

Faithfully

W.S.C.

TO ROSCOE CATHER

May 2 [1931]
Las Encinas Sanitarium, Pasadena, California

Dear Roscoe;

Last summer in Paris I had a travelling case made exactly like Jan Hambourg's. The Knopfs gave me a very handsome one for Christmas, and as this one I got is really a man's case, and I have never used it, I am sending it to you. You may find it convenient for the many trips you take about the state. It has my initials on, but you can have those changed. My initials seem to be familiar ones now-a-days. An initialed cigarette case which I had used was lately sold for twenty-five dollars at a <u>Catholic church fair</u>. And for so many years my cigarette case was a family skeleton! Well, all things come to him who waits.

Did you see the ballad in the May Atlantic Monthly [Cather's poem "Poor Marty"]? It's said to be very good. Mother is well these days, but I got chilled after a hot walk and have had a tummy-ache for three days, like a colic[k]y baby!

With love to you all
Willie

TO DOROTHY CANFIELD FISHER

Sunday [June 14?,1931]
New York City

Dear Dorothy;

I got back a few days ago and go down to Princeton tonight for another of those degrees you are always joking me about. (How avoid 'em is the question? By sailing in May—but I can't sail every year.) Your letter reached me last night and makes me very happy. About this book I have no feeling at all—except the kind of gratitude you feel toward an old fur coat that has kept you warm through a long cold Atlantic crossing. It has been like a little tapestry tent that I could unfold in hotels and sanitariums and strange places and forget the bleakness about me. Quebec always gives me that sense of loyalty, of being faithful to something.

To recapture that feeling, and to get the sense of the North, was all I tried for. Every little detail of the way they lived is from some old book or letter. The search for all those little things helped me to hold my life together. How much it can mean to people who don't know the history of the period at all, I don't know. Jacques is the little nephew [Charles E. Cather] I love the best. I had him all that beautiful winter before Father died—he was only five (5) then. I stopped in Nebraska to see him for a day last week. He's just the same—remembers everything we did together. "I guess I liked when you used to pull me up the hill on my sled the best of all," he said softly. Such a faithful, loving little heart! Those late afternoon sled-rides were dear to me, too.

I'll be here for about 12 days (business matters) then Grand Manan!

Lovingly
Willa

TO PAVELKA BOYS, POSSIBLY EDWARD AND EMIL PAVELKA

June 26, 1931
Grosvenor Hotel, New York City

My dear Boys:

I expect you think I have forgotten all about you and your Commencement, but you are quite mistaken. I was delighted to get your pictures and have shown them to many of my friends in Pasadena and New York, telling them "That is the kind of fine Bohemian boys we have in Nebraska". It grieves me to think that Annie [Pavelka] hasn't any little boys any more, but I am very proud of all the big boys. My brother-in-law, Mr. [James William] Auld of Red Cloud, was here yesterday and he said he had seen one of you at some fair or athletic show not long ago, and that he was well pleased with you.

One reason you have not heard from me is that I have been graduating myself! I hurried on East to take a degree at Princeton and I had a very exciting time. At the President's dinner Colonel Lindbergh took me out to dinner and sat at my right, and the next day I lunched with him and Mrs. Lindbergh. I met a great many fine people, and they treated me well, I assure you.

It made me very sad to hurry through Nebraska and not see any of you, but I am coming to see you all before another year goes by. I promise myself that, every time I feel blue. You see, it is only the fact that my mother has been so ill and helpless in California that has kept me away from Nebraska. All the time I have for visiting must go to her.

With love to you both and a great deal of love to your mother and Elizabeth [Pavelka] and all your brothers, I am always

Faithfully your friend,
Willa Cather

TO FRANCIS TALBOT, S.J.

June 26, 1931
Grosvenor Hotel, New York City

My dear Father Talbot:

I don't think my book could have given you much more pleasure than your gracious letter of approval gives me. If you have been studying the early history of Quebec, you well know how contradictory their own histories are, and how difficult it is to come at a fair estimate of some of the men who are prominent in that period. I have been going to Quebec for many years and the thing that I always feel there, the thing that I admire, is a certain loyalty to language and religion and tradition. Some of those qualities are essentially French; but in Quebec they seem more moving and rather more noble than in France itself. Quebec seems to me more like a period than a place—like something cut off from France of 200 years ago, which, in some respects, was certainly finer than the France of today or America of today. I feel that the Rock still stands there, though so many generations have come and gone and cast their shadows in the sunlight for a little while.

There are some intentional inaccuracies; the King's warehouse, at that time, was at the mouth of the River Charles—it was not until some years later that it was placed where I put it in my story. But in all the larger matters I tried to be as accurate as I could.

Thanking you most cordially for your very heartening encouragement, I am

Most sincerely yours,
Willa Cather

PS: I think I ought to tell you that I made some rather grave errors in Catholic practice in the original manuscript (such as having Mass said for an individual soul on All Souls Day) and that these errors were corrected by an extremely intelligent and brilliant Catholic woman, Mrs. Garret McEnerney, the wife of the celebrated San Francisco lawyer.

TO ZOË AKINS

[June 21, 1931]
Grosvenor Hotel, New York City

Dearest Zoë

Princeton went off with a bang! I had Lindbergh for my dinner partner at the President's dinner, and lunched with him and Mrs. Lindberg[h] next day. All her photographs to the contrary, she is <u>fascinating</u>!

Lovingly
Willa

TO BLANCHE KNOPF

July 10 [1931]

Dear Blanche;

I'm still busy settling the house and drying all the linens and bedding in the sun. The little house sits on the very edge of the cliff, and the sea fogs come in just as they do into a boat. Besides, the place was not opened up at all last summer, so rust and mould got a good start. We'll be spick and span in a few days.

Please ask Alfred <u>not</u> to telegraph me the results of his correspondence with his London agent regarding "Shadows". No telegraph station on the island; all telegrams telephoned out under the Bay, and I have to go two miles to the nearest telephone to receive messages. I can easily <u>reply</u> to a letter by telegram, however.

Blanche, <u>please</u> get Charles the grocer to send me two cans of Italian Tomato Paste, two heads of garlic, and a pound of <u>wild rice</u>. It's the only shop that carries wild rice. Oh yes! please send me half-a-dozen small jars of Caviar (the 65¢ size keep best) ask Charles' salesman to under-value these things about half in his declaration, as the duty on food stuffs is now from fifty to eighty-five percent.

This is an interesting letter, surely! But I'll do better later.

With love
Willa Cather

Shadows on the Rock, *Cather's ninth novel, was published in August of 1931.*

TO ALFRED A. KNOPF

July 31 [1931]
Grand Manan Island

My Dear Alfred;

Because of the varying schedule of the one boat which is our only mail carrier, I got your letters of the 24th and 27th on the same day!

First, regarding the Heinemann situation [concerning negotiations for a collected edition in England]. I don't think their attitude very cordial or very promising, since they refuse to bind themselves to anything at all. I have made up my mind to let you go ahead with Cassell. I will have to write a letter to Evans, of course, and I will send you a copy of it. Meanwhile you may cable Salzberg to go ahead with Cassell, so far as I am concerned.

The news you write me about the initial distribution of the new book is delightful, and is a great surprise to me. I still see in that book only a story to please the quiet and meditative few. As it has got beyond that circle, I can only conclude that you and Blanche, and your office, and the "Archbishop" of four years ago, all had a good deal to do with bringing this bashful volume out before the curtain. I think the review in the Atlantic will make up the minds of a great many people who think they are intelligent, but unguided would probably have passed this book over as a dull one.

I have just finished the longest of the three stories I mean for the next volume, and have sent it down to my secretary to be typed. It will run about 23,000 words. We had spoken of "Obscure Destinies" as a title for that volume of three stories. Would you like "Out West" better? They are all western stories; one in Colorado, one in Kansas, one in Nebraska.

Tell Blanche the things from Charles came when much needed—especially the garlic and tomato paste, which you can't get in Protestant Canada; and yesterday [I] made a risotto that would make your mouth water. I can still get excellent champagne in St. John, Pol Roger 1919, that excellent year, which I couldn't get in Paris at all, nor anywhere but at Aix-les-Bains. This island is always beautiful, and the weather has been so wild and dramatic that I cannot stay at a desk very long. The climate is everything else in God's world,—but is <u>never</u> hot or sticky.

My love to you both, and my very deep gratitude to you and all your staff for the splendid way they have stood behind this book. It gives me a lighter heart for the books to come.

Faithfully yours
Willa Cather

TO MARY VIRGINIA BOAK CATHER

August 10 [1931]

My Dearest Mother;

The weather has been all sun and blue sea for the last week, and I have been taking some splendid long walks along the high cliffs where there are no houses for many miles and one never meets a soul. The islanders keep that stretch wild to pasture their cows in. Next week I won't have time to walk much, for hundreds of letters have been pouring in about my new book. My secretary in New York answers most of them, but there are many from old friends and important people that I must answer myself—enough to keep me very busy all next week.

I'm sorry that horrible picture of me got onto the front page of the magazine called "Time", but I couldn't help it. One just has to grin and bear such things. If I mourned about accidents like that, and about the things jealous, disappointed newspaper men write about me, I could just mourn my life away—which I don't intend to do. When the "Archbishop" first came out, all the reviews were unfavorable and many of them savage. Now those same newspapers call it a 'classic'.

My dearest love to Elsie, and I will write her as soon as I get caught up with my mail.

With my dearest love,
Willie

Dear Elsie and Douglass; please be sure to read the sketch and review in the Atlantic Monthly. It is in the "Atlantic Bookshelf", in the front advertising pages.

→ ←

The August 1931 Atlantic Monthly *published a glowing review of* Shadows on the Rock *by Ethel Wallace Hawkins. A review by Wilbur Cross, a former Yale English professor who became governor of Connecticut in 1930, was published in the* Saturday Review of Literature, *which later published, with permission, the following letter that Cather wrote to Cross in response.*

TO WILBUR CROSS

August 25 [1931]
Grand Manan Island

Dear Governor Cross;

I want to thank you most heartily for the first understanding review I have seen of my new book. You seem to be the first person who sees what a different kind of method I tried to use from that which I used in the "Archbishop". I tried, as you say, to state the mood and the view-point in the title. To me the rock of Quebec is not only a stronghold on which many strange figures have for a little time cast a shadow in the sun; it is the curious endurance of a kind of culture, narrow but definite. There another age persists. There, among the country people and the nuns, I caught something new to me; a kind of feeling about life and human fate that I could not accept, wholly, but which I could not but admire. It is hard to state that feeling in language; it was more like an old song, incomplete but uncorrupted, than like a legend. The text was mainly anacoluthon, so to speak, but the meaning was clear. I took the incomplete air and tried to give it what would correspond to a sympathetic musical setting; tried to develop it into a prose composition not too conclusive, not too definite; a series of pictures remembered rather than experienced; a kind of thinking, a mental complexion inherited, left over from the past, lacking in robustness and full of pious resignation.

Now it seemed to me that the mood of the mis-fits among the early settlers (and there were a good many) must have been just that. An orderly little French household that went on trying to live decently, just as ants begin to rebuild when you kick their house down, interests me more than Indian raids or the wild life in the forests. And, as you seem to recognize, once having adopted a tone so definite, once having taken your seat in the close air by the apothecary's fire, you can't explode into military glory, any more than you can pour champagne into a salad dressing. (I don't believe much in rules, but Stevenson laid down a good one when he said: you can't mix kinds.) And really, a new society begins with the salad dressing more than with the destruction of Indian villages. Those people brought a kind of French culture there and somehow kept it alive on that rock, sheltered it and tended it and on occasion died for it, as if it really were a sacred fire———and all this temperately and shrewdly, with emotion always tempered by good sense.

It's very hard for an American to catch that rhythm———it's so unlike us. But I made an honest try, and I got a great deal of pleasure out of it, if nobody else does! And surely you'll agree with me that our writers experiment too little, and produce their own special brand too readily.

With deep appreciation of the compliment you pay me in taking the time to review the book, and my friendliest regards always.

Faithfully
Willa Cather

TO DOROTHY CANFIELD FISHER

[September 1931]

Dear Dorothy;

My poor mother died on Monday the 31st. There was no boat out from here until Wednesday, so I could not even try to get to the services, which were held in Red Cloud on Thursday afternoon. My brother and sister left Pasadena with mother's body Monday night and two other brothers joined them on the way home. For mother's sake I am glad it is over—before her mind began to fail. The end was sudden—pneumonia. I shall stay on here through September and then I must go to my poor brother who has lived solely for his mother for three years and a half. I feel a good deal like a ghost myself, and I know it is much worse for him. Goodbye, I know you'll be sorry, my dear. It seems strange to me that you and I are now the "older generation." I never thought of that before.

Lovingly
Willa

→ ←

In a review of Shadows on the Rock *published in the September 1931* Forum, *Granville Hicks attacked both it and* Death Comes for the Archbishop *as "diffuse" and said it revealed why Cather was a "minor" writer. Hicks ended, "To-day, perhaps even more than in the past, it takes stern stuff to make a novelist. Miss Cather, one is forced to conclude, has always been soft; and now she has abandoned herself to her softness." Henry Goddard Leach was the editor of the* Forum.

TO HENRY GODDARD LEACH

September 1 [1931]

Dear Mr. Leach;

The article about which I wrote you is not exactly a review of my new book, but a general estimate of all my books and of me. From the letters I have received about it, I gather that it is accepted as your opinion and the <u>Forum's</u> opinion; Mr. Hicks is not mentioned. It is probably your policy to give your reviewers a free hand, but there are limits to all editorial policies. When I was editing McClures I would certainly not have allowed an article so generally derogatory to you to appear in the magazine. Had Mr. McClure and I both been abroad, the office staff would not have allowed an article so detrimental to an author for whom we had any regard to be printed, without first consulting us.

Granted that you felt the time had come to utter a few unpleasant truths, it is possible to say uncomplimentary things in a courteous and even a respectful way. But the tone of this article is sarcastic and contemptuous throughout, and no desk editor representing you in your absence would have printed such an article about any writer for whom you had much regard.

The <u>Forum</u>, I realize, has a right to put as low an estimate as you think just upon any writer's abilities, but I question the editorial ethics of printing a statement like the following [magazine text is literally cut out and pasted on the letter]:

> Like most of her books, it is elegiac, beguiling its readers with pictures of a life that has disappeared, and deliberately exploiting the remoteness of that life in order to cast a golden haze about it.

To "deliberately exploit" is certainly to use things or persons rather craftily for one's own advantage. Those words have a bad history, and their connotation is worse than their literal meaning. You must know that I am not an opportunist or a trickster. If you wished to tell the public a few plain truths about me, you could surely have given the job to someone who was not malicious.

A good many reviewers do not like this book very well. Dr. Cross, who reviewed it for Mr. [Henry Seidel] Canby, is, I gather, somewhat disappointed in it. But he has enough scholarship and literary background to see just what I was trying to do, and he gives me credit for an honest effort even though he wishes I had done something else.

An article in this tone, appearing in a magazine of <u>The Forum's</u> standing, does one harm, certainly, as it was intended to do. But I think the hurt it gives my feelings, coming from a publication with which I had always had most pleasant and friendly relations, far outweighs any other harm. This is the first letter of protest I have ever written an editor concerning a review, and I am very sad that it is to you I am addressing it.

Sincerely yours
Willa Cather

TO ALFRED A. KNOPF

September 3 [1931]

Dear Alfred;

With this letter I am sending Miss Aaron two short stories for the volume of which "Neighbor Rosicky" will make a third. I hope that you and Blanche will read them both before Miss Aaron starts out to sell them. "Old Mrs. Harris" is the more interesting, perhaps; but I think "Two Friends" is the best short story I have ever done. It's a little like a picture by [Gustave] Courbet; has that queer romantic sort of realism. It is so 'American' of thirty years ago that when I look it over I quite forget who wrote it. When you do a thing that is so indigenous that the greatest foreign master couldn't have done it, then, it seems to me, you bring home the bacon, even though it's but a sketch—a painter's subject done in a painter's way.

"Mrs. Harris", too, is very Western, and it's much more of a story; but it's the two "business men" I'm proud of.

I sent you a wire about the jacket for the fourth edition. I don't want to play the Atlantic article too hard, and as the third edition jacket will be small type and close set, why not have the fourth made up of short extracts with more space? I wish you would send me a proof of that drawing of a black rock you said you might sometime use on a jacket. It rather struck me at the time, and I'd like to see it again.

I suppose that awful Good Housekeeping portrait is good publicity; it's bringing in a flood of letters from the queerest kind of people, splashy ladies on Park Avenue and farmers' wives in Minnesota, all equally unable to write an English sentence.

Speaking of reviews, the worst I ever got were for "Antonia". I got them from a clipping bureau in those days, and read them. And in the whole United States there were just three enthusiastic ones; Fanny Butcher, Grant Overton in the <u>Sun</u>, and some Philadelphia paper. All the others said it wasn't a good story and it wasn't good English; it was a mass of notes to be read at a Grange meeting and not a book at all. "A Lost Lady" and "Youth and the Bright Medusa" were the only books that got good reviews. This time it's only the New York notices that are spiteful (publicity apropos of degrees and such things always antagonizes a lot of journalists). The papers in the chain of cities across the country are all cordial and friendly, even if they don't like this book as well as others.

With warmest regards to everyone in the office,
Willa Cather

Cather often remembered her reviews, especially of My Ántonia, *as having been much worse than they really were.*

TO MR. ALEXANDER STUART FRERE-REEVES, WILLIAM HEINEMANN, LTD.

September 9 [1931]

Dear Mr. Frere-Reeves;

During the last four months, because of the illness and death of my mother, I have not attended to business correspondence. I tell you this not as an explanation of my decision regarding the English publication of "Shadows on the Rock", but in apology for my discourtesy in not replying to your letters.

I have never had any fault to find with my treatment by the house of Heinemann in the past, and I have never bothered the house with letters urging them to push my books in England. I thought if the books were good the sale would in time take care of itself. But it seemed to me that with this book the time had come to push matters a little. I was disappointed in the terms offered by Heinemann, and the very small advance offered, 250 pounds, as against 750 offered by another publisher. That offer seemed to me to express very little confidence in the book.

The thing that most influenced me to let this book try its fortunes with another publisher was the note of irritation and extreme annoyance in Mr. Evans' letter to Mr. Salzberg. I have never met Mr. Salzberg, but I cannot believe that Alfred Knopf would have a very unreasonable man for his English representative. When there is friction between two publishing houses, it is almost sure to make a certain amount of unpleasantness for the author whose interests depend on the co-operation of the two houses. I am very stupid in business matters, and a business transaction which would be very simple for most people causes me a great deal of worry and indecision. That is why, for years, I have let Alfred Knopf manage my business affairs for me, very largely. He did not, however, attempt to influence me in my decision regarding "Shadows on the Rock". He merely put the correspondence before me. I felt that I would rather have the book go to a publisher who was eager to do his best with it than leave it with Heinemann, where the advance offer was not encouraging and where there seemed to be some antagonism toward me, or Knopf, or both.

As for a collected edition, if Mr. Evans had said he would attend to it in three years, or four years, that would have been definite enough for me, but he was unwilling to set any date.

I have none but the most friendly feelings for Heinemann, and admiration as well. I let this book go elsewhere not because of any dissatisfaction with our relations in the past, but because the terms offered for this particular book indicated that Mr. Evans thought less of its possibilities than I did. Perhaps I made a wrong decision, but, at any rate, I beg you to believe that there is nothing piqued or offended in my attitude, and that my feeling for the house as a great business and a friend to Letters is what it was when I expressed myself fully to you in New York last winter. I did not transfer my books to the Knopf English branch, you will remember, though it would have pleased Alfred, I think. I believed that the time would come when, without interference from me, you would find it advantageous to push my books a little more. With this last book, I thought that time had come. I may, of course, be mistaken. If you are in New York this winter I hope I may have an opportunity to see you.

Very sincerely yours

Willa Cather

P.S. Please excuse the rough form of this letter. I am off on this little island in the Bay of Fundy, without a secretary or typist, and I type very badly.

TO MR. MEROMICHEY

October 5, 1931

My dear Mr. Meromichey:

Thank you for your kind letter. To be quite frank with you, I always shrink a little from the idea of my books being read in schools. At least, I don't like to feel that they are "assigned" to students as a part of the grind. If young people read me, I would like it to be because they want to—I would even like to be read on the sly. But this is not replying to your question. If one of my books has to be read year after year (as "Ivanhoe" was in the days when I went to school), I think that "Death Comes for the Archbishop" will stand the wear and tear better than the others, and perhaps "One of Ours" or "The Professor's House" would be more interesting to the young people than any of the others. "The Professor's House" and Tom Outland's Story seem to be especially popular with German and Scandinavian school boys.

Very sincerely yours,
Willa Cather

TO FANNY BUTCHER

October 14 [1931]
New York City

I was so glad to get your card from Aix-les-Bains. I was up on my Canadian island and glad of everything this summer, until my mother died suddenly in Pasadena, August 31st. Since then life has been a tough pull. A long illness does <u>not</u> prepare one for the end of it.

I'm just back in New York for a few weeks, and one thing you can do for me; which is to send me six copies of your review of my book, which certainly gave me a hand-up when I needed it—made me feel that I had been able to transfer to you the unreasonable and unaccountable glow that all those little details of life in Quebec gave to me. It's like a child's feeling about Christmas—no <u>reason</u> for it, it merely happens to one.

Of course most of the reviewers have cursed and scorned me for what I <u>didn't</u> write! No 'drama', nothing about Indian fights! As if one didn't have a perfect right to love a cream pitcher (of the early Georgian period) better than the Empire State Building. As if one could choose what one would love, anyway, or how one should love it.––––But, as I told you, I did this one to keep me going, and I'm well satisfied if a few old friends like yourself get a little happiness out of it, as I did. I'm just back yesterday—haven't seen Alfred Knopf yet, but he telephoned yesterday that it keeps on selling like anything, 92,000 actual shipments from the office, besides the two Book Clubs. I think that's because he himself liked it, and he and all his staff have worked awfully hard for it. I am so glad <u>you</u> liked it. You're so much like Miss Roullier [?] that I almost feel as if you <u>were</u> French.

Affectionately
Willa Cather

Despite harsh reviews by some of the younger critics—such as Granville Hicks—
*Shadows on the Rock *was a top-selling novel, second only to Pearl S. Buck's *The*
*Good Earth *in 1931.*

TO READ BAIN

October 22, 1931

My dear Mr. Bain:

I have just returned to New York for a few days and your kind letter has been brought to my attention. This, I think, is the second time you have written me, and if we are going to be correspondents, I must beg you to either drop my middle name or spell it correctly. It is not Siebert, but Sibert. (I haven't used it myself for years.)

Yes, of course, most of the reviewers are indignant because I did not write a conventional historical novel with all the great characters up and doing, and behaving themselves in the traditional manner. This does not bother me in the least, and if it bothers the reviewers, I only wish they would write the kind of book they like about old Quebec. It is a subject open to all—has been standing there for three hundred years.

No, I am not a Catholic, and I do not think I shall become one. On the other hand, I do not regard the Roman Church merely as "artistic material". If the external form and ceremonial of that Church happens to be more beautiful than that of other churches, it certainly corresponds to some beautiful vision within. It is sacred, if for no other reason than that is the faith that has been most loved by human creatures, and loved over the greatest stretch of centuries.

Very cordially yours,
Willa Cather

➵ ➴

*While *Shadows on the Rock *was selling, Cather was thinking about her next book, *Obscure Destinies, *a collection of three stories. One of those stories, "Old Mrs. Harris," was first published in the *Ladies' Home Journal *under the title "Three Women"; it appeared there serially starting with the September 1932 issue. The following letter seems to be a transcription made by Knopf staff.*

TO MANLEY AARON, ALFRED A. KNOPF, INC.

October 27, 1931

My dear Miss Aaron,

I notice that in his very cordial letter Mr. [George Horace] Lorimer speaks of the story they have just bought for the Journal as "Old Miz Harris." Please call his attention to the fact that this is a very small variation from my text but it is an important one. In the first place it sounds as though the story were a Southern dialect story, which it isn't. In the second place it gives to anyone acquainted with the South a very wrong impression of the old lady's social status. Poor mountain people would certainly call her "Miz" but her neighbors and people of her own station would always call her "Mrs." and that is the designation of her respectable middle class position.

I hope of course, that the editors will be careful to see that there is no change in the text anywhere without my consent.

Yours sincerely,

[No signature present]

→ ←

M. A. DeWolfe Howe, author and editor of Memories of a Hostess, *wrote Cather in October of 1931 to ask if she might reconsider her earlier suggestion that he destroy the letters she wrote to Annie Adams Fields. The Fields materials in Howe's possession were now to be obtained by the Huntington Library in Pasadena, California, and he thought Cather might want to reconsider her previous position.*

TO M. A. DEWOLFE HOWE

November 11, 1931

My dear Mr. Howe:

Yes indeed, I beg you to destroy all my letters before you dispose of Mrs. Fields' correspondence. There are very special reasons why I wish this to be done.

In the first place, those letters are entirely artificial and unrepresentative of me. Your feeling that they might be of some guidance to a future biographer is mistaken; they would only mislead him. Mrs. Fields was so new a type in my experience that I was never at ease in writing to her. I was always afraid of touching upon one of her prejudices, or in some way letting the noisy, modern world in upon her. So I always tried to write her long sentences that meant nothing. I remember perfectly well how I used to struggle to fill out a few pages and say nothing at all.

Of course, when I was with Mrs. Fields herself, I never felt any constraint; in fact, there were few people with whom one could be so unguarded. That was because she was the soloist and I the accompanist. How delightful it was to have her look up from the morning paper and ask gravely: "My dear, who is this Rex Beach, has he to do with letters?"

But there was none of this genuineness and spontaneous pleasure in my letters to Mrs. Fields. They were written from a sense of duty—just because she enjoyed opening the morning mail. So if you will just put them in the furnace, I shall be greatly obliged to you.

Always faithfully yours,
Willa Cather

P.S. It has just occurred to me that the most satisfactory arrangement would be to ask you to send the letters in question to me, at the Grosvenor Hotel, 35 Fifth Avenue, New York, where I shall be stopping for a week or ten days. I will glance at them, and if there are any that seem to be more than mere formal evasion, I will return them to you for your collection.

Though it is unknown how many letters Howe had, he did send them to Cather to look over, and four letters from Cather to Fields are now found in the collections of the Huntington Library.

TO FERRIS GREENSLET

November 26 [1931]

Dear Mr. Greenslet;

I'd be very pleased if you did get out a new edition [of *Song of the Lark*], with a new jacket minus the Breton picture. I'm just leaving for a family reunion in Red Cloud, and could not possibly write a preface now. I've thought a good deal about prefaces, Knopf suggested one for a certain book of his, and I've decided not to write any more prefaces at all. They stimulate a temporary interest and curiosity, but in the long run they are a mistake, for an author still living and still working. I shall leave various comments on some of my books, out of which you can make prefaces after my decease.

If the writers of various novels I like had written prefaces to them, it would rather spoil the books for me. I think even stupid people like to puzzle over a book. A slight element of mystery is a great asset. The explanation of the "Archbishop" which I wrote for The Commonweal has been much used and quoted; but it would be a great mistake to use it as a preface to the book. It is too much like selling my own goods. One has to follow one's instinct in these matters, for that is the only guide one has. I know you will not misunderstand my refusal. I don't mean to be disobliging, and I am glad to help my publishers in any way that seems to me the right way <u>for me</u>. I am sure, for instance, that the article I wrote for the Colophon ["My First Novels (There Were Two)," published in June 1931], which has been so much quoted, stimulated interest in "O Pioneers" and "Antonia". Indirect methods are the best, I am sure.

I have not a copy of "The Song of the Lark" at hand, but I think of one change I beg you to make. Leave the dedication to Isabelle McClung, but please cut out the limping verse which follows it,—an idiotic attempt to immitate the metre of Walther's 'Prize Song' [from Richard Wagner's opera *Die Meistersinger von Nürnberg*].

Yes, the new book is doing wonderfully well. I really think the feeling in Knopf's office had a lot to do with it. They were all keener about it than about any other book of mine, even the salesmen. Mr. Stimson thought better of it than I did, a good deal. I turned in the first two-thirds of the manuscript to him when the Knopfs were abroad. I was feeling rather low about it, and he gave me a tremendous hand-up. I could see at once that it was personal, not publishing, enthusiasm. He and his staff did a lot for it.

Faithfully yours
Willa Cather

PART NINE

A Troubled Time

1932–1936

It's a brutal fact, Zoe, that after one is 45, it simply rains death, all about one, and after you've passed fifty, the storm grows fiercer. I never open the morning paper without seeing the death of someone I used to know, East or West, staring me in the face. And in the days when I first knew you, people didn't use to die at all; the obituary page never had the slightest connection with our personal life. Death just becomes a deep, be-numbing fact in one's life long before it ends one.

—WILLA CATHER TO ZOË AKINS, November 21, 1932

Willa Cather in 1936. Photograph by Carl Van Vechten

IN 1932, Cather published *Obscure Destinies*, a group of three stories set in the west—"Neighbor Rosicky," "Old Mrs. Harris," and "Two Friends"— that are among her best-loved fiction. "Old Mrs. Harris" is highly autobiographical, featuring a family much like the Cathers in a town much like Red Cloud, Nebraska. It is a deeply moving story that could only be published after the death of Cather's mother, for the character inspired by Virginia Boak Cather, Victoria Templeton, is complex and not altogether attractive. Three years later, in 1935, Cather published her eleventh novel, *Lucy Gayheart*, about a young musician from the West. She described the book as "modern, western, very romantic, non-Catholic." The central character of *Lucy Gayheart* is in many ways a darker counterpoint to the triumphant Thea Kronborg of Cather's 1915 novel *The Song of the Lark*. In 1936, her first book of nonfiction prose appeared, a collection of essays titled *Not Under Forty*. The preface to that volume, which claimed that the book was "for the backward, and by one of their number," signaled Cather's growing sense of emotional and intellectual isolation from the contemporary world. And yet she felt such isolation while also living as one of the most famous and celebrated authors of the day, one who attracted many fan letters and inquiries from people around the world.

→ ←

In February of 1932, Ferris Greenslet wrote Cather trying to convince her to sell the motion picture rights to The Song of the Lark. *He thought she might get as much as $15,000 to $25,000. He pointed out very politely that Houghton Mifflin* *was contractually able to sell the rights to the novel without her approval should they wish to.*

TO FERRIS GREENSLET

March 13 [1932]

Dear Mr. Greenslet;

If you can get a very high price for the film rights of "The Song of the Lark" I'll consent to the sale. But I wish you would send me a letter, signed by several members of the firm, assuring me that you will never ask me to consider a film proposition <u>for "Antonia"</u>. I would like to feel entirely safe where that book is concerned. You can do this for me, can't you?

I don't for a minute believe that a film production would do more than give the sale of the book a temporary punch. The production of "A Lost Lady" brought in hundreds of letters from illiterate and sloppy people, which gave me a low opinion of "movie" audiences.

I notice that you are advertising the new edition very handsomely, and I hope it will bring you a good return. Please let me know if you are in New York before the end of April, as I expect to be here until then.

Faithfully yours
Willa Cather

TO HELEN MCNENY SPRAGUE

March 20 [1932]

My Dear Helen;

We have had all our winter since I got back! I don't mind—I like a long, cold spring. I was so glad to get your letter, and to hear that your father [Bernard McNeny] and Louise had been punished for laughing at us. I hope they got good and cold, too!

I've been going to lots of concerts and operas since my influenza left me. I do hope we can hear some music together some day. I'd love to take you to some of my favorite operas. I've not seen as much of Virginia as usual, though we manage to get together once a week, at least. Tonight she is to dine with me at Sherry's. Last Saturday we lunched together and went shopping.

Oh Helen I am in dispair about the Lindbergh's baby! I don't believe they will ever see it again. The New Jersey & New York police magnates meet and "deplore the situation" and then go out to lunch. If I were the Lindberghs, I'd just go and live in another country where the right to privacy is recognized. Here they steal your baby and ruin your life and trample on all your decent feelings.

Don't you let anybody kidnap young Sprague when he arrives. I'll be awfully keen about him, and I know you'll bring him up in a natural, easy, unsentimental way, without making a martyr of yourself or a victim of him. Oh these pale, wistful looking plants that have grown up under the shadow of the heavy-weight "mother love" pose! You weren't brought up that way, and that was why you were such a dear child and such a pleasure to us all.

With love to you & your mother
Willa Cather

→ ←

On September 1, 1931 (see above), Cather had written to Leach, the editor of Forum, *complaining about a review by Granville Hicks that she considered unusually harsh.*

TO HENRY GODDARD LEACH

May 25, 1932

My dear Dr. Leach:

Both of your letters eventually reached me, and I thank you for bearing my hurt feelings in mind. The review about which I wrote you was the only review that ever gave me a case of hurt feelings; and my grievance was entirely a personal one. I mean by that that I was hurt as a person, not as a writer. I had always looked upon The Forum as personally friendly to me in this City where personal friendships have almost ceased to exist under the rush of business relations. I felt that such a review was not at all in the line of 'controversy', since a writer cannot with any shred of dignity defend his own work.

But I am the last person in the world to suffer very long from a case of wounded vanity or to brood upon it. I have long ago forgotten my surprise and indignation, and I beg you to forget that I was for a moment indignant. I am just leaving New York for Canada but if I am in the City next winter, please let us have tea together and drink to Mr. Hicks—if that was his name.

Very cordially yours,
Willa Cather

→ ←

The original version of the following letter has not been found, but two slightly differing transcriptions, probably made by Knopf or his staff, have survived in the Knopf papers. Where there are minor differences between the two, we have privileged the one dated by the transcriber July 12, 1967, which seems to evince greater fidelity to transcriptional details.

TO ALFRED A. KNOPF

June 20 [1932]

Dear Alfred:

If I had been told that one of my friends was soon to die, your father [Samuel Knopf] would have been almost the last for whom death seemed possible—unless in an accident of some kind. He simply seemed to me one of the strongest people I knew, in body and in purpose. (I am astonished to learn his age.) I didn't see him very often during a winter, but I always felt he was "there", in a very positive sense, and even five minutes with him invariably set me up. I had absolute confidence in him. He was my kind—by that I mean that he was one of the persons whom I admire, respect, understand, at once and without reservation, by instinct. There are not many of the younger men in whom I feel that kind of confidence; that in art, or business, or merely in human behavior, they will always <u>see</u> that the straight thing and the crooked thing are not the same, even if they do not shout about it. That mere perception is the thing that counts: without it human life would be too unutterably dull and filthy. If all the great "loyalties" are utter lies—why then, they are simply ever so much better than the truth. And that was what brought ideals out of the dung heap in the first place—because creatures weren't content with dung, though it is always there and, in a sense, more "real". I don't mean to be writing you this way, but you are, thank God, one of those few younger men in whom I do believe. Though in you it takes a different form than in your father, in its essence it's the same quality. I think it's the best thing you got from him, and I hope you'll always cherish it. (If you don't you'll be unhappy, I can tell you that!) I don't expect you to be a reformer, I merely expect you to preserve intact and to make better still that delicate instrument inside one which knows the cheap from the fine. The recognition of the really fine is simply one of the richest pleasures in life.

When I began this letter I did not foresee that it would take this turn (rather sermon-ish) but I usually write as I feel, and the shock of your father's death brings up the old question:—What do I really admire in people, and what is worth saving in a time when so much is being scrapped. But we needn't save it: it has an artful dodge of saving itself. It has survived all the "realities" and "discoveries" and has been through times much worse than ours. It can well rest a hundred years or two.

With my love and sympathy and confidence,
Willa Cather

→ ←

Cather's story "Two Friends" was first published in the Woman's Home Companion *in July 1932 with illustrations by Walter Everett. The magazine paid her $3,500 for it. One of the central characters, R. E. Dillon, was inspired by Carrie Miner Sherwood's father, James L. Miner.*

TO CARRIE MINER SHERWOOD

July 4 [1932]

My Dear Carrie;

I don't know if "Two Friends" is out yet, but I saw proofs of it before I left New York and ever since have wanted to prepare you for the dreadful illustrations. The editor gives a western story to some nut who has never been west of Hoboken, and who thinks that all Western men are rough-necks. I hate publishing stories in magazines, anyway, and only do it because they pay me very well.

Elsie wrote that when she went through Red Cloud the home yard looked lovely; I wish I could see it. Our little place here is so green and fresh this year, and though it is so primative and has no bath room, we find it very comfortable. I have invited Mary Virginia [Auld] to spend her month's vacation as my guest here. I expect her the middle of July. I shall put her up at the little colony about a quarter of a mile across the pine woods, where I used to stay before I had a house and where we still go for our meals. She will have more freedom there than here, and she can run down here when she wishes. There is not much gaiety here, but I hope she will enjoy the beauty of the place.

Please tell Helen Mac. [McNeny] that I was delighted to get her letter about young Bernard [Sprague]. I have just unpacked and oiled my typewriter, so you must pardon a messy, oily letter. When you think of it, Carrie, please send me the letter from Borneo, and that from the nice priest, I sent you some time ago; I am trying to file some of my papers up here.

I do hope you and Mary liked "Two Friends", at least that there was nothing in it that struck you as false. It is not meant to be a portrait of the two men, but a picture of something that they suggested to a child.

With love always
Willie

→ ←

The version of "Two Friends" published in Woman's Home Companion *included a description of an astronomical event called, in the story, a "transit of Venus." William Lyon Phelps, a professor of English at Yale University, promptly wrote telling Cather that the proper term for what the characters witness is an "occultation of Venus." The following was a Western Union telegram.*

TO ALFRED A. KNOPF

July 30 [1932]
Grand Manan Island
CHANGE TRANSIT TO OCCULTATION STOP I SAW IT WHATEVER IT WAS

WILLA CATHER

TO WILLIAM LYON PHELPS

August 16 [1932]
Grand Manan Island
Dear Mr. Phelps;
I am everlastingly grateful to you for calling my attention to my astronomical blunder. I knew that in the summer of 1893, sitting on a board sidewalk in a little Nebraska town, I did see the planet Venus go behind the moon and reappear. The neighbors said it was a "transit" of Venus. When I wrote the story last year, I could easily have checked up on this point, but I knew I had seen the planet behave in such a manner, and it did not occur to me that I had better make sure that I was giving the correct name to its behaviour.

Since your letter was forwarded to me I have had the matter looked up by the Knopf office, and we find that there was an occultation of Venus in the summer of 1893. The correction has been made in the second printing; your kindly letter will probably save me from writing many letters to indignant scientists, and has saved me from making the same blunder in the English edition; we cabled Cassells at once to make the change.

Very gratefully yours
Willa Cather

Knopf published Obscure Destinies *in August 1932. Unusually, "Old Mrs. Harris" was published in a magazine after the book appeared—in the* Ladies' Home Journal *of September, October, and November 1932, under the title "Three Women." For this long story, she was paid very well indeed: $15,000.*

➤ ✦

Cather's friend Zoë Akins married the British set and costume designer Hugo Rumbold in 1932, at age forty-six.

TO ZOË AKINS

September 16 [1932]
Jaffrey, New Hampshire

My Very Dear Zoë;

I am so glad to have a letter from you! Of course, marriage is always a gamble, except with children of eighteen, perhaps, who learn everything together—and therefore never learn much but how to get on with each other. But the worst thing is to be bored to death by a smiling, pale personality—and you have escaped that fate by a wide margin, I gather! What with a new husband and a new house, you ought to find life pretty interesting. The pictures of the house reached me at Grand Manan, Canada, and I got a great thrill out of them. I was able to pick out many of the changes you have made. Most of all I loved the picture of that heavenly room with so little in it, so that one felt the room itself and not an assemblage of things. It surely requires a much finer sense of form to make a room without things than with them—also, I imagine, more money. It's the proper spaces that are expensive, in any art. I love Green Fountains for a name. It's so very different from other "place names".

I'm awfully glad you like Mrs. Harris. Of course that's much the best of the three. The right things came together in the right relation, I thought. You know the types, but I wonder what it can mean to people who don't know the charming and untruthful South.—

I'm going back to New York next week, and will be at the Grosvenor while I look for an apartment. I almost hope I won't find an apartment! Zoë, I've just happened to read "Colomba" [by Prosper Mérimée] over, very slowly. What [a] beautiful and splendidly poised thing it is: the most terrific happenings slide easily and noiselessly into the narrative, <u>as they always do in life</u>, when the stage is never set for the moment that uplifts us or destroys us. The un-expectedness of life is what makes it interesting; the events are logical, but we never see the cause and effect until after the events have happened. That quality of unexpected developments which are at the same time logical, has almost disappeared from modern writing. I wish I could get rid of "atmosphere" and be another kind of writer for awhile. I'm tired of being my kind!

My love to you, dear Zoë.
Willa

TO THOMAS MASARYK

September 23 [1932]
Jaffrey, New Hampshire

Dear President Masaryk;

Some weeks ago I wrote my publisher to send you my new book. I could not autograph it, for I was then travelling in a remote part of Canada. The book has probably reached you before this, and if you have had leisure to read it you probably agree with me that one of the stories at least, "Old Mrs. Harris", strikes a more authentic note than the Quebec story I sent you a year ago. A book which grows out of admiration and study never has the authentic ring of a book that grows out of early experiences. Nevertheless, I do believe in a rotation of crops,—in writing as well as in agriculture.

You asked me, after I sent you the Quebec story, whether I were on the road to becoming a Catholic. By no means! I do, however, admire the work of the Catholic missionary priests on this continent.

I find I have a copy of a letter I wrote Governor Cross of Connecticut, after his review of the book appeared. I am enclosing it, as an explanation of how I happened to write "Shadows on the Rock". The work of the French Catholic missionaries was unique in that they brought with them a kind of culture and a way of living. These endure to this day—in the Province of Quebec, at least.

Please let me say in closing that your interest in my books is one of the most deeply satisfying things that have come to me as a writer. I don't believe they would have caught your attention if there were not something genuine and indigenous in them. The longer I live the more I feel that I am willing to be ever so little, if only I can be ever so true.

Faithfully yours
Willa Cather

TO JOHN SEXTON KENNEDY

November 1, 1932

My dear Mr. Kennedy;

I am sorry if I wrote you an unenthusiastic letter a year ago; but sometimes when one has to reply to a great many letters at one sitting, one's enthusiasm does get pumped rather dry, you know. I surely can thank you very warm heartedly for your appreciation of the stories in "Obscure Destinies". Those three stories are, every one of them, very near to my heart, for personal reasons. Moreover, I want to do all I can to overcome the provincial American prejudice against stories of that length. This is the only country in which stories of that length are dismissed rather lightly as minor pieces, simply because they are short. It is the custom here to rank a novel like the "Arrow of Gold", which is distinctly Conrad's second best, as more important than a masterpiece like "Youth", which could scarcely be better than it is—and which, of course, would have been quite ruined had he tried to expand it into a long narrative.

The long short story has always held such a dignified and important place in French literature that I wish it might command that same position in our own country.

No, it does not distress me at all to hear that a young man in Baltimore is working on a thesis, but if you know him, I suggest that you warn him to approach his subject in a more rational manner than that employed by young Mr. MacNamara, whose article ["Phases of American Religion in Thornton Wilder and Willa Cather"] in the [May 1932] Catholic World you may have seen. It is absurd to measure "spiritual growth", or even intellectual growth, chronologically. Our great enlightenments always come in flashes. The spirit of man has its ups and downs like his body, and the Roman Church of all others, it seems to me, has always had the wisdom and the kindliness to realize that instability in us.

Very cordially yours,
Willa Cather

TO ZOË AKINS

November 21 [1932]

My Darling Zoë;

I have just come back from the country and find your telegram, and the account of Hugo's death in the Sunday papers. What a dreadful shock for you, to have a big strong man go out like that! It makes one catch one's breath to think of it. Wasn't it fortunate that you had that jolly honeymoon together in Mexico, since this was going to happen? But why did it happen so soon,—less than a year after you were married. It's a brutal fact, Zoe, that after one is 45, it simply rains death, all about one, and after you've passed fifty, the storm grows fiercer. I never open the morning paper without seeing the death of someone I used to know, East or West, staring me in the face.

And in the days when I first knew you, people didn't use to die at all; the obituary page never had the slightest connection with our personal life. Death just becomes a deep, be-numbing fact in one's life long before it ends one.

Keep up your routine, dear Zoë, keep your life going as you've always done: you'll be less lonely that way than if you sit and think about things. And, just for the time, cut out alcohol. One's very apt to over do that when one is hard hit, and no ordinary human being can keep up with Jobyna [Howland] without disasterous results. I'm <u>not</u> knocking Jobyna, but she is rather spacious in capacity, as she is in size. I wish I could run out to see you for a week, but I've come back to town with a rather bad eye, (which now has a bandage on it) otherwise very well. I've just signed a lease for an apartment at 570 Park Ave. but I won't be moving for several weeks yet—can't even think of it until my eye clears up. It's merely a slight infection, but painful. I'll soon get the better of it. Do get the most you can out of your house and mind and thoughts. Personal life is rather a failure, <u>always</u>; biologically so. But something rather nice does happen in the mind itself as one grows older. If it hasn't begun with you yet, keep your courage, <u>it will happen</u>. A kind of golden light comes as a compensation for many losses. You'll see!! I wish I could have saved you this hard knock, my dear.

Willa

TO JENNIE C. MORSE CARSTENS

November 21, 1932

My dear Mrs. Carstens:

Of course, I have not time to reply to all the letters that come in to me; it is rather an unfair contest in correspondence, one against many.

But your letter has a nice friendly, neighborly ring that makes me wish to answer it, though it lay on my desk a long time unread while I was traveling. On reading it I feel as if I had been to a Sunday evening service in my own town of Red Cloud and heard some one talk about somebody's books—not mine. You say you wonder why I have never written anything sympathetic about religion, and this rather astonishes me. I have had so many, many letters from clergymen, both Protestant and Catholic, telling me that they find a very strong religious theme in at least two of my books.

Perhaps you think that because "Death Comes for the Archbishop" is about the work of Catholic missionaries, it is not concerned with religion as you know it.

Now, my dear lady, I am not a Roman Catholic. I am an Episcopalian, as were my father and mother. Bishop Beecher of Hastings, Nebraska, confirmed me. I am a Protestant, but not a narrow minded one. If you make a fair minded study of history you cannot be narrow. What organization was it that kept the teachings of Jesus Christ alive between the year 300 A.D. and the days of Martin Luther? I am sure that your minister will admit that nothing but a powerful organization could have brought the beliefs of the early church across to us through the anarchy and brutality that followed the fall of the Roman Empire.

This is a rather solemn and pedantic reply to your pleasant and neighborly letter, but I do think all Christians ought to know a little more history before they decide that there is only one kind of religion. I am sure I need not tell you, dear Mrs. Carstens, that this letter is entirely personal and confidential, and is not for quotation or publication. I have no objection, however, to your showing it to your minister; perhaps he can prove to me that there were "Protestant" churches before Martin Luther, but I have never yet been able to find any convincing evidence that there were.

Very sincerely yours,
Willa Cather

❧ ❦

The five peripatetic years Cather and Edith Lewis spent with no home address but the Grosvenor Hotel ended in the late fall of 1932 when they moved into an apartment at 570 Park Avenue, Cather's last address in New York. That year also saw the publication of Mary Austin's memoir Earth Horizon, *in which she criticized Cather for celebrating French priests in* Death Comes for the Archbishop, *a book Cather partially wrote in Austin's house.*

TO MABEL DODGE LUHAN

November 22 [1932]
Grosvenor Hotel, New York City

Dear Mabel;

Great news—we have at last taken an apartment, and are terribly busy fitting it up. I got back from Canada October 10th, but had to dash out to Chicago almost at once. I came back and signed the lease and began shopping for rugs and curtains, then had to go to Chicago again! But now most of the shopping is done, furniture got out of storage and set in place, cabinet-makers at work on bookshelves etc. We are staying right on at the Grosvenor and set-tling the new place slowly. Edith is desperately busy at the office, and if I shop for more than a few hours at a time I buy the most absurd things. We expect to move in about two weeks from now.

<u>What</u> do you think of Mrs. Austin's book? It's amazing how everybody mis-understood her and nobody ever "got the point". It's a big job to set out to be a genius in this ruthless age when even kings have to watch their step and pay their tailor bills. As for my base conduct—you know why I went to the house for a few hours every day for about a week—merely to be polite. I had two perfectly good rooms at La Fonda. And how the devil could I help it that the first archbishops of New Mexico were French? As I don't wear a Spanish comb in my hair I didn't mind it a bit that Bishop Lamy was a Frenchman.

H. G. Wells threatened H. & M. [Houghton Mifflin, publishers of *Earth Horizon*] with a libel suit, sent furious cables, and they had to knock out his confession on Hampstead Heath and make new plates, but some thirty thou-sand had already got out.

Have you read Hemingway's book [*Death in the Afternoon*]—of course you have. Don't you find it quite stunning? I don't see us getting to Mexico this winter. I simply <u>have</u> to have a dwelling place and my own books and things about me. <u>Then</u> I can travel in comfort and not feel like a tramp. Edith has wanted to write to you for a long while, but holding an important business job in N.Y. these days means working like fury. I hope she'll resign soon. She had a good long summer in Canada, about four months. At Grand Manan, and at Jaffrey N.H. where I spent two weeks, all my friends were reading "Lorenzo" [Luhan's *Lorenzo in Taos*]. I'd have been bothered to death by the curious, so I shut 'em off by saying you had said what you wanted to say, and I had no authority to add an oral appendix.

Please write me again before you go away. I'm awfully excited about getting an apartment.

With love
Willa

New address is 570 Park Avenue
(That's at the corner of Park & 63rd, just behind the Colony Club)

➤ ❮

In the early 1930s, many of Cather's old friends in Webster County, Nebraska, were, like most Americans, facing economic hardship.

TO CARRIE MINER SHERWOOD

Sunday [December 11, 1932?]
Grosvenor Hotel, New York City

Dearest Carrie;

Thank you for sending the book of reviews so promptly. Alfred Knopf wanted to use some extracts from them. They got here in plenty of time.

Now I want you to relieve my mind a little. The enclosed letter tells its own sad story.

1st Won't the Bladen bank come back and pay at least part of what it owes its depositors?

2nd What about the Inavale bank?

Why in thunder don't these people bank with Walter [Sherwood]—where they have a chance? What's the matter with the Lambrechts?

Now will you be my Santa Claus? I want them to have a good Christmas dinner. I know they won't buy prunes or dried apricots, they felt too poor to get them last year.

Please have Mrs. Burden pack a box:

2 dozen of the best oranges,
3 pounds of dates,
5 pounds best prunes
3 cans Texas figs
3 pounds cranberries
3 bunches celery
1 peck red apples

If there is any money left over after you get these things, get some Butternut coffee—I <u>know</u> they will cut the old lady down on her coffee, so put whatever is left into coffee.

I've already sent Mrs. Lambrecht a Christmas box, a lovely sweater and a lot of toys, but that was before I got Lydia's letter.

I'm sitting in the middle of a pile of trunks, dear Carrie. We move today. I think the new apartment will be lovely, but I'd have waited another year if I'd known so many of my old friends were going to be hard hit. I do want to help.

Lovingly
Willie

New address:
570 Park Avenue
(not far from [Mary] Virginia, I'm glad to say!
Roscoe's Virginia is to spend the Christmas holidays with me.

TO FERRIS GREENSLET

[Around December 29, 1932]

Dear Mr. Greenslet;

Excuse old machine,—only one at hand.

This morning I received from a Miss Hahn, with no sort of letter or apology, a barbarously reconstructed version of "Antonia." You spoke to me of using a portion of the book, some twenty pages; you did not mention such a horror as a skeletonized version of the whole novel. The lady has tried to make it a story of action; now it was never meant to be a story of action.

I had decided, after your talk with me, to allow your educational department to use the first thirty pages of the book, minus the introduction. If it would be an accommodation to you, personally, I would still be willing to allow that, on condition that there shall be no cuts at all in the text, and that this lady shall not write the introduction.

Can't we just drop the whole matter, anyway? You tell me they want something of 'mine'. Then your educators go and make this text as much like Zane Grey as possible. The reconstruction by Miss Hahn has neither Zane Grey's merits nor mine.

Really, my dear F.G., you've never treated "Antonia" very gallantly. You are always trying to do her in and make her cheap. (That's exaggeration, of course, but I'm really very much annoyed.) And you know how you've suggested cheap editions, film possibilities, etc. Antonia has done well enough by her publishers <u>as she is</u>, not in the cut rate drugstores or re-written by Miss Hahn. She made her way by being what she is, not by being the compromise her publishers have several times tried to make her. Even a cut in price would be a compromise in the case of that particular book, I think. And as to a cut in text, reducing the whole book to some few thousand words—! Those horrible boil-downs of "Notre Dame de Paris" and "Adam Bede" which are handed out to children are poison, as you well know.

I'm in my new house, but not unpacked, hence this untidy machine letter.

You see I don't want to go into a book that is made up of reconstructions of this kind, where the text is boiled down. It doesn't give youngsters even a chance to come in contact with the writing personality of a single one of the writers presented to them in this packing-house form. I think it's the lowest trick ever put over on young people.

Enraged though I am, I'm still your very good friend, and I send you good New Year wishes from my heart. Only let me hear no more of Miss Hahn and her stupid, brutal trade.

Faithfully (and affectionately) yours
Willa Cather

My new apartment will be ever so nice when it's done.

TO ZOË AKINS

New Year's Eve [December 31, 1932]
570 Park Avenue, New York City

My Darling Zoë;

On Christmas Eve, when the two little nieces were sitting before the fire and the new apartment was trimmed with greens, Josephine [Bourda] (the same old Josephine) came in bearing a tall tree all blossoming with spring, and announced "Un pommier, mademoiselle. Il faut faire les apple-pies!" ["It's an apple tree, miss. We can bake apple pies!"] Thorley must have sent the best he had for you, and the sudden advent of such a spring-time thing had something quite magical about it. There was just the right place for it, against my new french damask curtains, of which I am awfully proud. It is just as graciously blooming on New Year's eve as it was on Xmas eve, and I know you'd be glad for all the pleasure I've had from it.

Yes, the same Josephine! You must remember her, the big frenchwoman who was such a good cook. Last winter I heard by chance that her husband was very ill and her two daughters out of work, so I sent her a check to cover hospital expenses. When I took this apartment I sent for her to help me arrange things. She has not been in service since she left me, but she says she'd like to stay on, and God grant she may continue to feel thus. Such food, my dear, as she gives me! It's very amusing—I find I learned most everything in "Shadows on the Rock" from five years of Josephine! And I, conceited donkey, found that knowledge of pots and pans there in my head when I needed it (french pots and pans, which are very different) and I never gave a thought as to why I found myself able to write about french household economics with ease and conviction.

Well, tomorrow begins a new year. I wish you might have had it with your Hugo, dear Zoe. But really, our measurements of time are foolish—correct for business officers only—In our real, personal lives a week is often longer than ten years. I remember one summer that was longer than the twenty-five years that have followed it. Personal life can't be measured by the calendar. So I wish you a New Year full of growth and the best things that help one over hard places.

Lovingly
Willa

❧ ❦

The February 1933 issue of Atlantic Monthly *published Cather's essay "A Chance Meeting," which told the story of Cather's serendipitous 1930 meeting with Madame Grout, the niece of Gustave Flaubert, in Aix-les-Bains, France.*

TO DOROTHY CANFIELD FISHER

January 11 [1933]
570 Park Avenue, New York City

[Written in the top margin:] Telephone Regent 4–8354

My dear Dorothy;

It has been so long since I have written a letter because I wanted to that I scarcely know how to go about it. I've never even thanked you for your telegram last Christmas, or told you that the two winter months at home in the old house, among the old neighbors were more perfect than things often are—they meant more than years and years of life in other places. This winter I've at last found and taken a quiet apartment, got my things out of storage, and I think I'm going to love it when the long grind of "settling" is over. Edith Lewis is with me, and I have the same frenchwoman from the Basque country whom I had all through the war. When you are next in town won't you please make a date with me and come to see me—for tea if you can.

I want you to look in the February <u>Atlantic</u> for an account of a delightful adventure which will mean more to you than to most people who read it. I couldn't tell all the story without saying too much about myself—but you already know what I did not include. Wasn't it funny that it happened to me? I so well remember when I began to read Flaubert in Red Cloud, and when I dug through <u>Salammbô</u> and all the Letters with George Seibel, the German proofreader in Pittsburgh. Do read the Letters to Caroline over again! <u>What</u> a wonderful woman. For those few thrilling days at Aix-les Bains I had the whole group of her time in my two hands—they were more real than anything on earth to me. No work of art can recall and reproduce a period as a living human person can—if it's the right person.

I'm as well as anybody could be who went through moving in the Christmas shopping storm, with a Wyoming niece [Virginia Cather] on my hands for her college vacation. I parked her at a dear little hotel, and greatly enjoyed the time I could spend with her. I got off all my Christmas boxes to my old women on the farms out west. For three of them, thank God, I have been able to save their farms by paying their interest. About nothing ever gave me such pleasure as being able to help them keep their land—the land they've worked on since I was ten years old!

Now I've got to go to a business meeting, but I've had half an hour with you, anyway. I'm so glad you liked <u>Mrs. Harris</u>. I fussed with it a little, but I got very nearly the tone I was trying for.

With love always, even if I write so seldom.

Willa

❧ ☙

On February 2, 1933, Cather was ceremoniously awarded the first Prix Femina Americain for Shadows on the Rock. *The book was selected by French and American committees, and the presentation of the prize was made by the poet Edna St. Vincent Millay.*

TO IRENE MINER WEISZ

Thursday [January 1933?]

Dearest Irene;

The news won't be out until next week, but Alfred has just telephoned me that the Prix Femina (PRIX FEMINA) has been awarded to me for "Shadows", and that the French Ambassador will give a luncheon for me in New York, and that I'll <u>have</u> to go—or take a train for California! What a life!—when I want so much to give my time to the apartment. This will mean interviews, letters, telegrams etc, etc. Just at this time it's a real calamity. Meanwhile, it's a secret between you and me and Mr. Wise [Weisz] until you see it in the papers.

Lovingly

W.

❧ ☙

On May 28, 1933, Dorothy Canfield Fisher published a profile of Cather in the New York Herald Tribune *called "Daughter of the Frontier." The next letter anticipates the article.*

TO DOROTHY CANFIELD FISHER

[Probably early 1933]

My Dearest Dorothy;

Of course I'd rather have you do such an article than anyone else, and they've been after me through several people who knew nothing at all about me. I'm fairly sick of this legend of a pale creature who has sacrificed her life to art. I never in my life made a sacrifice to 'art'. Even as to teaching, I simply taught because I found it less distasteful than newspaper work. All my life I've shoved away the less agreeable for the more agreeable. The things that really attracted me were so much more attractive that I never found it at all hard to push aside the minor attractions, even when they were very pleasant. I've lead a life of self-indulgence, if ever anybody did. I wanted to see the world a bit and meet all sorts of people, so I spent five years on McClure's doing it. When I'd had enough, I stopped. I expect I've spent as much time hearing music as most people spend on their profession———pure self indulgence. This is the truth, you know. So please don't make me either noble or pathetic. Of course, in youth, when one is poor, one struggles; but what else is youth for? If one were rich and buried under tutors and 'advantages', there would be another kind of struggle. And I never shut myself away from the people I cared for, you know that. I shut out the crowd to be 'all there' with my friends.

Hastily but lovingly
Willa

→ ←

Cather's repeated claims that she was born in 1876, as in the letter below, misrepresent her actual birth date of December 7, 1873.

TO DOROTHY CANFIELD FISHER

[February 16, 1933]

My Dear Dorothy;

You've certainly done this operation as gently as it could be done, and you've been noble about keeping away from trivial personal stories,—of which you could tell so many! I've corrected two dates; I was born December 7, 1876.

Any summing up of one's books sounds strange to one, because one was never conscious of doing things consistently,—each book seemed a totally new thing, an escape, indeed, from the others. But if there is a common denominator, it is Escape, and you've hit on it. When I get on a Santa Fe train now and swing west to the coast, I often waken in my berth with that glorious feeling I had in childhood, the certainty of countless miles of empty country and open sky and wind and night on every side of me. It's the happiest feeling I ever have. And when I am most enjoying the lovely thing[s] the world is full of, it's then I am often most homesick for just that emptiness and that untainted air.

I'm rushing this back to you with my deepest th[a]nks for your protecting arm.

Lovingly
Willa

→ ←

Smith College wished to bestow an honorary degree on Cather in June 1933, when her niece Virginia Cather was to graduate.

TO ROSCOE CATHER

April 3 [1933]
New York City

My Dear Boy;

Your letter came just in time. When I found I could not get a room at the Northampton Inn, I was seriously thinking of going down to Bermuda and side-stepping the Smith Commencement. (I won't stay with Professors and help them pay off their social debts, you know.) But since you think Virginia would be disappointed, I will manage to be there. I have written the hotel at Amherst to engage a room, but have had no reply. Of course everything is crowded at that season. I'm going not at all for the degree, which I certainly don't need, but on your account, and on Mother's. When I thought it over, I was sure that she would want me to be there. I have not even written Virginia since Christmas. I have not done a stroke of serious work this winter. My correspondence and business affairs have driven me to the limit all the time. I had lost a good deal of money on bonds going bad, so I've simply devoted my time to getting rid of the old municipals which used to be so good, and putting the money into Tel. and Tel, and into Government bonds. Of course I've had to sell at 60 to 75, but it was the only thing to do. I've had Alfred Knopf's lawyer to help me. But such transactions, together with the awful Income tax I have to pay, have broken up my winter completely.

I'll do the best I can to represent you at Commencement and keep Virginia from feeling lonely.

With a heartful of love,
Willie

TO ROSCOE CATHER

April 25, 1933

My dear Roscoe:

I ought to have sent you a telegram. I was so glad to hear that your bank stood firm through the storms—what storms they have been! I wonder what you think of all that is going on in the world now, especially in the banking world. As for me, I simply think anything is better than timidity and inactivity. I do not think Roosevelt is any giant of intellect and he may run us into a few snags, but at least we will be moving,—and for the first time since Theodore Roosevelt was in the White House we have a President who can speak French to the French Ambassador! The whole misunderstanding with [Pierre] Laval came about from the fact that when Hoover thought he was paying a compliment, Laval thought he was making a promise. I am simply driven to death with the yearly college torment and haven't much time to write, but I wish you would keep me posted on how affairs are going with you and the bank in Wyoming.

With special love to Twinnies,
Willie

TO S. S. MCCLURE

May 26 [1933?]
New York City

Dear Mr. McClure;

I have been hoping that I would see you again before the summer scattering, but now that the hot weather has come suddenly I am leaving town to stay with friends in the country. Later I go to Canada. When I come back in the fall we must have another evening together and talk over our old friends, and about those days when we worked so happily together. I was always eager to please you, and you were <u>eager to be pleased</u>. I still think that was the secret of your success with young people. You often thought them a little more able than they really were, but those who had any stuff in them at all tried to be as good as you thought them, to come up to your expectations. You had such a spirit of youth yourself that you knew how to strike a spark in young writers. We must talk over those years of comradeship when we meet again.

Until then, good luck to your book! And please wish me good luck with mine—just now it seems to me rather stupid.

Affectionately always,
Willa Cather

TO ELSIE CATHER

June 21 [1933]

Dear Sister;

Everything went well—Virginia graduated <u>cum laude</u>. I tried to do my whole duty—lunched with her and her dear friend Miss [Charlotte] Wilder (who seems a very nice person, awfully like her brother [Thornton Wilder]) paid a visit to Baldwin House and the house-mistress, etc. We stayed in a suite at Faculty House, Mount Holyoke, as it is quiet there. Virginia had dinner with us at the [George and Harriet] Whichers, who recalled your visit and begged to be remembered to you.

Virginia left with us as far as Springfield; from there she went on to Detroit. She seems a rather sad little figure to me—I wish I could do something to cheer her up. But these days most young people seem sad to me.

Your good letter reached me via Virginia—she came over to Mt. Holyoke to dine with us the night we got there, came over in Mary Lewis' car.

With love,
W.

TO DOROTHY CANFIELD FISHER

June 22 [1933]

My Dearest Dorothy:

At last the Herald Tribune article did reach me, and I sent it straight to Isabelle. A reply has just reached me. Both she and Jan are delighted with it.

Isabelle says she wishes to see you to tell you how much she likes it. She would certainly be the hardest person in the world to please in such a matter, so I think we may say "a good job" without reservation. As for me, there is nothing in it that I <u>don't</u> like, and much that I do, and I'm very grateful to have so good a front presented to the public. To me, myself, articles about myself never give me much delight, no matter how sympathetic and generous they are, simply because they make me for the moment self-conscious. My chief happiness (probably yours, too) is in forgetting the past as if it had never been. No, I don't mean 'the past', but myself in the past. As soon as I think of myself as a human figure in that past, in those scenes (Red Cloud, Colorado, New Mexico) the scenes grow rather dim and are spoiled for me. When I remember those places I am not there at all, as a person. I seem to have been a bundle of enthusiasms and physical sensations, but not a person. Maybe everyone is like that. How can anyone really see himself? He can see a kind of shadow he throws, but not the real creature. I have been running away from myself all my life (have you?) and have been happiest when I was running fastest. Those last three winters of my mother's life held me close to myself and to the beginnings of things, and it was like being held against things too sad to live with.

So Sally [Dorothy and John Fisher's daughter] is getting married, and my oldest nephew is getting engaged! My goodness, where have all the years gone to? It's all terribly perplexing, my dear. But I enjoy life immensely—when I forget it.

I'm off for Canada next week (Whale Cove, Grand Manan, New Brunswick) Please let me know where you are going this summer. Not Germany now, I think. Thank you dear for your kind judgments, and your loyalty to early memories—memories of early youth, when such little things could produce wonders of excitement and joy.

Lovingly
Willa

➜ ❮

When Cather wrote the following to the only son of Alfred and Blanche Knopf, Pat was fifteen years old.

TO ALFRED A. "PAT" KNOPF JR.

August 15 [1933]

My dear Pat;

What original ideas you have for a vacation pastime, to be sure! I like a retreat from the world, but not just in the way you have selected. Well, when you <u>do</u> go to New Mexico to ride, you'll be happier with your appendix out, I can tell you that. I am doing lots of walking up here, on rather rough trails that run along the edge of the sea-cliffs. There are few beaches, and anyhow it's too cold to bathe. We have had only one day when the thermometer went above eighty-two. The Italian air fleet on their return trip went right over this island, right over my little house at 2:15 in the afternoon and wrecked my afternoon nap. I thought them ugly beasts, with their ribs all showing, and shook my fist at them.

I hope you are over the uncomfortable part of an operation by this time. You must come to see me whenever you are in town next winter, and let's plan a theatre party on our own, without letting anyone chaperone us! I'd love that.

Have a good time while you are getting well, and make them give you good things to eat. I wish I could send you one of the lobsters we pull out here.

With much love, my dear boy,

Your special friend
Willa Cather

TO ZOË AKINS

[August 26, 1933]
Whale Cove, Grand Manan Island

Darling Zoë;

The book-ends did not reach me in time—I left town July 8th—but my secretary is holding them for me. Nothing can come into Canada now without the bill of sale. But the white and the green knitted jackets, which were presents from you, are here and are my constant companions on this breezy coast. They comfort my sore shoulder in the most friendly way.

I've had all kinds of a summer—some good, some bad. Mary Virginia spent her vacation with me here, and that I <u>did</u> enjoy.

I'm working on a book about a very silly young girl [*Lucy Gayheart*], and I

Willa Cather with her niece Mary Virginia Auld on
Grand Manan Island, 1933

lose patience with her. Perhaps I am too old for that sort of thing. At any rate,
it does not put me in a holiday mood as some books have done. My little hut
here looks very pretty, buried in roses and hollyhocks, and sitting on the cliffs
at the very edge of the sea. I'm fond of the place. I'm fond of Zoë, too, and
I wish you could drop down in this wild spot sometime. Newspapers always
three days late, maid three times a week, no radio on this island. World-affairs
never touch us.—Except that the damned Italian air fleet, on its return trip,
did go over this island, over this house at 2:30, and wrecked my afternoon nap!

Lovingly, dear Zoë
Willa

TO ALFRED AND BLANCHE KNOPF

October 26 [1933]

My Dear Blanche and Alfred;

I am certainly a pig, or I would have thanked you before this for the splendid package of books you sent me. I haven't looked into the Bullett, but all the others are good. Work and the fine weather have kept me from writing letters. My excuse for not thanking you for the books is——industry! This morning I finished the first draft of <u>Lucy Gayheart</u>. I'm by no means out of the jungle, but now I know there's a trail through, and a reason for going through—at least, there is to me. It will take a hard winter's work, and you, my good friends, will help to keep the dogs off me, I know. I know, because you've done it more than once. I haven't learned to work in that apartment awfully well; maybe I can arrange things better this winter. If I can't I'll come back to Jaffrey!

I had a cunning note from Pat last week.

The weather is glorious—my ankle does splendidly on a four mile walk, I've not tried it further. Wild clouds and very <u>low</u> ones, as in France; the mountain dark purple all day yesterday, the top of it powdered with snow, and the sky rolling masses of silver and purple and black from morning until night. (This sounds as if I were trying to work off some "writing" on you, but since you <u>know</u> the mountain, there's some point in mentioning it's present complexion.)

With love to the both of you
Willa Cather

→ ←

Cyril Clemens, founder of the Mark Twain Society and editor of the Mark Twain Quarterly, *was a distant cousin of the author, not his son.*

TO CYRIL CLEMENS

December 28 [1933]
570 Park Avenue, New York City

Dear Mr. Clemens;

It will give me great pleasure to receive the medal from the International Mark Twain Society, and I appreciate the honor which the Society confers in this award. I have always been proud of a story which Albert Bigelow Paine tells in his Life of Mark Twain. It seems that your father once found an early poem of mine ["The Palatine"] re-printed in a newspaper, and he showed it to Mr. Paine and commended it with some enthusiasm. I think Mr. Paine quoted several stanzas of the poem in his book—the third volume, if I remember rightly. I was a very young writer at that time, and a word from Mark Twain, spoken to a third person, meant a great deal to me.

Very sincerely yours
Willa Cather

Excuse my tardy reply to your letter; I have just returned from northern Canada.

→ ←

In the fall of 1933 Ida Tarbell, whom Cather knew from her days at McClure's, *wrote Cather as part of a campaign to raise money to provide a modest income for S. S. McClure, who was financially destitute.*

TO IDA TARBELL

January 7 [1934]

Dear Miss Tarbell;

I am so afraid I may forget the check for the fund for Mr. McClure, that I am sending it to you now, when I am writing a whole sheaf of checks.

Sometime we are going to meet together, aren't we? Why is it that one has less time for one's own as one grows older?

Affectionately
Willa Cather

TO CARRIE MINER SHERWOOD

January 27, 1934

My dear Carrie:

Mr. Cyril Clemens, son of Mark Twain, is President of the International Mark Twain Society, to which men of letters in all countries belong. The Society recently held a contest to decide what is the most memorable and representative American novel in the last thirty-five years, the writer of this novel to be awarded a silver medal by the Mark Twain Society. The majority votes were for Antonia, and the medal is waiting for me in St. Louis whenever I have time to go and get it.

Out of a number of reports on Antonia which were sent to the Society, there is one which I think you might like to have (chiefly because it is so well written) to keep in your copy of Antonia. Now, don't show it to the town cats or put it in the paper, or do anything to make [blacked out] and [blacked out] want to scratch my eyes out any worse than they do. Of course, I want you to show it to Mary, and you might show it to Helen Mac. [McNeny] some time, because I know neither of them wants to murder me. I want you to have it because it particularly takes notice of the fact that, though there have been many imitations of Antonia and some of them good, I really was the one who first broke the ground.

Oh yes, there is another reason why I don't want you to show this article about; a lot of our fellow townsmen would go chasing out to look poor Annie [Pavelka] over and would agree as to what a liar I am. You never can get it through peoples heads that a story is made out of an emotion or an excitement, and is not made out of the legs and arms and faces of one's friends or acquaintances. Two Friends, for instance, was not really made out of your father [James L. Miner] and Mr. [William Newman] Richardson; it was made out of an effect they produced on a little girl who used to hang about them. The story, as I told you, is a picture; but it is not the picture of two men, but of a memory. Many things about both men are left out of this sketch because they made no impression on me as a child; other things are exaggerated because they seemed just like that to me then.

As for Antonia, she is really just a figure upon which other things hang. She is the embodiment of all my feeling about those early emigrants in the prairie country. The first thing I heard of when I got to Nebraska at the age of eight was old Mr. Sadalaak's [Francis Sadilek] suicide, which had happened some years before. It made a great impression on me. People never stopped telling the details. I suppose from that time I was destined to write <u>Antonia</u> if I ever wrote anything at all.

Now I don't often write, even to my dearest friends, about my own work, but you just tuck this away where you can read it and when people puzzle you, or come at you and say that I idealize everything and exaggerate everything, you can turn to this letter and comfort yourself. The one and sole reason that my "exaggerations" get across, get across a long way (<u>Antonia</u> has now been translated into eight languages), is that these things were not exaggerations to me. I felt just like that about all those early people. If I had exaggerated my real feeling or stretched it one inch, the whole book would have fallen as flat as a pancake, and would have been a little ridiculous. There is just one thing you cannot fake or counterfeit in this world, my dear Carrie, and that is real feeling, feeling in people who try to govern their hearts with their heads.

I did not start out to write you a long lecture, but some day I might get bumped off by an automobile, and then you'd be glad to have a statement which is just as true as I have the power to make it.

My heart to you always,
Willie

P.S. I had a wonderful afternoon with Irene when she was here, and I am so happy that she and Mr. Weisz are going to escape from this troubled part of the world. Isn't he a good sport?

TO VILHJALMUR STEFANSSON

March 22, 1934

My dear Mr. Stefansson:

I am t[h]rilled to think you cast a ballot for me, but why in the world for membership in the Philosophical Society? Don't you know that I am the least philosophical person in the world? I cannot read five pages of Hegel, no not five paragraphs, without tying my head up in cold water. Santayana and Bergson are the only philosophers I can read with pleasure—and perhaps that is only because they both write well. However, I thank you warmly for your vote, and if I am actually made a member of this dignified body, I shall try to cultivate my mind a little. At any rate, I shall have had the pleasure of hearing from you.

Always cordially yours,
Willa Cather

→←

In the spring of 1934 Cather badly sprained her left wrist, marking the beginning of many years of pain and trouble with both of her hands.

TO ELSIE CATHER

May 7, 1934

My dear Sister:

I am so awfully sorry to hear that you have been sick and low spirited—any one who is sick is low spirited. Now you must not take all those rumors from Red Cloud too seriously. Will Auld's behavior may affect our fortunes, but it cannot affect our honor [Auld, a banker in Red Cloud, and Cather's sister Jessica divorced in 1933]. The more he shows himself up there, the more people will understand that we got a very bad deal—no, nobody wrote me what has been going on. Mrs. Rickerson's little card to Molly, which you yourself sent me, told me the whole story.

I had that pleasant evening with Bishop Beecher just about a week before I got my hand hurt. Of course I realize, my dear, that you had plenty of troubles of your own—and if I had only known that you had them, I might have sent you a few books or a few flowers or something to amuse you; but like you, I was pretty much concentrated on my own troubles. An absolutely smashed hand is such a serious thing for a writer,—and just now it proves to be a very serious thing for Alfred Knopf to have a writer with a smashed hand. I really cannot get the book done for fall publication, as I see things now. For two months I have simply put in the whole of every day with doctors, massage, electric treatments and hot water treatments. I have at last got out of splints, but my wrist and thumb are now very stiff as the result of being tied to a board for two months, and it will take a lot of massage to give them back any elasticity. However, I am working again now every morning by hand (of course, I cannot type), and as a result am feeling much more cheerful. Alfred Knopf read the first third of the new book last night, and telephoned me this morning that he would wait any number of months or years for the rest, and that he had "scarcely believed he had it in him any more to be so enchanted by the sheer grace of a character in a story". The book is about a very young girl and the title will be simply "Lucy Gayheart". It is modern, western, very romantic, non-Catholic. So there we are!

I have been sending a lot of books to the Red Cloud library—some very good ones—and if only I had known you were sick, I would have sent them to you. Don't hesitate for a minute to go back to Red Cloud this summer; it is full of our friends and there are very few friends of J. W. Auld there.

Lovingly,
Willie

P.S. Here is a little check I want you to spend on keeping up your yard. I always feel that if the yard is nice, people think pleasantly of father and mother when they pass by.

W.

TO LOUISE GUERBER BURROUGHS

Sunday [June 10, 1934]

My Dear Louise:

Your lovely roses have been such delightful companions to me all this day while I was mending the roads in "Lucy Gayheart". In these days one has to squeeze one's memory hard to remember <u>just</u> what it was like to walk over frozen country roads in certain weathers. Not very important, and I had side-stepped it. But this morning I sat down and made myself remember.

With love
W.S.C.

TO EARL AND ACHSAH BARLOW BREWSTER

July 1, 1934

My dear Brewsters:

I suppose Edith wrote you that I had a hurt hand for most of the winter, and that is why I have not written to tell you how much I enjoyed your book on Lawrence [*D. H. Lawrence: Reminiscences and Correspondence*]. I think the letters themselves show a much nicer side of him than most of those in the big collection, and oh, I <u>very much</u> like Earl's and Achsah's own words about their friend! It seems to me that they are almost the only honest words that have been written about Lawrence, except [Dorothy] Brett's funny little book [*Lawrence and Brett: A Friendship*] which was honest in its way, and I thought quite charming. But, as you know, most of his friends wrote about Lawrence to exhibit themselves and not at all to enlighten one about D. H. L. I had a letter yesterday from Isabel[le] Hambourg, telling me that your book gives her a better idea of Lawrence than anything she has ever read—but probably she herself has written you to that effect.

Edith and I hope to get away to Grand Manan in the second week of July. I have been kept in town through the heat by rather complicated business affairs. Moreover, I insisted upon finishing, before I left, the book which was interrupted for more than three months during the winter. I have got it done, but I expect it would have been a better "do" if I could have written it without interruption. For three months I really did nothing but take care of my hand—I made a career of it, and was a trained nurse with one patient.

How often we think and talk of you, dear friends, and wish we were on our way to see you. We had hoped to go abroad this spring, you know, but my hand changed our plans. One of these days we will be on our way to you, however, and God speed the time.

With all good wishes to you both,

Affectionately,
Willa Cather

→ ←

Cather's brother Roscoe was a successful banker, and she often turned to him for help with financial matters. When she needed to attend to some financial matters in Red Cloud, he generously traveled there as her representative.

TO ROSCOE CATHER

July 2 [1934]
New York City

My Dear Roscoe;

So nice a letter as yours deserved a speedy answer. I never thought of <u>not</u> paying the cost of that trip, my dear boy; I was asking enough of you in asking you to give the matter your attention. But since you want to do all that for me as a gift, I will take it in the high spirit in which you offer it. I don't know when a letter has pleased me so much as yours—it sounded a lot like your father. I think he left to all of his sons some of his fine courtesy. Even poor Jim has some of it. It makes you all just a little more chivalrous than the men around you. I am sure Virginia and the twins feel it.

The heat is very bad here, and I won't get away before the middle of

July. I stayed on in the heat to finish the interrupted book, and did it. More than that, I sold the serial rights for a good price. It will come out in the Woman's Home Companion from April 1935 to Sept 1935 [actually March–July 1935]. This, of course, delays the book publication—it will be out Sept 1st, 1935.

Scribners' wanted to serialize it, but their bid was only about half that of the Crowell people. They never pay much, as they have a very small circulation. There is nothing in serial publication now-a-days but money, so get all you can. Once there was "class" about appearing in good magazines, but now there are no good ones, so why bother?

Lovingly to you all
Willie

TO ELSIE CATHER

July 14 [1934]

Dearest Sister;

I am writing in bed after packing all day. Thank you for your letter from Hastings. I am so glad Bess [Seymour] is there and that she has no cancer. Oh that heat! Every morning for weeks I open the Tribune before breakfast and look at the temperatures reported from Omaha, Kansas City, and Denver, always hoping it will say "rain & cooler" and it never does. Minnesota and Wisconsin are just as bad. My heart is heavy for you all, and especially for the old people. If I were a Catholic I'd be sure this world is being punished for its new ways of thinking and behaving.

The heat was 100 to 110 here right along for the two weeks when I was finishing my book, but I did not mind it much. This apartment was usually cool in the mornings, and Josephine was always so jolly and resourceful. My poor typist could not keep my manuscript clean—the purple ink ran and smeared on the pages, and for the first time I sent in dirty manuscripts to both the magazine and to Alfred Knopf.

Both Alfred and the W. H. Companion are very much excited about the story. Three weeks ago I sent a rough draft to Jan Hambourg for musical corrections. Yesterday I got a cable which reads:

> "Lucy unquestionably your finest work. Beautiful, rich, inevitable complete. Like Brahms B major trio
>
> Isabelle Jan"

It's by no means my finest book; but the design is good, I think. The first part is written for the last. It would all be much better if I had not had to drop it entirely for nearly four months, just when I was going strong. I never got back the same enthusiasm.

Now I am sending you another check, for it takes days to get to Grand Manan, and some days to get settled after we arrive. You might need something for Doctor or hospital before I can write you again.

Virginia cried bitterly when I told her Bess was so ill. She said some of the best memories she had were connected with her Aunt Bessie.

I see by the paper that Charles [Auld] is at home! Pleasant, I should think. What <u>do</u> the townspeople think of Will Auld? Do you ever see any of them, of the Aulds, I mean? So it turns out that Bess has helped to pay for [Will and Jessica Cather Auld's son] Tom's schooling! I can never have much respect for that young man, I'm afraid.

Elsie, I wish you would use some of this check to get one of those new oscillating electric fans for your bedroom—they are almost noiseless and they saved my life in the hot stuffy rooms of the Grosvenor hotel. Changing the air does refresh the body.

I feel guilty to be going off to a cool place, dear Bobbie, but after two weeks I'll have my proofs to read, and I could never do that in Red Cloud in the heat. I expect you think I'm pretty selfish, but if you could read the hundreds of letters that come in to me all the time (to the office, too) you would have to believe that my books do give pleasure to the intelligent and the sick and the unfortunate, as well as giving fools and tonguey women something to talk about. They do more for more people than I could personally do if I were as strong as iron and devoted my whole life to good works. I don't write 'em with that purpose, but they have that result. <u>Any kind of integrity</u> helps in this world, and I have my own kind.

With love, dear sister, and thinking of you and what you are up against, every hour in the day,

Willie

TO ALFRED A. KNOPF

July 27 [1934]

My Dear Alfred:

I must seem very inconsistent to you—wanting big plain type for the "Archbishop," and not wanting it for "Lucy". But you see I wanted the "Archbishop" to look as if it were printed on a country press, for old people to read. I don't, of course, want "Lucy" to look like that. I do wish you could repeat the "Lost Lady" type, with it's sharp "W"s and "M"s. Perhaps a smaller size of this Caslon would do, but I honestly think this page you send me looks like a child's First Reading Book—It stares at me with open eyes and open mouth until it's actually hard to read. I can't see any text, I see only letters that look unnaturally large and commonplace on a page of this size.

If you will repeat the page of "A Lost Lady" exactly for me, I'll write you another romantic story, and a better one than Lucy! Now that's a fair offer, isn't it?

So far, glorious weather on the island, and I've never before enjoyed getting back to it so much. Today is the first rain and heavy fog. I love being on this mere pin-point in the North Atlantic, drowned in oceans of fog with the rain beating down, and no sound but the water and the bell-buoy. The Brittish Government sends out buoys with a lovely tone; this one is the G below middle C, I think, and the fog makes it deep and full and very soft—it seems to call from a great distance.

With love to you both,
W. S. C.

TO MARY MINER CREIGHTON

[Around August 15, 1934]
Grand Manan Island

My Darling Mary:

A week ago today I and my family lost the kindest of friends [Dr. E. A. Creighton], and you lost what very few people ever have at all, a life-long companion who cherished you and admired you and found complete happiness in his life with you.

You will tell me that this makes it only the harder to bear now. It will make your loneliness greater, I know. But you and I have lived long enough to know that it is possible for human beings to have only a very limited amount of real happiness in this world, and so many people miss it altogether. You had more than most of the people I know. I have known very few marriages as happy as yours. Your devoted care prolonged the Doctor's life for many years, and you made his home so pleasant for him that, as he often told me, he could be happier there than anywhere else in the world. I always loved to meet Doctor on the street because he always looked so happy. His kind, intelligent face glowed with an inner content. I liked to listen to his nice voice when he came to look mother over. When I was far away I always felt easy in mind about father and mother because Dr. Creighton was there. I knew if anything went wrong he would get there, and get there quick. You remember I kept his telephone number plastered in both bedrooms on sticky labels, so that they could see it <u>without</u> glasses. I wish you and he could have been in New York another winter; but I shall always feel grateful to fate that you were both there that one winter.

Sometime, Mary, I want to tell you about a kind thing he did for a young woman of this town. I promised him never to mention it, and I never did. He came to our home one morning and said he wanted to see me alone. A patient of his was going to have her second baby just after she had lost her first, and <u>would I please be nice to her</u>! He asked it just like that! Said she was nervous and felt every little thing, and when I met her would I please be cordial and jolly her up a little. He said he knew I didn't mean it, but that sometimes I <u>was</u> rather brusque with people. I promised, and I certainly never admired the Doctor so much as when I walked out to his car with him after that interview. Think of the delicacy of the man, to realize the importance of such little things, and to come directly to me and ask me to be a little more agreeable! I was complimented that he felt he could frankly ask me to "mend my manners"! Almost any doctor will try to help a hurt foot or hand, but how many will try to help hurt feelings? Not many.

I expect you can guess who the young woman was, but since he asked me not to mention his unusual professional call that morning, I never shall to anyone but you, and I had rather only you and Carrie and Irene knew about it. Of all my memories of the Doctor, that is the one I like most. It <u>took so many qualities</u> in a man to make him do that simple thing! Very few women have as much delicacy as that.

My heart bleeds for you, dear Mary, but how many proud and happy memories you have to comfort you. If I could have tried to plan a happy life for you when we were little girls, I could not have planned anything better than you have had. I never saw a <u>dis-</u>contented look on the Doctor's face. You made him perfectly happy. Only think, he might never have gone to Red Cloud at all! His going there meant so much good for my own family and countless others, as well as for you and for him. I shall just try to be thankful to God that he <u>did</u> go there.

So lovingly, dear,
Willie

TO LOUISE GUERBER BURROUGHS

August 29 [1934]
Grand Manan Island

Dear Louise;

I've thought of you often since I arrived here July 20th. My conscience was uneasy because I had never told you how much I enjoyed reading the diary of your ancestress about her terrible crossing of the Atlantic. The last weeks in town were hectic; I was arranging the serial publication of "Lucy" and doing what I could to help old friends in Nebraska who were actually in want.

Even here the summer has been unusually dry. Most of the time this island has been a shining gold spot in a blue sea. I have just finished reading the galley proofs of "Lucy" and I think better of it than I did when it was a messy corrected manuscript. The lines of a thing come out in type.

Last night came your letter with distressing news. However did Mr. [Bryson] Burroughs pick up that bug? I suspect it was by loafing too little and painting too much. But if you have your own bungalow, and he is writing, then he is living and not merely being sick. And he's doing the Pre-Raphaelites! They always seemed so beautiful and legendary to me when I knew their works in re-production only. But when I went to England first and saw their works! Such awful color, I've never got over the shock of it. I mean [Edward] Burne-Jones and [Dante Gabriel] Rossetti—seems as if they mixed a little mud in their paint. I remember awful greens, and ladies,—pure Virgins with mouldy complexions. These painters should be engraved, always, and their canvases kept in a locked gallery for students only.

I'm doing nothing, and thinking about nothing but the weather. I've been reading a lot of Anatole France over because I happen to have a lot of his books up here. Speaking of cycles of taste, he's despised in France now, you know. They shrug and say, "Oh yes, a virtuoso."

Oh you, I've only a few Shakespeares up here—not the "Merchant". A lost line torments me; what <u>is</u> the second line of Morocco's speech which begins,

> Mislike me not for my complexion,
> The – – livery of the – – sun
> To whom I am a neighbour and (near bred (?)

I try supplying various adjectives, but with him it's dangerous to substitute.

With love and good wishes to you both, and recommending toddy for the invalid,

Yours
W.S.C.

The line from Shakespeare's Merchant of Venice, *spoken by the Prince of Morocco, is:*

> *Mislike me not for my complexion,*
> *The shadow'd livery of the burnish'd sun,*
> *To whom I am a neighbour and near bred.*

TO EDWARD WAGENKNECHT

November 22, 1934

My unknown Friend:

Your first name I can read, but your last name begins with a swastika and ends with a king, so the Postmaster must use his discretion. I got back to New York some weeks ago, and working through an enormous accumulation of letters, I finally came upon yours and stopped for a breathing space, partly because of your difficult handwriting and partly because you began your letter with the name of someone I loved. What an inadequate book [*Sarah Orne Jewett*] that young man [Francis O. Matthiessen] did write about Miss Jewett! He misinterprets so many of the facts that he dug up, and she herself never for a moment graces his pages. It <u>seems</u> to me that even if I had never known her, I could have reconstructed her from her letters to Mrs. Fields and her published works. This young man is modern and abrupt. Before he wrote his book he sent me a letter which said simply: "At what date can I call upon you for information regarding Sarah Orne Jewett?" I think I told him January 1, 1990.

Thank you for the incident you tell me about Mary Jewett after she was paralyzed. I grew to know her very well after Sarah Jewett's death, and often visited her in the beautiful old house at South Berwick. It is a lasting regret to me that I was unable to go to see her during her long illness. My mother had a stroke in Pasadena, California, shortly before Miss Jewett's illness came upon her, and from that time on I had to be on the West coast. Her nephew, Dr. [Theodore] Eastman, kept me posted as to her condition. He, you know, was snuffed out only a few months after Mary Jewett's death, and now that whole family, and all the beautiful things which graced their lives, have vanished as if they had never been. (The one good thing about that young man's book is that it contains some very charming drawings and photographs of that beautiful New England interior.) It is a disgrace to New England that any of Miss Jewett's books should be out of print. It will be a long while before New England produces such another writer.

My friendliest greetings to your mother and yourself. It is a pleasure to hear from any true lover of Sarah Orne Jewett.

Very cordially yours,
Willa Cather

TO EGBERT SAMUEL OLIVER

December 13, 1934

My dear Mr. Oliver:

Twenty-eight professors are writing books on "Creative Writing in College Courses." I know that, because I have written answers to twenty-eight men, and with the twenty-eighth, I made a resolution that I would answer no more letters on that subject. You are twenty-nine, and you come too late.

I think it is sheer nonsense to attempt to teach "Creative Writing" in colleges. If the college students were taught to write good, sound English sentences (sentences with unmistakable articulation) and to avoid hackneyed platitudinous, woman's-club expressions, such as: "colorful", "the desire to create", "worth while books", "a writer universally acclaimed"—all those smug expressions which really mean nothing at all—then creative writing would take care of itself. Nothing whatever should be done to stimulate literary activity in America! [I]ts quality will never be improved by stimulation. I do wish the colleges taught people to write passably clear and correct English, however. More than half of the twenty-eight professors who have written to me within the last few months were quite unable to use "which" and "that" and "would" and "should" correctly—at least, they did not honor me by using them correctly in their letters of request. They made many other errors of the same sort, which a well-trained high school student avoids.

Very sincerely yours,
Willa Cather

(Dictated)

TO IDA KLEBER TODD

December 28 [1934]

Dear Mrs. Todd;

Happy New Year! People are always writing me (people I don't know) that I have "influenced" their lives. I wonder if you know that you have influenced mine? Once, long ago, in some discussion, you said, half under your breath, "Oh yes, of course, art simplifies." I had never thought of that before; I have been trying to live that remark ever since. It was the <u>way</u> you spoke, carelessly and yet as if there could be no doubt about the matter; and because I felt a kind of authority in you—didn't try to explain it, just felt it.

I have read thousands of pages that did not say as much to me as that sentence rather lightly dropped by a living voice—a very individual voice with a tempo and timbre distinctly its own. The sentence went home like an arrow—because of something in you and something in me. As I said, I've been trying to live it ever since.

With all my heart, Happy New Year!

Affectionately,
Willa Cather

TO THOMAS MASARYK

February 14 [1935]
New York City

My Dear President Masaryk;

As the date of your birthday approaches please allow me to send my heart-felt good wishes, and my congratulations on the quality of the years you have left behind you. And may I take this occasion to tell you that your friendly interest has been and is one of the most cherished rewards of my professional life? We live in a strange world, at a strange time. Public opinion just now means less than ever before, because it is re-actionary, without roots or background. It represents the spasm of a multitude of minds, not their natural judgement. We could almost say with <u>Macbeth</u> that "nothing is but what is not." We behave as though we could create a new scale of values by the mere act of besmirching the old. In such a time, the only satisfaction any reflective person can have is in the sympathetic consideration of a few individuals in the world; those whom one respects and admires. Your friendly interest in my books has grown the more precious to me as the times have grown stranger. Of the half-dozen so called "public men" from whom I used to hear by letter occasionally, you are the only one who is not now living in exile. They were not sentenced by any court, I believe; they simply are not allowed to live at home. Switzerland and America are rich in scholars just now, because they have nowhere else to go.

Greetings and salutations to you from my heart.

Willa Cather

TO ROSCOE CATHER

April 23 [1935]

My Dear Roscoe;

Don't think that I did not appreciate your long, understanding, letter about the English reviews. I hope I can sometime have a long talk with you about the peculiar satisfaction I get out of working occasionally in legendary themes. Rotation of crops is a good thing for gardens and writers.

Things have been pretty thick for me. When I was up in Montreal trying to get some work done in a quiet place I had an appendix attack and had to come home. Here I have had a second attack, and will have to go up for an operation before long. Isabelle McClung Hambourg, who has been very ill in Paris all winter, landed on March 26th with her husband who came over to tour Canada with his two brothers [Mark and Boris Hambourg]. They form the Hambourg Trio, playing chamber music. I called my doctor for Isabelle, who found her condition very serious; both kidneys much enlarged and incysted. Nothing malignant, but a condition which keeps them from performing more than half of their proper function, necessitates the strictest possible diet and an invalid life from now on. Three surgeons agree that the kidneys were mal-formed at her birth and, for the last eight years, have been growing rapidly worse with the natural changes of body tissue. I am not writing this to any other member of my family, as there are, alas, so many people who rather rejoice in the overthrow of the strong and the generous. Jan was with her for three weeks, while I got some work done in Montreal. Then he had to go off on his tour. I removed her to the Lennox Hill Hospital, about half a mile from me, and will have the whole responsibility until his return, June 1st. She is just as sweet and dignified and uncomplaining as an invalid as she was as a girl, but of course you will understand how sad all this makes me and how much it takes out of me. The doctors are devoted to her. With the strictest care she may live for some years. I have given up my trip to Italy this summer and am not trying to work now. I shut up my portefolio in Montreal. After Jan's return I shall have my appendix taken out. Worst of all my perplexities, my dear French woman [Josephine Bourda], who has been my prop and stay ever since I moved into this apartment (she used to be with me all during the war years, from 1914 to 1918) is going back to her native Pyrenees with her husband and daughter to stay for good. I'm glad she is to be again among her native mountains which she loves, but it will wreck my life, rather. No one else will ever so respect me and my calling. She sails on May 25th.

I am trying to live day by day, and not to worry; but when I'm very tired my philosophy fails me! Your love and interest is a help to me.

I will write you later about Virginia's letter. She seems to be finding her own way.

Devotedly
Willie

→ ←

Marie Meloney, who had a wide social circle, was a prominent journalist and editor of This Week *magazine.*

TO MARIE MATTINGLY MELONEY

May 29, 1935

Dear Mrs. Meloney;

I have just returned to town for a few days and find your letter awaiting me. I have been wanting to write you for a long while, to thank you for your kindness in delivering to me Mr. [James M.] Barrie's gracious message about My Antonia. Please accept my belated thanks for your friendly office in sending me an extract from his letter to you.

Regarding the suggestion you make to me, I am afraid I can only shake my head. I never have written, and I very much doubt if I could write, a story at the suggestion of another person. I have never tried to write a story that was not the outcome of some rather sharp personal experience; and, of course, you know as well as I, one cannot go out and hunt for personal experiences. Everything that one goes out and hunts for is second-hand—and second-rate. I have been very much interested in looking over the copies of This Week, and when I return to New York next November, I shall follow its career with every good wish in the world.

Very sincerely yours,
Willa Cather

➔ ❖

In the summer of 1935 Cather and Lewis sailed for Europe. They spent several weeks in Italy, and then went to Paris again, where Cather saw Isabelle Hambourg for the last time. This was her final trip to Europe.

TO MARY MINER CREIGHTON

August 8 [1935]
aboard the Rex

My Dear Mary;

Here we are, beyond the Azores, and the splendid autumn flowers you and Irene sent me still make our dinner table lovely day after day and turn my thoughts to my dear friends at home. So far we have had a rather rough passage, heavy seas with intense heat—a rather unusual combination. I was terribly tired when we left New York, but Mary Virginia came down to the boat with us and unpacked my steamer trunk and all my toilet things so deftly that I set off with a neat cabin. Before we were out of the narrows I went to bed and stayed there for 24 hours. For the first time in my life I had dinner and breakfast in bed on shipboard! Yesterday I began to feel like myself again, and today I am enjoying everything. I am never a sick [traveler], but to be terribly tired is about as bad.

This letter is for Irene as well as Mary, and it will be put off at Gibraltar and sent back on La Savoie, sister ship of the Rex. I want to tell Irene that the remedy against sea-sickness my doctor gave Edith has worked <u>perfectly</u>, and she has not been miserable, even in the very rough weather. It is a new German preparation, very effective, but one has to have blood tests and heart tests made before a physician will give it to one.

Irene kept urging me to make this trip, after I had rather lost heart about it, and if any spring comes back into me (as I begin to believe it will) I shall feel that I largely owe it to her. She was with me in the darkest hours of my discouragement about Isabelle, when I was too tired to decide anything for myself. The slippers she sent for Isabelle are in my big trunk, just as she did them up. My love to you both and to Carrie goes with this. I get so much comfort in thinking of our long friendship, and how it has grown so much stronger through the years, binding us all together. If I didn't have those things at the bottom of my heart I wouldn't get much out of blue seas or sunny lands.

Devotedly
Willie

TO ROSCOE CATHER

September 8 [1935]
Hotel Royal Danieli, Venice

Dear Brother;

Edith and I have been in Italy not quite a month—and it seems six months! We have both been well, and have had a most successful trip so far. After ten days in the high, cool Dolomites, we dropped down to Venice by motor. Of course foreign travel is never <u>all</u> roses, as people at home seem to think. In Venice the mosquitos <u>always</u> devour one, as they did when you drove us near Gray Bull [Greybull, Wyoming]; one sleeps under nets, and if a mosquito gets in there's an all-night struggle. If I go out on the Grand Canal to see the moonlight, I pay for it by such a horribly swollen face as is keeping me indoors today.

Sept 25th I go on to Paris to be with Isabelle, who is slowly losing ground.

"Lucy" is doing well, but not brilliantly—nothing like the "Archbishop" or "Shadows".

Lovingly
Willie

TO YALTAH MENUHIN

October 23 [1935]
Paris

My Darling Yaltah;

Your letter from South Africa got to Paris in record time and caught me just a few days before Miss Lewis and I sail for home. It seemed miraculous that a letter could come so far and get here on October 21st! I want to leave this little word, so that you will know that it did reach me and it was such a happy surprise for both Edith and me. I wish I had been one of your jolly mining party, although my experience of caves in the Southwest, and the underground prisons of Paris has made me dread all sub-terranean explorations. I like to be on <u>top</u> of the earth.

How in the name of all queer chances did you ever come upon Lucy Gayheart on the other side of the world! I meant to send it to you when you got back, but it never occured to me that book-post could catch up with you in Australia or New Zealand.

Edith and I are busy getting some warm clothes for the boat, and preparing to slip away without saying goodbye to Isabelle, as she has requested us to do. It's very hard to go when I know how ill she is, and yet I feel that I can not stay longer. I must get home and begin to pull my life together again. Marutha [Menuhin] will understand that. Living without work and without any particular purpose for so long has made me feel, not like the boy who lost his shadow, but like the shadow which lost the boy! That is more serious you know.

This short note is to greet you one and all when you reach Paris. If I were here then, I would give all five of you a hug as strong as a Russian bear's. I expect you have all grown very much, even Marutha has grown in <u>pounds</u>, I hope. (Excuse hotel pen.) I wish I could be here to hear Yehudi's first European recital after all the changes of thought and feeling that such a great experience must bring.

Lovingly to every one of you,
Willa Cather

→ ←

By late November of 1935 Cather was back in New York. One of the letters she had waiting for her was from an English professor at the University of Michigan, Carlton Wells, who identified a small detail about Cather's use of Felix Mendelssohn's oratorio Elijah *in* Lucy Gayheart.

TO CARLTON F. WELLS

January 7, 1936
New York City

My dear Mr. Wells:

I have just come back from a long stay in France and Italy, and the punishment of a holiday is that I have now to face a really terrifying mountain of letters which have been held for me here in my absence. I am working through this accumulation gradually and have just come upon your letter, to which I reply with real pleasure.

You are one in about seventy-five thousand, apparently, for you are the only person who has noticed that I changed the text of the famous aria in the Elijah; changed it for exactly the purpose you divine. The whole story verges dangerously upon the sentimental (since youthful hero worship is really the theme of the first two parts of the book), and if I had used the text of that aria as it actually stands, it would have been quite unbearable. Among the letters I have so far read, there are at least a dozen from concert musicians to whom this story seems to have appealed; but not one of them has noticed my variation of the text, although several are baritones who have sung the Elijah many times. I am delighted to have found one reader who did notice it because, of course, to a writer all those slight changes in language have great importance—perhaps an exaggerated importance. Please let me thank you for your friendly letter and wish you all good things for the New Year.

Very cordially yours,
Willa Cather

TO MRS. SIDNEY MATTISON

January 21, 1936

Dear Mrs. Mattison:

I don't usually welcome namesakes very cordially, for the simple reason that I never liked my own first name. I never like feminine forms of masculine names, in fact. If I had known, when I first began to write, that my name would be printed about a good deal, I would certainly have changed it to Mary or Jane, or Janet. I could not have changed my real name, out of respect to my parents: but I could have changed my writing name, and I often wish I had.

When I saw your little girl's pictures however, she seemed like such a real little person that I wanted to write to her and give her my good wishes. Perhaps she won't dislike the name as much as I do.

Cordially yours,
Willa Cather

[This accompanied the preceding cover letter:]

My dear Namesake:

Your mother has sent me several pictures of you, which makes me feel that you are a real little girl, and not just a name. She tells me that you are seven years old. That is a very nice age. I remember having enjoyed things very much when I was seven. Four years ago one of my dearest friends was seven years old—but, alas, that was four years ago, and now she is eleven. I hope your next four years will be as jolly as hers have been. The best thing I can wish for you is, that you will be absolutely sincere in your likes and dislikes—I don't mean violent, but sincere. If, when you grow older, my books bore you terribly, be honest about it and don't try to pretend to like them because some aunt or uncle tells you ought to like them, or that a great many people do like them. I would be ashamed of a namesake who did not know when she <u>really</u> liked a thing, and who did not stand up for her own tastes. I wish you lots of friends and happy vacations.

Cordially yours,
Willa Cather

➔ ❧

Professor Wells wrote back to Cather to ask if her letter to him about the text of Elijah *might be printed in a column by his friend William Lyon Phelps. He also mentioned that his students—to whom he had read the letter—enjoyed hearing it.*

TO CARLTON F. WELLS

January 23, 1936

Dear Mr. Wells:

I am sorry not to be able to oblige you, but I never allow quotations from personal letters to be printed. When, among a great number of the rather flat and dreary letters I receive, I come upon one that is alive and intelligent, I am rather prone to answer it in a somewhat intimate and unembarrassed tone. I take for granted that a person who writes a discriminating and intelligent letter is the sort of person who would not use any portion of my letter for publicity of any kind.

Very sincerely yours,
Willa Cather

I should like to oblige Mr. Phelps, but I shall do that at some other time, and in some other way. I did not even know that I was writing to your English class, Mr. Wells. English professors have many wiles, but I honestly thought you were interested in the question you asked me. O tempora, O mores! (The second "O" looks like a zero, certainly!) Enough: I become more cautious every day.

W.S.C.

TO WILLIAM LYON PHELPS

February 17, 1936

My dear Mr. Phelps:

I got home from Europe just before Christmas and have not yet got through the mountain of letters which accumulated in my long absence, but I want to skip a few hundred unanswered letters and drop a line to you, because last night I picked up the Yale Review and read your article on Mark Twain [published December 1935].

I knew Mark Twain during my first year in New York, when he was living on lower Fifth Avenue and spent most of his time in bed. Because I knew the man himself, Mr. [Van Wyck] Brooks' book [*The Ordeal of Mark Twain*] has always seemed to me one of the most glaring pieces of misapprehension that ever happened in a world full of mistakes. Mr. Brooks simply has no idea of what the real man was like; and I am afraid the imaginary Mark Twain, Mr. Brooks creates, would never have written "Huckleberry Finn". I don't know Mr. Brooks personally, but I have always heard good things about his scholarship and integrity. When he wrote about Mark Twain, he simply made a bad choice of subject, and I suspect from the general tone of his book that he could never have understood old Mr. Clemens at all: and if he had chanced to know him, I am afraid the intercourse would have been a series of mild, but painful, shocks!

This letter, you will understand, is confidential. It is not for me to contradict Mr. Brooks. But it is a great relief to me that some one has boldly refused to swallow this sentimental view of Mr. Clemens as a blighted genius, and you were certainly the man to do it. You could do it in the course of your usual activities; while I would have had to step so far out of mine, that it would have looked almost as if I had some personal grudge. I really feel very grateful to you. If Mr. Brooks could have seen that old lion in his bed telling stories to three or four young people, if he could have seen this for five minutes, he could never have written his book.

Cordially yours,
Willa Cather

❧ ❧

At some point Ferris Greenslet spoke with Cather about the possibility of Houghton Mifflin's publishing an edition of her complete works, the sort of edition that would be finely designed and marketed to collectors.

TO FERRIS GREENSLET

March 8, 1936

My dear Mr. Greenslet:

No, I have not so far had anything to do with influenza, and I am sorry to hear that you have had such a visitation. I have had plenty of sick friends however, and their many operations have kept me racing about among the hospitals until I sometimes think the only possible escape is to retire to a hospital myself.

I want to consult you about three things.

I. Are you still anxious to do a subscription edition in 1937 or 1938? Publishers sometimes change their minds as the times change. I hope to have time to run over some of the books and make corrections this summer, and that is why I ask you if you still adhere to the plan as we discussed it. If your proposition still holds, it was awfully considerate of you not to bother me about it at all in this past year when so many perplexing and unexpected things have come up. You remember the mild poet's remark "Only the sorrows of others cast", etc. Well, sometimes they can quite snow one under.

II. Tell me please, is there now a garage on the site of Mrs. Fields's old house at 148 Charles Street? Perhaps this is only a legend?

III. I am getting up a short book of essays for Alfred Knopf because we have been bothered with a good many requests to reproduce certain stray pieces of writing, which I think Mrs. Fields would have called "papers". I want to include a little sketch of Mrs. Fields which I did as a review of Mark Howe's "Memories of a Hostess", and following that a short article on Miss Jewett. The latter I haven't yet clearly planned, because I wanted first to know from you whether you would be quite willing that I should use a considerable portion of the preface I wrote for the Mayflower edition. I would, of course, state either in the article or in a note at the bottom of the page, that this was written as a preface, naming the book and publishers. You will remember that by my own wish there was no question of compensation when I did the preface for you, and I would not like to appear an "Indian giver" in asking your permission to use it again. I am asking you, really, because I said some things there about the quality of her work which I think I could not say quite so well again.

The times have changed so much that it might be wiser not to call forth Miss Jewett's shade into this present world, which would be so objectionable to her. The language in which she was such an artist has almost ceased to be. The brassy young Jews and Greeks from New York University have made the only language that is much heard in New York today. I may get discouraged and drop the notion altogether. It might be better if we could hide her away for awhile.

I suppose the thing that has made me rather want to do a little sketch of Miss Jewett, twenty years after, is that I get a good many letters from young people, both in this country and in England, asking me about her in a very reverent tone.

Faithfully yours,
Willa Cather

→ ←

Greenslet answered that, yes, Houghton Mifflin was still very interested in the "subscription edition" of her works, and asked that she deliver any revisions of the text to him by the fall of 1936 so that they could launch the new edition—eventually called the Autograph Edition—in the fall of 1937. He also approved of Cather's using her introduction to the Jewett book for her "short book of essays" Not Under Forty, published in 1936. Cather explains the curious title in the preface to the book: "It means that the book will have little interest for people under forty years of age. The world broke in two in 1922 or thereabouts, and the persons and prejudices recalled in these sketches slid back into yesterday's seven thousand years."

The following letter appears to be a transcription made by Knopf staff.

TO ALFRED A. KNOPF

May 1, 1936
New York City

Dear Alfred,

I was saving my projected title [*Not Under Forty*] as a surprise for you—possibly a shock. You see I think that to call a book of essays by any of the conventional titles such as <u>Personalities and Opinions</u> is foolish. Essays are dull enough anyhow. I have the hope that these papers are less dull than most, because they are mostly accounts of personal adventures with very individual literary personalities. However such a title would not be very satisfactory, as the best paper among them is certainly the one called <u>The Novel Demeuble</u>.

You would be much more reconciled to this title if you had gone through the text of the various essays. But you want a description of the book immediately and the paper on Thomas Mann [" 'Joseph and His Brothers' "] will not be finished and properly typed before the week after next. There will be, I fear, only five essays in all, and of these you have read only the one on Mme. Groux ["A Chance Meeting"]. It will have to be a small book and I suppose you would want to sell it at a dollar. I haven't the least idea to just how many words it will run, because this request for information for the catalogue has come suddenly. I had expected to give you an estimate of the length of the text, i.e., number of words, about the middle of May. I don't suppose you will need to know about details of that kind for the catalogue. I hope that Mrs. Kenyon may be able to convert you to this title for the essays. But if you think it really too outrageous I will, of course, listen to reason. Please think it over when you get back and call me up.

Yours,
[No signature]

➤ ⬅

In the spring of 1936 Annie Pavelka, Cather's old friend and the prototype for Ántonia in Cather's novel, wrote Cather thanking her for the Christmas check that she used to purchase a washing machine.

TO ANNIE PAVELKA

May 19, 1936

My dear Annie:

I have not written you because I have not been very well for the last five months and have been pretty badly overworked, trying to keep my business affairs afloat. But when I am not well, I especially enjoy letters from my old friends and your last one gave me great satisfaction, although not all the news was good. I am so happy that you got an electric washing machine with the $55 I sent you at Christmas. But the full price of the washer was $65, and I want to pay for it all. Therefore, I am enclosing a check for $10 to make up to you what you paid out, and now you can call it "Willie's Washer". You know, I am not very fond of my real name, Willa, and I always am pleased when Carrie and Mary Miner, and the people who knew me when I was little, call me "Willie," as my mother and father did. Nowhere else in the world do people call me by that name—just a few of the older people about Red Cloud.

In a few days, you will receive from me a box of winter clothing, which I do not need any more. One dress (the one with the plaid waist), I wore only twice, as I was ill then and not going out much. The striped silk dress (which looks like seersucker but is really silk), I think you may be able to wear yourself for Sunday best. However, I want you to dispose of these dresses just as you wish, and to give suitable ones to the daughters who have been the nicest to you. I have a good many little nieces to send clothes to, or I would send more to your nice girls. I always pray for your good health, just as I pray the Lord to send rain to Nebraska.

Your faithful friend,
Willa Cather

TO ALFRED A. KNOPF

July 18 [1936]

Dear Alfred;

I am more than pleased that Herr [Thomas] Mann liked my remarks about his wonderful book, and am grateful to you for sending me the excerpt from his letter. The weather has been so fine here that I have been out of doors most of the time with my dear little Wyoming nieces [Margaret and Elizabeth Cather, who were visiting Grand Manan]. (Nineteen is a grand age: I enjoy being in its company.) They leave the island on Monday, and I shall miss them terribly. I wish I could keep them all summer, but they have to go home for the wedding of an older sister.

Here are the contracts, in a queer envelope. Please ask Miss Rubin to send me half-a-dozen legal-size envelopes—none procurable on this island.

Mrs. [Sigrid] Undset's book has not come yet—but packages are always slow.

Please embrace Blanche for me, and tell her I shall write her as soon as I am nieceless.

Yours always
Willa Cather

TO ALFRED A. KNOPF

August 12 [1936]

Dear Alfred;

Thank you very much for the books you sent me some time ago. Mrs. Undset's book [*Gunnar's Daughter*] is surely one of her best—there is something awfully fine and fateful about it. It reads like a translation of a fine narrative poem—grandly Norse.

Conrad Richter is surely a man worth watching. When he writes of things that really interest him his sentences have a thrill, they flash into pictures, have a certain tone color. All this means of course that he has some real imagination,—and some red blood.

But I don't think you will ever get anything very interesting from Miss [Dorothy] Thomas. She has none of Richter's qualities. She never gets a thrill out of anything, never has any unusual perception or feeling. Dull, plodding, lifeless prose, as if she were packing a trunk <u>for someone else</u>, and trying conscientiously to put everything in. There is no fire in her, and no imagination. She says everything in the flattest possible way. Take a single sentence like that at top of page 126 of Richter's book [*Early Americana and Other Stories*]; Miss Thomas could never write a sentence like that, though its only merit is that the man saw something with interest and told it vividly. He is alive and writes with some vitality. You can't find one paragraph in her book [*The Home Place*] like that one—which, after all, merely communicates information about a dry autumn. She is of the [Ruth] Suckow breed, but much more limited.

If you have Mrs. Undset's "The Ax" and "The Snake Pit" in the old edition, <u>not</u> the one volume edition, will you please send them up to me?

I'll rush the page proofs back to you if they are sent properly by mail and reach me promptly.

I hope you and Pat had a splendid vacation.

Yours
W.S.C.

The sentences at the top of page 126 in Richter's Early Americana and Other Stories *(Knopf, 1936) read, "Before September the summer springs on the plain had dried up. The clear, running stream in Red Draw stopped flowing and turned up to the sun its light-colored sand like a dead snake's belly."*

TO ZOË AKINS

August 30 [1936]

Dear Zoë—

Thank you with all my heart for writing me about Jobyna [Howland]. I hadn't heard of her death and might not have heard for months. O Zoe, don't you sometimes wish we had been born in a kinder and less "progressive" age than this, when people lived closer together and stayed at home more and had a <u>deeper</u> and less scattered life? So many sad and bitter things are happening to my old friends in Nebraska that I can't feel very happy. I can send them canned fruit and vegetables and checks to buy clothes and fuel, but I can't bring their dead trees and ruined pasture land back to life. These five terrible years of utter drouth and frightful heat have ruined their farms and their health. In my own town [there were] <u>two months</u> when the heat did not drop below 100 for a single day, and went as high as 117, usually about 110! I feel wicked to be up here in this green flowery island in the north and to be wearing sweaters almost every day. Since I wrote you I've not been awfully well, but I think it's worry about my old friends that takes the enjoyment out of me. Keep well, my dear, and enjoy life—as you have a blessed gift for doing. One's life is all one has, and I want yours to be long and happy. You'll miss Jobyna, but I'm so glad she died on an up-grade and never went all to pieces as I had a fear she might do. And to think of her business affairs being in good order! Jobyna was always wiser than she let on to be—except about alcohol. Why do people guzzle, when a little wine is so good?

This is not a letter, dear, but a note to thank you for writing me at once. These days I dread a pen like a red hot poker.

Lovingly
Willa

TO MARGARET AND ELIZABETH CATHER

August 12 [1936]

My Darling Twinnies;

My rose is a curtain of bloom, from root to tip, and the hollyhocks are going strong. Now the golden rod on the edge of the cliffs waves against a purple sea, all the way up to the High Place. Last week the moon rose further and further north every night, first over the tip of fishhead, and finally right in front of our door—came up out of the water like a battered old copper kettle as it grew more and more lop-sided. It made such a bright, narrow path right to the foot of our cliff that one was tempted to walk across it. The weather here has been wonderful—blue and gold every day, with good rains at night.

Our lawn is very green now, and the monkshood makes a violet hedge against the gray house. It is so mild now, the weather, that we can sit out in our steamer chairs after dinner. The fire places have not been lit for a week. Mrs. Beal & Ralph [Beal] are here cleaning house today, and I am now writing in the attic. We read the proofs of the new book last week.

On Saturday we walked to Bright Angels, but no sweet twin did follow. We both miss you very much and often wish you were here. On Friday Miss [Winifred] Bromhall came for tea. She and Miss Jordan and Miss Glenning[?] and many others wish to be remembered to you—they also miss you. You must both come here again, my dears, before you do any desperate thing like getting married. If we all three wish it, we can make it come true. Next time it must be in August, when all the flowers are out, and the water warm enough to bathe in, and the whales due to arrive. The morning you left we got up early and waited on the shore, but we couldn't even see the boat. I wish your father and mother could have come on by airplane and dropped down on us while you were here. Perhaps they can, next time, and we can go to the Wolves and out to Gannet Light. Tomorrow we go to Southern Head if it is fine, and I shall remember the happy day we had there with you.

A world of love to you, my dears, from your
Aunt Willie

→ ←

The following is the only known surviving full letter from Cather to Edith Lewis.

TO EDITH LEWIS

Sunday 4:30 P.M. [October 5, 1936]
Shattuck Inn, Jaffrey, New Hampshire

My Darling Edith;

I am sitting in your room, looking out on the woods you know so well. So far everything delights me. I am ashamed of my appetite for food, and as for sleep—I had forgotten that sleeping can be an active and very strong physical pleasure. It can! It has been for all of three nights. I wake up now and then,

Edith Lewis, left, with Willa Cather in Jaffrey, New Hampshire, 1926

saturated with the pleasure of breathing clear mountain air (not cold, just chill air) of being up high with all the woods below me sleeping, too, in still white moonlight. It's a grand feeling.

One hour from now, out of your window, I shall see a sight unparalleled—Jupiter and Venus both shining in the golden-rosy sky and both in the West; she not very far above the horizon, and he about mid-way between the zenith and the silvery lady planet. From 5:30 to 6:30 they are of a superb splendor—deepening in color every second, in a still-daylight-sky guiltless of other stars, the moon not up and the sun gone down behind Gap-mountain; those two alone in the whole vault of heaven. It lasts so about an hour (did last night). Then the Lady, so silvery still, slips down into the clear rose colored glow to be near the departed sun, and imperial Jupiter hangs there alone. He goes down about 8:30. Surely it reminds one of Dante's "eternal wheels". I can't but believe that all that majesty and all that beauty, those fated and unfailing appearances and exits, are something more than mathematics and horrible temperatures. If they are <u>not</u>, then we are the only wonderful things—because we can wonder.

I have worn my white silk suit almost constantly with <u>no</u> white hat, which is very awkward. By next week it will probably be colder. Everything you packed carried wonderfully—not a wrinkle.

And now I must dress to receive the Planets, dear, as I won't wish to take the time after they appear—and they will not wait for anybody.

Lovingly
W.

I don't know when I have enjoyed Jupiter so much as this summer.

➤ ✦

In 1934 Warner Brothers released a second film based on A Lost Lady, *this one a rather freely adapted talkie starring Barbara Stanwyck. Cather's views on adaptation began to harden about this time, and she forbade dramatic adaptation of her works for the rest of her life and in her will.*

TO ZOË AKINS

December 15 [1936]

My Very Dear Zoë; (et tu, Brute!)

Please explain to Mr. [Daniel] Totheroh that if I would not allow an old friend like you to make a play of one of my books (and I wouldn't!) there is not much likelihood that I would let anyone else do it. I long ago made my decision about the question of dramatization, and it is absolute and final. Until I write a very different sort of novel, I shall never have one dramatized. I need make no explanation beyond the fact that I don't wish "A Lost Lady" dramatized. The legal aspect of my position I looked up long ago (Mr. Totheroh is by no means the first enthusiastic applicant) and I am, as you probably know, absolutely protected. The former sale of screen rights does not in anyway break down my ownership of the book. I am heartily sorry the young man wasted his time and energy, but he should not have built his bungalow on my land before informing himself whether it was for rent or for sale.

I will hold the ms. if you are coming on in January, as I am afraid I have defaced some pages by scrawling comments on the margins; these I will explain to you, and you can pass them on to the young man if you wish. I hear from several sources that he is [a] very fine fellow, and intelligent. This is a business letter, and I must be brief. There <u>are</u> a good many demands made on me, you know.

Devotedly always
W.S.C.

TO ZOË AKINS

Sunday [December 20, 1936]
New York City

My Very Dear Zoë;

I meant to write you a <u>non</u> business letter at once after I sent the other, but I've been overwhelmed by things.

No, <u>I am not cross </u>with you! I never have been. It would take a good deal to make me that. You simply let your natural kindness blind your judgment this time. The play you sent me is a stupid piece of work. If you aren't coming soon, I'll try to write you why I think so. This fellow never had the faintest idea of what Mrs. Forrester was like. Her lines are as common as mud—except when he quotes.

But I certainly don't hold his dumbness against <u>you</u>! That would be too petty.

Forgive this hurried scrawl, my dear. Alfred Knopf is sailing in a few days, suddenly, and a lot of business matters have come up to be arranged before he goes. The Christmas rush is on, and all the demands that one's family makes at this season. So forgive me if my letter sounded curt. I never feel annoyed with you. You have always been one of my real comforts, and one of the few people, of the <u>very</u> few people whom I trust. Wish me a happy Christmas in bed, and I'll come up smiling!

Yours
W.

PART TEN

Years of Grieving

1937–1939

As for me, I have cared too much, about people and places—cared too hard. It made me, as a writer. But it will break me in the end.
—WILLA CATHER TO ROSCOE CATHER, November 6, 1938

Willa Cather on Grand Manan Island, 1930s

IN 1937, Cather started writing a novel based in family lore that would challenge her artistry in new ways: *Sapphira and the Slave Girl*. Writing this book, set in antebellum Virginia, sent her both mentally and literally back to the region of her earliest childhood. She would need to conduct research—as she had many other times in her writing career—and learn as much as she could about the history of slavery and the lives of slaves in the American South, then write as empathetically and convincingly as she could about African American life. The writing of the novel was interrupted, however, by two devastating personal losses: her brother Douglass's death of a heart attack in 1938 and the death of Isabelle McClung Hambourg, her longtime friend and one of the great loves of her life, only a few months later after a long illness. These deaths, combined with the dark news of the rise of Nazism and the beginning of World War II in Europe, meant that the 1930s ended bleakly for Cather.

TO ROSCOE CATHER

January 7, 1937

My dear Roscoe:

Was there ever anybody who could always throw the monkey-wrench into the machine and add a spray of cypress to the holly wreath, like our sister Elsie? She wrote me from Casper that she was having such a delightful visit: I turned the page and on the other side, she says, "I am doubly glad to be here for if Roscoe is going to leave Casper as he intends, it may be many years before I see him again."

Now please tell me, where do you propose going—Alaska or South America or Tahiti? Even from Tahiti I get letters from James Norman Hall, who implores me to come to visit him and says it isn't a hard trip. Please enlighten me about your plans, my dear boy.

Hastily, but with all my love,
Willie

→ ←

Cyril Clemens wrote Cather in 1936 asking about her 1902 visit with poet A. E. Housman. In her reply, Cather wondered how he knew about it and dismissed its importance. Ford Madox Ford, in his 1932 memoir Return to Yesterday, *had jocularly told a false story that Cather, as president of the Pittsburgh Shropshire Lad Club, found Housman in Cambridge and delivered a golden wreath to him.*

TO CYRIL CLEMENS

January 30, 1937

Dear Mr. Clemens:

Are you sure it was in the <u>Forum</u> that you saw the article which you quote? I thought it was published in the Saturday Review, and it was written by the Prince of Prevaricators, Ford Maddox Ford.—Not a word of truth in it! I am sure that no group of ladies from Pittsburgh ever went to see Mr. Housman—and still more sure that I never headed such a group. When I met him it was not at his rooms in Cambridge, or in Cambridge at all. There was no golden wreath. It was simply an afternoon of conversation—conversation chiefly about other things than Mr. Housman's verses.

I have been greatly annoyed by this matter, Mr. Clemens, and have been besieged by demands to 'tell what I know about Housman'. In short, I am paying a heavy price for a very brief acquaintance. Alfred Knopf (who publishes <u>More Poems</u>) and I talked the matter over and he has suggested that at some time, probably in the distant future, I should write a very exact account of my afternoon with Housman, in much the same informal manner that I have used in the book of essays recently published under the title <u>Not Under Forty</u>. These essays are scrupulously truthful accounts of accidental meetings with very interesting people. This promise to Mr. Knopf will protect me from the almost threatening demands that have been made by a number of people. One's memories, after all, are one's own, and if one relates them to the public one prefers to do it in one's own way.

When I last wrote you about this matter I had determined never to give out any account of my impressions of Mr. Housman. But since so many false stories (like the one you quote on your postcard) have been started, I shall probably some day, when I am not so busy as I am now, write a statement of the very brief and simple facts.

Sincerely yours,
Willa Cather

TO ZOLTAN ENGEL

February 20, 1937

My dear Mr. Engel:

Please accept my heartiest thanks for the beautiful medallion of Rudyard Kipling which you have been gracious enough to send me. I have seen few portrait medallions which seem to me so successful, and it will be a great addition to my collection.

You ask me whether I know of any colleges that would be grateful for a medallion of Kipling: I am afraid I do not. I am led to believe that just at present most colleges would be more interested in a portrait medallion of Mr. T. S. Eliot!

Thanking you again for your kindness, I remain

Cordially yours,
Willa Cather

TO META SCHAPER CATHER

February 20, 1937

Dear Meta:

Roscoe may still be in the far west, in which case I beg a favor of you. If a package or any letters, addressed to me, come to you from the enclosed address, please forward them to me. This George Seibel is a Pittsburgh editor, and is one of the most persistent and tormenting of all my many curses.

Hastily, but with love to you all,
Willa

TO GEORGE SEIBEL

February 22, 1937

My dear Mr. Seibel:

I am glad to say that I haven't any New York address at present. I go to New York several times each year, but I stop at a different hotel every time. Just at present I am on my way to visit my brother in Wyoming. Anything you may wish to send me will eventually reach me if you will address it in care of—

Mr. R. C. Cather,
1225 N. Center Street,
Casper, Wyoming.

I am sorry to say that I have heard nothing of Francis Hill for many years.

I am delighted to hear that you and Mrs. Seibel are both well. As for me, I am well—whenever I am not in New York. The air there is so filled up with gasoline that a country bred person cannot get enough oxygen to breathe.

With best wishes always,
Willa Cather

→ ←

The following letter was written in response to a public debate in the pages of the Saturday Review of Literature *between the critics Bernard DeVoto and Edmund Wilson, particularly DeVoto's article "My Dear Edmund Wilson," published in the February 13, 1937, issue.*

TO BERNARD DEVOTO

March 10, 1937

Dear Mr. De Voto:

This letter is not for publication, and writing to editors is certainly not a habit of mine.

But I find that after several weeks have gone by I still feel a wish to thank you for your letter to Mr. Edmund Wilson, which appeared in the Review some time ago. I say thank you advisedly, because in that letter you stated clearly things that I have felt very strongly and have never been able to formulate, even to myself. One knows that our actual lives are very little made up of economic conditions. They affect us on the outside, but they certainly are not what life means to you or to me or to the taxi driver, or to the elevator boys and hall boys (all of whom I know very well) in the house where I live. Theories of economic reform and social reconstruction really seem to interest nobody very much—except the men who write about them and the men who have made it a profession to be interested in them. Most, if not all of these students who burn with zeal to reconstruct and improve human society, seem to lose touch with human beings and with the individual needs and desires which make people what they are.

You probably remember that as an empiricist Tolstoi went even further than you go in your letter to Mr. Wilson. After spending most of his life in pondering how to make life better for men of high and low estate, he decided that the European desire to organize society efficiently was a mistake. And he repeats down through the years that "the state of a man's mind has always been more important to him than the conditions of his life. It seems as if there were some antithesis between efficient organization and the best there is in mankind; as though, in a highly organized, extremely efficient society, men cease to think truly or feel deeply." Of course, Tolstoi tried to be a Marxist and failed; of course, he is very much out of date and out of fashion now, but certainly no one ever took the puzzle of human life more to heart or puzzled over it more agonizingly,—not even the New Republic.

It quite heartens one to have a man come out and say frankly, as you did, that it seems natural to regard the world immediately about one as made up of individuals rather than of "masses": and that human history and human experience, and the human needs we know to be strongest in ourselves and in our friends, make the most reliable data we have as to what really comprises happiness and well-being in individuals and large collections of individuals.

Please excuse me if I seem to be trying to write your editorial back at you, for I know very well I could not improve upon it.

Very sincerely yours,
Willa Cather

→ ←

When the Canadian critic E. K. Brown sent Cather his essay "Willa Cather and the West" from the University of Toronto Quarterly, *she was favorably impressed.*

TO E. K. BROWN

April 9, 1937

My dear Mr. Brown:

I recently returned from a long absence, and among the many reviews and articles awaiting me I find your interesting and very friendly pamphlet. You have certainly brought a friendly and unprejudiced mind to my books, and though I do not always agree with you I am interested in all your opinions.

I think you make a very usual mistake, however, in defining a writer geographically. Myself, I read a man (or a woman) for the climate of his mind, not for the climates in which he has happened to live. The places in which he has lived do, to a certain extent, color his mind. But to me the Kipling of <u>Captains Courageous</u> is just as vigorous and keen and full of his subject, as the Kipling of the early Indian stories.

You say that the Southwest of the <u>Archbishop</u> is not so much my country as the West of Nebraska. I think in your zeal to make your case, you have fallen into error. I knew the Southwest early, and knew it long and well. I did not write about it earlier for one reason only: the Southwest is so essentially and at its roots a Catholic country, that it seemed to me no Protestant could handle material properly. (You understand that I am speaking here of the <u>real</u> Southwest, the Mexicans and the Indians and the workers on the railroads. I am not speaking of the tourists and cheap artists and dude ranches which have infested that country and overwhelmed it since I first knew it.)

To go back to the other side of my parenthesis, I waited fifteen years for some Roman Catholic to write a book about the real New Mexicans, their religion and country, and some of those early French missionary priests who left such a fragrant tradition of tolerance and insight and kindly sympathy. Isn't it possible after all, that one may admire quite as sincerely a man of Father Latour's type as a man of Father Vaillant's? I am asking you to read a letter which I wrote concerning the actual writing of <u>Death Comes for the Archbishop</u>. You will find it on page 17 in the pamphlet enclosed.

Very cordially yours,
Willa Cather

I must apologize for the enclosed pamphlet:—it is one my publisher uses as a reply to colleges and clubs who write to him for information.

Willa Cather

➜ ❮

The following letter continues a correspondence with Akins about a dramatic adaptation of A Lost Lady *that began at the end of 1936.*

TO ZOË AKINS

April 19, 1937

My dear Zoë:

You will forgive me if I say [a] word in typewriter about Mr. [Daniel] Totheroh's play, which I am sending back to you.

Take Mrs. Forrester's first entrance in Act I. What does she say when she comes into the Judge's office? <u>My, your stairs are steep</u>! That is what the scrub woman says when she arrives. Did you ever, Zoe, know a woman with any spunk or sparkle who used "my" as an exclamation? I remember a fat old Methodist neighbour who used to drag out "My, but the days are warm, Mr. Cather!" In her first sentence, Zoe, he shows her up for a common, dreary thing. In her next sentence, she refers to her (1) age and to her (2) travelled state! Two things she would never have done. (1. Her particular weakness, 2. Bad taste.)

A little later she trills to this lumping Swede that his little boy's eyes are "blue as a mountain lake". Ho-Ho! When she doesn't talk like a corsetless old Methodist woman, she talks like a darling club woman, and says she "would die" to have such eyes etc. That expression stamps her socially. So does "you can help me out". Everything she says stamps her socially, except when she brazenly quotes me. She says Niel will be "a great asset" to Sweet Water society. Lord, they needed assets—some future, with Marian as the social leader!

Everything that Niel says is the speech of a cotton-mouthed booby. As to Mrs. Forrester's smirking about "drinking here alone, with two men"–––the dining-room girls in our little town-hotel might have said that; the common- est King's Daughter or Eastern Star sister would have refused the sherry, or drunk it and said nothing. On page 13, the playwright becomes unbearable because he makes the Judge bring out discreditable insinuations about Cap- tain Forrester. The integrity of the book really rests on Captain Forrester.

My dear Zoë, I read no further than the first act. Nothing could induce me. The language he puts in Mrs. Forrester's mouth shows that he hadn't the least idea of the kind of woman she was. I snatched up the book, which I hadn't read for years. I could find no excuse for him. As you know, Mrs. Forrester was done from life, an absolutely truthful portrait. Her speech was always a delight to me. She never said anything very wise, or even very witty, but her voice and eyes spoke together—it was quick spontaneous staccato, usually a little mocking. She never used bromidic expressions, such as "I hear Niel is back", or "You can help me out." One can't judge what one writes I suppose, but if I let her down and made her talk like a common slut, may I suffer for it!

Zoë, I pray you turn to page 8 of Act I and see what that rather nice boys' picnic becomes. Nothing great, those few pages, but something rather fresh and rather genuine about it. And this is what he does with that nice morning!

Now, my dear Zoë, I don't care how many grand situations he may have built up in the acts I did not read, or how "dramatic" he may be, and I don't care what might happen to the common woman that he has made of Mrs. Forrester. We'll forget this episode forever, but I do <u>want you to refer to the passages I have mentioned in the first act</u> and judge as to whether you think I have been unreasonable.

I do thank you for the verses you sent me. Of course, I like the one about your own room very much the best—in fact, I like it very best. The one on Jobyna [Howland] I would like, if you hadn't put her name under the title. I just, somehow, cannot in my mind connect Jobyna with the out-of-doors or the quiet things of nature. And yet, you know, I liked her very much.

Now that I've explained myself a little, my mind is clear of wrath against this young man. It's the only quarrel ["quarrel" is crossed out] no, discord, that has jarred you and me in so many years—and I've been a goose to take it seriously. Forgive me.

With my love to you
Willa

→ ←

In the spring of 1938, Roscoe Cather wrote his sister at length explaining his impending move to Colusa, California, and his purchase of a bank there.

TO ROSCOE CATHER

May 19 [1937]
Jaffrey, New Hampshire

My dear Brother:

I am not a good enough writer to tell you how much I appreciate your long confidential letter with its account of all you have been doing. You put the situation to me so clearly that I feel as if I had been through your adventures with you. I am so glad, oh so glad, that you and Meta are to be released at last from those long, hard Wyoming winters which you have borne so bravely: and that now you are to spend your time in that northern part of California, which to me is so much more beautiful than the southern part. Even though you should not make a great deal of money, it will be a grand move. What can money buy that is so worth while as beautiful country and the pleasant things of every-day life which so often go with beautiful country? Your picture of Colusa seems to me just the sort of town I would like myself. I like everything about northern California, except the fact that there are a great many idle, drifting, shallow people there. Just the kind of people among whom Jim's wife [Ethel Garber Cather] cuts a simper in the South [of California]. But you and Meta will find your own kind of people, even in California.

I am so glad that you have had this wonderful visit with Douglass. I love to have you two men happy together. Yes, you are quite right; he has more of Father in him than any of us, and he has kept so remarkably young in face and feeling. (But wasn't it funny that I was the only one who got Father's hands? And the older I grow, the more they are like his.)

I must say again, dear boy, that nothing could please me more than to know that you and Meta are going to live in a mild climate, and that you are going to be near Douglass. And when I go out to stay with the Menuhins, I can come to visit you. Your town cannot be very far from Los Gatos.

With all my love to you,
Willie

[Written on the back:] I return to N. Y. a week from today.

→ ←

Pat Knopf ran away from home in the spring of 1937 after learning that he did not get accepted into Princeton, determined to make good before he returned. Police found him hungry and penniless in Salt Lake City, and he came back to New York.

TO ALFRED A. KNOPF

August 9 [1937]
Grand Manan Island

Dear Alfred;

My Herald-Tribunes come in bunches, and I don't always open them at once. So for me, Pat was lost, found, returned, all in one bunch of news, like a "continued story". I'm glad he is back again, but more glad that he ran away. I'm glad he wanted to run away. He has had too much petting, and it's a good sign that he felt like kicking it all over. People are always (on your account and because you are a publisher) paying more attention to him than they naturally would to a lad of his age. Their overtures are more potent than your efforts to counteract them: (bad English, but you will understand.) All this wouldn't matter if the boy were just a silly ass. But there is another side to him, and you'll agree with me that the other side hasn't had much chance. We all like flattery, and most young people like to stand out from the crowd and be exceptional. The son of a successful and prominent man always has a hard time. But the only son of a conspicuously original and successful publisher, in these times when every society girl and every school boy wants to "write"—well, he's pretty nearly damned from childhood. I've sometimes wished you'd sent him to school in Switzerland, where his name would not suggest getting next to a publisher. I don't think you can realize what a handicap "Alfred A. Knopf Inc." is to him. We'd have to be of heroic ["heroic" is rewritten here three times] mould to stride over it. (I wrote Blanche several weeks ago about getting a black spider sting on my right hand—had a nasty time with it. Now I'm free of bandages, but my hand remains stiff and awkward, as you can see when I have to write the word "heroic" over three times to make it at all decipherable!) I hope you and Blanche didn't worry too much about Pat's running away.

My love to you both, and a great deal to Pat—though, I shan't tell him so.

Devotedly to you all
W.S.C.

P.S. Just a word: why don't you ask Greenslet to let you see the [crossout] (failed again!) prospectus they are preparing for the subscription edition? A rumor is going round that you have left me, or I have left you.

W.S.C.

→ ←

Cather's twin nieces made a second visit to Grand Manan in the summer of 1937.

TO MARGARET AND ELIZABETH CATHER

Tuesday [August 1937?]

My Darling Twinnies;

Yesterday a wild north-easter—wish you could have seen it. Bitter cold, and breakers of black water pounding up on the Giants' Graves under a very low black-gray sky. Today, fair and dreamy—all off on boat trips.

I finished the autographs on Friday morning and sent them over to East-port by special messenger (Ralph!) on Saturday boat. He bore himself like a King's messenger! Hadn't been to Eastport for years. We left the box in back hall, he came for it at six a.m. bore it off without waking us. Took it on boat as personal baggage, got it through American customs, drove in a taxi to express office at the far end of Eastport, got it on the train for Boston. Such a proud man he was. Happy thought: if I take Ralph for my island secretary, then per-haps we may have Willie [Thomas] for gardener?

Willie went for Miss [Sarah] Jacobus to cut the alder thickets on the Dim-ple Downs with his double-edged ax. Ax rebounded from a dead alder and cut his knee to the bone. He walked home but was unable to work for some days—lost blood, of course, and such dirty clothes rubbing it as he walked home! Inflammation gone, however, and the wound has healed.

I was almost as much disappointed as you, my dears, about your being shut out of the comfortable Frontenac. I didn't realize that after prohibition it would be crowded. I should have written the management two weeks before you went away, and demanded rooms as a personal favor. Ah, I wish you could see Quebec in Winter!

I am sending a very interesting book on G. Manan on to Colusa. My hand is still stiff, as you can see—autographing didn't do it any good. I must get a note off to Stephen [Tennant] who cabled yesterday from Aix-les-Bains to know where I am and whether I am ill. So now I must stop this letter. Every-one misses you, my dear children, but no one misses you so much as I do.

Your very loving aunt.

P.S. Oh delight! Yesterday Miss Bonnell telephoned Gannet Light [Gannet Rock Lighthouse] keeper to ask if she might come to spend night first fair day.

Keeper replied his wife away on visit for two weeks, and he was afraid Government Inspectors would not approve Bonnell's visit! These are the actual facts. She had engaged motor boat.

TO ZOË AKINS

October 28 [1937?]

My Very Dear Zoë;

The book [*The Hills Grow Smaller: Poems*] came, some days after your letter. If the gracious inscription on the front page is true, I thank God for it—and your own generous mind. I read the book through in bed, after tea, which is an hour I save for things I really want to read. If I told you I liked it as much as I like your first book of verse written long ago, you'd know I was lying. For you yourself know it's not so good. It's not so <u>singing</u>. The lyric———something isn't here. Single lines don't echo and stay in one's mind just because they somehow had the rhythm one's heart had then. You've gone and got thoughtful, as Edna Millay has! You've grown wiser in almost every way, my dear, but wisdom doesn't seem to have much to do with Poetry.

Yes, you've grown wiser in every way except in the matter of self-protection. You <u>will</u> give the people who hate you a chance to vent their spite. I hope you won't offer a new play in New York this season. Is there <u>no</u> place to put on plays except New York or some place where New York press men are taken thither by force? You'll never get a fair showing from them—your plays are not the kind they like. You're a romantic, and your hue is not the wear just now. The young men who "cover the theatre" have a grudge—and I'm afraid you have played into their hands a little. You have been indiscreet enough to write articles or letters to the paper explaining yourself—which always means defending oneself. The safe thing would be to present a hard and stony face to critics, not to take them into your confidence—and that is what you do when you reply to them. I, too, have my haters—they go for me every time they can; Messers [John] Chamberlain, [Lionel] Trilling, Kronborg [presumably Louis Kronenberger], Kaysmere [possibly Alfred Kazin?]—oh there are a lot of them. If ever I replied to them, or wrote articles setting forth my views and defending the kind of "art" I believe in, I think even Alfred Knopf would soon be trying to pass this brick along to another publisher, for he would come in for some of the ridicule. The nearest I have come to such a break was that article on Miss Jewett in <u>Not Under Forty</u>. It wasn't a near break, (I may as well be truthful) it was a <u>whole</u> break. Nearly a hundred furious letters, and sly digs from the press generally, have shown me how foolish it is to make public a credo—one's articles of faith ought to be the most protected of one's secrets. Some of these horrid New York University graduates, all with foreign names and more foreign manners, had been publishing some of the most horrid articles about her and about "sex-starvation" in New England writers generally. Provincial ladies and lady-like men. It made me angry and I broke out. Silly performance. Now I have learned that if one is consistently silent where one's own self is concerned, one must be silent when one's friends are attacked. They reflect one's point of view, one's admirations—to speak for them is, in a manner, to speak for one's self.

With you the case is more serious than with me. New York book reviewers have very little influence outside New York. Those in the "New Republic" and the "Nation" have, I suppose, but I really don't care. The theatrical first night reviews are read everywhere by the small city Sunday editors and repeated—in print. I may be wrong, but I feel you ought not to bring out a new play here for a year or two. You don't have to—so why not keep out from under the ax? Of course, if you show this letter to George [a mistake for Eugene?] O'Neill or any other theatrical persons, they'll tell you it's all nonsense. But they would be letting themselves off easy, and I am telling you an unpleasant truth—never an easy or pleasant thing to do. The New York theatrical writers have a grudge, have it in for you. Since you are certainly prosperous and don't have to submit to punishment, why do you? A book, if it's universally damned as the "Archbishop" was, can go quietly on and sell its five hundred thousand and keep selling. But a play can't go quietly on by itself. There's a big overhead. It can be kicked of[f] the stage and buried in a week—a night, for that matter.

My dear Zoë, I'll put you on your honor to show this letter to no one. In preaching discretion to you, I've been indiscreet myself. I've been to honest because I want to save you pain, and because I feel it must be better for your reputation on the Pacific coast not to have these knocks coming back from New York. I've been thinking for a year about writing this letter. If a friend knows you're up against a clique of prejudice and spite, it's that friend's business to tell you so, even if it is a mighty unpleasant job. As for the letter (now it's written), read it, destroy it, forget it if it is painful. And let the next Willy-boy actor or Russian Prince you talk to persuade you that every play you write will have a fair greeting by the New York Press.

Now I'm tired, my dear, and must say goodnight.

Your True though Tactless friend
W.S.C.

TO ZOË AKINS

[Written in the top margin:] I remember your room at the Ritz was full of your own garden flowers

November 8 [1937]

Dearest Zoe;

The flowers reached me three days ago, and tonight they are as fresh as if they had just come out of your garden. And how did you know that I especially love the leaves and the balls of the eucalyptus tree? Do send me some of the balls or nutlets in late November. They keep fragrant all the winter through.

I hope these white flowers mean forgiveness, Zoë. I doubt if I had a right to write you as I did. Maybe you don't mind being pummelled by a lot of New Deal boys who are out to knock you! Anyway, I mind it for you. Chiefly because it's a frame-up, and I doubt if you could get a newspaper notice that was not a foregone conclusion.

I'm afraid my way of saying things is a little more crabbed than usual. I'm working on a new book [*Sapphira and the Slave Girl*] which is such a pleasure to me, and God and man seem agreed that I shan't get ahead with it. Nothing is more disturbing to me than to work with Houghton Mifflin, and I have got into their net again with the subscription complete edition. Knopf has no subscription department, and he wanted me to do this—said it had to be. It's given me the Hell of a spring and summer, and now it's breaking into my winter and my new book. I don't want <u>anything</u> but quiet and a fairly pleasant place to write in, and to be <u>let alone</u>. Do you think I can get it? I'd be glad to live on a crust if I could get just that. I can't!! Now the Goddam movies are after "Antonia". I'm in terror for fear Houghton Mifflin may sell me out; they can, you know. Isn't it hard luck!

Lovingly
W.

TO ELSIE CATHER

December 22 [1937]

My Precious Sister;

How kind you were to write me a lovely long letter and tell me all about the ceremony for the windows, and about the old folks at home! I don't deserve it. But this year I tried to send cards to every one of mother's old friends, and all those of "our crowd" at home. I did forget Mrs. Warren, but I sent one with a little note to dear Mrs. Macfarland in California.

Life has been crowded, for the Menuhins arrived only a few days before Douglass came, the mother very ill and forbidden to leave her bed, and I tried to be with the little girls (who are no longer little, but as lovely and loving as ever) until Yehudi and his father arrived from New Orleans and other Southern engagements. But I arranged so that I could be with Douglass as much as if I had no other ties, and he went to Yehudi's first concert here—I gave him my seat, and I sat in the Menuhin's box. I am sure he enjoyed the splendor of Carnegie Hall and the almost theatrical welcome and triumph New York gave Yehudi.

Douglass was here for my birthday dinner—poor M.V. had to work at the Library that night and could not come, and I wouldn't ask anyone not "family", so he and Edith and I had a wonderful evening to ourselves.

I don't know if you know that he came on largely to see a doctor. The best heart specialist in New York pronounced his heart <u>absolutely</u> all right. What a relief that was to both of us. The pain in his left arm comes from some form of neuritis. Please dear use this little check for something jolly.

A merry Christmas to you, dear.
Willie

TO FERRIS GREENSLET

January [really December?] 29, 1937
New York City

My dear Ferris Greenslet:

Thank you for your letter bearing good wishes, and may I send you all possible good wishes for the coming year?

I have been a long time in replying to your letter of December 4th. I have thought your proposition over carefully and I am still, as I was when I first read your letter, strongly against any plan to make an illustrated edition of <u>Antonia</u> for next year, or for any other year.

Certainly, I like Grant Wood's work, but his whole view of the West, and his experience of it, is very different from my own. Our geographical background was different. Iowa is a black-loam and heavy-clay state: too much rain and plenty of mud. In Central and Western Nebraska the soil is sandy and light, not nearly so productive as in Iowa,—that is why the farms were so much further apart. Settlers in Nebraska were seventy per cent from overseas.

Foreign population in Iowa was much smaller—though there were a good many Czechs there.

Why can't we let <u>Antonia</u> alone? She has gone her own way quietly and with some dignity, and neither you nor I have reason to complain of her behavior. She wasn't played up in the first place, and surely a coming-out party, after twenty years, would be a little funny. I think it would be all wrong to dress her up and push her. We have saved her from text books, from dismemberment, from omnibuses, and now let us save her from colored illustrations. I like her just as she is.

I would, of course, be pleased if I could feel sure that the Benda illustrations will never be ripped out again, and I would be greatly gratified if one of the excellent proof-readers at the Riverside Press would run through the book and mark the broken letters and illegible words which should be replaced. In case you should ever decide to reset the book, I beg you to use just the same type and the same slightly tinted paper now used.

By the way, I think very well of a book you have recently published, but I would not dare tell you which, lest one of your enterprising young men should manage to work my name into an advertisement.

Faithfully yours,
Willa Cather

TO SINCLAIR LEWIS

January 14, 1938
New York City

My dear Lewis:

I have had a grand time reading <u>The Prodigal Parents</u>—all through it I had the sense of coming home again to my own people. Even the sawdust son and the detestable Sara are unmistakably American—couldn't be mistaken for anything else. Maybe it's the fact that they are so easily taken-in that makes them seem so much our own kin. With a world-wide reputation for being smart and on-the-make, aren't we just about the most gullible and easily taken-in of all peoples? It's our incurable optimism and sweet trustfulness that have got us into all this mess. When this country is chock-full of solid people who always come up to the scratch without any rhetoric, like Fredk. Wm. and Hazel [Cornplow, characters in Lewis's novel], will you tell me why we lie down and take a booting? I half believe that it's because we can't seriously believe evil of anyone. We don't like to believe evil. It's more comfortable not to believe it. We think that Stalin must have very good points, and we know Mussolini has made Italy <u>so</u> comfortable for tourists. I don't believe we'll waken up to the situation we've drifted into until the knife is at our throat. There are Howard Cornplows in every country, but I think in other countries they have more meanness and sharper claws than this poor dub. The reason I so enjoyed this book is, that it fairly glows with that peculiar and generally misplaced and unintelligent kindness which is so peculiarly American. (For a hundred years we have been begging all the crooks and incompetents in the world to come over to us and be happy. Well, we've got them). What is worse is that we've got their grandsons, and with the right kind of political manipulation they'll do us all in very nicely. Anyhow, I'd rather live and die in such a silly soft-hearted country than in any other. Wouldn't you? All the same we are in a tight fix just now, though not many of the people you meet on your lecture tour will realize it. They will tell you that "things will come out all right", just because they always have.

Please come and have tea with me when you get back.

Your obliged
Willa Cather

TO YEHUDI MENUHIN

January 22 [1938]

My Dear Yehudi;

It is impossible to get these letters here in German. Travellers cannot carry big books about, so I send this tiny little one, which contains all the preserved letters of a young man who died at thirty-one [Franz Schubert]. They are rather heart-breaking, these letters, when one thinks of all that lay behind them. (I like to think that if you had been living in his time you would have seen what the others did not see, and would have helped him.) But put all the hardships and disappointments together in one heap, and match against it all the lovely things he made in fifteen years,—can one then say that he had an unhappy life? Being hungry wouldn't matter much if one's mind were blooming every day like that, would it?

Happy Birthday, dear and noble artist. God send you many years of achievement and happiness.

Your loving and grateful
Aunt Willa

→ ←

Stephen Tennant, a flamboyant British artisocrat, writer, and artist, began a correspondence and friendship with Cather after reading My Mortal Enemy *in 1926.*

TO FERRIS GREENSLET

January 24, 1938

My dear Ferris Greenslet:

I am going to ask a favor of you and I have put it off a long time. Under another cover I am sending you a book of drawings by young Stephen Tennant, the fourth son of Baron Glenconner. Anne Douglas Sedgwick wrote to me some twelve years ago and asked if she might give this boy permission to write to me. Since then Stephen and I have been good friends, and two years ago he spent the winter at the Shattuck Inn in Jaffrey and gained thirty pounds. (I sent him there for a three weeks' stay, to recover from a cold he caught on landing. He stayed there the winter, all alone with his valet.) He is a very handsome fellow, with great talent, but very frail health. I enclose with this letter two of the notices which greeted his book in England. The review by Connolly is really very discerning.

Of course, since the book has attracted attention in England and has delighted Margot Asquith, Stephen's publishers do not see why they should not be able to export a few hundred sheets to the States. I promised Stephen that I would present his book for the consideration of the only two publishers with whom I have direct relations. I made this promise before I saw the book! He warned me that the tone was ribald. But when it arrived I saw at once that it wasn't the kind of ribaldness that goes in America (I think myself that these sketches, done in 1929, were a natural reaction of the young man's upbringing, which was very puritanical). Viscount Grey was a firm stepfather and his feeling about "Nature" was certainly very different from young Tennant's; I should liked to have heard their breakfast table conversation.

You will enjoy looking through this book,—the drawings are really remarkable, you know. All I beg of you is to write me a personal letter, telling me how the book strikes you and giving me a few words of explanation as to why it would be rather impossible for an American publisher to handle this book. (Of course, if you know of any publisher who would be able to use imported sheets, I would be delighted to send the book to him.) It is difficult to explain to Stephen why, when we are so indecent in some things, we draw the line at others: certainly we simply won't stand for any "lyrical beauty", as Mr. Connolly calls it. We want Hemingway and words of four letters, without any perfume.

I hate to bother you about this, but you see I promised the young man (he is twenty-nine, but he seems about nineteen) that I would show you and Alfred his book, and I have to keep my word. Alfred wrote me a nice letter to send him and I don't feel that I am imposing on you greatly when I ask you for one, because I think you will really enjoy running through the book some evening. Please return the two press cuttings and mail the volume back to me when you have looked it over.

Faithfully yours,
W.S.C.

On second thought I decide to enclose a letter in which Stephen comments on, and explains, the book himself. Please return it to me. All his letters are illustrated like this—he does them at top speed—in a few minutes.

Tennant's book, Leaves from a Missionary's Notebook, *was never published in the United States.*

TO MARGARET AND ELIZABETH CATHER

January 24, 1938

My darling Twinnies:

I must tell you how splendidly the moving pictures that Edith took at Grand Manan came out. We have no projector, but we took Hephzibah and Yaltah Menuhin into a kodak shop and had them run off. They were perfectly splendid of you, and even of me! And the woods and water were grand. Yehudi was away on tour, but he wants to see them before he sails, because the girls gave him such a good account of them. If there is such a thing as a good projector in Colusa, we will mail the films to you sometime and then you can show your father and mother just what Grand Manan is like.

The champagne that I like best is Louis Roederer and 1929 is a grand year, also 1926 is very fine. I am having a busy life these days, for when Yehudi is in town the girls and I usually walk with him, and when he is away on tour we walk without him, and also go to the art galleries. Last Thursday night we had a grand Opera party; Yehudi took his two sisters, Edith and me to hear Lohengrin. On January 29th we have another opera party to hear Tristan and

Isolde. [Written in the margin next to above paragraph:] If you listen in on Saturday you can here it too! Afternoon performance will be evening with you, will it not?

Anything about my doings with the Menuhins is confidential, my dears, I know you understand that. People are always trying to make themselves important by using their name. I think you know that it is because they are such beautiful and <u>good</u> human beings that I love them, and not because they are "celebrities." Yehudi happens to be the kindest and noblest human being I have ever happened to know at close range, and to me his nature is more interesting and beautiful than his talent. Of course, I am forced to believe that in his case a great talent and a lofty nature are one; neither could exist without the other. We had a wonderful walk round the reservoir one day last week when the thermometer was only eight above zero and the wind very keen. After an hour and a half out there we were so warm and jolly that we none of us wanted to go in, and were late for lunch.

Your tactful Aunt Jessie tried to crowd herself in on the Menuhins when they were in Los Angeles. She wrote the father [Moshe Menuhin] a letter that she must see him in order to send a message to <u>me</u> (ME!) since he was going to New York!!! Little did the lady know that I had many times warned both the mother and father that they must never receive any relative of mine whom I had not asked them to receive. I am not going to have this family tormented simply because they have been nice to me. It is a measure of Aunt Jessie's intelligence that she could think she might put such a dodge through.

Now my dears, forgive me for getting in a temper about Aunt Jessie. Good-by and heaps of love to you all.

Your devoted
Aunt Willie

[Enclosed and written on a page from *Book Week* for January 8, 1938, with a column by Sinclair Lewis praising Cather's work:] I've never met Lewis but twice, yet he's always doing these "big brother" acts for me. Nice and friendly of him.

TO HENRY SEIDEL CANBY

March 2, 1938

My dear Mr. Canby:

I am just back in town after a long absence, and hasten to reply to your letter. Of course, you have my permission to keep my name in the P.E.N. Club through 1939, if it will oblige you. I warn you, I shall be on the other side of the world in 1939, and as for the "distinguished group" which you propose to bring over, I had rather they stayed at home and wrote something interesting! I do not believe you could look me in the eye and tell me that you think all this getting together and talking with the mouth, has anything but a bad effect on writers. I wonder, indeed, whether it has anything but a bad effect on human beings in general? I wish the Tower of Babel would happen all over again.

Now, another thing: I want to thank you for your review of Katharine Anthony's book on Miss Alcott [titled *Louisa May Alcott*]. I see the Freud fanatics are getting on your nerves, as they are on mine. It happened that my old friend Mrs. James T. Fields, born a May, was a cousin of Louisa May Alcott. Several years before she died, Mrs. Fields asked me to destroy a great number of more-or-less family letters, which she did not wish to leave among her drawers-full of correspondence. There were a great many from Miss Alcott, who used often to come for long New England visits at her cousin's house. Anything more lively and "pleasant" and matronly you could not imagine. She was often a good deal fussed about money, because, apparently, she was practically the only earning member of the family. You know the tone and conversation of the warm-hearted distinctly "pleasant" New England woman. The later letters showed her warm pleasure in "getting on" with her work and earning money that was so much needed. If the "naked bodies" of the men she nursed in her hospital experience left any "wound", it was certainly not perceptible to her relatives, or in her letters—or in her very jolly books, as I remember them. Catherine the Great might be called fair game for Miss Anthony's obsession, but certainly that warm-hearted and very practical New England spinster was not. I wish now that those letters to Mrs. Fields had not been destroyed. All these remarks, of course, are entirely confidential and are meant for you and Mrs. [Marion] Canby alone, but the tone of your review is so <u>right</u> that I want to add my hearty word of confirmation.

I am going to write to Mrs. Canby very soon, and I hope that we three can get together again before this almost-gone winter is over.

With my warmest greetings to you both,
Willa Cather

➔ ←

Both of Roscoe's twin daughters, Margaret and Elizabeth, were married in 1938.

TO ROSCOE CATHER

March 26 [1938]

My Dear Boy;

Oh, they are all headed for matrimony, I can see it! You and Meta had better adopt <u>me</u>, I wont go back on you.

Please take your motor trip. Go to Tuscon, and go out to the <u>very</u> old mission of St. Xavier del Bac, go again and again. It's about the loveliest thing on this side of the Atlantic. It's Franciscan—read up a little on St. Francis. Everything about the place is lovely

I'll write you about the Lake Placid plan later. Edith Lewis is a Delta Gamma, and greets her "sister in the Bonds"

Hastily
W.

→ ←

Cather often took a keen interest when her work was being translated into French, as it was a language she knew well.

TO ALFRED A. KNOPF

April 19, 1938

My dear Alfred:

You will see by reading the enclosed letters from Madame [Marguerite] Yourcenar (the first written before she came to see me, the second afterward), that our interview greatly cooled her enthusiasm.

1. Unfortunately, Madame Yourcenar made her translation from the Tauchnitz edition [in English, though published in Germany], which contains many errors. She was no farther away than New Haven; had she applied to either you or me, a recent and corrected edition would have been sent her promptly.

2. Madame Yourcenar has never been in the Southwest at all, and seems to have no conception of how very different that country is from any other part of the United States. She has not informed herself about its people or customs—which, after all, are today very much as they were in Archbishop Lamy's time. In so far as that country and people are concerned, her mind is an utter blank. Yet she says that there are some descriptive passages in the

book (I don't know how many) which she must "paraphrase." How can one paraphrase descriptions of a landscape which one has never seen, or even informed oneself about? You will notice she speaks of these passages as descriptions of "American landscape"; as you know, it is Mexican landscape, not "American".

3. Madame Yourcenar further told me that it would be impossible to use in her translation the local names of things—i.e., nouns such as burro, mesa, adobe (both a noun and adjective), casa, arroyo, hacienda, etc., etc. These words were, of course, originally Spanish, but they are now common words everywhere in the southwest. All the American farmers and railroad workmen use them without knowing that they are Spanish. There are simply no other names for these things. You cannot call an arroyo a ditch or a ravine.

4. I had of course thought that Madame Yourcenar would do what all the other translators of this book have done—simply employ these native words as they are used in my text. She declared that this was impossible, as the use of foreign words was very objectionable to the French taste and, moreover, they would not be understood by French readers. Explanatory footnotes, she said, were very objectionable to a French audience, and in such bad taste that she could not use them. I reminded her that the pages of <u>Carmen</u> [by Prosper Mérimée] are peppered with Spanish words, and whole sentences in the Gypsy language which are translated in footnotes. This is equally true of <u>Colomba</u> [also by Mérimée]. She said this would merely make a book look old fashioned, and with great decision dismissed the suggestion. She consented to use the word <u>pueblo</u> in her translation, but would promise nothing further.

5. Since my meeting with Madame Yourcenar I have been running through the very excellent Italian translation made by Alessandra Scalero, and I find that in every instance she uses the New Mexican nouns and adjectives, those I have listed above in paragraph 3 and many others, exactly as I used them myself. The only difference being that she puts all these foreign words, even such simple ones as "poker," "rancheros" and "hacienda", in italic. She has very clear and enlightening footnotes on such words as "trapper," "gringo," and very short footnotes telling clearly what a "mesa" is, a "hogan," "wampum," etc. The Italian translation clearly and faithfully reproduces the English text of the book.

6. Now we will get to the heart of the matter. Madama Yourcenar feels that this book accurately translated would not make, as she says, "beautiful French". I have every admiration for the writer who wishes to write his own language beautifully, and I am afraid she has chosen a book which is not suited to the kind of French she wishes to write. My apprehensions have to do with:

<u>First</u>, her absolute refusal to make use of the local New Mexican-Spanish words for which there are no English or French equivalents.

<u>Second</u>, the fact that she wishes to paraphrase the passages describing a country which she has never seen and about which she has read very little.

Paraphrasing in this case would certainly be improvising. And how many improvisions, one would like to know? Madama Yourcenar told me that some of these words were "not in the dictionary". I find very clear definitions of the several she mentioned in the unabridged Webster's Dictionary, published 1935.

After going through the Italian translation and seeing how possible it is to make a faithful translation, I think it is not unreasonable in me to ask that I should be allowed to see proofs of Madama Yourcenar's translation before it is published.

Excuse this long letter.

Faithfully yours,
Willa Cather

→ ←

Douglass Cather died suddenly in June 1938, at the age of fifty-eight.

TO ELSIE CATHER

June 21, 1938

My darling Sister:

There is nothing I can say—nothing I can say at all. When Edith told me she had bad news for me, I thought of almost every one in the family—except Douglass. Nothing in my life has ever hit me so hard. Father's death and Mother's seemed natural. They had lived out their lives, but this seems unnatural altogether, and I cannot get used to it or feel reconciled to it. Anyone so full of the joy of life, and so full of energy and hope—no, I can't seem to accept it at all. A good deal of the time I cannot believe it's true.

One thing I do feel humbly grateful for, that it was so quick, that he died without the consciousness of dying.

I hoped that you would not undertake the long journey to California, that you would feel reconciled to remember him as you saw him last, but I did not write or wire you because I think in such matters one has to decide for oneself.

I was grateful to Roscoe for letting me know the hour of the service. Since it took place at two o'clock there, it was six o'clock here. I wanted to spend that hour in a church, but was unable to find any Episcopalian Church which would be open at that hour. They close at six. So I went to the Church of the Dominican Fathers, which is only a few blocks from this house and where I have quite often gone for service. The Catholics seem to be the only people who realize that in this world grief goes on all night, as well as all day, and they have a place for it to hide away and be quiet.

Now, my dear, for your sake and for mine, do not try to write me about your trip out there or about the services, or very much about the family meeting. It would be too hard on you to write, and on me to read. We are, both of us, so deeply torn and moved by such things, and I do not want to ask you to go through the ordeal of writing to me. It will only make the wound bleed again—I mean bleed afresh. It will always be there for both of us, that wound. Nothing that has ever happened to me has hurt me or discouraged me like this.

Willie

TO ROSCOE CATHER

June 29, 1938

My dear Roscoe:

I can be of little help to you, but I think there are some things which I should confide to you.

1. I am enclosing a letter from Mary Virginia [Auld Mellen]. Please read marked passage. Neither Edith nor I can remember that Douglass said anything about a will on that occasion. The three of us were laughing and talking here together, and it is very possible that he may have said something that neither Edith nor I caught. Mary Virginia must have heard him make some such statement—she would not lie, but neither Edith nor I heard it. He might have said some such thing merely as a figure of speech—to illustrate the fact that he had been really worried. But in quoting a man who can no longer speak for himself, I must state exactly what I remember hearing him say and what I do not remember.

2. Douglass asked me to go down with him to Tiffany's to select a present for Miss Rogers—he had already been there himself. He took me to a show case full of bracelets, but they all happened to be extraordinarily ugly. There really was not a very pretty bracelet in the place. I noticed, however, a case full

of really beautiful rings—not the awfully expensive kind—prettily blended stones and lovely settings. I said quite innocently, "Why not get a ring?"—I really was not pumping him; I am a poor detective. But he shut one eye and screwed up his face a little and said, "No, no, that's a little too, too pointed." I laughed and said, "Oh, you mean decisive." "That's it," he replied, and I laughed and said, "same old fox", which seemed rather to please him. For the two summers when I saw a good deal of Miss Rogers at the sanitarium, I honestly saw nothing objectionable about her. She was competent at her job, not stupid, had good manners and was more attractive than Douglass' other girls. (Wait till you see the Edith to whom he made a bequest!) Douglass was rushing Miss Rogers pretty hard, and she admired him very much. His lovely way with his mother was enough to win any woman's heart. He told me, when he said good-bye to me the spring before Mother died, that he thought he might marry Miss Rogers, and I told him I could see nothing against it.

Now, six or seven years of courtship is pretty hard on any young woman who has to make her own living. I think she lost her position at Las Encinas because there was "talk", owing to Douglass. When I knew her I certainly believe that she was no "gold digger", but she was like any other girl who has found the man she wants (I should say loves, not "wants") and tries to make him believe she can make him happy. In the six or seven years which have elapsed since I first knew her and used to take long trips with the two of them, she may have deteriorated very much. That constant demand for sympathy and affection-which-gets-nowhere, is very hard on a young woman. Her position now is certainly much worse in every way than when she first knew Douglass. She has lost several positions, has been "talked about", has passed from the twenties into the thirties, which is against her professionally and matrimonially. I hope he was very generous to her during his lifetime, for the bequest in his will seems to me insufficient recognition. During the years when Jessica and Elsie were giving him lots of perplexity (these seem to be the two persons most offended), Miss Rogers was giving him the kind of companionship and sympathy he liked. If Douglass was very generous to her, I am glad. She did more than any of us to make him comfortable. I think we ought to look at the matter as human beings. How would you like one of your daughters to be played with like that, always expecting to be married next year? I am enclosing a letter from Elsie which needs no comment. When I knew Miss Rogers, she was a nice, straight girl, and she believed altogether in Douglass' affection—which was undoubtedly real affection,—though it led nowhere for her.

3. Now there is something I hate to tell you, and yet I feel I ought to. In every letter that Jim has written me since he left Kearney and joined Douglass, there has been a strong taint of disloyalty—except in the last letter, written after Douglass was dead. At first and for years after, he was always complaining that Douglass had given him a few hundred dollars to throw sand in his eyes and cheat him out of his share of FATHER'S ESTATE—which he seemed to think very large indeed! I wrote trying to reassure him, telling him I would give Douglass the management of my own savings at any moment. Secondly, all his later letters—there were not many, he wrote about twice a year—were full of complaints of his being held down and made a mere hired man, when he knew as much about the oil business as anybody. He said repeatedly that the oil business required no knowledge, no intelligence of any kind. It was pure luck, and he intended to play around with the little fellows, the under-dogs who had not had the luck of Douglass and his partners.

I know, Roscoe, these letters from Jim would have great influence with you if I had only saved them, but that little taint of ingratitude and disloyalty was like an ugly smell to me. I would keep the letters for a few days, try to answer them, then tear them up. There are many good qualities about Jim. When I am with him, I always feel a peculiar and special tenderness for him. But he tremendously overrates his own ability, and he is continuously nagged on by a wife [Ethel Garber Cather] who is full of petty ambitions, and who has developed a much more venomous nature than ever her old mother had. Ethel was patient with Jim for a long time, I know; but when she turned, she turned not to vinegar but to hydrochloric acid. I am not judging her, but it is up to you, your father's son, to see that these furious and self-seeking women do not attack Miss Rogers tooth and nail and do her more harm than our family has already done her. Father would not have dealt fiercely with her. If she has another will tucked away somewhere, properly executed, as an honorable man you will have to see justice done. I am almost sure she hasn't. Elsie's hypothesis, that she encouraged him to drink these last five or six months, is so absurd. We know now that he knew he had a bad heart and the game might be up any time. One sort of man would lie in bed and read and eat toast. He wasn't that sort. When he had drunk a few cocktails or a bottle of champagne, that dark shadow withdrew to a distance—did not seem so close, and he could talk to Miss Rogers about his rosy plans for the future and how he meant to go abroad on the Queen Mary. I think it was to get rid of that fear that he has been using himself up for the last year or so.

4. Now Roscoe, usually I keep peoples' secrets, especially when they are

secrets I am ashamed to read. But I think you ought to know how vacillating and unappreciative of favors and how weak Jim is—under his queer kind of conceit. I hope you will not try to give either him or Jack much authority, but will trust rather to the experience and to the possible, even probable, integrity of Douglass' partners—whom he trusted so much. Jack is a dear fellow but—feels no responsibility, happy-go-lucky. You can't make men over after they are thirty-five. Don't put Jim up against any important men—Roy Oatman, Russell Amack, etc., etc. were always his kind. I know Doug's partners are not exactly Harvard men, but <u>they know their business</u>, have proved it. Jim says there is nothing whatever about the business to know.

This is the last letter I shall write you on this subject. As soon as I am well enough, I will get off to Grand Manan, where I have no typewriter and nobody who can take dictation from me. But when you talk about "developing" Jim and Jack, I think I ought to ask you to sit down and consider awhile, and I feel that I ought to give you this important sidelight on Jim; that he is not loyal, and never while Douglass was living did he write a nice letter about him—only fault finding and distrustful ones.

Jim is sweet with his children, poor lad, but I don't believe he is much fonder of them than Douglass was. Doug's face used to glow and his voice was just full of feeling whenever he spoke of those children.

When I knew her Miss Rogers was not looking about for a man—most of the young men at the sanitorium disliked her. She was extremely good at her job, and wanted to make a real career of it. When I went off on a three day trip down to Caliente she never said or did anything that made me feel that she was a cheap sort. She was then a frank, fresh, rather intelligent Western girl; I never saw her throw a soft look at Douglass, or hold his hand in the car, or languish. She behaved like a well brought up girl. I am (oh this <u>pen</u>!) I am sorry if her life has been spoiled. Deal in this case as Father would have done.

Lovingly
Willie

<u>Destroy Elsie's letter after you have read it</u>

❧ ☙

Cather's first book, April Twilights, *began with a poem titled "Dedicatory," dedicated to her two oldest brothers, Douglass and Roscoe. It remembers the "three who lay and planned at moonrise, / On an island in a western river, / Of the conquest of the world together."*

TO MARGARET CATHER

[Postmarked July 13, 1938]
Admiral Beatty Hotel, Saint John, New Brunswick, Canada
My Darling Margaret;

We are here in this old town again—great showers of rain and bitter cold. We left New York in intense heat, both of us exhausted by packing. Here we will shop a little and rest in bed a great deal. So many hard and sad things have come down on me in the last six weeks that I am rather a wreck. I didn't quite know whether I could take the noon train for Boston on Sunday. Just as I was putting on my hat to take the cab, a box of great gardenias dropped down into my lap—sent by Yehudi's darling little new wife [Nola Nicholas Menuhin] with such a tender message. Somehow it did hearten me. I can't feel utterly knocked out so long as the young love me. Nola is just the right wife for my boy,—and just the kind no one would ever have selected for him. I am hard to please, and I was very jealous <u>for</u> Yehudi. I might have thought she wasn't brilliant or picturesque enough for him. But he sees the souls of people—that is his peculiar gift. She is the right one.

Dear child, I was and am so glad your kind mother thought of giving me a little place in the service for Douglass by having that first dedication read. It would never have been taken out if it hadn't been such very weak verse. But I'm glad I wrote it and felt it, if it is poor verse, and glad that we three loved each other so dearly in our youth and always, though it breaks my heart now, and it seems to me that I never can care very much about living again.

Give a warm and loving greeting to Elizabeth when you write

Lovingly
W.

TO ROSCOE CATHER

[Probably September 1938]
Grand Manan Island
My Dearest Brother;

Your long letter from the clinic brought me great peace of mind; first, because it gave good report of your physical state, secondly because you confessed a weakness, and that enables me to confess mine. The reason I have not written you oftener is that after I write a letter to any of the family, I lie awake all night, and all my past failings and failures go through my head like a horrible cinema film: Why did I not do more for mother and father when they were living? Why did I give up one evening of Douglass' short stay in New York to an English publisher, and send Doug to a show alone? My life seems to have been made up of mistakes of this kind. And yet, I have never been "ambitious". I drove ahead so hard because I wanted never, never to come back on Father for anything, nor to ask any of my family to put up a dollar to back a game they didn't understand. But in doing that, I let a good deal of life slip by. I was at home on three different summers when Jim was coercing, tormenting father to "set him up in a business". Father used to hide in the bath room for hours. I got a great disgust for that form of parent-torture. Perhaps in trying so hard to be quit and clean of that sort of wheedling, I neglected some things that mattered more.

You ask for a report of health. Better than when I left town. Then I had not been sleeping without med[i]cine for sometime, and had a very unpleasant trembling of the hands. All nerve reactions were bad, and, funniest of all, my hair was coming out in great bunches—it seems that sometimes results from nervous disorders.

I am much better now, of course. My hands are steady again, I sleep fairly well, but I am not very happy.

[This paragraph marked in margin: "copy for Elsie"] It seems strange that Alfred Knopf, who has been always such a dear and loyal friend to me, in music and in art, not to speak of our happy business relation, should turn up with the only recent picture I have of Douglass. One day when I took Douglass into his office, Alfred snapped him with his little Leica camera, invisible and soundless. Douglass never knew he was snapped, and I didn't know it. They were not very good, so Alfred didn't offer them until after Douglass' death.

Please send on[e] of the prints I enclose to Elsie, with a Copy of this explanation. Keep one for yourself, and give one to Jack and one to Jim; to no one else.

Elsie says you have Douglass' copies of my books. You may give one to Jack and one to Jim, but see that they are copies which are clearly inscribed to Douglass. Even so, they may be used for club purposes by the women. All the other copies you will please take to your own home.

Tell my darling little Margaret that I am very happy that she is happy, and that every one of our lovely places on this island make me think of her. Last summer I had five gay companion[s] who made me love life; the twins for summer, and the Menuhins for winter. Within six months they have all married. Just now I must try to work a little every day on the book I began in the last autumn. It's lost its pep, but it is the only thing that will bring me back to myself; regular work hours, I mean. Alfred and Dr. Garbat agree on that. Letter writing disintegrates me. Margaret will get a little wedding present some day.

I shall not be here after September 15th, but I don't yet know just where I shall be.

This is the old typewriter Doug bought for me from the busted gambler in Cheyenne thirty year[s] ago, when we three were there together. It has lain up here in the damp sea air for six years, so please excuse mistakes. Ralph [Beal] has tried to mend it with automobile tools.

Very lovingly to you all

Willie

→ ←

Isabelle McClung Hambourg, who was very ill with kidney disease, was living in Sorrento, Italy, with her husband, Jan, at the Hotel Cocumella.

TO EDITH MCCLUNG

September 26, 1938

My dear Edith:

I do not wonder that you are feeling anxious about Isabelle's situation in Italy, but in so far as I can tell, Mussolini's aim in expelling a great number of Jews from Italy is to give more jobs to the native Italians. His action seems to arise from the unemployment situation, rather than from personal hatred as it unquestionably does with Hitler. As Jan is not engaged in any business which would take a job away from an Italian, I think there is a very good chance that he will not be troubled. I understand that Jewish tourists are admitted to Italy and courteously treated. Mrs. [Elizabeth Moorhead] Vermorcken of Pittsburgh has lately gone over to Italy, and is at the present time at the Hotel Cocumella. If she saw anything threatening, I think she would write or cable me.

I got back from Canada, where I have been all summer, only the day before yesterday, and found a short letter from Isabelle awaiting me here. She has never given me any indication of feeling alarm about the Jewish situation in Italy. But in this last letter, the last paragraph reads as follows:

> "If we should be going away from here, I'll cable you. As long as I do not cable, you will know that we are here in the shelter of this simple and comfortable room with the kind Garguilos".

I believe the G–s are the proprietors of the hotel.

This summer (July 1 to September 15) I have heard from Isabelle less often than usual, and I know that she was less well than in the winter. But when she did write, she always told me that there were some nice Americans staying at the Cocumella, and that she enjoyed their company when she was well enough to see them. One of these people was Miss [Florence] Overton, director of the branches of the New York Public Library, and as soon as I get my trunks unpacked, I shall go to see her for information. Miss Overton was in Sorrento in the early part of the summer, and I think the Jewish question had not yet arisen when she sailed for home. If, from her or from any other source, I get any information about the Hambourgs' actual position there at the present time, you may be sure that I will let you know at once.

Very cordially yours,
Willa Cather

TO THORNTON WILDER

October 9, 1938
New York City

Dear Thornton Wilder;

For nearly a year I have been wanting to write to you. I truly think "Our Town" is the loveliest thing that has been produced in this country in a long, long time—and the truest. From several technical points of view it is highly important, as nearly everyone recognized at once. But of course its great importance is something that everyone feels and nobody can define: we can only vaguely say the "spiritual quality" of the play. Two hearings of it are not enough. I must hear it once again before I leave for Jaffrey New Hampshire to spend a few weeks on Monadnock. I have been going there in the autumn for fifteen years, and in your play I find a complete expression of everything I have ever seen and felt and become friends with in that countryside and in all the little towns scattered about the foot of that mountain. Something enduring and resigned and gracious lies behind the details of your play, as the mountain lies behind (and permeates) all those little towns and farms, and the lives of all those people. Exiled Americans, living abroad, to whom I have sent the book of the play, write me that it has made them weep with homesickness.

I love everything you have ever written, but you have done nothing so fine as this. I am not only happy about it, but thankful for it.

Faithfully yours
Willa Cather

TO FERRIS GREENSLET

October 12 [1938]

Dear F.G.

No, please. By no means let <u>Antonia</u> go on the air. Thank you for letting me know about this proposition, as I have a strong feeling against it.

Isabelle McClung Hambourg died yesterday, in Sorrento, Italy. I need scarcely tell you that this [is] another great change in life for me. It is only four months since my brother Douglass, the one closest to me in my family, died of a heart attack, in California. They were the two people dearest to me.

Faithfully
Willa Cather

TO IRENE MINER WEISZ

October 14 [1938]

Dearest Irene;

Isabelle Hambourg died in Sorrento, October 10. Her last letter to me was dated September 24. It was written in the garden, looking out on the bay and Vesuvius; she was in her wheelchair enjoying the autumn weather.

With Douglass and Isabelle both gone out of my life, I scarcely know how I shall go on. Please tell Carrie.

Lovingly
Willie

You and Mr. Weisz were so nice to her. I shall not forget, ever.

TO EDITH MCCLUNG

October 24, 1938

My dear Edith:

Please excuse my typing this letter. My hand-writing grows more and more difficult to read, and I don't wish you to puzzle over it.

I feel very remorseful that I did not telegraph you when I received a cable from Jan a few days after Isabelle's death. I thought, of course, that he would have cabled you at the same time. On the same afternoon that I got Jan's cable I got a long distance telephone call from my sister-in-law in Sacramento, telling me that my older brother [Roscoe] was having dangerous hemorrhages after an operation, and asking me whether I could come on by air at short notice. His condition remained dangerous for four days, and during that time I was in a half-stupified condition. This house was full of paperers and painters, so I went to the Lowell Hotel and took the rooms which Isabelle used to occupy, awaiting the issue. If conditions had been otherwise, I would naturally have written to you at that time, even though I took it for granted that Jan had cabled you word of Isabelle's death. He should have done so, but I cannot blame the poor distracted man for anything he did not do; there is so much red tape to be gone through when a foreigner dies in Italy and is buried there.

Jan's letter to me about the last days of Isabelle's illness probably came on the same boat as his letter to you, and it tells practically the same story. In one paragraph he says:

"During nearly five days I watched her strong, loyal and loving heart resist death. Not more than half a dozen times did her face show anguish or anxiety, then only for a few minutes. She slept as though under the influence of a potent anaesthetic. As she died her face took on a perfectly calm remote look. After three hours her lips shaped into a gentle gracious smile. The parish priest came on Saturday and prayed for her. The Nuns (who had been at her bedside day and night) dressed our Darling in her favorite lace dress and she looked so handsome—her distinguished self."

Isabelle's last letter to me was a short one, dated September 24th. It was written on her knee as she was sitting in the garden. She says: "These September days are soft and warm and lovely. We are down on the terrace, so this untidy note is being written on my knee." All the first part of September she was able to walk with Jan down to the end of the garden and sit looking at the sea. I think September 24th must have been her last walk to the terrace. The letter is short, but the tone of it very cheerful.

Everyone who saw Isabelle during her stay at the Hotel Cocumella speaks of the beauty and dignity of her life there; how she never oppressed anyone with a sense of her illness, and how everyone loved to be with her and felt privileged to have a little private conversation with her. When she did not feel strong enough to see people (which was often) she stayed in her room or sat on her little balcony in the sun. She did not go down to dinner except when she could appear with graciousness and ease of manner.

I had made all arrangements to go to Sorrento in July, but on June 13th my brother Douglass died in Los Angeles of coronary thrombosis—having had no previous illness. After that I felt unequal to the voyage, but had planned to spend a part of this winter in Sorrento.

Surely, when you saw Isabelle last you must have realized that her time was short. Her doctors at the Lenox Hill Hospital thought she could scarcely hold out through the year. That was why I followed her a few weeks after they sailed for France, and rejoined them there, and spent the autumn there at a nearby hotel, so I could be with her every day. Nobody ever bore a long and fatiguing illness with more courage and more dignity. When I went over to Paris in 1930, she was already very ill. I went over in April and stayed until late November. She was even then struggling under a dragging fatigue which almost never left her. She had lived for years on the strictest diet, cutting out everything that increased blood pressure, except weak tea in the afternoon and a few cigarettes. She knew nothing definite about her kidneys being wrong until she came back to New York. Perhaps that was just as well. As you know, when people have that particular defect of the kidneys, they are born with it, and it develops slowly all through their lives. Nothing can be done about it, and I think it was better that she was spared the knowledge of an incurable defect as long as possible. It seems just too cruel that such a thing should fall upon her, of all people. But even that slow poisoning could not take away anything of the beauty, or charm, or great heartedness she had for the people who loved her,—and they were many. Jan's absolute devotion to her during her long illness was very precious to her, and even people who sometimes found him a little difficult could never find anything to criticize in him as a husband. She hated being handled by nurses. She loved having him give her her bath, lift her when it was hard for her to rise, and by so many delicate attentions disguise her actual infirmities from everyone.

You probably do not realize, Edith, how much it pleased her that you took the trouble to come down to New York and see her several times when she was in the hospital. Her uncle Will's going to Cherry Valley to see her was another thing that warmed her heart—she could never speak of it without tears.

Poor Jan; I am very impatient with him sometimes—he is so impractical in some things, but Heaven knows he loved and admired Isabelle every day they lived together, and that was her one great solace in the cares and anxieties and suffering that she lived through during these last twelve years. I think I can say that she was never really unhappy, and I know that she had times of great happiness. She made many warm and beautiful friendships, and even on the date of her last letter, September 24th, she was still loving life. You can understand that living will never be the same for me again. I don't yet know where I am or what kind of future there will be for me in a world in which there is no Isabelle to write to or to go to. It will take me a long while to get used to things as they are now.

I have written at greater length than I intended, Edith, and I will ask you to regard this letter as confidential to you. I don't wish to be telling more about Isabelle than she would have told about herself. To anyone who truly loved her you might wish to quote from this letter, but not to anyone else, please. Near of kin are not always kind of heart. I feel sure she would not wish her cousins, the Lees, to know anything about her life, though she was very fond of their mother, her "Aunt Beck". I know she was truly fond of her cousin Mary Griswold (?) I am not sure about the name, though I remember the girl very well. I think she and her brothers now live in Florida.

Sincerely yours
Willa Cather

TO ROSCOE CATHER

November 6 [1938]
Shattuck Inn, Jaffrey, New Hampshire

My Dear Brother;

How can I help worrying when you let yourself be carved up by a smooth talking insurance man? The surgeon whom I consulted in N.Y. said quietly that your hemorrhages were the result of bad technique or bad judgment, probably both, on the part of your doctor. You would have saved time in the end, and much vitality, if you had gone to the Mayo Clinic where thousands of similar operations have taught the men to guard against possible consequences, and where the surgeons aren't looking for operations but looking toward the long afterwards. I have a hard appendix, but they refused to operate because it would take too much out of my vitality and working power. For the same reason they refused to remove Dorothy Canfield's very disfiguring goitre.

Your one fault, my dear boy, (the only one I know of) is that you have always been too willing to trust people—you think too well of them. It's an engaging fault. I don't mind when it concerns your mind and estate, but for heaven's sake dont let the persuasive talkers practice on your body. You have but one, you know. You are trusting the ability of your two well-meaning brothers much too far, I think. But that concerns only money losses, it doesn't endanger your life.

I am up here alone at this hotel in the woods where I have done most of my best work and where the proprietors are so kind to me. I finished "Antonia" here, finished "A Lost Lady" and began the "Archbishop". The best part of all the better books was written here. It was Isabelle who first brought me here. You cannot imagine what her death means to me. It came just four months after Douglass' death, before I had got my nerves steady again. No other living person cared as much about my work, through thirty-eight years, as she did. As for me, I have cared too much, about people and places—cared too hard. It made me, as a writer. But it will break me in the end. I feel as if I couldn't go another step. People say I have a "classic style". A few of them know it's the heat under the simple words that counts. I early learned that if you loved your theme enough you could be as mild as a May morning and still make other people care—people in countries who read it in the strangest languages—Hungarian and Roumanian are the latest. Some day you must come and see my whole bookcase full of translations. It's the one thing that simple <u>really</u> caring for an old Margie, an old cat, an old anything. I never cultivated it, from the age of twenty on I did all I could to repress it, and that effort of mind did, after years, give me a fairly good "style"—style being merely the writer, no the <u>person</u> himself; what he was born with and what he has done for himself. Isabelle watched me every step of the way. But the source of supply seems to be getting low. I work a little every day (1½ hrs.) to save my reason, to escape from myself. But the sentences don't come sharp and clear as they used to—the pictures are a little blurred. Perhaps it's fatigue only—I hope so. This book [*Sapphira and the Slave Girl*] has been twice interrupted by death, and twice by illness. I keep it up not for the book itself, but for the peace it brings me to follow old activities that used to be so happy—so rapid and so <u>absolutely</u> absorbing.

Goodbye dear. I've not written so long a letter in a long time—except to Isabelle's poor devoted and now desolate husband.

W.

TO MARGARET CATHER SHANNON

Wednesday [probably November 9, 1938]
Shattuck Inn, Jaffrey, New Hampshire

[Written in the top margin:] The <u>Parker</u> House is where I always stop—very picturesque part of Boston.

Yes, little Dear; I am here, and hope to be all this month. I want to be alone as long as I can. That is the only way I can pull out of things. You see there are some people one loves and is proud of, as I was of Douglass. Then there are some people who have been a part of one's inner and outer life for so long that one does not know how to go forward without them. Thirty eight years ago Isabelle McClung, Judge [Samuel A.] McClung's daughter, took me into her father's comfortable well-ordered house in Pittsburgh. I was a poor schoolteacher, at sixty dollars a month, living in a boarding house. I was a raw, densely ignorant, but very happy girl from the west—found everything jolly. I knew something about books. Isabelle knew very little about books, but everything about gracious and graceful living. We brought each other up. We kept on doing that all our lives. For most of my life in Pittsburgh (five years) Isabelle and, I think, your father, were the only two people who thought there was any good reason for my trying to write—was it merely an excuse for not getting married? Isabelle has always been my best and soundest critic,—in some ways better than Edith, who knows much more about the technique of writing. I have sent Isabelle every manuscript before I published [part missing?] were always invaluable. Her husband is returning to me three hundred of my letters which she carried about with her from place to place all the time. She had lived abroad for fourteen years, but I often went to her, and in mind we were never separated. Now we have no means of communication; that is all. One can never form such a friendship twice. One does not want to. As long as she lived, her youth and mine were realities to both of us.

Goodbye, my precious girl, be young, be happy, as my Yehudi and Nola are.

Lovingly
W.S.C.

TO ROSCOE CATHER

Sunday, December 25 [1938]

My Dear Roscoe;

Potted plants kept coming in all day yesterday until the apartment was full of them. Then we went tea with the Menuhins at five. When I came home at seven, for dinner, a box from Irene Hays, the very smartest New York florist was on my desk. "Yehudi, of course: he often sends me flowers from there["]. When I opened the box I took out the richest purple violets I have seen this winter—and your card. I simply burst into tears. It was instantaneous. Disappointment? Exactly the opposite. Surprise and delight. It was an emotion made up of many things. One's family do not see one in a "romantic" light. That is natural. Douglass always sent me a gunny sack full of walnuts at Christmas time. It was nice of him. But no man of my own family ever sent me flowers before, and though flowers come to me so many, so many and so often, these violets broke me all up for a moment—and filled me with a strange kind of pride. They were on my breakfast table this morning, and are before me on my table as I write. My pleasure seems out of proportion to the cause. But the cause is everything; from the days when we used to sleep up in the old attic with the snow blowing in, and listen to trains whistle in that bitter cold air, and it matters more to me to have you throw me a bouquet than to have all the other flowers that come to me on my birthday and Christmas. You brought back to me something of Christmases long ago, when I had <u>so much</u> hope—and so little to found it on. But we three older ones did love each other, and we found life pretty thrilling when we went to the South Ward school.

A Happy New Year, dear, to you and Meta.

Willie

[On back of envelope:] Please let me know where you will be two weeks from now.

→ ←

Cather's claims about her early stories in the following letter are not backed up by any available evidence and are likely fabrications constructed to convince Wagenknecht to leave her alone. When "A Death in the Desert" was published in 1903, she had already published thirty-two other short stories and hundreds of articles and reviews; it was hardly the "first published story which was altogether my own work."

TO EDWARD WAGENKNECHT

December 31, 1938

My dear Mr. Wagenknecht:

Thank you for your kind words about the Autograph Edition. I think Mr. [Bruce] Rogers did a very fine piece of work—indeed, he never does anything that has not distinction.

I never received the copy of the Sewanee Review. I was abroad during most of '29 and '30, and my publishers cannot forward second class mail to me. There is too much of it.

Now to the object of your letter. You will see that in returning the list you sent me I have crossed out six of the early stories you attribute to me, because they are not really genuine; some of them are wholly spurious. I cannot give you the history of each of these, but let us take the first one, "On the Divide". It was a college theme written for a weekly theme class. The professor was a very young man, just out of college himself, and was one of those mistaken young men who think they can reflect credit upon their department by rushing their students into print. As the <u>Overland Monthly</u> did not pay for contributions, he was able to get it printed there. Before he sent it there, he touched it up very considerably and added what he called "color". My theme was a short account of a Swede farmer who carried off a girl in a storm. I forget now how much the professor added, but I remember I was amazed when he attributed to this Swede some skill in wood carving—said he did this in his lonely hours, or something of that sort. I have only the dimmest recollection of this theme, but I remember that he put in several high spots which amazed me. Incidently, he had the story printed quite without my knowledge. I was not in the least offended, and thought he had been very kind to dress up a dull college theme.

The story "Eldorado" ["El Dorado: A Kansas Recessional"], though it was written much later, was sent to the same professor and highly retouched by him. He was older by that time, and so was I,—but we were neither of us any wiser. I will say for myself however, that I had no intention of publishing the story. It was the result of a kind of correspondence course which I kept up with this young man after I left college. The other stories which I have marked out as wholly or partially spurious, were the collective effort of a club of four youngsters, of whom I was one, who worked on Pittsburgh newspapers. The reason that the stories were sent about under my name was that, thanks to the young professor to whom I have just referred, I had had several stories printed in magazines while the other members had not. The <u>New England Magazine</u>

did not pay for contributions, any more than did the <u>Overland Monthly</u>, so there were no profits to be shared. I had almost entirely forgotten about this little club of newspaper youngsters, but we had a jolly time collaborating, and the results, though worthless enough, did nobody any harm.

The first published story which was altogether my own work was "A Death in the Desert", published in Scribner's. I forget the date. The remaining titles on your list, beginning with 1907, are all protected by copyright, which I am very careful to renew at proper intervals, as I wish to keep the stories out of print. They are all immature work, most of them carelessly written in the intervals of very exacting editorial work. I became an editor on the staff of McClure's magazine in 1907, and managing editor in 1908. Several attempts have been made to print collections of these stories by small publishing houses in the West, but we have always been able to prevent it. An instructor in one of the western colleges had several of the stories made up in mimeograph sheets, which he used in his class room. But some copies were circulated outside the class room, and I was able to stop it and have all mimeograph copies destroyed. In many states the law rules that any form of reproducing a writer's work without the writer's consent is a form of publishing. I do not know what the law may be on this point in the State of Washington, and I do sincerely hope that I shall not have occasion to ask my attorney to investigate.

My dear Professor Wagenknecht, your quotation from the publisher who put out the early essays of George Eliot is simply a publisher's salesman talk. There is no interest or profit for any "scholar" in examining immature and labored productions. There is no profit in it even for this sales-talking publisher. When an American publisher put out a volume of Kipling's very early work which had run out of copyright, he made nothing on it at all—I believe he lost money.

I am sorry to say that I cannot by any twist of thinking, construe your wish to call attention to these long forgotten stories, signed with my name, as a friendly wish.

It seems to me a rather indelicate proceeding on your part. I cannot imagine myself doing such a thing with Mr. Hemingway's early work, for instance.

Suppose I were an apple grower, and, packing my year's crop, I were very careful to put only the apples I thought reasonably sound into the packing boxes, leaving the defective ones in a pile on the ground. While I am asleep or at dinner, a neighbour comes to the orchard and puts all the worthless apples into the boxes that are to go to market. Would you call that a friendly action, or the neighbour a friendly man? Writing is subject to outside conditions; to drought, crow-peckings, wasps, hail storms, just as much as apples are. The honest writer, like the honest fruit grower, sorts his work over and tries to keep only what is fairly sound. Everyone has that right of supervision over their handiwork—the carpenter, the dressmaker, the cabinetmaker. He can put his flimsy work in his cellar and forget it, and our copyright laws give the writer the same privilege.

Very truly yours,
Willa Cather

TO ROSCOE CATHER

[Probably January 1939]

No, my dear Roscoe, it was not business trouble that I meant to write you about when I asked where you would be in January. Sometimes I wish to speak to you "personally", as you do to me in your letter which just came.

Since I have lost Isabelle there is now no one to whom I can show things to—no one who will take pleasure in pleasant recognition that comes my way. Of course Alfred Knopf is always interested, but he takes the lofty stand that whatever I do is pretty good, and it's no matter what people say, while to me it does matter what some people say. People like Tweedsmuir [John Buchan, Lord Tweedsmuir]—because his book on Augustus Caesar [*Augustus*] seems to me the best piece of historical writing that has come along in years, and because he is a finished scholar.

The Swedish review is a fine piece of critical work because it tells exactly <u>why</u> the book was written as it was; the low tone, the respectful distance which I tried to keep between the characters and myself. And he is equally good on [D. H.] Lawrence, whom I knew very well.

So if you are not too busy, I would like to send you such things from time to time. The Menuhins are like Alfred—they think high praise comes naturally to me, as to them. A few years ago Yehudi told a reporter that his favorite authors were <u>Victor Hugo</u> and Willa Cather!

But you know it's a long road from Red Cloud to any sort of finish.

Look the enclosures over when you have leisure and a good cigar, and when you and Meta have read them, mail them back to me, registered post.

Lovingly
Willie

TO BURGES JOHNSON

January 12, 1939

My dear Mr. Johnson:

Certainly, you may quote anything you wish from "Not Under Forty" and anything you select from my letter to "Pat" Knopf, provided you don't select a statement that is too informal or rather exaggerated. I don't remember now just how informal my letter was, but I remember that I gave him my real reasons for writing "The Professor's House" in the form I did. I thought the unusual structure was sufficiently bound together by the fact that the Professor's life with Tom Outland was just as real and vivid to him as his life with his family, and because Tom Outland was in the Professor's house so much during his student life. He and the atmosphere he brought with him became really a part of the house—that is, of the old house which the Professor could not altogether leave. If I had happened to write the book in a very modernistic manner, letting everybody's thoughts and memories and shades of feeling tumble into the book helter-skelter, I could have made a rather exciting color study. But the trouble is, these stunts, while they are very exciting, seem to leave nothing behind—no after taste for the writer. They go up, and out, like rockets.

May I say, Mr. Johnson, that I am very happy that "Pat" is so interested in his work under you? I think it is a genuine interest. There is good material in "Pat", but he has been under very poor teachers and had the misfortune in early boyhood to be thrown among a lot of very showy and rather clever people. That is the almost inevitable fate of the only son of a publisher in this particular time. A great many very cheap people come and go in a publisher's office these day[s], and young lads cannot very well judge which are the wise ones and which are the wisecrackers.

Very cordially yours,
Willa Cather

TO YALTAH MENUHIN STIX

Monday [January 23, 1939]
New York City

My darling Yaltah,

We have had wonderful cold weather and lots of snow. I have been walking around the Reservoir alone—but pleasant memories kept me company. There

[are] very few people that I like to walk with—only <u>three</u> whom I like very much to walk with!

I am overwhelmed with business—trying to keep a very poor French translation of the "Archbishop" from being published in Paris. The Swedish, Danish, Norwegian, and <u>Slovak</u> ones are said to be very good, so why should the French one be so dull and plodding! Isn't it stupid!

My precious, if you have a Bible in the house (and maybe you have the one dear Marutha bought from the agent long ago—so characteristic of her!) anyway, if you have one, please read the First and Second Books of Samuel, so that you can enjoy a beautiful book I am going to send you; J. M. Barrie's last play "The Boy David". It failed in London, because nobody there reads the Old Testament now-a-days. But I think you will see how wonderfully Barrie does the future man in the boy. And I think Marutha will love it, too. Maybe you would like to know that, like you, Barrie had a special fondness for the "Archbishop". I am so glad I was able to interest him (to give him some distraction, I mean) when he was old and ill.

Goodnight, my dear, my especially dear Yaltah.

Your Aunt Willa

P.S.

Tuesday [January 24, 1939]

Oh Yaltah, the boy David, the young shepherd, is such an <u>enchanting</u> creature! I have just read the 1st & 2nd Books of Samuel over again with delight. One must have the unadorned facts in one's mind to see what Barrie was trying to do in his lyrical play. I wish some one would select the best Psalms of David and publish them in a small volume. They are <u>great</u> <u>poetry</u>. No one alive on this earth today can write such poetry.

TO DAYTON M. KOHLER

March 16, 1939

My Dear Mr. Kohler;

What is the use? Hitler entered Prague last night. President Masaryk was an old friend of mine. He was a scholar and a lover of letters. In my childhood I had many Czech friends. I love their way of life. And what about "British honor", which I have always believed in? However much we may try to live in a nobler past, this thing has come upon us and lowers our vitality and our wish to live.

Thank you for your kind and friendly letter. Those books were written in better times than this.

> Sincerely yours
> Willa Cather

TO ELIZABETH CATHER ICKIS

March 30 [1939]

My Darling Elizabeth;

I am proud as a peacock to be a great aunt! And I am so glad you have named the baby Margaret. Her aunt Margaret was here in this apartment the day after she got the news and was in a flutter of excitement. She so hoped you would name the baby for her, but said it would probably be named for you and Lynn's [Ickis] mother. She said she didn't see how she <u>could</u> wait for months to see you and the baby. I should just like to go and see that baby myself! Mary Virginia was here for dinner last night and was thrilled to hear about your having a daughter. Poor little M.V.—I sometimes fear she has had to wait too long to start a family—and worked too hard. It's a wise girl who marries a man with a job, who can go and "get the little rabbit skin". Kiss Margaret on her black head for me. I send you a world of love, dear.

> Your Aunt Willie

TO CARRIE MINER SHERWOOD

June 28, 1939

My dear Carrie:

You have probably already been surprised by receiving a fat book from the Channel Book Shop. I wanted to send it to you in the early part of last winter, but I thought then you would be getting ready for Christmas. Then I thought I would send it sometime during February or March, but for both of those two months I was too ill with influenza to do anything, and I got so behind in replying to important letters that I have only just now caught up.

And now it is early summer, when every housekeeper is too busy to read anything. So I'll just ask you to tuck this book away and read some portions of it next winter, when the days are quiet. I send you the book, of course, because of the rather interesting and original articles on modern writers—though I like the chapters on Jane Austen, the Brontë sisters, and George Eliot.

Two years ago a French scholar at the University of Toulouse wrote a study of all my books, which I want some day to have translated for a few of my American friends. It is some four hundred pages long, and I have been too busy to bother to get a translator for it. But next to that book, I think the short chapter on my books in Margaret Lawrence's "School of Femininity" is the one I would most like you to read—and to keep. I like the article not chiefly because it is flattering, but because the writer says what she has to say in few words, and without rambling. If there is any real merit in my books, she puts her finger on the root of it. I once sent you a lot of English reviews, and you will remember that even the most enthusiastic reviewers never attempted to say why they got a special pleasure out of this or that book. They talk about "atmosphere", "style", "form", etc., but Miss Lawrence puts it in a very few words. She seems to understand that I can write successfully only when I write about people or places which I very greatly admire; which, indeed, I actually love. The characters may be cranky and queer, or foolhardy and rash, but they must have something in them which gives me a thrill and warms my heart. Now this is something I would never have said myself to anyone, but since Miss Lawrence has said it for me, I want you to have this confession of faith in her words. I hope that both you and Mary will at some time find time to read it, and I hope you will agree with me, that it would not be wise to show it to other people in my home town. I do not believe there is anyone but you and Mary who would not feel a little,—well, a little spiteful, you know. Nevertheless, I would like one person in my home town to have such a clear explanation of the way in which my books really were written, and I would like you to be that person. You, more than any other one person now living, know a great deal of the material that went into some of the books. And those things we will keep to ourselves. They do not belong to the gossips. I have heard that Verna Trine considers herself the original of <u>Lucy Gayheart</u>, and that another so-called friend at home considers that I thought I was writing about myself when I wrote Lucy's story: that I dressed myself out in brown eyes and red cheeks and a bewitching personality, and quite believe that I was like that! You and I know who the girl was who used to skate in the old rink, dressed in a red jersey. But please tell me, Carrie, <u>did</u> Sadie Becker have golden-brown eyes? The picture was perfectly clear to me when I was writing the book, but since then a queer doubt has come over me, and I sometimes think they were gray! But I can hear her contralto laugh today, as clearly as I did when I was twelve.

A great many things have happened in my life, dear Carrie, since I last wrote you a long letter. I have often wanted to write, but my heart always failed me. I am now looking at the very spot on the rug where Douglass stood, so big and strong, when he gave me a last hug before he dashed off to catch the plane that took him westward. I want you to know that during the ten days he spent here, we had almost a lifetime of happiness. On my birthday I stuffed the turkey for him myself, because my very excellent French cook could never make the kind of stuffing Grandma Boak used to make, and that was the kind he liked best. A great many flowers always come in on that day, and he spent the afternoon helping me to arrange them. The only interruption in his visit was that I had to send him to the theater alone one evening, because I had an important engagement to dine with an English publisher who was sailing the next day. I bitterly regret that lost evening, but the date had been arranged early in October.

I have lost many friends within the last few years, but losing Isabelle and Douglass within four months has made me a different person, and I shall never be the same again.

This past winter was a hard one to live through. The brightest thing in it was the solicitous affection and loyalty of the Menuhin family, and my great happiness in learning to know and truly love Yehudi's wife. She has all the directness and firmness of her solid Scotch ancestry. She is sweet, yet decided; the more I know her, the more I feel she is right for him in every way. Marriage is apt to make or mar a young artist, but Yehudi has been as fortunate in this as he has been in other things. It was her character and the direct, clear look in her eyes, that first drew him to her. They came to see me when I was ill, and when I was well we were often together, the three of us. I loved being with the two of them almost more than I used to love being with Yehudi alone. You know, splendid young people can always make me very happy—they seem to give me something to live for. And these two fill my heart with joy, even when I am sad. Cablegrams and long letters from Hephzibah, in Australia, bring her very close to me. And I enjoy her life in wild Victoria, on a ranch with twenty-five thousand sheep, as much as I enjoyed her professional success. Think of the courage and high-heartedness of a girl who could lightly drop a career and cancel her engagements in all the capitals of Europe, to go to Australia and live "a much realer life", as she writes me. I have not met her husband, but I love him from his letters, and because he is Nola's brother and Hephzibah's husband.

This is a long letter, dear Carrie, but so many things have been happening to me, and I have been out of your life so long, that I want to get back into it again.

                                        Lovingly to you and Mary
                                                            Willie

I was so truly disappointed to miss Father [Dennis] Fitzgerald [of Red Cloud].
I was in New Hampshire when he was here. The people at the Knopf office were sorry I missed him—they liked him at first sight. Thank Mary for her letter. I always love to hear from her.

    I shall be leaving for Canada soon.

TO EDNA ST. VINCENT MILLAY

                                                    October 10 [1939?]

Dear Edna Millay;

    I'm not fond of writing letters, but may I thank you for the glow of pleasure your last volume [*Huntsman, What Quarry?*] has given me? Nobody ever sings anymore—and when someone does (someone with a lovely voice) it makes one feel quite young for a moment, even for a whole day, and following days. More than a month ago I first got the book, in Canada, but I have read it many times since. Did you, perhaps, in your childhood have a painted picture-book with a large picture showing red robins dropping russet leaves over the Babes in the Wood? I had such a book. It's a beautiful allusion—quite melts one's heart. You wouldn't have done it twenty years ago. Perhaps you will smile and say that you <u>did</u> write it twenty years ago,—but I should find it hard to believe. Nearly everything in the book is very lovely. Just to hear anybody sing again——If one has an authentic right to sing, one can gratify the ear as much in "Inert Perfection" as in "Not So Far as the Forest". Again, thank you.

                                                        Sincerely yours
                                                        Willa Cather

TO FERRIS GREENSLET

                                                    October 19, 1939

Dear F.G.:

    The Swedish books have just come, and I thank you. Also, I want to thank you for the copy of the "College Reader" you sent me.

Will you be annoyed if I call your attention to some errors in the biographical notice of William Archer? Mr. Archer and I were friends from 1908 until the time of his death. When I went to London every year for McClure's, and he was my guide and advisor while I was there. He took me to George Meredith's funeral. We saw the Abbey Theatre Company the first night they ever played in London, sat in [William Butler] Yeats' box with Lady Gregory. When I came back from a stay in Italy in January 1921, "The Green Goddess" was in full swing in New York. I found a letter from Archer awaiting me at my house, had dinner with him as soon as possible, and he told me the whole story of "The Green Goddess". He had written me the story of his work on the play, indeed, in 1916 or 1917. The play was written in those years, <u>not in</u> 1920, as this biographer states. He wrote the play to relieve the boredom of his position as censor of the Dublin, Ireland, post office. Archer's interest was always in plays with a spiritual motive, and a burning purpose. He was one of the first, if not <u>the</u> first English critic to feel the poetry of [John Millington] Synge's plays when they were produced in London. But he had also been interested in the pure mechanics of the drama, though he had no admiration for carpenter-made plays. He enlivened his routine in Dublin by making a purely mechanical play, where the interest was produced by time honored situations dressed in modern clothes. Play carpentry, he called it. He thought its success was due to the fact that [George] Arliss played it more than to any other reason. He rather liked making so much money, of course.

The introductory notice speaks casually of his interest in Ibsen. Ibsen was the great enthusiasm of his life. He not only pushed Ibsen's plays in England, and "edited" them as your biographer says; he was the sole translator of many of the best plays, among them "A Doll's House", "Pillars of Society", "Ghosts", "An Enemy of Society". He and Edmund Gosse translated "The Master Builder". These are the only Ibsen plays I happen to have in my bookcase, but I know that Archer translated still other Ibsen plays. I wonder why your editors chose to use "The Green Goddess" in the "Reader". But since they did, I think the introductory note should have been more accurate. Of course, the play was first produced in Philadelphia, December 27, 1920, but Archer had written me an outline of it in '16 or '17, and it was written in those years.

I do not suppose you have much to do with the text book section of the publishing house, so perhaps it is foolish in me to trouble you. One does, however, hate to see an old friend presented in such a misleading fashion. The man who first translated and popularized Ibsen in English, did a great service to the English stage. That work was important and formative, and it was the serious work of Archer's life. "The Green Goddess" was the diversion of a dull year or two.

Faithfully yours,
Willa Cather

[Included is the brief biography of Archer to which Cather refers. She underscored the word "edited" in a sentence about Archer and Ibsen, drew a line from it to the margin, and wrote:] A very different job from translating.

TO HELEN LOUISE CATHER

December 20, 1939

My dear Helen Louise:

Here is just a little check for a Christmas card. I am sending very modest Christmas cards this year because great misfortunes have happened to some of our friends at Grand Manan. Our carpenter is very ill because he can't get over the shock of his son's death. His son just went out in the woods and shot himself after a quarrel with his very gentle old father. A week later, one of our most faithful helpers, Willie Thomas, suffered a great loss. His house burned down at night. He and his brother and his old mother escaped in their night clothes. No insurance—lost everything. One neighbor gave enough timber for a new house, and the Island fishermen volunteered to build it. A half dozen of us pooled together and supplied the money for all the iron fittings, the cement, doors, windows, furniture, bedding, etc., etc. The twins would tell you what a fine old fellow Willie is. He is over sixty years old, and is still one of the best tree hewers on the Island.

It seems absurd to have both West Virginia and Margaret as near as Boston, and yet never to see them. But I am trying awfully hard to finish a book that has been dragging on for a long while. I quit it altogether when you[r] Uncle Douglass died, and four months later, when I was just picking it up again, Isabelle died in Italy. So this book has had very bad luck. Books are just like people; some have good luck in their making and some have bad.

I am so glad you can be near the grandparents Garber. I am ordering some carnations for Mrs. Garber's Christmas. I chose those because she can smell them, even if she can't see them very well.

Heaps of love to you, dear, and don't forget me. We shall see one another again some day, and then it will be as if we had not been separated for so long.

Your very loving
Aunt Willie

PART ELEVEN

The Culmination of a Career

1940–1943

The rush of Virginia memories, when once I began to call them up, was heavy upon me. I wrote many chapters of Virginia ways and manners, just as things came back to me, for the relief of remembering them in a time of loss and personal sorrow. That "eased" me, and comforted.
—WILLA CATHER TO FERRIS GREENSLET, November 25, 1940

Willa Cather, about age five, Winchester, Virginia

*S*APPHIRA AND THE *S*LAVE *G*IRL, the novel Cather had been working toward in the last years of the 1930s, was published on December 7, 1940, her sixty-seventh birthday. As she emphasized in many letters from those years, this, her last completed novel, had its origin in something she witnessed when she was only five years old: the reunion of two women, a mother who remained with the white family that had once enslaved her and a daughter who escaped slavery before emancipation and fled to Canada. Working on it was essentially a retreat into memory, a way to find comfort as death and war clouded her world. And yet the novel is by no means a comfortable, sentimental book. It is a complex story of danger, injustice, and fear—yet another example of Cather's consistent desire to make her work reflect an honest and thoughtful view of humanity.

TO ROSCOE CATHER

January 8 [1940]

Dear Brother;

It's hard to keep in touch—hard for me to tell you much about the realities of my life. I don't send you fan letters. But a writer's relations to his or her publisher is a very vital fact—means happiness or constant anxiety. Last spring I happened to mention to Alfred that I thought it was very kind of Jan, among other things to send me the copy of an unpublished story which Isabelle had at her death.

"Do you mean to say that you have a completed manuscript that I have never seen?"

"But this is only a short story—you couldn't possibly publish it alone. I sent a copy to Isabelle because she is an invalid—to amuse her. I call it "The Old Beauty". Of course, if you'd like to see it———"

"I would."

So I sent it over to his apartment. The first letter came, and I acknowledged it. Then came the second, which gave me great pleasure.

Somewhere I still have a letter from him, dated "Christmas morning, 4 oclock." I had been at his house for a Christmas Eve party (awful English, excuse!) and I took with me the ms. of "A Lost Lady" thinking he might read it over the holiday. He sat up after the party that night and read it, and wrote me that night at 4 a.m. The letter reached me by special messenger on Christmas morning. So it began:

> "Christmas morning,
> four oclock.
>
> My dear Miss Cather.
>   I think you are a very great writer. ——————

The story struck him hard; and he was there at the bat when I pitched him a ball. (This figure is bad baseball, I know, but it expresses the relation between a writer and a live publisher, who isn't afraid.)

A scrappy letter, my dear boy, but I've been in bed for a week, bronchitis, missing all the jolly things I would otherwise be doing with Yehudi and Nola. So I am taking my dullness out on you, and, writing in bed, I cannot write very clearly.

Please send Alfred Knopf's two letters back to me. I thought you might like to see them.

> With my love
> Willie

Remember; we have a rendezvous. We will meet this spring or summer. If this damned Virginia book hadn't made me so much trouble I'd be foot-loose now. But I want to get it done for Knopf's sake, because he never nags or hurries me.

The short story referred to here did not appear until after Cather's death, when Knopf published The Old Beauty and Others *in 1948.*

TO PENDLETON HOGAN

February 5, 1940

My dear Mr. Hogan:

You[r] letter has lain unanswered on my desk for a long time. When I returned from a vacation in the West, I found so many letters awaiting me that it has taken me three weeks to answer them. I cannot reply to yours very fully, simply because there are many letters still ahead of yours. You ask me one or two questions which I can touch upon briefly.

I am always glad when people tell me they like "My Mortal Enemy", because it was a rather difficult story to write. You ask me why Ewan Grey and Esther do not come into the story again. Simply because their only use was to flash into the story for a moment, as one of the many examples of Myra's extravagant friendships. To have mentioned them again in the latter part of the story would have been both confusing and misleading. She could not possibly keep all these people in her life, especially after she was ill and, so to speak, in exile. And I, who was merely painting a portrait of Myra, with reflections of her in various looking glasses hung about the room, would have been very foolish to try to account for any of these people whom Myra had loved and left behind. And it was the extravagance of her devotions that made her, in the end, feel that Oswald was her mortal enemy—that he had somehow been the enemy of her soul's peace. Of course, her soul never could have been at peace. She wasn't that kind of woman. I knew her very well indeed, and she was very much as I painted her. At least, many of her friends and relatives wrote to me that they recognized her immediately, although the story was not written or published until fifteen years after her death.

I think it is better to answer one question fully than to say a word in reply to half a dozen questions. I heartily appreciate your friendly and cordial letter, and I declare you a thoroughly well-posted reader. As to writing, you will do well at it <u>if you enjoy it</u>. I advise you, as I do many young writers, to devote a good deal of your leisure to a study of the French language and literature. They are the best correctives for the faults to which we American[s] are prone. Good luck, and believe me,

Very cordially yours,
Willa Cather

Cather did not explicitly name the prototype for Myra Henshawe in My Mortal Enemy, *and many theories have been put forward, inspired in part by this letter.*

The most convincing case, made by Charles Johanningsmeier, is that Myra was based on Hattie McClure, the wife of editor and publisher S. S. McClure.

TO ZOË AKINS

February 15, 1940

My dear Zoe;

I am so glad that you have a place you love, with gardens and fountains, and that beautiful view of the mountain ridge. It always brings me peace to think that when the world is full of misery and madness, you can shut yourself up there and forget that the heritage of all the ages is being threatened. I have not succeeded in providing myself with such a retreat, and I realize that not to have done so is one kind of failure. For years and years an escape to a wild little island in the North Atlantic (with plenty of hardships, but absolute freedom) satisfied me absolutely. I love raw fogs and heavy storms from the sea better than a mild climate like yours—Oh, much better. But the hardships have grown to be a little more of a strain, and there is no way to "civilize" and modify the place without spoiling the very thing I love there.

Yes, I am glad you have a safe kingdom in this terrifying world. But, Zoe, I am not glad that you wrote <u>Starvation on Red River</u>. It is the only play of yours that I have ever read with no pleasure at all. I read it carefully, and I could not once detect your voice—it all sounded like something through a loud speaker. I don't think you <u>belong</u> in the Dust Bowl. The characters just don't come through to me as individuals; they seem made to fit certain situations. I cannot believe that a successful business man, a grown up man of the world, would ever find any pleasure in hiding a roll of money away in a niche where he used to put his pennies as a little boy. The situation which results from his doing such a thing, seems to me forced and improbable, as does the behaviour of the small boy, <u>Harry</u>.

No matter how many melodramatic situations a play flashes on one, I doubt whether it can have a very strong dramatic interest unless the audience can have a very strong personal interest, either admiration or affection, <u>for at least one of the characters</u>. Lately we have had ever so many plays which tried to get on without this, and they have none of them been good plays. "The Little Foxes" is the most recent example. Nobody cares a hang what happens to any of the characters in that shocking play—one would like to see the whole bunch massacred, so that one could go home. And in this play, from you of all people, I can't find a single person who either you or I can get worked up about. <u>Pearl</u>, least of all.

She just doesn't seem to me a real person. And the lion doesn't seem to me a real lion. Why, pages of dialogue are wasted on that damned Lion!

What I am trying to say, Zoe, is that you were trying to write a play against your natural sympathies. I can't help feeling that you hated writing it. So much of the dialogue is devoted to explaining and apologizing (accounting) for illogical situations; one action does not develop naturally out of another, and somehow the action never seems to go with the word. You never before wrote a play with no real feeling in it, and I hope to Heaven you never will again. Don't do it, write your own kind of thing. Leave bloody lion tamers to skirts like Lillian Hellman. Please don't be angry with me, but this play really hurt my feelings and made me sad.

Lovingly
Willa

➢ ➣

On February 20, 1940, Greenslet wrote Cather about an unusual request: a book dealer in Utah would purchase a thousand copies of My Ántonia *if a bull in the novel had its name changed from "Brigham Young" to something more suitable for a Utah readership.*

TO FERRIS GREENSLET

February 24 [1940]

My Dear F.G.

Why not Ferdinand? Seriously, I am willing to change the name of my bull to <u>Andrew Jackson</u>, for this edition of one thousand only. I do it as an accommodation to you. Not for five hundred dollars, but because you helped me to save "Antonia" from Grant Wood. Please, when you return from Florida, write me an agreement signed by yourself and another officer of the company, to the effect that the bull's name is to be changed for 1,000 copies only. My father's two bulls were named Gladstone and Brigham Young. I like both names—one refers to disposition (stubborn,) and the other to physical adequacy.

Here's wishing you a pleasant vacation

Willa Cather

P.S. Of course I am in accord with you on the suggested proposal regarding the sale of a set of the autograph edition for the Finland fund.

W.S.C.

TO HELEN LOUISE CATHER

Easter Sunday, March 23, 1940

My Dear Goddaughter;

(How solemn that sounds!) I wanted to send you something in remembrance of the day when you are to be confirmed, having seen you through your baptism, but I couldn't think of the right thing. Well one night I dreamed the right thing. I dreamed about you and your grandmother Cather on the upper front porch of Grandfather's house. So the moment I was awake, the meaning of that very pleasant dream flashed into my mind. I got up immediately, went to the box where I keep my trinkets and took out a little marquise ring which Douglass gave mother long ago. When he came to New York six months before his death, he brought the ring to me. I had it cut down to fit my little finger and have often worn it. Marquise rings, unless they are very large ones with many stones, are usually worn on the little finger: Of course on the third finger when they are engagement rings. (verb understood, please!)

I know your Grandmother would want you to have this ring from her and from me, on this occasion. I want you to have something near you to remind you often of her. She loved you and Mary Virginia the best of her granddaughters. She used to tell me that you two did many thoughtful little things for her, and never seemed to think that it was silly for her to like pretty clothes just because she was old. How often I feel sad now because I always found something else to do when she wanted me to go to Mrs. Burden's to "look at hats". People can be very cruel in this world without meaning to be. I know she would want you to have her little ring as well as if she had told me so, and it gives me pleasure to send it to you. Sometime I will tell you some of the loving things she said to me about you.

Goodbye my dear, this is the first letter I have written by hand in many a long day. I think the Nicene Creed the most beautiful prose in the world. If I am wakeful in the night and <u>think</u> it through to myself, slowly, I can nearly always go to sleep. There is such authority and majesty in it.

Lovingly, my dear,
Your Aunt Willie

P.S. The ring will be too small for your little finger, perhaps. If so get Mr. Trickey (or his successor) to fit it properly and send the bill to me. The ring will reach you later than the letter, since registered packages are always long on the way.

✦ ✦

Cather's old friend Carrie Miner Sherwood was, along with her husband, involved with Red Cross fund-raising for Webster County, Nebraska.

TO CARRIE MINER SHERWOOD

June 5 [1940]

My Dear Carrie;

I think this a pretty heavy quota for Webster County under the present conditions, so I would like to make my contribution to the Red Cross fund as a citizen of Webster County. As I see that Walter [Sherwood] is treasurer I send my check to you. If it is turned in to the Red Cross solicitors, they will accept a check on the Chase Bank as cash.

I own land in Webster County and pay taxes there, so I should think I would be allowed to contribute my donation from there and help to bring the quota up to the stipulated amount.

I have been out of the French Hospital for nearly three weeks, but I am not very energetic. There was [nothing] very serious the matter—a sore throat that kept hanging edge of quinsy but never quite got there. You remember mother used to have those bad throat attacks. This was the first time for me. It made me think a lot about her.

Lovingly
Willie

P.S. I do not check on my account in Walter's bank, because if my Chase Bank check is sent to the Red Cross Headquarters it will be returned to me and can be filed among my contribution checks for the Income Tax examiner. I'm writing indistinctly because I'm tired, my dear.

The Red Cross is the one charity I know that does what it pretends to.

TO CARRIE MINER SHERWOOD

Thursday [June 8, 1940]

Dear Carrie;

I forgot the most important thing—that I want my Red Cross check to be anonymous.

[Mary] Virginia said today she was afraid I'd made a blunder: that it would discourage others from contributing, and that persons who knew about it would say I was trying to show off. I think she meant her father [J. W. Auld] would.

Hastily
Willie

→ ←

June 10, 1940, was "dreadful and discouraging" because, as Germany was overwhelming France and on the verge of taking Paris, Italy abandoned its neutrality and declared war on France and Great Britain.

TO FERRIS GREENSLET

June 10, 1940

Dear Ferris Greenslet:

Ever since the first number of John Buchan's autobiography [*Memory Hold-the-Door*] came out in the Atlantic, I have wanted to tell you how fine I think it is and to congratulate you upon having secured such a book of sanity and comfort for us all. On this most dreadful and discouraging of days, June 10th, I had the chapter "Bright Company" for my companion at teatime. The world and life he brings before me seems almost as far away as the world of Vergil's Eclogues. As you know, I have been blamed as an "escapist",—indifferent and selfish. But there are things one cannot escape. And I think none of the personal sorrows I have lived through have ever shaken my days and nights as has the gloom (doom?) which has been gathering for the last few months over almost everything that has made the world worth living in or living for. You are one of the people who I know feels as I do; but the strange thing is that almost everyone feels it in some degree. My doctor tells me that the patients in the hospitals are very much affected by it, and their wish to get well seems to flag. He will not let me go over to Philadelphia on the 12th to take a degree from the University of Pennsylvania, because I am so slow in recovering from a recent illness. But I write chiefly to thank you for telling me about Buchan's autobiography, which I might have missed when so many distracting and devastating things are happening in the world, and to all my friends abroad.

Faithfully yours,
Willa Cather

P.S. This seems a foolish personal request to make when I really care so little about personal things just now: but since <u>Antonia</u> is still selling, and since I am still perpetually receiving letters about her, I do wish you would send to the Riverside Press for a copy of the current edition. I lately sent for several, to present to my nurses at the French Hospital, and I was shocked to find on what poor, thin paper the book is now printed. The trouble is that since the letters on page 5 show through the paper and cloud the text on page 6, the book is now very hard to read. I have always found that the principal objection to cheap editions, like the old Dent "Everyman" books, and the "Giants" of the Modern Library, is that one side of every leaf shows through the paper and clouds the next, so that there is not a clear page on which the eye can rest with satisfaction or read without a certain amount of disquieting effort.

W.S.C.

TO ROSCOE CATHER

July 11, 1940

My Dear Roscoe:

Yesterday I arrived home from Jaffrey, New Hampshire, where I spent several week[s], trying to get over the results of a severe illness which I had in May. I was in the French Hospital for a week at that time. I did not write you because I did not wish to alarm you, and my doctor said it would be a slow recovery. I had accepted an invitation to take an honorary degree from the University of Pennsylvania June 12th, but I was too ill to go to Philadelphia. They gave me the degree <u>in absentia</u>, however. I have come back able to work steadily at my desk, which I have not been able to do for some time. I am determined that Alfred Knopf shall have this book (title <u>Sapphira and the Slave Girl</u>) this autumn. I have broken half a dozen dates with him, and I feel that it is a question of honor not to break another.

I wonder what I ever said that made you think I was ready to read proofs!! Why, when I went up to Jaffrey some weeks ago, two of the most important chapters were still unwritten. But there, in the quiet country, in my old attic rooms, I wrote them in two weeks time—worked two and one-half hours every morning, and stayed in bed all afternoon as my doctor had directed. But these chapters, scrawled in pencil, have to be rewritten several times before they are ready for the press and the whole story, which has been interrupted so many times, must be gone over and welded together, so to speak.

The story was going strong and I was full of enthusiasm for it when Douglass died. After that I did not work any more at all for four months. Then Isabelle died. When I went back to the manuscript, I was almost a different person. I had lost my keen interest in the story. I have done all I can to mend that break in the story, and to make the latter part like the first, but the break will always be there.

Among the many letters I found waiting for me when I got back from Jaffrey, I find one from Margaret, and I shall communicate with her just as soon as I can. She has no telephone, so I must wait until I have time to write a letter and make an appointment. I have not unpacked my trunk, but today I began my new schedule by working two hours, and I intend to do this every day until the book is ready for Alfred Knopf. I am going to get this book done if I have to stay in town with it all summer. If you read my sketch about Alfred Knopf in the book I sent you ["Portrait of the Publisher as a Young Man," in *Alfred A. Knopf Quarter Century*], you may understand why I feel this way. The sketch gave no hint of the thousand personal kindnesses I have had from him, or of his constant interest in my comfort and welfare. It's a matter of honor with me not to disappoint him by delaying this book again. If I can get it done in time to go to Grand Manan, I can of course read the proofs there. But the proofs are still a long way ahead. Mary Virginia always helps me a lot when she is in town—does bits of shopping, etc., for me—but she is away on her vacation for one month. There are other difficult features in the situation, but I am certainly going to finish this book before I leave town, unless some serious accident should befall me.

Now forgive me for telling all my troubles. The results of a high blood pressure are sometimes terribly hard to bear. The thing I mind most is a kind of clouded memory, especially regarding very recent happenings, engagements etc. You know, I used to have a real good memory.

Lovingly
Willie

P. S. The letters from my friends in France and England are heartbreaking. Those letters alone would be enough to take all the drive out of one.

July 12th

Your letter about the State of California vs. the Ocean Front just reached me. I'm sorry you had to write it, but I certainly call it a well composed letter—you made this technical tangle as clear as it can be made. I'm sure I don't know what a process server could do to me. If he starts to drag me to some court or other just now, he won't get me very far. Too bad I didn't get off to G. Manan some weeks ago. He'd have had some chase finding me!

I love to think of your happy family reunion, dear brother.

W

TO ROSCOE CATHER

August 26 [1940]

My Dear Roscoe;

What a <u>darling</u> granddaughter you have! Tell dear Elizabeth that everyone at Whale Cove Cottage is delighted to see a picture of her little daughter and they send their love to her.

Last week I wrote the last chapter of "Sapphira and the Slave Girl" (It had been hand-written three times before, but this time I copied it off on the machine in final form) and telegraphed Knopf. I enclose his reply, which you may mail back to me.

"Sapphĭra" is pronounced with a short "i", as in Madeira, Zamira etc. It is not the Bible "Sapphīra" with long "i", but an old English name made from the Bible name with the "i" made short.

I will write you when I get back to a comfortable typewriter. The old one I keep up here year after year is the same old machine I bought for $30.00 in Cheyenne that summer I was there with you and Douglass (we got it from a fellow who was dead broke, you remember. All my early books were typed on it.) I always write a book through the first time by hand. This book I have written twice by hand—some chapters of it three and even four times. It is technically the most difficult book I ever wrote, and it has had very hard luck. I've tried an experiment in form which most people will not like, and which, I admit, rather gives the show away. The fact (which only a very few people will notice) is that in this case there is a concealed show behind the first show. This second show, coming on the stage in the Epilogue, is the reason for, and the authority for, the first show. Without that literal account of something that happened to me when I was between five and six years old, the whole book would be <u>constructed, not lived</u>, like a hundred other stories of the South and of slavery: the old costumes, the old high-stepping language and "mansions", the old Uncle Remus dialect. This is <u>true</u> Virginia negro speech, which was much modified "Uncle Remus" talk. When I began the story that speech was in my brain like a phonograph record. I hadn't a moment's hesitation.

Half-way through the story I went South to verify it. <u>Not</u> with a note-book my ear is my notebook—it is the only one I have ever carried.

Please save this scrawl until you read the book. I have not written a word of comment or explanation to anyone else about the book. You are the only one in my family who cares a damn. I never used to mind that, but as one grows older one wishes there were some one of one's blood kin who was deeply interested. However, better no one than the wrong kind like those poor D. H. Lawrence left behind him. [James M.] Barrie and Thomas Hardy, thank God, left no "representatives" but their own books,—and that is best. You can't keep your cake and eat it too.

I'm tired, so I'm writing foolishness—so excuse

Lovingly
W

TO ALFRED A. KNOPF

August 29 [1940]
Grand Manan Island

My Dear Alfred;

I did not write you until I had something definite to report. Living on our island was never so perplexing and inconvenient as it has been this summer. I will report my amusing misadventures when I see you. Miss Bloom's vacation came at the worst possible time for me. She will not be in New York until the Tuesday after Labor Day.

However, within a few days I shall be able to send you the rest of the manuscript, all of it except one chapter, the insert chapter of about 3,700 words which follows page 82 of your manuscript. That insert is completed, and I will send it to Miss Bloom to copy as soon as she returns. I will ask her to do it as quickly as possible and hold it until my return for my final corrections. That chapter has a good deal of interesting dialect and native idiom, and I want to go over her copy of it before I give it to you. I will do this as soon as I reach New York on September 17th or 18th. You would surely have the corrected copy on the 20th.

I am leaving the island earlier than I expected, because the cook (a mighty poor one!) is going then.

I am taking the sketch for the jacket to the post office today, as a boat goes out tomorrow—the first boat out for two days. I like this design, though I really like Mr. [Rudolph] Ruzicka's more conservative style better than this rather violent departure from his usual manner. This is confidential, I would not admit it to anyone else.

Please mail me a bunch of the reviews of Thomas Mann's long awaited "Return" [*The Beloved Returns*]. It's a great book, of course, if you approach it from the right angle, but how many of our esteemed fellow citizens have ever read Goethe, even in translation? And what will the author's complete saturation with his subject mean to those who haven't read Werther or Wilhelm? I wonder how many of "pure Nordics" of the present Germany have read them?

I never thanked you for the wine you sent me just before I left town—I didn't even open the package. It was not ingratitude but heat that made me so ill-mannered. It was 99 degrees on the day Miss Lewis and I left town.

Thank you for ordering the candy, which I hope will come on tonight's boat.

With love to you both
Willa Cather

TO BISHOP GEORGE ALLEN BEECHER

September 28, 1940

My Bishop and my very dear Friend:

You never had a kinder impulse than that which led you to write me a beautiful letter about the dedication of the altar rail at Grace Church. This letter, which I will keep all my life, brought tears to my eyes and peace to my heart. There are few spots in the world that I love as much as I love that little church in Red Cloud. And when I read your letter, I feel that I am there myself. I know that to me, too, the windows would speak like voices, and many precious memories would come back to me. How well I remember the evening when you confirmed me, with my father and mother, in that dear little church. That evening meant a great deal in the lives of all three of us.

It seems almost like one of the miracles of old that dear Molly Ferris was able to be present at that service and once more bear witness to her "faith that has been a light to many." I feel grateful, my dear Bishop, that in your busy life you took the time to write me of that Sunday service while your heart was still full of it. Your good letter brought to my heart an uplift and a warmth which could express itself only in prayer. I felt as if I had been with you all on that happy day.

It will not be long, I hope, before I am with you in person as well as in thought. I feel very hopeful that I can be in Red Cloud and Hastings sometime this coming winter, and then I can explain to you some of the many things which have kept me away so long.

 With loving good wishes to Mrs. Beecher and yourself,

Faithfully and affectionately yours,

Willa Cather

→ ←

Sapphira and the Slave Girl *was designated a "main selection" of the Book-of-the-Month Club in January 1941, which meant large sales for the novel.*

TO ROSCOE CATHER

October 5, 1940

My dear Roscoe:

 Before I left Grand Manan I wrote you a rather hysterical letter, and I am ashamed of it. Please forget it and forgive me. Sometimes, at the end of a long pull of work, people get shaky and wonder what it is all about. Unfortunately, I had a severe toothache nearly all the while I was up there, and with our queer boat service I would have lost a whole week getting to a dentist on the mainland and returning. I had only six weeks to finish the book, and could not lose a week. The local doctor gave me codeine when my sleep was too badly broken up, but codeine leaves a mean hang-over. On the whole it was a fairly nerve-racking experience. I got the book done, however, and apparently with considerable success.

 In these days any kind of success brings its own problems. I am enclosing a letter from Alfred Knopf which will explain some of them to you.

 The Book of the Month Club (their selection of the book for January has not been publicly announced and is a secret) will make their payment to both Alfred and me at the end of January. I always make up my income tax <u>from January 1 to January 1.</u> Mr. [Joseph] Lesser, in Alfred's office, does it for me. I have been four years writing the book and most of the financial returns will come in during the year 1941, when the tax on what is called "unearned income" is to be greatly increased. You see, Alfred has taken the trouble to worry about that, and is willing to advance me half of what the Book of the Month Club pays, in order to get that amount into my 1940 tax return. I had been thinking rather mournfully of the income tax problem that would confront me next year, but I had not spoken to him about it.

I have in my safe deposit box a letter received from you some time before I went away for the summer. In this letter you said that you had a check for me from the Ocean Front Oil property, but that you were holding all such checks to use in some litigation with the State of California. If, without any injustice to the other participants to whom checks are due, you could send me my check before the first of December, it would certainly help me out very much in my tax report, by increasing my income for this year (this year it (my income) happens to be lower than it has been for many years) and reducing it for 1941, when it will be larger than it has ever been before in any one year. Knopf never made as big a first printing as he is making for Sapphira. The next largest first printing was of Shadows on the Rock, which the Book of the Month Club had also accepted. As you probably know, the Book of the Month Club makes its own books. It simply buys from the author and publisher the right to print the book in their own cheap way, and send it to the subscribers. They cut into Alfred Knopf's sale somewhat, but he feels that the wide advertisement they give the book fully compensates. Moreover, the Book of the Month Club members are made up of people who practically never buy books—they want something to read but don't know how to go about getting it. As Alfred says, very few of the members are in my "natural audience" at all.

God knows, my dear brother, why such a quiet book, dealing with old fashioned people and the long ago, should set a bunch of young men like the office staff on fire, but it seems to have done so. The form (structure) of the book is fairly good, but the Epilogue and the approach to it are pretty daring, and I was very much afraid it would give the reader a jolt. Fortunately, I wrote the Epilogue before I wrote beyond the first few chapters of the book—I like to see my end from my beginning. That was before Douglass died and before Isabelle died, and I was full of enthusiasm for my idea. Every word in the scene of Nancy's Return is true, my boy, even the weather. The excitement of that actual occurrence seemed to change me from a baby into a thinking being. For years I had wanted to write that actual scene, but I could never see a way to use it except in a personal autobiography, and I hate autobiographies.

With my love
Willie

P.S. I am sending you a copy of a letter to Elsie, which will explain some of the problems which puzzle me at present, quite as much as the income tax! I'm only half way through the page proofs.

TO DOROTHY CANFIELD FISHER

October 14, 1940

[Written in the top margin:] <u>Confidential</u>

My dear Dorothy:

I wish I could write you just a note by hand, but my right hand is in a bandage just at present (sprains). Now at last, my dear Dorothy, we are quits about titles. I have always been ashamed that I called your last book "Seasoned Wood" [really *Seasoned Timber*]! You see, I had left the book at Grand Manan, where I have a considerable library, and I was writing from memory. Now you write me about "Sapphira and the Slave <u>Maid</u>"! my dear, which is "Sapphira and the Slave Girl". You see, I like the doubling up of s's and r's, just as you like "timber" better than "wood".

It gives me very special pleasure, my dear Dorothy, to know that you really like the book, though you must have read some very incomplete version of it, for I am just handing back the galley proofs of one chapter which I brought down from Grand Manan with me, and the galley proofs of the rest of the text were unusually slovenly. Douglass and Isabelle died when I was in the middle of the book, and I threw it aside for nearly a year. When I picked it up again, I had not much enthusiasm left. However, I had written the Epilogue before that break—because the Epilogue was where I was going. I think it is bad manners to jump from the third person to the first person in a narrative, but that meeting between Nancy and Aunt Till, which took place just as I tell it, was one of the most moving things that ever happened to me when I was little. And it was from the long talks between my grandmother and Till and Nancy, that I got my strongest impressions of how things had been in the old days before the War. This grandmother was really a "Rebel", since she lost two sons in the Confederate Army. But she was a lover of justice. In a beautiful old map in the Society Library, made in 1821, I found the actual ferry by which my grandmother took Nancy over the Potomac River. My father's people were all "Republicans", and the post-mistress was my great-aunt, Sidney Gore, born Sidney Cather.

I cannot tell you how much pleasure I had in listening to those voices which had been non-existent for me for so many years, when other sounds silenced them. I loved especially playing with the darkey speech, which was deep down in my mind exactly like phonograph records. I could remember exactly what they said and the quality of the voice. Just wait till our wise young reviewers, such as Clifton [Fadiman] and Louis [Kronenberger], sadly call attention to the inconsistency in Till's and Nancy's speech,—never knowing that all well trained house servants spoke two languages: one with white people and one with their fellow negroes. But when they were very much excited or in sorrow, they nearly always reverted to the cabin idiom.

Once I had dropped the book for good. It was only after this unspeakable war began that I took it up again. I am an "escapist", you know, and by this means I could truly escape for two hours every day,—from the newspapers, and the letters from my friends in London which shattered my nerves,—not by their complaints but by their sheer splendour.

Good-bye and thank you, dear Dorothy. I expect I should have put off writing to you until my hand was well, but so many things crowd in nowaday, that one is almost afraid to wait.

Yours always,
Willa

TO FERRIS GREENSLET

Sunday [probably November 25, 1940]

Dear F.G.

Despite coincidental misfortunes (secretary out of town and the thumb of my right hand badly sprained), I must venture a scrawl to tell you what deep pleasure the letter from you and Mrs. Greenslet gives me. I prefer to think it is from both of you—indeed, you practically say so. The rush of Virginia memories, when once I began to call them up, was heavy upon me. I wrote many chapters of Virginia ways and manners, just as things came back to me, for the relief of remembering them in a time of loss and personal sorrow. That "eased" me, and comforted. Then I cut what was too solidly "manners and customs" and re-wrote the story according to the design I had in mind when I wrote the first chapter—a pleasant breakfast table, and incidental discussion of disposing of a gentle and affectionate girl—(not <u>slave</u> girl really, but a member of the family). The real Nancy's real mother was a real member of my family when I was little. The stories about that strange relation (those I have happened to read) were all so partisan for or against. The institution was neither a torture prison, nor a benevolent training school. It had its pleasant domestic surfaces. Underneath? Well, "down with us" we didn't think much about the underneath. Aunt Till was no pitiable figure to me—nor to herself. Dignity, personality!

But a sore thumb can't go into these matters seriously, analytically. It (the original conception) was all light and shade, was meant to be neither wise nor instructive—certainly not heavy. Some weeks ago I put the discard (the excised chapters & paragraphs) on the bathroom scales, and they weighed six pounds. I was very pleased.

Affectionately to you both
W.S.C.

P.S. Certainly, I am perfectly willing you should place the note on names where Alfred places his notes on design. I <u>placed</u> it out of <u>place</u> in 1st edition because I feared some people of the same name used in [the] story, Frederick County people, might feel hurt. Second edition will probably change that.

Do you know there is nothing at all to a hand <u>but</u> a thumb?

TO ROSCOE CATHER

November 28, 1940

My dear Brother:

How long it is that I have wanted to write you. All kinds of pleasant things have been happening, but they happen much too fast. One of the pleasantest was a luncheon that I finally managed to arrange at Sherry's, with your Margaret and Virginia, and Mary Virginia. After a long and very conversational luncheon we went to see the colored moving pictures, which Edith took of the twins at Grand Manan, thrown on a Kodak screen. Not one of the three nieces had seen these before. The pictures really are beautiful and do justice to the splendid cliffs and the blue sea.

Two weeks before this I had shifted round a lot of dates to get a free space, and telegraphed Margaret asking her to lunch with me two days following receipt of the telegram. She has no telephone and it is difficult to reach her on short notice. I, just at this time, can't make any engagements otherwise than on short notice. When she sent me the enclosed note, turning me down for a bridge party, I felt a little hurt. But the moment I met her in the restaurant, I was so delighted to see her dear little face again that I forgot all about my astonishment at being turned down. Of course, the child could hardly have had any idea of how many calls there are on me just now from the printing office, from the business office, the editorial office and from newspaper offices. Anyhow, I expect it is good for me to be turned down occasionally.

I only hope the three girls enjoyed those 3 ½ hours at Sherry's as much as I did. I was delighted to see West Virginia again, and felt immediately that there was a very interesting personality behind her blue eyes. Mary Virginia told me when I first came home from Canada that Virginia decidedly had "poise"—a thing which Mary Virginia admires very much. To "poise", I would add, ease and relaxation. They are delightful qualities to find in young people and not at all common in the young people of today. In time, these three qualities become "distinction". Dear little Margaret was just as sweet and appealing as ever, in a very becoming poke hat and black veil, just the kind of hat I used to find in grandmother Boak's chests, in Virginia. It was quite the right shape for Margaret, and she looked very cunning.

I have never even had time to thank you for your dear letter from Grass Valley. I put it (the letter) in my "Lost Lady", even though I had never heard of Grass Valley when I wrote the book. I thought she [Lyra Wheeler Garber] came from San Francisco, and it was not until Douglass told me, in California, that I knew Mrs. Garber's grandmother was a Spanish woman. I am glad I did not know it, for I wasn't a very practised writer when I did that book and I might have been tempted, as poor [Joseph] Hergesheimer always was, to use the charm of the "exotic". But I was able, just by being truthful, to do her "from life", as the painters say, and still give her that quality which several French reviewers caught and in describing the character said that "the portrait had a reminder of Spanish women."

Now I must stop, my dear boy, for just at present my right hand is in a sling and I am behind in everything. Perhaps I wrote you that I autographed the édition de luxe (500 copies) in three days, and it sprained the big tendon in my thumb, which has gradually grown worse. If I have to have it strapped to a splint, I shall go to the French Hospital and let the nuns take care of me, for without a right thumb one is utterly helpless. However, I am not going until after Yehudi's concert, on December 2nd, even if I have to sit in the box with my hand in a white scarf. Good-bye, my dear boy. I do love your three daughters, and Margaret has a particular charm for me. I can't tell you just why, but one never can tell the why of particular affinities, you know.

Lovingly
Willie

TO FANNY BUTCHER

January 9 [1941?]
New York City

Dear Fanny Butcher;

You ask me what book I would rather have written than all others: I suppose you mean what novel? Well, since it's a wishing game, why be modest? I imagine you expect me to name some neat obscure book, by some neat obscure talent. To be really <u>chic</u> I ought to say that I'd love to be responsible for the high-flying rhetoric of "Moby Dick", where one metaphor about the Musèe de Cluny and the human soul runs to the length of a page and a half.

Thank you! If I can choose, I won't meekly say that the neck of the chicken is my favorite portion. I'd rather have written "War and Peace" than any other novel I know. I am not sure that I admire it more than any other, but I'd rather have written it; Simply for the grand game of making it, you understand, quite regardless of the result. I would like to be strong enough to have, and to survive, so many gloriously vivid sensations about almost everything that goes to make up human society. I would like to have had that torrent of life and things pour through me; and yet to be well-bred enough as an artist to unconsciously and unfailingly present it all in scale, with the proper perspective and composition and distribution of light; enough, at least, to hold the thing together. That much form, it seems to me, any satisfying work must have. From this you may infer that I wouldn't choose to be swept away in Dostoevsky's torrent, though it's as big and full as [a] heart could desire. The richer the welter of life, the more it needs a restraining intelligence. I choose "War and Peace", thank you, because it has both———and in what a degree! You remember what an experience it is to read that book for the first time; can you imagine anything more exciting than writing it? The actual writing of it, of course, was a much more concentrated and unadulterated and smooth-running form of excitement than all the many, the countless excitements, long forgotten, which enabled him to write it at all. But there, of course, I'm getting into a matter which isn't for general discussion. Every trade has its compensations; but it's wiser to keep quiet about them, or somebody turns up and tries to spoil them for you.

Sincerely yours
Willa Cather

TO MR. WATSON

February 12, 1941

My dear Mr. Watson:

Your very kind and interesting letter would have been answered long before this, except for the fact that all of the month of November I was suffering from an injury to my right hand. The month of December, I spent in the French Hospital having treatment for my hurt. I am still unable to use a pen and my hand is under constant treatment. It progresses very slowly. I wish I were able to answer your letter at length for it is a thoughtful one, much beyond the range of the usual intelligent reader.

I can best answer briefly by saying that I never try to write any propaganda—any rules for life or theories about the betterment of human society. I by no means despise that kind of writing. It can be very noble, at its best, and very useful. But I think it loses some of its strength <u>when disguised as fiction</u>. You mention Dickens. Of course, important reforms resulted from his books. But he did not write in the reformer's spirit, nor did he write in order to produce reformers. He wrote because his heart was touched, or his indignation aroused by certain abuses. In other words, he wrote about life itself, as it moved about him. He had no theories for the betterment of the world. So many of the books on social betterment which are written nowadays are written out of ill feeling; out of class hatred, or envy. Very often they are written out of a very great conceit and vanity, by young writers, who really think that the history of the world and the wisdom of the great statesm[e]n was all a very silly affair. These new writers think they can manage the age-old tragedies of life very neatly.

I am glad to have you tell me that some of your youthful friends can read my books with interest. My method of work is so simple that I have never had a conscious method. I never write about people or places that have not interested me intensely: that have not taken hold of me in some very personal way which I cannot explain. After a subject has hag-ridden me for a long time and the book is pretty well developed in my mind, then I begin to write it. The actual writing is usually a very pleasant experience. Accidents and incidents from the outside break in, of course, but the actual development of a story that has been carefully planned is the pleasantest occupation I know.

Let me thank you again for your friendly letter. The noble fortitude with which you bear those mischances, which in one way or another must come to us all, I shall not forget. If my hand is well enough tomorrow, I shall sign this letter myself.

Very cordially yours,
Willa Cather

TO VIOLA ROSEBORO'

February 20, 1941

My very dear Miss Roseboro:

My hand is still utterly out of commission and I am unable to write at all. The surgeon began mild exercise and massage too soon, and now I am back in splints again. I call this a terrible trial to patience.

It is awfully kind of you to be concerned about the reviews, but the truth is, Miss Roseboro, that this book has had a better "press" than any book I have written heretofore. For many years I have not had anything to do with a clipping bureau, but when the reviews are all in Alfred Knopf usually asks me to look them over. The New York reviewers always lament the fact that my new book (whichever it may be) is a marked decline from the previous book. Logically, I should have reached the vanishing point long ago. It might interest you to know that I did see practically all the reviews that followed the publication of Antoniá, and from coast to coast there were only two favorable ones. One by Fanny Butcher and one by Grant Overton. All the others said this book was formless and would be of interest only to the Nebraska State Historical Society.

I am asking Miss Bloom to send you the review by [Henry Seidel] Canby, which I really think is sound and discerning. He gives me credit for trying to do a definite thing, and doing it fairly well. Of course, most of the reviewers still want to know why I did not try to do a very different thing, which would have been more dramatic. This, however, applies only to the New York reviewers. After I got your letter I telephoned the office and asked them to send over a bunch of reviews from San Francisco to New Orleans. They were practically all very cordial, and I was astonished that the Southern cities seemed really enthusiastic. The personal letters that the book has brought in are a real source of satisfaction, as so many of the writers know the country and the conditions.

I hope this cold weather is not treating you too brutally. My hand is quite painful a good deal of the time, but what I mind most is the boredom of incapacity.

Lovingly yours
Willa Cather
per Sarah J. Bloom

TO ROSCOE CATHER

March 2, 1941

My dear Roscoe:

I am so sad to hear of your illness. I would have sent out inquiries, but all the time you were sick with the flu, I was in a particularly low and discouraged state about my hand. I am not writing any of this to Elsie because she is generally so communicative, and there are some people in Lincoln (people like the Pounds) who would be delighted to hear that my right hand was permanently out of commission. For the weeks while you were ill, it did seem as though I were not to have any right hand at all in the future, and the number of things you can do with your left hand are trivial and base. My surgeon here earnestly tried to persuade me to learn to compose by dictation—a thing absolutely impossible to me and against all my taste and habits. The Knopf office became as much alarmed about the situation as I. They entered into a correspondence with Dr. Frank Ober of Boston, who mended up so many of the English officers disabled in the World War. His New York patients generally fly to Boston for treatment, but he comes to New York once a month to see those who are not well enough to make the trip. He saw me just three weeks ago today. In his Boston shop he had constructed for me a metal glove reaching to the elbow, shaped metal underneath held on by leather straps across the top of my hand, wrist and arm. My own physician here thinks it a wonderful contrivance. I have worn it only one week, and while I cannot see any great improvement, I am not suffering from jars and little hurts all the time, as I was when I wore a wooden splint. Also, my wrist is absolutely immobile in metal, whereas in a wooden splint it would move about a little.

I have not written you very seriously about this before, because I am afraid that I have a rather bad reputation in my family—a reputation for howling about my ills. But somebody in the family ought to know the facts. Of course when a hand gets in this shape, a painful arthritis sets in, and the question is whether I can ever use it again to write books or even letters. The surgeons in the New York Orthopedic Hospital thought my only way out was dictation. Dr. Ober thinks I have a chance to write again, if I am very careful and never use my hand for anything but work on a manuscript—never write letters, or even sign them when I can avoid it.

You are perfectly right. I want to give the bank stock to Charles Edwin [Cather], but you can see that just now, with no preparation yet made for the income tax, I haven't the time to attend to it. I cannot describe this situation to you, but if you will tie your hand up in a handkerchief when you get out of bed and keep it tied until you get ready to go to the office, you will understand something of the laboriousness of caring for your body with one hand. Even then, you won't have to put up your hair! You know, with my metal glove, I feel just like Otto of the Silver Hand [from the children's novel by Howard Pyle]!

With love,
Willie

P.S. [written in the hand of S. J. Bloom] Dear Roscoe: Since I dictated this letter, a letter has come from Elsie charging me with inconsiderateness toward her and my friends in Red Cloud for not telling them on what date I will arrive there. I thought it best to let Miss Bloom write her how impossible it would be for me to travel under the circumstances. Miss Bloom wrote her on Friday.

Dictated by Miss Cather
S. J. Bloom

[Clumsily handwritten and enclosed in a small envelope:] The garden of spring flowers came last night! You are too good to me, dear boy.

TO CARRIE MINER SHERWOOD

March 22, 1941

My dear Carrie and my dear Friend:

I cannot write you as I wish to until I can write you with my own hand. But in these days when the weather is very bitter and I am confined to the house a good deal, my thoughts are often with you, going over the long, long past which we have shared together, even though we have so often been far apart in body.

Mary's telegram did not altogether surprise me, because only a few days before it came I had received a letter from her telling me that Walter [Carrie's husband] was very ill indeed. Of the wonderful care and nursing you were giving him I had heard again and again from Elsie, and Mary [Miner Creighton], and Trix Florance. I love to think that he died in his own home among those who loved and cherished him, and in a community that honored him. Do you know, it doesn't seem so long to me since you showed me a photograph of young Walter Sherwood inside your watch case, when you were going away to school in St. Mary's. I must not talk of these things to you, for it makes me cry and it will make you cry. But it is strange how, at this end of the road, everything is foreshortened, and we seem to possess all the stages of our life at the same time. The perplexities that I have with my hand and the perpetual inconvenience I suffer from it, are not half so real to me as mother-and-father's golden wedding, or your own wedding day, or Douglass' last visit with me here. Perhaps one reason that I enjoy so much remembering these things is that this winter I have been alone a great deal—my choice. I have seen almost no one but very dear friends, the true and tried ones. Yehudi and his lovely wife [Nola Nicholas Menuhin] came often while they were in New York, and Mary Virginia has been a great help in every way. Whenever we meet she always leaves me in better spirits than I was before. I often wonder how two such selfish people [Jessica Cather and J. W. Auld] ever came to have such a nice child.

You will hear from me very soon again, my dear, because within a few weeks I hope to be able to make plans. My general health is good and my hand seems to be making definite improvements since Dr. Ober, the surgeon from Boston, took hold of it. Some day I shall write Mary about his treatment. As a doctor's wife, I think it would interest her to know.

Now I have said so little of what I wanted to say! But, oh, how thankful I am that I had those two winter months with you in Red Cloud almost ten years ago! I can remember those evenings with you and Walter before your fireplace, and what good advice both you and he gave me.

I send my heart to you, Carrie
Willie

⇾ ⇽

Langston Hughes wrote Cather after the publication of Sapphira and the Slave Girl *thanking her for "the sympathy with which you have treated my people."*

TO LANGSTON HUGHES

April 15, 1941

Dear Mr. Hughes:

I wish to thank you for your friendly letter, and I am glad that the characters in the book seem to you truthfully presented. All of the colored people in the book are people whom I have known at one time or another, in Virginia or elsewhere. Some of them are people for whom I had an affection in my childhood.

Very cordially yours,
Willa Cather

TO MARY WILLARD

May 6, 1941

Dear Friend of Many Years,

It is bitter that I should be unable to write to you by hand. I have waited for some days to turn to you, because I seemed unable to utter anything but a cry of grief and bitter disappointment. Only Isabelle's death and the death of my brother Douglass have cut me so deep. The feeling I have, all the time, is that so much of my life has been cut away. May [Willard] has been my friend since I was twenty years old. She was the first person who was kind to me in Pittsburgh, and the first person there whom I had the joy of admiring. She dated back at least two years before Isabelle, and was the most vital and vivid part of my early years there. But you know all these things. I don't know why I am trying to tell you about them. As soon as I got Mr. Knapp's letter, I asked Edith Lewis to telephone Ethel Litchfield for me, as gently as she could. But Ethel hung up the telephone: she couldn't talk. That night, however, she called me and asked me please not to quit this world before she did. "I can't go through it again, Willa, I simply can't!" That was just what I had been feeling all day about Ethel herself. You see, that little group formed itself some years before you came to Pittsburgh, Marie—May and Ethel and Isabelle and I. We were all of us young then, and we melted together, as it were. People who came later were never a part of that very first design.

Later there was Cecil Sharpe and the glorious folk dancing period, when everybody seemed to recover their first youth. I was in New York then, working hard but, as you will remember, I went back to Isabelle for long visits, and used to attend the folk dancing classes. It seemed to me that all the dancers, men and women alike, really had taken a dip in the Fountain of Youth. Oh, those are beautiful days to remember! Isabelle often said that in the outdoor dances, May looked the youngest of them all and she was certainly by far the best dancer ———.

I haven't seen Ethel since I talked with her over the telephone that night. We both felt that it was better not to meet. She has gone down to Washington to take care of her Dutch grandchildren for a time, and their importunate activities will engage her mind for the present, I hope.

My brother Roscoe, as I think I wrote May, is ill in a very small and very hot California town, Colusa. He had a heart lesion as a result of neglected angina. Two heart men have been procured from a distance. They have written me intelligent letters and the two best heart men here have had the details from them. They all agree that my brother should not see me before the first of June. I hope he will then be well enough to be moved to San Francisco with me.

I beg you, don't try to answer this letter, Marie. Don't even acknowledge it. I know that letters like this are painful to receive and yet, I know it is true that it helps one just a little to know that one's old friends share one's grief———grief is a poor word anyhow; what I mean is that terrible sense of loss with which one wakens up in the morning and lies down at night. Something lost out of oneself and out of one's world and out of the very air one breath[e]s.

All this winter when I have been literally helpless and often so discouraged about my right hand, just thinking about May and all the things we had to talk about together would brace me up a little. I love my brother Roscoe dearly, and I am longing to see him, but it was with May that I wanted to talk about all of the strange things that have happened in the world. That was the thing I looked forward to with joy.

With Love and Happy memories
Willa Cather

TO IRENE MINER WEISZ AND CARRIE MINER SHERWOOD

May 16, 1941

Dear Irene and Carrie:

I wanted to write to both of you very often within the last few weeks, believing that Carrie is still in Chicago. I have been under great anxiety and stress since the middle of March. One of my oldest and dearest friends, of the Pittsburgh period, died suddenly in San Francisco. My brother Roscoe, since the first of March, has been in the hospital at Colusa with a very serious heart condition (angina pectoris), so severe that it caused a lesion in the heart muscle. The doctor in Colusa is not very intelligent, evidently, but he did call in a man from Marysville, of whom the best heart man in New York thinks very well. The local doctor, however, let Roscoe go for several months with a blood pressure of 220/120 before he called in any assistance. My doctors here think the eventual attack could have been averted, had the proper measures been taken earlier. I am sending you a copy of a letter from one of the older heart specialists here. This will make his case clear to you, and you will understand the dread and anxiety in which I have been living. I am going to Roscoe as soon as his doctors think wise—probably early in June. For the present they wish to avoid any emotion for him.

I think Elsie has not been informed as to the seriousness of Roscoe's condition, and I am not sending her a copy of this letter. Indeed, I don't wish anyone to know how serious Roscoe's case is, except Carrie and Irene and Mary. Roscoe's wife would rather Elsie did not know his actual condition, as she (Elsie) is very excitable and would probably go to see him immediately. His best chance for the time being is to avoid any emotional fluctuation.

During these last weeks I have so often thought of you two, and I often wished that I could enjoy with you the great exhibition of French paintings in Chicago. I felt sure that Irene would persuade Carrie to go to that exhibit with her. All the time that it was in New York I was unable to see it. Doctors and massage and the care of my right hand have taken all the time and strength I had. Like my poor brother, I have been under a pretty heavy emotional stress, and much of the time have been very tired. The letters which poured in after the publication of Sapphira have touched me very deeply. It is impossible to answer all of them, but I have tried to dictate appreciative replies to the letters from people who loved Douglass and from old friends of my father and mother.

I am sad to tell you that when I go West to Roscoe, I shall probably go from Montr[e]al, by the Canadian Pacific. My doctor can get special arrangements for me over that road. Miss Lewis will go with me, as I still wear a metal gauntlet, and must continue to wear it for several months. I cannot dress myself without help, and therefore could not travel alone. My hand is constantly improving, even though the gain is so slow. I now firmly believe that I shall be able to write again, though probably not using my hand in the old fashion—I have known other writers who worked with a penholder held between the first and two middle fingers in order to save the thumb. Sigrid Undset and the dear Menuhins have been bright spots in this trying time. Sometime, my dear Carrie, I want to tell you all about Madame Undset. She was here last night and spent the evening. Every time I see her she brings a large peace and relaxation. She is just all a great woman should be—and on a giant scale. She is a wonderful cook, a proficient scholar and has the literature of four languages at her fingers ends. There is nothing about wild flowers and garden flowers that she doesn't know, and she is able to make plants thrive and bloom in her very humble and gloomy little hotel rooms. Besides all this, there is in the woman a kind of heroic calm and warmth that rises above all the cruel tragedies and loss of fortune that the last three years have brought. She simply surmounts everything that has been wrecked about her and stands large and calm;—she who has lost everything seems still to possess everything, and the small pleasures can still make her rather cold eyes glow with marvelous pleasure. She combines in herself the nature of an artist, a peasant, and a scholar. She is cut on a larger pattern than any woman I have ever known, and it rests me just to sit and look at the strength that stood unshaken through so much. Of course, of her son's murder in a German concentration camp, she never speaks.

Good-bye, my darling friends. This is for the three of you, Mary and Irene and Carrie. I wish I could share with you the pleasure and support I have found in this undaunted exiled woman, as I wish I could share with you whatever else is good in my life.

With all the old love to the three of you,

Devotedly
Willie

P.S. What I write you about Madame Undset, of course, is confidential. She wouldn't like me to advertise her, even in praise. She is self-sufficient, and would never think of trying to make a good impression on anybody. But I want you three to share with me the pleasure of realizing someone who is so meticulous about her cookery and her scholarship, and whom the German Army could not break.

When the Nazis invaded Norway in April 1940, Undset was forced to flee her home. The elder of her two sons died that same month, and she had also lost her daughter to illness shortly before the war.

TO ROSE ACKROYD

May 16, 1941

My dear Mrs. Ackroyed:

Your letter has awakened many pleasant memories. Your grandmother, Mary Ann Anderson, was a very special favorite of mine when I was a little girl of five to eight years old and lived at Willow Shade on the Northwestern Turnpike. When I was shut up in the house with colds, I used to watch out of the front windows, hoping to see Mrs. Anderson coming down the road. My family usually sent some word to her when I was sick, because she was so tactful and understanding with a child.

Years after we moved West, when I graduated from college, I went immediately back to visit my great-aunt, Mrs. [Sidney] Gore. At that time I had several happy meetings with Mary Ann Anderson. She came down to Auntie

Gore's to see me, and I several times walked up that beautiful Hollow Road, up to Timber Ridge, to see her in her little house where she lived all alone, and where she was as happy as the day was long. She had a most unusual interest, you understand, in following the story of peoples' lives and knowing everything that happened to them. She got great pleasure out of other peoples' good luck, and was deeply sympathetic when they had bad luck. At this time I was twenty-one years old, but of course I remembered all the people I knew in my childhood. Mary Ann and I talked for hours at a time, and she would tell me all about what became of the people whom I remembered—how they lived, if they were still alive, and how the older people had ended their days.

Your Aunt Marjorie [Anderson] and your Uncle Enoch [Anderson] both went to Nebraska with us. Enoch was with us for two years and then, when my father decided to leave the farm, he and two boys from Winchester went to California to hunt work in the big wheat fields there. He once sent us a picture of himself driving a big threshing machine, but after that we never heard of him. Your Aunt Marjorie died in 1928. She was in our family continuously after we left Virginia until the day of her death. She was greatly beloved by all of us,—children and grandchildren. Her love of children was one of her outstanding qualities. I have lived in New York for thirty years, but while my parents were living I went home for long visits, at least every other summer. I used always to spend many happy hours with Marjorie in the big sunny kitchen or on the shady back porch. She liked to talk about old times in Virginia, and my father always told her the news that came in the weekly Winchester paper. I shall always remember those hours with Marjorie on the shady back porch or in the sunny kitchen with especial pleasure. She died from a short illness in the autumn of 1928, when I was in New England. She is buried in our family lot in Red Cloud, Nebraska.

I have had many pleasant letters since the publication of "Sapphira and the Slave Girl", but few of them have called up so many happy memories as yours, which brought once more my dear Mary Ann Anderson to my mind. How glad I would be to have the croup again, if I could watch out of one of those windows at Willow Shade and see Mrs. Anderson coming briskly around the turn of the road! Here is a photograph lately taken of all that is left of the once beautiful Willow Shade, and I have marked a circle around the window where I used to sit to watch for my dear Mrs. Anderson coming down the road.

Very cordially yours,
Willa Cather

P.S. The real name of the woman who wove our carpets was Mrs. Kearns, but there may have been a Mrs. Cowper also.

[Included is this appended note:] Miss Cather asks me to explain that the signature affixed to this letter is genuine but unlike her natural signature. Because of an accident to her right hand. It is still in splints and she can make only a very poor attempt with her left hand.

S. J. Bloom, Secretary

TO ROSCOE CATHER

September 17, 1941
New York City

My dear Roscoe:

This must be a love letter, short and sweet. I have been down to the French Hospital for a week getting over some of the shocks and difficulties of the trip home, and the unpleasant surprise that very extensive and noisy repairs were going on in our apartment house.

When I was packing my bags to come down here I threw in one of my six copies of Shakespeare's Sonnets. I always carry a copy of the Sonnets about with me. I memorized most of them many years ago and when I occasionally forget a line, I like to have the text at hand so that I can look it up quickly. The copy which I happened to bring down here I had not opened or even seen for many years. It turned up by chance. When I was looking up something in it yesterday, I noticed this blank end-page. The writing on it set me thinking. I must have carried this same book when you and I went to Dale Creek Canyon [in Wyoming] on a "pass" so many years ago! I remember we rode home on the rear platform of some little passenger train. It was a very starry night and fairly chilly, but we sat out there and wondered about the future and how we could ever manage to hang together, and make a living in a world which seemed to [be a] good deal like a greased pole, or a huge slippery glass sphere—so slippery that one might slip into space at any moment—we seemed to have no way of hanging on to it, really.

This little end-page brought that time and its perplexities back to me very vividly. You and Douglass and I felt awfully responsible for the younger brothers and sisters, didn't we? We surely wanted to help.

Well, we have managed to hang on to the slippery globe a good while, and we have had our compensations as well as our disappointments.

Roscoe, my dear boy, I won't nag at you and I won't fuss over you, but I do think you ought to consider me a little bit and be careful. In so far as I am concerned, <u>you are absolutely the only bit of family I have left</u>. You are the only one who goes back and understands. I love all the nieces, to be sure, but that is quite [a] different matter. You are the only prop I've got.

Lovingly
Willie

[Enclosed is a blank end page from a book with the following written on it.]

Dale Creek Canon, Wyo
Summit of the Rockies
August 30, 1898 XXIX

The "XXIX" on the end paper is a reference to Shakespeare's Sonnet 29:

When in disgrace with fortune and men's eyes,
I all alone beweep my outcast state,
And trouble deaf Heaven with my bootless cries,
And look upon myself, and curse my fate,
Wishing me like to one more rich in hope,
Featur'd like him, like him with friends possess'd,
Desiring this man's art, and that man's scope,
With what I most enjoy contented least:
Yet in these thoughts myself almost despising,
Haply I think on thee,—and then my state
(Like to the lark at break of day arising
From sullen earth) sings hymns at heaven's gate;
For thy sweet love remember'd such wealth brings
That then I scorn to change my state with kings'.

TO ROSE ACKROYD

December 27, 1941

My dear Mrs. Ackroyd:

I got many lovely Christmas gifts and Christmas cards, but yours is the only one that brought tears to my eyes. Of course, I shall keep it and love to have it, and I thank you very much for it. What a wonderful old face! She is older here than when I saw her last. I know that chiefly because her hair is so much thinner, but the eyes have all their old fire. In the time of my first memories of her, she had the most wonderful reddish auburn hair, so wavy that it was almost crinkly. And her skin, too, was brown, or had a brownish shade. I think it is very kind of you to send me this photograph. You must have realized from my letter that I was very fond of dear Mrs. Anderson.

Your Uncle Snowden, too, I remember very distinctly. I do not wonder that he was your favorite uncle. There was something very fine about Snowden. I always liked to see him. Once, when I was about five years old and somebody had driven Marjorie and me up to your grandmother's house on Timber Ridge, a violent rainstorm came up. Marjorie and I were supposed to walk home, because the road was downhill all the way. Marjorie had stout shoes, but I wore little slippers. Snowden came up from his house on the Hollow Road, on a gray horse, and took me home in front of him, holding the reins with one hand and keeping his other arm around me to steady me on the old cavalry saddle. He had on an old gray Confederate overcoat, which I suppose had been his father's. I remember how contented and safe I felt. Children know when people are honest and good. They don't reason about it, they just know.

Thank you again, dear Mrs. Ackroyd, for this photograph of that dear old face. I shall keep it as long as I live, and I only wish such a photograph had come to us while my mother was still living. She would have loved to see it.

Very cordially yours,

Willa Cather

➜ ⬅

With the following letter to the Norwegian novelist Sigrid Undset, Cather included a clipping from the Red Cloud Commercial Advertiser, *January 5, 1942, which quotes Bob Smith's cable to his father: "Just arrived from Kunming. Came through both battles of Rangoon safely. Knocked down four ships personally. Happy New Year."*

TO SIGRID UNDSET

Saturday [January 24, 1942]

Dear Sigrid Undset;

I hope this will reach you on Sunday morning. I have been thinking about you a great deal because I have just read a book I had not seen before. The translation appeared in '37 [actually 1935], and I was in France all that year. I believe the title in the original is Elleve Aar [published in English as *The Longest Years*]. There are many things in it I would like to ask you about. In one thing I surpassed you: I could sew quite well when I was seven!!

Since Christmas life has been full of people and events—many old friends from the West in town.

I was pleased when I read that a Nebraska boy had brought down four Jap planes on Christmas day. When I found he was Bob Smith, from my own little town of 1200 people, a lad with whom my nieces went to school, I felt more than pleased. I like his cable to his father. I like "personally"—nice little adverb, nothing showy about it.

We have millions of boys like Bob, but not in big cities.

The Western friends who storm New York every year in mid-winter, will soon be going home and I hope that you can come to us for a long evening.

Devotedly yours
Willa Cather

➙ ←

The following to Roscoe was written after several long, exasperated letters to him about the bothersome behavior of their siblings, especially their sister Elsie.

TO ROSCOE CATHER

April 22, 1942

My dearest Brother:

Aren't we a pair to draw to? Just as soon as I heard that you were sitting up, I myself retired to a hospital. I don't fail to see the humor of it, however. I am getting out from under now, and yesterday boldly went forth and had my hair washed with no ill effects. When we first heard that you were ill, pretty much everything went wrong. Edith had various woes and I have various woes, but now we are both getting straightened out.

A long time ago you wrote me such a dear letter trying to explain Elsie's erratic conduct. In that letter you struck off a great sentence. My mind has vibrated with it ever since. You said: "We must take each other as we are." That doesn't sound very profound, but it is profound. If all families lived up to it there would be a good deal more peace in the world. I really think the Miner family have lived up to it. But ever since I got that letter I have been ever so much nearer, and more tolerant, to all my kin.

Jack wrote me such kind and comforting letters while you were ill. Indeed, Jack was never at fault. It was I who was at fault, because I dragged him into a kind of world that he was not fitted for. I did that not so much because I was ambitious for him (<u>this is really true</u>), but because he was at that time very unhappy at home. Jim and Ethel were both using him like a little hired boy. Jim was building a house for himself on the Crowell place, and Jack was doing all the work—pretty heavy physical work. This is just a word of explanation because I remember I spoke to you rather hardly of Jack. I do not feel that way now, and I never shall again.

I expect you are finding, just as I do, that getting well is rather slow and tedious work. There are lots of friends here whom I would like to see, but haven't yet the strength to see people, so I have made a game of having my four o'clock tea every afternoon <u>with Winston Churchill</u>! I don't think there is anybody on earth who knows better how to get every possible pleasure out of every single day, from his first egg at breakfast to his last highball at night. I find that an imaginary tea with him, meditating on his unfailing buoyancy, really does me a great deal of good. I am sending you a little book which I got from the British Library of Information, and I hope it will amuse you as much as it has amused me. His speeches are too long and too many for me to remember, but these little extracts from the speeches one can remember—and the mere vitality of them helps me along.

My dearest love to you both

Willie

TO MARGARET CATHER SHANNON

October 16 [1942]

Williams Inn, Williamstown, Massachusetts

My Dear Little Margaret;

I have been here now for one week. Quiet college town—nothing but college and houses, no shops. One has to go to North Adams to buy anything.

Good hotel, good food and <u>wonderful</u> milk; from cows not from the grocer's! I hope to pick up a few pounds. All food has been hateful to me since July 24th, but here I get really hungry and want my dinner.

I haven't heard from your father for many weeks. Sometimes I worry and am afraid he may be ill. Meta has never written me since I have been a "post-operative". I wish she would. Yesterday I walked half a mile in the lovely autumn sunshine and was very much encouraged.

I am registered here as

Winifred Carter (CARTER)

Horrid name, but <u>all</u> feminine names beginning with W are horrid. In a college town I can't very well use my own name—this is an all-year-open in[n] and a dozen of the Professors live here. This hotel sits right in the campus. The students are just back. One nice senior caught me studying the stained glass in the chapel. He asked if I were not I in such a nice way that I admitted it. He promised not to give me away, and I'm really sure he won't.

Please let Winifred Carter know how you are, dear. I have no Miss Bloom here, and I shan't write letters until I rise above one hundred and ten pounds—ridiculous weight for me!

Lovingly

Your Aunt Willie

or

Winnie!!

TO ALEXANDER WOOLLCOTT

December 5, 1942

Dear Alexander Woollcott:

I, too, have very lately come out of a hospital, and it was <u>not</u> the French hospital. That it was not my favorite hospital, was due to the fact that Dr. Allen Whipple decided to rob me of my gall bladder, and he operates nowhere on earth except at the Presbyterian Hospital—and in Rome, I believe!

I am grateful to you for the letter from the Nolan family which you enclosed. Oh, I think there are thousands of families like the Nolans in America, and many boys like Robert B! I am glad that he found a church and "served Holy Mass in the small mission chapel". I am not a Catholic, but I do believe that when young people are held together by something which we might call "spiritual", they make better citizens and better friends.

Now for the chief point in your letter. If you and I were sitting at a table in your study discussing the matter of the proposed anthology for young soldiers, I think we should try to put ourselves back to our eighteenth or nineteenth year and try to remember what we really liked to read then—what we read from pleasure, not from duty.

You ask me whether I think anything of Miss Jewett's should go into such an anthology. When I was nineteen, I was not in the least interested in Miss Jewett. I found nothing in her stories that I wanted from a book. I was blind alike to their elegance and their truthfulness. At that age I was reading Balzac furiously, and reading everything of Tolstoy's that had been translated. Very young people don't care a hang about anything between the covers of a book but one thing—vitality. Young people, even those who are destined to become more or less critical in their tastes, are hungry to read about "life" and about characters who are in the midst of the struggle. They don't care at all <u>how</u> a thing is done; refinement simply goes over their head, form doesn't mean anything. They like high color, they like to be "thrilled", and they want excitement in a book. I am speaking now of young people with intelligence and the rudiments of taste. It is my honest conviction that Miss Jewett, much as I admire her, would have no proper place in such an anthology as you are making.

Oh, I could tell you a lot about what to keep out of your anthology! But when I try to suggest what you might put in, I seem to face a pretty blank wall. I cannot see many "American classics" which would not be cold comfort for lively young Americans in a foreign land. Nearly all the "classics" are too mild, and so many of the new books are too "strong" and are passionately devoted to the ugliness and baseness of American life. Strange to say, I think we come out rather better in poetry than in prose. There are lots of country boys who have a shy liking for some of Longfellow's ballads and who take "The Building of the Ship" seriously. Many American boys like to read the younger Robert Frost—"A Boy's Will" and "North of Boston". "The Death of the Hired Man", for example. I have known a great many young people who loved verses in "A Boy's Will".

I am greatly pleased that you liked "Sapphira", and I am especially pleased that you liked the last chapter. Many people didn't. But in this book my end was my beginning: the place I started out from. I don't really know whether I was five years old or six years old when Nancy came back to us from Canada, but the event was so important to me that all through my life, whenever I happened to remember it, I found a little echo of the thrill that went through me when she entered the room where her old mother and my grandmother and I were all waiting for her. That chapter is an unornamented and literally truthful account of Nancy's return———and the afternoons I used to spend in the big kitchen where Nancy and Till and my grandmother discussed almost everything that had happened since Nancy went away, are among the happiest hours I can remember.

Always faithfully and admiringly yours,
Willa Cather

P.S. I almost think that if I were making an "Anthology" for American soldiers, I would make a neat edition of Huckleberry Finn, and let it go at that!

Thousands of them have never read it, and the thousands who have read it will read it with a different feeling in a foreign land. Times have changed, I know. But anyhow, I think it is still the most American of any.

TO MR. PHILLIPSON

March 15, 1943

Dear Mr. Phillipson:

The high school teacher whom you mention must have been more than "sensitive and kindly"; she evidently had a feeling for sound sentence structure. I get hundreds of letters from college students, friendly and enthusiastic, but the weakness of their sentence structure is often appalling. They seem convinced that friendly and enthusiastic clauses need have no particular relation to each other or to the main stem of the sentence. Sometimes these letters show insight and a real feeling for literature. But how can these boys expect to play sonatas when they cannot play scales? I am chiefly interested in your letter because you seem to have a feeling for the English sentence. In writing, that is the beginning of everything.

You ask me about "Paul's Case". I once had in my latin class a nervous, jerky boy who was always trying to make himself "interesting", and to prove that he had special recognition and special favours from members of a stock company then playing in the town theater. You will recognize one part of Paul. The other part of Paul is simply the feeling I myself had about New York City and the old Waldorf Astoria (not the horrid structure which now stands on Park Avenue), when I first left college and was teaching latin in the Pittsburgh High School. I used to come to New York occasionally then, and that is the way the City seemed to me. Of course, I never ran away, or jumped under a railway train: neither did the real Paul, in so far as I know. But that is the way stories are usually made—a grafting of some outside figure with some part of the writer's self.

You speak of a "universal longing for a world beautiful". In the first place, this longing is by no means universal. It is rather exceptional. And don't, please, speak of a "world beautiful"! That is the only bad phrase in your letter. But it is bad. It is what I call "women's club phraseology". You could have said that better, had you tried. But a desire for beauty—a strong desire—is the important thing, is the real gift. And it is a blessed gift which cannot be altogether thwarted or starved, because there is beauty everywhere. I have never stayed in Rochester, but I have been through it, on the train, in the winter-time, and

I thought the snow-covered country around it glorious. If you will ask at the public library for a book of mine called "The Song of the Lark", you will find out how I feel about this desire which is so hard to name. Rebecca West calls it "the strange necessity". If one has that desire, no circumstances can keep him from the treasure house of the world. All the great literature and the great music and the great art are his. As much of these things, I mean, as his desire can reach. And after all, we deserve only what we can reach—though the process of reaching it may be slow.

Very cordially yours,
Willa Cather

TO MISS MASTERTON

March 15, 1943

My dear Miss Masterton:

What a delightful letter you wrote me! My secretary has just asked me <u>why</u> it was such a delightful letter; the only answer to that is that there was a delightful person behind the letter. If you had to read such hundreds of letters as I have to read every year—letters from people entirely unknown to me, you would acquire a fortune teller's mystic skill in reading personality. When I get a real human letter like yours, it is just as if a charming person came into the room and sat down and began to talk to me.

I seem fated to send people on journeys. Not long ago I had a letter from a Boston schoolteacher who was started for Quebec by a sentence in "Shadows on the Rock". As for the number of people who have gone a-journeying in New Mexico on the trail of the <u>Archbishop</u>—well, the managers of the Harvey House system have repeatedly invited me to come and stay at the Bishop'[s] Lodge indefinitely, as their guest! The great disadvantage about writing of the places you love is that you lose your beloved places forever—that is, if you are a quiet person who doesn't like publicity. I have not been back to Virginia since <u>Sapphira</u> was published, nor to Quebec since "Shadows on the Rock" was published, nor to New Mexico since the <u>Archbishop</u> was written,—except on the train. I have been through New Mexico many times on the train, for that is the country I love best.

Isn't the part of Virginia beyond Timber Ridge and the Capon River lovely? Such simple, honest, earnest people live there. It would have been the same forever if motor cars had never been invented. I was actually present when they were tearing to pieces the Double S road leading from the village of

Gore up to the top of Timber Ridge. It was the most beautiful piece of country road that I have ever found anywhere in the world. I never found anything in the Swiss or Italian Alps so beautiful as that road once was.

I am sorry you saw that desolate ruin [the house Willow Shade, near Gore, Virginia] which forty years ago was such a beautiful place, with its six great willow trees, beautiful lawn, and the full running creek with its rustic bridge. It was turned into a tenement house long since, and five years ago the very sight of it made me shiver. Of course, it still lives in my mind, just as that March day when Nancy came back still lives in my mind. Even her dress is described in more detail than I could ever remember about any dress I saw last week. She was just exactly like that, and old Till was just like that. I was between five and six years old when the return happened, and it was the most exciting event in my life up to that time. I had heard so much about Nancy, and my mother often sang me to sleep with that old song. Mrs. Blake was my grandmother [Rachel Elizabeth Seibert Boak], and she really took Nancy across the Potomac. Well, those were old times, but they were beautiful.

I am so glad you are a Scotch woman. I have always loved the Scotch, in Canada as well as abroad.

Very cordially yours,
Willa Cather

TO META AND ROSCOE CATHER

noon, Tuesday [March 23, 1943]

Dear Meta and Roscoe;

I've seen him, all right! Though his dear little [mother] hasn't. He [Richard Shannon] is now <u>almost</u> 24 hours old. I don't know why the nurse had pity on me, but she waylaid me after I had spent nearly an hour with Margaret, took me down the hall, and brought him to the <u>closed</u> door of his little glass house. He was not red, just rosy, wide awake, and he gave me the once-over, deliberately. He's an individual, just as I am an individual—a trifle less experienced. I don't know his name. You see I didn't meet him until I <u>left</u> Margaret; then he was not an individual, and I didn't feel interested in his name. The mere abstract idea of grand-nieces and nephews does not violently appeal to one who dislikes getting old.

Margaret looked just like herself, and I loved being with her once again. I think she'd like to <u>see</u> her baby. I shall patent a crib enclosed in glass, so that babies can be wheeled in for their mothers to look at them, even if the intimacy goes no further.

Love and Congratulations to you both
Willie

TO DOROTHY CANFIELD FISHER

March 31 [1943]

Dear Dorothy;

The Yale Review is the one magazine I do get regularly; because, as your old Vermonter said, it doesn't come "too reg'elar". I had read your article (excuse new pen) before the copy you sent me arrived, and I wanted to write you about it. But what is there to say? What is there to say about anything that is happening now? There is no spot on the earth's surface that one can rest one's mind against any more. I knew you had many ties in France and I have often wanted to write to you. But again, what is there to say? Besides, I got a little behind with life, I allowed the celebrated Doctor [Allen] Whipple to "remove", no, to <u>take out</u>, my appendix and gall bladder last July. August and September were nasty months to recover in: horrible heat, and the humidity of Singapore. Bad news from every quarter of the world always pouring in. I got so behind in my correspondence, in normal vitality, in <u>weight</u> (16 pounds) that I thought I could never catch up again. Slowly one comes to life again—but one wonders why, when most of the world one loved is being destroyed and so many of the friends one loved have been destroyed. We wont live to see the beautiful new world they talk about emerge. We see only a thousand years of glorious endeavour wrecked and wiped out. Anyhow, I don't want to live in the new world they promise me—it's not to my taste.

Affectionately
Willa

Isn't Churchill a great old boy? Isn't England a great old land?

TO ROSCOE CATHER

May 22, 1943

My dear Roscoe:

Extract from a letter written by Mary Virginia Mellen on her return to Colorado Springs:

"I do wish that you could see Uncle Roscoe now. He looks perfectly splendid! Mother had said that he looked almost cadaverous after his severe sickness of a year ago, so I was prepared for that. What was my most happy surprise when this erect, very healthy looking man walked briskly across the lobby and kissed my hand! Truly, he seemed in much better physical health than when I saw him last, five years ago. He said he had been feeling much better for the past month or so than he had for a long time. It would have done your heart good if you could have been with us that evening, for we had the jolliest kind of dinner party."

Mary Virginia has done many, many kind things for me in the last ten years, but she has never done a kinder thing than when she wrote me the above. You see, my dear, brother, when I knew that you were going South to go through with that tedious lawsuit, my heart sank. I suppose one judges others by oneself—especially the few "others" who are dear to one. I just can't, as yet, stand up to a tedious business meeting, not even at the Knopf office where everyone is so friendly. (That same acute sensitiveness to personalities which got me along in my own work, now simply threatens to destroy me.) Ever since your letter came, telling me that you were going South, the dread of what it might do to you has interfered a good deal with my sleep. You see, you were a very frail man when I saw you last. Mary Virginia's letter arrived only a few days ago, and when I read it I just broke down and cried. As soon as I was really sure of my voice, I called up little Margaret by telephone and read that portion of Virginia's letter to her. I feel completely reassured, because Virginia has never deceived me—even when she had to tell me unpleasant truths—and there is certainly the ring of truth in the above extract. She was glad for you, and for me.

Lovingly to you and Meta,
Willie

TO WILLIAM LYON PHELPS

May 29, 1943

Dear, friendly, Mr. Phelps:

I recognized your handwriting before I opened your letter. You have so often been kind enough to send me friendly comments that I otherwise would not have seen. I am especially pleased to have this word from J. M. Barrie about "A Lost Lady". My intercourse with Sir James was very singular, because he was so shy and indirect in personal intercourse. I first knew that he liked my books from a message he sent by a young Englishman who was travelling in this country—a message about "Death Comes for the Archbishop" which was very pleasant to hear. Then, through another friend of his, he began to use gentle pressure upon me for an autographed copy of "My Ántonia". I did not take it seriously, for I don't think writers often care about autographed copies. (After all, isn't the one real and only autograph in the book itself, on every page of it?) Another friend in England wrote me that Barrie was ill, and that he really wanted an autographed copy. I, of course, sent one. I sent it through a Mrs. [Marie M.] Meloney, whom you probably know.

When young Stephen Tennant was travelling in this country about eight years ago, I saw a good deal of him, since we had intermittently corresponded for a long time. While he was here Thomas Hardy's widow wrote him such a charming letter, asking him to tell me how much pleasure Hardy got out of "A Lost Lady". Mrs. Hardy herself died within a year or two afterward.

I think there is nothing quite so satisfying as having given pleasure, in their old age, to some of the writers who fascinated one in one's youth.

We have grown to be old friends by this time and I may sign myself

Faithfully yours,
Willa Cather

TO HARRISON T. BLAINE

June 9, 1943

Dear Harrison Blaine:

What a nice letter you wrote me! I am glad you did not repress your first impulse. I think you will be interested to know that there is a singular connection between "My Ántonia" and High Mowing [near Jaffrey, New Hampshire]. Before Mrs. Blaine bought that lovely place, Mrs. Robinson let it for two summers to old friends of mine. A considerable part of "My Ántonia", from page 163 through 263, was written in a little tent which I put up at the bottom of the hill which slopes from your mother's house toward Stony Brook Farm. The tent was very simple—no floor—pegged down to the ground. Inside it there was nothing but a table and a camp chair. I was living at the Shattuck Inn that summer and autumn, and every morning, after a very early breakfast, I used to go up the Stony Brook Farm road and cut through the hedge into

Mrs. Robinson's property and to my tent. I carried a little portfolio with my papers and pens. I always left my ink-bottles in the tent. No one disturbed me. I had two good hours of work and then, in the heat of the day, I used to climb the stone wall and go back to the Inn through the shady wood which still lies at the foot of the hill. The wood was well kept in those days. Lady's-slipper and Hookers' orchid used to grow there. Once, in the late autumn, I met an agreeable fox in the wood.

Of course, some of the people at the hotel knew that I went to the tent to write, but no one knew what I was writing. After the book was published I never happened to tell anyone that part of it was written in the tent at High Mowing. It is not my habit to talk about any piece of work I have in hand—that would spoil the fun of it for me. I finished the book in New York that winter, and I think you are the only person to whom I have ever confided the fact that a portion of that particular book was written in the tent. But since you love High Mowing (as I do) and since you really care for the book that was partly written there, it seems to me you ought to know that there is a very real connection between the book and the place.

The next summer and autumn I was working in the same tent upon "One of Ours", but I stayed too late into October and got a bad touch of influenza. It was a very rainy autumn and the tent, having no floor, used to get pretty wet. After that year the Shattucks were kind enough to let me have several rooms on the top floor of the hotel, where there was no clattering of feet over my head, and I worked very happily there on other books. Since the hurricane altogether destroyed the beautiful wood behind the hotel, I have not gone there so often. My favorite walk for the afternoon was through that wood as far as the Ark, and then back again to the Shattuck Inn. The next time I am in Jaffrey I will certainly go to see your mother at High Mowing, and I hope you will be there to have tea with us.

You say you have a personal reason for writing to me about Ántonia. But have I not an even more personal reason for replying to you? That book and that place are always associated in my mind, though the actual scene of the Western book was so far away.

Cordially yours,
And hoping that we shall meet in Jaffrey
Willa Cather

TO ALFRED A. KNOPF

July 29 [1943]
Asticou Inn, Northeast Harbor, Maine

Dear Alfred;

Two weeks ago I reached this very satisfactory refuge, after travelling up and down the Maine coast in an unsuccessful search for comfortable quarters. All the old pleasant places of five years ago are deserted. Bar Harbor is a ghost town. All the big houses of the rich are now inhabited by one caretaker. The good shops of former times are shut down—main street a row of dirty windows.

Here Miss Lewis and I have a very comfortable cottage with a lovely garden. Absolute quiet. We take our meals at the Inn which is a short block away. We walk to it over green turf and fine trees and hedges keep it out of sight. The food is not very good, certainly, but better than I have found anywhere else except in Boston.

Next week Miss Lewis goes up to Grand Manan to look after some repairs that are to be made on her cottage there, but I shall be here for the next fortnight at least. The weather is always cool here. One needs a wood fire every evening. We have a good deal of rain and heavy weather, but there is a good library, and after the horror of Portland and it's war industries I am very willing to sit indoors by the fire and read forgotten books—or botanize a little. This place is not nearly so interesting as Grand Manan but it is much more comfortable (in the conventional way) and not so reduced in food supplies.

I hope you are out of New York and its preposterous "heat waves."

On any day that you are not too busy I'd be glad to hear from you about anything you're interested in. I'm delighted that Ezra Pound is a "traitor"—though I can't believe him very genuine even in that role. It has been the Hell of a summer, hasn't it? In every way.

Languidly but faithfully
Willa Cather

The remark about the poet Ezra Pound is a reference to his anti-semitic, fascist turn during World War II.

TO ROSCOE CATHER

August 25 [1943]
Hotel Statler, Boston

My Dear Roscoe;

Your telegram came and I wrote Crowell at once. We have been held up in this very dirty hotel for 8 days waiting for two seats in a chair car from Boston to New York,—a five hour journey! We leave tomorrow. The heat here has been terrible. After seven weeks at the Asticou Inn where no spirits are served and the food was very poor, I now dine at the good old Parker House, drink a cocktail every night and go to a movie show every afternoon!

My love to you and your two ladies.
W.

TO ZOË AKINS

December 4, 1943

My dear Zoe;

You will remember that while you were in New York last summer I telephoned you that I was going into the Presbyterian Hospital for a few weeks. In reality I was going in to have the celebrated Doctor Whipple take out my gall bladder and appendix. The operation was a brilliant success (no drainage tubes or any of those horrid things) but the recovery was very slow and pretty awful. I weighed one hundred and twenty-six pounds when I went into the hospital and I came out weighing a little under one hundred and ten. For most of the month of August and all of September, I was lying in bed, in the apartment, too ill to move, and the heat was outrageous. To make matters worse, it rained every day. I sweated pounds off, just as English jockeys do when they are in training. I kept on hating food and there was an undercurrent of nausea all the time, until about the first of December. Since then I have been pulling up rapidly. I now weigh a hundred and fifteen pounds, have a good appetite and enjoy food. I rather hope I will gain a little more because I am not strong enough to go shopping and all the dresses that hang in my closets are preposterously too big for me!! Even my shoes are much too big. My hair all came out and I have frightful neuralgia in my head—unless it is tied up in woolen scarves at night.

I am relating these tiresome details because I am sure that you have known for some time that something was the matter with me. You asked me once over the telephone if you had offended me. Of course, my dear Zoe, we have always had different "ideologies" (horrid word!) and as people grow older their beliefs, like their arteries, grow harder—we are less and less able to sympathetically comprehend the other fellow's point of view. But something more than this, something physical which I could not understand, was making me more and more short-tempered and irritable, unable to bear my own shortcomings and those of my friends. Now that I am pigeon-livered, maybe I will have more patience with the "new poetry" (manufactured by mathematicians and politicians) and with the distorting processes with which the film makers attack the old masterpieces, drag them out of their secluded niches, and use them for their horrid purposes. I [the rest of the typewritten letter cut away; then handwritten on the back:] Here let me insist that when an intelligent man makes a good film (Noel Coward, for example) I enjoy it as much as anybody. But these cheap hash-overs of really great literature (<u>Anna Karenina</u>, <u>Notre Dame de Paris</u>, <u>Wuthering Heights</u> etc) show the poverty of the minds behind the camera. Who would steal music if he could write music of his own? Novels of action can be dramatized. Novels of feeling, even if it is only feeling for a city or a historic period, cannot be.

Well, as Mrs. [Florence] Arliss cabled "Happy New Year anyway!"

Affectionately
Willa

TO SIGRID UNDSET

[December 25, 1943]

Dear Sigrid Undset;

This is Christmas day, and the lovely callas you sent me are standing white and tall on the table beside me. They have been good company for me ever since they came. This is such a terrible Christmas—it seems like a preparation for horrors unexampled and unguessed at. For the first time in my life I feel afraid—afraid of losing everything one cherished in the world and all the finest youth of the world. The address from the Vatican does not cheer one much. The new evils we all know, but in their nature they destroy our power to combat them. The cold pride of science is the most devilish thing that has ever come into this world. It is the absolute enemy of happiness. The human mind, not the spirit, has disinherited human nature.

This is a maudlin note to send out on Christmas day. Please forgive me. The time is very dark.

Affectionately always
Willa Cather

TO IRENE MINER WEISZ

December 31, 1943

My very dear Irene:

The pudding came so wonderfully wrapped and decorated that I hated to separate it from its beautiful box. Believe me, the friendship and kind thoughts that go into the making of a gift like this, which is done with your own hands, and brings your mother's favourite recipe for a sauce, means more to me than you can perhaps imagine. I do thank you, dear—it warms my heart that you thought of me.

I hate to write gloomy letters, but this has been a rather stern year for me. I have lost three very dear old friends of the Pittsburgh circle within the last year; their death was most unexpected. Some of my friends seem to have lost patience with me, at last. I have had no word from Carrie this Christmas or for a long time back, and I think she might be sorry if she knew how sad it has made me. I don't know how I can have hurt her. Perhaps I wrote her too many long letters about the revival of interest in "Antonia" and the new edition of it in England. Or perhaps she was very much disappointed that I did not go out to Red Cloud in October or November. I had planned to go, and looked forward to it so eagerly—that was while I was up in northern Maine. But when I got back to town and had to struggle with getting the apartment cleaned and the terrible problem of domestic help, my courage sank little by little. We had no maid at all until the first of November, but did our own housekeeping and went out to most of our meals. Edith had absolutely promised to go back to the office the first of November. After she went we had two unfortunate experiments with help. Of course, all phases of housekeeping have been very trying. By the time Mary Virginia wrote me that she was coming East, I felt sure that she could help me out a little, and she did. She helped me principally by living at an hotel and coming to see me very rarely. She saw at once that any kind of excitement, particularly pleasurable excitement, simply used me up. It uses me up more than the drudgery of washing dishes and cleaning house. For instance: when I had Virginia and Helen Louise (who lives away off in Jersey) lunch with me at Sherry's and then took them up to the Frick Art Gallery, we had an awfully jolly time and I was very proud of both my nieces. They pleased me very much. But I had a bad night after the party, and had to stay in bed and be very quiet all the next day. Virginia caught on to all those things at once, and never came to see me without a special message from me, and never stayed long when she came. I was so afraid she would not understand this queer state of bad nerves, but she did. We didn't go to a single play or movie together while she was here—not even to a concert.

You know, I think, how hard things always hit me (you are very much like that yourself, my dear!) Well, they hit me just as hard as ever, but I can't stand up under them. That confounded operation did something to my nerves.

Now, you can see how difficult it would be for me to go back to Red Cloud, where there are so many pleasant and painful associations. I think I could stand the scorn of the scorners (such as Helen Mac [McNeny]), but seeing the people whom I really care for in the old surroundings, would be pretty difficult. Why, I am afraid I would go around weeping, as dear Mollie used to!

Then Elsie, you know, has made things pretty difficult. However, we will not go into that. But, you see, all things put together when one is very weak and wobbly, make one timid. I wish I had asked Mary Virginia to talk to you about this phase of her visit here. She caught on to the state of things at once, and saw that she had to touch on things very lightly. Didn't you think, Irene, that she looked awfully well and seemed very tactful and "experienced"? I mean in the right way.

Mary Creighton wrote me an awfully nice letter acknowledging a little check I sent the Guild. As Mary wrote me once, "there are always two sides to every story." She tries to give both sides consideration. Carrie is more violent,—just as I am, or used to be. I am much milder now—and more cowardly. I am afraid she has given me up for a quitter. It makes me very sad. I am not whining, I am simply quietly telling you the truth. Please don't cut me off, my dear! Just now I am wearing my right hand in a brace again—result of having to answer too many letters from splendid soldier boys. But this letter I shall sign myself.

Have a happy Winter in Mexico, and when you come back in the Spring you must come on to New York, and you will see the situation and understand.

My love to you and Mr. Weisz. It is snowing here today, and I love to think of you going toward that sunny land.

Lovingly and Faithfully
Willie

(Excuse hand in brace!)

PART TWELVE

The Final Years

1944–1947

Now I know that nothing really matters to us but the people we love. Of course, if we realized that when we are young, and just sat down and loved each other, the beds would not get made and very little of the world's work would ever get done.

—WILLA CATHER TO IRENE MINER WEISZ, October 25, 1945

Cather and S. S. McClure in New York, May 19, 1944

Cather's last years were painful as she battled the physical strain of illness and the emotional strain of loss, as well as the daily news of the war, which saddened her profoundly. But there were bright spots, too: she took great pleasure in her nieces and nephews, she wrote a few stories, and she began work on another novel. Set in the fourteenth century around the Papal Palace in Avignon, France, this final novel, never finished, was to be called *Hard Punishments*. The story concerned the friendship of two young men who suffered medieval kinds of punishments—one had his tongue torn out, the other his thumbs stretched. Only fragments of the manuscript remain.

TO HARRIET FOX WHICHER

January 24, 1944

Dear Mrs. Whicher:

I am so glad to hear from you again. I know I don't deserve it. But when one drops out of everything for nearly two years, one gets so behind that it seems impossible to catch up with life again.

Isn't this an amazing and unsatisfactory world, to us even though we are in the least tormented corner of it? Nobody belongs anywhere any more, and nobody, either old or young, is living the kind of life they intended to live and are prepared to live. I don't wonder that you and Mr. Whicher fled away from Amherst for your Christmas.

All the young people in my family are in the war in one way or another.

Mary Virginia is with her husband, Dr. [Richard] Mellen, at the Station Hospital, Camp Carson, Colorado. They have been there for more than a year now. Virginia was in New York for six weeks this winter, and it seemed lovely to have her back again. I parked her at the Hotel New Weston, which isn't far away, and we did a good many pleasant things together. Her brother Tom [Auld] and his wife are in a hospital camp at Goldfield, Arizona. I love the Southwest, but Goldfield is certainly one of the dreariest spots in it. My brother Roscoe's oldest daughter (the one who graduated from Smith when I had my last visits with you) [Virginia Cather Brockway] is staying with my brother in California, as her husband [John Hadley Brockway] is commander of a plane carrier somewhere in the Pacific. When all family relations are broken up, and so many friends of mine don't even know where their husbands or sons are, the result seems to be that nothing in our life is very real at any time. There is a scramble for food, and one reads the war news: that's about all.

Your lovely Christmas card of Beacon Street in winter, I am pasting in Mrs. Fields' book, "Memories of a Hostess". I used to love Boston. But now that they are trying to make the region around Trinity Church look like the ugliest part of New York, Boston, to me, seems like a jig saw puzzle all broken up—it hasn't any character now.

Miss Lewis and I spent last summer at Northeast Harbor, Maine. We stayed at the Asticou Inn and lived in great comfort, though the food was poor, as it was everywhere: was and is! Wouldn't it be wonderful if we could drop back and live as we did fifteen years ago? This sort of suspense really isn't life at all.

It is good to hear from one's friends, and I do thank you for writing me a letter which I did not deserve. And I wish a Happy New Year to you and Mr. Whicher.

Affectionately
Willa Cather

I hate to send you a dictated letter, but in doing up so many packages at Christmas time (for boys in the army and for friends no longer very young or very well) I sprained my right hand—the one Dr. Ober kept in a brace for six months several years ago. So I am back in the brace again. Very difficult to guide a pen with a steel brace attached to one!

TO VIOLA ROSEBORO'

February 12, 1944

Very dear Miss Roseboro':

I expect you will wonder why I have not written to you when I tell you that scarcely a day has gone by this winter that I haven't thought of you. No, not because of dear Miss Tarbell's death. I have been thinking of you in connection with the death of the world—the death of the world you loved so well, and roamed about it so much. Oh, I am so glad you did roam about—roamed as far as Constantinople and saw the Saint Sophia—which I shall never see. What a grand old sailor you were!—just drinking your fill of that beautiful old world which we thought would last forever. Why should the beautiful cities that were a thousand years a-making tumble down on our heads <u>now, in our short lifetime</u>? What is the sense of it? We saw one war, and there was sorrow a-plenty. But why do we have to see our world destroyed? See countries sponged off the map, as we used to erase them from the blackboard—after we had drawn them at school?

Sir James Jeans said in a lecture I heard him give: "Next to man's longing for personal immortality, he longs to feel that his world is immortal and will go on indefinitely as he has known it." This has been the feeling of human beings in all ages. Why on earth do we, in all the countless stretch of years, just in our little moment, have to witness everything laid waste? I write to you in this strain because you were one of the few people I knew who cared intensely and personally about—well, about Saint Sophia for instance.

The reason that I haven't written to you before is that two of my younger brothers, all my nieces and nephews, and the children of my friends in the many States I have lived in—these young people are all uprooted and some of them quite lost. None of the young people are doing what they wanted to do, or prepared themselves to do, or were already accomplishing with great happiness. Two young professors of Amherst, such nice boys, write me from the mud of Guadalcanal. My dearest young niece only knows of her husband that he is commanding an airplane carrier "somewhere in the Pacific". I feel bitterly because so many of the boys from my own little town in Nebraska have been shunted out to those terrible Pacific Islands, where the hardships are so much greater than they can be anywhere in Europe. To be killed may be uncomfortable, but to lie in slime and be eaten up by bugs is a punishment no boy deserves. I somehow am sure that you feel these things more than most people, and that maybe you would like an expression from an old friend who also feels the outrageousness of fate. Of course, we have brought it all on ourselves—or, rather, our smart scientists have brought it on us.

Good-by, my friend, and I hope you are more successful than I in keeping calm. It is bad enough to have all our splendid young men die. But even they, plucky fellows, <u>do not want the world to die!</u> I think of you often, dear friend. I would come to see you if I could. I haven't been very well since that miserable gall bladder operation was put over on me.

Affectionately
Willa Cather

❖ ❖

The 1943–44 production of Othello *starring Paul Robeson, José Ferrer, and Uta Hagen was a popular and critical success. Robeson's performance as Othello is also notable because he was the first black actor to play the part with an otherwise white cast in a modern production. He made his debut in the role in London in 1930.*

TO HELEN LOUISE CATHER

February 12, 1944

Dear Helen Louise:

I have made three unsuccessful efforts to telephone you—two of these on successive Sundays. I think you must have disappeared altogether in the Murk. I forget for what date you got your tickets to <u>Othello</u>. In the meantime Yehudi made a second desperate effort and succeeded. He played a concert in Washington, got the midnight train, found that his stateroom had been commandeered for an ambassador, sat up all night, and got in here at about 10 o'clock in the morning. He had a nap, and marshalled Edith and me to the theater that evening. He had already seen the play twice, but he was determined that we should see it.

You see, it was at his mother's apartment that I first met Paul Robeson. Yehudi was a boy of fourteen then and the family spent every winter in a big apartment in the Ansonia Hotel. Marutha (Yehudi's mother) invited Robeson and [*New York Times* music critic] Olin Downes and me for dinner one evening. She had just come back from Switzerland, where Mrs. Robeson was living (because Paul's son was in school there). She wanted to give him tidings of his wife. On my way across the park I was wondering whether I might feel a bit "Southern" in such mixed company. But the moment one meets Robeson, one loses everything except the flash that always comes when one first meets a truly great personality. His manners are perfect, because he is so natural—<u>he never thinks about himself</u> or what effect he will make. In "domestic" conversation he has the most beautiful speaking voice I can remember. In <u>Othello</u> he has very little opportunity to use this intimate voice, but you do get it when he lands in Cyprus and greets Desdemona—a very short scene but one of the most beautiful in the play.

Of course, I knew Robeson's impersonation was a very fine one. Before this war it made a great sensation all over Europe. His reading of the part was about what I felt sure it would be. But for me, the real surprise and thrill of the evening was Uta Hägen. Although so young, she is a celebrated Scandinavian actress [actually German American], and I expected a little of that thick accent. But she speaks the most <u>beautiful English</u>, and her interpretation was a revelation. I had never seen the stage play before, though I have heard Verdi's opera many times and I have heard good vocalists sing Desdemona. They were always distinctly mature, if not matronly. And when this lovely young thing came in, terrified before the Doge, my heart took a double beat. The fact is she is not lovely at all—a rather plain, peaked, starved little thing, like [ballerina Alicia] Markova. But her beautiful conception of the part is so strong that it shines through her, like a candle through a horn globe. And she grows lovelier with every act, until the last terrible one. When, after the arrival of the deputation from Venice, Othello strikes her, she does the most beautiful fall I have ever seen on the stage. And it isn't a trick fall, either. I am sure that she must have taken lessons from some of the Russian ballet people, because she <u>acts with her whole body</u>. It is no mixture of "gestures" and "elocution". I would have gone to the theater again to see her before this, if I didn't have my right hand in its little aluminum brace once more. It has been strapped up ever since New Year's. It is a hard punishment to bear, and inhibits me in almost everything. I haven't done anything wicked, except that I was having a good fling at work about Christmas time.

Good night, and my love to you.

Your Aunt Willie

TO BISHOP GEORGE ALLEN BEECHER

March 28, 1944

My dear Bishop:

What a beautiful Christmas present you sent me! A letter which told me of your wonderful two-weeks trip through western Nebraska, holding services day and night in the scattered missions, with all the members of your so-widespreading flock gathering to bring children and grandchildren to their beloved Bishop.

Your letter has lain for all these weeks on a little table beside my bed where I always keep about half a dozen letters which I like to read over and over. Not many of them have such a triumphant lift as yours. It is a letter I shall always keep, because it is such strong testimony that good things triumph and fine effort is recognized <u>even in a world which is now so darkened</u>. Your Christmas letter awakens joy in my heart, and will always be treasured by me. I am glad you remembered the little church in Red Cloud where you confirmed me with my father and my mother. I think of that service and that church very often. I haven't many friends left in Red Cloud now, and I hear the little town is very much changed. Perhaps it is better to remember it as it was in those days of happy family reunions, when everything breathed love and confidence.

Just after the New Year came in, my right hand collapsed again, just when I had been working so happily on my new book. I am allowed to take off the brace for one hour a day to sign letters and business papers. <u>Please</u> ask your doctor to explain to you the results—and causes—of inflammation of the <u>sheath of the big tendon</u> of the right thumb. Then you will understand the true condition of my annoying disability, and you will not be deceived by the rumors which float about Red Cloud, to the effect that I have been paralyzed in the right arm. I'll tell you something, my Bishop; when no man rejoices in his neighbour's misfortune, then there will be no more wars.

Lovingly to you both
Willa Cather

→ ←

"Col. Harvey's party," referred to in the following letter, was a celebration orchestrated by Col. George Harvey, editor of the North American Review, *at Delmonico's in New York City on December 23, 1905, for the seventieth birthday of*

Mark Twain. The "rose bower" is what Cather sometimes called her small attic bedroom in her childhood home, which was papered with a pattern of red and brown roses. "Grandmither" is one of her early poems, "Grandmither, Think Not I Forget."

TO ROSCOE CATHER

May 13 [1944]

My dear Brother

What a precious letter came from you last night! I am so glad that this "publicity" amuses and pleases you. It was all news to me—(I take no periodicals, never turn on the radio except for Churchill.) So Life has dug up some of the pictures of Col. Harvey's party! I was teaching in the Pittsburgh High School then! "Paul's Case" had been published in "McClures", and somebody told Col. Harvey I had a future. A kind Pittsburgh woman took my classes at the High School for four days to enable me to come to New York for the party, and she loaned me fifty dollars to have a good dress-maker make the dress in which I appear. (I had money in bank, but wouldn't use it for anything so frivolous.)

Yes, I was young then. I hit the road pretty early and worked terribly hard. I was never conceited, thank God, and never very hopeful. I expected to teach hard all my life in order to get time to write just a little. I did not complain, because everything interested me, even teaching. Now I have to avoid being much interested—it simply uses me up. That is the natural result.

Well, father and mother both got something out of it, and you have always seen that there was something in it, ever since that hot afternoon in the "rose bower" when I first read "Grandmither" to you.

I have three suit cases of letters from the wise and the great, from J. M Barrie, Thomas Hardy among them, but none are so precious as this one from father. I have never shown it to anyone before.

Lovingly
Willie

→ ←

On May 19, 1944, Cather was awarded the prestigious Gold Medal of the American Academy of Arts and Letters for her lifetime's work. Theodore Dreiser, Paul

Robeson, and her old boss S. S. McClure were given awards at the same ceremony. When McClure was presented with the Order of Merit for his contributions to journalism, Cather spontaneously walked across the stage and embraced him.

TO S. S. MCCLURE

May 26, 1944

Dear Mr. McClure:

I cannot tell you how happy it made me to see you again on last Friday afternoon. The sight of you awakened such a torrent of happy memories and stirred in me such a flood of gratitude, that I kept asking myself, "<u>Why</u> have I let such a long time go by without seeing my Chief?" I want to see you again, before I go away for the summer, to tell you all the <u>whys</u>. For the last ten years I have been in New York City so little—so many unexpected things have happened in my family, sad things and pleasant things. I want to tell you all about it.

Where, I wonder, can I meet you? Miss Lewis and I still keep our apartment at 570 Park Avenue, southwest corner of 63rd Street and Park Avenue. Like many of my friends, I have no maid—when I am out there is no one even to answer the telephone. I suppose women are not permitted to call on you at your club, but if you can drop me a line telling me where I could call on you, I would be glad to come. Or, if you can come to see me here at our apartment, I will always be here to receive you if you can let me know beforehand the day and the hour. I shall not be happy until I have a talk with you and try to clear myself of negligence.

Affectionately and, in heart, always faithfully yours,

Willa Cather

TO ROSCOE CATHER

June 30 [1944]
Asticou Inn, Northeast Harbor, Maine

[Note at the top:] Written in the yard of our cottage here.

Dear Roscoe;

I do want you to read both these articles. They are very truthful and exactly like Mr. McClure! After all he was the best friend I ever had, and I've neglected him shamefully for ten years. He has no home, but lives quietly at the Union League Club. The week before I left town I spent such a happy afternoon with him there. He is 86 years and has grown so gentle. Courteous and kind he always was. He is no longer a whirlwind, but a summer breeze. He took me into the Library of his Club, sat down beside me and held my hand and began: "Miss Cather, do you happen to remember the economic reforms of Edward the First when he got home from Palestine?"

Just like him! He always expected me to "remember" whatever was on his mind.

Ten years ago we nearly quarrelled when he came to dinner. He was just back from Italy and insisted that Moussolini had developed "a perfect government." He now generously recalled that I had called it a "perfect abscess" and said "why, Mr. McClure, you couldn't run an office that way, much [less] a Government!" Nice of him, wasn't it? I mean to see him from time to time this winter. I have had to cut out so many people since I have not been well, but I ought not to cut out the man who gave me my first chance.

Willie

TO JAMES CATHER

Monday, October 30 [1944]

Dear Jim;

I thought you might like to see this account of the Army's first game, and probably Charles [Jim's son, who was at West Point] will not think to send it to you—youngsters seldom do think to send things———they have jobs of their own to look after. Charles came to my apartment as soon as the game was over. I took him to Sherry's for dinner—it is the last really attractive restaurant left in this city. I had reserved a table a week ago. After dinner we came back to this apartment and chatted about the world until midnight. Charles' boat with 2500 cadets aboard sailed at 12:30. I thought best not to turn a fine looking lad out on the streets of New York on a Saturday night until he had just time to catch his boat—too many vamps about. He seems very happy in his work, and he won't think of much else for awhile.

November 18th the Army plays Notre Dame and Charles will again be my guest. My secretary, Miss Bloom, says that is the one game she never misses, and that when the cadets stand at attention during the National Anthem she always <u>weeps</u>! I would like to see that game, but if I taxi-ed out six miles to the Polo grounds, fought my way through struggling crowds, and <u>wept</u>, I fear I would be a pretty flat hostess to your son at six oclock.

By the way, I respect the family prejudices and never order cocktails when Charles is dining with me. I never drink them myself—don't like them—but I order them for my men friends. I think you can trust me to be a discreet hostess. I have become very fond of the lad. I surely think you and Ethel have been lucky in your children!

Affectionately to you both
Willie

[Felix "Doc"] Blanchard, the Army's white hope, is Charles' room mate I understand!

Army was the national champion in college football in 1944 and '45, and "Doc" Blanchard won the Heisman Trophy in 1945.

→ ←

The following letter was first published in Talking Book Topics *in June 1948 as part of their announcement that a recording of* Death Comes for the Archbishop *was now available. The editors thought Cather's letter "an excellent statement by a first-rate artist of the essence of* Talking Book *reading" but four years later printed an apology in the magazine for unintentionally violating the prohibition on the publication of her letters.*

TO ARCHIBALD MACLEISH

December 11, 1944

Dear Mr. MacLeish:

You have already heard from Alfred Knopf that I am quite willing that you should put three of my books into records for the blind.

I would never have been unwilling to have such records made had I been sure that the recording was done by people who read simply, as our mothers and grandmothers did when they read aloud to us in our childhood. My refusal was largely the result of a singular coincidence. Some months or weeks before I received your original request, I was dining with an old friend in a little Italian restaurant where the radio was turned on for the evening. Over this radio I heard several chapters from My Antonia read by a young woman who had all the airs and graces of a small town elocutionist. They were quiet chapters from a very quiet book—a mute on the strings. This reader certainly removed the mute, and with all her physical powers she put into the text what was not there.

When a book is read for recording, the reader is not only a collaborator but an interpreter of the writer. It is the reader who decides the tempi and the stresses. He is even able to attempt a personification of the characters, and to make them declamatory where the writer has kept the dialogue casual and low in tone. I am afraid that people who have worked for the radio find it hard to refrain from virtuosity, and I really do not think all books should be read in an elocutionary way.

Very cordially yours,
Willa Cather

TO FRED OTTE

December 12, 1944

My dear Fred Otte:

How nice it is to hear from you again! I think the steel industry and oil country must be grand for keeping up one's enthusiasms. Oh, dogs are nothing new to me. I have several friends who have gone to the dogs. In social relations (relations with humans), dogs of different breeds seem to have very special and individual effects. I never knew a fancier of Collie dogs who was not very companionable and sympathetic. Perhaps that is because they are all Scotchmen. (I think most Scotchmen are sentimental underneath their grouch.) But, Oh, beware the Norwegian Elkhounds! Social relations with them will contaminate almost any man. One friend of mine who began raising Elkhounds, and taking prizes for them, has become as savage as they are—a biter and snapper of the first order! Beware the Elkhound! And write to me on my next birthday.

Very cordially yours,
Willa Cather

TO ROSCOE CATHER

[December 1944]

POETRY!!

There was an old writer who lived in a stew,
'Cause she had so many nieces she didn't know what to do!
And they lived so many places she just lost her wits,
So she siezed her address book and tore it to bits!!

P.S. Please send me present addresses of Elizabeth and Margaret. Have something for them and can't send even a card.

My right hand has gone back on me and is very lame.

Merry Christmas and love
Willie

→ ←

The postscript of the following letter suggests that Cather may have had a different publishing arrangement in mind for the novel Hard Punishments, *though the details of these plans—and of Knopf's role in them—are unknown.*

TO ROSCOE CATHER

December 29 [1944]

Dear Brother;

If I had the wellest hand in the world instead of a very sick hand I could never tell you the pleasure these beautiful violets have given me. They came on the morning of Christmas Eve, among the first to come, so I had long joy of them before I got tired. They were more gorgeous this year than ever before and filled my room and my sitting room with that moist spring-like fragrance which is like nothing else on earth. They were the Parma Violets this year (they are not always to be had in winter) and they are much the sweetest of all.

On the same evening, from the same florist, came a box of yellow jonquils from Charles Edwin. He has been sending them to me at Christmas time since he first came East, two years before he ever met me. Where did he ever learn nice ways and gentle manners? I often wonder.

Lovingly,
Willie

My wretched hand went back on me because I had been working hard on a story for my London publisher, Cassell, to be printed for next Christmas with illustrations—my legendary kind of theme—Time about 1340 A.D. Interests me very much. I hope my hand will get better and let me go on with it. My hand (not the story!) is more painful than it has been before.

Lovingly, and <u>so gratefully</u>, dear.
Willie

So glad that Virginia will have her husband for awhile.

TO ZOË AKINS

January 5, 1945

My dear Zoe:

Never worry about the turkey. Don't think I could have managed him if he had arrived. We have only a part time cook—not very expert.

But the plant from Thorley's was, and is, a great success: a cyclamen, deep rose color, with the beautiful leaves all fresh and strong. I enjoy beautiful plants just as much as I detest ratty ones. This one has given me great pleasure. I would love to write you by hand, but just in the middle of a piece of work which I was enjoying very much, my right hand went back on me complete and is tied up in a brace again. It cannot even get out to wish you a Happy New Year with a pen.

Thinking about years, Old and New, (in a period of enforced inactivity, one does think, you know) it has occurred to me that you have had the things you most wanted out of the years, and that I have got a good deal of what I wanted. Above all, I have pretty well escaped the things I <u>violently did not want</u>, some of which were: too much money, noisy publicity, the bother of meeting lots of people. While I was editor of McClure's I had to meet a great many people, both here and in England. I enjoyed it, but after I had enough of it, I wanted to be absolutely free—and I have enjoyed that much more.

Affectionately and with a thousand good wishes,
Willa Cather

>→ ←

It is unclear who Cather is referencing when she refers to the "Hicks brothers" in the letter below; certainly critic Granville Hicks wrote critical reviews of her works, but he had no brother who also wrote criticism.

TO IRENE MINER WEISZ

January 6, 1945

Darling Irene:

I have hoped my hand might get better so that I could write you with my pen. But when I had been working very happily on a story that interests me very much, my right hand suddenly collapsed (about the 16th of December) and has been tied up in its metal brace ever since—a terrible disappointment. I am afraid I will lose all of the joy of the story in the long wait which will now come.

Irene, I have read your dear letter over many times, and each time I read it I cry. It is because I have put my real feelings and real heart into my books that they speak to you. You may remember that I had to make my own living and help those at home until I was twenty-five years old: teaching, (I was a good teacher—took it seriously) newspaper work, writing for small magazines. I often wonder why I went on writing, for I wasn't very ambitious. I think I can honestly say that I wrote for pleasure, and not from vanity. When I wrote about the people I loved and the places I loved, they came back to me so vividly, that it was like having them all over again. They warmed me and excited me, as their actual presence would have done—perhaps more so. So, no matter how hard I worked at my job all through the week, I always wrote for my own pleasure on Saturday and Sunday.

I have managed to recapture a good many of the pleasures of the past, in one book or another, but I have had to pay for my pleasures as I went along. The writers whom I most admire have been very kind to me. You remember President Masaryk, former President of Czechoslovakia. I have a bundle of his letters to me, running over a period of eight years—the last one written shortly before his death. He was a great linguist and a fine critic. Some day I would like to tell you about him.

Yes, the world has been kind. But certainly my home town has not been very kind, nor some of the people who go out from there. Helen Mac, when she was in New York, espoused the cause of the Hicks brothers—two not-very-successful reviewers, who have made almost a career explaining to people what a second-rate scribbler I am, after all. I was amused when I noticed in the Red Cloud paper that on two occasions Helen McNeny had reviewed and lectured on a book by Granville Hicks, in the Auld Library [in Red Cloud]!! These books would not necessarily attack me personally, but would ridicule everything I believe in. Of course, all this is gratifying to the little group at home who sit around and do fine detective work on "where she got this, and where she got that". I could tell you in confidence, Irene, that so often I do not remember at all where I "got" them. After Ántonia was published, Father pointed out to me half a dozen incidents—things I had done or seen with him (the two crazy Russians, etc.), and I honestly believed that I had invented them. They simply came into my mind, the way things do come when one is interested. When one is writing hard, one drives toward the main episodes and the detail takes care of itself. <u>Unless the detail is spontaneous</u>, unsought for by the writer, he isn't much of a writer—has mistaken his job.

Let me break this serious discussion by a little fun. Mrs. Fred Garber, out in California, was very indignant about <u>A Lost Lady</u>, because, when the early chapters of the story came out in the Century Magazine, she went around boasting that Mrs. Forrester was her daughters' grandmother. Then when the plot thickened up and Frank Ellinger appeared, she was very angry. She once told Douglass, much later, that she should have tried to stop that book in some way. Douglass was too polite to tell her that the book has already been translated into French, Dutch, German and Norwegian, and that she would have had a hard time stopping it. Mrs. Charley Platt would certainly have liked to stop it. I was perfectly square about that book. I was staying with Isabelle in Toronto when the Red Cloud paper came, announcing Mrs. Garber's death in Oregon. It shook me up more than I would have thought. The day was very hot. I went to my room and laid down to rest. I had never once thought of writing about Mrs. Garber, but within an hour the story was all made in my mind, as if I had read it somewhere. Mrs. Platt didn't agree with my portrait, but that was what Mrs. Garber seemed to me, and what she meant to me. If a story has any real vitality, if it goes on being printed and sold in half a dozen languages, the root of it must be a real feeling—a strong personal feeling. It takes skill, of course, to get that feeling across to many people in many languages, but the strong feeling that comes out of the living heart is the thing <u>most necessary—and most rarely found</u>.

I beg you, dear Irene, never to show this letter to anyone, unless it might be Carrie or Mary. What a scream Helen Mac and the Hickses (and probably Mr. Leighton) would get out of it!

I am grateful for your understanding that I am not a smart trick writer. I have always felt that you felt something <u>human and</u> affectionate in my books.

Lovingly
Willie

Hand very bad today.

→ ←

As Cather indicates in the following, it was her third and final letter to Carl Weber about the Housman visit. She did not in fact have any plans to go to Mexico in 1945.

TO CARL J. WEBER

January 31, 1945
New York City

Dear Mr. Weber:

Please disregard any suggestion I may have made that you trace some of the erroneous statements about my visit to Housman. The world is full of erroneous statements, and I notice that they seldom do any one serious harm.

"By misdirections find directions out"? That is a successful method, until it is carried too far. In your first letter you stated that you had heard that I called upon Housman, and that "probably he was rude, as always." I replied to your letter only because I thought silence might mean acquiescence to your supposition that the man was rude. He wasn't rude at all, but very courteous. I felt that I should say so.

In answer to your second letter I went a good deal farther than I should have gone, and told you exactly where I met Housman and how I obtained his address.

Now comes your third letter, which is practically a questionnaire. To these questions I do not feel that it is incumbent upon me to reply. You even ask me to expose a second person to cross-examination. After all, this is not a case for the Federal Bureau of Investigation. One can dilate upon one's personal experiences, or one can be reserved about them.

I am leaving for Mexico City within a few days, and this is an opportune time to bring our correspondence to a close.

Very sincerely yours,
Willa Cather

TO ROSCOE CATHER

February 8, 1945

My dear Brother:

I have wanted to write this letter to you for five years, and I have simply never had the time to write or dictate anything that seemed so little important. I am always away behind in answering my mail. The subject matter of this letter really isn't important in itself, but it is important to me that you should know these facts which have pleased me very much.

If you are ever near a library where they have the <u>fourteenth edition</u> of the Encyclopedia Britannica, please spend a little time looking up these things. I bought the fourteenth edition five years ago, because my old eleventh edition was bound in soft suede and the limp backs were difficult for my lame hand.

When I bought the fourteenth edition my bookseller sent me Volume I for inspection, and in it he put a little mark. I opened it at the mark, naturally, and found an article on American Literature with a full page illustration made up of small photographs of American authors: all the old boys we used to study in school, and a few of the newer boys. But there were only three women—Harriet Beecher Stowe, Emily Dickinson and myself. I was pleased, of course, but did not think much about it. The five years went by and a few days ago I happened to be looking up the animal <u>caribou</u>; his habitat. In turning over the pages I saw something that looked familiar on the left-hand page. It really was my name—rather startled me. I read the article—short but extremely well written. I would have been well pleased with even a less pleasing article in that encyclopedia.

Press agent stuff is pretty well guarded against in the Britannica. A committee of experts, on all subjects covered, is appointed by the British Museum, to read the copy and pass upon it. The literary and historical material has been very much condensed for the fourteenth edition (a new edition is made every twenty-five years) because of the enormous development in mechanics and scientific studies. This little article, however, pleases me very much, and I think it will please you.

Lovingly always

Willie

TO YALTAH MENUHIN

April 20 [1945?]

My Dear Yaltah;

I was so pleased to have a word from you at Easter time, and to know that the Good Friday music recalled to you with pleasure the afternoon when you and Hephzibah and I heard Parsifal together. I still love the opera and the legend—though so much of Wagner has been rather spoiled for us by being boisterously played for very un-musical purposes.

Miss Lewis and I had a wonderful evening with your mother and father when they were here this winter. It really seemed as if you three, as you were ten years ago, might come bursting in at any moment. We all heard Yehudi's Bach concert with [Wanda] Landowska. I think that was the most beautiful and lofty music I have ever listened to.

With love and happy memories
Your "Aunt Willa"

TO CARRIE MINER SHERWOOD

April 29 [1945]

My Dear Carrie;

The Easter storm that was a break for you was a break for me also. I haven't had such a letter from you for years—a letter which sounded as if you were talking to me and sitting close beside me. So I want to begin this letter in my own hand, though I can't carry on very far. The tendon in my right thumb has never properly healed; bad weather, too much exercise——and it has to go back in its metal brace again. Last fall, when we first got home from Maine (where I had been writing steadily and very happily with no bad results) I started in with enthusiasm to help with the house-cleaning. No bad results at first———then, smash! I had to put on the brace again and wear it for four months straight. Only took it off to write a few Christmas cards and the Christmas checks I always send. You, too, seem to have a hand which gets sick. Don't drive it! Be careful. Dictate, you would soon get used to giving dictation. Of course I can't dictate in my own work—I have to see the picture shape itself on the page before me—the sound of my own voice would make me self-conscious. But I dictate all my letters, even those to old and dear friends.

Everything you tell me about your grandchildren interests me very much. I have often wondered where they all were, and what they were doing. Of course, the younger ones I do not remember very much, but I remember John Sherwood and Betty very well, indeed. Malvina Hoffman is generally said to be more interesting as an ethnologist than as an artist, but I have not seen any of her work and cannot have an opinion. Mabel Dodge's Indian husband simply took the name of Luhan because his Indian name would not be understandable among white people. A good many of the more sophisticated Indians do that. The name used for the owner of the white mules is Lujon [in Death Comes for the Archbishop]. I varied the spelling purposely, so that it would not look like Tony's name. Both, the name Lujon and Luhan, are very common Mexicans names—about as common as Smith is in this country. The white mules were named Contento and Angelica. Mabel Dodge's husband, of course, had no such mules. The ones I know were owned by Mexicans.

And am I to believe, my dear Carrie, that you are actually directing the management of all five farms! And this with all your Red Cross work! Yes, I wish Walter [Sherwood] could have known how his judgment would be justified by future events. One of the best things that President Roosevelt ever did was to establish that bank moratorium—which certainly weeded the sheep from the goats, and threw a spotlight on the men who were crooked and the men who were straight.

I am not exaggerating, Carrie, when I confide to you that I would rather go home to Red Cloud than to any of the beautiful cities in Europe where I used to love to go. But so many sad things have happened—and so many painful things. I am sure you will remember the pleasant morning when I said good-by to you, both of us sitting in the back parlor of my father's house, where everything was still the same. Ever since my gall bladder operation I have been pretty weak on the emotional side. I am sure you realize, as my brother Roscoe always did, that things have always hit me very hard. I suppose that is why I never run out of material to write about. The inside of me is so full of dents and scars, where pleasant and unpleasant things have hit me in the past. I do not so much invent as I remember and re-arrange. And I remember unconsciously. Faces, situations, things people said long ago simply come up from my mind as if they were written down there. They would not be there if they hadn't hit me hard. My working faculty does not seem to be knocked out, because last summer, up in Maine, when I could first use my right hand again, I worked very happily, and enjoyed it <u>so much!</u>. But I still have to lead a very quiet life and avoid getting too much excited. If I get stirred up, the reaction is very bad physically. It isn't my blood pressure—blood pressure perfectly normal—but I don't sleep, get awfully weak, and begin to weep, just like poor Mollie [Ferris] used to do!! I laugh at myself, but I just weep on! If Dr. Creighton were there, he would tell you it is nervous exhaustion, and that's what my doctors say.

I am writing dear Mariel Gere that I can not come to her for the fiftieth anniversary of our class graduation. She has written me such a lovely letter asking me to come and stay with her, in their dear old house that was a second home to me all through the days when I went to the university. I shall have to answer her affectionate letter in the negative—just because the excitement and emotional stir-up of such a reunion would take the strength out of me from head to foot. It doesn't at all grieve me to be unable to attend this reunion (though I would love to be with Mariel Gere in her house again), but it does grieve me very deeply to feel that I would really not be well enough to go down to Red Cloud.

I have had a very quiet but very happy winter, in spite of the shortage of help. We have an excellent woman who can give us only four hours a day, but she is a fine person and does a wonderful lot of work in four hours. All my friends have been kind and considerate—I see "as much company as I can enjoy", and no more. Yehudi and his wife have been so kind and thoughtful, and come to sit by the fire and have a cup of tea with me, though I cannot now have jolly little dinners for them, as I used to, simply because we have no cook. Our maid comes at ten, gets us an excellent lunch, and leaves at two. Sometimes I have Helen Louise for lunch. I think Mary wrote me that you all liked her. I think her a very sweet girl, and I like her husband.

This is only the beginning of a letter, you will get Volume II one of these days.

Very lovingly, and with happy memories,
Willie

❧ ❧

In a short note at the end of April accompanying her royalty check, Greenslet wrote how impressed he was at the continued steady sales of Song of the Lark *and* My Ántonia.

TO FERRIS GREENSLET

May 9, 1945

Dear F.G.,

Thank you for your kind letter. I am naturally pleased that the two books you mentioned hold up so well. Probably <u>O Pioneers</u> would do just as well, if Houghton Mifflin had not seen fit to sell many hundred copies at one dollar apiece some fifteen or twenty years ago. You remember your business office was then very keen for selling <u>Antonia</u> in Liggett's Drug Stores at one dollar a copy, and I managed to save <u>Antonia</u> by substituting <u>O Pioneers</u>. I think my judgment has been supported by subsequent developments.

Now to the real purpose of this letter. Can you tell me whether Ford Madox Ford is still living? He wrote and circulated a very false and silly story about a visit which Isabel[le] McClung and I made to Housman long ago, when I was twenty-four and Isabel[le] twenty-one. This entirely untrue story has been repeated in many articles and prefaces which have been floating about lately. As for myself, I never thought it worth while to deny any of this gossip, but the surviving members of Isabel[le]'s family object to it and blame me for not having refuted it. I think there is nothing for me to do but to write a truthful and accurate story of that innocent visit (made on a summer afternoon), which was really very pleasant.

I know you do not like to admit unpleasant facts about anyone—and you prefer to turn them off with a joke, which is a comforting philosophy to live by. But you must admit that Ford Madox Ford was seldom able to tell the truth about anything. I found that out once during a long stay in London. The Galsworthys warned me as to this failing of his, apropos of his yarns about his intimacy with Conrad. If the man is alive, I would not wish to say flatly that the original story was started by an irresponsible person.

Faithfully yours,
Willa Cather

Ford Madox Ford died in 1939. Cather never published an account of her visit to A. E. Housman.

TO SIDNEY FLORANCE

May 16, 1945

Dear Sidney Florance:

When I asked my niece, Helen Louise, whether she thought I had one real friend left among the business men of Red Cloud, she thought for a moment and then said very decidedly, "I do believe Mr. Florance is a real friend." Now to a real friend, I would like to explain briefly why my investments in Nebraska real estate turned out so unfortunately.

As soon as my books began to make money, I sent nearly all of it to my father to invest for me in Nebraska farm loans. I thought he knew the land and the farms pretty well, and it gave him so much pleasure to invest for me. At that time, I think, none of his other children were sending any money home. While he liked to read my early books, it was a matter of great pride to him to feel that they were worth real money to a considerable number of people. That went further with him than pleasant press notices, and it was a great pleasure to me to have him feel that satisfaction. I remember that the first check I sent him (I think it was for the first year's royalties on "One of Ours") was twenty-five thousand dollars. Father made a number of loans for me and always saw that the interest was kept up. I did not realize that it might be a burden to him, to attend to these farm loans. I did not realize, indeed, that he was every year growing older. Whenever I went home he was just the same.

One summer he remarked to me quite casually that he had handed all my mortgages over to Will Auld [James W. Auld], as his own memory had failed very much and Mr. Auld could take care of them much better than he.

I have always been proud of myself that I took this information with perfect calmness until I got to my own room, then I sat down and wondered what I could do. I had always distrusted Mr. Auld—not that I would then have accused him of outright dishonesty, but I knew that he was small and mean and I hate to do business with people of that kind. I could see no course of action open for me. If I had taken the papers out of the State Bank, it would have made Father very unhappy and it would have created further friction between Mr. Auld and my sister [Jessica; she and Auld were divorced in 1933]—where the situation was already bad enough. There just was nothing that I could do without making unhappiness in my family. I was well and strong and was doing the sort of work I loved, so I decided to take no action at all and let the matter ride.

Now I am telling you all this, Mr. Florence, because I would hate to have you think that I am such a natural-born idiot, or that my father was so stupid as to have loaned fifty-seven hundred dollars to Guy Henderson on land where there never was a well—nor enough real soil to raise beans. Neither Father nor I ever loaned Guy Henderson a penny. Other loans which Father made were paid off to the State Bank, and reinvested for the exclusive convenience of the Bank. I am burdening you with these details because I really don't want my friends to think me more stupid than I am.

Publishing, too, has its business side, and I have never had any trouble with it.

Now I can come to the point. I want to get rid as quickly as possible of any land I own or hold under mortgage in Nebraska. One reason is that the Internal Revenue people make so much trouble about accepting my statements on the income and output on these few farms that the tax ordeal, even with the help of an attorney, cuts into my own professional work. My working hours have been cut down considerably by illness, but I would have had a new book out this fall if the income tax people had not bothered me so.

Clearly, the thing to do is to get rid of the farms in Nebraska on which I now hold mortgages. My brother Roscoe has for some time urged me to do this. If you and Mr. [Willard] Crowell will be kind enough to look into my box, you can soon find on which farms I hold a mortgage. And I will be deeply grateful if you will advise me how to proceed with the disposition of these farms. Mr. Crowell has been the kindest of friends in looking after the places for me, and I trust his judgment absolutely. But I feel sure that looking after these places has become quite a burden to him, since the serious accident which kept him in the hospital so long.

Although it may have been tedious for you to read this long letter, it will not be tedious for you to answer it. What I really want is the name of some institution or person who would be willing to undertake the disposal of these farms for me. You have a progressive real estate agent in Red Cloud, I gather from the paper, Mr. Frame, but I do not like his style of advertising very well.

I am sure Howard Foe would be able to give us all sound advice in this closing-up. Perhaps he would be willing to take charge of any legal matters in connection with the foreclosures or sale of these farms.

I will be very glad to not only pay the usual charges for services of this kind, but to pay a liberal bonus in order to get the farms off my hands as quickly as possible.

Faithfully yours,
[Unsigned carbon copy]

TO ROSCOE CATHER

July 30 [1945]
Asticou Inn, Northeast Harbor, Maine

Dear Brother;

I have been here for three weeks but I have been working awfully hard and enjoying it. That is why you haven't heard from me. Work takes more out of me than it used to—a great deal more. But I enjoy it more than anything else. I have a funny little room in the attic here, with a sloping ceiling, like my "rose bower" in our old first house. Do you remember? I can always work best in a low room under the roof. All my best books were written in Jaffrey N.H. in a little room where I could almost touch the ceiling with my hand. I feel afraid in a big room. I like to be snug.

Lovingly
Willie

TO SIDNEY FLORANCE

August 11 [1945]
Asticou Inn, Northeast Harbor, Maine

Dear Sidney Florance;

I have written Mr. Crowell according to your kind suggestion—asking him to get three thousand two hundred for the Osborne place if he can, otherwise to let it go for three thousand.

Since I wrote Mr. Crowell the atomic bomb has sent a shudder of horror (and fear) through all the world, and one's own little affairs seem scarcely worth thinking about.

Perhaps the enclosed clipping was syndicated in the Chicago papers. Do not return it. Throughout this war I have found Major [George Fielding] Eliot the best commentator and the best forecaster.

Faithfully & Gratefully yours
Willa Cather

→ ←

Roscoe Cather died on September 4, 1945. The following letter was written before Cather received the news of his death.

TO ROSCOE CATHER

September 5, 1945
Asticou Inn, Northeast Harbor, Maine

My dear Roscoe,

I am sending you a letter from young? Joe Pavlick, who has bought the Osborn farm. I do not think I ever got a fan letter that pleased me so much as this funny honest scrawl from the son of old Joe Pavlick. You will remember him and his father well. You will also remember the time when old Joe and his son bought their first buggy, and young Joe drove over to our house to take me buggy riding. I had seen a good deal of him in Father's office and always tried to be friendly toward the poor clumsy lad. But, you know, in Red Cloud, in those days, taking a young girl buggy riding was a very definite gesture. On this occasion I ran up and hid in the attic and left poor Mother to deal with

Joe. She always had great tact and presence in handling the common people so I expect she gave me a pretty good alibi. You must send me back Joe's letter as I want to keep it for the nice things he says about Father. I am sure he means that with all his hard-working, honest nature.

I won't have any very definite address for a couple weeks—it depends on weather and various things—but I will be in New York before the first of October and I will telegraph you as soon as I get there. So keep Joe's funny letter and sen[d] it to me when you know I am again at 570 Park Avenue.

Lovingly
Willie

TO META SCHAPER CATHER

September 7 [1945]
Asticou Inn, Northeast Harbor, Maine

There is nothing I can say, dear Meta. Several times in my life I [had] bitter losses, but never before have I felt heart-broken—felt that things were done for me. Roscoe was the only one of my family who felt about things as I did, and he was the only one who saw, from the beginning, what I was trying to do. He was my best critic, because he knew both ends of the process; knew the material, and what I had been able to do with it, or had failed in the handling. He knew me better than I knew myself. He knew all his family better than I did, but he was more wise and charitable about them. The fact is that now I have no one to judge me, no one to tell me if I am off the true pitch—no other judgment that I care a bang about.

I got your telegram on the same afternoon that the typist brought me back the letter I had dictated to Roscoe in the morning. I am sending it to you.

At the same time the typist brought the typed copy of the new story she had just finished ["The Best Years"]. It was to go to him by the next mail. It is about our childhood. I can't bear to look at it now.

When you can, please write me what you are going to do.

Don't act too quickly. Since he was ill you have lived so entirely for him——you won't know what you do want for awhile. Call on me for anything that I can do—for me it will be just as if I were doing it for Roscoe. If ever a man was <u>one</u> with his wife, he was.

I just can't bear it, dear, this using the past tense to write about him. I would have been with you this summer, or on the way to you, if Roscoe hadn't written me again and again not to try west-bound trains.

I shall never forget all you did for him.

Lovingly
Willie

TO VIRGINIA, MARGARET, AND ELIZABETH CATHER

September 10, 1945
Asticou Inn, Northeast Harbor, Maine

Dear Virginia, Margaret, and Elizabeth:

I write you because I knew your father so much longer than you knew him, so much longer than even your mother knew him. We were close together in years and close together in sympathy from the beginning. There was a time when I first graduated from the University of Nebraska (and a poor school it was!) when Roscoe and I were put in a hard position for young people. You have heard, probably, that in the year 1893 all the crops in the state were burned up. My father had a big farm under cultivation. Fortunately he gave up operating it, for this drought continued for nearly ten years. And then was the time when things were very hard at home in Red Cloud. Your grandfather took an office position with the Security Investment Company in Lincoln. Your grandmother spent a good deal of time up there with him. I got my first newspaper job in Pittsburgh and sent home as much of my salary as I could. Your father stayed on in Red Cloud as Principal of the South Ward School. He was practically the father and protector of the younger children. I am quite sure your Aunt Elsie and your Uncle Jim and Uncle Jack can never forget his protecting kindness.

While I was working in Pittsburgh, the newspaper people always managed to get my transportation back to Lincoln in the summer so that I always had a few weeks at home in the summer time and Roscoe was always there. We shared our responsibilities and talked over the prospects for the younger ones and wondered how we were to get along through the world at all. Things looked very dark but we were always so happy to be together that we carried the troubles rather lightly.

When I had any free time I was always writing a little, simply because it interested me more than any other form of recreation—I wrote just as people who are really fond of music love to strum on the piano. Your father was always then and ever afterward my soundest and best critic. I used to think he knew the inside of my head better than I did. We always met at home every summer until your father married and went to Wyoming. Then there were several years when we were separated,—but only by distance. I went to England and to France working my way along by newspaper correspondence. By this time I had a fairly good position in the Pittsburgh High School as head of the English Department.

Roscoe and I were not much together again until some years after his marriage although we wrote to each other very very often and never in the least felt apart. I was not able to spend any long time with him until I went for that never-to-be-forgotten visit at Lander when the twins were just one year old. That was a long visit and it was one of the happiest chapters of my life. I do not think I have ever been in a house anywhere which seemed quite so attractive as the home Roscoe and your mother built for themselves in Lander, with the Wind River Mountains against the sky, and the little River flowing in the backyard—if I had ever settled in a place like that, I could never have left it. Your mother and father and I made wonderful trips up into the Wind River mountains which were then unspoiled by automobile roads and traffic. We went to a great many places on horseback and I remember how your father's critical eye was upon me to see whether I would flinch when a horse swam with me for the first time. Those were glorious days and I shall always remember them with pleasure and gratitude.

But what I remember best, and value most, is that your father was always such a fine gentleman toward every member of his father's family and in his own family. He simply couldn't be anything else.

His early business career was in a free world, and there was something joyful and romantic about it. The whole setting at Lander had something of the Old West. But though he lived on into times when business had become more systematized and had hardened into "high pressure salesmanship" <u>he never became in any sense a salesman</u>. The dirt of it never touched his finger tips. He never tried to put anything through or put anything over. He let "business" come to him; he didn't go after it. His father was just like that, and his grandfather. This inheritance ought to make you always a little prouder than many of the people with whom you will be thrown, and a little more careful to keep yourselves up to that level.

I am afraid this is a queer kind of letter of condolence but it is the only consolation that I can find, now that my comradeship with your father is cut off. I had just written him a long letter and signed it, when the telegram came from your mother. And when I wrote her, I sent also the letter which I had written to him.

Good-bye, my dears, you will, I am sure, always remember your father's gentleness—and gentility.

I am cutting my stay here short and will go down to New York in about ten days from now. I'll have to stay over for a few days in Boston.

I am sending all three letters to you, dear Margaret, because I am not so sure of the address of either of your sisters. Please forward them for me.

Lovingly to you all, always
your aunt Willie

TO MARGARET CATHER SHANNON

October 3, 1945

Dear Little Margaret:

What a wonderful thing it was of you to take your baby and hop onto a plane and go to San Francisco! If there is a place in another world for good people, your father is surely in it, and he will surely know how his little daughter tried to get to him. I think you must know yourself that you have always been a special favorite with me, dear Margaret. And once, in Casper, when I was walking home from the bank with your father, you came running down the sidewalk toward us and Roscoe said, "She will look me over! She is always the first one to notice if I am especially tired or if one of my bad headaches is coming on." I tell you this, dear, because you ought to know it, and ought always to remember it. There are few things in one's life so precious as to have given that magical kind of perception and sympathy toward someone we love. The knowledge that he felt that so keenly ought to be a precious thing for you to remember.

I wish he could have seen your little girl. Meta wrote me that she is such a lovely child, and I know your taking the baby out there was a greater comfort to your mother than anything else could have been.

Lovingly
W.S.C.

October 5th

I have been quite ill since I wrote this note and the doctor kept me flat in bed. Much better now.

TO IRENE MINER WEISZ

October 22 [1945]
New York City

My Darling Irene;

I know these are anxious days for you, and I want you to know that I think of you very very often and hope all goes well. I have been ill ever since I got home from Maine. I don't even try to do anything. I brought a new book home with me, but I have not had the energy to put it in order for Alfred Knopf to see, and I don't care whether it is ever published or not. Roscoe's death broke the last spring in me. He was always the closest of my brothers to me, in years and in feeling. Douglass and I twice had a little quarrel, but Roscoe and I never. We always felt the same way about things. The three summers I spent in Wyoming with him and his wife were among the happiest of my life. Now I don't care about writing any more books. Now I know that nothing really matters to us but the people we love.

Of course, if we realized that when we are young, and just sat down and loved each other, the beds would not get made and very little of the world's work would ever get done. For years, two weeks never went by that I did not get a jolly letter from Roscoe. I loved his three daughters and was able to do nice things for them. That gave him such great pleasure. When I last saw him in San Francisco he laughed and said "You know, the two summers you gave the twins in Grand Manan were the happiest summers of <u>my life</u>! I was so proud that you wanted them."

Goodbye, dear Irene. God bless you.
Willie

TO SIDNEY FLORANCE

November 21, 1945

Dear Mr. Florance:

Ever since your tribute to Fred Maurer appeared in the home paper I have wanted to write you and thank you for it. But troubles came thick and fast at that time, and after them a heavy correspondence. May I take this opportunity to thank you? I still have the article and shall continue to keep it in my scrapbook.

In my first year in the Red Cloud High School I sat very near the Maurer boys,—two brothers, I think. They sat next the north wall, where there were no windows—almost no light at all—and I used to see one boy always struggling to read his textbook. Their parents must have been terribly poor, for the two boys came all through the winter wretchedly clad. They had no overcoats and seemed to have little underneath their jackets and long pants. Those boys never had a fair chance.

I tried to keep up some correspondence with Fred as long as the lovely Gurney girl was taking care of him. But after she, so young and happy, died, I felt there was no one with him whom I knew or could reach. This note is just to tell you that one old friend of yours deeply appreciated your appreciation of him.

Cordially yours,
Willa Cather

TO META SCHAPER CATHER

Thursday [fall 1945]

My Dear Meta;

This morning, (what is left of it) belongs to you. Yesterday I got down to my bank and turned in my bank stock exactly according to Mr. Rutedge's letter of instruction. I had been kept in bed for several days by a slight heart attack—nothing serious.

Dear sister, I think you are mistaken about our being so very clannish. The truth is that Roscoe and Douglas and I were the "clan". Jess and Jim and Jack were, in a sense, the wards of the clan. We, the three Virginians, tried to look after the younger ones. Ever since that summer I spent with you and Roscoe when the twins were one year old, I have felt that you were more truly my sister than either Elsie or poor Jess. I felt that because we were very companionable, and liked to do things together. That is what makes companionship. Do you remember when we started out to find Pete's Lake—and never found it at all? I always loved to see Roscoe on a horse, and I love to remember him so. I often dream about him as he was when he rode with us then———in the days of the other world war! In Casper we went round in a car—went farther, but it wasn't quite so much fun. However, I rejoiced in that car, because I realized how much it saved Roscoe's strength. You remember we went up to Sheridan, and the next day crossed the mountains near Gray Bull and had a long, hard drive home—by the worst part of the old road to Lander, if I remember right.

Meta, I would love to have one of the photographs of Roscoe with Elizabeth's daughter on his shoulder. Margaret had one, and I liked it so much. He always <u>kept his figure</u>, which most men do not after fifty.

Jim was always a problem child. He was terribly ashamed of his gentle mannered father, and went with a tough crowd. There is a nice side to him, and his children have seen only that side. Whenever I have seen that side, I am weak to him. His greatest fault is that he thinks he has great business ability. He made the last twenty years of Father's life unhappy by trying one disastrous experiment after another.

Jack is just always Jack. He is loyal, true, and loving. But he married rather queerly. Even Father, who was too courteous to dislike any woman, didn't like his wife [Irma Wells Cather].

So you see, dear Meta, <u>the clan was</u>, but is no more. I am the only one left, and God knows I aint no clan! I should think you and I, together, represented the spirit of the old clan more than anybody else. So let us, in loyalty to those others, who are gone, try to keep together and be our own clan.

Jessie will always be mild and appreciative of any kindness. Elsie I have had to cut out. She followed me up with so much abuse that I just ceased writing to her. An old friend of mine who lives in Lincoln wrote me "why <u>does</u> Elsie let her jealousy of you spoil her life? It has become an obsession with her, and embarrasses her friends."

Now my dear, you and I are simply the only clan there is. We can adopt Jack when he is good and is not tyrranized over by Jim. I mean to draw a little closer to poor Jessie. Really, Father was to blame for her marrying Will Auld. Didn't he turn all my securities over to Will Auld? When Helen Louise was here one day last year helping me go over my accounts she exclaimed, "why, Will Auld simply stole twenty thousand dollars from you! Can't you do <u>anything</u> about it?" "Nothing—except not to let him steal my peace of mind." When I first found out how much I was stung, I sat down the next day and began work on <u>Sapphira</u>. Those old memories were a good cure for worry.

Now that my sprung tendon is bad again, I must stop, dear. But you and your dear daughters are more in my mind than any other people in the world.

Lovingly & gratefully

Willie

TO META SCHAPER CATHER

April 13 [1946]

My very dear Meta;

I want to tell you why I could not see Margaret when she and her two children were in New York for a week. It nearly broke my heart to miss her, but I was very ill all the week that she was here. This strange nervous collapse began with Roscoe's death. I was never well afterward. I was below normal when it seemed necessary to go in for a surgical operation. After three weeks in the hospital I came home and I tried <u>very</u> hard to carry on. At last I began to cry a great deal. I broke down more completely over pleasant things than for sad ones. I really didn't dare see little Margaret for that reason. I am too fond of her; of all my nieces she has always crept closest to my heart. I didn't want her to see me when I was such a wreck.

Two weeks ago my oldest friend, doctor Taylor, came home and took a strong hand with me. For the present he will not let me see anyone at all. Even Miss Bloom, my secretary, broke down and is now in a hospital in Albany. So I am absolutely isolated and see no one but Miss Lewis. Time and being very quiet are the only things that will help me. It seems that if one has, for many years, cared a great deal for a great many people and a great many things, one suffers a kind of emotional exhaustion in the end, and has to rest one's power to care.

I have [not] seen any friends since November, not even Yehudi, nor heard any music. I have simply had, for the present, to cut out all the things I loved most—and I want you to know.

Devotedly,
Willie

TO SIGRID UNDSET

May 20, 1946

Dear Sigrid Undset:

How many times I have read over your letter, which tells me so much about what you are doing and how you are in mind and heart. Of course, there were sad things about your home coming; of course, your little town cannot be the same place, and many of the young men have died. The big losses in wars do not hurt us so much as does the death of a friend's son or a neighbour's son.

But it must be an inspiration for you to be at home, where everyone is working for one purpose and working together. I think nothing puts hope into one like that feeling of working together.

We are in a very sad way here in the United States. There has never been such confusion before. Well may you say, "Oh, if Roosevelt were still alive". John Lewis, President of the United Mine Workers, seems to be the most powerful man we have, because he can stop the entire coal output and all manufactures and public utilities, including railroads. Coal, of course, is the basic generator of so many sorts of power. Just now wheels are standing still everywhere. I am not even sure that Miss Lewis and I can get up to Maine this summer. In Washington nothing is ever done, and nothing is ever settled. If we were up against great difficulties and shortages, I think we would not be so disheartened. But our troubles seem all to come from mismanagement and disagreements. We absolutely dread the morning newspaper. If you, in Norway, find anything hopeful in the American news, your reporters must spare you the worst. I think that everybody here feels the paralysis of a bitter disillusionment.

How fortunate you are to be where there is no "bigness" except that of the spirit! Where everyone stands shoulder to shoulder, and everyone is doing the best he can. I am glad that you saw this country when you did see it, and not as it is now.

Instead of living in the present, I have been trying to live in old Histories and in great books, which are always a source of strength. I am so gratified that your great trilogy, Kristin Lavransdatter, has appeared again in three volumes, as it should be, and not crowded into one unwieldy tome. I hope you will never let those horrible producers at Hollywood put any of your books into films.

This is a sorry answer, dear friend, to your splendid letter, but one must have a spirit of hope to be anything but dull. Perhaps if we get up into the country again, the forests and the big tides on the Maine coast may put some heart into one. Then you will hear from me again, and I shall be a very different person, I hope.

Since you sailed I had a rather severe illness and was in the Roosevelt Hospital for several weeks. I think I am fairly well physically now, but there is a stagnation in the air which rather chokes one.

[Unsigned]

TO TRIXIE MIZER FLORANCE

June 12, 1946

My dear Trix:

I was so glad to hear about you and your family and your summer plans. I am grateful to have good news of Carrie Sherwood. I have known her a long, long time—a precious friendship of many years. My first memory of her dates back to the arrival of my family in Nebraska. We moved at once out to my grandfather's farm, some eighteen miles northwest of Red Cloud. On the first trip I made to Red Cloud in the farm wagon, I was taken by some member of my family to the frame building which was then Miner Brothers General Store. I remember a young girl who came up to me, held my hand for a few minutes and talked to me. She had very bright eyes and looked interested. That was Carrie. The better you know her, the better you will like her.

With love to you and yours,
Willa

TO ELIZABETH SHEPLEY SERGEANT

August 16, 1946
Asticou Inn, Northeast Harbor, Maine

My dear Elsie:

I wrote you a hasty note to tell you that I could never be persuaded to submit to a "Portable Cather" published by Viking. These "Portables" seem to be the last derivative of the torrent of anthologies which very nearly wiped out all the dignity and nearly all the profits of the legitimate publishing business. After the war everybody wants to "get by" easy; schools, teachers and pupils. Nobody wants to toil through "For Whom the Bell Tolls" when they can read the worst chapters of the book and say "Hemingway? Oh, yes, sure!"

Why are you (telling me that you are working on a new book in which you are very much interested) willing to squander your time and scatter your attention for a miserable collection which means to get by as a "Portable" when other forms of the Anthology have become a little stale??? Such a waste of energy!!

I think Alfred Knopf is still in England but I am quite sure that he would not have any dealings with a "Portable" when his entire list of any writer's books are selling steadily all the time.

So let me wish you happy days and good luck on your new book and ask you to forget this insidious "Portable" suggestion.

Yours
Willa Cather

TO HELEN LOUISE CATHER SOUTHWICK

September 17, 1946
Asticou Inn, Northeast Harbor, Maine

My dear Helen Louise,

I sent you a telegram last night asking you to telegraph your father for me. I had at home in my desk three small address books, one for foreign addresses, one for family addresses and another for friends in this country and in Canada. Miss Bloom packed my papers for me and I suspect she thought two address books were enough. She neglected to include the family address book so I was unable to reach your father direct. I will be glad if you will send me his present address when you write.

I am sending you a funny little clipping because it gave me pleasure, and I think it might give you pleasure. This cutting was sent me by an unknown person in Indianapolis—probably some writer on the Indianapolis Star. Just at the end I think there is a nice word to come from my old chief—the man who published my first short story in his magazine and afterward my first book of short stories—which I hope you haven't seen for most of it was bad enough. For the next three years after he had published that first book, I worked hard on Mr. McClure's magazine and he sent me abroad twice to arrange some important contracts in England for him. Of late years I simply have not had time or strength to keep up my connection with him as I should have done. He has been more faithful and loyal than I. I wrote him a long letter not long ago and shall see him as soon as I go back. I send this little clipping to you, my dear, because now that Roscoe is no longer alive, there is no one left to whom it would mean anything. You could send it to Charles if you wished,—but Jack's daughters whom I have never seen, do not seem to be very discreet though I am sure they are nice girls. They once sent me some poetry written by a high school teacher of theirs. The teacher, if not the girls, evidently had bright hopes that I could get it published for him, so I don't feel that Jack's family are safe confidants.

With love to you
W.S.C.

→ ←

In 1946 E. K. Brown published "Homage to Willa Cather" in the Yale Review. *This work, combined with his previous essay "Willa Cather and the West," so impressed Cather and Edith Lewis that, after Cather's death, Lewis and Alfred Knopf chose Brown to be her first biographer.*

TO E. K. BROWN

October 7, 1946

My dear Mr. Brown:

I have been delayed in writing to you by a whirlwind of repairs in this apartment house—repairs not requested by me and over which I had no control. Moreover, this is a difficult letter to write. It is hard for me to tell you in temperate language how deeply I appreciate your careful and sympathetic reading of my books.

The fact that I have not been writing much lately is largely due to the fact that I rather lost enthusiasm. Four years ago my brother Douglass, who loved the Southwest and with whom I used to knock about in that part of this country, died very suddenly of a heart seizure in California. Just one year ago this past September my brother Roscoe, who was in the sheep business in western Wyoming for many years, and with whom I used to spend long vacations in the summer time, died in his sleep at Colusa, California, where he had retired to escape the severe winter climate of Wyoming.

As for my books, I think I agree with your estimate in almost every instance. Of course, I know that "Death Comes for the Archbishop" is my best book. I was seven years in getting the material for it, but I never made notes because I did not expect to write a book about the Southwest. It was too big and too various. But it gave me more pleasure than any other part of this continent, and I made many trips down there simply as a matter of self-indulgence. You see, the story of the Southwest involved too many individuals—little related to each other. Strange: how long and pleasantly one can reach after a design, and how quietly and simply it comes to one at last. I shall always remember the late afternoon when I was sitting in a very gravelly, uncomfortable spot up by the Martyr's Cross, east of Santa Fé, watching the Sangre de Cristo Mountains color with the sunset. I suddenly, without any questioning, said to myself:

"The real story of the early Southwest is the story of the missionary priests.

They all came from France, and came here with a background: cultivated minds and a large vision—and a noble purpose."

From that evening on I began to find out what I could about those missionary priests—and everything I found out about them made me admire them the more. Even then I made very few notes, because the material stayed with me. Poor Mary Austin always claimed that the "Archbishop" was written in her house, in Santa Fé. Now I hear that a mad woman, called [Mary Cabot] Wheelwright, claims that it was written in her house. In truth, the book was written in the course of one year, most of it was written in a house near Jaffrey, New Hampshire. (Jaffrey lies at the foot of Mount Monadnock)—It was finished in my own apartment on Bank Street, in New York. I read the book through last spring (when I was recuperating from an illness)—the first time I have read it through since it was published. And I was pleased with it because it reflected some of the pleasure I used to feel when I wandered about that country by railroad and spring wagon and on horseback. I never used the automobile very much because I got more pleasure out of closeness than speed.

Now let me tell you a story, because I think I can always write better in narrative. I was very much disappointed in "O Pioneers", not disappointed in the reviews but in my own review of it. My credentials were honest, but I had made a mistake. I loved the Norwegian colony in Nebraska. They were rather stiff and severe—and very exclusive. And I loved the French colony up North, because they were gay and spirited and had such an attractive religion. But the Norwegian and the French people never liked each other. They didn't fight—but they didn't mix. Now, in "O Pioneers", I tried to blend what God himself had put asunder,—and I saw that I had been an idiot. I had then an excellent opportunity to make my residence in London, getting interesting matter for American publishing houses. Mr. McClure had sent me over twice for that purpose and I brought him back good material. I had two good friends in London who would always help me to get such material—William Heinemann and William Archer.

In the early spring of 1913 (it must have been), the spring after "O Pioneers" was published, I was taking a walk on Riverside Drive of a Sunday morning when I saw someone waving to me from across the street. It was Louis Brandeis. His wife was a Miss [Alice] Goldmark, and the Goldmarks then lived on Riverside Drive. He came across the street, shook hands with me and said:

"Miss Cather, I have read your book."

I was delighted to see him, but I answered rather grumpily: "I'm sorry."

He gave me one of those searching looks of his and said:

"Now, that's not quite sincere. But the book is."

Then we had a long talk, walking up and down. What he had to say was that whatever faults the book had, there was real feeling in it <u>for some places and some people</u>, and the thing that he, personally, did not find in contemporary writers was just that thing. He named three, I remember. Mrs. Wharton was one of them. (She being no longer living, I can use her name.) I know now that this talk was in the middle of Brandeis' terrible struggle about the railroads. You would have thought that he would be worn to a thread, but he was as handsome and gay as when I used to go to his house in Boston, in 1910 and 1911. The very scholarly and thorough book by Professor [Alpheus Thomas] Mason of Princeton, explaining all of Brandeis' great work, <u>never lets the living man, so witty and gay, once walk across the page</u>!

The truth is that after that talk with him, I changed my plans. I blundered on and didn't do much better, but I kept myself free from editorial work and was learning by failures. I never saw Louis Brandeis again. He probably took a glance at my two subsequent books and sighed and gave up the quest. It takes people (some people) a long while to learn what they really love, and what they love best.

I think you underestimate, a little, Mr. Brown, the pioneers among the early railroad builders in the West. Some of them were men of imagination——imagination of a high order. When I was very young—a child, indeed—I saw Jim Hill, and stood respectfully listening to him as he talked to a group of Burlington operatives. I think he was a great dreamer and a great man.

If one is any judge of one's own processes, I never conscientiously paid much attention to language. If the language tells more in the "Archbishop" than in other books it isn't due to any painstakingness on my part, any more than there is a design when the lid of a saucepan begins to hop because the water underneath it is boiling. When one cares <u>enough</u>, the language for that feeling comes. Good Heavens, we have language enough behind us! No other people has such a glorious heritage of language. We have the King James translation of the Bible and Shakespeare, and Chaucer—(not below either of them in his humor and his strange kind of tenderness). If a writer cares <u>enough</u> and is too self-respecting to be willing to make a fool of himself, the language comes as naturally as people laugh or cry.

This is a long, wandering letter, Mr. Brown, and maybe it isn't at all to the point. But it tells you the why of some things, at least. May I say that I am glad you had a good word for "My Mortal Enemy". It was lucky that by that time I had got into the hands of a broad-minded publisher. Houghton Mifflin would surely have sent that story back to me for extensive revisions.

I don't think much of "Lucy Gayheart" either. But, strangely enough, I think it picks up after all the Gayhearts are safe in the family burial lot. I think the last chapters, which deal entirely with the effect of Lucy on the hard-boiled business man, are rather interesting.

It has been a great satisfaction to me to find in your article how the various books struck a thoughtful and scholarly man. It takes a long while to learn to do anything passably well. And when the material was so exciting (and exhausting to one), maybe it took longer than it would have done if one had only had a cooler head and a better sense of form.

With deep appreciation,

Yours
Willa Cather

TO E. K. BROWN

January 24, 1947

Dear Professor Brown:

I have been tardy in answering your letter because I have as yet no definite plans for the spring or summer. I must be in California for a part of the spring and probably all of the summer. I have two brothers living there and a number of nieces and nephews scattered between San Diego and San Francisco. If I am in the city when you come on for your lectures in the Graduate School of New York University, I will certainly arrange a meeting. There are a great many things I would like to talk to you about—things more important than would directly concern you or me. What about the new edition of Shakespeare, arranged by that terrible teacher at Middlebury, Vermont, who retains what he considers the important scenes and cuts out what he considers superfluous or dull? I never feel apprehensive about Dos Passos and his kind, and I don't believe it is wise for the law to interfere with them, but I wish there were some way by which the law could interfere with an expurgated Shakespeare!

No, it will be a long time before we have another Brandeis on the Supreme Court bench. During the three years I spent in Boston, I was often at Mr. Brandeis' house in the evening. He was then working on one of his most difficult cases (one of his secretaries told me that his morning's mail would usually fill a peck measure); but during all this time I never heard him talk about anything that related to his professional life. Those were the days of the opera in Boston, and I used often to see Mr. and Mrs. Brandeis in the audience. It was Mrs. [Alice Goldmark] Brandeis who first took me to see Mrs. James T.

Fields, the widow of the great Boston publisher. The Brandeises lived on Otis Place and Mrs. Fields' house, 148 Charles Street, was just around the corner. I haven't happened to know another great man who was so fortunate in his wife as Mr. Brandeis. She was very handsome, very intelligent, and 'worldly' in a good sense—she had an instinctive knowledge of people, and she loved people and life—found everything interesting, even the absurd. She did not survive the Justice long.

Life stretches out as being rather long when one stops to remember all the fine people one has known and admired in this country and abroad. I used to spend a good deal of time in London. I remember how William Archer and I sat in Lady Gregory's box on the night that the Abbey players made their debut in London. They played <u>The Rising of the Moon</u> [by Lady Gregory] for the curtain raiser—and then <u>The Playboy</u> [*of the Western World*, by John Millington Synge]. It was a puzzled audience,—and I was puzzled. When we went afterward for some supper, Archer asked me what I thought of the performance. I said I thought it was interesting but not very dramatic. Mr. Archer said very gently, "To me, anything that is interesting in the theater belongs there —and is dramatic."–––We learn a great deal from great people. The mere information doesn't matter much–––but they somehow strike out the foolish platitudes that we have been taught to respect devoutly, and give us courage to be honest and free. Free to rely on what we really feel and really love–––and that only.

I shall look forward, then, to some discussion of our values when you come to New York in the spring.

Faithfully yours
Willa Cather

TO BISHOP GEORGE ALLEN BEECHER

March 12, 1947

Dear Bishop Beecher:

I just want to tell you how often I have thought of you since I had your son's telegram which told me such sad news. There is nothing in this world that can comfort one for the loss of a lifetime companionship. I saw all that after the death of my father. My mother was simply never again the same person, although she always had great courage.

I have delayed writing to you because I like to write very personal letters by hand and I have lately had a severe sprain to my right hand, which makes the use of the pen impossible for the present. I am glad that not very many weeks before Christmas, I did snatch the time to write you and Mrs. Beecher a Christmas letter (with pen and ink), while my hand was normal. I had a feeling that I wanted to write you both by hand——It was a kind of homesickness for you and all your work, and the visits I used to pay Mrs. Beecher when you were out on your diocese. I don't have many correspondents in Red Cloud now, but Carrie Sherwood and Mrs. Creighton have always been true friends, and so have Sidney Florance and his wife [Trixie]. I have been trying to help the hospital board make a pleasant hospital of the dear old house where my father and mother were so happy for many years, and where they made the house dear to their children by beautiful memories. The house was sold without my knowledge and had for some years a rather degraded existence. But now kind and truly friendly people, like Mr. and Mrs. D. B. Burden, are doing all they can to make it a homelike hospital. Even some of the poor little sewing societies out in the western part of the county are selling hand-pieced quilts and raising little contributions for the hospital. Some of the country people have written me how kindly and hospitably they were always entertained by my mother when they went to town to do their shopping or to have their teeth fixed. Those memories outlast the short term of human life.

I pray for you that you may have strength to bear the loneliness which faces you, and I am always devotedly and gratefully yours.

Willa Cather

TO E. K. BROWN

March 23, 1947

Dear Mr. Brown:

I am happy to have your letter telling me more or less of your plans, and I shall write my plans to you as soon as I have a clear head and plain sailing.

Yesterday this apartment was stormed by impetuous and loving friends, who were to sail on the Queen Elizabeth at one o'clock. Hepzibah, her Scotch husband, Lindsay, and her two little boys arrived first. Soon after, Yehudi's two children arrived. Later Yehudi himself—always a quieting influence, even where there is a crowd of excited children. Here we all were (the children only were new), the rest of us were sitting in these rooms just as we used to meet here every week ten and twelve years ago. Concert-trained people have perfect relaxation. They never think about what they are going to do in the next hour until the present hour is entirely spent. At eleven-thirty my guests quietly rose, got the children into their wraps, without any flurry, dropped down in the elevator to the street floor, where cabs were waiting, and drove to the North River docks at 56th Street to have lunch before the boat sailed at one. All their luggage had been placed on board, in the proper stateroom, the day before.

Yehudi and Hepzibah are going over to give a series of concerts together, not only in London but in other large cities throughout England as well—admission prices so little that even poor people can hear good music again. For sixteen years ever since they first came to me with letters of introduction from old friends in France and England, the Menuhin children have been one of the chief interests and joys of my life. There is just an inherent beauty in their natures that goes far beyond any "giftedness"—––and yet natural beauty of mind and heart is a very great part of the "giftedness". I would rather have almost any other chapter of my life left out than the Menuhin chapter which has gone on so happily over so many years. That is why I find that I cannot write any proper answer to your letter—cannot write anything today except about the wonderful yesterday with those dear children (as they still are to me) and their children. Today these rooms seem actually full of their presence and their faithful, loving friendship.

Willa Cather
by Sarah J. Bloom

TO SIGRID UNDSET

April 8, 1947

Dear Sigrid Undset:

If you knew how many times I have read over your letter and enjoyed it, I think you would be glad you took the pains to write me. The latter part of the winter has been very bad for me. I overstrained a tendon in my right hand—the same tendon which I injured eight years ago. I had thought it completely cured but it had a relapse in January, and since then I have been carrying it in a steel and leather brace to keep it absolutely still. The brace was made by an expert surgeon, is very light and comfortable, and my thumb lies in a neat little trough, apart from the rest of my hand. I sleep with it on, without any discomfort.

Isn't the world behaving very strangely, after all? Miss Lewis lunched this week with half a dozen very advanced Hindus, introduced to her by old friends (artists) who live out in the East. Their talk was really absurd, and very boastful and exultant about India's release from English rule. "Out from under the heel of the despot at last"! Wait until a few thousands are dieing of famine in the streets of their cities, when there is no [Archibald] Wavell to go down to Calcutta and supervise the rescue squads in the streets.

England has certainly been hard hit. Aside from the shortage of coal and food, the regimentation has been very severe—I suppose necessary. An aged friend of mine, who petitioned for a permit to buy enough lumber to mend his veranda floor, fell and broke his hip before he could get permission to buy the necessary lumber. At his age, he will scarcely survive such an accident.

Yes, Madame Undset, the winter has been mild here with us, drearily and demoralizingly mild—soft and damp. You probably know the Irish proverb, "A green Christmas makes a full graveyard." We had a three-day blizzard which roused false hopes; after that, sloppy, pale spring weather.

I think New York has become the most foolish city in the world—to live in. All the old women have had their hair dyed yellow—or cut short and violently frizzed. One rarely sees a really well-dressed woman.

I am glad that you remember with pleasure the shadbush and the dogwood. I wonder whether you happened to be in the South when the Judas tree (cercis canadensis) was in blossom? In Virginia when I was a child, the dogwood and the Judas tree and the white locust tree always blossomed at the same time. (The shadbush thrives only further North, I think.)

Dear and kind friend, this is a foolish letter but you must forgive me. The warm, soft winter, and <u>the strange deterioration in human beings</u> take all one's spirit. Every American now seems to want to live in New York City, drink cocktails and wear outrageous clothes. Miss Lewis and I have both had a good winter in so far as general heath is concerned. My right hand has been a great drawback for the last six months, but it is getting better and I hope to escape from New York before very long. When I go North you shall hear from me.

Always affectionately and deeply admiringly yours,
Willa Cather

TO E. K. BROWN

April 12, 1947

Dear Professor Brown:

I can't give any definite plans as to where I will be in the early summer, but I am now quite sure that I will not be going West in the middle [of] June. I expect, indeed, to go straight North to a cottage in Northeast Harbor, Maine, where I have often been very comfortable and where I can work a little.

I warmly agree with you about the benefits of our young people going abroad, especially to France. But I am sure you will agree with me that one has to choose the kind of young people. Once when I was in France for a year, I had an opportunity to observe some of the young Americans who flocked about Gertrude Stein. One couldn't very well tell whether they were youths of promise or not; they certainly thought they were, and fearlessly stated that opinion. But not one of them in the years that have gone by has done anything that took hold of one very hard. One of them, Steinbeck I think, wrote a play set in Norway, called "The Moon is Down". I read that with great interest and felt a real throb of life in it. I was a little disappointed when the last act and the climax of the play was a long quotation from Plato. The quotation was very fine . . . belonged where the American put it and was effectively introduced. But to me it threw a backward shadow on the earlier part of the play. Perhaps, if I were to read it again, I would feel differently.

What I mean is, that it takes the right kind of young American to go to France. He must have character and depth, and a passion for the things that lie deep behind French history and French art. I wish I could have had a comfortable boardinghouse near Chartres when Henry Adams used to prowl about the cathedral. Young people who flocked about Gertrude Stein were a rather soft lot. Some of them wore bracelets!! I hope you have had better luck with your students who have gone over.

As soon as I have arranged my dates for Northeast Harbor, Maine, and Nova Scotia, I will certainly let you know, Mr. Brown.

Faithfully yours,
Willa Cather

TO DOROTHY CANFIELD FISHER

April 17, 1947

My dear Dorothy:

I have wanted to write to you for a long while, but I hate to send you a typewritten letter. Early in the winter I "pulled" the tendon of my right thumb, and since then have been carrying my right hand in a light metal and leather brace which comfortably isolates my thumb. It has responded to its vacation and I hope soon to get it out of the brace altogether.

This is a letter of inquiry, merely. I long ago promised an editor to sometime furnish him with an account of the short call which you and Isabelle and I paid on Houseman. In such an article I would wish to admit that you saved the day (which might have been embarrassing) by the blessed and time-honored avenue of Latin scholarship! You had a bridge for approach, congenial approach, to Professor Houseman, which Isabelle and I had not. If I make such a statement about you, I want to be accurate. As I remember it, you had come from studying for your Ph.D. degree with Gaston Paris, in France? That fact interested Professor Houseman and turned the conversation in safe and impersonal channels. Several rather mushy boys (young men they were, apparently) have sent rather horrid manuscripts on Houseman to me. I could not destroy them, but if they should ever get them published I should like to leave a plain statement of an uninvited call upon a scholar and a gentleman—a stiff and angular gentleman at that! Why do all these Willie boys sigh for him so, and claim him for their own? The word 'lad' seems to hypnotize them.

You may remember that Isabelle and I had just come from Ludlow, where we had spent two weeks. We were on friendly terms with the bookseller there, Mr. Woolley, who often sent us things which he thought might interest us. He would say: "You must not carry these books; I will send them up to your hotel by my lad." At that date "lad" was the common name for errand-boy—for any young man who was hired by a merchant or by the old Feathers Hotel.

Our punishments are strange in this world. Why should a severe Latin teacher (a real scholar) be made the apologist for lazy youths who whine that the world owes them a living—a living with laurel and roses!

Affectionately always
Willa

Houseman taught Latin at the university of London did he not? Do you remember what branch of Latin? <u>Curse my metal thumb</u>!

➜ ❖

Willa Cather died of a cerebral hemorrhage on April 24, 1947, at her apartment in New York. Edith Lewis remembered, "She was never more herself than on the last morning."

VIRGINIA CATHER BROCKWAY TO META SCHAPER CATHER

Wednesday, April 30 [1947]

Dearest Mother–

Just got home & I'm having some coffee before I clean up, bathe, etc. Later I'll have to buy food & want to mail this when I go in.

I got to N. Y. early Monday morning & called Aunt Elsie and MV [Mary Virginia] at their hotel, & then walked over & joined them for breakfast. Then MV went to the apartment to help with the flowers, but Miss Lewis preferred to have the rest of us wait until the funeral. Uncles Jack & Jim were to arrive during the morning & Charles was to meet them, but they missed each other so all ended up at the apartment. Aunt Elsie & I got there at 1:15.

The funeral was very small, about twenty four people I guess, all old friends. Mrs. [Ethel] Litchfield whom Aunt Willie had known from the days in Pittsburgh was there. Yehudi's wife [Nola Nicholas Menuhin], a really beautiful girl, was also there. Beyond that I don't know, & I somehow didn't feel like asking. Uncle Jack can probably tell you.

The apartment was very little disarranged. Aunt Willie was in front of the windows and looked very lovely. There were masses of flowers. MV had busily torn bows off everything as Aunt Willie had always been allergic to bows on flowers & had always snatched them off. MV mentioned flowers from Maude Bradley, Zoe Akins, and Margery Sharp had cabled flowers from London.

Since Aunt Willie had known no minister in N.Y., Edith chose the only one she knew—a Unitarian minister who had conducted funeral services for Edith's mother. Edith & MV both thought Aunt Willie would be highly amused at having the Unitarian minister, but I'm afraid poor Aunt Elsie doubted that any but an Episcopalian minister could give one the right start toward heaven. However she felt better when she saw that he wore a very rich & elaborate vestment. She thought they were against such trappings. He just read from the Bible and offered a short prayer—nothing to conflict with our church. It was all very simple and dignified. He asked if he should read something Aunt Willie wrote, & evidently had an appropriate passage in mind, but Miss Lewis preferred just the Bible.

After the services Miss Lewis asked me to stay for a while and have a cup of tea with her. She told me all about Aunt Willie, and then her sister and Miss Bloom (Blum?) joined us for tea. It really did not seem at all inappropriate for Aunt Willie to be present, though it does sound odd.

She said it was very sudden. At 2PM Thursday Aunt Willie was well and cheerful, and was going to rest for a while. She was troubled with rheumatism or lumbago and was to see the doctor the next day. At three she came out and said she was very ill and had such a terrible pain in her head. Before four it was all over. They were unable to get a doctor until too late—one arrived ten minutes after Aunt Willie died. However she was not unattended. Their maid was a registered nurse until she got too old for such a strenuous life so she was able to do just about all that could be done.

Miss Lewis said she sometimes wondered if Aunt Willie had felt it coming for so often of late she had said that she hoped she could die as quickly and easily as Roscoe and Douglass had. Of course it's a blessing that she did rather than having the helpless years grandmother had.

Aunt Willie had not been well since her trip to California. And since her operation she had been very weak and tired. But she wasn't an invalid. She rested a great deal and had to eliminate most social life, but she was up and around every day and would do things like walking to the hardware store and coming back with mops & kitchen equipment. And she was making hopeful plans for the future. She would ask Edith how she would feel about packing up and going to California right away. And they were planning to go to Maine as Aunt Willie was most anxious to get back to work and thought she could there. Of late Aunt Willie had been talking and thinking more and more of the family, particularly the nieces and nephews because they were young and Aunt Willie apparently found something hopeful in youth.

In all, I guess, it was all for the best. As with dad, a little less severe attack and there would have been a long period of invalidism, which seems the most tragic end for a life.

After I left Miss Lewis I went to the station to get a reservation & pick up my bag & then to Aunt Elsie's hotel. She had them bring in a cot for me so I shared the room with Aunt Elsie and M.V. Uncle Jack & Jim were there and all the family had a most pleasant dinner together. Whenever I looked quickly at Uncle Jack I was almost certain that he was dad. He said that you seemed well and cheerful and that they were so happy to have you near them.

Yesterday MV, Charles, Uncle Jack, Uncle Jim & Miss Lewis took Aunt Willie up to Jaffrey for burial. Since one of Jaffrey's main charms for Aunt Willie was the fact that it was almost inaccessible it seemed better not to have everyone go. So I stayed with Aunt Elsie. We spent the day at the Metropolitan Museum and saw the Cathedral of St. John the Divine. It is very beautiful. After dinner we just talked and I left for the station at 9:30. Got here at seven and John met me. I took him to work & then drove home.

Aunt Elsie says she feels much better. The doctors never learned just what had been wrong with her. She wasn't ill in bed but she had been definitely not well. She did no housework at all, but she got up every day and then just rested and got caught up on her "3 Rs"—reading, resting, and radio.

John just called to tell me that there was mail in a desk drawer—two letters from you. I didn't know Aunt Willie felt any bitterness toward Aunt Elsie but I did know that they hadn't been too close, and was sure that Miss Lewis & MV would know what Aunt Willie would think of having the Unitarian minister while Aunt Elsie's opinion was just her own prejudice. Understand she (Aunt Elsie) is very <u>strictly</u> religious, and she is really rather prim.

I wrote to Aunt Willie a short time ago—a dull letter I thought—just about the garden and my birds as I had nothing else to say. But I just somehow felt I should write & I'm so glad I did. Miss Lewis said the letter made Aunt Willie very happy and she read the letter to Miss Lewis.

Yes, the family seems to have disintegrated. To me, Uncle Jack is the only real Cather left. Perhaps it's his resemblance to dad, and the fact that they have always been so good to me. Uncle Jim seems kind of prim and opinionated, as Aunt Elsie is. And Aunt Jessie just doesn't seem to belong.

I am glad that Edith was the one to arrange everything for she knew all of Aunt Willie's little quirks, and I'm sure the dignity and simplicity would have pleased Aunt Willie. It has of course been most terribly hard for Edith. She will be really lost, I fear.

I will be very careful of everything of Aunt Willies—books, pictures, letters. M. wanted me to take charge of all the letters but now I think they should be divided up—just in case of a fire or something unexpected.

It's eleven, so I must buy food & straighten the house a bit—then write to E & M.

Love,
Virginia

Biographical Directory

> ⭥

This biographical directory does not list every person mentioned in the letters by Willa Cather included in this volume. Focusing on individuals most readers will not be familiar with, it omits, for example, well-known writers, artists, politicians, and other people for whom basic information is readily available elsewhere (such as Charles Dickens, Winston Churchill, or Prosper Mérimée). People mentioned in the letters whose identities are not known beyond a name or a partial name are also not included, and identifications made in the text are often not repeated here.

ABBOTT, EDITH (1876–1957): Graduated from the University of Nebraska in 1901; became dean of the University of Chicago School of Social Service Administration.

ACKROYD, ROSE: Granddaughter of Mary Ann Anderson, of the Back Creek area in Virginia; niece of Enoch and Marjorie Anderson, who accompanied the Cathers to Nebraska.

ADLER, ELMER (1884–1962): Book designer and master of fine printing; designed and supervised the printing of some of Cather's books.

AKINS, ZOË (1886–1958): Playwright and also writer of poetry, fiction, criticism, screenplays, and radio and television scripts; winner of the Pulitzer Prize in 1935 for her adaptation of Edith Wharton's *The Old Maid*.

AMES, MARY H. (MAYSIE): Classmate of Cather and of Mariel Gere.

AMES, WINTHROP (1870–1937): American dramatist, producer, director, and theater owner.

ANDERSON, EDWIN H. (1861–1947): Director of the Carnegie Library in Pittsburgh while Cather lived there; director of the New York Public Library, 1913–1934.

ANDERSON, MARJORIE (MARGIE) (1854–1924): Accompanied the Cathers from Virginia to Nebraska as household help; prototype for Mahailey in *One of Ours* and Mandy in "Old Mrs. Harris."

ANDREWS, SARAH ("AUNTIE" OR "AUNTIE SISTER") (1834–1925): Sister of Mary Virginia Cather, Willa Cather's mother.

ARCHER, WILLIAM (1856–1924): Scottish playwright and drama critic.

ARLISS, GEORGE (1868–1946) and FLORENCE (1871–1950): Well-known British actors who had major successes in American theater and film.

AULD, CHARLES: Son of Jessica Cather Auld and James William Auld.

AULD, JAMES WILLIAM: Banker in Red Cloud; married to Jessica Cather but divorced from her in 1933; often called "Will."

AULD, JESSICA CATHER (1881–1964): Sister of Willa Cather.

AULD, MARY VIRGINIA (b. 1905): Cather's adored niece, the daughter of her sister Jessica Cather Auld; married name Mellen.

AULD, WILLIAM THOMAS: Son of Jessica Cather Auld and James William Auld; sometimes called "Tom" or "Will."

"AUNTIE" OR "AUNTIE SISTER": *see* Andrews, Sarah.

AUSTIN, MARY HUNTER (1868–1934): American writer and naturalist, author of *The Land of Little Rain*, *The Ford*, and numerous other works.

AXTELL, JAMES W. (1852–1909): publisher and editor in chief of the *Home Monthly Magazine*.

BAIN, READ (b. 1892): A professor of sociology at Miami University, Oxford, Ohio; editor of the *American Sociological Review* from 1938 to 1942.

BAKST, LÉON (1866–1924): Russian painter and designer of stage sets.

BARR, AMELIA E. (1831–1919): British American writer of popular historical fiction.

BARRIE, JAMES M. (1860–1937): British playwright and novelist, best known for *Peter Pan*.

BATES, HERBERT (1868–1929): A professor of English at the University of Nebraska who placed some of Cather's earliest writings; later a music critic in Cincinnati.

BEACH, REX ELLINGWOOD (1877–1949): Writer of manly adventure novels.

BECKER, SADIE: A talented musician and accompanist who moved from New York to Red Cloud with her parents as a young woman; possible prototype for Cather's character Lucy Gayheart.

BEECHER, GEORGE ALLEN (1868–1951): Bishop of Western Nebraska from 1910 to 1943; confirmed Cather and her parents in the Episcopal Church.

BENDA, WLADYSLAW THEODOR (1873–1948): Magazine and book illustrator chosen by Cather for *My Ántonia*.

BENNETT, ARNOLD (1867–1931): English novelist.

BERNHARDT, SARAH (1844–1923): Celebrated French actress.

BESSIE: *see* Seymour, Elizabeth.

BLOOM, SARAH J.: Cather's personal secretary from about 1923; managed much of Cather's correspondence and typed some of her manuscripts.

BOAK, RACHEL ELIZABETH SEIBERT (1816–1893): Cather's maternal grandmother, the model for Mrs. Harris in "Old Mrs. Harris."

BOURDA, JOSEPHINE: Cather's housekeeper and cook for many years.

BOURNE, RANDOLPH (1886–1918): Influential progressive thinker, critic, and essayist; died at age thirty-two in the influenza epidemic of 1918–1919.

BREWSTER, ACHSAH BARLOW (1878–1945) and EARL (1878–1957): American expatriate painters who lived in Italy, France, and India; Achsah was Edith Lewis's Smith College roommate and friend.

BROOKS, VAN WYCK (1886–1963): Literary historian, critic, and biographer; won the Pulitzer Prize for History in 1937 for *The Flowering of New England*.

BROWN, E. K. (1905–1951): Canadian academic who wrote the first biography of Cather, completed by Leon Edel and published in 1953.

BURROUGHS, LOUISE GUERBER: Librarian at the Denver Public Library who later moved to New York and worked at the Metropolitan Museum of Art.

BUTCHER, FANNY (1888–1987): Bookseller and writer; reviewed books, music, and art for the *Chicago Tribune* for almost fifty years.

BUTLER, NICHOLAS MURRAY (1862–1947): President of Columbia University 1902–1945; president of the American Academy of Arts and Letters 1928–1941.

BYNNER, WITTER (1881–1968): Poet; worked as an office boy and editor at *McClure's* after graduating from Harvard in 1902.

CALVÉ, EMMA (1858?–1942): Popular French operatic soprano.

CANBY, HENRY SEIDEL (1878–1961): American editor, critic, and literary biographer; a professor at Yale, helped launch the *Yale Review*; edited the *New York Evening Post Literary Review* and the *Saturday Review of Literature*; chaired the selection committee of the Book-of-the-Month Club from 1926 to 1954.

CANBY, MARION (1885–1974): American poet whose verses appeared in various magazines and were collected in *High Mowing* (1932) and *On My Way* (1937); wife of Henry Seidel Canby.

CANFIELD, FLAVIA (1844–1930): A painter and socialite greatly interested in the arts; mother of Cather's friend Dorothy Canfield Fisher; prototype for Flavia Hamilton in "Flavia and Her Artists."

CANFIELD, JAMES HULME (1847–1909): Chancellor of the University of Nebraska during Cather's student days; later president of Ohio State University; father of Dorothy Canfield Fisher.

CATHER, CHARLES EDWIN (1922?–2011): Cather's nephew, son of James Cather and Ethel Garber Cather; became Cather's literary executor.

CATHER, CHARLES FECTIGUE (1848–1928): Father of Willa Cather.

CATHER, DOUGLASS (1880–1938): Cather's brother, to whom she was very close.

CATHER, ELIZABETH (1915–1978): Cather's niece, daughter of Roscoe and Meta Schaper Cather, twin to Margaret Cather and sister to Virginia Cather; married Lynn S. Ickis in 1938.

CATHER, ELSIE (1890–1964): Cather's sister; sometimes called "Bobbie."

CATHER, ETHEL MAY GARBER (d. 1975): Cather's sister-in-law, married to brother James; related through her father to Silas Garber.

CATHER, FRANCES (FRANC) SMITH (1846–1922): Strong-minded aunt married to Cather's father's brother George.

CATHER, GEORGE P. (1847–1938): Cather's paternal uncle, the first member of the family to migrate from Virginia to Nebraska; married to Frances (Franc) Smith Cather.

CATHER, GROSVENOR P. ("G. P."): (1883–1918): Cather's first cousin, son of George and Frances (Franc) Smith Cather; died in France during World War I; prototype for Claude Wheeler in *One of Ours*.

CATHER, HELEN LOUISE (1918–2004): Cather's niece; daughter of James Cather and Ethel Garber Cather, sister to Charles Edwin Cather.

CATHER, JAMES (1886–1966): One of Cather's younger brothers, married Ethel Garber.

CATHER, JOHN (JACK) (1892–1959): Cather's youngest brother.

CATHER, MARGARET (1915–1996): Cather's niece, daughter of Roscoe and Meta Schaper Cather, sister to Virginia Cather and twin sister of Elizabeth Cather; married Richard Shannon in 1938.

CATHER, MARY VIRGINIA (JENNIE) BOAK (1850–1931): Mother of Willa Cather.

CATHER, META SCHAPER (1884–1973): Cather's sister-in-law, married to brother Roscoe; graduate of the University of Nebraska–Lincoln; taught high school before marrying Roscoe in 1907.

CATHER, ROSCOE (ROSS) (1877–1945): Cather's brother, to whom she was very close; her next younger sibling.

CATHER, VIRGINIA (b. 1912): Cather's niece, the daughter of Roscoe and Meta Cather; sometimes called "West Virginia."

CHANDLER, WILLIAM E. (1835–1917): Government official and U.S. senator from New Hampshire.

CLEMENS, CYRIL (1902–1999): Founder of the International Mark Twain Society and editor of the *Mark Twain Quarterly*.

COATES, FLORENCE EARLE (1850–1927): A poet from Pennsylvania.

CRAWFORD, F. MARION (1854–1909): Financially successful American novelist.

CREIGHTON, MARY MINER (b. 1873): Second daughter of James and Julia Miner of Red Cloud; married Red Cloud physician E. A. Creighton; a lifelong friend of Cather's and prototype for Sally Harling in *My Ántonia*.

CROSS, WILBUR (1862–1948): Professor at Yale and editor of the *Yale Review*; governor of Connecticut from 1931 to 1939.

DAMROSCH, WALTER (1862–1950): German American conductor and composer, elected to the National Institute of Arts and Letters in 1898 and to the American Academy of Arts and Letters in 1932; president of the Academy from 1941 to 1948.

DELAND, MARGARET CAMPBELL (1857–1945): American writer of fiction, poetry, and autobiography.

DEVOTO, BERNARD (1897–1955): Historian, essayist, and literary critic; faculty member at Harvard; edited "The Easy Chair" for *Harper's Magazine* from 1930 to 1955; editor of the *Saturday Review of Literature* from 1936 to 1938.

DORÉ, PAUL GUSTAVE (1832–1883): Successful French painter, engraver, and illustrator with a highly dramatic style.

DOS PASSOS, JOHN (1896–1970): American novelist of the post–World War I period; associated with the Lost Generation.

DUCKER, WILLIAM: A well-educated Englishman who worked in his brother's dry-goods store in Red Cloud when Cather was a child; read Latin and Greek with her and encouraged her curiosity about many subjects.

DUNNE, FINLEY PETER (1867–1936): Creator of popular newspaper character "Mister Dooley."

DWIGHT, HARRISON G.: Writer of fiction and poetry whose work Cather accepted (and sometimes declined) for *McClure's*.

EDDY, MARY BAKER (1821–1910): Founder of the Christian Science movement and the Church of Christ, Scientist, in Boston.

ENGEL, ZOLTAN: A graduate of Columbia University, a collector of artworks, rare books, and manuscripts; donated a rich collection to Columbia.

FARRAR, GERALDINE (1882–1967): American soprano and film actress.

FARRAR, PRESTON COOKE: A friend of Cather's in Pittsburgh and teacher at Allegheny High School; later a professor at the University of North Carolina, Chapel Hill.

FERRIS, MOLLIE (c. 1864–1941): A friend of the Cather family in Red Cloud.

FEUILLERAT, ALBERT G. (1874–1953): Born in Toulouse, France; Sterling Professor of French at Yale, 1929–1943.

FIELDS, ANNIE ADAMS (1834–1915): Celebrated hostess, widow of the noted Boston publisher James T. Fields; wrote poems, edited *Life and Letters of Harriet Beecher Stowe*, and was active in reform efforts.

FISHER, DOROTHY CANFIELD (1879–1958): A prolific writer of both fiction and nonfiction, a member of the original editorial board of the Book-of-the-Month Club, and a friend of Cather's from her student days on.

FISKE, MINNIE MADDERN (1865–1932): Noted actress interviewed by Cather in 1899.

FLORANCE, BEATRIX ("TRIX") MIZER (1875–1963): Childhood friend of Cather's, studied music in Chicago; a possible model for the character Lucy Gayheart's music career.

FLORANCE, SIDNEY: Banker in Red Cloud; married to Beatrix Mizer Florance.

FOE, HOWARD: Lawyer in Red Cloud with whom the Cather family worked.

FOERSTER, NORMAN (1887–1972): A student of Cather's in Pittsburgh who became a professor and critic; established a creative arts doctoral program at the University of Iowa.

FOOTE, KATHARINE (later Katharine Foote Raffy) (b. 1881): Daughter of American musician and composer Arthur William Foote; began correspondence with Cather after reading *The Song of the Lark*.

FOOTE, MARY HUBBARD (1872–1968): A painter well known for her portraits; a frequent visitor at Mabel Dodge Luhan's home in Taos, New Mexico.

FORD, ELSIE MARTINDALE: Wife of Ford Madox Ford (Hueffer); separated from him in 1908 but never officially divorced.

FORD, FORD MADOX (PSEUD.) FORD MADOX HUEFFER (1873–1939): British novelist and critic.

FREMSTAD, OLIVE (1871–1951): Swedish American soprano; made her Metropolitan Opera debut in 1903; specialized in Wagnerian roles.

GALE, ZONA (1874–1938): Essayist, novelist, and playwright; won the Pulitzer Prize for Drama in 1921 for *Miss Lulu Bett*; active in social issues and Progressive politics.

GALSWORTHY, JOHN (1867–1933): British novelist and playwright.

GARBER, LYRA WHEELER (1855(?)–1921): Second wife of Silas Garber; social leader in Red Cloud during Cather's childhood and adolescence; the model for Marian Forrester in *A Lost Lady*.

GARBER, SILAS (1833–1905): Captain of Company D, the 27th Iowa Infantry, during the Civil War; homesteaded in Nebraska in 1870 and in 1871 founded the town of Red Cloud; governor of Nebraska, 1874–78; the model for Captain Forrester in *A Lost Lady*.

GARNETT, EDWARD (1868–1937): Influential British critic, editor, and writer.

GAYHARDT, ANNA: A teacher at the Blue Hill School when Cather met her, a graduate of Peru Normal School.

GEOGHEGAN, HAROLD: Art history professor at Carnegie Technical School (later Carnegie Mellon University) in Pittsburgh in the 1910s, where he taught Jack Cather.

GERE, CHARLES (1860–1904): Publisher of the *Nebraska State Journal*; befriended Cather during her years at the university.

GERE, MARIEL: Friend of Cather's from her college days in Lincoln, Nebraska.

GERE, MARIEL CLAPHAM: Wife of Charles Gere and mother of Mariel, Frances, and Ellen.

GERWIG, GEORGE: Cather's predecessor as drama critic for the *Nebraska State Journal*; in 1892 moved to Allegheny, Pennsylvania, where he became secretary to the city's board of education.

GILDER, JEANNETTE LEONARD (1849–1916): Pioneering woman journalist who cofounded and edited the *Critic*.

GOLDMARK, JOSEPHINE (1866–1939): Protective labor law activist, research director of the National Consumers League; author of *Fatigue and Efficiency*, which advocated shorter labor hours.

GOLDMARK, PAULINE (1874–1962): Secretary of the National and the New York State Consumers Leagues, and assistant director of social research for the Russell Sage Foundation; adviser on the employment problems and health of women for AT&T from 1919 to 1939; author of *Women and Children in the Canning Industry* (1908).

GORE, JAMES HOWARD (1856–1939): Cather's cousin, son of her great-aunt Sidney

Cather Gore; a professor of mathematics at Columbian University in Washington, D.C., and author of many books on mathematics, politics, art, and travel; married to Lillian Thekla Brandthall (1868–1913), daughter of a former Norwegian ambassador.

GORE, SIDNEY CATHER (AUNTIE GORE): Willa's great-aunt, sister of her grandfather William. The town of Gore, Virginia, is named for her and she appears briefly in *Sapphira and the Slave Girl* as Mrs. Bywater.

GOUDY, ALEXANDER K.: Principal of Red Cloud High School when Cather attended; later superintendent of Nebraska public schools.

GOUDY, ALICE E. D.: A friend from Cather's youth, wife of Alexander K. Goudy.

GRANT, JUDGE ROBERT (1852–1940): Member of the Department of Literature, American Academy of Arts and Letters, elected in 1915.

GREENSLET, FERRIS (1875–1959): Associate editor for the *Atlantic Monthly* 1902–1907; then, for thirty-five years, literary editor at Houghton Mifflin, where he championed Cather's early novels; author of *Under the Bridge*, a memoir of his life in publishing, among other works.

GRIGGS, NELLY (1875–1943): A singer from Nebraska; later married Hartley Burr Alexander, a writer, scholar, and iconographer also from Nebraska.

GUINEY, LOUISE IMOGEN (1861–1920): American poet and essayist and a friend of Annie Adams Fields and Sarah Orne Jewett.

GUND, MARGIE MINER (1875–1936): Third daughter of James and Julia Miner of Red Cloud; married Blue Hill banker Charles Frederick Gund; prototype for Julia Harling in *My Ántonia*.

HAMBOURG, ISABELLE MCCLUNG: A socialite from a prominent Pittsburgh family and Cather's devoted longtime friend.

HAMBOURG, JAN (1882–1947): Violinist and husband of Isabelle McClung Hambourg.

HARRIS, SARAH (1860–1917): Newspaperwoman Cather met while a student at the University of Nebraska; co-owner and editor of the *Lincoln Courier* in the late 1890s.

HENDRICK, BURTON J. (1870–1949): Writer at *McClure's* and later editor and writer of many books of nonfiction and biography.

HESS, MYRA (1890–1965): Well-known British concert pianist who toured in the U.S.

HOGAN, PENDLETON (b. 1907): Writer of fiction and nonfiction.

HOWE, MARK ANTONY DEWOLFE (1906–1967): Writer, editor of the memoirs of Annie Adams Fields.

HOWLAND, JOBYNA (1880–1936): Actress and "Gibson Girl" who starred in silent films in the 1910s; famous for her role in the Broadway production of *The Gold Diggers*; friend of Cather's friend Zoë Akins.

HRBKOVÁ, ŠÁRKA B.: Czech American translator, writer, and educator; head of the University of Nebraska's Department of Slavonic Languages and Literature from 1908 to 1919.

ICKIS, LYNN S. (1913–2003): Married Cather's niece Elizabeth Cather in 1938.

JEWETT, MARY RICE (1847–1930): Sister of Sarah Orne Jewett.

JEWETT, SARAH ORNE (1849–1909): New England writer; mentor to whom Cather dedicated *O Pioneers!*

JOHNSON, BURGES (1877–1963): A professor at Vassar and Union colleges, an editor, and an author.

JOHNSON, ROBERT UNDERWOOD (1853–1937): Editor, poet, and ambassador to Italy under President Woodrow Wilson; edited the *Century* and *Scribner's* magazines; secretary of the American Academy of Arts and Letters.

JONES, WILL OWEN (1862–1928): Managing editor of the *Nebraska State Journal* and Cather's mentor there.

KALEY, CHARLES W. (1846–1917): From Red Cloud; president of the Board of Regents of the University of Nebraska at the time Cather sought a teaching job there.

KEEBLE, GLENDINNING: Music critic with the *Pittsburgh Gazette-Times*; read and provided advice for *The Song of the Lark* before its publication.

KOHLER, DAYTON M. (1907–1972): Longtime professor of English at Virginia Tech University.

KNOPF, ALFRED A. (1892–1984): Founder of New York publishing house in 1915; published all of Cather's works from *Youth and the Bright Medusa* (1920) on.

KNOPF, BLANCHE (1894–1966): Wife of Alfred A. Knopf and a partner in the publishing house; traveled widely and was inducted into the French Legion of Honor.

LA FARGE, OLIVER (1901–1963): American anthropologist and novelist; won the Pulitzer Prize for novel *Laughing Boy* (1929).

LAMBRECHT FAMILY: German immigrant family (including husband Fred Lambrecht, wife Charlotte Preussner Lambrecht, and daughters Pauline and Lydia) who lived near the Cather family homestead outside of Red Cloud. Lydia and Pauline were Cather's first playmates in Nebraska.

LAVAL, PIERRE (1883–1945): Prominent French politician; served as premier from 1931 to 1935 and later as prime minister.

LEE, VERNON (PSEUD.) VIOLET PAGET (1856–1935): British essayist and fiction writer.

LEMAÎTRE, JULES (1853–1914): French critic and dramatist.

LEWIS, EDITH (1882–1972): Cather's companion and housemate for nearly forty years; a professional woman in magazines and advertising.

LINDBERGH, CHARLES (1902–1974) and ANNE MORROW LINDBERGH (1906–2001): The celebrity aviator and his wife were both acclaimed authors. Their son, Charles Lindbergh III, was kidnapped and murdered in 1932 in what was called the "Crime of the Century."

LITCHFIELD, ETHEL JONES: Accomplished Pittsburgh pianist; friendship with Cather began in 1902.

LOTI, PIERRE (PSEUD.) JULIAN VIAUD (1850–1923): Well-traveled French novelist.

LOWELL, AMY (1874–1925): American poet and critic.

LUHAN, MABEL DODGE (1879–1962): A patron of the arts and literature who maintained a salon on Fifth Avenue in New York before moving to Taos, New Mexico, where she hosted many artists and intellectuals.

LUHAN, TONY: Member of Taos Pueblo; married Mabel Dodge in 1923.

MACKENZIE, CAMERON (1882–1921): Son-in-law of S. S. McClure, hired at the magazine in 1906, became general manager in 1908.

MAGEE, CHRISTOPHER L. (1848–1901): Pittsburgh businessman who became one of the most powerful political figures in the city in the late nineteenth century.

MARLOWE, JULIA (1866–1950): English actress.

MASARYK, TOMÁŠ (1850–1937): Czech patriot and philosopher; a founder of Czechoslovakia and its president from 1918 to 1935.

MASTERS, EDGAR LEE (1869–1950): American poet, known for *Spoon River Anthology* (1915).

MATTHIESSEN, FRANCIS O. (1902–1950): Scholar and critic noted for *The American Renaissance* (1941); also published books on Sarah Orne Jewett, Henry James, and Theodore Dreiser.

MCCLUNG, EDITH: Sister of Cather's friend Isabelle McClung Hambourg.

MCCLUNG, SAMUEL (1845–1915): Pittsburgh judge and father of Isabelle McClung Hambourg.

MCCLURE, HATTIE: Wife of S. S. McClure and likely prototype for Myra Henshawe in Cather's *My Mortal Enemy*.

MCCLURE, S. S. (1857–1949): Founded and ran the widely circulated *McClure's Magazine*, where Cather worked as a member of the editorial staff from 1906 to 1911.

MCDONALD, JAMES (1870–1968): Classmate of Cather's from North Platte, Nebraska; one of the founders of the *Lasso*.

MCKEEBY, DR. G. E. (1844–1905): Cather family physician, mayor of Red Cloud in the late 1880s; prototype for Dr. Archie in *The Song of the Lark*.

MCNENY, BERNARD: Attorney in Red Cloud and family friend; husband of Helen McNeny.

MCNENY, HELEN SHERMAN: Friend from Red Cloud, married to Bernard McNeny.

MELLEN, RICHARD HAGER: Married Cather's niece Mary Virginia Auld in 1935; William Thomas Auld's roommate at Amherst College; a graduate of Harvard Medical School.

MELONEY, MARIE MATTINGLY (1883–1943): Editor and writer; edited the *Delineator* from 1920 to 1926, the *Sunday Magazine*, and *This Week Magazine*.

MENCKEN, H. L. (1880–1956): American editor and critic, noted for acerbic social comment and for *The American Language* (1918).

MENUHIN, HEPHZIBAH (1920–1981): American pianist who gave her first recital at age eight; later a linguist and author; sister of violinist Yehudi Menuhin and pianist Yaltah Menuhin.

MENUHIN, MOSHE (1893–1983) and MARUTHA (1892–1996): Russian immigrants to the U.S., parents of violinist Yehudi Menuhin and pianists Hephzibah and Yaltah Menuhin.

MENUHIN, NOLA NICHOLAS: First wife of violinist Yehudi Menuhin and mother of Zamira Menuhin; sister of Hephzibah Menuhin's first husband, Lindsay Nicholas.

MENUHIN, YALTAH (1921–2001): American pianist, poet, and artist, sister of violinist Yehudi Menuhin and pianist Hephzibah Menuhin.

MENUHIN, YEHUDI (1916–1999): American violinist, debuted with the San Francisco Orchestra at age seven.

MEYNELL, ALICE (1847–1922): British poet and essayist.

MICHELET, JULES (1798–1874): French historian; author of the nineteen-volume *History of France*.

MINER, HUGH (1871–1951?): Son of James and Julia Miner of Red Cloud; took over his father's store and later became postmaster in Red Cloud; married Cather's cousin Retta Ayre.

MINER, JAMES L. (1847–1905): A merchant in Red Cloud; the model for R. E. Dillon in "Two Friends" and Mr. Harling in *My Ántonia*.

MINER, JULIA ERICKSON (1844–1917): Norwegian-born wife of James L. Miner of Red Cloud; a good amateur musician; the model for Mrs. Harling in *My Ántonia*.

MONROE, HARRIET (1860–1936): Founder of *Poetry Magazine* and its editor from 1912 to 1936.

NANSEN, FRIDTJOF (1861–1930): Norwegian Arctic explorer.

NEIHARDT, JOHN (1881–1973): Writer about the Great Plains best known for *Black Elk Speaks* (1932); became Nebraska's poet laureate in 1921.

NEVIN, ETHELBERT (1862–1901): American composer of art songs.

NEWBRANCH, HARVEY (1875–1959): An 1896 graduate of the University of Nebraska; editor of the *Omaha World-Herald* for fifty-six years; won a Pulitzer Prize in 1919 for an editorial condemning lynching.

NORRIS, KATHLEEN THOMPSON (1880–1966): California newspaperwoman and a prolific writer of fiction.

OBER, DR. FRANK ROBERTS (1881–1960): Prominent orthopedic surgeon from Boston who treated Cather's tendinitis; responsible for Cather's hand brace.

OSBORNE, EVELYN: A friend and fellow graduate student of Dorothy Canfield whom Cather met in Paris in 1902; the prototype for Virginia Gilbert in "The Profile."

OTTE, FRED, JR. (1884–1956): One of Cather's students at Central High School in Pittsburgh, and privately tutored by her; later a businessman and occasional correspondent of Cather's.

OUIDA (PSEUD.) MARIE LOUISE DE LA RAMEE (1839–1908): English romantic novelist.

PATER, WALTER (1839–1894): English essayist and critic, known as a stylist.

PAVELKA, ANNIE SADILEK (1869–1955): Daughter of Bohemian immigrants to Nebraska, worked as the Miner family's hired girl in Red Cloud; married a Bohemian farmer and raised a large family in the northern part of Webster County, Nebraska; prototype for Ántonia Shimerda in *My Ántonia*.

PEATTIE, ELIA WILKINSON (1862–1935): Columnist for the *Omaha World-Herald* and literary editor of the *Chicago Tribune*; wrote fiction for adults and children.

PERSHING, JOHN J. (1860–1948): Leader of the American Expeditionary Force in World War I; taught mathematics at the University of Nebraska when Cather was a student there.

PHELPS, WILLIAM LYON (1865–1943): American critic; professor of English at Yale for forty years.

PHILLIPS, DAVID GRAHAM (1867–1911): A "muckraking" journalist and writer of novels of political and social criticism.

PHILLIPS, JOHN S. (1861–1949): Publisher and editor who cofounded *McClure's Magazine* with S. S. McClure.

POUND, LOUISE (1872–1958): College friend of Cather's who went on to gain recognition as a scholar of folklore; the first woman president of the Modern Language Association.

POUND, STEVEN AND LAURA: Parents of Louise, Roscoe, and Olivia Pound; prominent citizens of Lincoln, Nebraska, while Cather was a student there.

POUND, ROSCOE (1870–1964): Brother of Louise Pound, graduate of the University of Nebraska, and prominent legal scholar; dean of Harvard Law School from 1916 to 1936.

PUVIS DE CHAVANNES, PIERRE (1824–1898): French muralist.

RASCOE, BURTON (1892–1957): Editor, author, and critic of drama and literature whose column "The Day Book of a New Yorker" was syndicated in more than four hundred newspapers.

REYNOLDS, PAUL REVERE (1864–1944): The first literary agent in New York; founded his business in 1893 and represented many well-known authors; Cather's agent beginning in 1916.

RICHARDSON, MARGUERITE (b. 1918): Youngest daughter of W. N. Richardson, prototype for Mr. Trueman of "Two Friends"; half sister of Winifred (Freddie) Richardson Garber.

RICHARDSON, WINIFRED (FRED): Daughter of W. N. Richardson, prototype for Mr. Trueman of "Two Friends"; married Seward Garber, son of Silas Garber and his first wife.

RINEHART, MARY ROBERTS (1876–1958): Prolific American writer well known for her murder mysteries.

RITTENHOUSE, JESSIE B. (1869–1948): Poet, anthologist, and critic who helped found the Poetry Society of America.

ROBERTS, ALTHEA (ALLIE): Classmate of Cather and of Mariel Gere.

ROD, EDOUARD (1857–1910): French Swiss novelist and critic.

ROE, E. P. (1838–1888): A Civil War chaplain who became an author of popular novels with religious themes.

ROSEBORO', VIOLA (1858–1945): Fiction editor at *McClure's* from 1896 to 1906; author of short stories and novels.

SCAIFE, R. L.: Production editor at Houghton Mifflin.

SEDGWICK, ANNE DOUGLAS (1873–1935): American-born English novelist.

SEDGWICK, ELLERY (1872–1960): Editor of the *Atlantic Monthly* from 1908 to 1938.

SEIBEL, GEORGE (1873–1958): A literary and drama critic in Pittsburgh; married to Helen Seibel.

SERGEANT, ELIZABETH SHEPLEY (1881–1965): Author and journalist; wrote for the *New Republic* and others; met Cather in 1910 and wrote *Willa Cather: A Memoir* (1953).

SEYMOUR, ELIZABETH (BESSIE) (1857–1934): Cather's cousin; lived with half brother Will Andrews and their mother, Sarah Andrews, sister of Cather's mother, on a farm north of Bladen.

SHANNON, RICHARD S.: Married Cather's niece, Margaret Cather, in 1938.

SHARP, CECIL (1859–1924): Scholar and promoter of English folk music and dancing.

SHERWOOD, CARRIE MINER (1869–1971): Eldest daughter of James and Julia Miner, neighbors of the Cathers in Red Cloud; married Red Cloud banker Walter Sherwood; lifelong friend of Cather and prototype for Frances Harling in *My Ántonia*.

SILL, PEORIANNA BOGARDUS (1833–1921): Music teacher in Red Cloud who directed the 1889 production of *Beauty and the Beast* in which Cather took part.

SPRAGUE, HELEN MCNENY: Daughter of Bernard and Helen McNeny, married attorney Leon Sprague.

STEFANSSON, VILHJALMUR (1879–1962): Anthropologist and arctic explorer.

STEICHEN, EDWARD (1879–1973): Photographer famous for portraits, especially fashion and portrait photography for *Vanity Fair* and *Vogue*.

TALBOT, FRANCIS, S. J.: Literary editor of *America*, a Catholic magazine; positively reviewed *Death Comes for the Archbishop* in 1927.

TARBELL, IDA (1857–1944): Famous "muckraking" writer; preceded Cather as an editor at *McClure's*.

TAYLOR, CLARA DAVIDGE (1858–1921): Art gallery owner and promoter of modernist art; married to painter Henry Fitch Taylor.

TENNANT, STEPHEN (1906–1987): British aristocrat famous for his decadent lifestyle; his one novel, *Lascar*, was never completed.

TYNDALE, DR. JULIUS: Medical doctor in Lincoln during Cather's college years who also wrote theater reviews; brother of Emma Tyndale Westermann.

UNDSET, SIGRID (1882–1949): Norwegian writer; winner of the Nobel Prize in Literature in 1928.

VAN DOREN, CARL (1885–1950): American editor, critic, and novelist; author of *The American Novel* (1921).

VAN VECHTEN, CARL (1880–1964): American novelist, photographer, and music and drama critic.

VERMORCKEN, ELIZABETH MOORHEAD (1866–1955): An acquaintance from Pittsburgh who later wrote *They Too Were Here: Louise Homer and Willa Cather* (1950).

VINSONHALER, DUNCAN M.: A judge who represented a group of Omaha, Nebraska, citizens in commissioning a portrait of Cather.

WAGENKNECHT, EDWARD (1900–2004): American literary critic and biographer; wrote on Thoreau, Hawthorne, Sir Walter Scott, Mark Twain, Shakespeare, and Abraham Lincoln.

WALPOLE, HUGH (1884–1941): British novelist who wrote several bestselling books in the 1920s and 1930s.

WARD, ELIZABETH STUART PHELPS (1844–1911): Popular American novelist and proponent of clothing reform for women.

WARD, MARY AUGUSTA (ARNOLD) (1851–1920): Well-known British novelist who wrote under the name Mrs. Humphry Ward.

WEBER, CARL J. (1894–1966): Literary scholar, taught at Colby College for thirty-nine years; wrote a biography of Thomas Hardy.

WEISZ, IRENE MINER (b. 1881): Youngest daughter of James and Julia Miner of Red Cloud; married Chicago businessman Charles Weisz; a lifelong friend of Cather's and prototype for Nina Harling in *My Ántonia*.

WELLS, CARLTON F. (b. 1898): Professor in the Department of English at the University of Michigan; wrote or edited a number of books.

WEST, REBECCA (PSEUD.) CICELY ISABEL FAIRCHILD (1892–1983): English author, journalist, critic, and travel writer.

WESTERMANN, LOUIS AND EMMA: Acquaintances of Cather's in Lincoln; Mr. Westermann was the owner and publisher of the *Lincoln Evening News*; the family was the prototype for the Erlichs in *One of Ours*.

WESTON, KATHERINE (KIT): College friend of Cather's from Beatrice, Nebraska; daughter of the chairman of the University of Nebraska Board of Regents.

WHEELWRIGHT, MARY CABOT: Founder of the Wheelwright Museum in Santa Fe.

WHICHER, GEORGE FRISBIE (1889–1954): Graduate of Amherst College, where he subsequently taught from 1915 to 1954; author of a biography of Emily Dickinson (1935) and other literary studies.

WHICHER, HARRIET FOX (1890–1966): A graduate of Bryn Mawr and Barnard; professor of English at Mount Holyoke from 1918 to 1944; afterward a freelance copy editor at McGraw Hill.

WHITE, WILLIAM ALLEN (1868–1944): journalist, novelist, and editor of the *Emporia Gazette* in Emporia, Kansas; a national spokesman for the American Midwest in the early twentieth century.

WIENER, CHARLES F. (1846–1911): Merchant who lived near the Cathers in Red Cloud; conversant in French and German; he and Mrs. (Fanny Meyer) Wiener (1853–1893) allowed Cather the use of their fine library and were prototypes for the Rosens in "Old Mrs. Harris."

WILCOX, ELLA WHEELER (1850–1919): American poet, sometimes called "the poet of passion," from the title of her book *Poems of Passion*.

WILLARD, MARY AND MAY: Friends of Cather's in Pittsburgh; May was a librarian.

WING, TOM: Classmate of Cather's at the University of Nebraska and a cousin of Edith Lewis; married Katharine Weston.

WOOLLCOTT, ALEXANDER (1887–1943): American critic and radio personality, known for his wit; a member of the Algonquin Roundtable.

WYATT, EDITH FRANKLIN (1873–1958): Novelist, journalist, and social reform activist; wrote for *McClure's* while Cather was an editor there.

YEISER, JAMES (JIM) (1878–1953): Youngest son of Judge George O. Yeiser, the prototype for Judge Pommeroy in *A Lost Lady*; became a reporter and worked in San Francisco.

YOURCENAR, MARGUERITE (1903–1987): French novelist and essayist, the first female member of the *Académie française*.

Note on Archives Holding
Original Cather Materials

⇴ ⇤

The existence of this book is due in large part to the excellent work of archivists in many different institutions both in the United States and in Europe. The attention they have given to Willa Cather's original letters, both to protect them from decay and to make them accessible for research, has been crucially important for this effort and to Cather scholarship generally. We heartily thank and honor the archives, libraries, and foundations that have made our work possible.

In the many years we have spent in research on Willa Cather letters, we have relied on the cooperation of the nearly eighty institutions that hold the original documents. In this volume, we include letters that are held in more than forty institutions. A complete list of all those whose originals were transcribed for this book appears below. The whereabouts of two letters included in this collection—the February 17, 1916, letter to Katharine Foote and the March 28, 1927, letter to Stephen Tennant—are unknown; they are assumed to be in private hands. As we considered our selections for this volume, we were able to consult photocopies or, in one or two instances, transcriptions of some letters whose locations are presently unknown.

Several of the institutions listed below have large and particularly important Cather collections, and we especially wish to acknowledge the cooperation of these institutions: the University of Nebraska–Lincoln, Harvard University, the Willa Cather Foundation, the Nebraska State Historical Society, the University of Vermont, the Morgan Library, Yale University, the Barbara Dobkin Foundation, Drew University, the Harry Ransom Humanities Research Center, the Newberry Library, the University of Virginia, and the Huntington Library.

Those interested in locating the original document of a letter included in this collection are invited to consult the list below and to visit the Willa Cather Archive at http://cather.unl.edu.

1. Allegheny College, Pelletier Library, Meadville, Pennsylvania
2. Amherst College, Amherst, Massachusetts
3. Barbara Dobkin Foundation, New York, New York
4. Bryn Mawr College, Bryn Mawr, Pennsylvania
5. Buffalo and Erie County Public Library, Buffalo, New York
6. Chicago Historical Society, Chicago, Illinois
7. Colby College, Miller Library, Waterville, Maine
8. College of the Holy Cross, Archives and Special Collections, Worcester, Massachusetts
9. Columbia University, New York, New York
10. Cornell University, Carl A. Kroch Library, Ithaca, New York
11. Dartmouth College, Hanover, New Hampshire
12. Drew University Library, Special Collections and Archives, Madison, New Jersey
13. Duke University, Durham, North Carolina
14. Enoch Pratt Free Library, Baltimore, Maryland
15. Georgetown University, Washington, D.C.
16. Harry Ransom Center, University of Texas at Austin, Austin, Texas
17. Harvard University, Houghton Library, Cambridge, Massachusetts
18. Historical Society of Wisconsin, Madison, Wisconsin
19. Huntington Library, San Marino, California
20. Indiana University, Lilly Library, Bloomington, Indiana
21. Jaffrey, New Hampshire, Public Library
22. J. P. Morgan Library, New York, New York
23. Library of Congress, Washington, D.C.
24. Massachusetts Historical Society, Boston, Massachusetts
25. National Library of Norway, Oslo Division
26. Nebraska State Historical Society, Lincoln, Nebraska
27. New Hampshire Historical Society, Concord, New Hampshire
28. New York Public Library, New York, New York
29. Newberry Library, Chicago, Illinois
30. Princeton University, Firestone Library, Princeton, New Jersey
31. Stanford University, Stanford, California
32. Texas Woman's University, Denton, Texas
33. University of Arkansas, Fayetteville, Arkansas
34. University of California, Bancroft Library, Berkeley, California

35. University of California, Los Angeles, Department of Special Collections, Research Library, Los Angeles, California
36. University of Chicago Library, Chicago, Illinois
37. University of Michigan, Bentley Historical Library, Ann Arbor, Michigan
38. University of Nebraska–Lincoln, Archives and Special Collections, University Libraries, Lincoln, Nebraska
39. University of Pittsburgh, Center for American Music, Pittsburgh, Pennsylvania
40. University of Vermont, Bailey-Howe Library, Burlington, Vermont
41. University of Virginia, Albert and Shirley Small Special Collections Library, Charlottesville, Virginia
42. Virginia Polytechnic Institute and State University, Blacksburg, Virginia
43. Wellesley College, Margaret Clapp Library, Wellesley, Massachusetts
44. Willa Cather Foundation, Red Cloud, Nebraska
45. Yale University, Beinecke Library, New Haven, Connecticut
46. Yale University, University Library, New Haven, Connecticut

Note on Works Cited and Consulted

Editorial notes and insertions throughout the book were written using several sources, both digital and print.

For general biographical information, in addition to the letters themselves, we regularly consulted James Woodress's *Willa Cather: A Literary Life* (Lincoln, NE: University of Nebraska Press, 1987), Edith Lewis's *Willa Cather Living* (Lincoln, NE: University of Nebraska Press, 2000), and Elizabeth Shepley Sergeant's *Willa Cather: A Memoir* (Athens, OH: Ohio University Press, 1992). Mildred Bennett's *The World of Willa Cather* (Lincoln, NE: University of Nebraska Press, 1961) was also useful, particularly in preparing the early sections of this book.

All of the reviews of Cather's work that we have quoted are from *Willa Cather: The Contemporary Reviews*, ed. Margaret Anne O'Connor (Cambridge: Cambridge University Press, 2001). Quotations from interviews are from *Willa Cather in Person*, ed. L. Brent Bohlke (Lincoln, NE: University of Nebraska Press, 1986). Joan Crane's *Willa Cather: A Bibliography* (Lincoln, NE: University of Nebraska Press, 1982) is an extremely helpful guide to Cather's long and diverse record of publication.

For information about individual works we have relied on the *Willa Cather Scholarly Edition* series published by the University of Nebraska Press.

The Willa Cather Archive (http://cather.unl.edu) and its collection of digital materials, including both original resources and digital forms of some works listed above, was consulted heavily. The Archive now incorporates *A Calendar of the Letters of Willa Cather*, ed. Janis P. Stout (Lincoln, NE: University of Nebraska Press, 2002), in *A Calendar of the Letters of Willa Cather: An Expanded, Digital Edition*, ed. Janis P. Stout and Andrew Jewell. See http://cather.unl.edu/index.calendar.html.

Bibliographic information for texts not authored by Willa Cather, both books and magazines, was found through various resources, but we would especially like to acknowledge the HathiTrust Digital Library, at http://www.hathitrust.org, for its fine collection of digital materials.

In addition to the works mentioned above, and to works explicitly cited in the body of the text, the sources listed below are quoted or have provided key information for editorial notes.

Cather, Willa. "Murger's Bohemia." *The World and the Parish: Willa Cather's Articles and Reviews, 1893–1902.* Edited by William M. Curtin. Lincoln, NE: University of Nebraska Press, 1970, pp. 292–96.

———. "My First Novels (There Were Two)." *Willa Cather on Writing: Critical Studies on Writing as an Art.* Lincoln, NE: University of Nebraska Press, 1988.

Jewett, Sarah Orne. *Letters of Sarah Orne Jewett.* Edited by Annie Fields. Boston and New York: Houghton Mifflin Company, 1911.

Johanningsmeier, Charles. "Unmasking Willa Cather's 'Mortal Enemy.'" *Cather Studies*, Volume 5. Edited by Susan J. Rosowski. Lincoln, NE: University of Nebraska Press, 2000.

Lyon, Peter. *Success Story: The Life and Times of S. S. McClure.* New York: Scribner, 1963.

"Miss Cather Wins French Book Prize." *New York Times.* February 3, 1933, p. 15.

Index

PHOTOGRAPHIC CREDITS

The Associated Press: 627

Charles E. Cather Collection, Archives and Special Collections, University of Nebraska–Lincoln Libraries: 206, 333

Roscoe and Meta Cather Colleciton, Archives and Special Collections, University of Nebraska–Lincoln Libraries: xiv

Library of Congess, Prints and Photographs Division, Carl Van Vechten Collection, LC–USZ62–42538 DLC: 463

Nebraska State Historical Society, RG2639–184: 13

Philip L. and Helen Cather Southwick Collection, Archives and Special Collections, University of Nebraska–Lincoln Libraries: Cover, frontispiece, 3, 31, 55, 66, 95, 149, 221, 269, 340, 360, 401, 489, 523, 575

Mrs. Josiah Wheelwright. From Theodore Jones, "Willa Cather in the Northeast (A Pictorial Biography) 1917–1947." UNB Masters Thesis, 1968. Archives and Special Collections, University of New Brunswick: 520

A NOTE ABOUT THE EDITORS

JANIS STOUT is the author of nine scholarly books, including *Willa Cather: The Writer and Her World,* and two books about Katherine Anne Porter, one (*South by Southwest*) to appear in 2013. She has also edited two volumes on Cather and has written a memoir about retirement, *This Last House.*

ANDREW JEWELL is an associate professor at the University of Nebraska-Lincoln, and the editor of the Willa Cather Archive (http:// cather.unl.edu). He is the coeditor of the book *The American Literature Scholar in the Digital Age,* and a member of the Willa Cather Foundation Board of Governors.

A NOTE ON THE TYPE

This book was set in Adobe Garamond. Designed for the Adobe Corporation by Robert Slimbach, the fonts are based on types first cut by Claude Garamond (c. 1480–1561). Garamond was a pupil of Geoffroy Tory and is believed to have followed the Venetian models, although he introduced a number of important differences, and it is to him that we owe the letter we now know as "old style." He gave to his letters a certain elegance and feeling of movement that won their creator an immediate reputation and the patronage of Francis I of France.

Composed by North Market Street Graphics,
Lancaster, Pennsylvania

Printed and bound by Berryville Graphics,
Berryville, Virginia

Designed by Cassandra J. Pappas